Special Edition

Using Java Server Pages and Servlets

Mark Wutka

201 W. 103rd Street
Indianapolis, Indiana 46290

Contents at a Glance

Special Edition Using Java Server Pages and Servlets

International Standard Book Number: 0-7897-2441-3

Library of Congress Catalog Card Number: 00-107931

Printed in the United States of America

First Printing: October 2000

02 01 00 4 3 2 1

Trademarks

All terms mentioned in this book that are known to be trademarks or service marks have been appropriately capitalized. Que cannot attest to the accuracy of this information. Use of a term in this book should not be regarded as affecting the validity of any trademark or service mark.

Warning and Disclaimer

Every effort has been made to make this book as complete and as accurate as possible, but no warranty or fitness is implied. The information provided is on an "as is" basis. The author and the publisher shall have neither liability nor responsibility to any person or entity with respect to any loss or damages arising from the information contained in this book.

Acquisitions Editor
Todd Green

Development Editor
Hugh Vandivier

Managing Editor
Thomas F. Hayes

Project Editor
Tricia A. Sterling

Copy Editor
Julie A. McNamee

Indexer
Deborah Hittel

Proofreader
Harvey Stanbrough

Technical Editor
Cliff McCartney

Team Coordinator
Cindy Teeters

Media Developer
Jay Payne

Interior Designer
Ruth Lewis

Cover Designers
Dan Armstrong
Ruth Lewis

Production
Steve Geiselman

CONTENTS

About the Author

Mark Wutka has been programming since the Carter Administration and considers programming to be a relaxing pastime. He managed to get a computer science degree while designing and developing networking software at Delta Airlines. Although he has been known to delve into areas of system and application architecture, he isn't happy unless he's writing code…usually in Java.

As a consultant for Wutka Consulting, Mark enjoys solving interesting technical problems and helping his coworkers explore new technologies. He has taught classes, written articles and books, and given lectures. His first book, *Hacking Java*, outsold Stephen King at the local technical bookstore. He's also known for having a warped sense of humor.

He plays a mean game of Scrabble, a lousy game of chess, and is the bane of every greenskeeper east of Atlanta.

He can be reached via email at `mark@wutka.com`. You can also visit his company Web site at `http://www.wutka.com`.

Dedication

To my Mom, Dr. Patricia Brown Graham

It is both an honor and an absolute joy to be your son and friend.

Acknowledgments

Writing a book like this is more than just a team effort. The team members are more than just the people whose names you see in the credits, they are also our family and friends.

The first person I would like to thank is you, the reader. Without you, there would be no need for this book. I sincerely hope that you enjoy and learn from this book, and that you find it useful enough to refer to it frequently.

I can't give enough thanks to my wife, Ceal. You have put up with me all these years and supported me in everything I do. Your love and encouragement help me get through every day.

I owe such a huge debt to my Mom for all that she has done for me. She always gave me encouragement and served as a wonderful role model. While I was working all day and writing in my spare time, my Mom was making me look like a slacker by working, writing a book, *and* writing her dissertation. I can't say enough to thank you, but…thank you! Thank you also to Dr. John Graham for supporting both of us!

I'd like to thank several of my colleagues, my two technical editors, Cliff McCartney and Chuck Cavaness, foremost. I really appreciate having two top-notch gurus to bounce ideas off of. It's like having a personal think-tank. Thanks to Mike "Dot-Com" Connor for his suggestions and also for several of the menu images I used in the book. I'd also like to thank Joe Weber for his excellent input on the original outline for this book. I put a lot of stock in what Joe says.

The folks at Que have been a pleasure to work with. I'd especially like to thank Todd Green, who probably thinks by now that I don't know how to read a calendar; Hugh Vandivier, who probably thinks I don't know how to work a fax machine; Julie McNamee; Lauren Dixon; and Tricia Sterling. I know there are a lot more people working on this book that I have never talked to and whose names I don't know. Thank you, too. I couldn't have done any of this if it weren't for you folks.

Finally, I would just like to say: Mandus Eats It! Thank you.

Tell Us What You Think!

As the reader of this book, *you* are our most important critic and commentator. We value your opinion and want to know what we're doing right, what we could do better, what areas you'd like to see us publish in, and any other words of wisdom you're willing to pass our way.

As an Associate Publisher for Que, I welcome your comments. You can fax, email, or write me directly to let me know what you did or didn't like about this book—as well as what we can do to make our books stronger.

Please note that I cannot help you with technical problems related to the topic of this book, and that due to the high volume of mail I receive, I might not be able to reply to every message.

When you write, please be sure to include this book's title and author as well as your name and phone or fax number. I will carefully review your comments and share them with the author and editors who worked on the book.

Fax: 317-581-4666

Email: `quetechnical@mcp.com`

Mail: Associate Publisher
Que
201 West 103rd Street
Indianapolis, IN 46290 USA

INTRODUCTION

In this introduction

WHO SHOULD BUY THIS BOOK

Special Edition Using Java Server Pages and Servlets represents a fairly unique approach to Java Server Pages and servlets. You'll find that most books focus on one or the other, but few, if any, present JSP and servlets as a pair of cooperating technologies. Java Server Pages are great for some aspects of Web design, while servlets are better for others. This book shows you how to use Java Server Pages and servlets in tandem with each other, enabling each technology to do what it does best.

If you are a Web designer with some knowledge of Java programming, this book will help you apply your Java knowledge to server-side programming. You can make Web pages that are mostly HTML with a smattering of Java here and there to include dynamic content. By including custom tag libraries, you can even make Java Server Pages without coding a single line of Java.

If you are a software developer looking to write Web applications, this book will speed you on your way. You will learn how to display Web pages, interact with a database, and even use Enterprise Java Beans to get the content you want to display. If you want to write XML, *Special Edition Using Java Server Pages and Servlets* shows you how. You'll not only see how to generate XML, but also how to write servlets that accept XML files—a handy way to conduct business-to-business communications.

If you are a software architect looking to see how Java Server Pages and servlets fit in to an application architecture, this book explains the common uses of servlets and Java Server Pages and how these technologies fit in with common infrastructure components such as CORBA, RMI, and EJB. When you finish with this book, you'll know how to put JSP and servlets to their best use within your architecture and how to tailor your architecture to get the best results from JSP and servlets.

If you don't know Java at all, this is not the book for you. This book assumes that you know at least some Java. If you only know a little Java, you can get by pretty well if you stick to Java Server Pages. After you get more comfortable with Java and you know how to create classes and compile them, you can start creating servlets.

HOW THIS BOOK IS ORGANIZED

PART I: BASIC SERVLETS AND JAVA SERVER PAGES

The first 10 chapters are your basic training. When you finish these chapters, you'll know almost everything you need to know when you create servlets and Java Server Pages. The key concepts introduced in this first part are applied throughout the rest of the book. What you learn first will constantly be reinforced.

Part II: Core Components In-Depth

This part gives you more background into servlets and Java Server Pages. Part I shows you how to do things, Part II shows you why things work the way they do and gives you a deeper understanding of the major parts of JSP and servlets.

Part III: Java Web Application Architecture

Part III takes your newfound knowledge of JSP and servlets and begins to apply it to various applications. You'll learn how to use a database to get data for your servlets and Java Server Pages. You'll see how to access CORBA and RMI-based application servers. You'll even see how to access Enterprise Java Beans. If you aren't familiar with some of the higher-level application design concepts, you'll learn some of those, too.

Part IV: Taking JSP and Servlets Beyond HTML

Part IV shows you that JSP and servlets aren't just for HTML pages. You'll see how to create XML documents with JSP and servlets, and how to receive XML files. You'll also learn how to use JSP and servlets to create an application for the wireless Web. You'll even see how to use JSP and servlets to do server-side image processing, something you don't see very often.

Part V: Advanced Techniques

Part V covers some of the more advanced topics that you don't encounter as often. You'll see how to package your Web applications to make them easy to install. You'll also learn how to create new tags that can be used in a JSP. With enough custom tags, you can write a JSP without a single line of Java code! Part V also covers some of the security features of JSP and servlets and also touches on internationalization.

Appendixes

Appendixes A, "JSP Syntax and API Reference," and B, "Servlet API Reference," give you a handy API reference guide to the entire JSP and servlet API. Appendix A also summarizes the JSP syntax. Appendixes C, "Apache and Tomcat," D, "JRun," E, "ServletExec," and F, "Resin," show you how to install and configure several popular JSP and servlet engines.

Conventions Used in This Book

This book uses the following typographic conventions to make reading easier:

- New terms appear in *italic*. The *italic* attribute also is used for emphasis.
- All code listings and commands appear in a special `monospace` font.
- Replaceable elements and placeholders use *`italic monospace`*.
- The **`bold`** attribute is used for the text you type at the command prompt or into text boxes.

- In those occasions when a line of code is too long to fit on one line of this book, it is broken at a convenient place and continued on the next line. A code continuation character (➥) precedes the continuation of a line of code. (At the command prompt, you should type a line of code that includes this character as one long line, without breaking it.)

Note

Notes explain interesting or important points that can help you understand significant concepts and techniques.

Tip

Tips describe shortcuts and alternative approaches to gaining an objective. Tips often help you in real-world situations.

Caution

Cautions appear where an action might lead to an unexpected or unpredictable result, including possible loss of data or other serious consequences.

Most chapters contain a "Troubleshooting" section in which you can find answers to problems that can arise.

PART I

Basic Java Server Pages

CHAPTER 1

The Evolution of the Web Server

In this chapter

It has been a long journey from the original Web page to Java Server Pages. This chapter gives you a brief overview of the evolution of the Web server and Web programming. If you are really anxious to jump into JSP programming, skip ahead to Chapter 2, "Getting Started with Java Server Pages," because this chapter doesn't introduce any technical details required for the rest of the book. It is nice, however, to understand how things came to be the way they are.

THE BASIC WEB SERVER

Originally, the World Wide Web was a network of hypertext pages. Back when the Web was born, "hypertext" was one of the big industry buzzwords. All the computer magazines were calling hypertext a revolution. I must confess that when I first read descriptions of hypertext I thought it was really neat, but I never imagined that anything like the Web would come along. Fortunately, Tim Berners-Lee and the rest of the folks at CERN, the European nuclear research organization in Switzerland, had the vision to turn hypertext into a world-changing phenomenon.

The beauty of the Web lies in its simplicity. At its core, the Web consists of a browser requesting files from one or more servers using a simple protocol. The key is that the user doesn't need to know where the files are. The browser keeps track of where to fetch the files. Figure 1.1 shows an example of the interaction between a browser and some Web servers.

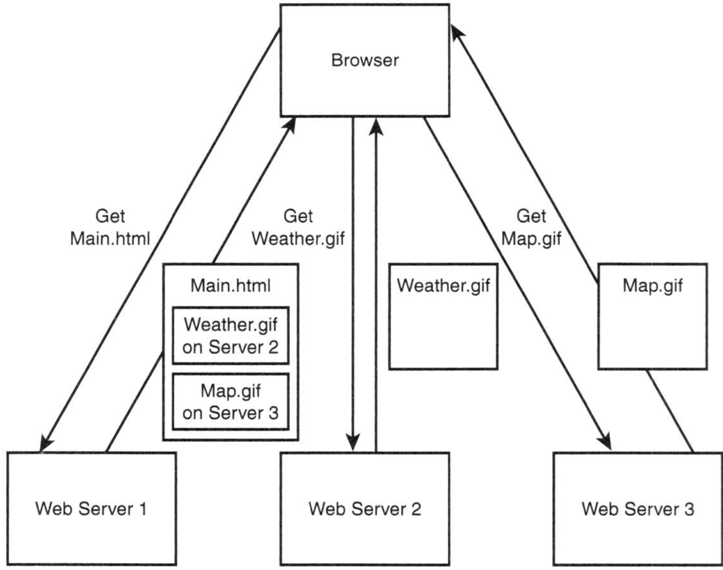

Figure 1.1
The browser fetches pages and images from different servers.

Originally, Web pages were mostly text files with occasional images. Although there were some graphical browsers, text-only browsers were more popular because most Web users were using text terminals. The original Web servers only needed to serve up these pages, and thus were little more than simple file servers. Even today, the vast majority of Web access is still based on fetching files from the server and displaying them.

CGI: THE COMMON GATEWAY INTERFACE

Although hypertext is a key component in the success of the Web, the capability to create interactive forms certainly enhances its popularity. Of course, to accept input from a form, the Web server must do more than just serve files. It must be able to receive the data entered in the form, process it, and return results.

The tricky part of form handling is that the Web server needs to handle new input forms with a minimum of effort. It would be quite difficult to change the Web server every time a new form was added, so the original Web pioneers came up with a simple way to handle forms: the Web server now launched an external program to handle a form.

Had the original Web server been written for Microsoft Windows, it might have used a dynamic link library (DLL) to handle forms. Windows programs frequently rely on DLLs to load code dynamically at runtime. As it was, most Web servers were originally written for Unix, where spawning an external program is a common way to handle network operations. The Web server just needed a way to pass the data from the form to the external program, giving rise to the Common Gateway Interface, or CGI. CGI is still one of the most common ways of handling forms and generating dynamic content.

The basic feature of CGI is that information from the Web server is passed to the external program through environment variables. When the browser sends a form to the Web server, it adds the values of the various form fields to the end of the URL specified in the form's `ACTION` field. For example, consider the HTML form shown in Figure 1.2.

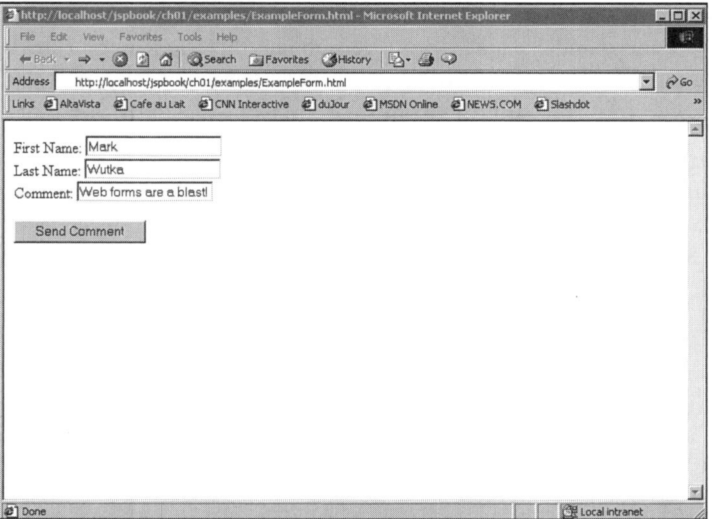

Figure 1.2
A Web form has data fields that must be sent to the server.

The HTML source for the form is shown in Listing 1.1.

LISTING 1.1 SOURCE CODE FOR ExampleForm.html

```
<html>
<body bgcolor="#ffffff">
<form action="HandleExampleForm.jsp" method="get">
First Name: <input type="text" name="firstname"><br>
Last Name: <input type="text" name="lastname"><br>
Comment: <input type="text" name="comment"><br>
<p>
<input type="submit" value="Send Comment">
</body>
</html>
```

When the user clicks the Send Comment button, the browser first performs a special encoding on the values in the form variables to restrict them to a limited character set. The encoding for the form shown in Figure 1.2 would look like this:

```
http://localhost/jspbook/ch01/examples/HandleExampleForm.jsp?
firstname=Mark&lastname=Wutka&comment=Web+forms+are+a+blast%21
```

When the Web server runs the form handler, it sets a number of environment variables, including one called `QUERY_STRING`. The `QUERY_STRING` variable contains the encoded form variables passed by the browser. Most CGI libraries now contain routines to parse the `QUERY_STRING` variable and extract the individual form variables.

After the form handler starts, the Web server takes the output from the form handler and passes it back to the browser. The form handler can use simple print statements to send its results back, as if it were writing the results to the screen. The Web server is able to capture this output and redirect it back to the browser. Figure 1.3 illustrates how the Web server exchanges data with a CGI program.

A limitation is involved in sending a form to the server. Namely, many browsers and Web servers cannot handle a URL over a certain length. The general rule of thumb is that the total length of the URL cannot be longer than about 4 kilobytes. To send more than 4KB, the browser must transmit the form variables using a slightly different method.

Normally, the browser sends a form to the server using a command called `GET`, which is also the command used to display a normal Web page or an image. Remember, the Web server is usually acting like a file server, and the `GET` command asks the server to get a file. The Web server also supports a command called `POST`, which expects the browser to send the additional form data in a different format. The browser does not set the `QUERY_STRING` variable when performing a `POST`.

When a form is sent using `POST` instead of `GET`, the CGI form handler must read the form variables as if they were typed in from the keyboard. As it does with the output, the Web server redirects the data from the browser to make it appear like keyboard input. Again, most CGI libraries are able to parse the posted data into individual variables.

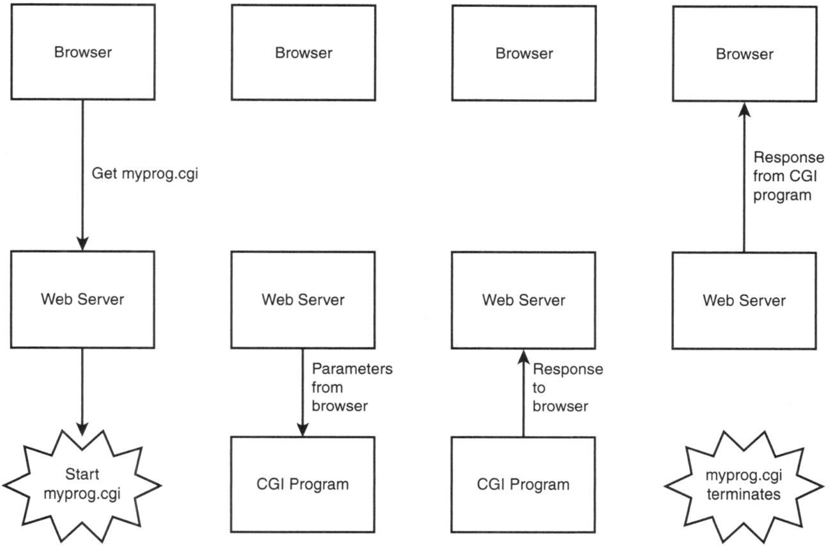

Figure 1.3 The Web server starts a CGI program, passes it data, and sends the program's output back to the browser.

NSAPI, ISAPI, AND OTHER LOADABLE MODULES

Although CGI is flexible, it does have one major limitation: Spawning an external program is an expensive process. The Netscape Web server introduced a much faster alternative to CGI, called the Netscape Server API, or NSAPI. Essentially, NSAPI uses the dynamic link library concept often used in Windows programs. Typical NSAPI libraries are written in C, using a well-defined set of functions.

After it's loaded, the NSAPI library acts like part of the Web server. The advantage over CGI is that the Web server doesn't have to wait for another program to start up, and it can pass in the form variables as parameters to a function rather than stuffing them into an environment variable. One of the hazards of NSAPI is that an NSAPI library can cause the Web server to crash if it has a severe bug. If a CGI program crashes, it affects only the user who was running the CGI. The Web server recognizes that the CGI program crashed and returns an error message. When an NSAPI library causes a Web server to crash, it affects all users of the Web server because they won't get any response from the server.

Because NSAPI requires a dynamic link library, only a limited number of languages can be used to create an NSAPI library. This makes it more difficult to write the form handler in a common scripting language such as Perl or Python. Figure 1.4 illustrates how the Web server interacts with an NSAPI library.

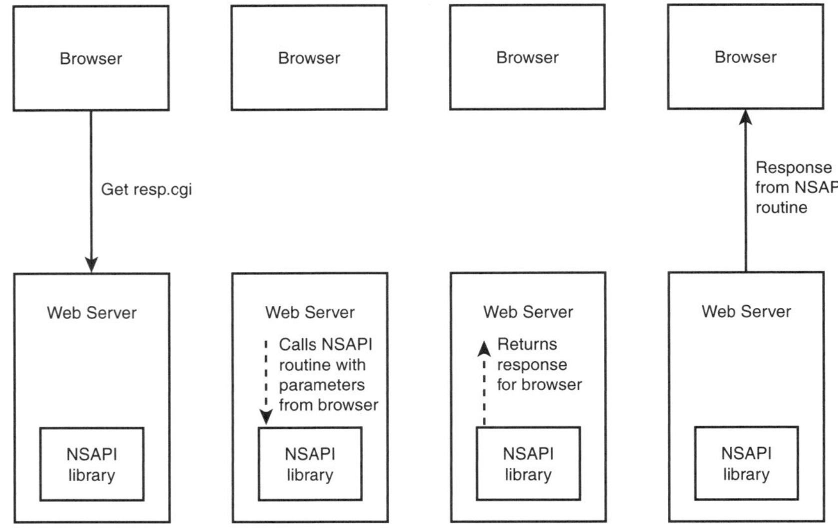

Figure 1.4
An NSAPI routine runs as part of the Web server.

Microsoft's Web server, Internet Information Server (IIS), has its own equivalent to NSAPI, called the IIS Server API, or ISAPI. Although it is functionally the same as NSAPI, ISAPI is a little more flexible in the number of languages it supports. You can, for example, write ISAPI form handlers in Visual Basic or in Microsoft's flavor of Java.

The Apache Web server, currently the most popular Web server on the Internet, has the capability to run Perl programs, without starting an external process, through an extension called `mod_perl`. Perl has long been a popular language for writing CGI programs. `mod_perl` helps make Apache an attractive platform for Web developers.

Recently, there has been an alternative to the proprietary NSAPI and ISAPI APIs. Building on the basic concept of CGI, the FastCGI protocol defines a method for CGI programs to run continuously, rather than starting up for every request. Basically, the Web server starts the FastCGI program the first time it is accessed, and afterwards the Web server passes form variables and other information to the FastCGI program using a network connection. When the FastCGI program has finished processing the request and sent a response to the browser, it waits for another request. The next time a request comes in, the FastCGI program is already running and can handle the request much faster than if it had been a regular CGI program. Figure 1.5 shows how the Web server interacts with a FastCGI program.

While FastCGI appears to solve some of the problems of CGI, it introduces some additional problems. First, FastCGI is not an accepted standard. Although standardization is not a requirement, the presence of a standard often encourages multiple implementations, giving you a better choice of software vendors.

Second, you can't really take advantage of multiple execution threads. Each FastCGI server program can handle a single request at a time. While the architecture allows you to spawn multiple copies of a server, the server itself is somewhat limited. You end up wasting memory by starting a separate server.

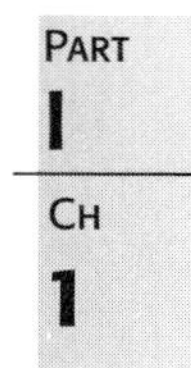

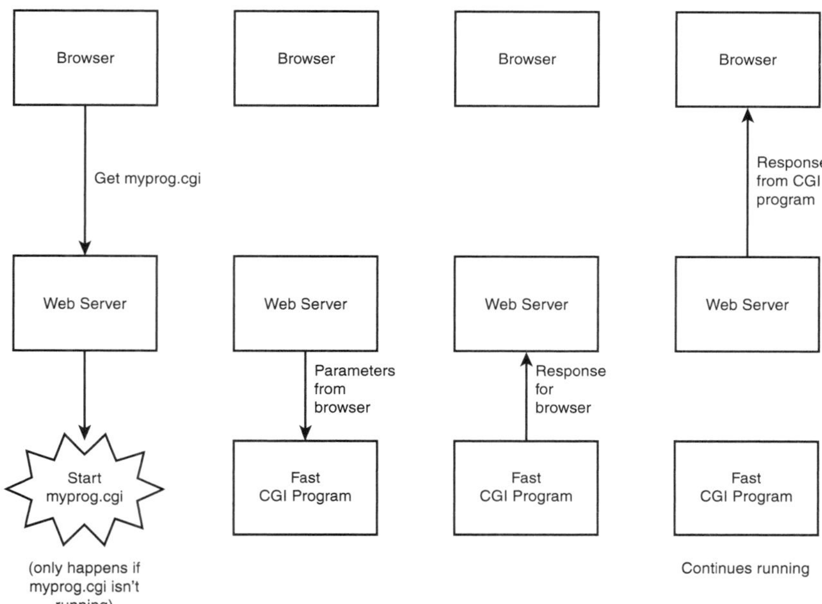

Figure 1.5
A FastCGI program continues to run after handling a request.

ACTIVE SERVER PAGES

Active Server Pages (ASP) represents a departure from the traditional way of processing Web forms and generating dynamic content. The difference between ASP and its predecessors is that an Active Server Page is a Web page with code embedded inside it that runs on the Web server. If you've ever written a CGI program, you know that generating well-designed Web pages is a tedious task.

Like many programmers, I am terrible at designing a Web page that is pleasing to the eye. My brain just doesn't see things the way some of the more artistically inclined people do. When a company wants professional-looking Web pages, it typically hires graphics design people to lay out the Web site and the individual Web pages. Many times, these designers use a Web editor that shows the pages as they would appear on the browser. When the page needs to display information that comes from a CGI program, the CGI programmer must write a program that prints out the same HTML that the graphics designer originally created. Not only is this a tedious process, but when the designers change the page, incorporating those changes into the CGI program is just plain depressing.

Other more resourceful programmers have written complex filtering programs that allow their CGI programs to use the original pages from the designers. The filters insert the dynamically generated information where it is needed. Although these filters help relieve some of the pain of CGI, they still fall short of the mark.

Active Server Pages solve the problem of mixing graphics design with Web programming in a unique way. Through the use of special HTML tags, you can insert VBScript or JavaScript code into the Web page for execution on the server. Many Web page editors recognize the Active Server Page tags and ignore them when rendering a page on the screen. Now the graphics designers can hand off a Web page to the programmers who insert the Active Server Page code. If the designers need to make changes, they can edit the page without harming the existing ASP code, making maintenance of the Web page considerably easier.

Note

The Active Server Pages processor uses the Active Scripting API when executing ASP code. Any language that supports this Active Scripting API can be used within an Active Server Page. There is a version of Perl for the Windows platform that supports the Active Scripting API and can be run within Active Server Pages.

Microsoft wisely gave Active Server Pages the capability to access databases and communicate with other applications within the Web server. You can do almost everything with an ASP page that you can with a CGI program. Also, because the ASP processor runs within the Web server, you get all the speed benefits of the dynamic library solutions such as NSAPI and ISAPI. The speed benefits of running the ASP code within the Web server are offset somewhat by the fact that the code typically runs through an interpreter as opposed to being compiled ahead of time.

Being interpreted at runtime is a hindrance to Active Server Pages from a performance standpoint, but when it comes to development, it's a real boon. When you develop an ASP, you can edit it, save it, and immediately run it. There is no compilation involved, so the development cycle is much shorter.

One aspect of Active Server Pages proves to be a real hindrance to its general acceptance: ASP is available only on Microsoft's IIS Web server. In fairness, non-Windows versions of ASP are available from other companies, but these versions are not typically available from major Web providers.

SERVLETS

After Java came on the scene, Sun needed a way to support Web server development. Although Java made its initial splash as a tool for enhancing the Web browser, it was obvious that Java would be quite useful on the server. Unfortunately, Java and CGI didn't mix well. For one thing, spawning an external program meant starting the Java Virtual Machine, and that could be an expensive process in terms of memory and CPU time. Also, Java had no standard way to fetch environment variables, so a Java program couldn't even see the `QUERY_STRING` environment variable.

Sun attacked this problem head-on by developing a Web server in Java. After a Web server was created that was Java friendly, it was simple to make a Java class that could handle form input. Because Java had the notion of an *applet*, which was like a little piece of an application, Sun created the *servlet*, which is a little piece of a server.

A servlet can do everything that a CGI program can, but because it runs inside the Java Virtual Machine along with the Web server itself, it does not require the spawning of an external program. Because Java has the capability to load classes at runtime, the servlets can be loaded when needed.

Sun also had the foresight to design the servlet API so that it is not tied specifically to the HTTP protocol used by Web browsers and servers. Instead, Sun created a generic servlet API and a specialized subclass called `HttpServlet`. As other forms of client-server protocols come along that fit into the servlet architecture, Sun can add other specialized servlet classes to handle those protocols. Figure 1.6 illustrates how a Java Web server interacts with a servlet.

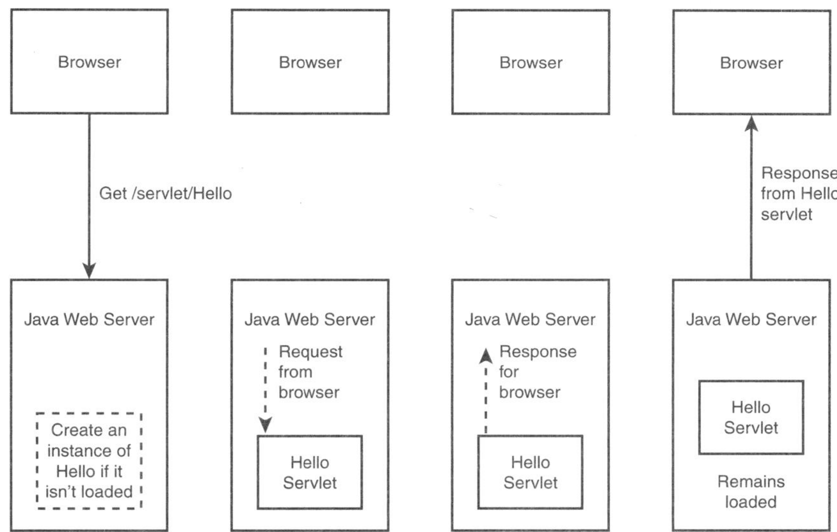

Figure 1.6
A servlet looks just like another Java class to a Java Web server.

Several companies offer Servlet implementations that plug into existing Web servers. Typically 100% of Java Web servers are not as fast as Web servers written in C or C++—at least not yet. Although it is possible to make a Web server extension that runs a servlet within the same process as the Web server, most implementations tend to run the servlet engine as a separate process and use a network protocol to communicate with the server. Figure 1.7 shows a typical servlet engine implementation.

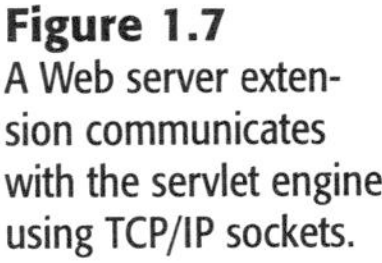

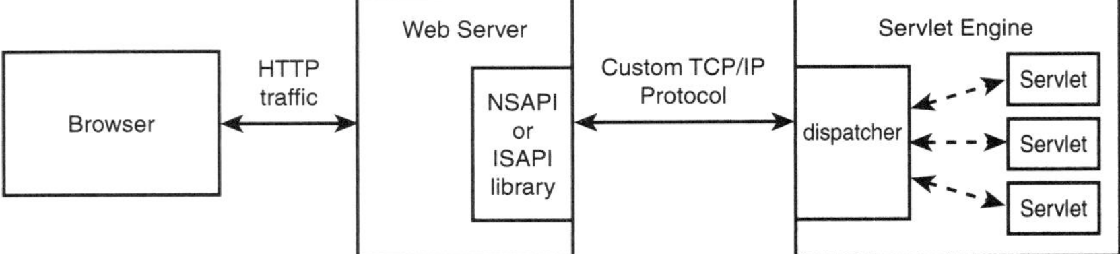

Figure 1.7
A Web server extension communicates with the servlet engine using TCP/IP sockets.

XML AND XSL STYLESHEETS

Within the past few years, the Extensible Markup Language (XML) has been gaining popularity. XML provides a framework for standardizing the way data is represented. Although XML does not specifically say how to represent data items, such as an employee or an invoice, it does provide a standard way to read and write these data items.

In the past, you might store employee information as a record in a file containing a long sequence of characters. Maybe the first 30 characters are the name, followed by 10 characters representing the phone number, and so on. Unfortunately, other companies probably represent an employee record with a slightly different format. XML defines a standard way for you to specify the data items contained in an employee object. For example, you might define an employee like this:

```
<employee>
   <first-name>Mark</first-name>
   <last-name>Wutka</last-name>
   <employee-number>123456789</employee-number>
</employee>
```

Of course, other companies might choose different names for the fields, but you can at least write a program that can read in all the fields without worrying about any custom formats. As XML matures, standards will develop that define the structure of commonly used data items.

When it comes to Web programming, you can use a special formatting language called XSL (Extensible Stylesheet Language). The idea is that instead of writing programs that generate HTML, you write programs that generate XML. An XSL file tells the browser how to format the XML that your program generates.

At the moment, most browsers do not understand XSL. Instead, special translation programs on the server perform the conversion automatically and send HTML back to the browser. The combination of XML and XSL allows Web programmers to concentrate on getting the correct data and allows graphics designers to concentrate on a pleasing stylesheet.

One of the drawbacks of the XML/XSL combination is that you end up generating XML that is passed to another program that must parse the XML and then process it. If you already have a representation of the data in your program, it would be better if you could generate HTML directly from that internal representation rather than sending it to another program.

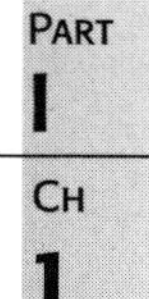

JAVA SERVER PAGES

Sun saw that ASP was a good idea and decided that a Java version of ASP would be useful. Java Server Pages provide many of the same capabilities as Active Server Pages, but have distinct differences:

- Java Server Pages are available on non-Windows platforms and in greater numbers than the non-Windows ASP implementations.
- The current JSP implementation is limited to Java as a scripting language. The design of JSP does allow for other scripting languages to be supported in the future, however.
- JSP enables you to create new tags that are understood by the JSP processor, allowing you to extend the language itself.

If your company is moving toward XML, you can generate XML from a Java Server Page and then pass that XML to an XSL formatter. JSP offers some interesting formatting possibilities, however, that would enable you to keep your data in its original form instead of transforming it into XML.

One of the strengths of Java Server Pages is that they are compiled into servlets. If you already know the servlet API, you don't have to learn much more to do Java Server Pages. Java Server Pages and servlets can also interact easily. Of course, there is much more to learn about JSP and servlets, and that's what this book is all about.

CHAPTER 2

Getting Started with Java Server Pages

In this chapter

A "HELLO WORLD" JAVA SERVER PAGE

Java Server Pages are, in the most basic sense, Web pages with embedded Java code. The embedded Java code is executed on the server before the page is returned to the browser. If a picture is worth a thousand words, in this case an example is worth a thousand explanations. Listing 2.1 shows a basic Java Server Page.

LISTING 2.1 `HelloWorld.jsp`

```
<HTML>
<BODY>
<%
    out.println("<H1>Hello World!</H1>");
%>
</BODY>
</HTML>
```

Although you can probably guess what the browser will display when this page runs, Figure 2.1 should remove any doubt since it shows the output from this page.

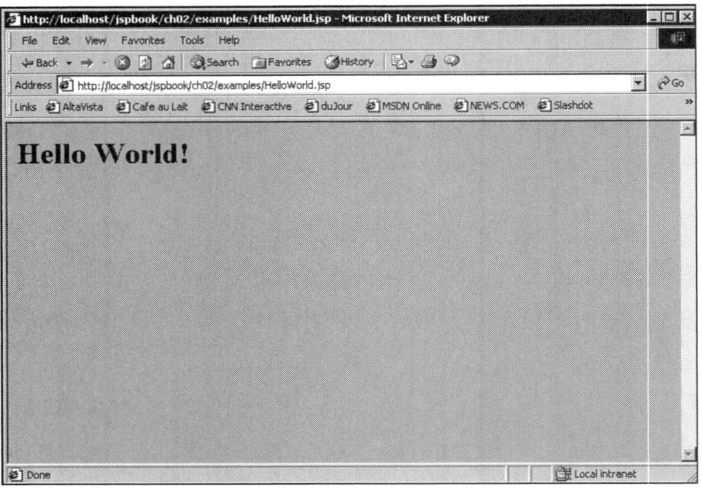

Figure 2.1
A Java Server Page can generate HTML output.

Note

If you want to try out the "Hello World" Java Server Page, treat it like an HTML page. Put it in the same place that you would put an HTML page and point your browser to it. You will also need to install a JSP engine like Tomcat or Resin. See Appendixes C-F for instructions on installing a JSP engine.

If you are having trouble displaying the "Hello World" JSP, refer to the "Troubleshooting" section at the end of this chapter.

When the browser asks the Web server for a Java Server Page, the Web server invokes the JSP engine. This JSP engine converts the Java Server Page into a servlet that displays the HTML code in your JSP file and executes any of the Java code embedded in the JSP file.

After the code has been translated, the JSP engine compiles the servlet, loads it automatically, and then executes it. Typically, the JSP engine checks to see whether there is already a servlet for a JSP file and whether the modification date on the JSP is older than the servlet. If the JSP is older than its generated servlet, the JSP engine assumes that the JSP hasn't changed and that the generated servlet still matches the contents of the JSP. Because it takes some time to generate a servlet and compile it, the JSP engine wants to minimize the number of compiles it has to perform, so it tries to avoid unnecessary compiles.

The other interesting piece of this equation is the actual HTML code that was sent to the browser. Most browsers enable you to view the HTML source for the Web page you are viewing. Listing 2.2 shows you the HTML code generated by the JSP in Listing 2.1.

LISTING 2.2 HTML SOURCE CODE FOR `HelloWorld.jsp`

```
<HTML>
<BODY>
<H1>Hello World!</H1>

</BODY>
</HTML>
```

As you can see, the text from the `out.println` statement in the JSP file is inserted directly into the HTML output. Of course, printing out a text string is not a practical use for JSP. Typically, you want to print out things that might change every time you run the JSP. The current time and date are trivial examples of items more suited for a JSP.

The `out` object used to write the "Hello World" string is an object of type `JspWriter`. For now, you just need to know that this `out` object has approximately the same methods as `PrintWriter`, which is similar to the older `PrintStream` class. There are `print` and `println` methods for writing out various types of data. One word of caution, however, `JspWriter` is neither a `PrintStream` nor a `PrintWriter`, so you cannot pass the `out` object to methods that expect either of those two classes. You'll learn more about the `JspWriter` object in Chapter 14, "Core Java Server Page Components."

When the browser asks the Web server for HelloWorld.jsp, the JSP engine (the software responsible for handling Java Server Pages) first checks to see if HelloWorld.jsp has already been compiled into a servlet. If not, it creates a servlet that prints out the HTML in your JSP file and executes the code contained within the JSP file. Listing 2.3 shows the portion of the generated servlet that produces the HTML code in Listing 2.2.

LISTING 2.3 JAVA CODE TO PRODUCE THE HTML FROM LISTING 2.2

```
// begin
out.write("<HTML>\r\n<BODY>\r\n");
// end
// begin
[file="D:\\ch02\\examples\\HelloWorld.jsp";from=(2,2);to=(4,0)]
out.println("<H1>Hello World!</H1>");
// end
// begin
out.write("\r\n</BODY>\r\n</HTML>\r\n");
// end
```

Typically, you won't need to look at the generated servlet; however,sometimes it is useful. If your JSP throws an exception and you print out the Java stack trace from the exception, the line numbers displayed in the stack trace will be line numbers from the generated servlet. There is no standard indicating where the generated servlets must be placed. It varies from JSP engine to JSP engine.

USING THE <% %> TAGS IN A JAVA SERVER PAGE

As you saw in the HelloWorld.jsp example, the `<%` and `%>` tags in a JSP file are used to indicate the presence of Java code within the HTML. The JSP specification allows for languages other than Java to be used for scripting. At the present time, few servers support languages other than Java; however, eventually there will be more support for other scripting languages. Until that time, and certainly for the rest of this book, the focus is on Java as the JSP scripting language.

Note The Resin JSP engine from Caucho, discussed in Appendix F, "Resin," has support for using JavaScript in a JSP instead of Java.

You can intermix the `<%` and `%>` tags with other HTML tags in just about any combination you can think of. The rules are simple. Any text outside the `<%` and `%>` tags is rendered verbatim. Any Java code within the `<%` and `%>` tags is executed. If you want to generate HTML from the Java code between the `<%` and `%>` tags, use the `out` variable, which is a `JspWriter` object. Listing 2.4 shows a somewhat ridiculous example of mixing the `<%` and `%>` tags with regular HTML.

LISTING 2.4 SOURCE CODE FOR `Greeting.jsp`

```
<HTML>
<BODY>
Good
<%
    java.util.Calendar currTime = new java.util.GregorianCalendar();
    if (currTime.get(currTime.HOUR_OF_DAY) < 12)
    {
%>
        Morning!
<%
    }
    else if (currTime.get(currTime.HOUR_OF_DAY) < 18)
    {
%>
        Afternoon!
<%
    }
    else
    {
%>
        Evening!
<%
    }
%>
```

```
</BODY>
</HTML>
```

If you are totally unfamiliar with either Active Server Pages or Java Server Pages, the code in Listing 2.4 probably looks absolutely bizarre to you. First, remember that the code outside of the `<% %>` tag pair is sent verbatim. Of course, that might lead you to conclude that the three strings, `Morning!`, `Afternoon!`, and `Evening!`, should all be sent in the response. What really happens is that items outside of the `<% %>` tag pair are converted into Java statements that print out the HTML verbatim. Because the `Morning!`, `Afternoon!`, and `Evening!` strings occur within an `if` statement, they are only printed when their section of the `if` block is true.

Note

Listing 2.4 deliberately avoids importing `java.util.*` just to keep the example simple. Importing Java packages is discussed in Chapter 10, "Performance," but if you can't wait, the syntax for importing `java.util.*` is `<%@ page language="java" import="java.util.*" %>`.

Listing 2.5 shows you a portion of the Java code generated by the JSP in Listing 2.4. (Don't worry, you won't have to look at the Java code for every JSP in this book, or even in this chapter.)

LISTING 2.5 JAVA CODE GENERATED BY LISTING 2.4

```
// begin
    out.write("<HTML>\r\n<BODY>\r\nGood\r\n");
// end
// begin [file="D:\\ch02\\examples\\Greeting.jsp";from=(3,2);to=(8,0)]
    java.util.Calendar currTime = new java.util.GregorianCalendar();
    if (currTime.get(currTime.HOUR_OF_DAY) < 12)
    {
// end
// begin
        out.write("\r\n\t\tMorning!\r\n");
// end
// begin
[file="D:\\ch02\\examples\\Greeting.jsp";from=(10,2);to=(14,0)]
    }
    else if (currTime.get(currTime.HOUR_OF_DAY) < 18)
    {
// end
// begin
        out.write("\r\n\t\tAfternoon!\r\n");
// end
// begin
[file="D:\\ch02\\examples\\Greeting.jsp";from=(16,2);to=(20,0)]
    }
    else
    {
// end
// begin
        out.write("\r\n\t\tEvening!\r\n");
```

LISTING 2.5 CONTINUED

```
// end
// begin
[file="D:\\ch02\\examples\\Greeting.jsp";from=(22,2);to=(24,0)]
    }
// end
// begin
    out.write("\r\n</BODY>\r\n</HTML>\r\n\r\n\r\n");
// end
```

The Java code in Listing 2.5 looks ugly, and those `//begin` and `//end` comments make it tough to read. After you start comparing it to Listing 2.4, you should begin to get the idea of how the `<% %>` tags relate to the rest of the file.

> **Tip**
>
> It's easier to read through a JSP if you remember that any text outside of the `<%` and `%>` tags is really just shorthand for an `out.write` statement containing that text.

When I referred to Listing 2.4 as a ridiculous example, I meant that it is fairly difficult to follow and not a good example of how to make a clear, readable JSP file. It does, of course, show you how `<% %>` and HTML text can be intermixed.

DISPLAYING A VALUE WITH <%= %>

The earlier example in Listing 2.4 could have been written in a much more compact way that determined the time of day first and printed out its greeting near the end of the file. Listing 2.6 shows a much more compact version.

LISTING 2.6 SOURCE CODE FOR `Greeting2.jsp`

```
<HTML>
<BODY>
<%
    java.util.Calendar currTime = new java.util.GregorianCalendar();

    String timeOfDay = "";

    if (currTime.get(currTime.HOUR_OF_DAY) < 12)
    {
        timeOfDay = "Morning!";
    }
    else if (currTime.get(currTime.HOUR_OF_DAY) < 18)
    {
        timeOfDay = "Afternoon!";
    }
    else
    {
        timeOfDay = "Evening!";
    }
%>
Good <% out.write(timeOfDay); %>
```

```
</BODY>
</HTML>
```

As you can see, Listing 2.6 is much easier to read because it doesn't jump back and forth between Java and HTML so rapidly. Down at the bottom of the file, you can see where the `timeOfDay` variable is written out as part of the display. Notice that even though it is a single statement on the same line as some HTML text, `out.write(timeOfDay)` must still end with a semicolon because it must be a legal Java statement.

JSP provides a shorthand for printing out variables to save you from having to put `out.write()` all over the place. The line that prints out the greeting in Listing 2.6 can be replaced with the following line:

```
Good <%= timeOfDay %>
```

The `<%=` tag indicates that you want to write out a Java expression as part of the output sent back to the browser. Notice that you still close the tag with `%>` and not `=%>`. You can include any Java expression; just make sure you don't put a semicolon after the expression. The following line shows you a more complex expression:

```
<%= 2*3+4-5*6+7*8-9 %>
```

As you can see, it's just as valid to print out a numerical expression as it is to print out a string. In fact, you can also print out an entire object. For example, you can print out the string representation of a calendar object using the following line:

```
<%= new java.util.GregorianCalendar() %>
```

Of course, the result of printing out an object might not be what you expect. Figure 2.2 shows how the `GregorianCalendar` object looks when displayed using the `<%=` tag.

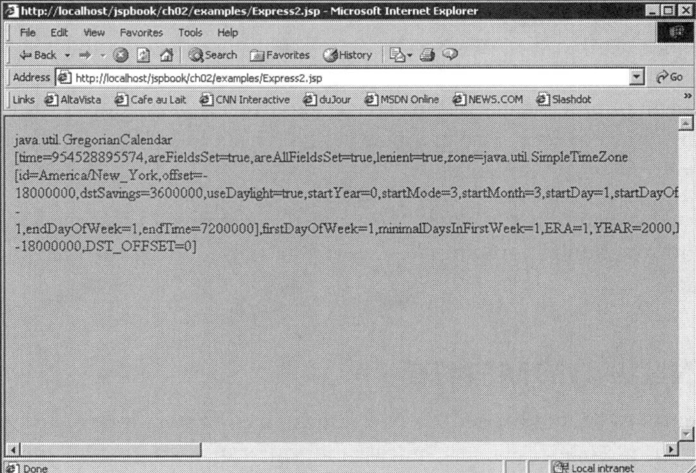

Figure 2.2
The `<%=` tag can print out an entire object.

Note

Make sure you don't put any space between the `<%` and the = sign.

When you display an object using the <%= tag, the result is the same kind of output you would see if you wrote out the object to `System.out` in a regular program. Basically, the output routine calls the `toString` method in the object and displays the results of the method call.

Tip

> Anything you put between the <%= and %> ends up inside an `out.write()` expression. In other words, think of <%= as shorthand for `out.write(` and its closing %> as shorthand for `);`.

Listing 2.7 shows a somewhat more practical combination of <% and <%= to display the current date.

LISTING 2.7 SOURCE CODE FOR ShowDate.jsp

```
<HTML>
<BODY>
<% java.util.Calendar currDate = new java.util.GregorianCalendar();
// add 1 to month because Calendar's months start at 0, not 1
   int month = currDate.get(currDate.MONTH)+1;
   int day = currDate.get(currDate.DAY_OF_MONTH);
   int year = currDate.get(currDate.YEAR);
%>
The current date is: <%= month %>/<%= day %>/<%= year %>
</BODY>
</HTML>
```

The <%= tag is often useful when graphics designers are creating the Web page and Web programmers are adding the server-side Java code. Typically, the Web programmers encase their code in <% %> tags somewhere near the beginning of the JSP file. They put all the interesting data (the data interesting to the graphics designers) into Java variables. Then, the graphics designers can lay out the page the way they want it and use the <%= %> tags to insert the data where they want without having to write any Java code. Listing 2.7 is a basic example of this very concept. The graphics designers can insert the `month`, `day`, and `year` variables anywhere they want.

As you will see later in this book, there are additional ways that the Web programmers can supply information for graphics designers when different groups must maintain the same JSP page.

INSERTING COMMENTS

Comments are generally used for two things: making notations about the code and removing sections of code. There are at least four different ways to add comments to a Java server page, each with its own advantages and disadvantages. If your JSP is generating HTML, you can use HTML comments, which use the <!-- and --> tags like this:

```
<!-- This is an HTML comment -->
```

In general, only use HTML comments in a JSP if you want the comment to be visible on the browser. Most of the time, you don't care whether the user can see any of your comments, so the HTML comments are usually not used in a Java Server Page. You might find yourself using the HTML comments if you have a large section of HTML in your JSP and you want to remove a section temporarily. Although you could remove it with the JSP comment tags (which you will learn about in a moment), it's nicer to keep the block pure HTML rather than turn it into a mixture of HTML and JSP tags.

Because any code you place inside the <% %> tags is Java code, you can use both of Java's commenting mechanisms. For example, you can do a one-liner comment like this:

```
<% // This is a one-line JSP comment %>
```

You can also use the /* */ comment tags within separate <% %> tag pairs. This method is difficult to follow, and fortunately there is a better way. Here is an example of using the /* and */ comment tags:

```
<% /* %>
  This is actually commented out
<% */ %>
```

Not only is the commenting method confusing, it's also wasteful. When the JSP is compiled into a servlet, the text within the /* */ tags is still converted into Java statements that emit the text. Because the Java statements are surrounded by /* */, they are ignored by the compiler.

Java Server Pages have a special comment tag pair recognized by the JSP compiler. You can surround your comments with <%-- --%> to place a comment in your JSP code. The <%-- --%> prevents text from even being placed into the Java servlet generated by the JSP compiler. Here is an example of a JSP comment:

```
<%-- This comment will not appear in the servlet --%>
```

If you need to remove a section of code from a Java Server Page, the <%-- --%> tags are the best way to do it. They take priority over the other tags. In other words, if a <% %> tag pair occurs within the comment tags, the <% %> tag pair is ignored, as the following example shows:

```
<%--
<%
    out.println("You will never see this.");
%>
--%>
```

Declaring Methods and Variables with <%! %>

So far you have seen how to insert Java statements and Java expressions into your code. In case you haven't realized it yet, all the code within the <% %> tags and all the expressions within the <%= %> tags belong to one big Java method in the generated servlet. That is why you can use the <%= %> tags to display a variable that was declared inside the <% %> tags.

You might want to put an entire Java method into a JSP. If you try to declare a method within the `<% %>` tags, the Java compiler reports an error. After all, Java doesn't like it if you try to declare a method within another method. Use the `<%! %>` tags to enclose any declarations that belong outside the big method that generates the page. Listing 2.8 shows a JSP file that declares a separate method and then uses the `<%= %>` tags to display the result of calling the method.

LISTING 2.8 SOURCE CODE FOR DeclareMethod.jsp

```
<HTML>
<BODY>
<%!
    public String myMethod(String someParameter)
    {
        return "You sent me: "+someParameter;
    }
%>
<%= myMethod("Hi there") %>
</BODY>
</HTML>
```

Since it may not be obvious, Figure 2.3 shows the results of the DeclareMethod.jsp as they are displayed on the browser.

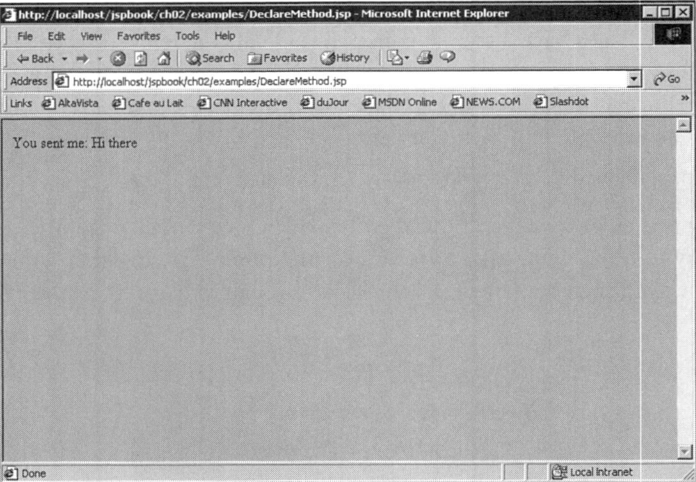

Figure 2.3
You can declare Java methods in a JSP and display results returned by those methods.

Tip

The `out` variable is not available inside any methods you declare using the `<%!` tag. If you need to send data back to the browser from within a method, you must pass the `out` variable in as a parameter of type `JspWriter`.

In addition to declaring methods, you can also use the `<%! %>` tags to declare instance variables. These instance variables are visible to any methods you declare, and also to the code within the `<% %>` tags. Declaring an instance variable is as simple as this:

```
<%! int myInstanceVariable = 10; %>
```

After this variable has been declared, you can use it in other methods declared with `<%! %>` or within the `<% %>` and `<%= %>` tags. For example, you could display the value of `myInstanceVariable` this way:

```
<%
    out.println("myInstanceVariable is "+myInstanceVariable);
%>
```

Likewise, you can display the variable using the `<%= %>` tags this way:

```
MyInstanceVariable is <%= myInstanceVariable %>
```


Note

Several implementations of Java Server Pages still use the older Java Server Pages specification version 0.92. In the older specification, the `<%! %>` tags did not exist. Instead, you had to start the embedded methods and declarations with `<SCRIPT RUNAT=SERVER>` and close them with `</SCRIPT>`.

HANDLING MULTIPLE THREADS IN A JSP

Even though Java is a fairly thread-friendly language, many Java developers are not comfortable dealing with a threaded application. If you are developing Java Server Pages for a production system, you need to become comfortable with threading. By default, the JSP engine assumes that your Java Server Pages are thread-safe and might invoke the same page from multiple threads.

If all your Java code is enclosed within the `<% %>` tags and you don't use any external objects, your code is probably already safe. Remember, because each Java thread has its own execution stack (where local variables are stored), any method that only uses local variables should already be thread-safe. If you do use external variables, or if you declare instance variables with the `<%! %>` tags, you might run into threading issues.

Note

Just in case you're worried, the `JspWriter` class (that is, the `out` variable) is properly synchronized. You don't have to worry that your `out.print` and `out.println` statements will fail when multiple threads try to call them at the same time.

Listing 2.9 shows an abbreviated example of a real-life situation in which threading issues became an ugly problem. In this example, the Java Server Page is formatting name and address information for a customer. As you look it over, see if you can spot where the threading issues occur.

LISTING 2.9 SOURCE CODE FOR `Address.jsp`

```
<HTML>
<BODY>
<%!
// Holders for the various portions of the address
    String firstName;
    String middleName;
    String lastName;
    String address1;
    String address2;
    String city;
    String state;
    String zip;
%>

<%
// Copy the information passed into the JSP
    firstName = request.getParameter("firstName");
    middleName = request.getParameter("middleName");
    lastName = request.getParameter("lastName");
    address1 = request.getParameter("address1");
    address2 = request.getParameter("address2");
    city = request.getParameter("city");
    state = request.getParameter("state");
    zip = request.getParameter("zip");

// Call the formatting routine
    formatNameAndAddress(out);
%>
</BODY>
</HTML>

<%!
// Print out the name address
    void formatNameAndAddress(JspWriter out)
        throws java.io.IOException
    {
        out.println("<PRE>");
        out.print(firstName);
// Only print the middle name if it contains data
        if ((middleName != null) && (middleName.length() > 0))
        {
            out.print(" "+middleName);
        }
        out.println(" "+lastName);
        out.println(address1);

// Only print the second address line if it contains data
        if ((address2 != null) && (address2.length() > 0))
        {
            out.println(address2);
        }
        out.println(city+", "+state+" "+zip);
        out.println("</PRE>");
    }
%>
```

Can you see the problem? If you can't, don't feel to bad. In the real-life program, the error was not discovered until the program was being tested with multiple users. The problem is that the variables holding the name and address information are instance variables. Typically, only one instance of a JSP class is loaded at one time. Each time a browser asks a Java Server Page, the Web server spawns another thread to handle the request. It's possible to have multiple threads executing the same Java Server Page at the same time.

In the case of Listing 2.9, the problem is that the instance variables are shared across all the threads. One thread could set all the variables, and then before it has a chance to call the formatting routine, another thread comes along and changes the values. Figure 2.4 illustrates how this happens.

Figure 2.4
Multiple threads can modify the same member variable in a JSP.

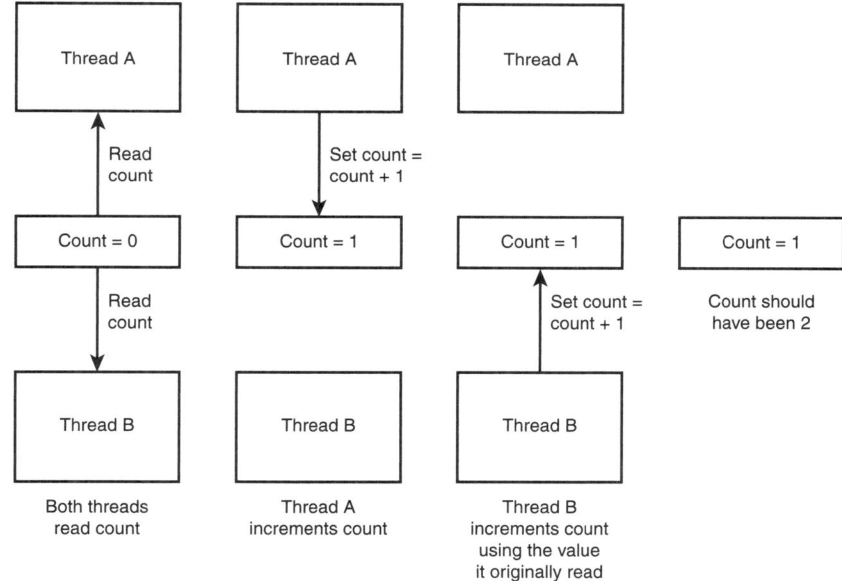

As I said before, the root of the problem is that the data is being passed to `formatNameAndAddress` via instance variables instead of as parameters to the method. Although it seems like an obvious thing to just pass parameters, in the real-life program this example was pulled from, the formatting routine needed about 30 different values. It would have been more than a little cumbersome to pass 30 parameters around, especially if they must be passed to several different methods. One solution for this problem is to synchronize the variable assignments and the method call, like this:

```
// Copy the information passed into the JSP
    synchronized (this)
    {        firstName = request.getParameter("firstName");
        middleName = request.getParameter("middleName");
        lastName = request.getParameter("lastName");
        address1 = request.getParameter("address1");
        address2 = request.getParameter("address2");
```

```
        city = request.getParameter("city");
        state = request.getParameter("state");
        zip = request.getParameter("zip");

// Call the formatting routine
        formatNameAndAddress(out);
    }
```

Although synchronization can prevent threading problems, it does so at the cost of performance. The reason the server tries to use multiple threads to call a JSP is to try to service as many requests as possible in a short amount of time. If you suddenly create a bottleneck in which a large amount of work can only be done one thread at a time, you are defeating the performance enhancements of threading. There is nothing wrong with using the `synchronized` keyword here and there to prevent errors, but synchronizing all or more of the work in one large block is usually not a good idea.

The solution for the problem posed in Listing 2.9 involves passing the data as method parameters rather than through instance variables. Although the example could be rewritten to pass each data item as 8 separate parameters, the original code from which this example was taken had 30 separate parameters and a more elegant solution. All the parameters can be encapsulated in a Java class, and the Java class can be declared within the JSP as a nested class. Listing 2.10 shows the thread-safe solution.

LISTING 2.10 SOURCE CODE FOR `AddressGood.jsp`

```
<HTML>
<BODY>
<%
// Allocate a holder for the data
    NameAndAddress data = new NameAndAddress();

// Copy the information passed into the JSP
    data.firstName = request.getParameter("firstName");
    data.middleName = request.getParameter("middleName");
    data.lastName = request.getParameter("lastName");
    data.address1 = request.getParameter("address1");
    data.address2 = request.getParameter("address2");
    data.city = request.getParameter("city");
    data.state = request.getParameter("state");
    data.zip = request.getParameter("zip");

// Call the formatting routine
    formatNameAndAddress(data, out);
%>
</BODY>
</HTML>

<%!
// The holder for the formatting data
    class NameAndAddress
    {
        public String firstName;
        public String middleName;
```

```
        public String lastName;
        public String address1;
        public String address2;
        public String city;
        public String state;
        public String zip;
    }

// Print out the name address
    void formatNameAndAddress(NameAndAddress data, JspWriter out)
        throws java.io.IOException
    {
        out.println("<PRE>");
        out.print(data.firstName);
// Only print the middle name if it contains data
        if ((data.middleName != null) &&
            (data.middleName.length() > 0))
        {
            out.print(" "+data.middleName);
        }
        out.println(" "+data.lastName);
        out.println(data.address1);

// Only print the second address line if it contains data
        if ((data.address2 != null) &&
            (data.address2.length() > 0))
        {
            out.println(data.address2);
        }
        out.println(data.city+", "+data.state+" "+data.zip);
        out.println("</PRE>");
    }
%>
```

The example in Listing 2.10 avoids thread collisions by allocating an object to hold the data it passes to another routine. Because each thread allocates its own copy of the data object, the threads cannot overwrite one another's data.

TROUBLESHOOTING

ERRORS WHEN ACCESSING THE PAGE

Why do I get a `404 (File Not Found)` error when I access the Java Server Page?

You are probably putting the JSP in a directory that the Web server can't get to. If you have an HTML page that you can access from the Web server, put the JSP in the same directory and see if you can get to it. Also try using the default directory for your Web server (for Microsoft Web servers it's usually c:\InetPub\WWWRoot).

Why do I get a `500 (Internal Server Error)` error when I access the Java Server Page?

Usually a 500 error is caused by a miscommunication between the Web server and the JSP engine, or an error in the JSP engine. First check to make sure that you have configured your JSP engine properly. Many JSP engines come with a pure-Java Web server as well as an interface to an existing Web server. Usually these pure-Java servers run on port 8000 or 8080. Try hitting the JSP using the pure-Java server (if you type `http://localhost/HelloWorld.jsp`, try `http://localhost:8000/HelloWorld.jsp`). If the JSP displays correctly, the interface between the JSP engine and your regular Web server is broken. Try reconfiguring it. Another possibility is that you don't have a Java compiler set up correctly. See the next troubleshooting tip to see how to solve that problem.

Why do I get an error saying `No Compiler Available` *or* `unable to locate "com.sun.tools.javac.Main`*?*

The JSP engine converts your Java Server Pages into Java classes and then compiles them. To compile them, it needs a Java compiler. You need to install either a full JDK or at least get the tools.jar file from an existing JDK installation and put it in your classpath. This error occurs mostly when you have only installed the JRE (Java Runtime Environment), which does not come with a Java compiler.

COMPILER ERRORS

Why do I see bizarre compiler errors like `expected }` *or* `no catch/finally clause`*?*

You probably forgot an opening `<%` or a closing `%>`.

DOESN'T SHOW HTML

Instead of seeing an HTML page, why do I see the source code for my JSP?

You don't have the JSP engine set up correctly. The Web server doesn't understand that the JSP engine is supposed to handle filenames ending in .jsp. You might need to reinstall your JSP engine.

CHAPTER 3

Getting Started with Servlets

In this chapter

A "HELLO WORLD" SERVLET

Servlets are a little more involved than Java Server Pages, but in simple cases they aren't too bad. Listing 3.1 shows you the "Hello World" program in servlet form.

LISTING 3.1 SOURCE CODE FOR `HelloWorldServlet.java`

```
package usingjsp;
import javax.servlet.*;
import java.io.*;
public class HelloWorldServlet extends GenericServlet
{
    public void service(ServletRequest request,
        ServletResponse response)
        throws IOException
    {
// Tell the Web server that the response is HTML
response.setContentType("text/html");

// Get the PrintWriter for writing out the response
        PrintWriter out = response.getWriter();

// Write the HTML back to the browser
        out.println("<HTML>");
        out.println("<BODY>");
        out.println("<H1>Hello World!</H1>");
        out.println("</BODY>");
        out.println("</HTML>");
    }
}
```

The HTML portion of the `HelloWorldServlet` is probably the most recognizable part. For the sake of completeness, the browser's view of the `HelloWorldServlet` is shown in Figure 3.1.

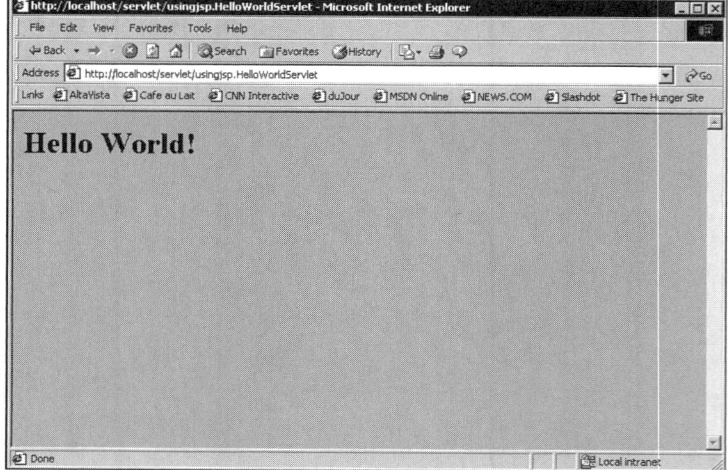

Figure 3.1
A servlet can generate HTML code.

Unlike Java Server Pages, servlets are pure Java classes. The good news is that you don't have to learn any additional syntax to create a servlet; the bad news is that you have to do a bit more work in your programs. As you can see from the "Hello World" servlet, the amount of work isn't really that great.

COMPILING THE SERVLET

Before you compile the servlet, make sure the servlet classes are in your classpath. The location of the servlet classes varies depending on which servlet engine you are using, but typically they are in a file called servlet.jar. If you are using the Resin servlet engine, the servlet classes are in a file called jsdk22.jar (for version 2.2 of the Servlet API). The location of the jar file also varies depending on the servlet engine, but you usually find it in the lib directory. Appendixes C-F in this book contain configuration information about several popular Web servers. If all else fails, consult the documentation for your servlet engine. In fact, you should probably consult the documentation first.

If you are having trouble compiling your servlet, see the "Troubleshooting" section at the end of this chapter.

RUNTIME CLASSPATH

Unlike Java Server Pages, servlets must be in the servlet engine's classpath. When a Java Server Page runs, the JSP engine ensures that the servlet it generates is visible to the JSP engine. Unfortunately, you don't have the luxury of the JSP engine to help you out when you write servlets. Most servlet engines enable you to modify the classpath for the purpose of loading servlets, so you won't have to add all your servlet directories to the system classpath.

Listing 3.1 showed that you can put your servlet into a package. The name of the servlet becomes the fully qualified classname of the servlet. The URL used to load the servlet specifies the pathname for the servlet as `/servlet/usingjsp.HelloWorldServlet` (refer to Figure 3.1). Most servlet engines contain a special URL mapping for the `/servlet` directory, which signals that you want to run a servlet. When the Web server sees this special URL, it passes it on to the servlet engine. This `/servlet` directory usually picks up servlets from the classpath, so you can easily run any servlet that is in your system classpath just by appending the classname to `/servlet/`.

Note

You almost always have to set up a specific URL pattern for running servlets (such as `/servlet/`) or you need to set up a full URL that points to a servlet. Unlike a JSP, a servlet doesn't have an extension on the end of its name to indicate what kind of a file it is.

If you are having trouble running your servlet, see the"Troubleshooting" section at the end of this chapter.

THE HelloWorldServlet IN-DEPTH

The first thing your servlet must do is implement the `Servlet` interface. There are two ways to do it: subclass from a class that implements the `Servlet` interface or implement the `Servlet` interface directly in the servlet. The `HelloWorldServlet` takes the easier approach by subclassing an existing class that implements `Servlet`. There are other classes that also implement the `Servlet` interface, and they will be discussed shortly.

When a request comes in for a particular servlet, the servlet engine loads the servlet (if it has not yet been loaded) and invokes the servlet's `service` method. The method takes two arguments: an object containing information about the request from the browser and an object containing information about the response going back to the browser.

Tip

Currently, most servlet engines don't automatically reload a servlet after it has been loaded. If you recompile a servlet, you usually need to restart the servlet engine to pick up the changes. This problem should slowly disappear over time as vendors create special class loaders to reload servlets when needed.

Next, the servlet must tell the Web browser what kind of content is being returned. Most of the time, you will be returning HTML content, so set the content type to `text/html`. As you will see in Chapter 24, "Creating an XML Application," you can also set the content type to `text/xml` and return XML data back to the browser. Earlier in this chapter, Listing 3.1 showed that you set the content type of the response by invoking `setContentType` in the response object.

After you have set the content type you are ready to start sending text back to the browser. Of course you need some sort of output object to send the text back. Again, the response object has the methods necessary to get an output stream for writing a response. Because the "Hello World" servlet is writing out text, it only needs a `PrintWriter` object, so it calls the `getWriter` method in the response object. If you need to send binary data back to the browser, you should use the `getOutputStream` method in the response object.

The final part of the "Hello World" servlet should be the most obvious, and if you paid attention in Chapter 2, "Getting Started with Java Server Pages," this part should be the most familiar. The "Hello World" servlet uses the `println` method in the `PrintWriter` to send HTML back to the browser. Remember, in Chapter 2 you saw a portion of the servlet code generated by the "Hello World" Java Server Page. Aside from some extra comments, that code is almost identical to the code at the end of the "Hello World" servlet. After all, Java Server Pages eventually become servlets and there are only so many ways to send output from a servlet, so why shouldn't they be similar?

THE ANATOMY OF A SERVLET

As you just saw in the `HelloWorldServlet`, a *servlet* is a Java class that implements a few important methods. You can choose to implement these methods yourself or create a subclass of an existing servlet class that already implements them. The `Servlet` interface defines the methods that are required for a Java class to become a servlet. The interface definition is shown in Listing 3.2.

LISTING 3.2 THE DEFINITION OF THE `Servlet` INTERFACE

```
package javax.servlet;

public interface Servlet
{
    public void destroy();
    public ServletConfig getServletConfig();
    public String getServletInfo();
    public void init(ServletConfig config)
        throws ServletException;
    public void service(ServletRequest request,
        ServletResponse response)
        throws ServletException, java.io.IOException;
}
```


Most of the time, you will create a servlet by subclassing either `GenericServlet` or `HttpServlet`. Both of these classes implement the `Servlet` interface, but they provide a few handy features that make them preferable to implementing the `Servlet` interface yourself.

THE `service` METHOD

The heart of any servlet is the `service` method. As you just learned, the servlet engine calls the `service` method to handle each request from a browser, passing in an object containing both information about the request that invoked the servlet and information about sending back a response. The `service` method is the only method that a servlet is actually required to implement. The `service` method is declared this way:

```
public void service(ServletRequest request,
    ServletResponse response)
    throws java.io.IOException
```

THE `init` METHOD

Many times, a servlet needs to perform some initialization one time before it begins to handle requests. The `init` method in a servlet is called just after the servlet is first loaded, but before it begins to handle requests. Listing 3.3 shows a simple `init` method that initializes a database connection.

LISTING 3.3 `init` METHOD FROM `JDBCServlet.java`

```
protected Connection conn;

public void init()
{
    try
```

LISTING 3.3 CONTINUED

```
    {
// Make sure the JdbcOdbcDriver class is loaded
        Class.forName("sun.jdbc.odbc.JdbcOdbcDriver");

// Try to connect to a database via ODBC
        conn = DriverManager.getConnection(
            "jdbc:odbc:usingjsp");
    }
    catch (Exception exc)
    {
// If there's an error, use the servlet logging API
        getServletContext().log(
            "Error making JDBC connection: ", exc);
    }
}
```

Notice that the `init` method in Listing 3.3 does not take a parameter like the `init` method in the `Servlet` interface. One of the convenient features of the `GenericServlet` and `HttpServlet` classes is that they have an alternate version of `init` that doesn't take any parameters. In case you're wondering why it even matters, the `init` method in the `Servlet` interface takes a `ServletConfig` object as a parameter. The servlet is then responsible for keeping track of the `ServletConfig` object. The `GenericServlet` and `HttpServlet` classes perform this housekeeping chore and then provide the parameter-less `init` method for you to do any servlet-specific initialization.

Caution

If you override the `init(ServletConfig config)` method of `GenericServlet` or `HttpServlet`, make sure you call `super.init(config)` as the first statement in your `init` method so that the housekeeping will still be performed.

THE destroy METHOD

Sometimes, the servlet engine decides that it doesn't need to keep your servlet loaded anymore. This could happen automatically, or as the result of you deactivating the servlet from an administration tool. Before the servlet engine unloads your servlet, it calls the `destroy` method to enable the servlet to perform any necessary cleanup. The cleanup usually involves closing database connections, open files, and network connections. Listing 3.4 shows the `destroy` method that is a companion to the `init` method in Listing 3.3.

LISTING 3.4 destroy METHOD FROM JDBCServlet.java

```
public void destroy()
{
    try
    {
// Only try to close the connection if it's non-null
        if (conn != null)
        {
```

```
            conn.close();
        }
    }
    catch (SQLException exc)
    {
// If there's an error, use the servlet logging API
        getServletContext().log(
            "Error closing JDBC connection: ", exc);
    }
}
```

THE getServletInfo AND getServletConfig METHODS

If you are subclassing `GenericServlet` or `HttpServlet`, you probably won't need to override the `getServletInfo` or `getServletConfig` methods. The Servlet API documentation recommends that you return information such as the author, version, and copyright from the `getServletInfo` method. Although there is no specific format for the string returned by the method, you should return only plain text, without any HTML or XML tags embedded within it.

The `getServletConfig` method returns the `ServletConfig` object that was passed to the servlet in the `init` method. Unless you are keeping track of the `config` object yourself, your best bet is to leave this method alone and let the superclass handle it.

SENDING A RESPONSE TO THE BROWSER

Probably the biggest difference between Java Server Pages and servlets is in the way responses are sent back to the browser. In a JSP, most of the response is embedded in the JSP in the form of static text. In the servlet, however, the response is usually in the form of code—mostly calls to `out.print` and `out.println`.

A minimal servlet needs to do two things to send a response: set the content type and write the response. If you are new to Web programming, you are probably unfamiliar with the notion of *content type*. Even though every request you make to a Web server involves a content type, it has probably been invisible to you. Whenever a browser asks the server for a file, the server sends back a content type along with the file. The content type tells the Web browser how it should display the file. For instance, if the file is an HTML file, the content type is `text/html`, whereas a JPEG image file has a content type of `image/jpeg`.

Most Web servers determine the content type by looking at the extension on the filename (for example, .htm and .html indicate HTML files, whereas .jpg indicates a JPEG image). In the case of a servlet, however, the Web server can't guess what the servlet is going to send back. It could be sending back HTML, XML, WML, or even a JPEG image! Instead, the Web server relies on the servlet to tell it what is being returned.

As you saw earlier in Listing 3.1, you set the content type by calling the `setContentType` method in the `ServletResponse` object. If you already know the exact length of the response, you can also call the `setContentLength` method. If you are just sending an HTML response, you don't need to send the content length. The browser can figure it out.

After you have set the content type, you are ready to send the response. If you are sending a text response, as is the case with HTML and XML, you should use the `PrintWriter` object returned by `response.getWriter()`. If you are sending a binary file, such as a JPEG image, an audio file, or an animation file, you should use the `ServletOutputStream` returned by `response.getOutputStream()`.

Note

Although the `ServletOutputStream` class also contains print and `println` methods such as the `PrintWriter` class, you should use the `PrintWriter` object when sending text output. Some content types require a slightly different character set, and the `PrintWriter` object automatically adjusts the character set based on the content type. In fact, the general rule of thumb with Java I/O is that you should always use a `Writer` object when writing character data.

You don't need to worry about closing the output stream when you are done writing out the response; the servlet engine knows you are through when the `service` method has finished executing. In addition to giving you the output streams, the response object performs other interesting tasks. You can control the amount of buffering, flush the output stream, and even clear the output stream. The `ServletResponse` is discussed in detail in Chapter 13, "Core Servlet Components."

Caution

Make sure you set the content type before you call `getWriter`. Because the servlet engine modifies the character set mapping depending on the content type, it needs to know the content type before it creates the `Writer`.

THE `HttpServlet` CLASS

You've seen that two prebuilt servlet classes are available for you to subclass, but so far you don't know why you would choose `HttpServlet` over `GenericServlet`. The main difference between the two is that `HttpServlet` has extra methods and special request-and-response objects that are geared toward the HTTP protocol. The `HttpServlet` provides separate methods for handling the different type of HTTP requests (`GET`, `POST`, `PUT`, and so on). The two most common types of HTTP request are `GET` and `POST`, which are handled by the `doGet` and `doPost` methods:

```
protected void doGet(HttpServletRequest request,
    HttpServletResponse response)
    throws ServletException, java.io.IOException;

protected void doPost(HttpServletRequest request,
    HttpServletResponse response)
    throws ServletException, java.io.IOException;
```

As you can see, the `doGet` and `doPost` methods are of the same general form as the `service` method. The `service` method of `HttpServlet` looks at the type of the HTTP request and then calls the appropriate handler methods. The `HttpServletRequest` and

`HttpServletResponse` classes contain extra methods for dealing with the HTTP protocol. These classes are introduced more fully in the next few chapters and discussed in detail in Chapter 13.

CHOOSING BETWEEN JAVA SERVER PAGES AND SERVLETS

Although you've just barely scratched the surface of JSP and Servlets, now is a good time to talk about when to use servlets, when to use JSP, and when to use both. To make such decisions, you need to weigh the advantages and disadvantages of each. Remember, too, that because Java Server Pages are translated into servlets, they can't be all that different when you get right down to it.

THE ADVANTAGES AND DISADVANTAGES OF JSP

The biggest strength of JSP is that it looks like HTML (or XML or whatever kind of content you are generating). You can give a JSP to someone who is familiar with HTML and expect that person to be able to make changes in a fairly short amount of time. It is also quite obvious what the HTML will look like when it is sent to the browser. It is not always so obvious when the HTML is generated by Java code.

An add-on to this strength is the fact that people who are weaker with Java can use Java Server Pages. You don't need to know too much Java to do at least basic things with JSP. You don't even need to know how to declare a Java class. As vendors begin to support other languages with JSP (some already support JavaScript) you will have people who don't even know Java writing Java Server Pages!

A much more subtle advantage of JSP, one that you have not really encountered yet, is that when the JSP is turned into a servlet, that servlet is automatically loaded into the servlet engine. When the JSP changes, its corresponding servlet is automatically regenerated and reloaded. When you are doing rapid development, it's great to be able to make quick changes and see them without having to restart the server. If you make a lot of changes to a lot of files, you don't have to worry about reloading all the changed files; the JSP engine picks them up automatically.

Because Java Server Pages eventually become servlets, it's difficult to point to any technical disadvantages of a JSP that aren't also present in servlets. The greatest disadvantage I've seen in practice is related to the greatest strength of JSP: the capability to mix in Java code with HTML. If you aren't careful in organizing your code, you can end up with an ugly mess: huge JSP files with HTML interspersed between huge blocks of Java code. Things only get worse if you do a lot of JavaScript in the page, too. It can be terribly confusing to look at a page and not know whether you are looking at server-side Java code or client-side JavaScript. Fortunately, you will learn ways around this in the next few chapters.

The Advantages and Disadvantages of Servlets

For the most part, the advantages of servlets are the disadvantages of JSP and vice versa. Because servlets are Java classes, you don't end up with a huge mess of Java, HTML, and JavaScript. Everything in your servlet is Java. Of course, when the servlet is generating HTML or XML, you might find that you still have a huge mess in the form of ugly `out.print` and `out.println` statements.

Servlets are not always automatically reloaded by the servlet engine, although that situation will hopefully change in the future. You also need to specify a special URL or at least a URL pattern (such as `/servlet/`) for executing a servlet, although for a JSP you only need to have a filename that ends with .jsp. This makes your site configuration a little more tedious to maintain.

It probably sounds like I'm biased in favor of JSP, and I can't really dispute that. Because a JSP eventually becomes a servlet, you have the entire servlet API available to you from within the JSP.

There is an interesting combination of servlets and JSP that has been used by many people around the world. When the initial request comes in, it is handled by a servlet. The servlet performs any business logic (fetching data from the database, doing computations, pulling data in from other sources). When it's time to send a response back to the browser, the servlet calls a JSP to render the output. This uses the strength of each of these technologies: The servlet is a simple Java class, whereas the JSP is a template geared towards generating output. You will learn more about this technique in Chapter 7, "Organizing Your Application."

If you take a little extra time, you can create a JSP that doesn't contain any Java code at all. It might seem a little strange to make a JSP with no Java code, but throughout the rest of this book you will learn about built-in JSP tags that let you access Java objects, and also a tag-extension mechanism that lets you create new JSP tags. Using these features, you can easily eliminate embedded Java code, which some would argue is the best way to use JSP.

It probably sounds a little too simplistic, but you should use the technology that best fits your requirements, or at least your comfort level. If you have a lot of static HTML, XML, WML, or other textual markup language, use a JSP. If you are sending back binary data, such as an image or an audio file, a servlet is probably a better bet (not from a technical standpoint, just an aesthetic one). If you aren't comfortable with your Java skills, start playing with JSP to get your feet wet.

Troubleshooting

Can't Compile the Servlet

Why won't my servlet compile? The compiler reports that it can't find the `javax.servlet` *package.*

Your classpath isn't set up correctly. You need to locate the servlet.jar file (it might have a different name) and add it to your classpath.

THE SERVLET WON'T RUN

Why does the Web server gives me a `404 (File Not Found)` error or a `500 (Internal Server Error)`?

This is usually either an installation problem or a classpath issue. One way to check the installation is to run one of the default servlets that comes with the servlet engine. Check Appendixes C-F to find out which default servlets your servlet engine comes with. If you can't run one of the defaults, you need to check the configuration of your servlet engine and possibly reinstall it. If you can run the default servlet, but not your own, your classpath probably doesn't point to your servlet. Also, if you change the classpath after you have started the servlet engine, you need to restart the servlet engine to pick up the changes.

CHAPTER 4

Creating HTML Forms

In this chapter

Up to this point, you have only learned how to send output back to the browser. One of the key points of the Web is the fact that you can create forms to send data from the browser to the server. You are finally ready to begin creating forms with JSP and servlets, and that's where the fun really begins!

A SIMPLE HTML FORM

To start off the exploration of HTML forms, it's best to start with a small form and expand from there. Also, it's better to start with a Java Server Page rather than a servlet, since it is easier to write out the HTML. Most of the form handling for JSP and servlets is identical, so once you know how to retrieve form information from a JSP, you know how to do it from a servlet. Listing 4.1 shows an HTML file containing a simple input form that calls a JSP to handle the form.

LISTING 4.1 SOURCE CODE FOR `SimpleForm.html`

```
<HTML>
<BODY>

<H1>Please tell me about yourself</H1>

<FORM action="SimpleFormHandler.jsp" method="get">

Name:    <INPUT type="text" name="firstName">
    <INPUT type="text" name="lastName"><BR>
Sex:
    <INPUT type="radio" checked name="sex" value="male">Male
    <INPUT type="radio" name="sex" value="female">Female
    <INPUT type="radio" name="sex" value="alien">Alien<BR>
<P>
What Java primitive type best describes your personality:
<SELECT name="javaType">
    <OPTION value="boolean">boolean</OPTION>
    <OPTION value="byte">byte</OPTION>
    <OPTION value="char" selected>char</OPTION>
    <OPTION value="double">double</OPTION>
    <OPTION value="float">float</OPTION>
    <OPTION value="int">int</OPTION>
    <OPTION value="long">long</OPTION>
</SELECT>
<BR>
<INPUT type="submit">
</FORM>
</BODY>
</HTML>
```

The `<FORM>` tag in Listing 4.1 sends the input from the form to a JSP called SimpleFormHandler.jsp. Figure 4.1 shows this form running in a browser.

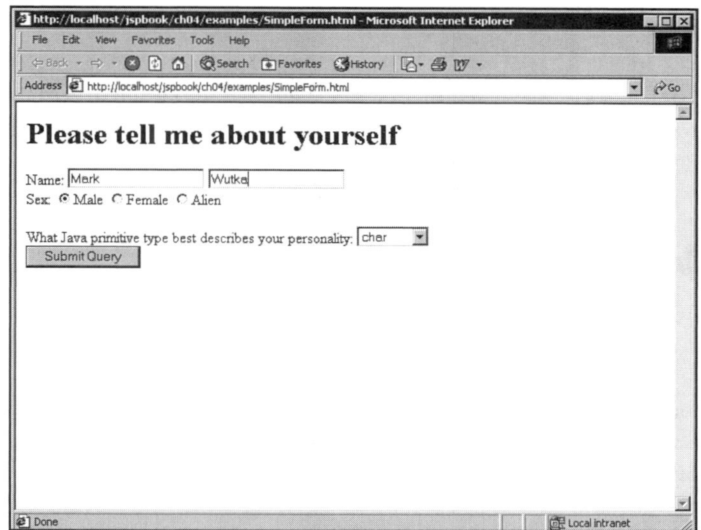

Figure 4.1
HTML forms frequently serve as the frontend for a JSP.

The `SimpleFormHandler` JSP does little more than retrieve the form variable and print out their values. Listing 4.2 shows the contents of SimpleFormHandler.jsp, which you can see is pretty short.

Listing 4.2 Source Code for `SimpleFormHandler.jsp`

```
<HTML>
<BODY>

<%

// Grab the variables from the form
    String firstName = request.getParameter("firstName");
    String lastName = request.getParameter("lastName");
    String sex = request.getParameter("sex");
    String javaType = request.getParameter("javaType");
%>
<%-- Print out the variables --%>
<H1>Hello, <%=firstName%> <%=lastName%>!</H1>
I see that you are <%=sex%>. You know, you remind me of a
<%=javaType%> variable I once knew.

</BODY>
</HTML>
```

If you are having trouble displaying the form, or some of the form results, see "Form and Form Variables Names," in the "Troubleshooting" section at the end of this chapter.

Most of SimpleFormHandler.jsp should seem pretty familiar to you. It is very similar to an example in Chapter 2, "Getting Started with Java Server Pages," that assigned some variables and printed out their values using the `<%= %>` tags. The only new thing introduced in

Listing 4.2 is the built-in `request` object. Every Java Server Page has a few built-in objects. The most common ones are `out` and `request`.

The `out` object was introduced in Chapter 2 and is the output stream used to send data back to the browser. The `request` object contains information about the request from the browser and although it contains quite a bit of information, the `request` object is most commonly used for retrieving the values of form variables.

Tip

The `request` object is really just an instance of `HttpServletRequest`. Once you know how to use the `request` object in a JSP, you are ready to use the `HttpServletRequest` object in a servlet.

As you look at the `SimpleFormHandler` JSP, it should be pretty obvious what the output would look like. Just to make sure you've got it, Figure 4.2 shows how `SimpleFormHandler` looks when displayed in a browser.

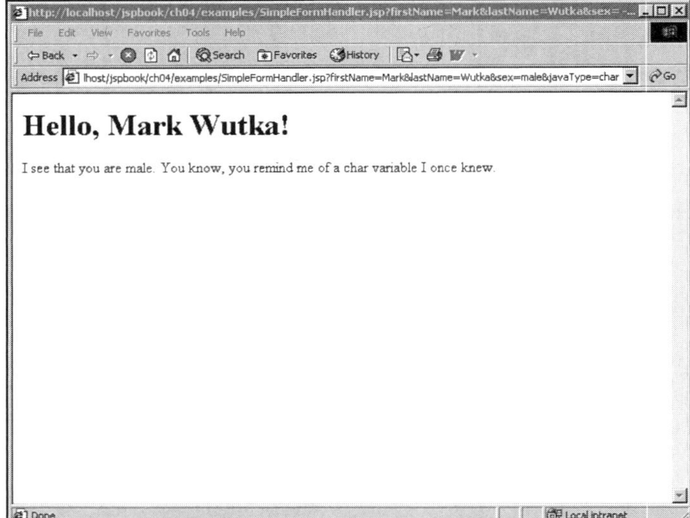

Figure 4.2
A JSP can read form input and embed the form data in its output.

USING THE `request` OBJECT

As you saw in Listing 4.2, the `getParameter` method in the `request` object retrieves the values of the form variable. The lone argument to `getParameter` is the name of the form variable as it was defined in the HTML form, and must match the case exactly. In other words, if you called a form variable `firstName` in the HTML file, you must pass `firstName"` to `getParameter` and not `firstname"` or `FIRSTNAME`.

If you ask the `request` object for the value of a form variable that does not exist, it will return `null`. Note that `getParameter` always returns a string. If you are expecting a number, you will have to convert it yourself.

Note

> There is a difference between a form variable that is empty and a form variable that does not exist. The value of an empty text box is `""` (a string with a length of `0`). The `getParameter` method should only return `null` if a form variable does not exist at all.

Although I have been using the term *form variable* to describe the parameters passed to the JSP, these parameters technically have nothing to do with forms. When you press the Submit button on an HTML form, the browser encodes the form variables and passes them one of two ways: using an HTTP `GET` command or an HTTP `POST` command. Without getting down into the nitty-gritty of the HTTP protocol, parameters in a `GET` command are passed in the actual URL, while in a `POST` command they are passed in a different part of the request.

➔ For a detailed explanation of `GET` and `POST`, **see** "`GET` Versus `POST`," **p. 221**.

You may notice while surfing the Web that the URL displayed by the browser has a `?` and some values of the form "name=value" separated by "`&`" characters. In fact, if you look back at Figure 4.2, you can see exactly that. If you wanted to, you could run SimpleFormHandler.jsp directly without going through the initial HTML form. All you need to do is add the parameters to the end of the URL.

Note

> URLs have a special encoding for many characters. For example, a space is represented by "+". Many characters are represented by "%" followed by the character's ASCII value in hex. The "=" sign, for instance, is represented by `%3D` because its ASCII value is `61` decimal or `3D` hex. You may want to stick to characters and numbers when entering parameters by hand.

Why is this important? Well, you will often need to test a form handler, and rather than typing in the form values every time, you will find that manually passing the parameters straight to the form handler is a big timesaver. Also, because all of the form variables are encoded directly into the URL, you can bookmark the JSP in your browser and display the form output whenever you select that bookmark.

Bookmarking a Java Server Page is not always useful, especially when the JSP is just accepting form input. When the JSP is displaying updated information like sports scores, weather, stock quotes, or other frequently changing data, bookmarking the page is quite useful. Unfortunately, if the data is sent to the server via an HTTP `POST` request, bookmarking doesn't work. The bookmark only contains the URL, and when form data is sent via `POST`, the URL does not include the form data.

Handling Multiple Form Values

The browser passes parameters to the server as a series of name=value pairs, like `firstname=Sam` or `"lastname=Tippin`. When there are multiple values for the same form variable name, the browser sends multiple name value pairs. Listing 4.3 shows a simple input form with several text input fields.

Listing 4.3 Source Code for `MultiForm.html`

```
<HTML>
<BODY>

<H1>Please enter a list of names</H1>

<FORM action="MultiFormHandler.jsp" method="get">
    <INPUT type="text" name="names"><BR>
    <INPUT type="text" name="names"><BR>
    <INPUT type="text" name="names"><BR>
    <INPUT type="text" name="names"><BR>
    <INPUT type="text" name="names"><BR>

    <INPUT type="submit">
</FORM>
</BODY>
</HTML>
```

Figure 4.3 shows the form running inside a browser.

Figure 4.3
You can prompt the user with multiple values for the same form variable.

Notice that in Listing 4.3 the names of each of the fields are the same. If you were to use the `getParameter` method to fetch the names, you would only get the first one. When you need to fetch multiple parameters, use the `getParameterValues` method. Listing 4.4 shows a Java Server Page that retrieves the values from the page in Listing 4.3.

LISTING 4.4 SOURCE CODE FOR MultiFormHandler.jsp

```
<HTML>
<BODY>
The names you entered are:
<PRE>
<%
// Fetch the name values
    String names[] = request.getParameterValues("names");

    for (int i=0; i < names.length; i++)
    {
        out.println(names[i]);
    }
%>
</PRE>

</BODY>
</HTML>
```


Two things you need to know about the `getParameterValues` method:

- If the parameter value doesn't exist at all (that is, there was no form variable with that name), `getParameterValues` returns `null`.
- If there is exactly one parameter value, you still get back an array. The length of this array will be `1`.

You will usually know the names of all the parameters you are expecting, but for cases where you need to discover the names of all the parameters passed in you can use the `getParameterNames` method. The method signature for `getParameterNames` in the `request` object is

```
java.util.Enumeration getParameterNames()
```

The `getParameterNames` method returns an enumeration of the string objects. Each of these strings is the name of a parameter and can be used as an argument to `getParameter` or `getParameterValues`. Listing 4.5 shows a Java Server Page that dumps out the names and values of all the parameters passed to it, including multiple values.

LISTING 4.5 SOURCE CODE FOR ShowParameters.jsp

```
<HTML>
<BODY>
You passed me the following parameters:
<PRE>
<%

// Find out the names of all the parameters
    java.util.Enumeration params = request.getParameterNames();

    while (params.hasMoreElements())
    {
// Get the next parameter name
        String paramName = (String) params.nextElement();

// Use getParameterValues in case there are multiple values
        String paramValues[] =
            request.getParameterValues(paramName);

// If there is only one value, print it out
        if (paramValues.length == 1)
        {
            out.println(paramName+"="+paramValues[0]);
        }
        else
        {
// For multiple values, loop through them
            out.print(paramName+"=");

            for (int i=0; i < paramValues.length; i++)
            {
// If this isn't the first value, print a comma to separate values
                if (i > 0) out.print(',');

                out.print(paramValues[i]);
            }
            out.println();
        }
    }
%>
</PRE>
</BODY>
</HTML>
```

Figure 4.4 shows the output from the JSP shown in Listing 4.5. You can easily play around with the `ShowParameters` JSP by passing parameters directly in the browser. One such set of parameters is shown at the top of Figure 4.4.

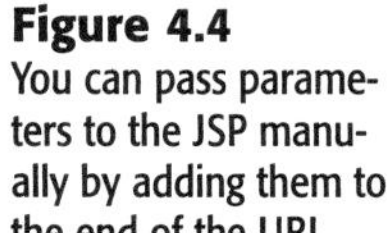

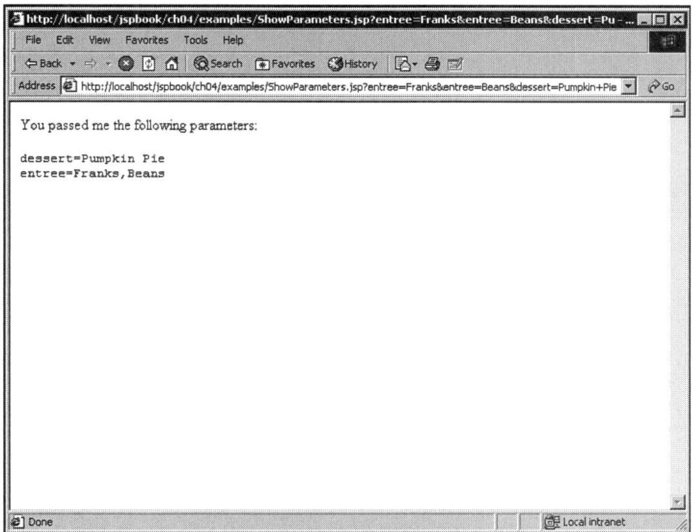

Figure 4.4
You can pass parameters to the JSP manually by adding them to the end of the URL.

RETRIEVING FORM VARIABLES IN A SERVLET

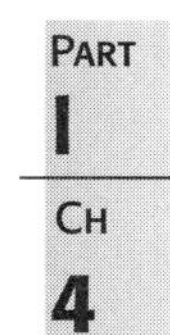

Up to this point, the discussion has centered around the `request` object in Java Server Pages. In case you missed it, the `request` object in a JSP is an instance of `HttpServletRequest`. If you recall from Chapter 3, "Getting Started with Servlets," an HTTP servlet receives an instance of `HttpServletRequest` when its `service` method is invoked. This means, of course, that you already know how to retrieve form variables in a servlet because you do it the same way you do in a Java Server Page.

Listing 4.6 shows a servlet version of the `ShowParameters` Java Server Page you saw in Listing 4.5. Again, you can test it out by passing parameters directly in the URL.

LISTING 4.6 SOURCE CODE FOR `ShowParametersServlet.java`

```
package usingjsp;

import javax.servlet.*;
import javax.servlet.http.*;
import java.io.*;
import java.util.*;

public class ShowParametersServlet extends HttpServlet
{
    public void service(HttpServletRequest request,
        HttpServletResponse response)
        throws IOException
    {
// Tell the web server that the response is HTML
        response.setContentType("text/html");
```

LISTING 4.6 CONTINUED

```
        PrintWriter out = response.getWriter();

        out.println("<HTML>");
        out.println("<BODY>");
        out.println("You passed me the following parameters:");
        out.println("<PRE>");

// Find out the names of all the parameters
        Enumeration params = request.getParameterNames();

        while (params.hasMoreElements())
        {
// Get the next parameter name
            String paramName = (String) params.nextElement();

// Use getParameterValues in case there are multiple values
            String paramValues[] =
                request.getParameterValues(paramName);

// If there is only one value, print it out
            if (paramValues.length == 1)
            {
                out.println(paramName+
                    "="+paramValues[0]);
            }
            else
            {
// For multiple values, loop through them
                out.print(paramName+"=");

                for (int i=0; i < paramValues.length; i++)
                {
// If this isn't the first value, print a comma to separate values
                    if (i > 0) out.print(',');

                    out.print(paramValues[i]);
                }
                out.println();
            }
        }

        out.println("</PRE>");
        out.println("</BODY>");
        out.println("</HTML>");
    }
}
```

The output from `ShowParametersServlet` is identical to the output from the `ShowParameters` JSP. In fact, the core part of both programs is the same. The only difference is the code to print out the beginning and ending HTML tags.

JavaScript and Java Server Pages

Although a few Web sites use Java applets on the browser for client-side automation, the majority of client-side browser code is written in JavaScript. One of the most frequent questions I hear is, "How can I access JSP variables from my JavaScript code?" The answer is not a simple one, and the question indicates a basic misunderstanding about when and where the various types of code execute.

Always keep in mind that Java Server Pages execute only on the server, and JavaScript executes only on the client. The only information the client and server can share is in the form of HTTP parameters and generated Web pages. In other words, you can't access JSP methods or attributes directly from JavaScript.

Tip

Always assume that the Java Server Page will execute completely and then vanish before the browser receives the page's output. Although it is not technically true, the assumption should remind you that server-side data is not accessible from JavaScript.

Passing Data to JavaScript

Although JavaScript cannot access JSP data, a JSP can insert data into a Web page that the JavaScript can access. Chances are the JavaScript is embedded inside the JSP to begin with. You can use the `<%= %>` tags to pass data to JavaScript.

Note

Java Server Pages are designed to support scripting languages other than Java. The Resin JSP server from Caucho supports JavaScript as an alternative to Java on the server. Don't let that confuse you. You still cannot access server-side variables directly from client-side JavaScript, even if you are using the same language on the client and server.

In addition to the `<%= %>` tags, you can also write out JavaScript code using any of the other methods for generating output. In other words, you can also use `out.println` or `<% %>`. Listing 4.7 shows a Java Server Page that initializes a JavaScript variable.

Listing 4.7 Source Code for JavaScriptData.jsp

```
<HTML>
<HEAD>

<%

// Set up a Java variable that will be placed into
// a JavaScript routine
    String jsDataItem = "Hello, JavaScript!";
%>

<SCRIPT>
```

LISTING 4.7 CONTINUED

```
// jsVar holds data that came from a JSP
var jsVar = "<%=jsDataItem%>";

function handleLoad()
{
    alert("jsVar = "+jsVar);
}

</SCRIPT>
<BODY onload="handleLoad()">
</BODY>
</HTML>
```

Notice that even though the `jsDataItem` variable is a string, you still need to put quotes into the JavaScript program. The JSP processor has no idea that the page contains any JavaScript. As far as it is concerned, anything outside the `<% %>` tags is just pure text.

If you have trouble running your JavaScript functions or you get compile errors when you include JavaScript, see "JavaScript Problems," in the "Troubleshooting" section at the end of this chapter.

DIFFERENT WAYS TO DO FORMS

As with most flexible programming tools, you can arrange your JSP form handling code in a number of ways. Three of the most common ways to handle forms are

- A static HTML input form calling a JSP form handler
- A JSP input form calling a separate JSP form handler
- A single JSP page that displays the form and handles the input

Note

You can organize your Java Server Pages in many other ways, especially when you mix servlets with JSPs. You will see several other examples in Chapter 7, "Organizing Your Application."

The HTML page way back in Listing 4.1 and the JSP in Listing 4.2 are examples of a static HTML form calling a JSP form handler. This form of Web programming has been the most popular for years—dating back to the origin of CGI programs. Many developers prefer to keep their Web site as pure HTML, using JSP, servlets, or other server-side technologies only for handling form data.

A PRACTICAL HTML AND JSP COMBINATION

So far, the examples you have seen are not very practical. That is, they illustrate certain core concepts, but they don't really give you a feel for how they might be used in the real world. It's about time you get something you can relate to. One of the difficulties in presenting real-world applications is that they can get pretty complex.

A questionnaire is a simple example application that you can do using only the techniques discussed so far, with a little bit of pure Java mixed in. The problem is this: You want to present the user with a fill-out form asking various questions. Some of these questions may be simple radio buttons; some of them may be text fields, and others may be check boxes. Figure 4.5 shows just such a form. Once the user fills out the form and presses the Submit button, you need to store the survey information in a file.

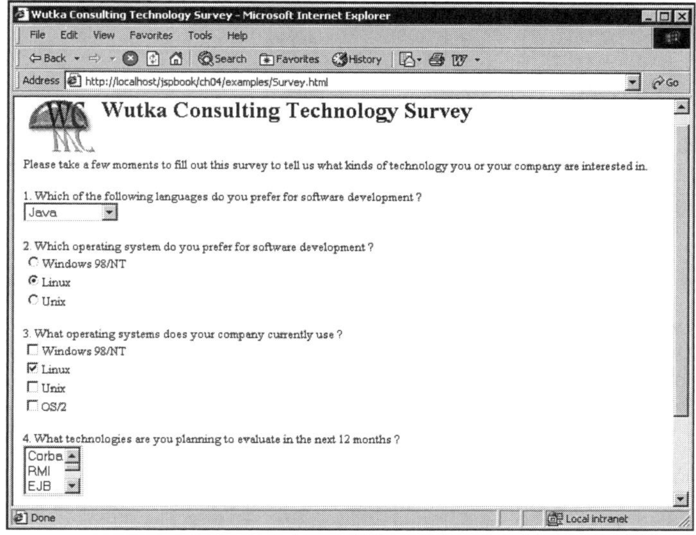

Figure 4.5
Java Server Pages are great for creating survey forms.

Listing 4.8 shows the HTML source code for the page. As you can see in the source code and in Figure 4.5, the survey supports several different types of input.

LISTING 4.8 SOURCE CODE FOR `Survey.html`

```
<HTML>
<HEAD>
<TITLE>Wutka Consulting Technology Survey</TITLE>
<STYLE>
<!--
H1 {font-size: large}
P {font-size: x-small}
TD {font-size: x-small}
OPTION {font-size: x-small}
INPUT {font-size: x-small}
-->
</STYLE>
</HEAD>
<BODY bgcolor="#ffffff">
<IMG SRC="wclogo99.gif" align=left width=75 height=60>
<H1>Wutka Consulting Technology Survey</H1>
```

LISTING 4.8 CONTINUED

```
<BR>
<P>
Please take a few moments to fill out this survey to tell us what
kinds of technology you or your company are interested in.
<P>

<FORM action="Survey.jsp" method="POST">

1. Which of the following languages do you prefer for software development ?
<BR>
<SELECT name="langpref">
    <OPTION value="c++">C/C++</OPTION>
    <OPTION value="java" SELECTED>Java</OPTION>
    <OPTION value="delphi">Delphi</OPTION>
    <OPTION value="vb">Visual Basic</OPTION>
    <OPTION value="ada">Ada</OPTION>
</SELECT>
<P>
2. Which operating system do you prefer for software development ?
<BR>
<input type="radio" name="osdevpref" value="windows">Windows 98/NT<BR>
<input type="radio" name="osdevpref" value="linux" checked>Linux<BR>
<input type="radio" name="osdevpref" value="unix">Unix<BR>
<P>
3. What operating systems does your company currently use ?
<BR>
<input type="checkbox" name="osuse" value="windows">Windows 98/NT<BR>
<input type="checkbox" name="osuse" checked value="linux">Linux<BR>
<input type="checkbox" name="osuse" value="unix">Unix<BR>
<input type="checkbox" name="osuse" value="os/2">OS/2<BR>
<P>
4. What technologies are you planning to evaluate in the next 12 months ?
<BR>
<SELECT name="technologies" multiple size=3>
<option value="CORBA">Corba</OPTION>
<option value="RMI">RMI</OPTION>
<option value="EJB">EJB</OPTION>
<option value="COM">COM</OPTION>
<option value="XML">XML</OPTION>
<option value="WAP">WAP</OPTION>
</SELECT>
<P>
<P>
<TABLE>
<TR>
<TD>Name:<TD><INPUT type="text" name="name">
<TD><FONT SIZE=-1 COLOR="#ff0000">*</FONT>E-Mail:
    <TD><INPUT type="email" name="email">
</TABLE>
<FONT SIZE=-1>*We will not give your e-mail address to anyone else
<P>
<INPUT TYPE="submit" value="Submit Survey">
</FORM>
</BODY>
</HTML>
```

Processing the survey form is a matter of calling `getParameter` and `getParameterValues` to fetch the various form variables. Use `getParameter` for the form fields that can have only one value, and `getParameterValues` for the ones that can have multiple values (check boxes and multivalue select). Listing 4.9 shows the JSP form handler for the survey.

LISTING 4.9 SOURCE CODE FOR `Survey.jsp` (ORIGINAL VERSION)

```
<%@ page language="java" import="java.io.*" %>
<HTML>
<BODY bgcolor="#ffffff">

<%
// First, get all the entries from the survey

// langpref is a select box, there should be a single value
    String langpref = request.getParameter("langpref");

// osdevpref is a radio button, there should be a single value
    String osdevpref = request.getParameter("osdevpref");

// osuse is a checkbox, there are multiple values
    String[] osuse = request.getParameterValues("osuse");
    if (osuse == null) osuse = new String[0];

// technologies is a multi-values select, there are multiple values
    String[] technologies = request.getParameterValues(
        "technologies");
    if (technologies == null) technologies = new String[0];

    String name = request.getParameter("name");
    String email = request.getParameter("email");

// Now write out the survey results to a file
    try
    {
        PrintWriter fileOut = new PrintWriter(
            new FileWriter("survey.out", true));

        fileOut.println(langpref);
        fileOut.println(osdevpref);

// Loop through the osuse array and
// print the values separated by commas
        for (int i=0; i < osuse.length; i++)
        {
            if (i > 0) fileOut.print(", ");
            fileOut.print(osuse[i]);
        }
        fileOut.println();

// Loop through the technologies array and
// print the values separated by commas
        for (int i=0; i < technologies.length; i++)
        {
```

LISTING 4.9 CONTINUED

```
            if (i > 0) fileOut.print(", ");
            fileOut.print(technologies[i]);
        }
        fileOut.println();
        fileOut.println(name);
        fileOut.println(email);
        fileOut.println("-----");

        fileOut.close();
%>

<H1>Thanks!</H1>
Thank you for participating in our survey.  Your feedback is important!

<%
    }
    catch (IOException ioExc)
    {
        application.log("Error saving survey results", ioExc);
%>
<H1>Sorry!</H1>
Due to a server error, we were unable to save your survey results.
We are sorry for the inconvenience and appreciate the time you took to
enter the data. Please try again later.
<%
    }
%>

</BODY>
</HTML>
```

As you can see, the form handler just fetches the form variables and dumps them out to a text file. It prints a series of dashes after each entry so a person reading the survey file can tell where one entry stops and where another begins. Listing 4.10 shows the output file after two entries.

LISTING 4.10 SAMPLE OUTPUT FROM `Survey.jsp`

```
java
linux
linux
EJB, XML, WAP
Mark Wutka
mark@wutka.com
-----
vb
windows
windows
COM
Noah Magination
noahmag@fierymail.com
-----
```

When Survey.jsp opens its output file, it opens it in the Current directory. Each servlet engine has its own notion of a current directory which may be different with each new version and also different across operating systems. Working with files is a difficult thing when it comes to servlets and Java Server Pages. The problem is that you usually want your code to be portable, so you don't want to put an absolute filename like c:\surveys\survey.out or /home/surveys/survey.out in your program. This problem especially becomes ugly when you want to run the same code on Unix and Windows because Unix doesn't support drive letters.

If you don't use an absolute filename, you are at the mercy of the servlet engine. It will put your files where it wants to. The good news is that once you figure out where it is putting them, it should always put them in the same place (at least until you upgrade to a newer version).

Tip

Each JSP/Servlet engine has a different *Current* directory. If you can't find any mention of it in the documentation, write a JSP or a servlet that creates a file with a fairly unique name, and then just search for that file.

Setting Configuration Parameters

Obviously, using absolute pathnames is not an ideal solution, nor is using the current directory. Fortunately, there is another solution. You can set a property that your code can read to determine where to save its files. You may have to modify the startup script for your servlet engine in order to set the property, but once that is done, you have a platform-independent way of specifying a directory (or any other configuration parameter).

Tip

If you have many configuration items, consider setting a property that points to a configuration file. That way you only need to set up a single property.

Listing 4.11 shows the changes made to Survey.jsp to support a property called `"survey.dir"`. You can set the property by adding a parameter like `-Dsurvey.dir=c:\surveys` to the Java command used to run the servlet engine.

Listing 4.11 Excerpt from `Survey2.jsp`

```
// See if there is a property pointing to the output directory
        String outputDirectory =
            System.getProperty("survey.dir");

        File outputFile = null;

// If there is an output directory, create a File that points there
        if (outputDirectory != null)
        {
```

LISTING 4.11 CONTINUED

```
            outputFile = new File(outputDirectory,
                "survey.out");
        }
        else
        {
// Otherwise, let the file be a relative path based on the current dir
            outputFile = new File("survey.out");
        }

// Open the output file
        PrintWriter fileOut = new PrintWriter(
            new FileWriter(outputFile.getAbsolutePath(),
            true));
```

LOCKING OUTPUT FILES

Writing data to a file is simple, but writing data for multiple users to the same file at the same time is another story. Java doesn't support file locking, and you can't be guaranteed that two threads won't be running your JSP at the same time.

Take another look at that last statement because it's a lot scarier than you might have first thought. You might think you can just synchronize a section of code to make it single-threaded. While you can make a single instance of your JSP single-threaded, the servlet engine might actually run several copies of your servlet or JSP at once for performance reasons. If all the servlets ran within the same virtual machine, you could synchronize on some globally shared object so that the critical section of code would only be executed by a single instance of your JSP at any given time. Unfortunately, you can't even be sure that all the servlets or JSPs will be executed within the same virtual machine. The servlet engine might start up multiple instances of the Java Virtual Machine for performance or security reasons.

Fortunately, these issues occur only when you need to access resources that are outside of the Virtual Machine (files, database tables, and so on). Databases typically handle locking themselves, so you don't have to worry much about them. Files are one of the few remaining headaches.

The trick to locking a file in Java is that you don't lock it, you rename it. On most operating systems, renaming a file is an atomic operation. That is, only one process or thread can rename a particular file at a particular time and either the file will be renamed or it won't. You don't get into a situation where two threads have the file partially renamed and then both fail.

The idea, then, is to rename the file to something like blahblah.locked, work on the file, and then rename it back to blahblah. If your program tries to locate blahblah and it isn't found, it's probably being locked. The program just needs to sleep for a little while and then try again.

Listing 4.12 shows the changes made to Survey.jsp to support locking by renaming (also incorporating the alternate directory configuration). The locking code will try every second to lock the file, timing out after 30 seconds.

Listing 4.12 Excerpt from Survey3.jsp

```
// See if there is a property pointing to the output directory
        String outputDirectory =
            System.getProperty("survey.dir");

        File outputFile = null;
        File renamedFile = null;

// If there is an output directory, create a File that points there
        if (outputDirectory != null)
        {
            outputFile = new File(outputDirectory,
                "survey.out");
            renamedFile = new File(outputDirectory,
                "survey.lck");
        }
        else
        {
// Otherwise, let the file be a relative path based on the current dir
            outputFile = new File("survey.out");
            renamedFile = new File("survey.lck");
        }

        boolean renameSucceeded = false;

// Loop until the file is available or there have been too many tries
        for (int i=0; i < 30; i++)
        {

// First, make sure that the original output file exists
            if (outputFile.exists())
            {

// If the rename succeeds, exit the loop and write to the file jsp
                if (outputFile.renameTo(renamedFile))
                {
                    renameSucceeded = true;
                    break;
                }
            }
            else
            {
// If the output file didn't exist, try creating the renamed file
// directly. The file can only be created if it doesn't exist, so if
// the create fails, someone else is writing the file

                if (renamedFile.createNewFile())
                {
                    renameSucceeded = true;
                    break;
```

LISTING 4.12 CONTINUED

```
                }
            }

// Up to this point, the rename has failed. Sleep for 1 second
// and try again
            try {
                Thread.sleep(1000);
            } catch (Exception ignore) {}
        }

        if (!renameSucceeded)
        {
            throw new IOException("Unable to lock file");
        }

// Open the output file
        PrintWriter fileOut = new PrintWriter(
            new FileWriter(renamedFile.getAbsolutePath(),
            true));
```

After the file has been written and the output stream is closed, the JSP needs to rename the file back to the original name so another thread can access it. The change involves adding a line after the stream is closed.

```
        fileOut.close();

// After the file is closed, rename it back to the original
        renamedFile.renameTo(outputFile);
```

If your file locking doesn't work or stops working, see "File Locking Problems," in the "Troubleshooting" section at the end of this chapter.

A JSP INPUT FORM CALLING A JSP FORM HANDLER

While static HTML forms are nice, you sometimes need to generate the input form dynamically. For example, you might want to conduct online polls. Rather than creating an HTML form for each poll, you can create a data file containing the poll information and then let a JSP page format the poll question into an input form. Figure 4.6 shows an example of an online poll.

Listing 4.13 shows the Java Server Page that creates the poll using some of the techniques from the Survey JSP. Specifically, it lets you specify a directory where the poll description and results files live.

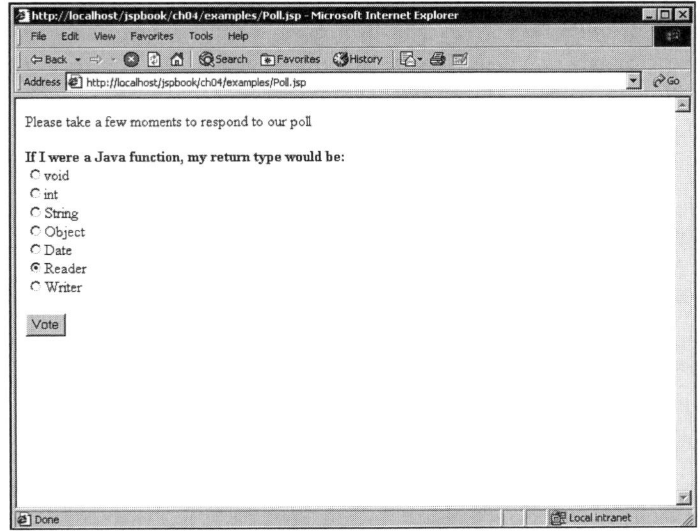

Figure 4.6
The dynamic nature of JSP makes it easy to create online polls from an input file.

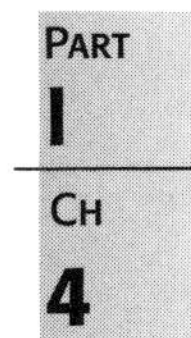

Listing 4.13 Source Code for Poll.jsp

```
<%@page language="java" import="java.io.*" %>
<%@page language="java" import="java.util.*" %>

<HTML>
<BODY bgcolor="#ffffff">
<%

    try
    {
// See if there is a property pointing to the poll directory
        String pollDirectory = System.getProperty("poll.dir");

        File pollFile = null;

// If the directory has been specified, look for the poll
// file there (the poll file describes the question and possible
// answers for the poll)

        if (pollDirectory != null)
        {
            pollFile = new File(pollDirectory, "poll.in");
        }
        else
        {
            pollFile = new File("poll.in");
        }

// Open the poll file
        BufferedReader in = new BufferedReader(
            new FileReader(pollFile));
```

LISTING 4.13 CONTINUED

```
// The poll question should be on the first line
        String question = in.readLine();

        String line;
        Vector answers = new Vector();

// Now read each possible answer, one per line
        while ((line = in.readLine()) != null)
        {
            answers.addElement(line);
        }

        in.close();

// Now display the question and the possible answers
%>
<%-- First display the question --%>
<P>
Please take a few moments to respond to our poll
<P>
<FORM action="PollVote.jsp" method="POST">
<B><%=question%></B>
<BR>
<%-- Now loop through the possible answers --%>
<%
        Enumeration e = answers.elements();
        while (e.hasMoreElements())
        {
            String answer = (String) e.nextElement();
%>
<INPUT type="radio" name="answer" value="<%=answer%>"><%=answer%>
<BR>
<%
        }
%>
<P>
<INPUT type="submit" value="Vote">
</FORM>
<%-- Now handle the case of an IOException while reading the poll file --%>
<%
    }
    catch (IOException exc)
    {
%>
<H1>Sorry</H1>
The poll is currently unavailable. Please try again later.
<%
    }
%>
</BODY>
</HTML>
```

The online poll is just one example of a very common use of JSP. In essence, the JSP is a template: You provide the data, and it formats the data the way you want.

Tip

Notice how the Java Server Page tries to do all the non-display work up front and then displays the data at the bottom? Your code is easier to maintain if you can keep the display code in one place. In Chapter 5 you'll see how to move the non-display code out into a servlet and let the JSP just handle the display.

The vote-taking portion of the online poll is another example of dealing with multiple threads accessing a file. In this case, though, you aren't just appending to the end of a file, you're rewriting the file. It turns out that rewriting is a little easier than locking the file.

To update a file, you create a new, temporary file that will contain the updated version of the file. When you create the file, you check to make sure that the creation was successful. If the creation fails, you can assume that another thread has already created the file and is in the process of updating the file.

Once you create the temporary file, you copy the original file into the temporary file, making whatever changes you need to make. For the poll example, you need to find the line that contains the answer the user chose and update the vote count for that answer. When you are done writing the new file, you close both files, delete the original file, and rename the temporary file to the name of the original.

For example, if the online poll is stored in a file called poll.dat, you would create a temp file with a name like poll.tmp, You read lines out of poll.dat and copy them into poll.tmp, and then delete poll.dat and rename poll.tmp back to poll.dat.

When you rename the temporary file back to the original name, that signals any waiting threads that you are done with the file. One of those threads can now create a temp file to make the updates it needs to make. Again, the other threads that need to make updates have to wait until that thread completes its changes and renames its temp file back to the original.

Listing 4.14 shows a Java Server Page file that updates the vote counts for the online poll and displays the current poll results in a bar graph.

Listing 4.14 Source Code for `PollVote.jsp`

```
<%@ page language="java" import="java.util.*" %>
<%@ page language="java" import="java.io.*" %>

<HTML>
<BODY bgcolor="#ffffff">
<%

    String answer = request.getParameter("answer");

    if (answer == null)
    {
%>
<H1>Oops!</H1>
You tried to vote without voting on anything!
```

LISTING 4.14 CONTINUED

```
</BODY>
</HTML>
<%
        return;
    }

    try
    {
// See if there is a property pointing to the poll directory
        String pollDirectory = System.getProperty("poll.dir");

        File pollFile = null;
        File tempFile = null;

// If the directory has been specified, look for the poll
// file there (the poll file describes the question and possible
// answers for the poll)

        if (pollDirectory != null)
        {
            pollFile = new File(pollDirectory, "poll.dat");
            tempFile = new File(pollDirectory, "poll.tmp");
        }
        else
        {
            pollFile = new File("poll.dat");
            tempFile = new File("poll.tmp");
        }

// To add an entry to the poll, this program just creates a new
// version of the poll data file, updating the count for the answer
// provided

        boolean createSucceeded = false;

// Loop until the file is available or there have been too many tries
        for (int i=0; i < 30; i++)
        {

// Only one process or thread can create the temp file, others fail
// if the file exists. In other words, only one thread can be updating
// the poll data.
            if (tempFile.createNewFile())
            {
                createSucceeded = true;
                break;
            }

// Up to this point, the create has failed. Sleep for 1 second
// and try again
            try {
                Thread.sleep(1000);
            } catch (Exception ignore) {}
        }
```

```
        if (!createSucceeded)
        {
            throw new IOException("Unable to lock file");
        }

// Create a temporary holder for the counts and answers
        Vector counts = new Vector();
        Vector answers = new Vector();
        int totalVotes = 0;

        try
        {

// Try to read the poll.dat file
            BufferedReader in = new BufferedReader(
                new FileReader(pollFile));

// Output will go to the temp file
            PrintWriter pollOut = new PrintWriter(
                new FileWriter(tempFile));

            String line;

            boolean foundAnswer = false;

            while ((line = in.readLine()) != null)
            {
// The poll.dat file should have lines in the form count:answer
// Split out the count and the answer here
                int colonPos = line.indexOf(':');
// If there is no colon, just skip the line
                if (colonPos < 0) continue;

                String countStr = line.substring(0,
                    colonPos);
                String answerStr = line.substring(
                    colonPos+1);

                int count = 0;
                try
                {
                    count = Integer.parseInt(
                        countStr);
                } catch (Exception ignore) {}

// Compare the answer sent from the user with the answer on this
// line. If they are the same, increment the count
                if (answerStr.equals(answer))
                {
                    foundAnswer = true;
                    count++;
                }

                totalVotes = totalVotes + count;

                pollOut.println(count+":"+answerStr);
```

LISTING 4.14 CONTINUED

```
// Save the answer and the current count
                answers.addElement(answerStr);
                counts.addElement(new Integer(count));
            }

            pollOut.close();
            in.close();

// Now replace the original poll file with the new one
            pollFile.delete();
            tempFile.renameTo(pollFile);

// If the answer from the user was nowhere in the file, tell the
// user there has been an error. This implies that a poll.dat needs
// to be set up ahead of time with all the possible answers and initial
// counts of 0.
// This program could dynamically add answers if they are not found, but
// that would allow someone to put phony answers in by manually calling
// this page with something like:
// http://blahblah/PollVote.jsp?answer=MyPhonyAnswer

            if (!foundAnswer)
            {
%>
<H1>Unexpected Answer</H1>
You entered an answer that the vote taker doesn't recognize.
</BODY>
</HTML>
<%
                return;
            }

        }
        catch (IOException ioExc)
        {
// If there's an error, just delete the temp file, meaning that this
// vote won't be counted and another process can try recording a vote
            try {
                tempFile.delete();
            } catch (Exception ignore) {}
%>
<H1>Sorry!</H1>
The vote taker is unable to record your vote. Please try again later.
</BODY>
</HTML>
<%
            return;
        }
%>
<%-- Now display the poll results --%>
<H2>Thank you for your vote!</H1>
<P>
<B>Here are the current poll results:</B>
<P>
<TABLE>
<%
```

```
        int numAnswers = answers.size();

// The counts and answers were saved in a temporary vector

        for (int i=0; i < numAnswers; i++)
        {
            String currAnswer = (String) answers.elementAt(i);
            Integer count = (Integer) counts.elementAt(i);

            int countPct = 0;
            if (totalVotes > 0)
            {
                countPct = (100 * count.intValue()) /
                    totalVotes;
            }

%>
<%-- Show each answer as a table row. Stretch out a GIF image horizontally
     to make a bar graph of the various answers, then print the answer,
     the total count and what pct of the total votes the count represents.
     Since the percentage only goes to 100, multiply by 3 so the image can
     Go from 0 to 300 pixels.
--%>
<TR>
<TD><IMG SRC="pollbar.gif" HEIGHT=20 WIDTH="<%=countPct*3%>">
<TD><%=currAnswer%>
<TD><%=count%> (<%=countPct%>%)
<%
        }
%>
</TABLE>
There have been <%=totalVotes%> votes so far.

<%-- Now in case there was an error trying to create the temp file,
     handle any exception that came up --%>
<%
    }
    catch (Exception exc)
    {
        application.log("Error recording vote", exc);
%>
<H1>Sorry!</H1>
The vote taker is unable to record your vote. Please try again later.
<%
    }
%>
</BODY>
</HTML>
```

The technique of stretching out an image to display a bar graph is fairly common. The pollbar.gif file is only 1 pixel wide and 20 pixels high. It doesn't need to be any larger since it will be stretched horizontally. Figure 4.7 shows a bar graph generated by PollVote.jsp.

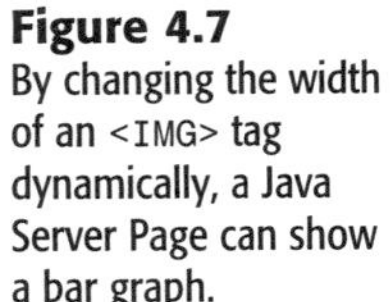

Figure 4.7
By changing the width of an <IMG> tag dynamically, a Java Server Page can show a bar graph.

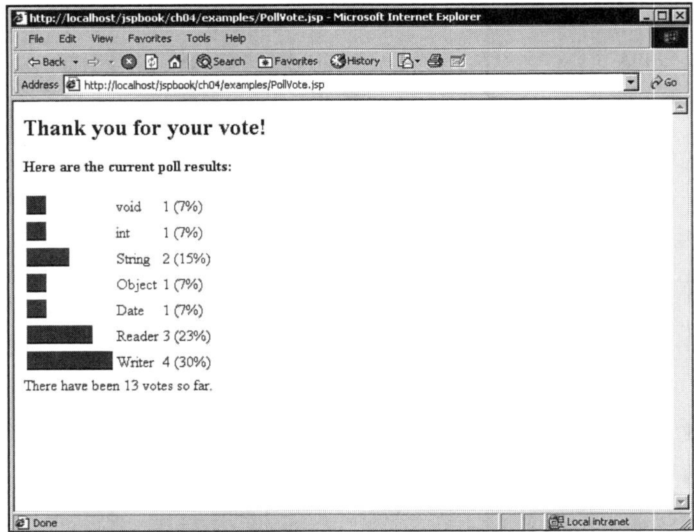

USING THE SAME JSP FOR THE INPUT FORM AND FORM HANDLER

You might think it's a little strange, but putting the input form and the form handler in the same JSP page is sometimes a good idea. Typically, you would combine the input form and form handler when the user needs to use the form multiple times, possibly seeing the results of the previous form submission.

For example, you might have a page for entering an order where you display the current order and allow the user to enter new items for the order. At the beginning of the page you handle the new order items entered by the user and then display the current order. At the end of the page you display the form to add new entries.

The first time the user hits the page, you can detect that there is no form data to process and just present the initial input form. After that, when you detect the presence of previous form data you can process it. There are a few different techniques you can use to detect the form data:

- Simply look for the presence of form variables.
- Pass a special variable indicating that this is a form submission.
- Submit the form using the HTTP `POST` method and examine the request method in your form.

Looking for the form variables is the easiest of these methods. You may occasionally find times when it doesn't suit you. For example, you may pass in a set of form variables to the input form the first time it is displayed. The seed values might be embedded in the URL, passed from the Web page that led the user to the current input form. You wouldn't be able to tell the difference between the initial seed values and a form submission. Even so, this method should work for you most of the time.

In the case where you pass initial values to the input form, you can create a hidden variable on the form with an additional parameter, like `"isSubmitted"`. The declaration in HTML would look like this:

```
<INPUT type=" hidden" name=" isSubmitted" value=" yes">
```

When the user accesses the form for the first time, you won't see this variable because they haven't submitted the input form. You can simply check to see if `request.getParameter("isSubmitted")` returns `null` or not. If it is null, the form was not submitted.

Sometimes you don't even want to go through the hassle of testing to see if the form variables are there. You want to know right away if the form was submitted. If the initial form is accessed using a hyperlink (i.e. the browser accesses the form with an HTTP `GET`) and you declare the method for the `<FORM>` tag to be `"POST"`, you can use `request.getMethod()` to determine if the user actually submitted the form.

In other words, you set up your form like this:

```
<FORM action="someaction.jsp" method="POST">
```

You then use `request.getMethod` to see whether the form was submitted, like this:

```
if (request.getMethod().equals("POST"))
```


AN EXAMPLE INPUT FORM AND FORM HANDLER JSP

Suppose you want to create a page that allows the user to enter their name, address, and possibly other information and then control how they want the information formatted. The user might be ordering personalized stationary with various formatting options. You can display the current formatting information and then allow the user to change the information all from the same page. You can also detect that the user hasn't entered a required field or marked the required fields in some way. Figure 4.8 shows how the initial input form might look. Figure 4.9 shows the form asking for the user to supply values for the required fields. Figure 4.10 shows the form displaying the formatted data.

The form in Figure 4.8 is certainly a lot simpler than a typical form of this type. You would probably have additional information like phone numbers, email addresses, and Web addresses. Listing 4.15 shows the single JSP that generates the input form and displays the formatted data. The program uses the `request.getMethod` technique to determine whether the user has submitted any data.

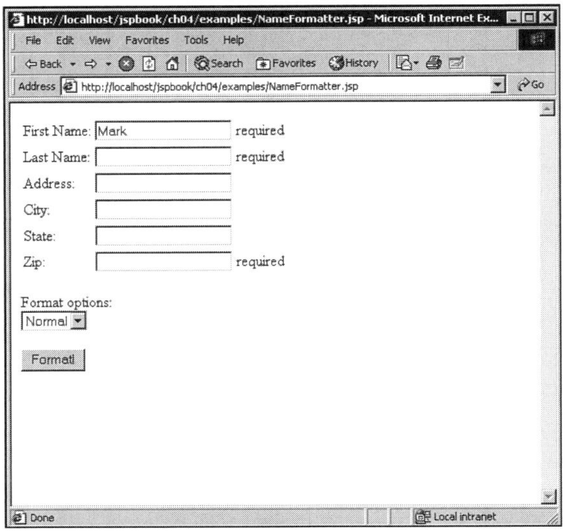

Figure 4.8
A JSP can be called multiple times with extra output appearing at different times.

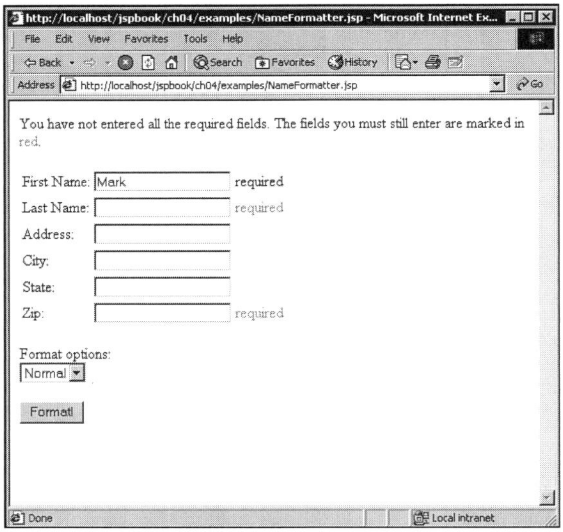

Figure 4.9
A JSP can display required fields that the user has neglected to enter.

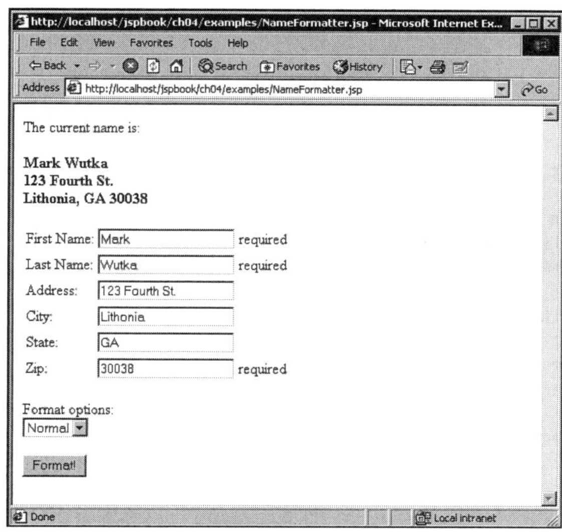

Figure 4.10 You can also display formatted text and allow the user to change the values being displayed.

Listing 4.15 Source Code for `NameFormatter.jsp`

```
<HTML>
<BODY>

<%
    String firstName = request.getParameter("firstname");
    if (firstName == null) firstName = "";

    String lastName = request.getParameter("lastname");
    if (lastName == null) lastName = "";

    String address = request.getParameter("address");
    if (address == null) address = "";

    String city = request.getParameter("city");
    if (city == null) city = "";

    String state = request.getParameter("state");
    if (state == null) state = "";

    String zip = request.getParameter("zip");
    if (zip == null) zip = "";

    String formatOption = request.getParameter("formatoption");
    if (formatOption == null) formatOption = "";

// Since some fields are required, set the default style for the "required"
// labels
    String firstNameRequiredColor = "black";
    String lastNameRequiredColor = "black";
    String zipRequiredColor = "black";
```

LISTING 4.15 CONTINUED

```
    String requiredNotifyColor = "red";

// When this form is originally shown, it is fetched by an HTTP GET
// request, but in the METHOD option in the FORM tag below, the form
// is fetched using an HTTP POST command.

// See if this form was submitted (i.e. the user filled in the form
// and pressed the submit button)
    if (request.getMethod().equals("POST"))
    {
        boolean allRequiredFieldsPresent = true;

// See if any of the required fields are blank
        if (firstName.length() == 0)
        {
            firstNameRequiredColor = requiredNotifyColor;
            allRequiredFieldsPresent = false;
        }

        if (lastName.length() == 0)
        {
            lastNameRequiredColor = requiredNotifyColor;
            allRequiredFieldsPresent = false;
        }

        if (zip.length() == 0)
        {
            zipRequiredColor = requiredNotifyColor;
            allRequiredFieldsPresent = false;
        }

// If the user hasn't entered the required fields, tell them that the
// fields are marked in a separate color.
        if (!allRequiredFieldsPresent)
        {
%>
You have not entered all the required fields. The fields you must still
enter are marked in <font color="<%=requiredNotifyColor%>">
<%=requiredNotifyColor%></font>.
<%
        }
        else
        {
// Display the name and address as it has been entered

            String nameString = firstName+" "+lastName+
                "<BR>"+ address+"<BR>"+city+", "+
                state+" "+zip;

            out.println("The current name is:<P>");

            if (formatOption.equals("bold"))
            {
                out.println("<B>"+nameString+"</B>");
            }
```

```
            else if (formatOption.equals("italic"))
            {
                out.println("<I>"+nameString+"</I>");
            }
            else
            {
                out.println(nameString);
            }
            out.println("<P>");
        }
    }
%>
<%-- Always allow the user to update the data and submit --%>
<FORM action="NameFormatter.jsp" method="POST">
<TABLE>
<TR><TD>First Name:<TD><INPUT type="text" name="firstname" value="<%=firstName%>">
<TD><FONT color="<%=firstNameRequiredColor%>">required</FONT>

<TR><TD>Last Name:<TD><INPUT type="text" name="lastname" value="<%=lastName%>">
<TD><FONT color="<%=lastNameRequiredColor%>">required</FONT>

<TR><TD>Address:<TD><INPUT type="text" name="address" value="<%=address%>">
<TR><TD>City:<TD><INPUT type="text" name="city" value="<%=city%>">
<TR><TD>State:<TD><INPUT type="text" name="state" value="<%=state%>">

<TR><TD>Zip:<TD><INPUT type="text" name="zip" value="<%=zip%>">
<TD><FONT color="<%=zipRequiredColor%>">required</FONT>
</TABLE>
<P>
Format options:<BR>
<SELECT name="formatoption">
    <OPTION value="normal">Normal</OPTION>
    <OPTION value="bold">Bold</OPTION>
    <OPTION value="italic">Italic</OPTION>
</SELECT>
<P>
<INPUT type="submit" value="Format!">
</FORM>
</BODY>
</HTML>
```

Many of the examples you have seen so far can be a bit difficult to follow because of the mixture of Java code and HTML. Chapter 5, "Saving Data Between Requests," will show you how to better organize your code and eliminate some of these problems.

TROUBLESHOOTING

FORM AND FORM VARIABLE NAMES

I press the Submit button, but the form won't load. What am I doing wrong?

Aside from the obvious spelling errors in the action attribute of the `<FORM>`, you must also make sure that the capitalization action attribute matches the name of the form JSP. Even if you are running under Windows, Java is case sensitive, so you can run into problems if you try to invoke a JSP using capitalization that is different from the actual filename.

Why are the form variable values null?

Usually the reason you can't get the value of a form variable is because the name of the variable in the form doesn't exactly match the name you use in the `getParameter` method, either because of a spelling difference or a capitalization difference.

JAVASCRIPT PROBLEMS

Why won't JavaScript function run or report errors?

When mixing Java and JavaScript, it is often very easy to accidentally mix some Java code into the JavaScript. In some cases, you just won't get the results you expect. Most of the time you get JavaScript errors. An editor that does syntax colorization often helps separate the Java from the JavaScript and points out any errors.

Why does JSP compile errors occur when adding JavaScript functions?

Although there are many causes of compile errors, accidentally mixing JavaScript into the Java code is a common one. An editor with syntax colorization can also help reduce these errors.

FILE LOCKING PROBLEMS

Why doesn't locking ever work?

Chances are that you are not allowed to rename the existing file or you have misspelled the name of the file.

Why does locking work only for a while and then stop?

If your program crashes while it has the file locked, the file remains locked (that is, it never gets renamed). You will need to rename the file manually to get locking to work again.

CHAPTER 5

SAVING DATA BETWEEN REQUESTS

In this chapter

Web programmers often need to keep track of data between user requests. Given what you already know about JSP, servlets, and HTML forms, you already have the ability to keep track of data between requests. You can store user data in hidden form variables.

STORING DATA IN HIDDEN FORM VARIABLES

Although not the most elegant solution, form variables are used by many applications to store user data. The idea is that every time the user submits a form, it contains some hidden variables that contain information about the user. These variables might be a login ID and password or the user's name. The big hassle with this method is that all your forms must preserve these hidden variables and continue to pass them around.

The best way to illustrate this technique is with an example. Listing 5.1 shows a login form that calls a JSP to handle the login.

LISTING 5.1 SOURCE CODE FOR `Login.html`

```
<HTML>
<BODY bgcolor="#ffffff">
<H1>Login</H1>
Please log in

<FORM action="Login.jsp" method="POST">

<TABLE>
<TR><TD>User Name:<TD><INPUT type="text" name="username">
<TR><TD>Password:<TD><INPUT type="password" name="password">
</TABLE>
<P>
<INPUT type="submit" value="Login!">
</FORM>
</BODY>
</HTML>
```

The goal of this example is to preserve the username across multiple pages. Obviously the Login.jsp page will have the username because it's passed as a form variable from Login.html. Listing 5.2 shows Login.jsp. Notice that it inserts the username as a hidden form variable.

LISTING 5.2 SOURCE CODE FOR `Login.jsp`

```
<HTML>
<BODY bgcolor="#ffffff">

<%
// Get the login information
    String userName = request.getParameter("username");
    String password = request.getParameter("password");

%>
Welcome, <%=userName%>!
```

```
<FORM action="/servlet/usingjsp.ColorServlet" method="POST">

<%-- Save the username in a hidden form variable --%>
<INPUT type="hidden" name="username" value="<%=userName%>">

<P>
Please enter your favorite color:
<SELECT name="color">
    <OPTION value="blue" SELECTED>Blue</OPTION>
    <OPTION value="red">Red</OPTION>
    <OPTION value="green">Green</OPTION>
    <OPTION value="yellow">Yellow</OPTION>
    <OPTION value="mauve">Mauve</OPTION>
</SELECT>
<P>
<INPUT type="submit" value="Choose color!">
</FORM>
</BODY>
</HTML>
```

Figure 5.1 shows the output from Login.jsp.

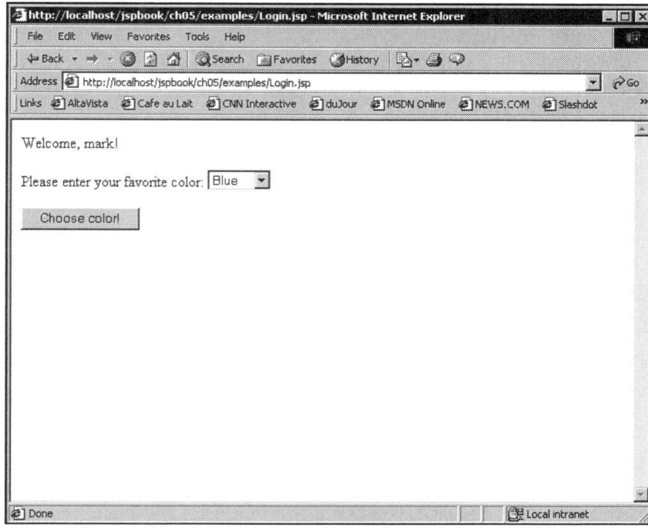

Figure 5.1
A page can contain hidden form variables that the user can't see.

Just so you don't think servlets have been cut out of the loop here, the third part of this example is a servlet that receives the hidden form variable along with the user's color choice. Listing 5.3 shows the servlet.

LISTING 5.3 SOURCE CODE FOR ColorServlet.java

```
package usingjsp;

import javax.servlet.*;
import java.io.*;

public class ColorServlet extends GenericServlet
{
    public void service(ServletRequest request,
        ServletResponse response)
        throws IOException
    {
// Tell the Web server that the response is HTML
        response.setContentType("text/html");

// Get the PrintWriter for writing out the response
        PrintWriter out = response.getWriter();

// Fetch the username and color parameters
String userName = request.getParameter("username");
        String color = request.getParameter("color");

// Write the HTML back to the browser
        out.println("<HTML>");
        out.println("<BODY bgcolor=\"#ffffff\">");
        out.println("Well, I see that "+userName+
            "'s favorite color is "+color+".");
        out.println("</BODY>");
        out.println("</HTML>");
    }
}
```

SECURITY CONCERNS WITH HIDDEN VARIABLES

One of the reasons you don't see hidden variables used very often in commercial Web sites, especially e-commerce sites, is that they are inherently insecure. Suppose Login.jsp actually verified the username and password. You would assume that the username passed to `ColorServlet` is valid. There is nothing to stop someone from inserting their own username and even a bizarre color by passing it in the URL for the servlet. Figure 5.2 shows an example of how the system can be tricked. Notice that the phony username and color are embedded into the URL.

Changing a username is bad enough, but imagine what could happen if someone did this with a bank account or credit card number! Certainly this technique needs some work. You could get clever and choose a variable name that is far less obvious than "`username`". Suppose, for example, that you changed the name of the hidden variable to "`xpq7564HHgk`". Surely no one would guess the variable name! Unfortunately, all someone needs to do is ask the browser to display the source for the page, as shown in Figure 5.3.

Another big concern with hidden form variables is that the user might accidentally bookmark the secure information. When you submit a form using an HTTP `GET` method (setting `method="get"` in your `<form>` tag), the form variables all appear in the URL and will be part of a bookmark if the user bookmarks the page. Even hidden form variables show up in the URL. If you use hidden form variables, even storing a single value, make sure you use an HTTP POST to keep the hidden information from being bookmarked.

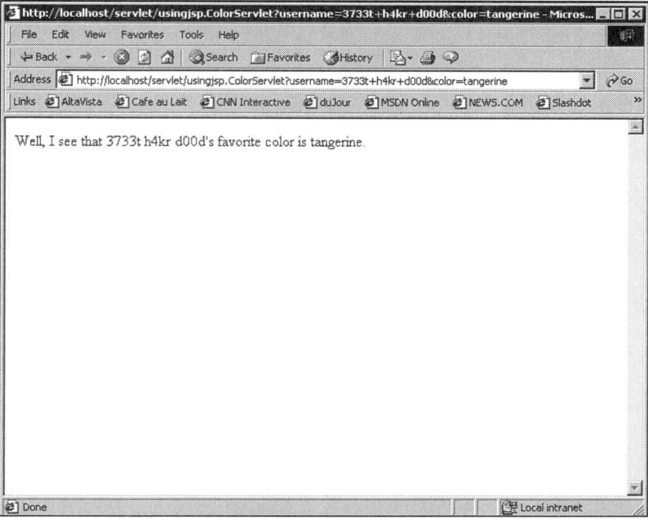

Figure 5.2
A malicious user can send phony values for hidden form variables.

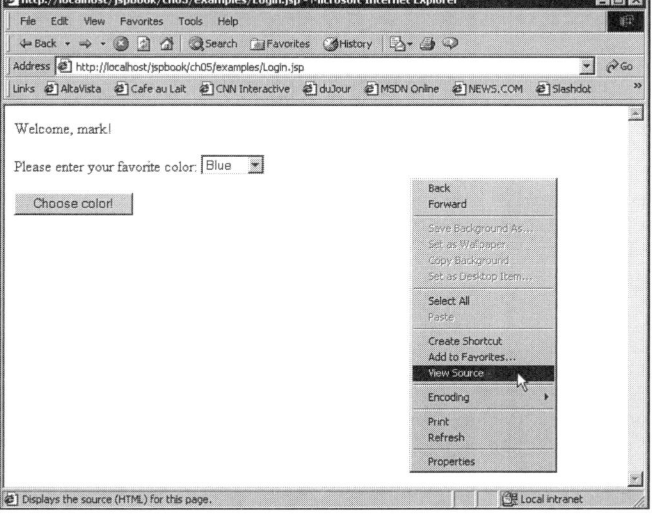

Figure 5.3
Because a user can view the source to a page, you can't safely hide anything in the page.

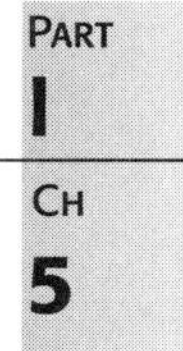

Now, suppose you decide to store information on the server instead of trying to save all the data in hidden form variables. When a request comes in from a browser, how will you know what information goes with which client browser? To solve this problem, the browser must identify itself somehow.

You need to store one piece of data on the client: a key that uniquely identifies the browser and helps you remember where the user's data is stored. In other words, you get some data from the client, you store it in a hash table using some random key, and then send that key back to the browser in a hidden field. The next time the user fills out a form, the browser sends the server the hidden key field along with the other form variables. Your code on the server takes that key, looks in the hash table, and pulls out the user's data.

Storing data this way is much more secure than putting the data straight into hidden fields. Now if someone wants to break the system and tamper with the data, the best he can do is change the key. If the key value is large enough, it's unlikely that the hacker will be able to guess someone else's random key. He certainly won't be able to send you phony data, because the data stays on the server.

Listing 5.4 shows you a Java class that implements the key generation and data storage for keeping track of user data.

LISTING 5.4 SOURCE CODE FOR UserDataTable.java

```
package usingjsp;

import java.util.*;

public class UserDataTable
{
    protected static Hashtable userData = new Hashtable();
    protected static Random keyGenerator = new Random();
/** Creates a new table for a user's data and returns the key for
 *  the user's data.
 */
    public static String createUserData()
    {
// Create a random key for the user's data
        String userKey = ""+keyGenerator.nextLong();

// Create a hash table for the user's data and store it
        userData.put(userKey, new Hashtable());

        return userKey;
    }

/** Returns the user data table for a particular user */
    public static Hashtable getUserData(String userKey)
    {
        if (userKey == null) return null;
        return (Hashtable) userData.get(userKey);
    }

/** Destroys the user data table for a particular user */
    public static void clearUserData(String userKey)
    {
        if (userKey == null) return;
        userData.remove(userKey);
    }
}
```

To make use of this new `UserDataTable` class, you need to change the Login.jsp file to store the username in the user data table instead of a hidden frame. Listing 5.5 shows how Login.jsp can support this new storage method with very few changes.

Listing 5.5 Source Code for `Login2.jsp`

```
<%@ page language="java" import="java.util.*,usingjsp.*" %>

<HTML>
<BODY bgcolor="#ffffff">

<%
// Get the login information
    String userName = request.getParameter("username");
    String password = request.getParameter("password");

    String userKey = UserDataTable.createUserData();

    Hashtable userData = UserDataTable.getUserData(userKey);

    userData.put("username", userName);
%>
Welcome, <%=userName%>!
<FORM action="/servlet/usingjsp.ColorServlet2" method="POST">

<%-- Save the username in a hidden form variable --%>
<INPUT type="hidden" name="userkey" value="<%=userKey%>">

<P>
Please enter your favorite color:
<SELECT name="color">
    <OPTION value="blue" SELECTED>Blue</OPTION>
    <OPTION value="red">Red</OPTION>
    <OPTION value="green">Green</OPTION>
    <OPTION value="yellow">Yellow</OPTION>
    <OPTION value="mauve">Mauve</OPTION>
</SELECT>
<P>
<INPUT type="submit" value="Choose color!">
</FORM>
</BODY>
</HTML>
```


The main difference between Login.jsp and Login2.jsp is that Login2.jsp creates a user data table and stores the key for that table in a hidden field. Notice that Login2.jsp does not send the username back to the browser in a hidden field. All you need now is to modify the `ColorServlet` program to fetch the username from the user data table instead of from the hidden field. Listing 5.6 shows the modified `ColorServlet` that uses the user data table.

Listing 5.6 Source Code for `ColorServlet2.java`

```
package usingjsp;


import javax.servlet.*;
```

LISTING 5.6 CONTINUED

```
import java.io.*;
import java.util.*;

public class ColorServlet2 extends GenericServlet
{
    public void service(ServletRequest request,
        ServletResponse response)
        throws IOException
    {
// Tell the Web server that the response is HTML
response.setContentType("text/html");

// Get the PrintWriter for writing out the response
        PrintWriter out = response.getWriter();

// Fetch the user key and color parameters
        String userKey = request.getParameter("userkey");
        String color = request.getParameter("color");

        Hashtable userData = UserDataTable.getUserData(userKey);

// If the user data table isn't found, someone probably monkeyed with
// the key value.
        if (userData == null)
        {
            out.println("<HTML><BODY>");
            out.println("<H1>Sorry</H1>");
            out.println("The system is experiencing problems.");
            out.println("</BODY></HTML>");
            return;
        }

// Now try to get the username from the table
String userName = (String) userData.get("username");

// Write the HTML back to the browser
        out.println("<HTML>");
        out.println("<BODY bgcolor=\"#ffffff\">");
        out.println("Well, I see that "+userName+
            "'s favorite color is "+color+".");
        out.println("</BODY>");
        out.println("</HTML>");
    }
}
```

This method of storing data makes one assumption that you can't overlook: The servlet and Java Server Page must be running within the same Java Virtual Machine (JVM). The key to preserving the data is that the `UserDataTable` class uses static data. If the servlet runs in one JVM while the Java Server Page runs in another JVM, they will be using separate copies of the `UserDataTable` class, and thus will not share any data. If you ever decide to use a technique like this, make sure that everything is running within the same JVM. Most servlet and JSP engines on the market today run within a single JVM.

The hidden form variable approach seems to work fairly well except for one thing: the hidden variable itself. First of all, putting the hidden variable in every form is a hassle. Second, it requires the browser to use forms only as a method of accessing server-side pages. If you use a hyperlink, there are no form variables to pass. You must either rewrite your hyperlinks to include something like "?userkey=9345837479" or find a better alternative. That alternative is the session object.

STORING DATA IN A session OBJECT

One thing you need to realize when dealing with the Web is that there is no permanent connection between the browser and the Web server. If you have done database programming or socket programming, you are familiar with the concept of a session: an active connection between two participants.

The HTTP protocol used by the browser and the Web server is not session-oriented. When the browser needs a page from the Web server, it opens a connection, retrieves the page, and then closes the connection. Because there is no active connection, the Web server has no idea what is happening on the browser. The browser could crash or the entire client computer could be turned off, and the Web server would be oblivious.

That being said, servlets and Java Server Pages do have a notion of a session. Near the end of the discussion on hidden form variables, you saw a technique in which data is stored on the server, referenced by a single key that was stored on the client. Servlets and Java Server Pages use a very similar technique, which is implemented by the HttpSession object.

The beauty of the HttpSession object is that it does not rely on hidden form variables and works even if a servlet or JSP is accessed via a hyperlink. The reason HttpSession is able to work without hidden form variables is that it uses something called a *cookie* to store the user's session key. A cookie contains a piece of data that the server sends to the browser and that the browser sends back to the server with each request. You will learn much more about cookies in Chapter 8, "More About Saving Data."

➔ To learn more about cookies, **see** "Storing Data in a Cookie," **p. 170**.

USING THE session OBJECT IN A JSP

The Java Server Pages API has several built-in objects. You have already seen two of them: request and out. The next important one is called session, and it's an instance of HttpSession. The three methods that you use the most in the session object are getAttribute, setAttribute, and removeAttribute. The declarations for these methods are

```
public void setAttribute(String name, Object value)
    throws IllegalStateException
public Object getAttribute(String name)
    throws IllegalStateException
public void removeAttribute(String name, Object value)
    throws IllegalStateException
```

These methods act much like the get and put methods in the Hashtable class. That is, setAttribute associates a name with a value, and getAttribute returns the value associated with a name or null if there is no value associated. For example, to store some data in a session, you would do something like this:

```
session.setAttribute("someKey", "here is my data");
```

To retrieve the data back out of the session, you would do something like this:

```
String myData = (String) session.getAttribute("someKey");
```

Note

The `getAttribute`, `setAttribute`, and `removeAttribute` methods were added to the Servlet API in version 2.2. Prior to version 2.2, these methods were called `getValue`, `putValue`, and `removeValue` (with the same parameters). Although `getValue`, `putValue`, and `removeValue` are supported under version 2.2 of the Servlet API, they are deprecated. Only use them if your servlets must run under Servlet API version 2.1 or earlier.

`IllegalStateException` is thrown when you try to get or set an attribute on an invalid session. A session becomes invalid either when you call its `invalidate` method or after the session has timed out. The servlet engine keeps track of how long it has been since a session has been accessed; after a certain period of inactivity, the session is marked as invalid. You can configure the amount of time it takes to time out a session, either on a per-session basis or for all sessions.

Note

The Servlet API specifies a way for you to control the timeout period on a per-session basis. Most servlet engines also provide a way for you to specify a default timeout length, but they are not required to by the Servlet API.

Listing 5.7 shows the Login.jsp page modified to support the `session` object instead of the `UserDataTable` class. Notice that it no longer needs to use the hidden form variable.

LISTING 5.7 SOURCE CODE FOR `Login3.jsp`

```
<%@ page language="java" import="java.util.*,usingjsp.*" %>

<HTML>
<BODY bgcolor="#ffffff">

<%
// Get the login information
    String userName = request.getParameter("username");
    String password = request.getParameter("password");

// Store the username in the session
session.setAttribute("username", userName);
%>
Welcome, <%=userName%>!
<FORM action="/servlet/usingjsp.ColorServlet3" method="POST">

<P>
Please enter your favorite color:
<SELECT name="color">
    <OPTION value="blue" SELECTED>Blue</OPTION>
    <OPTION value="red">Red</OPTION>
    <OPTION value="green">Green</OPTION>
    <OPTION value="yellow">Yellow</OPTION>
```

```
    <OPTION value="mauve">Mauve</OPTION>
</SELECT>
<P>
<INPUT type="submit" value="Choose color!">
</FORM>
</BODY>
</HTML>
```

If you are having trouble storing or retrieving your session information, see "Storing and Retrieving Data," in the "Troubleshooting" section at the end of this chapter.

USING THE session OBJECT IN A SERVLET

You have probably guessed this already, but the `session` object you use in a servlet is identical to the one you use in a Java Server Page. The only difference is that it isn't already conveniently sitting around in a variable named `session`. Instead, you must get the `session` object from the `request` object.

Note

Java Server Pages also get the `session` object from the `request` object. The only reason you don't notice is that the JSP compiler automatically generates code to fetch the `session` object and put it in a variable named `session`.

To get the `session` object from the `request` object, just call the `getSession` method:

```
HttpSession session = request.getSession();
```

Inside a servlet, you use the same `getAttribute` and `setAttribute` methods to update session variables as you do in a Java Server Page. After all, the `session` object is an instance of `HttpSession` in both a servlet and a JSP.

Caution

Because the servlet engine needs to send a session cookie back to the browser, make sure you get the `session` object before you start sending a response back to the browser. Otherwise, it might be too late for the servlet engine to send back the cookie, because the cookie must be sent back in the header portion of the response. In a JSP, the `session` object is usually available immediately. You really only need to worry about this inside a servlet.

Listing 5.8 shows the modifications necessary to `ColorServlet` to make it use `HttpSession` instead of the `UserDataClass`. Also notice that unlike the previous versions of `ColorServlet`, this one is a subclass of `HttpServlet` (the others were subclasses of `GenericServlet`). The method signature on the service method is a little different now, too, because the `request` and `response` parameters are now instances of `HttpServletRequest` and `HttpServletResponse`.

LISTING 5.8 SOURCE CODE FOR `ColorServlet3.java`

```
package usingjsp;

import javax.servlet.*;
```

LISTING 5.8 CONTINUED

```
import javax.servlet.http.*;
import java.io.*;
import java.util.*;

public class ColorServlet3 extends HttpServlet
{
    public void service(HttpServletRequest request,
        HttpServletResponse response)
        throws IOException
    {
// Tell the Web server that the response is HTML
response.setContentType("text/html");

// Get the PrintWriter for writing out the response
        PrintWriter out = response.getWriter();

// Fetch the color parameter
        String color = request.getParameter("color");

// Get the username from the session
HttpSession session = request.getSession();

        String userName = (String) session.getAttribute("username");

// Write the HTML back to the browser
        out.println("<HTML>");
        out.println("<BODY bgcolor=\"#ffffff\">");
        out.println("Well, I see that "+userName+
            "'s favorite color is "+color+".");
        out.println("</BODY>");
        out.println("</HTML>");
    }
}
```

Note

Because the `HttpSession` object relies specifically on features of the HTTP protocol, you can only use it in servlets that are subclasses of `HttpServlet`.

HOW SESSIONS WORK

Now that you see that servlets and Java Server Pages can support sessions, you can take a step back and look at how the sessions work. When the servlet engine creates a session, it sends a session identifier (also referred to as a session key earlier in this chapter) back to the browser in the form of a cookie. Again, the cookie is just a piece of information that the browser sends back to the server whenever it asks the server for a page.

Usually, for a session, the cookie disappears when the Web browser is shut down. As you will see in Chapter 8, a browser can save cookies to disk, so when the browser starts up again it still knows about the cookies it had when it shut down. Because sessions are typically short-lived, and because shutting the browser down is an action that warrants the termination of a session, the session cookie is usually not saved to disk. Remember, the server has no idea when the Web browser shuts down. Figure 5.4 illustrates the interaction between the browser and the servlet engine as it relates to cookies and sessions.

Note You must enable cookies in your browser for these examples to work.

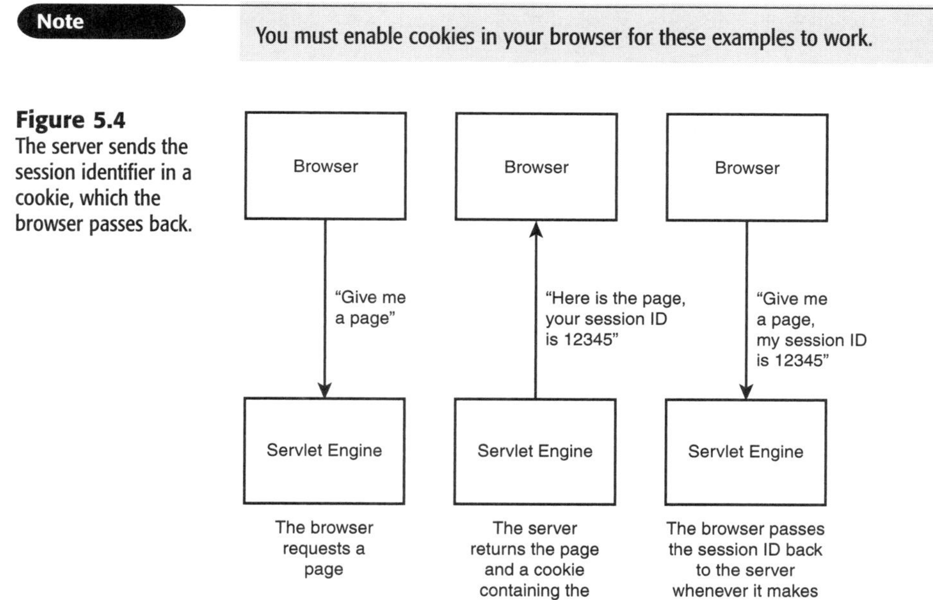

Figure 5.4 The server sends the session identifier in a cookie, which the browser passes back.

When the browser asks the server for a page, the server looks at the session cookie, and then finds the session corresponding to that session identifier. Occasionally, the servlet engine looks through its sessions and gets rid of those that haven't been accessed in a long time. If it didn't do this, eventually the servlet engine would be wasting a lot of memory holding onto sessions that could never be accessed again because the cookies associated with those sessions are long gone (people shut down their browsers eventually, and that kills the session cookies).

Forcing a New Session

When you call the `getSession` method to retrieve the current session, the `request` object automatically creates a session if one doesn't already exist. In some JSP implementations, the session is created automatically even if you never use it. Most of the time, you don't really care when the session has been created. Other times, however, you need to explicitly reset the existing session and start over.

Suppose, for example, that you have implemented an online shopping site. A user logs on, visits a few pages, and selects several items to buy. You store these items in the user's session as they travel from page to page. Now, suppose the user decides that she doesn't want any of those items, and rather than go through the trouble of removing them from her shopping cart, she decides to just log in to your site again.

If a user comes back into your login page, you probably want to start her over with a clean slate. Although you could design a site that is smart enough to figure out what you were last doing and send you back to where you left off, most people assume that when they come in through the "front door," they are starting over.

Note

Users might go back to the login screen and walk away from the computer, thinking their order is now gone. Imagine their surprise if another user could walk up to the computer, log back in, and have the previous user's order, complete with credit card number.

The `getSession` method in the `request` object enables you to control the creation of new sessions. When you ask for a session, you can ask that the request object not create a new session if one doesn't already exist. The following segment of code automatically invalidates the previous session and then creates a new one:

```
// Get the old session, but don't create a session if
// one didn't already exist (passing true would allow
// creation of a new one).
    HttpSession oldSess = request.getSession(false);

// If there was an old session, invalidate it
    if (oldSess != null)
    {
        oldSess.invalidate();
    }

// Now create a fresh new session
    HttpSession session = request.getSession(true);
```

This code works for both JSP and servlets, except that for a JSP, you shouldn't re-declare a session. Instead, the last line should just read

```
session = request.getSession(true);
```

HANDLING SESSION TERMINATION

A session can be terminated in two ways: You force the termination by calling the `invalidate` method on the session, or the servlet engine times the session out. Depending on the kind of data you store in the session, you might need to perform some kind of cleanup of the session data. For example, you might have a database connection stored in the session, or a connection to an RMI or CORBA service on another machine. Although Java's garbage collector eventually eliminates these resources, you shouldn't keep them open any longer than you need to.

A `session` object has a callback mechanism to notify an object when it has been associated with a session and when it is no longer associated with a session. That is, when you call `session.setAttribute("someName", someObject)`, the `session` object can notify the object that it is being associated with a session. When the session terminates, the `session` object can notify the object that it is no longer associated with the session.

This notification is on an object-by-object basis. Although it might seem strange at first, the notification technique is actually very flexible. You can write objects that are session-aware and can perform their own cleanup. If you are using standard objects, such as a JDBC Connection object, you can create a special session cleanup object that releases your database connection.

THE HttpSessionBindingListener INTERFACE

The HttpSessionBindingListener interface defines notification methods that the session object uses to notify objects when they are added to or removed from a session. There are two methods in the interface:

```
public void valueBound(HttpSessionBindingEvent event);
public void valueUnbound(HttpSessionBindingEvent event);
```

As you might have guessed, valueBound is called when an object is added to a session; valueUnbound is called when the object is removed from a session. Listing 5.9 shows an example class that listens for valueBound and valueUnbound messages and counts the number of sessions that are bound to it.

LISTING 5.9 SOURCE CODE FOR BINDLISTENER.JAVA

```
package usingjsp;

import javax.servlet.http.*;

/** Counts the number of sessions that are bound to this object. */

public class BindListener implements HttpSessionBindingListener
{
// The current session count
    protected int numSessions;

    public BindListener()
    {
        numSessions = 0;
    }

// Every time this object is added to a session,
// valueBound is called
    public synchronized void valueBound(HttpSessionBindingEvent event)
    {
        numSessions++;
    }

// Every time this object is removed from a session,
// valueUnbound is called
    public synchronized void valueUnbound(HttpSessionBindingEvent event)
    {
        numSessions--;
    }

// Returns the current number of bound sessions
    public int getNumSessions()
    {
```

```
        return numSessions;
    }
}
```

To test the `BindListener` class, you need to observe what happens when you access it from multiple sessions and also see what happens when you invalidate a session containing a `BindListener` object. You should expect to see the session count go up whenever the object is added to a session, and you should see the count go down when the object is removed from a session, or when the session it belongs to is invalidated.

Listing 5.10 shows a test harness JSP that exercises the `BindListener` class. By selecting various hyperlinks, you can remove the `BindListener` object from the session or invalidate the session.

LISTING 5.10 SOURCE CODE FOR BindTest.jsp

```
<%@ page language="java" import="usingjsp.BindListener" %>

<HTML>
<BODY bgcolor="#ffffff">

<%-- Set up a static BindListener shared by all instances of this JSP.

     There is probably only one instance, but just in case the server creates

     multiple instances, this page can handle it. --%>
<%!
    protected static BindListener listener = new BindListener();
%>

<%

    BindListener l = null;

// Allow the browser to pass a "removeListener" parameter to remove
// a listener from the session

    if (request.getParameter("removeListener") != null)
    {
        session.removeAttribute("listener");
    }

// Allow the browser to pass a "resetSession parameter to clear out
// the session
    else if (request.getParameter("resetSession") != null)
    {
// See if there is already a session
        HttpSession oldSession = request.getSession(false);

// If there was already a session, invalidate
        if (oldSession != null)
        {
            l = (BindListener)
                oldSession.getAttribute("listener");
            oldSession.invalidate();
```

```
// Tell the user that the session was reset and show that the
// bind counts have been updated. Make sure that there was a
// listener on the old session, too.

            if (l != null)
            {
%>
Your current session was reset. The listener now has <%=l.getNumSessions()%>
active sessions.<P>
<%
            } else {
%>
Your old session didn't have a listener.<P>
<%
            }

            l = null;
        }
    }
    else
    {
// See if the listener is already in the session
        l = (BindListener)
            session.getAttribute("listener");

// If not, add the global copy of the listener to the session
        if (l == null)
        {
// Put the global listener variable into the session
            session.setAttribute("listener", listener);
            l = listener;
        }
    }
%>
<%
    if (l != null)
    {
%>
You have a listener bound to your session.
<%
    } else {
%>
You do not have a listener bound to your session.
<%
    }
%>
There are currently <%=listener.getNumSessions()%> sessions holding onto the
bind listener.
<P>
<TABLE>
<TR>
<TD>
<A href="BindTest.jsp">Refresh Form</A>
<TD>
<A href="BindTest.jsp?removeListener">Remove Listener</A>
<TD>
<A href="BindTest.jsp?resetSession">Reset Session</A>
</TABLE>
```

```
</BODY>
</HTML>
```

Figure 5.5 shows several browser sessions running BindTest.jsp.

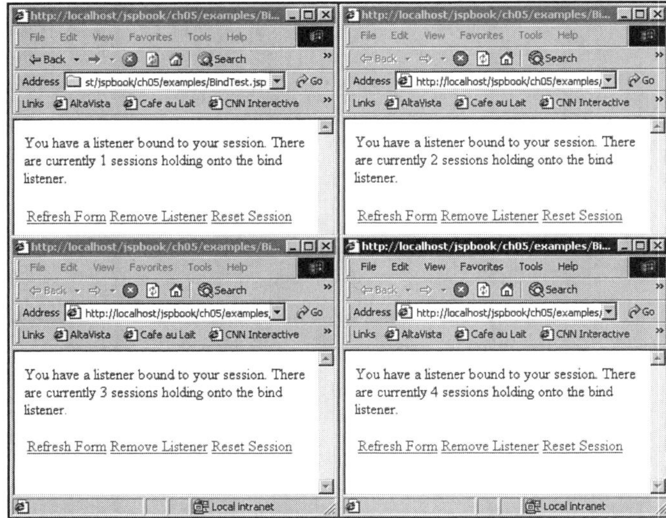

Figure 5.5
The `BindListener` object keeps track of how many sessions it belongs to.

HANDLING SESSIONS WITHOUT COOKIES

Normally, JSP and servlet sessions rely on the HTTP cookie mechanism to preserve the session identifier between requests. Cookies are really nice for doing things such as sessions and online ordering. Unfortunately, cookies have also been abused. Many Web sites store personal information in cookies, and many Web users don't like their personal information being sent to another Web server without their knowledge. To put it simply, cookie abuse has given cookies a bad name.

Many users now disable cookies within their browsers. You might think that with cookies disabled, the only way to keep track of session information would be the hidden field technique discussed at the beginning of this chapter. Fortunately, there is another solution.

If you knew the session ID, you could pass it as a parameter to all your servlets and Java Server Pages. The `HttpSession` object contains a `getId` method, so you could pass it around. Now all you need is a way to take a session ID and find the session with that ID. In version 2.1 of the Servlet API, there was a way to locate a session by ID (the `getSession` method in the `HttpSessionContext` object). Unfortunately, the `HttpSessionContext` class has been deprecated for version 2.2 of the Servlet API, meaning the class might be removed from future versions of the Servlet API.

You don't need to go through the trouble of tracking the session ID, however. The Servlet API provides a way for you to insert a session ID into a URL. The idea is, for every URL in your Web application that refers to a servlet or a JSP, you insert the session ID as a parameter to that servlet or JSP. Because the session ID is normally stored in a cookie, you only need pass the session ID as a parameter when cookies are disabled.

Note

Many Web sites that do session-oriented work require you to enable cookies. Although it's nice to be able to support sessions without cookies, users generally find them acceptable for applications such as online shopping. If you decide to require cookies, you might need to put a note on your Web site explaining the necessity of cookies.

The `HttpServletResponse` object (the `response` object in a JSP) contains two methods to help you pass the session ID around to different pages:

```
public String encodeURL(String url);
public String encodeRedirectURL(String url);
```

If you need to do session tracking but the browser doesn't support cookies, `encodeURL` and `encodeRedirectURL` return a modified URL containing the session ID as a parameter for that URL. If the browser supports cookies, the URL is returned unmodified. Listing 5.11 shows a JSP that presents a form, handles the submission of the form, and puts the form results into a session. It calls `encodeURL` and `encodeRedirectURL` to make sure that sessions are supported even with cookies turned off.

LISTING 5.11 SOURCE CODE FOR `RewriteDemo.jsp`

```
<HTML>
<BODY>

<H1>URL Rewriting Demo</H1>

<%-- See if the session already contains the name.
    If so, say "Hello" to the user --%>

<%
    String name = (String) session.getAttribute("name");


    if (name != null)
    {
// This user already has a session, show the name and show the list of
// items they have entered

        out.println("Hello, "+name+"!");
%>
        <A href="<%=response.encodeURL("RewriteDemo2.jsp")%>">
            Click here to continue</A>
<%

    }
// If name is passed in as a parameter, it must be as a response to
// the form input. Put it in the session and redirect it to the second
// page.
    else if (request.getParameter("name") != null)
    {
```

LISTING 5.11 CONTINUED

```
        session.setAttribute("name",
            request.getParameter("name"));
        response.sendRedirect(response.encodeRedirectURL(
            "RewriteDemo2.jsp"));
    }
    else
    {
%>
<FORM ACTION="<%=response.encodeURL("RewriteDemo.jsp")%>">
Please enter your name: <INPUT type=text name="name">
<P>
<INPUT type="submit" value="Login!">
</FORM>
<%
    }
%>

</BODY>
</HTML>
```

Figure 5.6 shows RewriteDemo2.jsp, which RewriteDemo.jsp redirects the user to. Notice that the address line contains an embedded session ID. The session ID appears because the browser in this situation has cookies turned off.

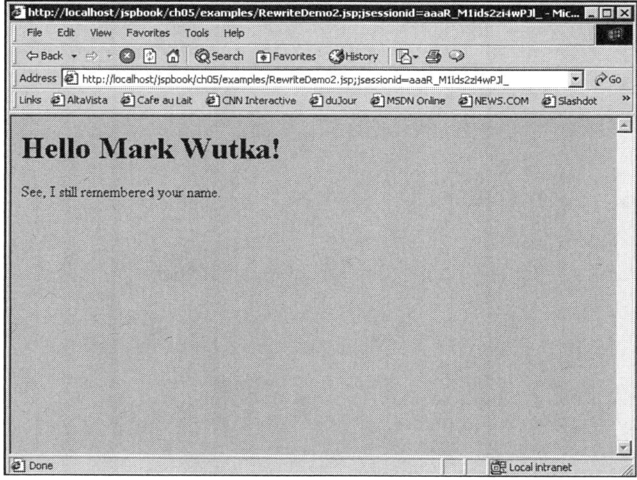

Figure 5.6
The session ID can be embedded in a URL.

If you are having trouble with URL rewriting, see "URL Rewriting" in the "Troubleshooting" section at the end of this chapter.

DISABLING COOKIES IN INTERNET EXPLORER

To disable cookies in Internet Explorer, you must change the security level for your Internet zone. Internet explorer groups Web sites into four zones: Local Intranet, Internet, Trusted Sites, and Restricted Sites. To change the security settings for a zone, go to the IE menu and select Tools-Internet Options and then click the security tab. You should see a dialog box like the one shown in Figure 5.7.

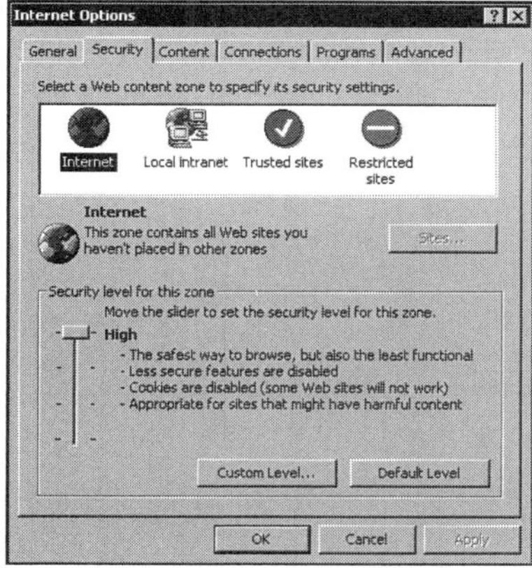

Figure 5.7
To change the cookie settings, go to the Security tab in the Internet Options.

You can change the setting on each zone to a different level (high, medium, medium-low, and low). The high setting disables cookies. If you are testing with the Web site on your own machine, you must change the setting for the Local Intranet zone. If you are testing with another machine, you will probably need to change the setting for the Internet zone. Just move the slider on the security dialog box up to high.

DISABLING COOKIES IN NETSCAPE

TO disable cookies in Netscape, click the Edit menu and select Preferences. Then, select Advanced in the dialog box. You should see a dialog box similar to the one shown in Figure 5.8. Click the Do Not Accept or Send Cookies button.

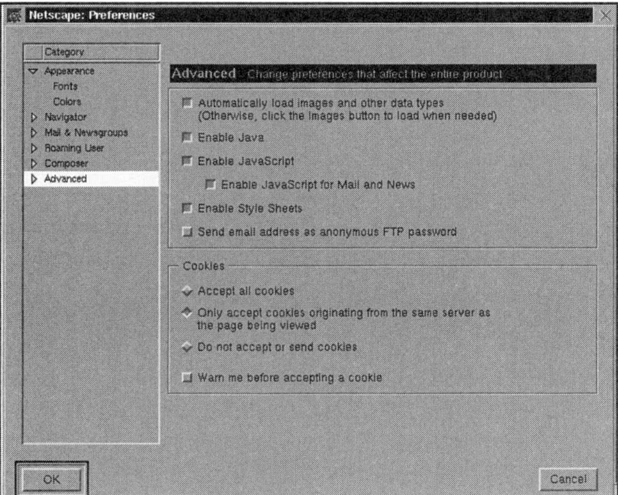

Figure 5.8
To change the cookie settings in Netscape, go to the Preferences dialog box and select Advanced.

If you are having trouble disabling or enabling cookies in your browser, see "Cookie Settings" in the "Troubleshooting" section at the end of this chapter.

Unfortunately, to make full use of URL rewriting, you must pass all your pages through the URL rewriting process. In other words, if you have a static HTML page with links to Java Server Pages or servlets that needs session information, you must turn these static HTML pages into Java Server Pages that use encodeURL to rewrite the HREF values for all the hyperlinks. So, in your HTML file where you have a line like

```
<a href="CallMe.jsp">
```

the JSP file would read

```
<a href="<%=response.encodeURL("CallMe.jsp")%>">
```

You also need to change the action attributes in each of your <FORM> tags. A <FORM> tag with an action of "HandleForm.jsp" appears in the JSP like this:

```
<form action="<%=response.encodeURL("HandleForm.jsp")%>">
```

Note

Modifying your Web site to rewrite all your forms and hyperlinks is a difficult task. Try to design your site so that you can minimize the amount of rewriting necessary.

STORING APPLICATION-WIDE DATA

The HttpSession class stores data items on a per-user basis. Sometimes, however, you have data that you need to share between various servlets and Java Server Pages that doesn't need to be stored for each user. For example, if you are writing a database application, you might need to share a database connection. From a Java Server Page, you can store data in the application object. The methods for storing data in the application object are identical to the ones for the session object:

```
public void setAttribute(String name, Object value)
public Object getAttribute(String name)
public void removeAttribute(String name, Object value)
```

From a JSP, if you want to store information in the application object with a name of myInformation, you make a call like this:

```
application.setAttribute("myInformation", "Here is the info");
```

To get the information back out of the application object, you call getAttribute:

```
String theInfo = (String) application.getAttribute("myInformation");
```

The application object is really an object that implements the ServletContext interface. The servlet context is also available from within the servlet. If your servlet is a subclass of GenericServlet or HttpServlet, as most are, you can call the getServletContext method:

```
ServletContext context = getServletContext();

context.setAttribute("myInformation", "Here is the info");
```

Remember that your servlet doesn't have to be a subclass of `GenericServlet` or `HttpServlet`. You could choose to write your own class that implements the `Servlet` interface. If you need to get hold of the servlet context in these cases, the context is contained in the `ServletConfig` object that is passed to your servlet's `init` method. You can always call `getServletConfig().getServletContext()` to get the servlet context.

WHY DO YOU NEED THE `application` OBJECT?

From all appearances, the `application` object seems like overkill. What is the difference between storing something in the `application` object and storing it in a static variable somewhere? You will see in Chapter 28, "Packaging a JSP Application," that it's possible to group a set of Java Server Pages and servlets into an application. The servlet engine knows what application a particular JSP or servlet belongs to. You could, for example, have a set of Java Server Pages deployed in a server under an application called "QA" and an identical set of JSPs under an application called "Beta". These two applications, although running in the same server and the same Java Virtual Machine, would have different `application` objects (that is, different `ServletContext` objects).

Now you can see how this differs from a static variable. If you tried to store a data item in a static variable, you would circumvent the notion of separate applications. There is only one copy of a static variable within a single Java Virtual Machine. You can't say that the "QA" application gets its own copy of a static variable and the "Beta" application gets another unless you are somehow able to run each application in a separate virtual machine. Because you can't count on a servlet engine to support multiple JVMs, you shouldn't rely on static variables for application-level data sharing.

TROUBLESHOOTING

STORING AND RETRIEVING DATA

I stored data in a session; why can't I find it in the session object?

There are many possibilities for this. The most common problem is that you mistyped the name of the item you want to retrieve. You might have stored it as `name` and you are trying to retrieve it as Name. If possible, create a Java class that contains a number of `public static final` string constants defining the names of the items you want to store in the session, and use these constants instead of hard-coding strings into the servlets and JSPs. Another possibility for this problem is that the browser has cookies disabled. Make sure you have cookies enabled or that you use URL rewriting to pass the session ID along.

Why do I get a compile error when I retrieve an item from a session?

The `session.getAttribute` method returns items of type `Object`. Even if you store a `String` object or another type, the return value is always `Object`. You must cast the result to the appropriate type when you retrieve it from the session.

COOKIE SETTINGS

I turned off cookies in Internet Explorer; why don't I see the session ID when I use URL rewriting?

Make sure you have turned off cookies for the security zone you are using. If you are accessing your local machine, you need to change the security setting for the Local Intranet zone, at least if you use `http://localhost` as the first part of your URL. Internet Explorer will not always notice that a URL is really part of the local intranet, however. It may consider `http://localhost` as being in the local domain, and think that `http://zinger.wutka.com` is in the Internet zone, even though it is the same machine as `localhost`. Try setting the security for the Internet and Local Intranet zones to be high.

URL REWRITING

Why does the browser seem to lose the session ID while navigating through my site using URL rewriting?

The problem is most likely the presence of an HTML page somewhere along the way. In order for URL rewriting to work, you must rewrite the URL for every link the browser might access. You must convert any static HTML pages into Java Server Pages, changing the hyperlinks so they use the URL rewriting routines.

CHAPTER 6

Debugging and Error Handling

In this chapter

WHY DEBUGGING IS TOUGH

Server-side programs are often tougher to debug than GUI programs. Although a GUI application can be more complex in terms of code structure and callbacks, server-side applications that are hosted by an application server are more difficult to debug because they are being hosted by another program.

If you want to debug a standalone Java program, you can usually start it up in a debugger and start tracing right from the start. When you need to debug a servlet, you must find a way to use a debugger with your servlet environment. It gets even tougher when you want to debug a JSP because you must first locate the servlet that was generated from the JSP and then debug it.

Server-side programs tend to have more threading problems and more database locking problems because they usually perform multiple services simultaneously. One person running an application is unlikely to try to edit the same record in two different windows, but two people might try to use the same server to edit the same record.

USING LOG FILES TO DEBUG AN APPLICATION

At one time, there were no symbolic debuggers. You couldn't bring up the source code and step through one line at a time, printing out variable values as the program changed them. The only thing you could do was write out debugging statements to indicate what the program was doing.

Believe it or not, logging is still one of the most common ways to debug a program. Debuggers, although very useful, often interfere with the debugging process in a number of ways. With other languages such as C++, programs could behave significantly differently when running in a debugger. It is not uncommon for a C++ program to run fine under a debugger and crash without the debugger.

Logging lets you display information at different points in the program without interfering too much with the overall running of the program. Obviously if you spend too much time writing to log files your program will slow down, but overall, logging is an excellent way to locate bugs.

USING `System.out` AND `System.err`

In a standalone Java program, you frequently write debugging information to `System.out` and `System.err`. When you call the `printStackTrace` method in a `Throwable`, for example, the stack trace goes to `System.err` unless you specify otherwise.

Because servlets and JSPs run inside a servlet/JSP engine, messages you write to `System.out` and `System.err` won't necessarily appear on your screen. Exactly where the messages appear depends on the servlet/JSP engine. Appendices C–F tell you where `System.out` and `System.err` messages go for various popular engines.

Not all servlet and JSP engines will support the use of `System.out` and `System.err`, so don't be surprised if you're using one that doesn't.

Using the Servlet Logging API

Recognizing that not all servlet engines can support `System.out` and `System.err` for logging, Sun added a pair of standard `log` methods in the `ServletContext` object. Using these methods, you can write log messages to a predetermined location. Again, the location of the log file is implementation-dependent. Appendices C–F tell you where the log files are located for several popular servlet engines.

> **Tip**
> If your servlet is a subclass of `GenericServlet` or `HttpServlet` as most are, the `log` methods are available as methods in the servlet itself.

The `log` methods in `ServletContext` are

```
public void log(String message)
public void log(String message, Throwable throwable)
```

The second variation of the `log` method lets you print the stack trace from an exception along with your message.

> **Tip**
> Using a Just-In-Time (JIT) compiler keeps the `printStackTrace` method from determining the exact line number where an exception occurred. You can turn off the JIT with either `-nojit` for the Java 1.1 JRE, or `-Djava.compiler=none` under Java 1.2. Other Java implementations might have similar options.

Logging to a File

When all else fails, you can always open up a file and write log messages to it. If you close the file after writing, remember to make sure you open it again with the `append` option set to `true`. That is, make sure you don't overwrite the existing file; otherwise, you'll lose the previous log message every time you write a new one.

Using Exceptions to Trace Execution

Sometimes when you're debugging, you want to find out what routine called a particular method. You could throw an exception, but you don't want to stop executing the method; you just want to write a log message indicating who called the method. For instance, one class might be calling a method with bad values and you want to locate the offending class.

You can throw an exception and catch it immediately to get an instant snapshot of the current thread's call stack, like this:

```
try
{
    throw new Exception("dummy");
}
```

```
catch (Exception exc)
{
    System.out.println("This method was called from:");
    exc.printStackTrace(System.out);
}
```

This technique isn't the prettiest thing in the world, and it isn't very fast, but sometimes it's the only choice you have.

USING A DEBUGGER

There are many different kinds of debuggers for Java. The JDK comes with a command-line debugger called `jdb`. Many people find `jdb` painful to use because it isn't a graphical debugger like you would find in a Java Interactive Development Environment.

Many times, however, you're working on a server in which you might not have access to a graphical environment anyway. When you have a lot of machines stored away in a machine room somewhere and you can't use the X Window system because of firewall restrictions, you might need to resort to using Telnet to access the machines. If you're using Telnet, `jdb` is probably your best bet.

Tip

If you can't use the X Window system because of firewall restrictions, you might try Virtual Network Computing (VNC) from `http://www.uk.research.att.com/vnc`. VNC often lets you go through firewalls that don't allow X traffic. It can also let you access a Windows NT machine the same way PCAnywhere does.

In general, there are two ways to debug a Java program: start the program from a debugger or run the Java program with remote debugging enabled and attach a debugger to the program. The advantage of remote debugging is that you don't need to figure out what class to run at startup. You let the server go through its normal startup and then attach the debugger and start running.

DEBUGGING A SERVLET WITH TOMCAT

The Tomcat JSP/servlet engine is fairly debugger-friendly. Several other servlet engines use Windows EXE files at startup, making it difficult to put them into debug mode. Tomcat's startup script, on the other hand, allows you to specify additional JVM options in the `TOMCAT_OPTS` environment variable.

To use remote debugging with any Java program, you must include the `-debug` flag in the `java` command. Most Java 1.1 Virtual Machines automatically turn off the Just-In-Time compiler when they see `-debug`, but the standard Java2 JVM does not. When you use Java2, you must include the `-Djava.compiler=NONE` flag before the `-debug` flag.

Also, turning on debug mode seems to mess up the built-in classpaths for the JVM, so you must specify a special boot classpath with `-Xbootclasspath`. The boot classpath must include the `rt.jar` file from Java's `jre/lib` directory and `tools.jar` from Java's `lib` directory.

Your TOMCAT_OPTS environment variable should look something like this (for JDK 1.2):

```
set TOMCAT_OPTS=-Djava.compiler=NONE -debug
➥-Xbootclasspath:d:\jdk1.2\jre\lib\rt.jar;
➥d:\jdk1.2\lib\tools.jar
```

Under UNIX your TOMCAT_OPTS variable should look something like this:

```
export TOMCAT_OPTS=-Djava.compiler=NONE -debug
➥-Xbootclasspath:/usr/local/java/jre/lib/rt.jar:
➥/usr/local/java/lib/tools.jar
```

Next, when you run Tomcat, you don't want it to open another window or run Tomcat in the background, so you must use the `tomcat.bat` or `tomcat.sh` script instead of using the normal `startup` command. Under Windows, type

```
tomcat run
```

For UNIX/Linux, the equivalent is

```
tomcat.sh run
```

When Tomcat starts, you should see a line giving you an agent password, as shown in Figure 6.1.

```
Command Prompt - tomcat run
rClient\interclient.jar;.;h:\mm-mysql\mysql_both_comp.jar;h:\IBMDebug\lib\dertrj
rt.jar;h:\jrun\lib\ext\servlet.jar;h:\jspbook\servlet;h:\tomcat\lib\servlet.jar
Agent password=3icfu4
Context log: path="/examples" Adding context path="/examples"  docBase="webapps/
examples"
Context log: path="" Adding context path=""  docBase="webapps/ROOT"
Context log: path="/test" Adding context path="/test"  docBase="webapps/test"
Context log: path="/jspbook" Adding context path="/jspbook"  docBase="h:/jspbook
"
Starting tomcat. Check logs/tomcat.log for error messages
Starting tomcat install=".." home="H:\tomcat" classPath="..\classes;..\lib\webse
rver.jar;..\lib\jasper.jar;..\lib\xml.jar;..\lib\servlet.jar;d:\jdk1.2\lib\tools
.jar;..\classes;..\lib\webserver.jar;..\lib\jasper.jar;..\lib\xml.jar;..\lib\ser
vlet.jar;d:\jdk1.2\lib\tools.jar;h:\InterClient\interclient.jar;.;h:\mm-mysql\my
sql_both_comp.jar;h:\IBMDebug\lib\dertrjrt.jar;h:\jrun\lib\ext\servlet.jar;h:\js
pbook\servlet;h:\tomcat\lib\servlet.jar"
Context log: path="/admin" Automatic context load docBase="H:\tomcat\webapps\adm
in"
Context log: path="/admin" Adding context path="/admin"  docBase="H:\tomcat\weba
pps\admin"
Context log: path="/example" Automatic context load docBase="H:\tomcat\webapps\e
xample"
Context log: path="/example" Adding context path="/example"  docBase="H:\tomcat\
webapps\example"
```

Figure 6.1
The agent password is a code that debuggers can use to access the Java Virtual Machine.

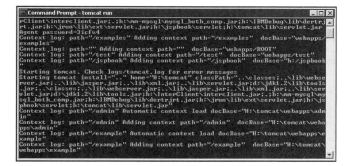

Now, to run `jdb`, just type

```
jdb -host localhost -password xxxx
```

Use the agent password from the JVM startup instead of *xxxx*, of course. You should now see a screen like the one shown in Figure 6.2.

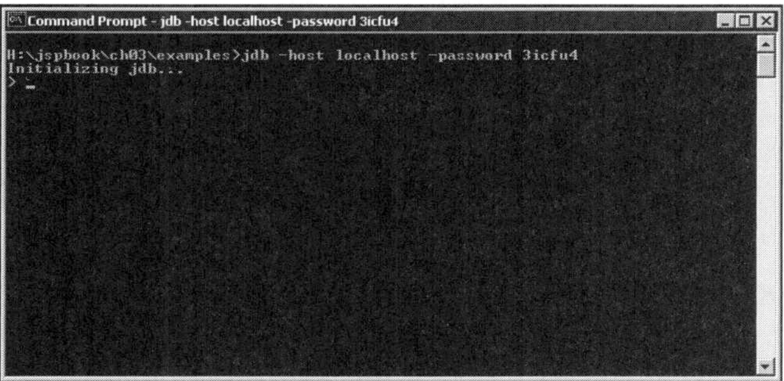

Figure 6.2
The Java Debugger can connect to a JVM running in debug mode.

To debug a servlet like `HelloWorldServlet`, just tell `jdb` to stop in the servlet's `service` method, like this:

```
stop in usingjsp.HelloWorldServlet.service
```

When you access the servlet, the debugger will notify you that a thread has reached the breakpoint, as you can see in Figure 6.3.

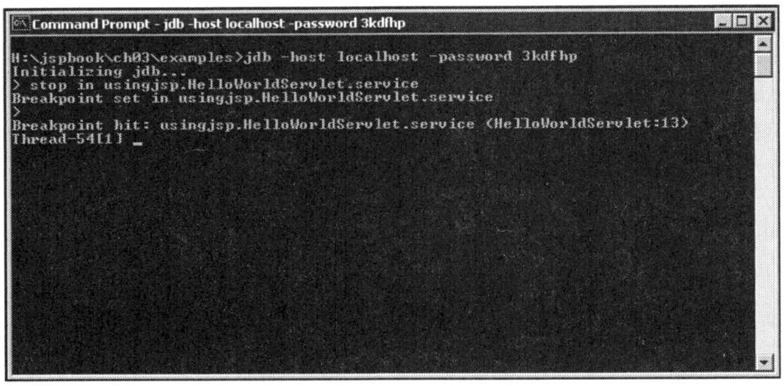

Figure 6.3
The debugger tells you when a thread hits a breakpoint.

You can use the `list` command to see the current line in the source code, but first you must tell `jdb` where to find the source code. Give `jdb` the full path to your source code, like this:

```
use h:/jspbook/ch03/examples
```

One thing you will discover with several of the Java debuggers is that they expect the source code to have the same directory structure as the packages. For example, `HelloWorldServlet` is in a package named `usingjsp`, so `jdb` looks for `HelloWorldServlet.java` in `h:/jspbook/ch03/examples/usingjsp` (it appends the package structure to the source code path).

After you have the source path set up, if you type `list` you should see something like the screen shown in Figure 6.4.

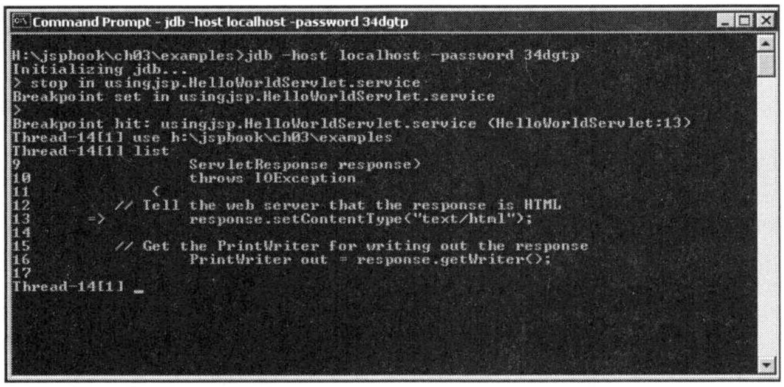

Figure 6.4
The Java Debugger can show you the source code that is executing.

The Java Debugger has many commands and includes some online help, which you can get by typing `help` or just `?`. Use the `cont` command to send control back to the program you're debugging and `quit` to exit.

Any debugger that supports the standard Java remote debugging protocol should be able to debug servlets running inside Tomcat.

Debugging a Java Server Page with Tomcat

Because Java Server Pages eventually become servlets, you can debug a JSP by following the same procedure you use to debug servlets. The only catch is that you must find out the name of the servlet first.

When Tomcat translates a JSP into a servlet, it puts the generated servlet code into the work directory underneath the main Tomcat directory. This is where you need to look for a JSP's servlet. Although the filenames and classnames of the servlets are roughly the same as the pathname for the JSP, you might find that tomcat represents some characters using a 4-digit hexadecimal code.

For example, the URL `http://localhost:8080/jspbook/ch02/examples/HelloWorld.jsp` is stored by Tomcat version 3.1 in a directory named localhost_8080%2Fjspbook. The servlet is in a file named _0002fch_00030_00032_0002fexamples_0002fHelloWorld_0002ejspHelloWorld_jsp_0.java. Although this might be a lot of typing, at least you can debug the JSP. Also keep in mind that when you debug a JSP, you're actually debugging a servlet. The generated servlet code might not match your JSP code exactly.

You might find a development environment that allows you to debug JSP files directly. As servlets and Java Server Pages become more popular, IDE developers will provide more support for them in the various development environments.

Error Handling

You usually won't be able to find all the errors in your Web application no matter how much debugging you do. Eventually, an error is going to crop up somewhere. In a servlet, you can put a try-catch block around your code to make sure the servlet doesn't throw an exception, but goes to an error-handling page instead.

Specifying an Error Page for a JSP

For a Java Server Page, you might be able to insert a try-catch block, but there's a better solution. You can specify an error page for each JSP. Whenever the page throws an exception, the JSP engine automatically invokes the error page. The error page can then log the exception (which is passed via the `exception` built-in variable) and display some sort of response to the user.

To set up an error page, use the `<%@ page errorPage="xxx" %>` directive. For example, Listing 6.1 shows a Java Server Page that intentionally throws an exception.

LISTING 6.1 SOURCE CODE FOR ThrowError.jsp

```
<%@ page errorPage="ShowError.jsp" %>
<html>
<body>
<h1> Hello World! </h1>
</body>
</html>

<%
// Throw an exception to invoke the error page
// Do a stupid expression to keep the compiler
// from generating "Statement Not Reached" errors
    int x = 1;
    if (x == 1)
    {
        throw new RuntimeException("Oh no!!!");
    }
%>
```

Listing 6.2 shows the error page that was specified in Listing 6.1. Notice that the error handling page includes the directive `<%@ page isErrorPage="true" %>`. This directive causes the JSP compiler to generate the `exception` instance variable.

LISTING 6.2 SOURCE CODE FOR ShowError.jsp

```
<%@ page isErrorPage="true" %>
<html>
<body bgcolor="#ffffff">
<h1>Error</h1>
Sorry, an error occurred.
<p>
Here is the stack trace:
<p>
<pre>
<% exception.printStackTrace(new PrintWriter(out)); %>
</pre>
</body>
</html>
```

Tip

When the JSP engine calls an error page, it is essentially doing the same thing as a JSP forward. If you have already flushed the output buffer, the JSP engine might not be able to display the error page, or the user might see the first part of the original output followed by the error page. Try to do the things that are likely to cause an exception first, that way the exceptions can be handled before any output is returned.

SPECIFYING ERROR HANDLERS FOR WEB SERVER ERRORS

Some errors occur in an application that you can't detect from a JSP or servlet. For instance, if you have a typo in one of your HTML hyperlinks, the Web server generates an HTTP 404 error. Because there is no servlet or JSP involved when the 404 error occurs, there is normally no way to know about the error other than when the user calls up on the phone asking about the error.

Fortunately, the servlet API specification provides a hook allowing you to specify an error handler for a specific Web server error or Java exception. The only difficulty you'll have in setting up these error handlers is that you must put them in a deployment descriptor, which is a file describing the contents of a Web application. Chapter 28, "Packaging a JSP Application" tells you everything you need to know about setting up a deployment descriptor and deploying a Web application on a server.

To add a handler for the 404 error, you just add the following information to the deployment descriptor:

```
<error-page>
    <error-code>404</error-code>
    <location>My404Handler.html</location>
</error-page>
```

Instead of a numeric error code, you can also specify a Java exception type for the error page. For example, whenever a `java.lang.NullPointerException` occurs in a JSP or servlet, you can invoke a special handler by adding the following information to the deployment descriptor:

```
<error-page>
    <exception-type>java.lang.NullPointerException</exception-type>
    <location>NullPointerHandler.jsp</location>
</error-page>
```

The location for an error page might be an HTML page, a JSP, a servlet, or some other kind of Web resource.

TROUBLESHOOTING

GENERAL PROBLEMS

Why are exceptions getting by my catch block even when I'm catching `Exception`*?*

In some fairly rare cases you might be getting an error instead of an exception. The `Error` and `Exception` classes are both subclasses of `Throwable`. If you catch `Throwable` you will definitely catch any possible exception or error.

LOGGING PROBLEMS

Where are my log messages going?

The location of the servlet and JSP log files is implementation-dependent. You should consult the document for the JSP/servlet engine. If you are using one of the packages documented in Appendixes C–F, you can find the location for log files in those appendixes.

Where are my `System.out` and `System.err` messages going?

Like the log files, the location for `System.out` and `System.err` messages is implementation-dependent. You should consult the documentation for your servlet engine, or refer to Appendixes C–F.

Why don't my messages show up in the log file?

While there are rare cases where the JSP/servlet engine delays writing output messages, most of the time you don't see the messages because you aren't really writing them. Exceptions are usually the root cause of these problems. You might want to try catching `Exception` to make sure there aren't unexpected exceptions, and in some cases you might even want to catch `Throwable`.

DEBUGGING PROBLEMS

Why doesn't the `jre` command recognize the `-debug` option?

You must use the `java` command for debugging. The `jre` command is intended as a production-level VM and doesn't include some of the extra baggage of the `java` command.

CHAPTER 7

Organizing Your Application

In this chapter

Up to this point, you have only seen the basic syntax and core features of Java Server Pages and servlets. Many of the examples you have seen are difficult to read because they frequently shift between Java and HTML. In fact, one of the biggest complaints about JSP is that the pages end up looking very messy and become very difficult to maintain. In this chapter you will see how to organize your Java Server Pages and servlets to make them much easier to read and maintain.

INCLUDING OTHER FILES

Splitting your code is one of the first techniques you can use to organize your code. Many sites have a consistent header on every page. You can put the header into a separate file and include it in every page. When you need to change the header, you only need to change one file.

Within a Java Server Page, you can choose to include another file at page compile time or at runtime. The advantage of including a file at compilation time is performance. At runtime, the JSP engine doesn't need to do any work since the file has already been included. Unfortunately, the servlet engine can only include files at runtime. After all, you are the one who compiles the server—how could the servlet engine include something at compile time?

To include another file at compile time, use the `include` directive, like this:

```
<%@ include file="includedFileName" flush="true"%>
```

Note

The path for the included file is relative to the path of the original JSP. That is, if the included file is in the same directory as the including file, you don't need to specify a directory name.

Listing 7.1 shows a JSP file that includes another file. Since the file is included at compile time, you can look at the generated servlet and see that the included code is there.

LISTING 7.1 SOURCE CODE FOR `CrazyWorld.jsp`

```
<HTML>
<BODY>
<%@ include file="Header.html" %>
<p>
Welcome to <i>It's a Crazy World</i>
<p>
</BODY>
</HTML>
```

By putting all of your header code in a single file, you can make sure that all of your pages have an identical header. When you change the header, you only need to change one file.

Listing 7.2 shows the Header.html file included by CrazyWorld.jsp.

Listing 7.2 Source Code for `Header.html`

```
<table bgcolor="#0000ff">
<tr><td><img src="face.jpg" align=left></td>
<td><h1><font color="#ffff00">It's a Crazy World</font></h1></td>
<td><img src="face.jpg" align=right></td></tr>
</table>
```

Figure 7.1 shows CrazyWorld.jsp as it appears in a browser. The image and header come from Header.html, while the welcome message comes from CrazyWorld.jsp itself.

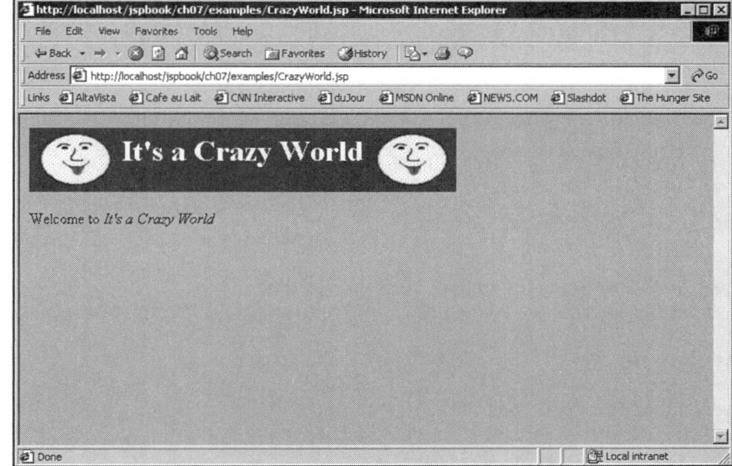

Figure 7.1 You can include header information at compile time using `<%@ include %>`.

When you include a file with the `include` directive, the JSP compiler processes the included file as if it were part of the JSP. You can use any JSP directives within the included file, and even include another file. Any variables and methods defined in the main JSP are available to included files.

> **Caution**
>
> The JSP specification does not provide a standard way for a JSP engine to learn that an included file has changed. Many JSP engines are able to detect that an included file has changed, but some may not. You should test your JSP engine to see if it can detect changes in included files and recompile automatically.

Although there is a potential speed gain by including files at compile time, you give up a lot of flexibility. When you include files at runtime, you are able to freely mix servlets and Java Server Pages.

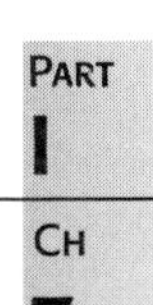

If you are having trouble including a file at compile time, see "Compile Time Includes," in the "Troubleshooting" section at the end of this chapter.

INCLUDING FILES IN A JSP AT RUNTIME

When you want to include a servlet or another JSP into your JSP, use the `<jsp:include>` directive, like this:

```
<jsp:include page=" includedFileName" flush=" true"/>
```

The `flush` attribute indicates whether the output buffer should be flushed before the file is included. According to version 1.1 of the JSP specification, this attribute is required but can only have a value of `True`.

Caution

Make sure you always include `flush=" true"` in your include tags. At least one JSP engine—ServletExec—will report an error if you omit `flush=" true"`.

Listing 7.3 shows a menu Java Server Page that displays a tab-style menu, highlighting a specific menu item according to a parameter that is passed to it.

LISTING 7.3 SOURCE CODE FOR `Menu.jsp`

```
<%
// See which menu item should be highlighted
    String highlighted = request.getParameter("highlighted");

// Set the names for the individual menu items

    String welcome = "welcome.jpg";
    if (highlighted.equalsIgnoreCase("welcome"))
        welcome = "welcomeS.jpg";

    String products = "products.jpg";
    if (highlighted.equalsIgnoreCase("products"))
        products = "productsS.jpg";

    String services = "services.jpg";
    if (highlighted.equalsIgnoreCase("services"))
        services = "servicesS.jpg";

    String support = "support.jpg";
    if (highlighted.equalsIgnoreCase("support"))
        support = "supportS.jpg";

    String aboutUs = "aboutUs.jpg";
    if (highlighted.equalsIgnoreCase("aboutUs"))
        aboutUs = "aboutUsS.jpg";
%>
<table cellpadding="0" cellspacing="0">
<tr>
<td><a href="welcome.jsp"><img src="<%=welcome%>" border="0"></a></td>
<td><a href="products.jsp"><img src="<%=products%>" border="0"></a></td>
<td><a href="services.jsp"><img src="<%=services%>" border="0"></a></td>
<td><a href="support.jsp"><img src="<%=support%>" border="0"></a></td>
<td><a href="aboutUs.jsp"><img src="<%=aboutUs%>" border="0"></a></td></tr>
</table>
```

Listing 7.4 shows a JSP that includes the Menu.jsp file using the `<jsp:include>` tag.

Listing 7.4 Source Code to support.jsp

```
<HTML>
<BODY bgcolor="#ffffff">
<%@ include file="Header2.html"%>

<jsp:include page="Menu.jsp" flush=" true">
    <jsp:param name="highlighted" value="support"/>
</jsp:include>
<p>
<h1>Frequently Asked Questions</h1>
<p>
<i>What in the world is a Zither?</i>
<br>
A zither is a stringed instrument that has between 30 and 40 strings.
<p>
<i>How do you expect to earn money if all you sell is zithers?</i>
<br>
We don't. This business is a tax write-off for our highly-successful
Amalgamated Golf Tees, Inc.

</BODY>
</HTML>
```

Note

Listing 7.4 uses the `<jsp:param>` tag (discussed later in this chapter) to tell the Menu.jsp file which item to highlight. It also uses the `<%@ include %>` tag to include a standard header.

Figure 7.2 shows the output of support.jsp. The menu items are generated by the Menu.jsp file.

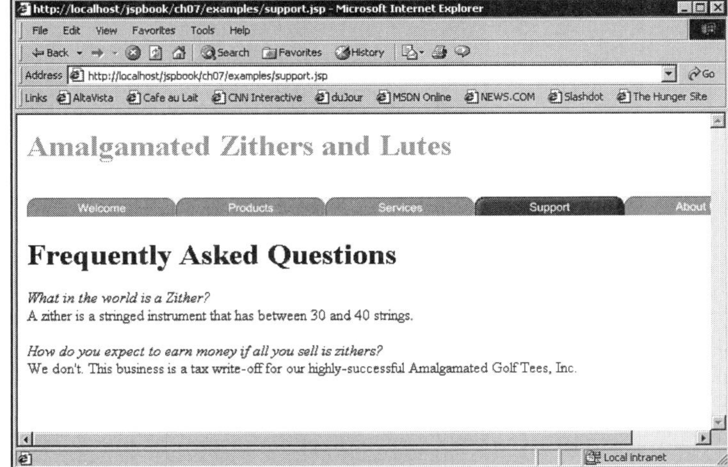

Figure 7.2 You can use the `<jsp:include>` tag to implement a menu.

There are a few restrictions imposed on files when they are included at runtime. These restrictions are not imposed on files that are included at compile time. An included file cannot change any header information sent back to the browser. Although you haven't had to change any header information yet, you will encounter headers in Chapter 8, "More About Saving Data," when you send a cookie back to the browser. You cannot set any cookie information from within an included file.

If you are having trouble including a file at run time, see "Run Time Includes," in the "Troubleshooting" section at the end of this chapter.

PASSING PARAMETERS TO AN INCLUDED FILE

Included files can access all the information in the `request` object, so they have access to any form variables passed from the browser. In addition, you can pass parameters to the included file using the `<jsp:param>` directive:

```
<jsp:include page=" someIncludedPage" flush=" true">
    <jsp:param name=" myParamName" value=" paramData"/>
</jsp:include>
```

Note

The `<jsp:include>` tag follows the XML standard of ending a tag with `/>` when there is no closing tag. When you include a file and don't pass any parameters, end the `<jsp:include>` tag with `/>`. When you pass parameters with `<jsp:param>`, you include a closing `</jsp:include>` tag. Notice too, that the `<jsp:param>` tag closes with a `/>`.

The included file fetches the parameters using `request.getParameter` and `request.getParameterValues` just as if the parameters were passed from the browser as form variables. Values from `<jsp:param>` take precedence over parameters already in the request. In other words, if you use `getParameter` to retrieve the parameter value, you will get the value specified in `<jsp:param>`. If you use `getParameterValues`, you will get both the value specified by `<jsp:param>` and the value passed from the browser.

Note

The parameters added with the `<jsp:param>` tag are only visible to the included page. They are not visible to the original page (that is, they don't affect the original set of parameters).

Listing 7.5 shows a page that includes another page while passing it a parameter value.

LISTING 7.5 SOURCE CODE FOR `MainForm.jsp`

```
<HTML>

<BODY bgcolor="#ffffff">

<jsp:include page="IncludedForm.jsp" flush=" true">

    <jsp:param name="myVar" value="I was passed from main"/>

</jsp:include>
```

```
</BODY>
</HTML>
```

Listing 7.6 shows the included page that prints out the values for `myVar` using `getParameter` and `getParameter` values.

Listing 7.6 Source Code for `IncludedForm.jsp`

```
<PRE>
<%
    String myVar = request.getParameter("myVar");
    String myVars[] = request.getParameterValues("myVar");

    out.println("myVar = "+myVar);
    out.println("The values for myVar are:");
    for (int i=0; i < myVars.length; i++)
    {
        out.println(myVars[i]);
    }
%>
</PRE>
```

Notice that the included form doesn't contain `<HTML>` or `<BODY>` tags. It always assumes that it is included from another page and that the surrounding page contains those tags. Figure 7.3 shows the output from MainForm.jsp. The original value for MainForm.jsp is passed as part of the URL, as you can see in the address line on the browser.

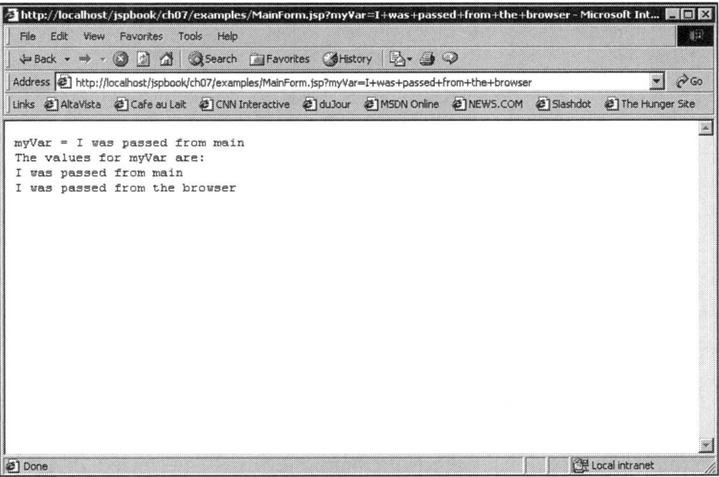

Figure 7.3 Included pages usually assume that they are included and don't contain `<HTML>` or `<BODY>` tags.

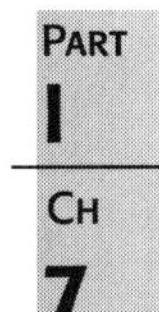

Including Files from a Servlet

The servlet API has a peculiar way to include files. While you might expect either the request or response objects to provide a method to include a file, it's not that simple. To include another servlet, JSP, or text file, you must obtain a request dispatcher for the resource you want to include.

Fortunately, you can obtain a request dispatcher quite easily. The fastest way to get a request dispatcher is to call `request.getRequestDispatcher` and pass it through the URL of the resource you want to include, like this:

```
RequestDispatcher d =
      request.getRequestDispatcher("destinationURL");
d.include(request, response);
```

Listing 7.7 shows a servlet that includes the IncludedForm.jsp from Listing 7.8.

LISTING 7.7 SOURCE CODE FOR `MainFormServlet.java`

```
package usingjsp;

import javax.servlet.*;
import java.io.*;

public class MainFormServlet extends GenericServlet
{
    public void service(ServletRequest request,
        ServletResponse response)
        throws IOException, ServletException
    {
// Tell the web server that the response is HTML
        response.setContentType("text/html");

// Get the PrintWriter for writing out the response
        PrintWriter out = response.getWriter();

// Write the HTML back to the browser
        out.println("<HTML>");
        out.println("<BODY>");

// Get the request dispatcher for the JSP to include
        RequestDispatcher dispatcher =
            request.getRequestDispatcher(
                "/jspbook/ch07/examples/IncludedForm.jsp");

        dispatcher.include(request, response);

        out.println("</BODY>");
        out.println("</HTML>");
    }
}
```

Notice that Listing 7.7 uses the full pathname for the included JSP. The servlet is not in the same directory as the JSP it is including. The `getRequestDispatcher` method takes a relative URL, so if you include another servlet that is in the same directory as your servlet, you don't have to specify the full pathname.

Tip

To pass parameters to a resource you are including, add the parameters to the URL when you call `getRequestDispatcher`. For example `getRequestDispatcher("MyForm.jsp?param1=blah")`.

Forwarding to Another Page

In addition to including another page, you can transfer to another page without returning to the original. This technique is called *forwarding*. When you forward the request on to another page (or servlet), the forwarding page is no longer involved in handling the request. You typically would use forwarding to handle an error, or if you need several different response pages that depend on the data in the request. In the latter case, you would use a JSP or a servlet to look at the incoming request, decide which response page to use, and forward the request on to that page.

Forwarding to Another Page from a JSP

The JSP syntax for forwarding is very similar to the syntax for including. You use the `<jsp:forward>` tag like this:

```
<jsp:forward page="destinationPage"/>
```

When you forward to another page or servlet, your original page is replaced with the new page. That is, any output you might have sent is cleared.

Note

If you get an `IllegalStateException` when forwarding to another page, you might not be buffering the page. Make sure you turn the buffering on.

Listing 7.8 shows a very simple JSP that forwards itself to another page.

Listing 7.8 Source Code for `MainForwarder.jsp`

```
<HTML>
<BODY>

You should never see me because my output is erased before forwarding.

<jsp:forward page="ForwardedPage.jsp"/>
</BODY>
</HTML>
```

As you can see in Figure 7.4, the text in the MainForwarder.jsp file doesn't show in the browser because it is erased before the ForwardedPage.jsp page executes.

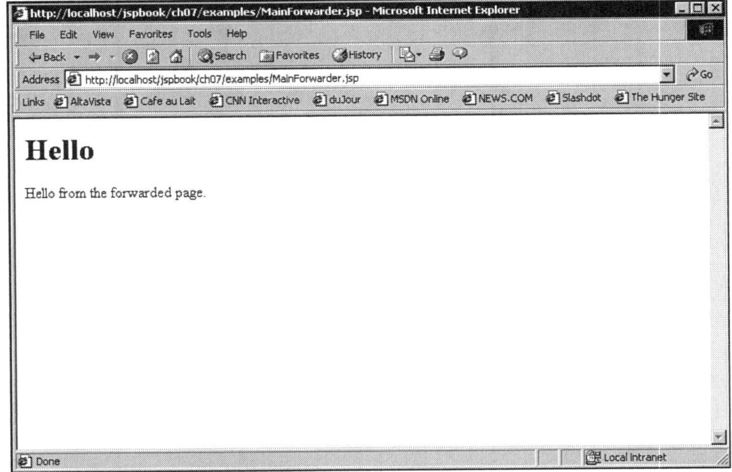

Figure 7.4
When a JSP forwards to another JSP, the output from the original JSP is lost.

FORWARDING TO ANOTHER PAGE FROM A SERVLET

Just as the syntax for forwarding from a JSP is similar to the syntax for including, the syntax for forwarding from a servlet is also very similar. You again use the `RequestDispatcher` object, only this time, instead of calling it `include` method, you call it `forward` method:

```
RequestDispatcher d =
            request.getRequestDispatcher("destinationURL");
d.forward(request, response);
```

Listing 7.9 shows an example servlet that forwards to the same ForwardedPage.jsp page used by the JSP in Listing 7.8. Again, the output from the servlet is erased before the forwarded page runs.

LISTING 7.9 SOURCE CODE FOR `ForwarderServlet.java`

```
package usingjsp;

import javax.servlet.*;
import java.io.*;

public class ForwarderServlet extends GenericServlet
{
    public void service(ServletRequest request,
        ServletResponse response)
        throws IOException, ServletException
    {
// Tell the web server that the response is HTML
        response.setContentType("text/html");

// Get the PrintWriter for writing out the response
        PrintWriter out = response.getWriter();

// Write the HTML back to the browser
        out.println("<HTML>");
```

```
        out.println("<BODY>");

        out.println("You should never see this");
        out.println("because my output buffer gets erased");

// Get the request dispatcher for the JSP to include
        RequestDispatcher dispatcher =
            request.getRequestDispatcher(
                "/jspbook/ch07/examples/ForwardedPage.jsp");

        dispatcher.forward(request, response);

        out.println("</BODY>");
        out.println("</HTML>");
    }
}
```

PASSING PARAMETERS TO THE FORWARDED PAGE

As you might have already guessed, passing parameters to a forwarded page works exactly like it does when you include another page. From a Java Server Page, you use the `<jsp:param>` tag, and from a servlet, you add the parameters to the end of the URL when you call `getRequestDispatcher`.

PASSING JAVA OBJECTS BETWEEN JSPS AND SERVLETS

While it is often convenient to just pass parameter strings between servlets and JSPs, you can't always fit everything you want into a string. If your servlet pulls some information from a database and you want to pass all that information to a JSP, you certainly don't want to convert all the information into strings. You are much better off just passing the Java objects containing the information.

In Chapter 5, "Saving Data Between Requests," you saw that you could store Java objects in a session by calling `getAttribute` and `setAttribute`. You could use the session to pass data to an included page or to a forwarded servlet, but you don't really want that data hanging around in the `session` once you are done with it. You also don't want to add housekeeping code to the included page to clean up the variables stored in the session.

Luckily, there is a better solution. You can store Java objects in the `request` object, using `getAttribute`, `setAttribute` and `removeAttribute`, just like you can with a `session` object. The methods are identical to those in the `session` object, except that they can't throw `IllegalStateException`:

```
public void setAttribute(String name, Object value)
public Object getAttribute(String name)
public void removeAttribute(String name, Object value)
```

Because the `request` object only exists as long as the request is being processed, you don't have to worry about performing any cleanup. When you finish handling the request and have sent a response back to the browser, the `request` object disappears. The next time a request comes in, there is a new `request` object.

MAKING YOUR APPLICATION MORE MODULAR

Maintaining a JSP-based application can be a lot of work when the Java Server Pages aren't well organized. Over time, they tend to grow and end up with an ugly mixture of HTML and Java code that can be almost unreadable. In most cases, you can reorganize the pages and make use of the `<jsp:include>` tag to split your page into manageable segments.

A REUSABLE HTML TABLE MODULE

One of the really handy things you can do with the `<jsp:include>` tag is create reusable modules. How many times have you had to take an array or a vector of objects and display them in an HTML table? Depending on the kind of applications you have done, you may have had to do this many times.

You could make a servlet or a JSP that takes an array or a vector of data and displays the data in a table. Then, every time you need to show a table, you can call the servlet. Listing 7.10 shows a servlet that uses the Reflection API to fetch data from either an array or a vector of objects and then displays the data in a table. It uses `request.getAttribute` to get the array/vector, but uses `request.getParameter` to retrieve any other options.

LISTING 7.10 SOURCE CODE FOR TableServlet.java

```
package usingjsp;

import javax.servlet.*;
import java.io.*;
import java.util.*;
import java.lang.reflect.*;

/** This class uses the Reflection API to fetch data from an array or
 *  a vector and put it in a table */

public class TableServlet extends GenericServlet
{
    public static final Class[] NO_PARAMS = new Class[0];

    public void service(ServletRequest request, ServletResponse response)
        throws IOException, ServletException
    {

// First, get the parameters for the TABLE, TR, TD and TH options
        String tableOptions = request.getParameter("tableOptions");
        if (tableOptions == null) tableOptions = "";

        String trOptions = request.getParameter("trOptions");
        if (trOptions == null) trOptions = "";

        String tdOptions = request.getParameter("tdOptions");
        if (tdOptions == null) tdOptions = "";

        String thOptions = request.getParameter("thOptions");
        if (thOptions == null) thOptions = "";
```

```
// Now, get the name of the object that contains the data to display
        String data = request.getParameter("data");

        if (data == null)
        {
            getServletContext().log("No data available");
            throw new ServletException(
                "No data parameter available");
        }

// Get the actual data object
        Object dataOb = request.getAttribute(data);
        if (dataOb == null)
        {
            getServletContext().log("No data object found");
            throw new ServletException(
                "Can't locate the data object named "+
                data);
        }

// Get the list of method/field names to display in each column
        String[] columns = request.getParameterValues("column");

// Get the types of each column field
        String[] columnType = request.getParameterValues("columnType");

// Get the headers for each column
        String[] columnHeaders = request.getParameterValues(
            "columnHeader");

// Create a table of column names and Fields/Methods for fetching data
        Hashtable columnAccessors =
            getAccessors(dataOb, columns);

// First print the table header
        PrintWriter out = response.getWriter();
        out.println("<TABLE "+tableOptions+">");

// If there are any headers, print them out
        if (columnHeaders != null)
        {
            out.println("<TR "+trOptions+">");
            for (int i=0; i < columnHeaders.length; i++)
            {
                out.print("<TH "+thOptions+">");
                out.println(columnHeaders[i]);
                out.println("</th>");
            }
            out.println("</tr>");
        }

// If the object is a vector, loop through the elements
        if (dataOb instanceof Vector)
        {
            Vector v = (Vector) dataOb;
```

LISTING 7.10 CONTINUED

```
            Enumeration e = v.elements();

            while (e.hasMoreElements())
            {
// For each row, print out the <TR> tag plus any options
                out.println("<TR "+trOptions+">");

// Print out the column values for the row
                printRow(out, e.nextElement(),
                    columns, columnType,
                    columnAccessors, tdOptions);
                out.println("</tr>");
            }
        }
// If the object is an array, loop through the objects
        else if (dataOb instanceof Object[])
        {
            Object[] obs = (Object[]) dataOb;

            for (int i=0; i < obs.length; i++)
            {
// For each row, print out the <TR> tag plus any options
                out.println("<TR "+trOptions+">");

// Print out the column values for the row
                printRow(out, obs[i],
                    columns, columnType,
                    columnAccessors, tdOptions);
                out.println("</tr>");
            }
        }
        out.println("</TABLE>");
    }

    protected void printRow(PrintWriter out, Object ob,
        String[] columns, String[] columnTypes,
        Hashtable columnAccessors, String tdOptions)
        throws ServletException
    {

// Loop through all the column names
        for (int i=0; i < columns.length; i++)
        {
// Get the value for this column out of the object
            Object value = getColumnValue(ob, columns[i],
                columnAccessors);

// Print the TD tag
            out.print("<TD "+tdOptions+">");

// If the column type is data, just print the data
            if (columnTypes[i].equalsIgnoreCase("data"))
            {
                out.print(value);
            }
```

```
// If the column type is "image", print out an <IMG> tag
            else if (columnTypes[i].equalsIgnoreCase("image"))
            {
                out.print("<IMG src=\""+value+"\">");
            }
            out.print("</td>");
        }
    }

/** Fetch a value from an object using either a Field or a Method object */
    protected Object getColumnValue(Object ob, String columnName,
        Hashtable columnAccessors)
        throws ServletException
    {
// Get the object used to fetch this column's value
        Object accessor = columnAccessors.get(columnName);

// If the column is a field...
        if (accessor instanceof Field)
        {
// .. fetch the value using the get method for the field
            try
            {
                Field f = (Field) accessor;

                return f.get(ob);
            }
// Log, the return the IllegalAccessException
            catch (IllegalAccessException exc)
            {
                getServletContext().log(
                    "Error getting column "+
                    columnName, exc);
                throw new ServletException(
                    "Illegal access exception for column "+
                    columnName);
            }
        }
// If the column is a Method...
        else if (accessor instanceof Method)
        {
// ... invoke the method
            try
            {
                Method m = (Method) accessor;

// The NO_PARAMS value is an empty array of Class defined at the top
// of this class.
                return m.invoke(ob, NO_PARAMS);
            }
// Log, the return any exceptions that come up while invoking the method
            catch (IllegalAccessException exc)
            {
                getServletContext().log(
                    "Error getting column "+
                    columnName, exc);
```

LISTING 7.10 CONTINUED

```
                throw new ServletException(
                    "Illegal access exception for column "+
                    columnName);
            }
            catch (InvocationTargetException exc)
            {
                getServletContext().log(
                    "Error getting column "+
                    columnName, exc);
                throw new ServletException(
                    "Invocation target exception "+
                    "for column "+columnName);
            }
        }
// If the column is neither a Field nor a Method, return null. You should
// never get to this point.
        return null;
    }

/** Creates a table mapping column-name to Field/Method */
    protected Hashtable getAccessors(Object ob, String[] columns)
        throws ServletException
    {
        Hashtable result = new Hashtable();

// First, get the Class for the kind of object being displayed
        Class obClass = null;

        if (ob instanceof Object[])
        {
// If the objects are in an array, get the first object in the array
            Object[] obs = (Object[]) ob;
// If there are no objects, don't bother filling the table
// it won't be needed
            if (obs.length == 0) return result;

            obClass = obs[0].getClass();
        }
        else if (ob instanceof Vector)
        {
// If the objects are in a vector, get the first element of the vector
            Vector v = (Vector) ob;

// If there are no objects, don't bother filling the table
// it won't be needed
            if (v.size() == 0) return result;

            obClass = v.elementAt(0).getClass();
        }

// For each column, look for a field and then a method with the column name
        for (int i=0; i < columns.length; i++)
        {
// First see if there is a field that matches the column name
            try
```

```
            {
                Field f = obClass.getField(columns[i]);
// If so, put it in the table and go to the next column name
                result.put(columns[i], f);
                continue;
            }
            catch (Exception ignore)
            {
            }

// Now see if there is a method that matches this column name
            try
            {
// The NO_PARAMS value is an empty array of Class defined at the top
// of this class.
                Method m = obClass.getMethod(columns[i],
                    NO_PARAMS);
// If so, put it in the table
                result.put(columns[i], m);
            }
            catch (Exception exc)
            {
                getServletContext().log(
                    "Exception location field "+
                    columns[i], exc);
                throw new ServletException(
                    "Can't locate field/method for "+
                    columns[i]);
            }
        }

        return result;
    }
}
```

Although the `TableServlet` servlet is pretty large compared with the amount of code it would take you to write out a single table, as you start using it in multiple Java Server Pages, it begins to pay off. Listing 7.11 shows a Java Server Page that invokes `TableServlet`.

LISTING 7.11 SOURCE CODE FOR `ShowTable.jsp`

```
<HTML>
<BODY>

<%
// Initialize an array with some data to display

    Person[] people = new Person[]
        { new Person("Samantha Tippin", 7, "770-123-4567"),
          new Person("Kaitlyn Tippin", 4, "770-123-4567"),
          new Person("Edward Alexander", 1, "No phone"),
          new Person("Norton Alexander", 10, "No phone")
        };
```

LISTING 7.11 CONTINUED

```
// Stick the array in the request where the servlet can get to it
    request.setAttribute("people", people);
%>
<%-- Invoke the Table servlet, tell it the name of the attribute
     where the data is stored (data=people), set the border size to 4
     on the <TABLE> tag, and describe each column to display --%>

<jsp:include page="/servlet/usingjsp.TableServlet" flush="true">
    <jsp:param name="data" value="people"/>

    <jsp:param name="tableOptions" value="BORDER=4"/>

    <jsp:param name="column" value="name"/>
    <jsp:param name="columnType" value="data"/>
    <jsp:param name="columnHeader" value="Name"/>

    <jsp:param name="column" value="age"/>
    <jsp:param name="columnType" value="data"/>
    <jsp:param name="columnHeader" value="Age"/>

    <jsp:param name="column" value="getPhoneNumber"/>
    <jsp:param name="columnType" value="data"/>
    <jsp:param name="columnHeader" value="Phone #"/>
</jsp:include>
</BODY>
</HTML>
<%!
// Define a class to contain information. This would normally not
// be defined within a JSP
    public class Person
    {
        public String name;
        public int age;
        protected String phoneNumber;

        public Person(String aName, int anAge,
            String aPhoneNumber)
        {
            name = aName;
            age = anAge;
            phoneNumber = aPhoneNumber;
        }

// Just to show that methods work as well as fields, only allow the
// phone number to be accessed via a method call
        public String getPhoneNumber()
        {
            return phoneNumber;
        }
    }
%>
```

Figure 7.5 shows the output from ShowTable.jsp.

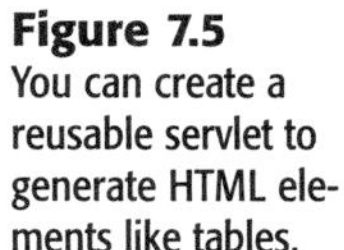

Figure 7.5
You can create a reusable servlet to generate HTML elements like tables.

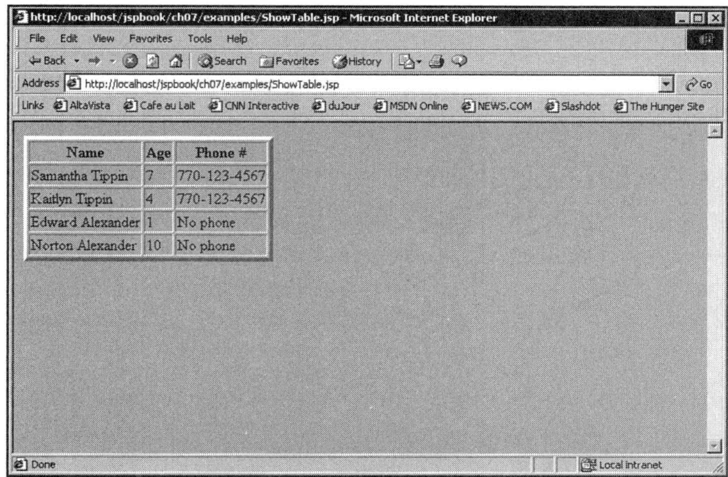

THE MODEL-VIEW-CONTROLLER PARADIGM

The Model-View-Controller (MVC) paradigm is a way of dividing an application into three distinct areas:

- The Controller, which is really the input that changes the system
- The Model, which is the data or the model of the system
- The View, which is the display of the data, whether it is graphical, textual, or even just information written out to a file

To put MVC into real-world terms, think of your application as a car. The gas pedal, brake, and steering wheel are *controllers*. They send input signals to the *model*, which is the engine, suspension, transmission, and so on. Your speedometer, tachometer, fuel gauge, and idiot lights are all examples of *views*. They give you some representation of what is happening in the model.

Most developers think of MVC in terms of a graphical user interface, since MVC really came from GUI development. With a little imagination, though, you can extend the MVC paradigm to Web development, in terms of servlets and JSP. The idea is that you split your application into three sections. A servlet handles any requests from the browser and acts as a controller. You put your business logic (the model) in Java classes that are neither servlets nor Java Server Pages. Finally, you use Java Server Pages to display the view, a representation of the model.

When applying MVC to a Web application, you have to make some concessions towards the way the Web works. When you use MVC in a GUI application, you can display as many views as you like at any time. You can pop up another window, or add some widgets to the screen. Pressing a button might cause only tiny changes in the view.

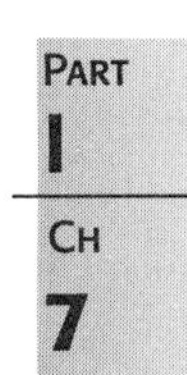

Because the browser and the Web server spend most of their time disconnected from each other, you can't have that kind of dynamic view or immediate feedback in a Web application. The important thing is that you concentrate on separating out the model, view, and controller into separate pieces.

HOW DOES MODEL-VIEW-CONTROLLER HELP?

Unfortunately, many applications are developed in a piecemeal fashion. Someone comes to a developer and says "Hey, can you write a JSP to display X on a browser?" A little while later, that person comes back and says "Great, now can you put X over here, compute Y, and display Z over here?" After a few rounds of this, the JSP might look beautiful to the user, but the source code probably looks hideous to the developer.

The sequence of tasks in the JSP can end up looking something like this:

1. Connect to the application server and get some data.
2. Display the data in HTML.
3. Go grab some information from the database.
4. If there's an error in the database, display error information.
5. Display the database information in HTML.
6. Go get the user's profile information from the security server.
7. If the user is a manager, erase the page and redraw it using the special manager's format.

No one ever intends things to be so convoluted; they just get that way sometimes. By applying MVC to this same sequence of events, you get a cleaner picture. The sequence would be something like this:

1. The controller servlet connects to the application server and gets some data and stores it in the `request` object.
2. The controller servlet grabs some information from the database and stores it in the `request` object.
3. If there is an error fetching data from the database, the controller servlet forwards to an error JSP.
4. The controller servlet fetches the user's profile information from the security server.
5. If the user is a manager, the controller servlet forwards to a JSP that displays the manager's view of the data.
6. If the user is not a manager, the controller servlet forwards to the regular display JSP.
7. The display Java Server Pages grab the information from the `request` object and display it.

AN EXAMPLE CONTROLLER

Listing 7.12 shows you an example controller that queries a database and then calls a view JSP to show the results. The database access code is not as robust as it should be. See

Chapter 19, "Building a Two-Tiered Web Application," for more information on accessing a JDBC database from Java Server Pages and servlets.

LISTING 7.12 SOURCE CODE FOR ControllerServlet.java

```
package usingjsp;

import java.io.*;
import java.util.*;
import java.sql.*;
import javax.servlet.*;

public class ControllerServlet extends GenericServlet
{
    protected Connection conn;

    public void init()
    {
        try
        {
// Make sure the JdbcOdbcDriver class is loaded
            Class.forName("sun.jdbc.odbc.JdbcOdbcDriver");

// Try to connect to a database via ODBC
            conn = DriverManager.getConnection(
                "jdbc:odbc:usingjsp");
        }
        catch (Exception exc)
        {
// If there's an error, use the servlet logging API
            getServletContext().log(
                "Error making JDBC connection: ", exc);
        }
    }

    public void destroy()
    {
        try
        {
// Only try to close the connection if it's non-null
            if (conn != null)
            {
                conn.close();
            }
        }
        catch (SQLException exc)
        {
// If there's an error, use the servlet logging API
            getServletContext().log(
                "Error closing JDBC connection: ", exc);
        }
    }

// This servlet isn't doing connection pooling, so just synchronize for
// thread safety.
```

LISTING 7.12 CONTINUED

```
// For production systems, don't do this, use a connection pool!

    public synchronized void service(ServletRequest request,
        ServletResponse response)
        throws java.io.IOException, ServletException
    {
        Statement stmt = null;

// Parse the minimum and maximum ages and go to an error page if they
// are invalid
        String minimumAgeStr = request.getParameter("minAge");
        int minimumAge = 0;

        try
        {
            minimumAge = Integer.parseInt(minimumAgeStr);
        }
        catch (Exception exc)
        {
            gotoPage("/jspbook/ch07/examples/BadAge.jsp?"+
                "reason=Invalid+minimum+age",
                request, response);
        }

        String maximumAgeStr = request.getParameter("maxAge");
        int maximumAge = 0;

        try
        {
            maximumAge = Integer.parseInt(maximumAgeStr);
        }
        catch (Exception exc)
        {
            gotoPage("/jspbook/ch07/examples/BadAge.jsp?"+
                "reason=Invalid+maximum+age",
                request, response);
        }

        try
        {
            stmt = conn.createStatement();

// Get all the people matching the criteria
            ResultSet results = stmt.executeQuery(
                "select * from person where age between "+
                    minimumAge+" and "+ maximumAge);

            Vector v = new Vector();

            while (results.next())
            {
// The person class can construct itself from a database row
                v.addElement(new Person(results));
            }
```

```
// Store the vector of person objects so the JSP can access it
            request.setAttribute("people", v);

            gotoPage("/jspbook/ch07/examples/ShowPeople.jsp",
                request, response);
        }
        catch (SQLException exc)
        {
            request.setAttribute("exception", exc.toString());
            gotoPage("/jspbook/ch07/examples/DatabaseError.jsp",
                request, response);
        }
        finally
        {
            try {
                stmt.close();
            } catch (Exception ignore) {}
        }
    }

// Since the servlet needs to forward to many pages, this method
// comes in handy as a one-liner for forwarding. It should really
// check to make sure it could get the dispatcher and do something
// predictable if it can't.

    public void gotoPage(String pageName,
        ServletRequest request, ServletResponse response)
        throws IOException, ServletException
    {
        RequestDispatcher d = getServletContext().
            getRequestDispatcher(pageName);

        d.forward(request, response);
    }
}
```

Note

The `Person` class used in the Controller servlet is a slightly more robust one than you saw in Listing 7.11. The big difference is that it is able to initialize itself from a JDBC `ResultSet` row. Although it is often quick and convenient to initialize an object from a `ResultSet`, it has its drawbacks. The object itself must know the names of the database columns and it depends on you performing a `"select *"` to get all the columns. You are often better off using an Object-to-Relational mapping tool like TopLink or JavaBlend.

AN EXAMPLE VIEW

The controller has done most of the work for this example. The view just needs to display the results. Since the controller passes the view a vector containing `Person` objects, it makes sense to reuse the `TableServlet` class from Listing 7.8. The view just needs to set up the proper parameters for the servlet. In fact, since the controller already stores the data in the `request` object, the view doesn't need to. It just needs to tell `TableServlet` where to find the data. Listing 7.13 shows the example view.

LISTING 7.13 SOURCE CODE FOR ShowPeople.jsp

```
<HTML>
<BODY bgcolor="#ffffff">

The following people matched your search criteria:
<P>
<%-- Invoke the Table servlet, tell it the name of the attribute
     where the data is stored (data=people), set the border size to 4
     on the <TABLE> tag, and describe each column to display.

     The "people" attribute was sent from the controller servlet
     and contains a vector of people objects. --%>

<jsp:include page="/servlet/usingjsp.TableServlet" flush="true">
    <jsp:param name="data" value="people"/>

    <jsp:param name="tableOptions" value="BORDER=4"/>

    <jsp:param name="column" value="name"/>
    <jsp:param name="columnType" value="data"/>
    <jsp:param name="columnHeader" value="Name"/>

    <jsp:param name="column" value="age"/>
    <jsp:param name="columnType" value="data"/>
    <jsp:param name="columnHeader" value="Age"/>

    <jsp:param name="column" value="city"/>
    <jsp:param name="columnType" value="data"/>
    <jsp:param name="columnHeader" value="City"/>

    <jsp:param name="column" value="state"/>
    <jsp:param name="columnType" value="data"/>
    <jsp:param name="columnHeader" value="State"/>

    <jsp:param name="column" value="country"/>
    <jsp:param name="columnType" value="data"/>
    <jsp:param name="columnHeader" value="Country"/>

    <jsp:param name="column" value="postalCode"/>
    <jsp:param name="columnType" value="data"/>
    <jsp:param name="columnHeader" value="Postal Code"/>

    <jsp:param name="column" value="email"/>
    <jsp:param name="columnType" value="data"/>
    <jsp:param name="columnHeader" value="E-Mail"/>
</jsp:include>
</BODY>
</HTML>
```

The front end to this Controller-View pairing is a very small HTML page that prompts for the minimum and maximum ages for the query. Listing 7.14 shows the source for the HTML page.

LISTING 7.14 SOURCE CODE FOR `PeopleQuery.html`

```
<HTML>
<BODY>

Please enter the minimum and maximum ages to view:
<P>
<FORM action="/servlet/usingjsp.ControllerServlet" method="POST">
Minimum Age: <INPUT type="text" name="minAge"><BR>
Maximum Age: <INPUT type="text" name="maxAge"><BR>
<P>
<INPUT type="submit" value="Perform Query!">
</FORM>
</BODY>
</HTML>
```

Finally, Figure 7.6 shows the output of the `view` class. Most of the view is actually generated by the `TableServlet` class.

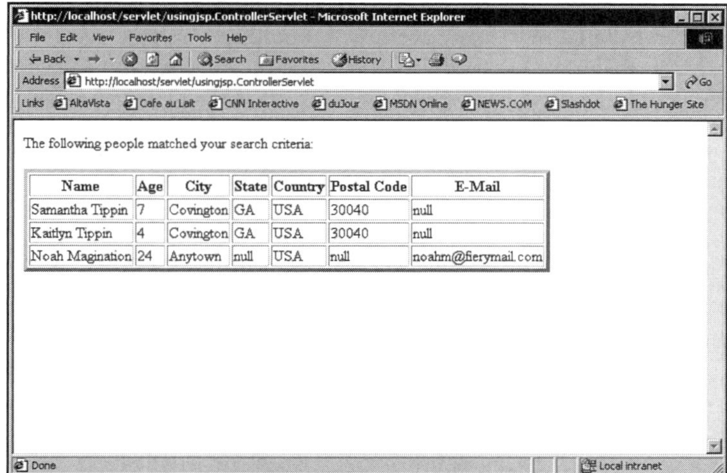

Name	Age	City	State	Country	Postal Code	E-Mail
Samantha Tippin	7	Covington	GA	USA	30040	null
Kaitlyn Tippin	4	Covington	GA	USA	30040	null
Noah Magination	24	Anytown	null	USA	null	noahm@fierymail.com

Figure 7.6 The View page is responsible for displaying the data retrieved from the model.

CALLING MULTIPLE CONTROLLERS AND VIEWS

One of the things you will notice in the controller servlet is that it has direct knowledge of the JSP that is handling the view. You should strive to break such dependencies whenever you can. What happens if you want to do things exactly the same way in the controller but display a different view of the data? The way things are right now, you have to make a separate version of the controller that displays the alternate view.

The controller should be concerned with sending input information to the model, and the view should be concerned with displaying the output. The only thing that ties the controller to the view at the moment is the fact that the controller contains the logic to forward the request on to the view. The way to completely separate the controller from the view is with a dispatcher servlet.

A dispatcher performs the crucial transition between the controller and the view. Instead of invoking a controller directly, you call the dispatcher and tell it which controller you want to call and which view to display. That way the controller doesn't have any specific view hard-wired into its code. Likewise, the dispatcher doesn't have a view hard-wired in, either.

Note

This is not the same dispatcher as the `RequestDispatcher` class that is part of the Servlet API. This section of the book refers to a dispatcher in the generic sense.

You can even have the dispatcher call multiple controllers before calling a view. That way, you can break your business logic down into fine-grained pieces. When the browser sends a request to the server, it may invoke several controllers to update various portions of the model before displaying the view.

One of the traditional problems in designing a Web application is the limited interaction between the browser and the server. You need to do as much as possible within a single request. In the past, this restriction has resulted in large, complicated servlets that perform many different functions. Many times, you would end up with several servlets that were more similar than they were different, because they needed to perform several common functions.

The dispatcher allows you to separate out common functions, put them each in their own servlet, and call them when you need them, even if you need to call several of them from a single request.

Listing 7.15 shows the dispatcher servlet. You pass the controllers using parameters (form variables) named `controller`. The path name for the normal view is passed in the `view` parameter, while the path name for the error handler view is passed in the `errorView` parameter.

LISTING 7.15 SOURCE CODE FOR `DispatcherServlet.java`

```
package usingjsp;

import java.io.*;
import java.util.*;
import java.sql.*;
import javax.servlet.*;

public class DispatcherServlet extends GenericServlet
{
    public void service(ServletRequest request,
        ServletResponse response)
        throws java.io.IOException, ServletException
    {

// Get the list of controllers to call
        String[] controllers =
            request.getParameterValues("controller");

// Get the name of the view to call
        String viewName = request.getParameter("view");
```

```
// Get the name of the view to call if there is an error
        String errorViewName = request.getParameter("errorView");

        try
        {
            for (int i=0; i < controllers.length; i++)
            {
                RequestDispatcher d =
                    getServletContext().
                        getRequestDispatcher(
                            controllers[i]);
                if (d != null)
                {
// Invoke the next controller
                    d.include(request, response);
                }
                else
                {
                    getServletContext().log(
                        "No controller named "+
                        controllers[i]);
                }
            }

            RequestDispatcher d = getServletContext().
                getRequestDispatcher(viewName);

// The dispatcher includes the other controllers, but it forwards to the view
            if (d != null)
            {
                d.forward(request, response);
            }
            else
            {
                getServletContext().log(
                    "No view named "+viewName);
            }
        }
        catch (Exception exc)
        {
// If there is an error, forward to the error view

            request.setAttribute("exception", exc.toString());

            RequestDispatcher d = getServletContext().
                getRequestDispatcher(errorViewName);

            if (d != null)
            {
                d.forward(request, response);
            }
            else
            {
                getServletContext().log(
                    "No errorView named "+errorViewName);
            }
        }
    }
}
```

If you want to use the dispatcher to call the `ControllerServlet`, you need to strip a few things out of the controller. You no longer need to include the calls to `gotoPage` since the dispatcher is handling that. Instead of calling the error page, make the controller throw a `ServletException` with the reason for the error.

You don't need to change anything in the ShowPeople.jsp page to make it work with the dispatcher. The only other thing you need to do is modify the initial HTML form so it passes the controller and view information to the dispatcher. You can insert the information as hidden form variables so it is automatically passed when the user submits the form. Listing 7.16 shows the modified HTML form.

LISTING 7.16 SOURCE CODE FOR `PeopleQuery2.html`

```
<HTML>
<BODY>

Please enter the minimum and maximum ages to view:
<P>
<FORM action="/servlet/usingjsp.DispatcherServlet" method="POST">

<INPUT type=hidden name="controller"
    value="/servlet/usingjsp.ControllerServlet2">
<INPUT type=hidden name="view" value="/jspbook/ch07/examples/ShowPeople.jsp">
<INPUT type=hidden name="errorView"
    value="/jspbook/ch07/examples/ErrorHandler.jsp">

Minimum Age: <INPUT type="text" name="minAge"><BR>
Maximum Age: <INPUT type="text" name="maxAge"><BR>
<P>
<INPUT type="submit" value="Perform Query!">
</FORM>
</BODY>
</HTML>
```

USING AN APPLET IN YOUR FORM

You can easily find dozens of Java books that tell you how to create an applet and put it in an HTML page. You are probably most familiar with the `<APPLET>` tag. The problem with the `<APPLET>` tag is that you don't have any control over which Java Virtual Machine runs the applet. If the user runs the applet from Internet Explorer, it will run using the Microsoft Virtual Machine. If you run it from Netscape, it will run under the version of Sun's JVM that came with your version of Netscape.

For simple applets that you use for flashy presentation, Sun's JVM is probably good enough. If you are writing an application to run on a corporate intranet, it may not be satisfactory. There are many incompatibilities between the various JVMs out there. Trying to run a Swing-based GUI under the Microsoft VM one time should convince you that there is a problem.

Sun's solution to the multiple VM issue is a part of the standard JRE (Java Runtime Environment) called the Java Plug-In. Using the `<EMBED>` tag in Netscape and the `<OBJECT>` tag in Internet Explorer, you can force the browser to run your applet using Sun's VM. Better yet, you can use the most recent version of the VM, in case you need some of the newer features.

The JSP environment provides a special tag for embedding an applet in a Web page that automatically detects the browser type and inserts the appropriate tag in the output. The JSP tag is called `<jsp:plugin>`. Listing 7.17 shows an example usage of `<jsp:plugin>`.

Listing 7.17 Source Code for `ShowApplet.jsp`

```
<HTML>
<BODY>
Here is the applet:
<BR>

<jsp:plugin type="applet" code="usingjsp.SwingApplet" codebase="."
    width="500" height="400">
    <jsp:fallback>
        <p>Unable to use Java Plugin</p>
    </jsp:fallback>
</jsp:plugin>

</BODY>

</HTML>
```

The text inside the `<jsp:fallback>` tag is displayed when the browser can't run the Java plug-in, either because the browser isn't capable or there are problems loading it. If you need to pass parameters to the applet, you can use the `<jsp:params>` tag, which encodes a number of `<jsp:param>` tags like this:

```
<jsp:params>
    <jsp:param name="myParam1" value="param1Value"/>
    <jsp:param name="myParam1" value="param1Value"/>
</jsp:params>
```

The `<jsp:params>` tag should be enclosed within the `<jsp:plugin>` in the same way that `<jsp:fallback>` is enclosed in Listing 7.17.

Listing 7.18 shows the generated HTML code when the ShowParams.jsp applet is run from within Internet Explorer.

Listing 7.18 `ShowApplet.jsp` Generated HTML for Internet Explorer

```
<HTML>
<BODY>
Here is the applet:
<BR>

<OBJECT classid="clsid:8AD9C840-044E-11D1-B3E9-00805F499D93"
```

LISTING 7.18 CONTINUED

```
        HEIGHT="400" WIDTH="500"
        CODEBASE="http://java.sun.com/products/plugin
        /1.1/jinstall-11-win32.cab#Version=1,1,0,0">
<PARAM NAME="code" VALUE="usingjsp.SwingApplet">
<PARAM NAME="codebase" VALUE=".">
<PARAM NAME="type" VALUE="application/x-java-applet;version=1.1">

        <p>Unable to use Java Plugin</p>

</OBJECT>


</BODY>
</HTML>
```

Listing 7.19 shows the code generated when the applet is run under Netscape.

LISTING 7.19 `ShowApplet.jsp` GENERATED HTML FOR NETSCAPE

```
<HTML>
<BODY>
Here is the applet:
<BR>

<EMBED JAVA_CODE="usingjsp.SwingApplet" JAVA_CODEBASE="."
TYPE="application/x-java-applet;version=1.1" HEIGHT="400" WIDTH="500"
PLUGINSPAGE="http://java.sun.com/products/plugin/1.1/plugin-install.html">
<NOEMBED>
<p>Unable to use Java Plugin</p>
</NOEMBED>
</EMBED>


</BODY>
</HTML>
```

The `<jsp:plugin>` tag accepts most of the common `<APPLET>` attributes like `code`, `codebase`, `archive`, `width`, and `height`. You can find all the options for the `<jsp:plugin>` tag in Appendix A.

TROUBLESHOOTING

COMPILE TIME INCLUDES

Why won't my included file show up?

If you entered the correct filename and the JSP engine didn't report an error while including the file, chances are that the place you included the file causes it to not show up. For example, if you include some tags within the `<head>` tag, they probably won't show up. Likewise, if you include the file within an HTML comment it won't show up. Do a "View Source" from your browser and see what's being sent from your JSP.

Why doesn't my JSP recompile when I change the contents of the included file?

The JSP specification doesn't require JSP engines to check included files to see if they have changed. Yours probably doesn't.

RUN TIME INCLUDES

My Java Server Pages have been running fine in other JSP engines; why does ServletExec report an error with my `<jsp:include>` tags?

ServletExec enforces the requirement that you put `flush=" true"` in the `<jsp:include>` tag. Many others JSP engines do not. Consider it a shortcoming of the other products that they did not report the error.

Why do I get an HTTP Error 500 when I try to access a JSP with an included file?

Most likely, the included file has some error that prevents it from being compiled. Check the log files of your JSP engine to see what the error is, or just try to access the included file directly. By accessing it directly you should see any errors on your screen.

CHAPTER 8

More About Saving Data

In this chapter

In Chapter 5, "Saving Data Between Requests," you learned how to store data between user requests using a session object. Although there are many uses for the session object, one of the most common uses is storing items for online shopping. When you shop online, you usually browse around the Web site, occasionally clicking an "Add to Shopping Cart" button to signal that you want to buy something. When you are done, you click "Check Out" and fill out your billing information.

The session object is a logical place to keep shopping cart data. You could, of course, keep the data on the client's browser. It can get pretty cumbersome trying to keep up with the shopping cart on the client when the user goes from page to page.

You could also store the shopping cart in a database and just keep enough data in the session to be able to retrieve the shopping cart out of the database. If the database is fast enough and you have so many sessions active at one time that you can't keep all the data in memory, the database might be a better solution. For most applications, however, the session is the ideal place.

Designing the Shopping Cart

Following the idea of the Model-View-Controller paradigm introduced in Chapter 7, "Organizing Your Application," you should concentrate on the model portion of the application first. In other words, create a Java class, or a collection of classes, that implement the behavior of the shopping cart. These classes should have no relationship to servlets or Java Server Pages. You should be able to use them in an entirely different kind of application if you want to.

First, ask yourself "What should I be able to do to a shopping cart?" For this example, you want to add items, remove items, list items, and purchase items contained in the cart. Next, ask yourself "What exactly is an item?" That's a good question. An item should have a description, a price, a quantity, and some kind of product code that you would use for your ordering system. Also, to purchase a product, the user must supply billing and shipping information. You should have one or more classes that represent this information.

Creating the Data Objects

To kick things off, Listing 8.1 shows the `Item` object that will be stored in the shopping cart. For good measure, it has `get/set` methods and implements the `Serializable` interface, so it is fairly well behaved as a bean.

Listing 8.1 Source Code for `Item.java`

```
package usingjsp.cart;

public class Item implements java.io.Serializable
{
    public String productCode;
    public String description;
    public double price;
```

```
    public int quantity;

    public Item()
    {
    }

    public Item(String aProductCode, String aDescription,
        double aPrice, int aQuantity)
    {
        productCode = aProductCode;
        description = aDescription;
        price = aPrice;
        quantity = aQuantity;
    }

// Make get/set methods so the attributes will appear
// as bean attributes

    public String getProductCode() { return productCode; }
    public void setProductCode(String aProductCode) {
        productCode = aProductCode; }

    public String getDescription() { return description; }
    public void setDescription(String aDescription) {
        description = aDescription; }

    public double getPrice() { return price; }
    public void setPrice(double aPrice) { price = aPrice; }

    public int getQuantity() { return quantity; }
    public void setQuantity(int aQuantity) { quantity = aQuantity; }
}
```

The next step is to create a class to hold the billing information. Because this is just an example, the billing is limited to credit card orders. All you need for a credit card order is the name of the person on the card, the card number, the type of card, and the expiration date. Listing 8.2 shows the `Billing` class.

LISTING 8.2 SOURCE CODE FOR `Billing.java`

```
package usingjsp.cart;

public class Billing implements java.io.Serializable
{
    public String nameOnCard;
    public String creditCardType;
    public String creditCardNumber;
    public String creditCardExpiration;

    public Billing()
    {
    }

    public String getNameOnCard() { return nameOnCard; }
```

LISTING 8.2 CONTINUED

```
    public void setNameOnCard(String aName) { nameOnCard = aName; }

    public String getCreditCardType() { return creditCardType; }
    public void setCreditCardType(String aCreditCardType)
        { creditCardType = aCreditCardType; }

    public String getCreditCardNumber() { return creditCardNumber; }
    public void setCreditCardNumber(String aCreditCardNumber)
        { creditCardNumber = aCreditCardNumber; }

    public String getCreditCardExpiration()
        { return creditCardExpiration; }
    public void setCreditCardExpiration(String aCreditCardExpiration)
        { creditCardExpiration = aCreditCardExpiration; }
}
```

Now, the shopping cart needs one more data object. You have the items, you have the billing information, now you just need to know where to ship the item. Listing 8.3 shows the `Shipping` class. Like the other two classes, the `Shipping` class has the `get/set` methods to make various bean tools happy.

LISTING 8.3 SOURCE CODE FOR `Shipping.java`

```
package usingjsp.cart;

public class Shipping implements java.io.Serializable
{
    public String name;
    public String address1;
    public String address2;
    public String city;
    public String state;
    public String country;
    public String postalCode;
    public String email;

    public Shipping()
    {
    }

    public String getName() { return name; }
    public void setName(String aName) { name = aName; }

    public String getAddress1() { return address1; }
    public void setAddress1(String anAddress1)
        { address1 = anAddress1; }

    public String getAddress2() { return address2; }
    public void setAddress2(String anAddress2)
        { address2 = anAddress2; }

    public String getCity() { return city; }
    public void setCity(String aCity) { city = aCity; }
```

```
    public String getState() { return state; }
    public void setState(String aState) { state = aState; }

    public String getCountry() { return country; }
    public void setCountry(String aCountry) { country = aCountry; }

    public String getPostalCode() { return postalCode; }
    public void setPostalCode(String aPostalCode)
        { postalCode = aPostalCode; }

    public String getEmail() { return email; }
    public void setEmail(String anEmail) { email = anEmail; }
}
```

CREATING THE ShoppingCart CLASS

Now, all that is left is the shopping cart itself. For the purposes of this example, the shopping cart doesn't do much with the order. Normally, you would insert the order in a database or send it to an application server. The important thing as it relates to JSP and servlets is that you are able to order some items and submit the order. To keep track of the order, you really don't need anything more than a vector of items. The billing and shipping information gets passed to the shopping cart when the order is finally completed. Listing 8.4 shows the source to the `ShoppingCart` class.

LISTING 8.4 SOURCE CODE FOR ShoppingCart.java

```
package usingjsp.cart;
import java.util.*;
import java.io.*;
public class ShoppingCart implements java.io.Serializable
{
// The shopping cart items are stored in a Vector
    protected Vector items;

    public ShoppingCart()
    {
        items = new Vector();
    }

/** Returns a Vector containing the items in the cart. The Vector
 *  returned is a clone, so modifying the vector won't affect the
 *  contents of the cart.
 */
    public Vector getItems()
    {
        return (Vector) items.clone();
    }

    public void addItem(Item newItem)
    {
        items.addElement(newItem);
    }

    public void removeItem(int itemIndex)
    {
        items.removeElementAt(itemIndex);
    }
```

LISTING 8.4 CONTINUED

```
// Warning! This order number is reset every time the server is
// restarted. This technique of generating an order number is
// just for demonstration
    protected static int nextOrderNumber = 1;

// Submits the order and returns a confirmation number
    public String completeOrder(Shipping shipping, Billing billing)
        throws ShoppingCartException
    {
// You would normally insert the order into a database or send
// it to an application server. For the sake of simplicity
// this shopping cart just writes the order to a file
        try
        {
            int orderNumber = 0;

// Make sure no other threads can be generating an order number
            synchronized (this)
            {
                orderNumber = nextOrderNumber;
                nextOrderNumber = nextOrderNumber + 1;
            }
            PrintWriter out = new PrintWriter(
                new FileOutputStream("order"+orderNumber));

// Print the shipping info
            out.println(shipping.name);
            out.println(shipping.address1);
            if (shipping.address2 != null)
            {
                out.println(shipping.address2);
            }
            out.print(shipping.city);
            if (shipping.state != null)
            {
                out.print(", "+shipping.state);
            }
            if (shipping.postalCode != null)
            {
                out.print(" "+shipping.postalCode);
            }
            out.println(" "+shipping.country);
            out.println(shipping.email);

// Print the billing info
            out.println(billing.name);
            out.println(billing.creditCardType);
            out.println(billing.creditCardNumber);
            out.println(billing.creditCardExpiration);

// Print out the items
            Enumeration e = items.elements();
            while (e.hasMoreElements())
            {
                Item item = (Item) e.nextElement();
```

```
                out.println(item.productCode+","+
                    item.quantity);
            }
            out.close();

// Return a confirmation number (the order number as a string in this case)
            return ""+orderNumber;
        }
        catch (Exception exc)
        {
            throw new ShoppingCartException(
                "Error saving order: "+exc.toString());
        }
    }
}
```

The `ShoppingCartException` used by the `ShoppingCart` class is just a subclass of `java.lang.Exception` and doesn't add any additional capabilities. It does help you organize your error handling, however, because you can catch `ShoppingCartException` instead of the more generic `Exception`. Listing 8.5 shows the `ShoppingCartException` class.

LISTING 8.5 SOURCE CODE FOR `ShoppingCartException.java`

```
package usingjsp.cart;
public class ShoppingCartException extends Exception
{
    public ShoppingCartException()
    {
    }
    public ShoppingCartException(String message)
    {
        super(message);
    }
}
```

DISPLAYING THE CONTENTS OF THE SHOPPING CART

So far, you have a lot of shopping cart code and not a single JSP or servlet. Like any technology, you should use Java's Web technologies where they are applicable. In this case, you are much better off with a shopping cart that doesn't care if it's on the Web. If you end up making some sort of standalone kiosk application where someone can walk up, select some items, and immediately make a purchase, you would still be able to use the `ShoppingCart` class even though the application is not Web-based.

Now it's time to put the shopping cart out on the Web by putting servlets and Java Server Pages on top of it. When it comes to displaying the contents of a shopping cart, you might need to show the contents at different times. For example, the user might click a "Display Shopping Cart" button and see just the contents of the shopping cart. Later, when the user clicks the "Check Out" button to make a purchase, you need to display the shopping cart again, but this time with other information on the page as well.

Because you need to display the shopping cart in different pages, it makes sense to create a separate JSP to display the shopping cart. The trick is, this JSP is not a complete Web page in itself. That is, it does not contain the <HTML> or <BODY> tags. Instead, it just contains the HTML tags necessary to display the shopping cart. That way, you can include it in other pages. Listing 8.6 shows the code for DisplayShoppingCart.jsp.

LISTING 8.6 SOURCE CODE FOR DisplayShoppingCart.jsp

```
<%@ page language="java"
import="usingjsp.cart.*,java.util.*,java.text.*" %>
<%-- Show the header with the shopping cart image --%>
<table border="0">
<tr><td><img src="cart4.png"><td><h1>Shopping Cart</h1>
</table>

<%
// Get the current shopping cart from the user's session
    ShoppingCart cart = (ShoppingCart) session.getAttribute("ShoppingCart");

// If the user doesn't have a shopping cart yet, create one
    if (cart == null)
    {
        cart = new ShoppingCart();
        session.setAttribute("ShoppingCart", cart);
    }

// Get the items from the cart
    Vector items = cart.getItems();

// If there are no items, tell the user that the cart is empty
    if (items.size() == 0)
    {
        out.println("<h3>Your shopping cart is empty.</h3>");
    }
    else
    {
%>
<%-- Display the header for the shopping cart table --%>
<br>
<table border=4>
<tr><th>Description</th><th>Quantity</th><th>Price</th></tr>
<%

        int numItems = items.size();

// Get a formatter to write out currency values
        NumberFormat currency = NumberFormat.getCurrencyInstance();

        for (int i=0; i < numItems; i++)
        {
            Item item = (Item) items.elementAt(i);

// Print the table row for the item
            out.print("<tr><td>");
            out.print(item.description);
```

```
            out.print("</td><td>");
            out.print(item.quantity);
            out.print("</td><td>");
            out.print(currency.format(item.price));

// Print out a link that allows the user to delete an item from the cart
            out.println("</td><td>"+
                "<a
href=\"/servlet/usingjsp.cart.RemoveItemServlet?item="+
                i+"\">Remove</a></td></tr>");
        }
    }
%>
</TABLE>
```

Figure 8.1 shows the shopping cart as it looks after you have added some items.

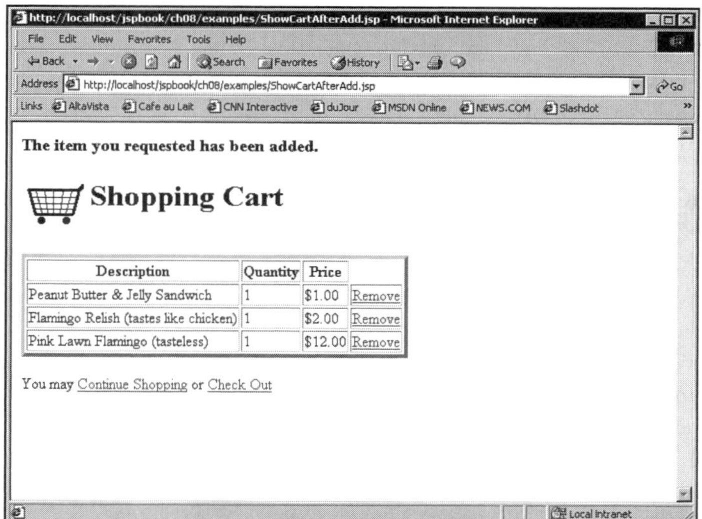

Figure 8.1
Many pages can use the same shopping cart display.

ADDING AND REMOVING ITEMS

Adding and removing shopping cart items are tasks that are nicely suited for servlets. When a user clicks the "Add to Shopping Cart" button, isn't that a job for a controller in the Model-View-Controller paradigm? It's an input signal that tells the data model (the `ShoppingCart` class, in this case) to change itself. The same thing goes for the remove task.

The `addItem` method in the `ShoppingCart` class seems simple enough. You just need to create an `Item` object to add. There are three basic approaches to creating the `Item` object:

- The client browser can send all the information necessary to create the item. This implies that you must pass all the necessary information to the client, even if it won't be needed.

- You can create the `Item` object ahead of time and store it in memory on the server in the `session` or `application` objects. When the user orders the item, you pull it out of the `session` or `application` object and put it in the shopping cart.
- You retrieve the `Item` information from an application server or a database. You only need enough information to uniquely identify the item you want to add.

Each of these approaches has advantages and disadvantages, and you might find yourself using different approaches for different types of systems. Although the `Item` class in this example contains only four data elements, the `Item` class for your real-world application might contain far more data elements. A complex item structure really requires the item information to stay somewhere on the server, either in the `session` object or in a database.

You might be wondering why you would create an `Item` object ahead of time and store it in memory. If you think about the way you shop for things online, you usually look at a page of items, each of which can be added to your shopping cart. The chances are good that the code that generated that page of items had to work with a bunch of `Item` objects. That is, when you generate the page you can order from, you probably need the `Item` object anyway. Why not just store it in the `application` object or the `session` and bring it back out when the user orders it?

Caution

If you allow the user to modify the contents of an `Item` object, such as changing the quantity or color, you must have a separate copy of the item for each user. If all the users share the same object, then when one user changes the quantity, it changes for everyone.

If you are able to store the objects in the `application` object, you will save a lot of memory. If you store the objects in the `session`, you end up saving many copies of the same object. If you have specialized items, however, it might be better to save the objects in the server. For example, if your pricing structure varies depending on the user, it might be better to keep track of items on a per-session basis. If you have several kinds of pricing, you can store one copy of an item for each price. There might be other attributes of the item that change depending on the user as well.

PASSING THE `Item` OBJECT FROM THE BROWSER

If your item is small enough that all its data can be passed easily from the browser, that's probably your best solution. After all, you won't have to worry about cleaning up the session when the user has finished placing the order.

Note

Remember, cleaning up after a session terminates is not a big deal. You just have to create objects that recognize when they have been unbound from a session and clean themselves up.

Listing 8.7 shows a Java Server Page that generates a page of items to order. Notice that the `"Add to Shopping Cart"` links each have all the information for the item embedded in their URLs. When the user clicks on a link, all the data elements for an item are passed to the server.

LISTING 8.7 SOURCE CODE FOR `ShowProductCatalog.jsp`

```
<%@ page language="java"
import="usingjsp.cart.*,java.net.*,java.text.*" %>
<html>
<body bgcolor="#ffffff">

<%
// Initialize the array of available products
    Item[] catalog = new Item[] {
        new Item("X-1", "Jet Plane", 2999999.95, 1),
        new Item("GWU-123876345-27B/6",
            "Graphite Writing Utensil", 12000.00, 12),
        new Item("BCT-12", "Bionic Cat Tongue", 3700.00, 1),
        new Item("EZ-1", "Professional Electronic Zither",
            699.95, 1),
        new Item("PF-101", "Pink Flamingo", 12.00, 1),
        new Item("LOD-7", "Lump Of Dirt (Medium)", 1.00, 1)
    };

%>

<a href="ViewShoppingCart.jsp">View Shopping Cart</a>
<p>
<h1>Available Products</h1>
<table border="1">
<tr><th>Description</th><th>Quantity</th><th>Price</th></tr>
<%

// Get a currency formatter for showing the price
    NumberFormat currency = NumberFormat.getCurrencyInstance();

    for (int i=0; i < catalog.length; i++)
    {
        Item item = catalog[i];

// Create the URL for adding the item to the shopping cart
        String addItemURL =
            "/servlet/usingjsp.cart.AddToShoppingCartServlet?"+
            "productCode="+URLEncoder.encode(item.getProductCode())+
            "&description="+URLEncoder.encode(item.getDescription())+
            "&quantity="+URLEncoder.encode(""+item.getQuantity())+
            "&price="+URLEncoder.encode(""+item.getPrice());
%>
<tr><td><%=item.getDescription()%></td><td><%=item.getQuantity()%>
    </td><td><%=item.getPrice()%></td>
<td><a href="<%=addItemURL%>">Add to Shopping Cart</a></td></tr>
<%
    }
%>
</table>
</body>
</html>
```

Figure 8.2 shows the product catalog as displayed by ShowProductCatalog.jsp.

Listing 8.8 shows the `AddToShoppingCartServlet` class that takes the items from the product catalog and adds them to the shopping cart.

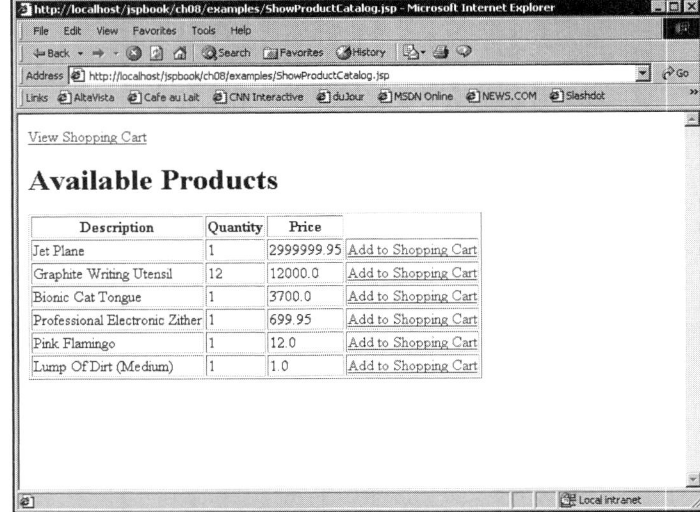

Figure 8.2
A catalog display contains links to add items to the shopping cart.

LISTING 8.8 SOURCE CODE FOR AddToShoppingCartServlet.java

```
package usingjsp.cart;
import javax.servlet.*;
import javax.servlet.http.*;
import java.io.*;
public class AddToShoppingCartServlet extends HttpServlet
{
    public void service(HttpServletRequest request,
        HttpServletResponse response)
        throws IOException, ServletException
    {

// First get the item values from the request
        String productCode = request.getParameter("productCode");
        String description = request.getParameter("description");
        int quantity = Integer.parseInt(
            request.getParameter("quantity"));
        double price = Double.parseDouble(
            request.getParameter("price"));

// Now create an item to add to the cart
        Item item = new Item(productCode, description, price, quantity);

        HttpSession session = request.getSession();

// Get the cart
        ShoppingCart cart = (ShoppingCart) session.
            getAttribute("ShoppingCart");
```

```
// If there is no shopping cart, create one
        if (cart == null)
        {
            cart = new ShoppingCart();

            session.setAttribute("ShoppingCart", cart);
        }

        cart.addItem(item);

// Now display the cart and allow the user to check out or order more items
        response.sendRedirect(response.encodeRedirectURL(
            "/jspbook/ch08/examples/ShowCartAfterAdd.jsp"));
    }
}
```

Keeping Items in Memory

If your shopping cart items are fairly complex, you are usually better off keeping them on the server and passing only a unique identifier for each item back to the client. For example, suppose you offer an item called "Pale Blue Japanese Guitar" with a product code of "PBJG-1." When the user clicks the "Add to Shopping Cart" link to buy the guitar, the browser just sends the product code "PBJG-1" to the server. The server looks up the product code and retrieves the object associated with that code.

Listing 8.9 shows a product catalog class that allows you to look up objects by product code, and also get a list of the available products. You might not want to display all the products on one page, so the product catalog allows you to display a certain number of objects at a time, starting at a particular position in the list.

Listing 8.9 Source Code for `ProductCatalog.java`

```
package usingjsp.cart;
import java.util.Vector;
public class ProductCatalog
{
    protected Item[] items;
    public ProductCatalog()
    {

// Set up an array of items that represents the catalog

        items = new Item[] {
            new Item("PBJG-1", "Pale Blue Japanese Guitar",
                700.00, 1),
            new Item("PBJZ-1", "Pale Blue Japanese Zither",
                1400.00, 1),
            new Item("PBJS-1", "Peanut Butter & Jelly Sandwich",
                1.00, 1),
            new Item("GCX", "Garlic Clove", 0.40, 1),
            new Item("XC", "Xenophobic Cat", 72.00, 1),
            new Item("BH", "Buttonhole", 0.05, 6),
            new Item("K9", "Dog", 100.00, 1),
            new Item("ATL", "Atlanta Airport", 9000000.00, 1),
```

LISTING 8.9 CONTINUED

```
            new Item("TEG", "Sheep", 75.00, 1),
            new Item("UPC", "Universal Price Code", 1.00, 1),
            new Item("ALL", "The Universe", 0.01, 1),
            new Item("ZYZZYVAS", "The last word in Scrabble",
                74.00, 1),
            new Item("SAM", "Urchin (aged for 7 years)", 0.0, 1),
            new Item("KATY", "Urchin (aged for 4 years)", 0.0, 1),
            new Item("FR44", "Flamingo Relish (tastes like chicken)",
                2.00, 1),
            new Item("PF44", "Pickled Flamingo (tastes like chicken)",
                2.00, 1),
            new Item("LF44", "Pink Lawn Flamingo (tasteless)",
                12.00, 1)
        };
    } java

/** returns an array containing all the items in the catalog */
    public Item[] getItems()
    {
        return getItems(0, items.length);
    }

/** returns an array containing a subset of items from the catalog */
    public Item[] getItems(int startingLocation, int numItems)
    {
// If the number of items to be returned is larger than the number
// in the catalog, adjust the number to be returned
        if (numItems > items.length)
        {
            numItems = items.length;
        }

// If by returning numItems items you would run out of items (if there
// are 5 items, you ask for 3, but give a starting location of 4),
// adjust the starting location backwards to insure that the proper
// number of items are returned.
        if (startingLocation+numItems >= items.length)
        {
            startingLocation = items.length - numItems;
        }

// Create an array for the returned items
        Item[] returnItems = new Item[numItems];

// Copy the items from the catalog into the return array
        System.arraycopy(items, startingLocation,
            returnItems, 0, numItems);

        return returnItems;
    }

/** Returns true if there are items at a particular starting location. java
    This is helpful in determining whether a page should show a "Next"
    button to see the next page of catalog items.
*/
    public boolean itemsAvailable(int startingLocation)
```

```
    {
        if (startingLocation >= items.length) return false;
        return true;
    }

/** Searches for an item by product code and returns it. If there is
    no such item, this method returns null.  */
    public Item findItemByProductCode(String productCode)
    {
// Linear searches aren't a good idea for big arrays, but this
// one is small
        for (int i=0; i < items.length; i++)
        {
            if (items[i].getProductCode().equals(
                productCode))
            {
                return items[i];
            }
        }

        return null;
    }
} java
```

Listing 8.10 shows a JSP that displays the contents of the product catalog, allowing the user to add items to the shopping cart. The user can also view successive pages of the catalog by clicking the Next button.

LISTING 8.10 SOURCE CODE FOR ShowProductCatalog2.jsp

```
<%@ page language="java"
import="usingjsp.cart.*,java.net.*,java.text.*" %>
<%!
// Declare a constant for the number of items to show on a page
    public static final int ITEMS_PER_PAGE = 5;
%>

<html>
<body bgcolor="#ffffff">

<a href="ViewShoppingCart.jsp">View Shopping Cart</a>
<p>
<h1>Available Products</h1>
<table border="1">
<tr><th>Description<th>Quantity<th>Price
<%

// Get the shared product catalog
    ProductCatalog catalog = (ProductCatalog) application.getAttribute(
        "ProductCatalog");

// If the shared product catalog hasn't been created yet, create it
    if (catalog == null)
    {

// Not that it matters since it would be okay for two threads to initialize
// the product catalog, but synchronize this anyway to make sure only one
```

LISTING 8.10 CONTINUED

```
// thread stores the catalog. Any other JSP or servlet that needs to store
// the product catalog in the application object must also synchronize
// on application

        synchronized (application)
        {
            catalog = new ProductCatalog();
            application.setAttribute("ProductCatalog", catalog);
        }
    }

// Get the next starting position for displaying catalog items
    String startingPositionStr = (String) request.
        getParameter("StartingPosition");

    int startingPosition = 0;

// If there is a starting position parameter, parse it as an integer
    if (startingPositionStr != null)
    {
        try
        {
// If there's an error parsing the number, the starting position will
// just remain 0
            startingPosition = Integer.parseInt(startingPositionStr);
        }
        catch (Exception ignore)
        {
        }
    }

// Get ITEMS_PER_PAGE items at a time
    Item[] items = catalog.getItems(startingPosition, ITEMS_PER_PAGE);

// Get a currency formatter for showing the price
    NumberFormat currency = NumberFormat.getCurrencyInstance();

    for (int i=0; i < items.length; i++)
    {
        Item item = items[i];

// Create the URL for adding the item to the shopping cart
        String addItemURL =
            "/servlet/usingjsp.cart.AddToShoppingCartServlet?"+
            "productCode="+URLEncoder.encode(item.getProductCode())+
            "&description="+URLEncoder.encode(item.getDescription())+
            "&quantity="+URLEncoder.encode(""+item.getQuantity())+
            "&price="+URLEncoder.encode(""+item.getPrice());
%>
<tr><td><%=item.getDescription()%></td><td><%=item.getQuantity()%>
    </td><td><%=item.getPrice()%></td>
<td><a href="<%=addItemURL%>">Add to Shopping Cart</a></td></tr>
<%
    }
%>
</table>
<table border="0">
```

```
<tr>
<%
    if (startingPosition > 0)
    {
        int prevPosition = startingPosition-ITEMS_PER_PAGE;

// Don't let the starting position go negative
        if (prevPosition < 0) prevPosition = 0;

// Write out a link to display the previous catalog page
        out.println("<td><a href=\"ShowProductCatalog2.jsp?StartingPosition="+
            prevPosition+"\">&lt;&lt;Prev</a></td>");
    }// Compute the next starting position in the catalog
    int nextPosition = startingPosition+ITEMS_PER_PAGE;

// Make sure that there are still items to display at that starting
// position (that is, make sure nextPosition isn't greater than the total
// catalog size)
    if (catalog.itemsAvailable(nextPosition))
    {
// Write out a link to display the next catalog page
        out.println("<td><a href=\"ShowProductCatalog2.jsp?StartingPosition="+
            nextPosition+"\">Next&gt;&gt;</a></td>");
    }
%>
</tr>
</table>
</body>
</html>
```

Figure 8.3 shows the paged version of the product catalog. The `<<Prev` and `Next>>` links allow you to scroll through the catalog.

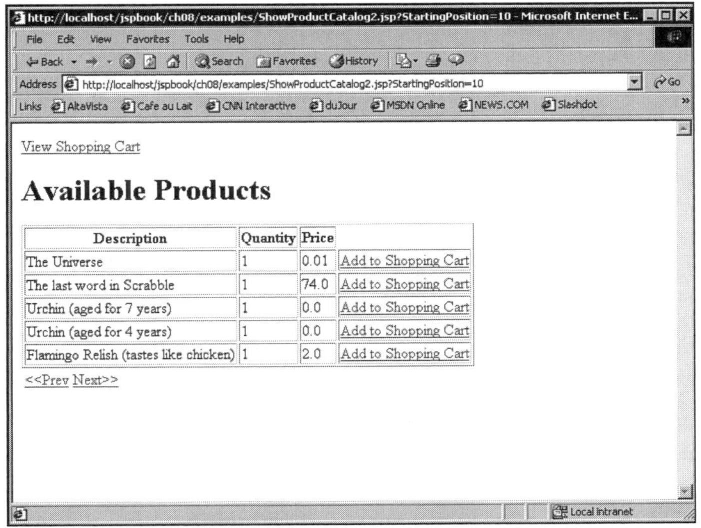

Figure 8.3
When you have many products, allow the user to scroll through the catalog.

If you are having trouble running the shopping cart examples, see "Shopping Cart Problems," in the "Troubleshooting" section at the end of this chapter.

ALLOWING MULTIPLE QUANTITIES

The current shopping cart code does not pay attention to the objects it contains. If you try to order two of the same item, it just keeps two copies of the item in its internal vector. You can enhance the shopping cart to keep track of item quantities. Whenever a user adds an item to the shopping cart, the cart should look through its list of items. When it finds an item that is the same as the one the user is adding, the cart increments the quantity on the item it already has instead of adding another item to its vector.

Because the `Item` class has a quantity that shows the number of items for one order (12 hot dogs, 6 colas, and so on), you need an order quantity that is the total number of items ordered. Every time you order another pack of 12 hot dogs, you add 12 to the order quantity. Your `Item` class should be something like the modified `Item` class shown in listing 8.11.

LISTING 8.11 SOURCE CODE FOR MODIFIED `Item.java`

```
package usingjsp.cart;
public class Item implements java.io.Serializable
{
    public String productCode;
    public String description;
    public double price;
    public int quantity;
    public int orderQuantity;

    public Item()
    {
    }

    public Item(String aProductCode, String aDescription,
        double aPrice, int aQuantity)
    {
        this(aProductCode, aDescription, aPrice, aQuantity, aQuantity);
    }

    public Item(String aProductCode, String aDescription,
        double aPrice, int aQuantity, int anOrderQuantity)
    {
        productCode = aProductCode;
        description = aDescription;
        price = aPrice;
        quantity = aQuantity;
        orderQuantity = anOrderQuantity;
    }

// Make get/set methods so the attributes will appear
// as bean attributes

    public String getProductCode() { return productCode; }
    public void setProductCode(String aProductCode) {
        productCode = aProductCode; }

    public String getDescription() { return description; }
    public void setDescription(String aDescription) {
        description = aDescription; }
```

```
    public double getPrice() { return price; }
    public void setPrice(double aPrice) { price = aPrice; }

    public int getQuantity() { return quantity; }
    public void setQuantity(int aQuantity) { quantity = aQuantity; }

    public int getOrderQuantity() { return orderQuantity; }
    public void setOrderQuantity(int anOrderQuantity)
    {
        orderQuantity = anOrderQuantity;
    }

    public boolean equals(Object ob)
    {
        if (ob == this) return true;
        if (!(ob instanceof Item)) return false;
        if (((Item)ob).getProductCode().equals(getProductCode()))
        {
            return true;
        }
        return false;
    }
}
```

Next, modify the `ShoppingCart` class to update the `orderQuantity` property when you add and remove items. Listing 8.12 shows the modified methods.

LISTING 8.12 MODIFICATIONS TO `ShoppingCart.java` FOR MULTIPLE ITEMS

```
public synchronized void addItem(Item newItem)
    {
        Enumeration e = items.elements();

// See if there is already an item like this in the cart
        while (e.hasMoreElements())
        {
            Item currItem = (Item) e.nextElement();

            if (newItem.equals(currItem))
            {
// Update the order quantity on the existing item
                currItem.orderQuantity = currItem.orderQuantity +
                    newItem.orderQuantity;
                return;
            }
        }

// Didn't find one like this one, so add this one to the cart
        items.addElement(newItem);
    }

    public synchronized void removeItem(int itemIndex)
    {
        Item item = (Item) items.elementAt(itemIndex);

// Remove 1 instance of this item from the quantity (an instance
// is the number of items in the quantity (1 car, 12 hot dogs)
        item.orderQuantity = item.orderQuantity - item.quantity;
```

LISTING 8.12 CONTINUED

```
// If the order quantity reaches 0, remove this item from the cart
        if (item.orderQuantity <= 0)
        {
            items.removeElementAt(itemIndex);
        }
    }
```

Also, you must modify the line in ShoppingCart.java that writes out the quantity from

```
out.println(item.productCode+","+
                    item.quantity);
```

to

```
out.println(item.productCode+","+
                    item.orderQuantity);
```

You must also make a few random changes in some of the Java Server Pages. Change ShowProductCatalog.jsp so it passes the order quantity to `AddToShoppingCartServlet`. Also change DisplayShoppingCart.jsp to show `orderQuantity` instead of quantity. Finally, change AddToShoppingCartServlet.java to get the order quantity passed in from ShowProductCatalog.jsp.

REMOVING SHOPPING CART ITEMS

In the example shopping cart class, you remove items based on the item's index in the shopping cart. One of the advantages of using the index is that you don't have to perform any searches. You can just ask the vector to remove the item with the specific index.

The shopping cart display Java Server Page automatically generates the Remove buttons for the items in the cart. Be very careful to insure that the view of the shopping cart is updated after the user removes an item. When an item is removed from the cart, the indices on the other items in the cart can change. If the view of the cart isn't updated to match the changed indices, the user might accidentally delete the wrong item from the cart. Listing 8.13 shows the servlet that performs the removal from the shopping cart.

LISTING 8.13 SOURCE CODE FOR `RemoveItemServlet.java`

```
package usingjsp.cart;
import javax.servlet.*;
import javax.servlet.http.*;
import java.io.*;
public class RemoveItemServlet extends HttpServlet
{
    public void service(HttpServletRequest request,
        HttpServletResponse response)
        throws IOException, ServletException
    {

// Get the index of the item to remove
        int itemIndex = Integer.parseInt(request.getParameter("item"));
```

```
        HttpSession session = request.getSession();

// Get the cart
        ShoppingCart cart = (ShoppingCart) session.
            getAttribute("ShoppingCart");

// If there is no shopping cart, create one
        if (cart == null)
        {
            cart = new ShoppingCart();

            session.setAttribute("ShoppingCart", cart);
        }

        cart.removeItem(itemIndex);

// Now display the cart and allow the user to check out or order more items
        response.sendRedirect(response.encodeRedirectURL(
            "/jspbook/ch08/examples/ShowCartAfterRemove.jsp"));
    }
}
```

COMPLETING THE ORDER

After the user has selected some items and decides to complete the order, you need to get the user's billing information and shipping address. Listing 8.14 shows the Java Server Page that displays the shopping cart and asks the user for billing and shipping information.

LISTING 8.14 SOURCE CODE FOR Checkout.jsp

```
<%@ page language="java" import="usingjsp.cart.*" %>
<html>
<body bgcolor="#ffffff">
<p>
<jsp:include page="DisplayShoppingCart.jsp" flush=" true"/>
<p>
<h1>Please enter your shipping information</h1>
<p>
<form action="/servlet/usingjsp.cart.CheckoutServlet" method="post">

<table>
<tr><td>Name:</td><td><input type="text" name="name"></td></tr>
<tr><td>Address:</td><td><input type="text" name="address1"></td>
</tr>
<tr><td></td><td><input type="text" name="address2"></td></tr>
<tr><td>City:</td><td><input type="text" name="city"></td></tr>
    <td>State:</td><td><input type="text" name="state" size=2
maxlength=2></td></tr>
<tr><td>Postal Code (Zip in U.S.):</td><td><input type="text"
name="postalCode"></td></tr>
<tr><td>Country:</td><td><input type="text" name="country"></td></tr>
<tr></tr>
<tr><td>E-Mail Address:</td><td><input type="text" name="email">
</td></tr>
</table>
<p>
<h1>Please enter your billing information</h1>
```

LISTING 8.14 CONTINUED

```
<table>
<tr><td>Name (as it appears on credit card):</td>
    <td><input type="text" name="nameOnCard"></td></tr>
<tr><td>Credit Card:</td>
<td><select name="creditCardType">
    <option value="amex">American Express</option>
    <option value="visa">Visa</option>
    <option value="mc">Mastercard</option>
    <option value="discover">Discover</option>
    <option value="bbbt">Billy Bob's Bank &amp; Trust</option>
    </select></td></tr>
<tr><td>Credit Card Number:</td><td><input type="text"
name="creditCardNumber"></td></tr>
<tr><td>Expiration Date:</td><td><input type="text"
name="creditCardExpiration"></td></tr>
</table>
<p>
<input type="submit" value="Complete Order">
</form>
</body>
</html>
```

Figure 8.4 shows a portion of the checkout page.

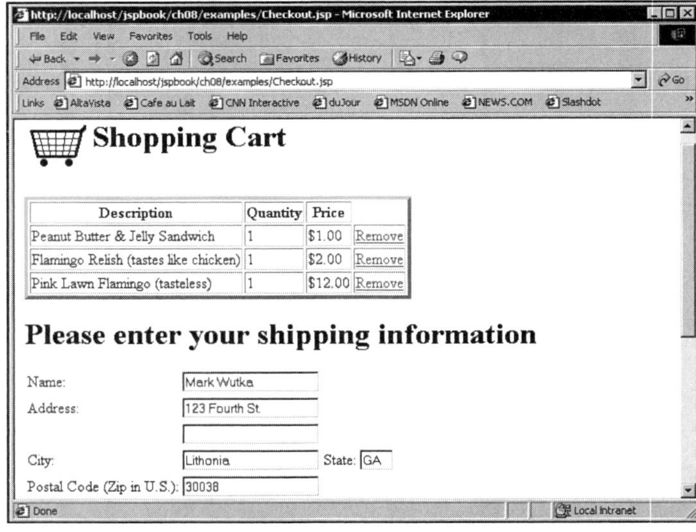

Figure 8.4
When checking out, you can show the cart again and then ask for additional information.

Listing 8.15 shows the servlet that takes the billing and shipping information and passes it to the shopping cart to complete the order. After the order has been submitted, the servlet calls a JSP to display the order confirmation.

LISTING 8.15 SOURCE CODE FOR CheckoutServlet.java

```
package usingjsp.cart;
import javax.servlet.*;
import javax.servlet.http.*;
import java.io.*;
import java.net.*;
public class CheckoutServlet extends HttpServlet
{
    public void service(HttpServletRequest request,
        HttpServletResponse response)
        throws IOException, ServletException
    {

// First get the shipping values from the request
        Shipping shipping = new Shipping();

        shipping.setName(request.getParameter("name"));
        shipping.setAddress1(request.getParameter("address1"));
        shipping.setAddress2(request.getParameter("address2"));
        shipping.setCity(request.getParameter("city"));
        shipping.setState(request.getParameter("state"));
        shipping.setPostalCode(request.getParameter("postalCode"));
        shipping.setCountry(request.getParameter("country"));
        shipping.setEmail(request.getParameter("email"));

// Next, get the billing values
        Billing billing = new Billing();

        billing.setNameOnCard(request.getParameter("nameOnCard"));
        billing.setCreditCardType(request.getParameter("creditCardType"));
        billing.setCreditCardNumber(request.getParameter(
            "creditCardNumber"));
        billing.setCreditCardExpiration(request.getParameter(
            "creditCardExpiration"));

        HttpSession session = request.getSession();

// Get the cart
        ShoppingCart cart = (ShoppingCart) session.
            getAttribute("ShoppingCart");

// If there is no shopping cart, create one (this should really be an error)
        if (cart == null)
        {
            cart = new ShoppingCart();

            session.setAttribute("ShoppingCart", cart);
        }

        try
        {
            String confirmation = cart.completeOrder(shipping, billing);

// Now display the cart and allow the user to check out or order more items
            response.sendRedirect(response.encodeRedirectURL(
                "/jspbook/ch08/examples/ShowConfirmation.jsp"+
                "?confirmationNumber="+URLEncoder.encode(confirmation)));
```

LISTING 8.15 CONTINUED

```
        }
        catch (ShoppingCartException exc)
        {
            PrintWriter out = response.getWriter();

            out.println("<html><body><h1>Error</h1>");
            out.println("The following error occurred while "+
                "processing your order:");
            out.println("<pre>");
            out.println(exc.getMessage());
            out.println("</pre>");
            out.println("</body></html>");
            return;
        }
    }
}
```

Listing 8.16 shows the order confirmation page.

LISTING 8.16 SOURCE CODE FOR `ShowConfirmation.jsp`

```
<html>
<body>
<h1>Order Submitted Successfully!</h1>
<p>
Thank you for your order. Your order confirmation number is:
<br>
<pre>
<%=request.getParameter("confirmationNumber")%>
</pre>
<p>
Please use this number when calling to check on your order.
</body>
</html>
```

STORING DATA IN A COOKIE

If you have been using the Internet for any significant period of time, you have probably heard of cookies. Cookies have been the subject of controversy for several years, although many people don't really understand how they work. A *cookie* is a piece of information that the server hands to the browser for safekeeping. The browser passes the cookie back to the server every time it asks for another page. The information is in the form `name=value`, although there are additional attributes that can be associated with the information.

> **Note**
>
> The source of the controversy surrounding cookies is the fact that various Web sites use cookies to share information about sites a user has visited. Many people consider the information sharing to be an invasion of their privacy.

For example, suppose the browser wants to store a cookie whose information is `UserID=Bob`. The server is essentially telling the browser, "From now on, every time you ask me for a page, I want you to say 'UserID=Bob'." Each cookie has an associated domain name. The cookie is only sent to servers within that domain name. You might have hundreds of cookies stored in your browser. Imagine if your browser had to send all those cookies to the server. The domain name helps the browser limit the number of cookies it needs to send. If the domain is set to `.wutka.com`, any server whose host name ends with `.wutka.com` would receive the cookie. In other words, the browser would send the cookie to `www.wutka.com` and also to `penguin.wutka.com`.

Note

Cookies can be associated with images instead of Web pages. It is this association that is the root of the cookie's bad rap. Banner ads can contain cookies and are used to track the sites you visit. A Web site can have its own cookies on the main Web page and allow the banner ad to have its own cookies as well.

In addition to restricting the cookie to certain domains, you can also restrict the cookie to certain pathnames in the URL. For example, you might have several different versions of your application running on a server. You might access the production system with a URL like `http://www.myhostname.com/prod/login.html`. Your QA system might have a URL of `http://www.myhostname.com/qa/login.html`. If you set a cookie just for the `.myhostname.com` domain, your QA and production systems might see each other's cookies. If you add the additional restriction of a pathname, you can tell the browser to only send a QA cookie when the URL path starts with `/qa/` and production cookies when the URL path starts with `/prod/`.

A cookie can also have an expiration time. The expiration time is specified in seconds. A negative expiration time means that the cookie stays around until the user shuts down the browser. An expiration time of 0 tells the browser to delete the cookie. When a cookie has a positive expiration time, the browser typically stores the cookie on disk to make sure it is available the next time the browser starts.

One other interesting aspect of a cookie is that you can specify that a particular cookie is only sent when the browser makes a secure connection (using https instead of the normal http in the URL). If a Web site sends sensitive information such as a credit card number in a cookie, it needs to tell the browser that the information is sensitive and should only be sent when the connection is encrypted.

Caution

You should try to avoid sending any sensitive information in a cookie if at all possible. Cookie files on the user's PC usually are not encrypted. Although someone might not be able to retrieve the cookie over the Internet, having unencrypted credit card data in a file on a PC is not very secure.

USING COOKIES IN SERVLETS AND JAVA SERVER PAGES

The `Cookie` class represents a cookie that needs to be stored on a browser or a cookie that has been sent from the browser. When you create a new cookie, you must supply an initial name and value for the cookie. You can change the value and any of the other attributes of a cookie after it has been created, but you can't change its name.

The following line of code creates a new cookie:

```
Cookie cook = new Cookie("UserID", "Bob");
```

You can use the `setDomain` and `setPath` methods in the cookie to restrict it to a specific domain and pathname. The following lines of code restrict the cookie to a domain of `".wutka.com"` and a path of `"/usingjsp"`:

```
cook.setDomain(".wutka.com");
cook.setPath("/usingjsp");
```

The `setMaxAge` method sets the number of seconds that the cookie should remain alive (how many seconds the browser should wait before deleting the cookie). A negative time means that the cookie lasts only as long as the browser is running, and a time of 0 deletes the cookie from the browser. The `setSecure` method marks the cookie as only being sent over HTTPS connections. If the browser accesses the server over a regular unencrypted HTTP connection, it won't send any cookies that are marked as secure. The method signatures for `setMaxAge` and `setSecure` look like this:

```
public void setMaxAge(int expirationLength)
public void setSecure(boolean useHttpsOnly)
```

To store a cookie on the browser, just add the cookie to the response by calling `response.addCookie`:

```
response.addCookie(cook);
```

Note

The cookie is sent back to the browser as part of the response header. If your JSP or servlet is not buffered, you must be very careful to send the cookie back before you write any part of the response. If you call `response.flushBuffer`, you will not be able to store any cookies after the buffer has been flushed.

If you are having trouble storing or retrieving cookies, see "Cookies," in the "Troubleshooting" section at the end of this chapter.

Listing 8.17 shows a servlet that sends a cookie to the browser.

LISTING 8.17 SOURCE CODE FOR `SaveCookieServlet.java`

```
package usingjsp;
import javax.servlet.*;
import javax.servlet.http.*;
import java.io.*;
public class SaveCookieServlet extends HttpServlet
{
```

```
    public void service(HttpServletRequest request,
        HttpServletResponse response)
        throws IOException, ServletException
    {

        Cookie cook = new Cookie("usingjspinfo", "Hello Cookie!");
        cook.setDomain(".wutka.com");
        cook.setPath("/servlet");

        response.addCookie(cook);

        response.setContentType("text/html");

        PrintWriter out = response.getWriter();
        out.println("<html><body bgcolor=\"#ffffff\">");
        out.println("Your cookie has been saved");
        out.println("</body></html>");
    }
}
```

To retrieve cookie values, use `request.getCookies`:

```
Cookie cookies[] = request.getCookies();
```

Listing 8.18 shows a servlet that retrieves all the cookies that have been sent to it and displays their contents.

Listing 8.18 Source Code for DumpCookiesServlet.java

```
package usingjsp;

import javax.servlet.*;
import javax.servlet.http.*;
import java.io.*;

public class DumpCookiesServlet extends HttpServlet
{
    public void service(HttpServletRequest request,
        HttpServletResponse response)
        throws IOException, ServletException
    {
        Cookie[] cookies = request.getCookies();

        response.setContentType("text/html");

        PrintWriter out = response.getWriter();
        out.println("<html><body bgcolor=\"#ffffff\">");

        out.println("Your browser sent the following cookies:");
        out.println("<pre>");

        if (cookies != null)
        {
            for (int i=0; i < cookies.length; i++)
            {
                out.println(cookies[i].getName()+": "+cookies[i].getValue());
            }
        }
```

LISTING 8.18 CONTINUED

```
        out.println("</pre>");
        out.println("</body></html>");
    }
}
```

TROUBLESHOOTING

SHOPPING CART PROBLEMS

Why do I get a `ClassNotFoundException` *when I try to use the* `ShoppingCart` *class?*

The JSP engine probably can't see the class in its classpath. The Tomcat and Resin JSP engines use the system classpath, so if `ShoppingCart.class` is visible somewhere in the system classpath, they should see it. JRun and ServletExec have their own classpath settings. See "Setting the Classpath" in Appendix D, "JRun," to see how to set the classpath for JRun and "Setting the Classpath" in Appendix E, "ServletExec," to see how to set the classpath for ServletExec.

I changed one of the shopping cart classes; why don't any of the servlets or Java Server Pages show the change?

Most servlet and JSP engines can't reload other classes automatically. You must restart the JSP/servlet engine to pick up changes in other classes.

COOKIES

I stored a cookie on the browser; why can't I see it?

First, check to make sure you spelled the cookie name right. Next, make sure the browser has cookies enabled. Also, if you specified a root path for the cookie, make sure that the JSP or servlet reading the cookie is in that path. Remember too, that if you don't give the cookie a specific expiration time, the cookie will vanish when the user shuts the browser down.

CHAPTER 9

INTERACTING WITH JAVABEANS

In this chapter

The <%, <%=, and <%! tags provide you with a way to access Java beans. Pages that use these tags, however, tend to look cluttered. You would be better off accessing Java bean properties in a Java Server Page using standard tags. That way, your page looks like a normal HTML page with a few extra tags. The `<jsp:useBean>` tag gives you the ability to create Java beans, and the `<jsp:getProperty>` and `<jsp:setProperty>` tags allow you to manipulate bean properties.

THE <jsp:useBean> TAG

When you want to use a Java bean within a Java Server Page, use the `<jsp:useBean>` tag to either create a new instance of the bean or use an existing bean. The idea behind the `<jsp:useBean>` tag and its associated helper tags is that you should try to move as much of your application logic as possible out of your JSP so all that remains is code to display the output.

When you encapsulate business objects or business logic into a Java class, you should make that Java class a bean. Many of Sun's Java APIs and tools revolve around the idea that you put your logic into beans and then use tools to help you create applications that use those beans. JSP is one of those tools.

ADDING THE BEAN TO THE PAGE

When you add a bean to a JSP, you can either create a new bean or use an existing one. The JSP engine determines whether it needs to create a new bean for you based on the bean's `id`.

When you add a bean to a page, you must at least give the bean an `id`, which is just a name, and the bean's class, like this:

```
<jsp:useBean id="myBean" class="usingjsp.TestBean"/>
```

The JSP engine first searches for an existing bean with the same `id` (`myBean` in this case). If it doesn't find an existing bean, the JSP engine creates a new instance of the class you specified. Where the JSP engine looks to find existing beans depends on the bean's `scope`.

> **Note**
>
> **The JSP compiler creates a variable with the same name as the `id` in the `<jsp:useBean>` tag. You can use this `id` in any Java code you put in your JSP. For instance, if you instantiated a bean with an `id` of `myBean`, you could write an expression like `<%= myBean.getFirstName() %>`.**

One of the other options you can use in the `<jsp:useBean>` tag is `scope`. The `scope` determines where the JSP engine stores a created bean and also where it looks to see if a particular bean `id` already exists. A bean can have a `scope` of `page`, `request`, `session`, or `application`. A bean with a `scope` of `page` is only visible on the current Java Server Page and disappears when the page finishes executing or forwards itself to another JSP or a servlet.

> **Note**
>
> **If you do not specify a `scope`, the default `scope` is `page`.**

A bean with `request scope` is visible to other Java Server Pages and servlets and is stored in the `request` object. You can use the bean's `id` to get it out of the `request` with the `getAttribute` method. For example, suppose you set up the following bean in a JSP:

```
<jsp:useBean id="myBean" scope="request" class="usingjsp.TestBean"/>
```

Now, suppose you want to include a servlet or forward the `request` on to a servlet, and the servlet needs to access your bean. The servlet would access the bean like this:

```
    usingjsp.TestBean theBean = request.getAttribute("myBean");
```


Because the `request` object disappears when the `request` completes, it should be obvious that a bean stored in the `request` is no longer visible.

Beans with `session scope` are stored in the `session` object. Suppose you created the following bean:

```
<jsp:useBean id="mySessionBean" scope="session" class="usingjsp.TestBean"/>
```

You could access this bean from a servlet like this:

```
    HttpSession session = request.getSession();
    Usingjsp.TestBean theBean =
          session.getAttribute("mySessionBean");
```

Finally, beans with `application scope` are stored in the `application` object, which is actually a `ServletContext` object. Like anything else stored in the `application` object, a bean with `application scope` is visible to any other JSP or servlet within the same "application."

Note

There is no servlet equivalent for accessing a bean stored with `page scope` because the `page scope` implies that the bean is only visible within the page. After you leave the page, you can't access the bean. If you need to access the bean within Java code in the JSP, use `pageContext.getAttribute("theBeanName")`.

If you are having trouble locating existing bean objects, see "Scope Problems," in the "Troubleshooting" section at the end of this chapter.

GETTING BEAN PROPERTIES

So far, you know how to put a bean on a page. Now you need to do something with it. Obviously, you must either put data into the bean, get data out of the bean, or both. Use the `<jsp:getProperty>` tag to get information from a bean. The syntax of `<jsp:getProperty>` is simple:

```
<jsp:getProperty name="beanId" property="propertyName"/>
```

The `<jsp:getProperty>` tag automatically inserts the property value into the output of the Java Server Page. It works like the `<%=` tag in that respect. In fact, for a bean stored in the `request` object, here are two identical ways to display one of the bean's properties:

```
<jsp:getPropery name="myBean" property="firstName"/>

<%= ((usingjsp.TestBean) request.getAttribute("myBean")).
    getFirstName() %>
```

As you can see, the `<jsp:getProperty>` tag takes care of fetching the bean from wherever it is stored, casting it to the appropriate type, and invoking the property's `get` method.

Because the `<jsp:useBean>` tag also creates a variable with the same name as the bean, you could also use the following expression:

```
<%= myBean.getFirstName() %>
```

The main reason you would choose the `<jsp:getProperty>` tag over the `<%=` tag is that the `<jsp:getProperty>` tag is language independent. Although the focus of this book is on using Java as the JSP scripting language, the JSP specification allows for other scripting languages such as JavaScript. Although the expression `<%= myBean.getFirstName() %>` works for JavaScript, it probably wouldn't work for other scripting languages. If you used Smalltalk as a scripting language, the expression would be something like `<%= myBean firstName %>`. You can be sure that `<jsp:getProperty>` will work no matter what scripting language you are using.

Setting Bean Properties

Obviously, if you can get bean properties from a JSP, you need to set them, too. The `<jsp:setProperty>` enables you to set bean properties and provides some useful shortcuts for copying parameter values into a bean.

The basic syntax for setting a bean property is

```
<jsp:setProperty name="beanName" property="propertyName"
    value="propertyValue"/>
```

You can even use the `<%=` tag inside the `<jsp:setProperty>` tag like this:

```
<jsp:setProperty name="myBean" property="name"
    value="<%=myName%>"/>
```

You can only use `<jsp:setProperty>` to set the value of string properties and certain data types that can be converted from a string. Table 9.1 lists the data types that are automatically converted and the method used to convert them.

TABLE 9.1 AUTOMATIC TYPE CONVERSIONS PERFORMED BY `<jsp:setProperty>`

Java Type	Conversion Method
`boolean` or `Boolean`	`Boolean.valueOf`
`byte` or `Byte`	`Byte.valueOf`
`char` or `Character`	`Character.valueOf`
`double` or `Double`	`Double.valueOf`
`float` or `Float`	`Float.valueOf`
`int` or `Integer`	`Integer.valueOf`
`long` or `Long`	`Long.valueOf`

For example, if your bean includes the following `set` method:

```
public void setAge(int age)
```

You can safely set the age like this:

```
<jsp:setProperty name="myBean" property="age" value="35"/>
```

The string `"35"` is automatically converted to an integer when the JSP engine sets the property.

SETTING PROPERTIES DIRECTLY FROM PARAMETERS

One of the great features of `<jsp:setProperty>` is that it recognizes the frequent need to copy values out of form variables and into beans. You can automatically copy a parameter into a bean property like this:

```
<jsp:setProperty name="myBean" param="paramName"
    property="propertyName"/>
```

If the property name is the same as the parameter name, you can omit the parameter name, like this:

```
<jsp:setProperty name="myBean" property="propertyName"/>
```

The presence or absence of the `value` keyword in `<jsp:setProperty>` determines whether the JSP engine uses a specific value or gets the value from a parameter. You can't have both a `value` and a `param` attribute in a single `<jsp:setProperty>`.

Note

If the value of a parameter is `null` or if it's an empty string, the `<jsp:setProperty>` method won't attempt to set the value. Although this behavior is normally good, it could trip you up if you expect to be able to clear out an entry by sending a blank value.

If your property is an indexed property (that is, an array of values), `<jsp:setProperty>` can handle it as long as it's an array of strings or one of the types previously listed in Table 9.1. To see how this works, imagine you have a class like the one shown in Listing 9.1.

LISTING 9.1 SOURCE CODE FOR `Group.java`

```
package usingjsp;
public class Group implements java.io.Serializable
{
    protected java.util.Vector members;

    public Group()
    {
        members = new java.util.Vector();
    }

    public String getMember(int which)
    {
        return (String) members.elementAt(which);
    }
```

LISTING 9.1 CONTINUED

```
    public void setMember(int which, String member)
    {
        members.setElementAt(member, which);
    }

    public String[] getMembers()
    {
// Convert the members vector into an array of strings
        String[] memberArray = new String[members.size()];
        members.copyInto(memberArray);

        return memberArray;
    }

    public void setMembers(String[] memberArray)
    {
// If there are no members, just clear out the vector
        if (memberArray == null)
        {
            members.setSize(0);
            return;
        }
// Copy the contents of the member array into the members vector
        members.setSize(memberArray.length);
        for (int i=0; i < memberArray.length; i++)
        {
            members.setElementAt(memberArray[i], i);
        }
    }
}
```

The Java Server Page shown in Listing 9.2 copies any `member` parameters it receives into the `Group` object, and then displays the contents of the object. Notice how easy it is to copy the values into the bean compared to the difficulty of getting the values out. The `<jsp:getProperty>` tag doesn't handle indexed properties well, so stick to single-value properties when using that tag.

LISTING 9.2 SOURCE CODE FOR `ShowGroup.jsp`

```
<HTML>
<BODY>
<%-- Create the bean --%>
<jsp:useBean id="group" class="usingjsp.Group"/>
<%-- Copy any member parameters into the bean --%>
<jsp:setProperty name="group" property="members" param="member"/><P>Group
members:<br>

<%-- Display the contents of the bean --%>
<%
    usingjsp.Group theGroup = (usingjsp.Group) pageContext.
        getAttribute("group");

    String[] members = theGroup.getMembers();
```

```
    for (int i=0; i < members.length; i++)
    {
        out.println(members[i]+"<BR>");
    }
%>
</BODY>
</HTML>
```

Figure 9.1 shows the ShowGroup Java Server Page in action, using values passed directly into the URL (look at the address line) .

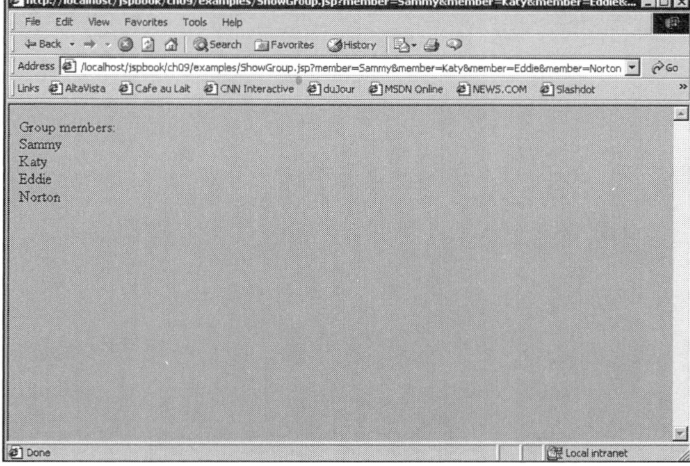

Figure 9.1
You can set multi-valued properties easily with <jsp:setProperty>.

In addition to the convenience of setting multiple values, the <jsp:setProperty> tag can also scan for matches between property names and parameter names. All you need to do is specify * for the parameter name, like this:

```
<jsp:setProperty name="myBean" property="*"/>
```

Listing 9.3 shows a simple test bean with a few properties.

LISTING 9.3 SOURCE CODE FOR TestBean.java

```
package usingjsp;
public class TestBean implements java.io.Serializable
{
    protected String firstName;
    protected String lastName;
    protected int age;

    public TestBean() { }

    public String getFirstName() { return firstName; }
    public void setFirstName(String aFirstName)
        { firstName = aFirstName; }
```

```
    public String getLastName() { return lastName; }
    public void setLastName(String aLastName)
        { lastName = aLastName; }

    public int getAge() { return age; }
    public void setAge(int anAge) { age = anAge; }
}
```

Listing 9.4 shows a Java Server Page that inserts values into a `TestBean` object and then displays the values again. One of the striking things about this JSP is that it does a fairly good bit of work but doesn't contain any explicit Java code.

```
<HTML><BODY><%-- Create an instance of the bean --%><jsp:useBean id="myBean"
class="usingjsp.TestBean"/>

<%--Copy the parameters into the bean --%>
<jsp:setProperty name="myBean" property="*"/>

The bean values are:<br>
First Name: <jsp:getProperty name="myBean" property="firstName"/><BR>
Last Name: <jsp:getProperty name="myBean" property="lastName"/><BR>
Age: <jsp:getProperty name="myBean" property="age"/><BR>

</BODY>
</HTML>
```

Figure 9.2 shows the output of ShowTestBean.jsp with parameters passed in directly in the URL.

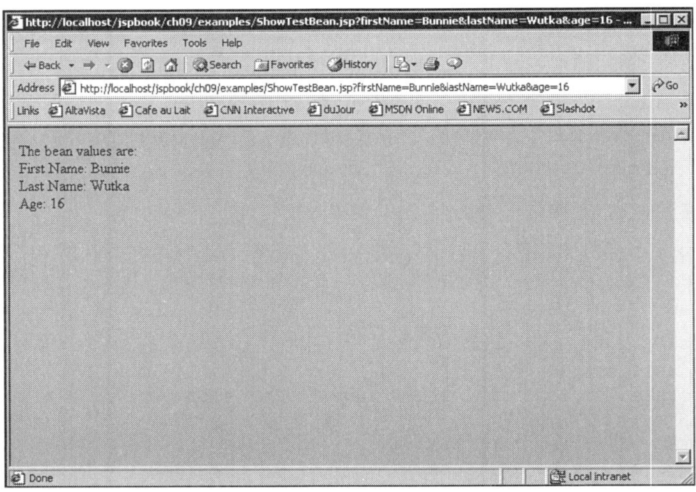

Figure 9.2
The `<jsp:setProperty>` tag makes it easy to set several bean properties from `request` parameters.

If you are having trouble accessing bean properties, see "Bean Property Problems," in the "Troubleshooting" section at the end of this chapter.

Initializing a New Bean

Frequently, you'll want to set only certain properties on a bean the first time it is created, but after that, you want to leave those properties alone. Rather than putting a `/>` at the end of <jsp:useBean>, you can use a closing </jsp:useBean> tag and put your initialization tags between the opening and closing tags for <jsp:useBean>. In other words, any code, HTML or JSP tags, between the <jsp:useBean> and </jsp:useBean> are only executed if the bean is created. If the bean already exists, any content between the opening and closing tags is skipped.

Listing 9.5 shows a variant of the JSP in Listing 9.4. This variant JSP changes the scope of the bean from page (the default) to session and executes some code when the bean is created.

LISTING 9.5 SOURCE CODE FOR TestInit.jsp

```
<HTML>
<BODY>
<%-- Create an instance of the bean --%><jsp:useBean id="myBean"
class="usingjsp.TestBean" scope="session">
    I initialized the bean.<BR>
    <jsp:setProperty name="myBean" property="firstName"
        value="blah"/>
    <% out.println("I ran some Java code during the init, too<P>"); %>
</jsp:useBean>

<%-- Copy the parameters into the bean --%>
<jsp:setProperty name="myBean" property="*"/>

The bean values are:<br>
First Name: <jsp:getProperty name="myBean" property="firstName"/><BR>
Last Name: <jsp:getProperty name="myBean" property="lastName"/><BR>
Age: <jsp:getProperty name="myBean" property="age"/><BR>

</BODY>
</HTML>
```

Figure 9.3 shows the output from the TestInit.jsp page when it is run for the first time from a browser.

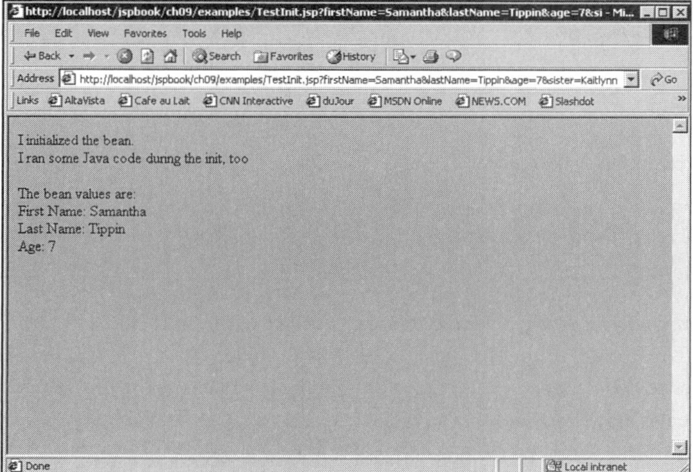

Figure 9.3
You can place initialization code between <jsp:useBean> and </jsp:useBean>.

Figure 9.4 shows the output from the TestInit.jsp page when you click the Refresh button on the browser after seeing the output from Figure 9.3. Notice that the initialization code isn't executed because the bean already exists and is stored in the `session` object.

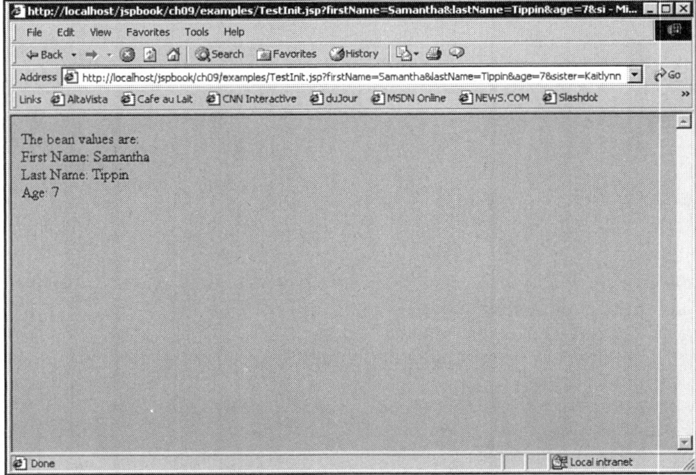

Figure 9.4
Initialization code isn't executed if a bean already exists.

THE TYPE OF AN EXISTING BEAN

Suppose you have a bean that implements a particular Java interface or is a subclass of some abstract Java class. Furthermore, suppose you want to refer to that bean using the interface or the abstract Java class. After all, you might be able to choose between several different subclasses of the abstract class when you first create the bean. Should all the following Java Server Pages have to figure out which subclass they are using and create separate `<jsp:useBean>` tags for each one?

When you need to refer to a bean using an abstract base class or an interface, you can use the `type` attribute instead of a `class` attribute in the `<jsp:useBean>` tag. For example, suppose you created a `Nameable` interface with a `getFirstName` and a `getLastName` like the one shown in Listing 9.6.

LISTING 9.6 SOURCE CODE FOR `Nameable.java`

```
package usingjsp;
public interface Nameable
{
    public String getFirstName();
    public String getLastName();
}
```

You want to write a JSP that prints out the first name and the last name stored in a bean, but you don't care about the actual classname of the bean. All you really care about is that it implements the `Nameable` interface. By specifying `type=usingjsp.Nameable` as opposed to `class=usingjsp.SomeBeanClass`, you can use any bean that implements `Nameable`. Listing 9.7 shows an example page:

Listing 9.7 Source Code for ShowNameable.jsp

```
<HTML>
<BODY>
<%-- Locate an instance of the bean --%>
<jsp:useBean id="myBean" type="usingjsp.Nameable" scope="session"/>

The bean values are:<br>
First Name: <jsp:getProperty name="myBean" property="firstName"/><BR>
Last Name: <jsp:getProperty name="myBean" property="lastName"/><BR>

</BODY>
</HTML>
```


If you need to create a bean, you must supply a classname. If you try to use the `type` attribute without a `class` attribute and the bean does not exist, the bean will be null. In other words, the JSP won't try to create a bean.

If you make changes to a bean and they don't appear to have any effect, see the "Making Changes" section in the "Troubleshooting" section at the end of this chapter.

A Bean-Based Web Application

In Chapter 8, "More About Saving Data," you learned how to make a shopping cart application by creating several core classes and then using servlets and JSPs to manipulate those core classes. The core shopping cart classes are all implemented as Java beans, making them ideal candidates for the `<jsp:useBean>` tag.

Many of the servlets used in Chapter 8 become very short Java Server pages, thanks to the `<jsp:useBean>` and `<jsp:setProperty>` tags. Listing 9.8 shows the updated ShowProductCatalog2.jsp file.

Listing 9.8 Source Code for ShowProductCatalog2.jsp

```
<%@ page language="java"
import="usingjsp.cart.*,java.net.*,java.text.*" %>
<%!
// Declare a constant for the number of items to show on a page
    public static final int ITEMS_PER_PAGE = 5;
%>

<html>
<body bgcolor="#ffffff">

<a href="ViewShoppingCart.jsp">View Shopping Cart</a>
<p>
<h1>Available Products</h1>
<table border="1">
<tr><th>Description</th><th>Quantity</th><th>Price</th></tr>

<%-- Get an instance of the product catalog class --%>
<jsp:useBean id="catalog" class="usingjsp.cart.ProductCatalog"
    scope="application"/>
<%
```

LISTING 9.8 CONTINUED

```
// Get the next starting position for displaying catalog items
    String startingPositionStr = (String) request.
        getParameter("StartingPosition");

    int startingPosition = 0;

// If there is a starting position parameter, parse it as an integer
    if (startingPositionStr != null)
    {
        try
        {
// If there's an error parsing the number, the starting position will
// just remain 0
            startingPosition = Integer.parseInt(startingPositionStr);
        }
        catch (Exception ignore)
        {
        }
    }

// Get ITEMS_PER_PAGE items at a time
    Item[] items = catalog.getItems(startingPosition, ITEMS_PER_PAGE);

// Get a currency formatter for showing the price
    NumberFormat currency = NumberFormat.getCurrencyInstance();

    for (int i=0; i < items.length; i++)
    {
        Item item = items[i];

// Create the URL for adding the item to the shopping cart
        String addItemURL =
            "AddToShoppingCart.jsp?"+
            "productCode="+URLEncoder.encode(item.getProductCode())+
            "&description="+URLEncoder.encode(item.getDescription())+
            "&quantity="+URLEncoder.encode(""+item.getQuantity())+
            "&price="+URLEncoder.encode(""+item.getPrice());
%>
<tr><td><%=item.getDescription()%></td><td><%=item.getQuantity()%>
    </td><td><%=item.getPrice()%></td>
<td><a href="<%=addItemURL%>">Add to Shopping Cart</a></td></tr>
<%
    }
%>
</table>
<table border="0">
<tr>
<%
    if (startingPosition > 0)
    {
        int prevPosition = startingPosition-ITEMS_PER_PAGE;

// Don't let the starting position go negative
        if (prevPosition < 0) prevPosition = 0;
```

```
// Write out a link to display the previous catalog page
        out.println("<td><a href=\"ShowProductCatalog2.jsp?StartingPosition="+
            prevPosition+"\">&lt;&lt;Prev</a></td>");
    }

// Compute the next starting position in the catalog
    int nextPosition = startingPosition+ITEMS_PER_PAGE;

// Make sure that there are still items to display at that starting
// position (i.e. make sure nextPosition isn't greater than the total
// catalog size)
    if (catalog.itemsAvailable(nextPosition))
    {
// Write out a link to display the next catalog page
        out.println("<td><a href=\"ShowProductCatalog2.jsp?StartingPosition="+
            nextPosition+"\">Next&gt;&gt;</a></td>");
    }
%>
</tr>
</table>
</body>
</html>
```


Most of the ShowProductCatalog2.jsp file is identical to the version in Chapter 8. The two main differences are the `<jsp:useBean>` tag that gets the `ProductCatalog` object and the link to add an item to the shopping cart. Instead of using a servlet to add an item to the cart, the new ShowProductCatalog2.jsp file uses a Java Server page.

Listing 9.9 shows the AddToShoppingCart.jsp file that adds an item to the cart. This file is significantly smaller and easier to read than its corresponding servlet from Chapter 8.

Listing 9.9 Source Code for AddToShoppingCart.jsp

```
<%-- Get a reference to the shopping cart --%>
<jsp:useBean id="cart" class="usingjsp.cart.ShoppingCart"
scope="session"/><%-- Create an item object --%>
<jsp:useBean id="item" class="usingjsp.cart.Item" scope="page"/>

<%-- Copy the request parameters into the item --%>
<jsp:setProperty name="item" property="*"/>

<%-- Add the item to the shopping cart --%>
<% cart.addItem(item); %>

<%-- Display the product catalog again --%>
<jsp:forward page="ShowCartAfterAdd.jsp"/>
```

AddItemToCart.jsp is much smaller for two reasons. First, the code to get an instance of the shopping cart is reduced to a single line. The servlet must check to see whether the cart already exists, and if not, create it. The `<jsp:useBean>` handles that.

Second, the servlet must copy each parameter into the `Item` object, converting the integer and double quantities as necessary. The `<jsp:setProperty>` tag copies all the parameters at once, because the parameters conveniently have the same names as their corresponding bean properties.

Likewise, the RemoveItem.jsp file, which replaces the `RemoveItemServlet` class from Chapter 8, is equally small. Listing 9.10 shows RemoveItem.jsp.

LISTING 9.10 SOURCE CODE FOR `RemoveItem.jsp`

```
<%-- Get the shopping cart --%>
<jsp:useBean id="cart" class="usingjsp.cart.ShoppingCart"
scope="session"/>
<%-- Ask the shopping cart to remove the item --%><%
cart.removeItem(Integer.parseInt(request.getParameter("item"))); %>

<%-- Display the shopping cart --%>
<jsp:forward page="ShowCartAfterRemove.jsp"/>
```

Again, the biggest savings here is the one-line creation/retrieval of the shopping cart.

Listing 9.11 shows the SubmitOrder.jsp file that handles the order submission in place of the `CheckoutServlet` from Chapter 8.

LISTING 9.11 SOURCE CODE FOR `SubmitOrder.jsp`

```
<%-- Declare a page to receive any errors that occur --%>
<%@ page errorPage="ShoppingCartError.jsp" %>
<%-- Get the shopping cart instance --%>
<jsp:useBean id="cart" class="usingjsp.cart.ShoppingCart" scope="session"/>

<%-- Create an object to hold shipping information --%>
<jsp:useBean id="shipping" class="usingjsp.cart.Shipping" scope="page"/>

<%-- Copy the shipping information into the shipping object --%>
<jsp:setProperty name="shipping" property="*" />

<%-- Create an object to hold billing information --%>
<jsp:useBean id="billing" class="usingjsp.cart.Billing" scope="page"/>

<%-- Copy the billing information into the billing object --%>
<jsp:setProperty name="billing" property="*" />

<html>
<body>
<h1>Thank you for your order</h1>
<p>
Your order confirmation number is
<%= cart.completeOrder(shipping, billing) %>.
<p>
Please use this number when calling to inquire about your order status.
</body>
</html>
```

Once again, the JSP realizes a huge savings over the servlet by use of the `<jsp:useBean>` and `<jsp:setProperty>` tags. The SubmitOrder.jsp uses a slightly different philosophy for displaying its results, too. The `CheckoutServlet` class is forwarded to a JSP to display the order confirmation. If it has an error submitting the order, it prints out an error message.

SubmitOrder.jsp prints out the order confirmation, and uses the `errorPage` option in the `page` directive to specify a page to handle the error. The error-handling page prints out an error message that is only useful for developers. Listing 9.12 shows the error-handling page.

LISTING 9.12 SOURCE CODE FOR SHOPPINGCARTERROR.JSP

```
<%@ page isErrorPage="true" %>
<html>
<body>
<h1>Error</h1>
<p>
Your order could not be processed because of the following error:
<pre>
<%= exception.getMessage() %>
</pre>
We are sorry for the inconvenience.
</body>
</html>
```

Note

The `isErrorPage=true` option in Listing 9.12 causes the JSP compiler to create a variable called `exception`, which contains the exception that caused the error page to be invoked.

As you can see, Java Server Pages make it easier to take advantage of Java Beans. When you add in Enterprise Java Beans (EJB), JSP becomes a very powerful scripting tool. You will learn more about the integration between EJB and JSP in Chapter 23, “Using Enterprise JavaBeans in a Web Application.”

TROUBLESHOOTING

SCOPE PROBLEMS

Why does it create a new object whenever I call `<jsp:useBean>`?

You probably forgot to specify a `scope` for the bean. Remember, the default `scope` for a bean is `page`, and all beans with `page scope` disappear when the page finishes executing.

I changed some bean properties in one page; why don't they show up on my other page?

You might have a `scope` problem on one of the pages. For example, if you set the properties on a bean with `session scope` and then you try to access the bean on another page but you give the bean `request scope` on the other page, you have two different beans. The second page looks in its `request` for the bean, and not finding one there, creates a new instance of the bean, ignoring the one in the session.

I checked to see that the `scope` is correct; why do I still not see the changes?

You should probably check the bean `id`s, too. Make sure they are absolutely identical, character-for-character. A bean `id` of `Fred` is different from a bean `id` of `fred`.

BEAN PROPERTY PROBLEMS

Why don't some of my parameters get copied into properties?

Chances are, you have a spelling difference between the parameter and the bean property name. Remember, unless you have a `BeanInfo` class that says otherwise, your bean property names are going to start with a lowercase letter (except when the first few letters of the property are capitalized). The property name looks capitalized in methods such as `getFirstName` and `setFirstName`, but the property name is still `firstName`. Make sure your parameter name matches the case of the property name.

MAKING CHANGES

I changed my bean class and recompiled it. Why don't my changes show up?

Many JSP engines don't reload associated classes when they change, only the JSP itself. If you are just testing and don't expect the bean to change in production, or at least not regularly, just restart the JSP engine. If you need to change the bean frequently, you might consider using a JSP engine that automatically reloads associated classes (such as Resin, for example) or write a custom class loader.

I know my bean class was reloaded; why do I still not see my changes?

Although new instances of the bean will pick up your changes, any existing beans are probably still using the older code. You need to clear the older beans out of whatever `scope` they belong to. In other words, if you have an old bean in a session, you need to get rid of it.

CHAPTER 10

Performance

In this chapter

When you're developing an application, your biggest concern is usually just getting it finished. Sooner or later, however, you have to work on optimizing performance. There are two parts to performance optimization. You can do things during development that you know will help improve performance. After development is complete, or at major milestones during the development cycle, you can do performance testing and isolate areas in which you need to concentrate on optimization.

Be careful about doing too much optimization work too early. You need to let the code stabilize before you go in and work on improving its speed or resource allocation. After all, you might make a change that really speeds things up today, but makes it difficult to add next week's new set of features.

MAKING JAVA SERVER PAGES AND SERVLETS THREAD-SAFE

One of the key features for high-performance server applications is the heavy use of threads. The Java networking classes do all their data transfer via blocking operations, meaning the executing thread waits until the data has been transferred. Many times, however, the server could be doing other things while waiting for the data to transmit. Most servers generally have one thread per client, with each thread listening for incoming requests. Some servers might also have a pool of threads to execute requests (the reader thread hands the request off to an execution thread and then looks for more incoming requests) .

Almost all JSP and servlet engines are multi-threaded, and by default, Java Server Pages are assumed to be thread-safe. Unless you specify otherwise, there might be multiple threads executing a Java Server Page at the same time. The `<%@ page isThreadSafe="false"%>` directive tells the JSP engine that a Java Server Page is not thread-safe. If you expect fairly high volume on your JSP, you should make sure it is thread-safe. Restricting a JSP to a single thread can really slow things down.

Servlets are also assumed to be multi-threaded, but there is no simple directive to mark the servlet as not being thread-safe. Instead, you must declare either the `service` method, or the individual `doPost` and `doGet` methods as being synchronized. Marking the whole method as synchronized is a brute-force method, just like marking an entire JSP as non–thread-safe. You are much better off finding the places where threading is a problem and fixing them.

There are certain things you can look for when searching for areas of your program that might not be thread-safe:

- Does the JSP access a variable defined with the `<%! %>` tag?
- Does the servlet access any member variables?
- Does the JSP or servlet modify the contents of an object stored in either the `session` or `application` (`ServletContext`) objects?
- Does the JSP or servlet use any libraries that might not be thread-safe?

Just because the answer to any of these questions is "yes," you don't necessarily have a threading issue. If you are always reading the value of a member variable, you probably don't have a threading issue. Sometimes you set up some variables during the initialization of a JSP or servlet and then don't change the value during execution. You can safely assume that multiple threads can read the value of the variables without any problems.

When you store an object in the `session` or the `application` object, you need to consider the circumstances in which multiple threads might be using the same data. For objects stored in the `session`, because each browser has its own session, the only threading issues will occur when the browser requests several JSPs or servlets at once. When you store objects in the `application` object, consider whether another thread might also be trying to store the same object.

Often you create an object that is shared across multiple servlets, but you only create the object if there isn't one already stored in the `application` object. When you discover that you need to create the object, synchronize on the `application` object, and then check again to see if the object needs to be created. Then, within the synchronized block, create the shared object. Listing 10.1 shows a segment of code that creates a shared object.

LISTING 10.1 CODE FRAGMENT TO CREATE A SHARED OBJECT

```
// See if the connection pool has already been created
    IConnectionPool pool = (IConnectionPool) context.getAttribute(
        "connectionPool");

// If not, the pool must be created
    if (pool == null)
    {
// Synchronize on the application object and check one more time
// for the pool just in case another thread is in the process
// of creating the pool

        synchronized(context)
        {
            pool = (IConnectionPool) context.getAttribute(
                "connectionPool");
            if (pool == null)
            {
// Make sure the database driver is available
                try {
                    Class.forName("org.gjt.mm.mysql.Driver").
                        newInstance();
                } catch (Exception exc) {
                    getServletContext().log(
                        "Error loading JDBC driver", exc);
                }

// Create the connection pool and store it in the application object
                pool = new SimpleConnectionPool(
                    "jdbc:mysql://localhost/usingjsp",
                    "", "");
                        context.setAttribute("connectionPool", pool);
            }
        }
    }
```

Because the test for the presence of the object is in the same synchronized block as the code that creates the object, you can be sure that only one thread actually creates the object.

You must also take special care with the objects you store in the `application` and `session` objects. If you store objects that aren't thread-safe, you must synchronize any method calls that modify the state of those objects. Most of the objects in the Java API such as `Vector`, `ResultSet`, `Connection`, and so on are thread-safe. If you use third-party libraries, consult your documentation to find out if any objects are known to be unsafe for threading.

Threading is more than just a programming issue, of course; it's also a tuning issue. The more threads your Java Virtual Machine or operating system must keep track of, the slower your overall performance. Many JSP/servlet engines let you configure the number of threads for performing various operations. You should have some idea of how many requests the server should be handling during a peak load, and the documentation for your JSP/servlet engine should give you an idea of how it uses threads and what numbers you can set for threading. You also need to decide whether you should gear your server for best performance under peak load, or better performance the rest of the time but some degradation at peak time. If you expect a huge load at peak time but peak time is only a small part of the day, and if gearing your server for peak time hogs resources the rest of the time, you might consider lowering your resource allocation.

If you create a car engine that can go 200 miles an hour using regular gasoline, you'll get terrible gas mileage. If you only need to go 200 miles an hour for 2 minutes, and 70 miles per hour the rest of the time, maybe you can set up the engine to do a peak of 180 miles per hour and get better gas mileage at 70. If you're doing a 500 mile race at 200 miles per hour, however, you need all the speed you can get.

Buffering Pages to Improve Performance

Buffering Java I/O is one of the biggest performance boosts any network-centric application can make. Without buffering, every time you write to an output stream you make a system call, which takes a lot of time. By buffering the output stream, you keep the data in memory until the buffer fills. Only when the buffer fills do you incur the time for the system call.

Buffering is a classic tradeoff between memory and speed. You use more memory for the buffering and improve the speed of your program. Some Java Server Pages and servlets might require different buffer sizes and deciding on the optimal buffer size will help you keep memory usage down while keeping your server running quickly.

From a speed standpoint, you want the buffer size to be as large as the page you are returning. That way, you only perform one system call to send the buffer back. When you look at memory usage, you want the pages with the largest buffers to execute as quickly as possible, so the memory can be reclaimed quickly. Unfortunately, it typically takes more time to generate the contents for a large buffer, especially if there is a lot of computation involved.

Optimization is an iterative process. You make changes and observe the results. You should only look at optimization when it looks like you have a problem. Before you deploy a large-scale production application, get a load-testing tool and see whether your application stands up under a heavy load. If not, look at the hot spots and try to reduce them.

As you start to tune your buffering, you can use `response.getBufferSize()` at the end of your JSP or servlet to find out how much buffer space you used. When doing this, set the initial buffer size to something much larger than you think you'll need. Otherwise, you might fill the buffer and then see a small buffer size because the buffer has already been flushed.

Caching Objects to Reduce Setup Time

Like buffering, caching is a speed-memory tradeoff. If an item takes a long time to create and initialize, you keep it in a cache and reuse it. Database connections are excellent examples of cached resources. It takes a relatively long time to establish a database connection, so most applications create the database connections when they start up and then store the connections in a connection pool, which is another form of a cache.

Some JSP and servlet engines even come with built-in database connection pools because they are so frequently used. In Chapter 19, "Building a Two-Tiered Web Application," you will learn more about connection pools, including how to implement your own pool.

The main difference between pooling and caching is that pooled objects are meant to be shared and reused. When you need a database connection, you grab it from the pool, use it, and put it back. With a cache, you typically create an object and put it somewhere for safe keeping until you need it the next time, but you don't necessarily want to share the object.

For example, when a user logs on to your application, you might query the database for information about the user. You might need this information every time the user makes a request, but you don't want to go back to the database every time to get it. Instead, you store the information in the user's `session` object. The `session` object makes an excellent cache.

Precompiling Java Server Pages

Converting a Java Server Page into a servlet and then compiling the servlet can be a time-consuming task for a JSP engine. Although the compilation only happens when the page has changed, you might want to compile all the pages ahead of time to make sure your users never see any delay when accessing recently changed Java Server Pages.

The JSP specification includes a special precompilation directive that asks the JSP engine to precompile a JSP rather than execute it. You just need to send a parameter of `jsp_precompile="true"` or just an empty `jsp_precompile` parameter to tell the JSP engine you want it to precompile a page.

Listing 10.2 shows a program that takes a base URL and a base directory and asks the JSP engine to precompile every JSP in the directory, including those in subdirectories. You can use this utility to eliminate compilation delays, and also to locate JSPs that no longer compile cleanly. Because you normally see compile errors only when you access a page, you often don't discover a broken JSP until a user stumbles upon it, especially when it's a rarely used page. The program in Listing 10.2 helps you locate those pages before the user does.

LISTING 10.2 SOURCE CODE FOR Precompile.java

```
package usingjsp;

import java.io.*;
import java.net.*;

/** A class to recursively visit JSP files and precompile them using
 *  a JSP engine
 */
public class Precompile
{
    public static FileFilter fileFilter = new PrecompileFileFilter();
    public URL rootURL;

    public Precompile(URL aRootURL)
    {
        rootURL = aRootURL;
    }

/** Precompiles an entire directory of files */
    public void precompileDirectory(File dir, String startDir)
    {
// Get all the files that are either directories or JSP files (the filter
// source code is at the bottom of this file)
        File[] files =  dir.listFiles(fileFilter);

        for (int i=0; i < files.length; i++)
        {
// If the current file is a directory, precompile its contents
            if (files[i].isDirectory())
            {
                precompileDirectory(files[i], startDir+"/"+dir.getName());
            }
            else
            {
// Otherwise precompile the current file
                precompileFile(files[i], startDir+"/"+dir.getName());
            }
        }
    }

    public void precompileFile(File file, String startDir)
    {
        try
        {
// Create the URL for precompiling
            URL precompileURL = new URL(rootURL, startDir+"/"+
                file.getName()+"?jsp_precompile=true");
// Create a URL connection to the JSP
```

LISTING 10.2 CONTINUED

```
            HttpURLConnection conn = (HttpURLConnection) precompileURL.
                openConnection();

// Check the response code (this also forces the connection to contact
// the Web server and precompile the JSP)
            int responseCode = conn.getResponseCode();

            System.out.println(startDir+file.getName()+": "+responseCode);
        }
        catch (Exception exc)
        {
            System.out.println("Exception: "+exc.toString()+
                " for "+startDir+file.getName());
        }
    }

    public static void main(String[] args)
    {
        if (args.length < 2)
        {
            System.out.println(
                "Please supply a base URL and a base directory");
            System.exit(0);
        }

        try
        {
            String startURL = args[0];
            File start = new File(args[1]);

            Precompile precomp = new Precompile(new URL(startURL));

            if (start.isDirectory())
            {
                precomp.precompileDirectory(start, "");
            }
            else
            {
                precomp.precompileFile(start, "");
            }
        }
        catch (Exception exc)
        {
            exc.printStackTrace();
        }
    }
}

class PrecompileFileFilter implements FileFilter
{
    public boolean accept(File f)
    {
        if (f.isDirectory()) return true;
        if (f.getName().endsWith(".jsp")) return true;
        return false;
    }
}
```

SIMPLE JAVA OPTIMIZATIONS

In addition to optimizing the performance of your servlet engine by manipulating the threads, or increasing throughput by modifying the buffering, you can do many simple things in your Java code to speed it up. These optimizations are always useful, no matter if you're writing a Web application, a GUI application, or an applet.

USE THE `StringBuffer` CLASS

Many Java programmers never take the time to use the `StringBuffer` class. I frequently ignore it even in situations in which I should use it. Most programmers concatenate two strings with a statement like this:

```
String foobar = "foo" + "bar";
```

When you look at this statement, you naturally assume that the Java Virtual Machine must have some built-in string concatenation operation. What most people don't realize, however, is that the Java compiler generates code similar to this:

```
StringBuffer a = new StringBuffer("foo");
a.append("bar");
foobar = a.toString();
```

Creating one string buffer isn't so bad, but things slow down when you have a series of concatenations like this:

```
String name = prefix;
name = name + " "+firstName ;
name = name + " "+middleName;
name = name + " "+lastName;
name = name + " "+suffix;
```

Each new assignment creates a new `StringBuffer` object. When you execute this code many times, you start creating a lot of `StringBuffer` objects. You are much better off creating a single `StringBuffer` object yourself and appending the strings to it, like this:

```
StringBuffer nameBuff = new StringBuffer(prefix);
nameBuff.append(" ");
nameBuff.append(firstName);
nameBuff.append(" ");
nameBuff.append(middleName);
nameBuff.append(" ");
nameBuff.append(lastName);
nameBuff.append(" ");
nameBuff.append(suffix);
String name = nameBuff.toString();
```

When you need to optimize your programs, start looking for places when you use `+` to concatenate strings. If you do several concatenations, replace them with `StringBuffer` and you'll see a reasonable performance increase.

PARSING NUMBERS

When you need to convert a string into a number, you use the various object wrapper classes such as `Integer`, `Double`, `Long`, and so on. There are several ways to convert a string into a number when using these classes, but there is only one optimal way (assuming that you want a native type as the end result).

When you want to convert a string into an `int`, for example, you might use one of the two following statements:

```
int i = (new Integer("12345")).intValue();
int i = Integer.valueOf("12345").intValue();
```

The problem with both of these statements is that they create a new `Integer` object first, and then extract the `int` value from the object. The most efficient way to convert a string into an `int` is by the `parseInt` method:

```
int i = Integer.parseInt("12345");
```

In fact, both the string constructor for `Integer` and `Integer.valueOf` use `parseInt` to first create an `int` and then wrap an `Integer` object around it. The other classes have their own parse methods, such as `parseDouble` and `parseLong`.

CREATING OBJECTS

As you might have noticed, the previous two optimization tips centered around reducing the number of objects you create. Object creation consumes time and memory, and the fewer times you do it, the faster your program runs. In fact, with a good just-in-time compiler, a Java program that doesn't create any objects can run about as fast as a C program that doesn't allocate memory. For example, Java programs that analyze chess moves recursively and reuse the same memory for the board tend to run about the same speed as their C counterparts. Although situations like this are rare in a typical business application, you can see that object creation does contribute to the relative slowness of Java.

TROUBLESHOOTING

THREADING PROBLEMS

I marked my pages as not being safe for threading; why do some users still see data belonging to other users?

Usually these situations happen because different servlets and Java Server Pages are sharing objects that aren't thread-safe. Remember that the JSP/servlet engine only ensures that a specific JSP or servlet will be accessed by one thread at a time. You might need to synchronize on any shared objects to make sure that only one user at a time can access the object.

Precompilation Problems

I asked the JSP engine to precompile a page; why didn't it compile the page?

The precompile option is only a hint to the JSP engine. It is up to the JSP engine whether or not to precompile the page.

PART II

CORE COMPONENTS IN-DEPTH

CHAPTER 11

JSP and Servlet Lifecycles

In this chapter

Now that you understand the major features of JSP and servlets, it's time to drill down into some of the underlying structure. It is important to understand the JSP and servlet lifecycle: when and how servlets and JSPs are loaded, executed, and unloaded. Because Java Server Pages are also servlets, it makes sense to start with servlets.

SERVLET LIFECYCLE

A servlet goes through four phases:

- Loading
- Initialization
- Execution
- Cleanup

SERVLET LOADING

A servlet can be loaded at three different times: when the server starts up, when the system administrator asks the server to load the servlet, or when a browser tries to access the servlet. Many servlet engines provide a way for you to list the servlets you want to load during startup. Although the actual loading of the servlet might take a reasonably short period of time, the servlet might have a costly initialization phase. By loading and initializing a servlet early, you can improve the response time of the server.

For example, suppose your servlet creates several database connections during initialization, and then reads and caches some data from the database. If you wait until a browser first accesses the servlet, the user will experience a much longer wait than usual while the servlet performs its initialization. If you load the servlet when the server starts, the server might take a little more time to start, but the users will not see any delays after everything starts. If you restart the server during periods of low usage, the users might never see the slowdown from initialization.

To load a servlet, the server needs to know the classname for the servlet. Normally, the classname is the name of the servlet that the browser asks for. When a servlet is within a Java package, the servlet name contains the fully qualified Java classname. For example, a servlet class named `HelloWorldServlet` in the package `usingjsp` would have a servlet name of `usingjsp.HelloWorldServlet`.

The tricky thing is, how does the servlet engine know that you are asking it to run a servlet? In the examples you have seen so far, the URL was something like `http://localhost/servlet/usingjsp.HelloWorldServlet`. It's not the word "Servlet" at the end of the classname that gives the server its cue, it's the `/servlet/` right before the servlet name.

A typical servlet engine recognizes a special servlet name called `invoker`. When you configure the servlet engine, you can map a URL pattern to a particular servlet. For example, the `/servlet` directory is typically set up by mapping `/servlet/*` to the servlet named `invoker`.

Whenever the servlet engine sees a URL starting with `/servlet/`, it extracts the servlet name from the URL and invokes the servlet. The servlet engine might not actually have a servlet named `invoker`, it usually is just a special name that the servlet engine recognizes.

You can also map specific URLs to specific servlets. For example, you could map the URL `/HelloWorld` to run the `HelloWorldServlet` program. You can save a little time by mapping servlet names directly, because the server doesn't have to extract a servlet name from the URL as it does when you use the invoker.

After the servlet engine knows it needs to run a servlet, it checks to see whether that servlet is already loaded in memory. If not, the servlet engine uses Java's dynamic class loading features to load the servlet into memory. After the servlet is loaded, the servlet engine initializes it and the servlet is ready to go.

Servlet Initialization

When the servlet engine initializes a servlet, it calls the servlet's `init` method, passing it a `ServletConfig` object. The `init` method is declared like this:

```
public void init(ServletConfig config)
    throws ServletException
```

The `ServletConfig` object contains initialization parameters and a `ServletContext` object. The initialization parameters are items that you can configure within your servlet engine. The following methods in `ServletConfig` let you find out what initialization parameters exist and the value of each parameter:


```
public java.util.Enumeration getInitParameterNames()
public String getInitParameter(String name)
```

The `ServletConfig` object also gives you access to the `ServletContext` object. A servlet is responsible for keeping track of its `ServletContext` object. Rather than dealing with the `ServletConfig` object and keeping track of the `ServletContext` yourself, you can just make your servlet a subclass of `GenericServlet` or `HttpServlet` (which itself is a subclass of `GenericServlet`).

`GenericServlet` and `HttpServlet` provide an `init` method that doesn't take any arguments:

```
public void init() throws ServletException
```

This simplified `init` method is provided as a convenience for servlets that need to perform initialization. Without this `init` method, you would need to override the normal `init` method and then call `super.init`, like this:

```
public void init(ServletConfig config)
    Throws ServletException
{
    super.init(config);

    // Perform servlet-specific initialization here
}
```

You should override the simplified `init` method to perform any servlet-specific initialization.

If you are having trouble with a servlet when there is an `init` method, see "Init Method Trouble," in the "Troubleshooting" section at the end of this chapter.

SERVLET EXECUTION

A servlet spends most of its time in the execution phase of its lifecycle. When a request comes in, the servlet engine invokes the servlet's `service` method, passing it the `ServletRequest` and `ServletResponse` representing a connection with a browser.

Although the execution phase of the lifecycle is fairly obvious, the full path of the request from browser to servlet might not be so obvious. Figure 11.1 shows the path a request takes from the browser all the way to the service method.

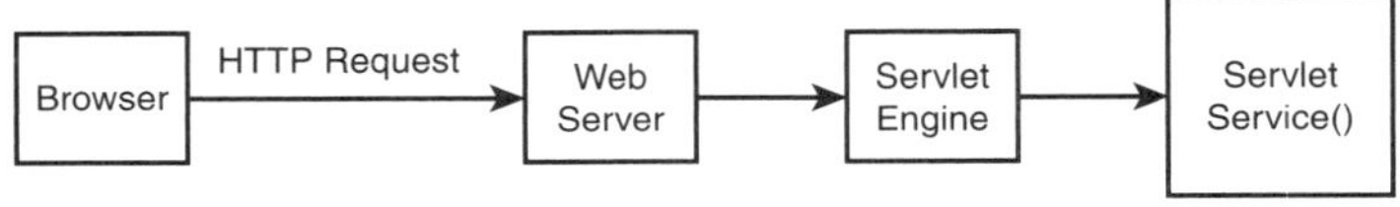

Figure 11.1
The Web server handles the communications with the browser while passing data to the servlet.

The fact that the Web server handles the communications with the browser might seem insignificant, but there is one interesting point. Until recently, there hasn't been an official Security Socket Layer (SSL) API from Sun, yet servlets and Java Server Pages have been able to support SSL since the Servlet API first came out. As long as your Web server supports SSL, you don't need SSL support in your Java environment.

The flip side of this is, just because you are able to access your JSPs and servlets from SSL, don't automatically assume that you have an SSL API available for use from your Java code. If you have a servlet that must make an SSL request to another server somewhere, you might still need to install the SSL package from Sun.

SERVLET CLEANUP

When the servlet engine decides to unload a servlet (either by administrator request, for performance reasons, or for system shutdown), it invokes the servlet's `destroy` method. The `destroy` method is a courtesy method to give servlets a chance to release any allocated resources that might be too precious to wait for garbage collection. For example, if your servlet allocates a large number of database connections, you want to release them when the servlet is destroyed. Otherwise, it might take a while before the system reclaims the connections during garbage collection.

Although you probably don't need to worry about cleanup if the whole servlet engine is shutting down, you still need to provide for the possibility that the servlet engine will want to unload the servlet, or that you might want to manually unload it.

JAVA SERVER PAGE LIFECYCLE

A Java Server Page has an extra phase in its lifecycle, because it must also be compiled. The phases of a JSP's lifecycle are

- Compilation
- Loading
- Initialization
- Execution
- Cleanup

JSP COMPILATION

When a browser asks for a Java Server Page, the JSP engine first checks to see whether it needs to compile the page. If the page has never been compiled, or if the JSP page has been modified since it was last compiled, the JSP engine compiles the page. The compilation process involves first parsing the JSP page, turning the JSP into a servlet, and then compiling the servlet.

You can circumvent the compilation process by manually generating a servlet for the JSP and compiling it by hand. As you saw in Chapter 10, "Performance," the Tomcat JSP engine provides a handy command-line tool for compiling a JSP.

Note

If you simply compile the JSP by hand, but then change the JSP source file later, the JSP engine will still recompile the JSP source. If you want to control the compilation totally, you must deploy your application with a Web Archive file (WAR), which is discussed in detail in Chapter 28, "Packaging a JSP Application." You can set up a URL mapping that forces YourPageName.jsp to run a specific servlet, avoiding the JSP compiler altogether.

JSP LOADING

Because a JSP becomes a servlet before it is actually loaded, the loading process for a JSP is similar to the loading process for a servlet. The main difference between a JSP and a servlet is that the class file for the JSP is always reloaded, even if a class file with the same name is already loaded into memory.

Note

Although a JSP class is always reloaded, any associated classes, such as Java beans or utility classes, are not always reloaded automatically. Some JSP engines might automatically reload other classes, but don't count on it.

JSP INITIALIZATION

Although a JSP is compiled into a servlet, JSP developers should not override the servlet `init` and `destroy` methods. If you need to perform JSP-specific initialization, override the `jspInit` method:

```
public void jspInit()
```

As with the servlet `init` method, you generally initialize database connections, open files, and create lookup tables in the `jspInit` method.

JSP EXECUTION

Whenever a browser requests a Java Server Page and the page has been loaded and initialized, the JSP engine invokes the `_jspService` method in the Java Server Page. The `_jspService` method takes an `HttpServletRequest` and an `HttpServletResponse` as its parameters.

Caution

Because the JSP compiler generates the `_jspService` method, you should never try to override this method yourself.

JSP CLEANUP

The `jspDestroy` method is the JSP equivalent of the destroy method for servlets. Override `jspDestroy` when you need to perform any cleanup such as releasing database connections or closing open files. The `jspDestroy` method is declared this way:

```
<%!
    public void jspDestroy()
    {
        // Your cleanup code goes here
    }
%>
```

RELOADING OTHER CLASSES

When you change a Java Server Page, the JSP engine automatically reloads it the next time a browser requests it. Some servlet engines even reload a servlet when it changes. Many engines, however, do not automatically reload associated classes. In other words, when you create a Java class that is a companion to a JSP and you change that companion class, it isn't reloaded even if the JSP itself is reloaded.

For example, the JSP in Listing 11.1 calls a static method in an external class to retrieve a message.

LISTING 11.1 SOURCE CODE FOR `ReloadTest.jsp`

```
<%@ page language="java" import="usingjsp.*" %>
<html>
<body>

The message is: <%= ReloadedClass.getMessage() %>
</body>
</html>
```

Listing 11.2 shows the `ReloadedClass` class that returns the message.

LISTING 11.2 SOURCE CODE FOR `ReloadedClass.java`

```
package usingjsp;

public class ReloadedClass
{
    public static String getMessage()
    {
        return "This is the original message";
    }
}
```


Now, when you run ReloadTest.jsp, you get the kind of result shown in Figure 11.2.

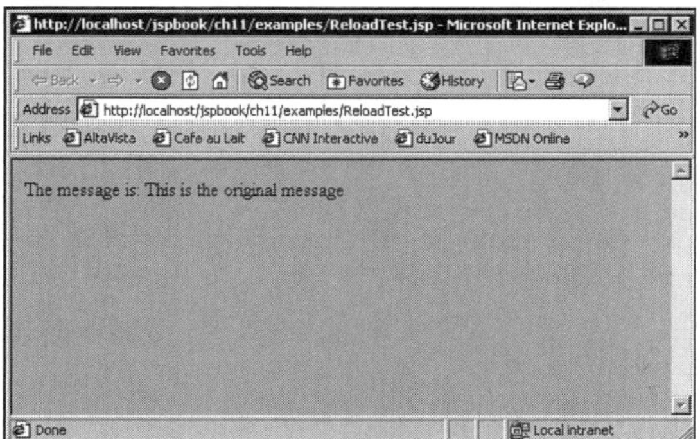

Figure 11.2 The JSP engine automatically loads the `ReloadedClass` Java class.

Now, suppose you change the message to return a different message, like this:

```
return "This is the new message";
```

When you recompile the Java class and reload the JSP, you will not notice any change because the JSP engine is still holding on to the original.

Now, suppose you change the `ReloadTest` class to have a slightly different message:

```
The new message is: <%= ReloadedClass.getMessage() %>
```

When you reload the JSP, the JSP engine recompiles the page, but the screen still looks the same. When the JSP engine loads the recompiled servlet into memory, it sees that it already has ReloadedClass in memory, so it doesn't bother to reload it again.

Now, if you restart the JSP engine and display the page again, you can see that the changed `ReloadedClass` class finally gets reloaded as shown in Figure 11.3.

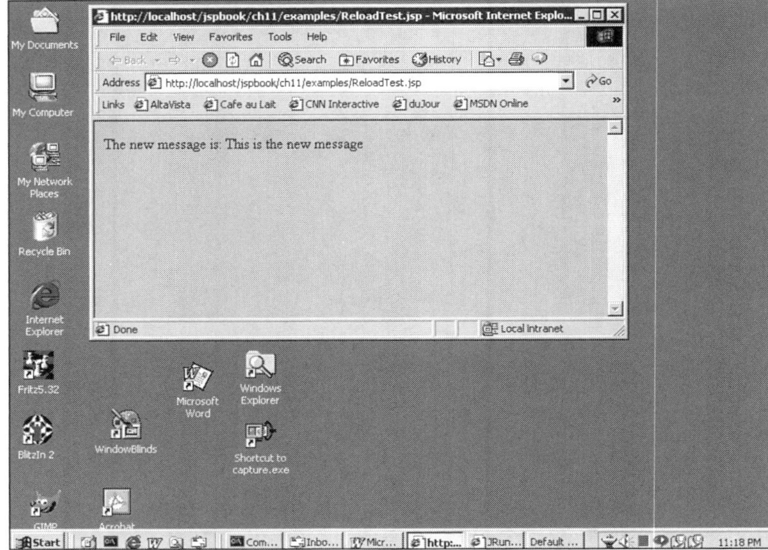

Figure 11.3
When the JSP engine is restarted it picks up the changed `ReloadedClass` class.

If you are having trouble reloading classes, see "Reloading Classes," in the "Troubleshooting" section at the end of this chapter.

Some JSP/servlet engines might automatically reload classes stored in Web Archive (WAR) files, which you will learn about in Chapter 28, "Packaging a JSP Application." Many, however, still require you to restart the Web server to pick up changed classes.

TROUBLESHOOTING

INIT METHOD TROUBLE

I added an `init` method to my servlet; why can't I run it now?

If your servlet was working before and the only thing you changed was the `init` method, there's a pretty good chance your `init` method is throwing an exception. If the `init` method throws an exception, the servlet engine will stop loading it and it won't run. Check your server's error logs to see if there are any exceptions there.

Why does my servlet act strange when I have defined an `init` method?

If you override the `init(ServletContext ctx)` method instead of the simpler `init()` method, and you forget to call `super.init(ctx)`, your servlet won't be properly initialized and might act strange.

RELOADING CLASSES

My JSP recompiled; why do I still see old data?

If your JSP depends on other classes that have changed, you must reload these classes. Most JSP engines must be restarted before they pick up changed classes.

I restarted my JSP engine; why didn't it pick up the changed classes?

Make sure that the class file the JSP engine is using has been changed. If you copy class files from one place to another, you might have an old copy of the class file somewhere else that is closer to the front of the classpath than the class file you just regenerated. Your operating system probably has a utility to search for files with a particular name (`Start->Search->"For Files or Folders...` under Windows, or `find` in Unix). Also, if you left any `.java` files in the directory where your JSP is, the JSP engine might have compiled those files and put them in its own class file directory. Again, searching for class files should locate any such files.

CHAPTER 12

How the Browser Interacts with the Server

In this chapter

Most of the time, a browser communicates with the Web server using the HTTP protocol. In some cases, the browser uses FTP and communicates with an FTP server, but overall HTTP carries the bulk of Web traffic. Most people wouldn't recognize the HTTP protocol if it bit them, and there's really nothing wrong with that. Even as a Java programmer, you don't need to know the specifics of HTTP because you have the `URL` and `URLConnection` classes to handle communications from the client side and servlets and JSP to handle the server side of things.

However, it's almost always better to know more than you absolutely need to, especially in the computer industry. That little extra bit of understanding can help you diagnose problems faster, understand the implications of architectural decisions better, and use all the capabilities a system has to offer.

THE HTTP PROTOCOL

An HTTP connection is a simple network socket connection. The Web server usually listens for incoming connections on port 80. After the connection is established, the browser sends a few lines of text indicating which Web page it wants to see, some request headers telling the Web server what kind of browser is making the request, and a few other interesting items, like the browser user's preferred language, the kinds of data the browser accepts, and even the kind of browser (Netscape, IE, Opera, and so on).

The only part of the request that is required is the first line that tells the server what file the browser wants. The rest is optional. Each line in the request is a human-readable text line, separated by a newline character. The request header ends with a blank line. The protocol is so simple that you can even interact manually with a Web server using the `telnet` command.

For example, you can view the HelloWorld Java Server Page from Chapter 2, "Getting Started with Java Server Pages," by telneting to port 80 on your Web server, entering `GET <the path of the JSP> HTTP/1.0`, and pressing Enter twice. The path in an HTTP request is the portion of the URL that comes after the host name and includes the leading `/`. Thus, if you access HelloWorld.jsp with `http://localhost/jspbook/ch02/examples/HelloWorld.jsp`, you enter `/jspbook/ch02/examples/HelloWorld.jsp` as the path.

Figure 12.1 shows a Telnet session requesting and receiving the HelloWorld JSP.

Note

You might need to turn on local echo in your Telnet window to see what you are typing. Also, if you make any typing errors, don't be surprised if the Web server doesn't understand the backspace key and complains that you sent it a garbled command.

Notice that the request to the server said that it was using version 1.0 of the HTTP protocol (the `HTTP/1.0` at the end of the `GET` request) and the server responded with version 1.1 of HTTP. HTTP version 1.1 adds a number of options that can optimize Web access and enable the browser to retrieve multiple pages over a single connection.

```
Command Prompt
GET /jspbook/ch02/examples/HelloWorld.jsp HTTP/1.0

HTTP/1.1 200 OK
Server: Microsoft-IIS/5.0
Date: Mon, 01 May 2000 18:30:16 GMT
Set-Cookie: jsessionid=34549957205816351;path=/
Expires: Thu, 01 Dec 1994 16:00:00 GMT
Connection: Keep-alive
Cache-Control: no-cache="set-cookie,set-cookie2"
Content-Type: text/html; charset=ISO-8859-1
Content-Length: 59

<HTML>
<BODY>
<H1>Hello World!</H1>

</BODY>
</HTML>

Connection to host lost.

H:\jspbook\ch12\examples>_
```

Figure 12.1
You can interact with a Web server directly by using the `telnet` command.

Under HTTP 1.1, an additional line must be present in each request. You must specify the name of the host you are accessing. This is important in multihome hosts in which a single Web server supports many host names.

Figure 12.2 shows a Telnet session that again fetches the HelloWorld.jsp file, this time using HTTP 1.1.

```
Command Prompt - telnet localhost 80
GET /jspbook/ch02/examples/HelloWorld.jsp HTTP/1.1
Host: localhost

HTTP/1.1 200 OK
Server: Microsoft-IIS/5.0
Date: Mon, 01 May 2000 18:32:11 GMT
Set-Cookie: jsessionid=20282695720593l747;path=/
Expires: Thu, 01 Dec 1994 16:00:00 GMT
Connection: Keep-alive
Cache-Control: no-cache="set-cookie,set-cookie2"
Content-Type: text/html; charset=ISO-8859-1
Content-Length: 59

<HTML>
<BODY>
<H1>Hello World!</H1>

</BODY>
</HTML>
_
```

Figure 12.2
HTTP 1.1 requires you to specify a hostname in the request.

Notice that the Web server did not automatically close down the connection as it did when you used HTTP/1.0. One of the optimizations of HTTP 1.1 is that a browser can make multiple requests using the same connection. Setting up a connection is a time-consuming process. You can force the server to close the connection by specifying `Connection: close` in the request. Figure 12.3 shows a Telnet session that asks the server to close the connection.

VIEWING THE REQUEST HEADERS MADE BY A BROWSER

A browser sends quite a bit more information than the minimum. The request object has methods that allow you to retrieve all the header values sent by the browser. Listing 12.1 shows a JSP file that displays all the headers sent to it.

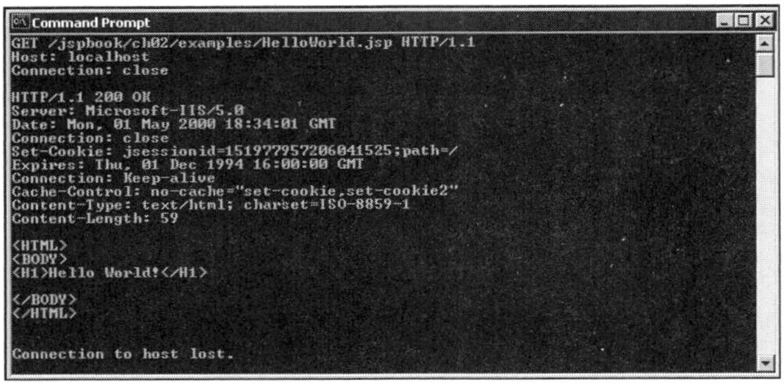

```
Command Prompt
GET /jspbook/ch02/examples/HelloWorld.jsp HTTP/1.1
Host: localhost
Connection: close

HTTP/1.1 200 OK
Server: Microsoft-IIS/5.0
Date: Mon, 01 May 2000 18:34:01 GMT
Connection: close
Set-Cookie: jsessionid=151977957206041525;path=/
Expires: Thu, 01 Dec 1994 16:00:00 GMT
Connection: Keep-alive
Cache-Control: no-cache="set-cookie,set-cookie2"
Content-Type: text/html; charset=ISO-8859-1
Content-Length: 59

<HTML>
<BODY>
<H1>Hello World!</H1>

</BODY>
</HTML>

Connection to host lost.
```

Figure 12.3
If you want the server to automatically close the connection in HTTP 1.1, you must explicitly say so.

LISTING 12.1 SOURCE CODE FOR `DumpHeaders.jsp`

```
<html>
<body>
<pre>
<%
    java.util.Enumeration e = request.getHeaderNames();

    while (e.hasMoreElements())
    {
        String headerName = (String) e.nextElement();
        out.print(headerName+": ");

        java.util.Enumeration h = request.getHeaders(headerName);

        while (h.hasMoreElements())
        {
            String header = (String) h.nextElement();
            out.print(header);
            if (h.hasMoreElements()) out.print(", ");
        }
        out.println();
    }
%>
</pre>
</body>
</html>
```

Figure 12.4 shows the headers sent to DumpHeaders.jsp.

How can you be sure that you are really seeing all the header values? Because HTTP works over a simple socket connection, you can create a program that accepts an incoming connection and dumps out anything sent to it.

Listing 12.2 shows the Dumper.java program you can use to verify that you are seeing all the header values.

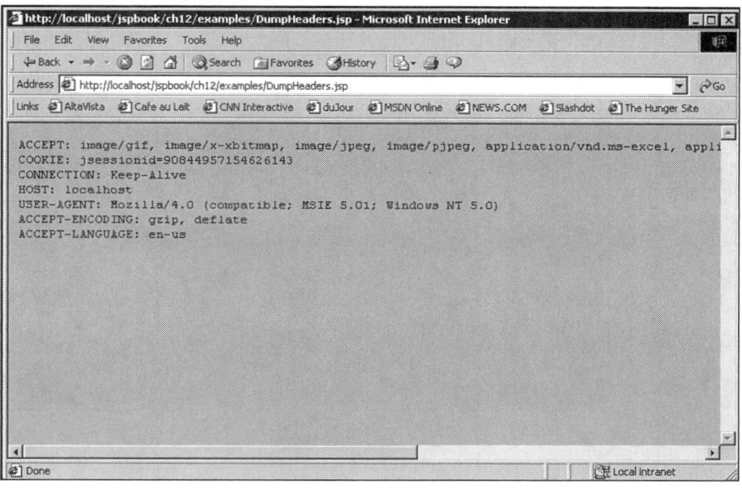

Figure 12.4
A JSP or servlet can examine all the request headers.

LISTING 12.2 SOURCE CODE FOR `Dumper.java`

```
import java.net.*;
import java.io.*;

public class Dumper
{
    public static void main(String[] args)
    {
        try {
            int portNumber = 1234;
            try {
                portNumber = Integer.parseInt(System.getProperty("port"));
            } catch (Exception e) {
            }
            ServerSocket serv = new ServerSocket(portNumber);

            for (;;) {
                Socket sock = serv.accept();
                InputStream inStream = sock.getInputStream();
                int ch;
                while ((ch = inStream.read()) >= 0) {
                    System.out.print((char) ch);
                }
                sock.close();
            }
        } catch (Exception e) {
            e.printStackTrace();
        }
    }
}
```

Figure 12.5 shows the output from the Dumper program. When you run Dumper on your local machine, point the browser to the URL `http://localhost:1234`. Because the Dumper program doesn't understand HTTP and doesn't know to shut down the connection, you'll need to either click the Stop button on your browser or terminate the Dumper program.

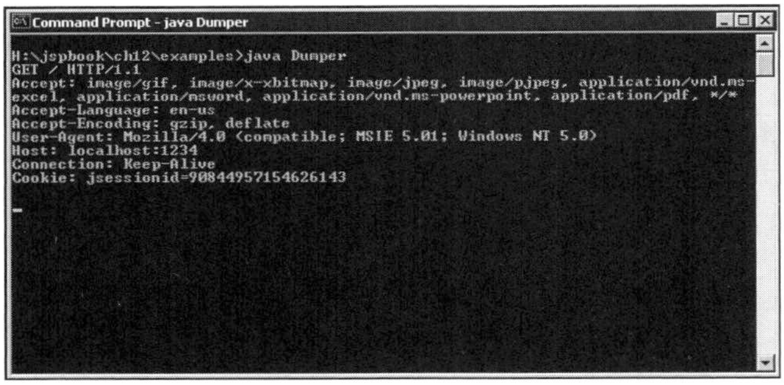

Figure 12.5
You can view the headers sent by a browser using a simple socket program.

If you are having trouble accessing the Dumper program, see "Running the Dumper Program," in the "Troubleshooting" section at the end of this chapter.

COMMON REQUEST HEADERS

The headers you saw in Figures 12.4 and 12.5 represent the most common set of request headers you'll receive. Netscape browsers might also send an `Accept-Charset` request header.

THE `Accept` HEADER

The `Accept` header indicates the kind of content the browser is able to accept. The order of the items is typically the order the browser prefers. In other words, when the browser lists `application/msword` before `application/pdf`, it says that it prefers MS Word documents to Adobe Acrobat documents (obviously this is a Microsoft browser!). Usually, you'll see `*/*` at the end of the list, meaning that the browser will accept anything, but it prefers those it has already listed.

If you look at the `Accept` header sent by a wireless phone (which you'll learn more about in Chapter 26, "Creating a Wireless Web Application"), you'll see that it lists HTML text and bitmap images after the `*/*`, indicating that it prefers just about anything to HTML or bitmaps! Here is the `Accept` header sent from a wireless phone:

```
Accept: application/x-hdmlc, application/x-up-alert, application/x-up-cacheop,
   application/x-up-device, application/x-up-digestentry, text/x-hdml;version=3.1,
   text/x-hdml;version=3.0, text/x-hdml;version=2.0, text/x-wap.wml,
   text/vnd.wap.wml, */*, image/bmp, text/html
```

THE `Accept-Language` HEADER

The `Accept-Language` header gives you a hint as to what language the browser prefers (actually, the browser's user, because the browser doesn't speak human languages). For English, you might see just `en` or you might see `en-us` or `en-uk` specifying English for a particular locale such as the United States or the United Kingdom. You can use this header to provide language-specific content automatically. You'll learn more about this idea in Chapter 30, "Internationalization."

The `Accept-Charset` Header

If present, the `Accept-Charset` header indicates the preferred character set(s) that the browser will accept. For Netscape running in an English-speaking locale, you'll most likely see this kind of header:

```
Accept-Charset: iso-8859-1,*,utf-8
```

The `User-Agent` Header

Of all the headers sent by the browser, the `User-Agent` header is probably the most useful because it indicates what kind of browser is making the request. Oddly, both Netscape and Internet Explorer identify themselves as Mozilla, which was the nickname for the Netscape browser.

Note

In case you're wondering where the name *Mozilla* came from, Netscape was founded by the folks who wrote the old Mosaic Web browser. Netscape Navigator was intended to be a monstrous version of Mosaic: the Godzilla Mosaic, or Mozilla.

When Internet Explorer first came out, it lagged behind Netscape in usage, and gradually added features to become a reasonable alternative by the time IE version 3 came along. By identifying itself as Mozilla compatible, IE is telling the Web server that it can handle anything Mozilla can.

If you want to figure out whether the browser is Netscape or Internet Explorer, only IE sends the `MSIE` string as part of it's `User-Agent` header. Thus, you can do the following test in your JSP or servlet:

```
if (request.getHeader("USER-AGENT").
    indexOf("MSIE") >= 0)
{
    // do Internet Explorer specific stuff here
}
else
{
    // do Netscape specific stuff here
}
```

You can perform similar tests to detect other browsers such as Opera.

If you are having trouble seeing request headers you are expecting, see "Request Headers," in the "Troubleshooting" section at the end of this chapter.

COMMON RESPONSE HEADERS

If you look all the way back to Figure 12.1, you'll see a typical response sent by a Web server. There are many variations of response headers, but relatively few that you need to worry about when you write Java Web applications.

THE `Content-Type` HEADER

The `Content-Type` header is the most important response header. It tells the browser how to interpret the data it receives. A JSP has a default content type of `text/html`, although you can use the `<%@page` directive to change the content type. If you are returning XML data, for instance, you use a content type of `text/xml`.

THE `Content-Length` HEADER

The `Content-Length` header is important for many types of content that contain binary data. It tells the browser exactly how many bytes are in the body of the response. That way the browser can read the full response without worrying about whether it has received everything.

THE `Cache-Control` HEADER

The `Cache-Control` header allows you to control how long the browser keeps a particular page cached. As you saw in Figure 12.1, a JSP normally isn't cached at all. You can request that a page be cached for 5 minutes (300 seconds) using the following response header:

```
Cache-Control: maxage=300
```

Note

The `Cache-Control` header controls only whether the browser uses the cache the next time it loads a page, it does not force the browser to reload the page when it expires. To reload a page after a specific period of time, include the tag

```
<META HTTP-EQUIV="Refresh" Content = "30; URL=YourJSPUrlHere.jsp">
```

in your JSP or HTL file. The 30 in the previous tag is the number of seconds to wait before refreshing.

THE HTTP POST COMMAND

So far, the only HTTP command you have seen in this chapter is the `GET` command. You are aware that there is another command, the `POST` command, that is frequently used to send form information to the Web server. Technically, the `POST` command might be used for more than just form data, but form data is by far the most common kind of data sent via `POST`.

When a browser sends a `POST` command, the first line of the request looks just like the `GET` request, except that instead of `GET`, the command is `POST`. The difference comes about just after the request header. In a `GET` request, there is no data after the request header. After the server sees the blank line indicating the end of the header, it processes the request. In a POST request, the browser sends the form data after the header.

Listing 12.3 shows a bare bones form that posts its data to the Dumper program so you can see what a POST request looks like.

LISTING 12.3 SOURCE CODE FOR PostForm.html

```
<html>
<body>
<form action="http://localhost:1234" method="post">
<input type="text" name="foo" value="Foo!"><br>
<input type="text" name="bar" value="Bar?"><br>
<input type="text" name="baz" value="<<BAZ>>"><br>
<input type="submit">
</form>
</body>
</html>
```

Figure 12.6 shows the output from the Dumper program after it receives a POST request.

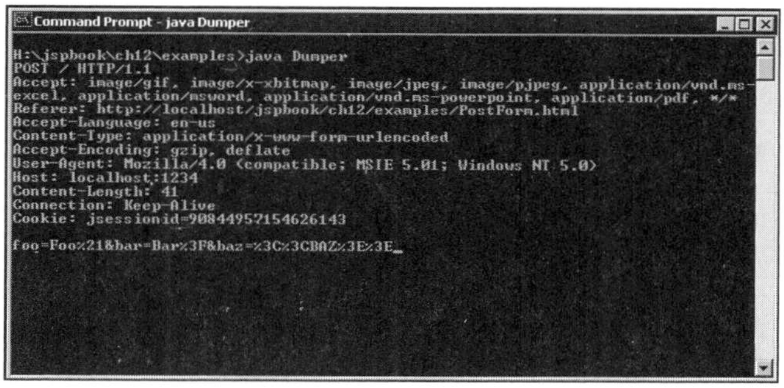

```
Command Prompt - java Dumper
H:\jspbook\ch12\examples>java Dumper
POST / HTTP/1.1
Accept: image/gif, image/x-xbitmap, image/jpeg, image/pjpeg, application/vnd.ms-
excel, application/msword, application/vnd.ms-powerpoint, application/pdf, */*
Referer: http://localhost/jspbook/ch12/examples/PostForm.html
Accept-Language: en-us
Content-Type: application/x-www-form-urlencoded
Accept-Encoding: gzip, deflate
User-Agent: Mozilla/4.0 (compatible; MSIE 5.01; Windows NT 5.0)
Host: localhost:1234
Content-Length: 41
Connection: Keep-Alive
Cookie: jsessionid=9084495715462614 3

foo=Foo%21&bar=Bar%3F&baz=%3C%3CBAZ%3E%3E_
```

Figure 12.6
A POST request sends form data in the body of the request.

If you are having trouble accessing the Dumper program, see "Running the Dumper Program," in the "Troubleshooting" section at the end of this chapter.

Notice that a content type and content length are in the request. No matter which direction the data is going, if you are sending content, you need to specify a content type and usually a content length.

GET VERSUS POST

You might wonder why someone would choose to do a GET instead of a POST or vice-versa. Why is there even a choice? When you send form data using the GET request, you're really taking advantage of a performance hack. By appending the form variables to the end of the pathname, you simplify the work that the server needs to do, because it takes a little more work to read posted data. For example, the corresponding GET request for the form data posted from the PostForm page looks like this:

```
GET /?foo=Foo%21&bar=Bar%3F&baz=%3C%3CBAZ%3E%3E HTTP/1.1
```

There is a limit to the length of the pathname for a `GET` request, however. So if the total length of your form variables is fairly long, more than 4KB, you can't use a `GET` request at all. Some servers won't even accept 2KB in a pathname. If you think the total length of your form data could be anywhere near the limit, you should use a `POST` instead of a `GET`.

Besides the size limitations, there are other reasons to choose `POST` over `GET` or vice-versa. If you submit a form using the `GET` request and then bookmark the resulting page, the bookmark contains the form variables because they are part of the URL. You might consider this a good thing because it saves the user from having to type in the data. It might also be a bad thing if one of the form items is a password. Not only is the password now saved as a bookmark, defeating the purpose of requiring a password, but also the password is visible in the browser's address window.

> **Tip**
> **If your form contains sensitive data like a password, use `POST` instead of `GET`.**

HTTPS: Secure HTTP

You might notice that when you visit a Web site that wants you to enter a credit card, the URL usually begins with `https` instead of `http`. The browser recognizes `https` as a request to use secure sockets to pass the data. The Secure Sockets Layer (SSL) allows you to send encrypted data back and forth between the browser and the server (technically, it just provides encrypted traffic between any two endpoints, not specifically browsers and servers).

The nice thing about using HTTP over SSL is that the HTTP protocol is still the same—it's just the transport layer that has changed. For example, if you had an SSL library that you could use with the Dumper program, you could connect to the dumper with `https` and still see the HTTP headers exactly as you see them with an unencrypted connection. Figure 12.7 shows the relationship between the HTTP protocol and the SSL protocol as compared to an unencrypted HTTP connection.

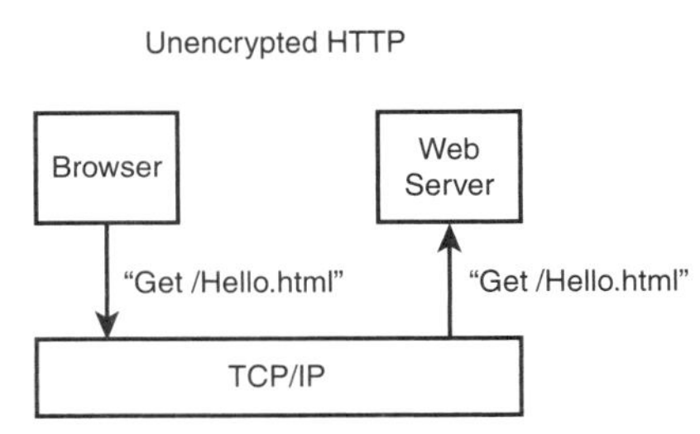

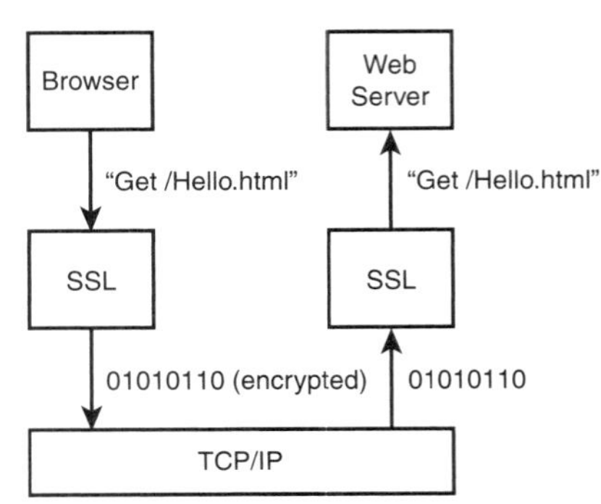

Figure 12.7
The Secure Socket Layer takes the place of a regular TCP/IP socket connection when sending encrypted HTTP traffic.

TROUBLESHOOTING

REQUEST HEADERS

Why don't I see the same headers coming from Netscape as I do from Internet Explorer?

Request headers are more like hints than required fields. The browsers aren't required to send any headers (although for HTTP `POST` they must send a content type). Without any requirements, there's no way to guarantee that different vendors will send the same information. You should write your application so it works even if there are no headers.

Why does Internet Explorer identify itself as Mozilla?

Internet Explorer identifies itself as Mozilla-compatible. Look for the string MSIE in the User-Agent header and you'll be able to identify Internet Explorer.

RUNNING THE DUMPER PROGRAM

I started the Dumper program; why can't my browser access it?

Did you remember to put the `:1234` after the hostname? The Dumper program operates on a port number other than 80 (the default HTTP port).

I remembered the `:1234` in the URL; why can I still not access the Dumper program?

Make sure you aren't using a Web proxy from your browser. Some proxies won't access non-standard ports. If the Dumper program is running on a separate host from your browser, make sure there isn't a firewall between your browser and the program. If you're running this from home, you probably don't have a firewall.

CHAPTER 13

CORE SERVLET COMPONENTS

In this chapter

THE ServletRequest CLASS

A ServletRequest object contains information about the request from the browser. In addition to obvious things such as form variables, the request object can give you information about the kinds of languages that the browser accepts and the character encoding used in the request. ServletRequest is actually a Java interface, not a class. Because you don't have to create the request object, however, it doesn't really matter whether it's an interface or a class.

> **Note**
> The built-in application object used by Java Server Pages is actually an instance of ServletRequest.

ACCESSING REQUEST PARAMETERS

Request parameters are values passed to the server two different ways. First, as you have already seen, you can pass parameters in the URL by appending a ? to the URL followed by parameters in the form name=value separated by &. Here's an example URL with parameters:

```
http://localhost/servlet/MyServlet?firstName=Kaitlynn&age=4
```

When the browser sends the server a form using an HTTP GET request, it automatically passes parameters as part of the URL. The browser can also pass parameters as part of the body of the request. To pass parameters in the request body, the browser must do an HTTP POST, because the HTTP GET request doesn't have a request body, just request headers.

➔ For a refresher on the HTTP protocol, **see** "GET Versus POST," **p. 221**.

> **Note**
> There is actually a third way for your JSP or servlet to receive a parameter. When you use the <jsp:include> or <jsp:forward> tag, you can supply parameters that are added to the set of parameters that were passed by the browser.

No matter how the server gets the parameters, you can access them using the ServletRequest object. You can use getParameter to retrieve a single parameter (or the first parameter if multiple ones are passed) and getParameterValues to retrieve multiple values:

```
public String getParameter(String name)
public String[] getParameterValues(String name)
```

If you request a parameter that doesn't exist, both getParameter and getParameterValues return null. You can find out all the parameter names by calling getParameterNames:

```
public java.util.Enumeration getParameterNames()
```

ACCESSING REQUEST ATTRIBUTES

When a Java Server Page creates a Java bean with the <jsp:useBean> tag and sets the scope of the bean to request, the bean is stored as an attribute of the request object. You can also store attributes in the request yourself. Typically, you need to store attributes in the request when you want to include or forward to another JSP or servlet. You can store, retrieve, and delete attributes using getAttribute, setAttribute, and removeAttribute:

```
public Object getAttribute(String name)
public void setAttribute(String name, Object attr)
public void removeAttribute(String name)
```

You can also get the names of all the attributes stored in the request by calling getAttributeNames:

```
public java.util.Enumeration getAttributeNames()
```

Note

Attribute names of the form java.*, javax.*, and com.sun.* are reserved for use by Sun.

When your servlet is called using the secure HTTPS protocol (HTTP over SSL), you can access the client's security certificate, if it is available, with the attribute javax.servlet.request.X509Certificate.

➔ For more information about client certificates, **see** "Accessing the Client Certificate," **p. 31**.

ACCESSING PROTOCOL-RELATED INFORMATION

You occasionally need to get protocol-related information, such as the kind of protocol or the network addresses of the server and the browser. Many Web servers can handle incoming requests for multiple network addresses and ports at one time. You can find out which host name and port received a request by calling getServerName and getServerPort:

```
public String getServerName()
public int getServerPort()
```

You can also retrieve the host name and IP address of the browser by calling getRemoteHost and getRemoteAddr:

```
public String getRemoteHost()
public String getRemoteAddr()
```

Listing 13.1 shows a servlet that displays the address of the client accessing the server.

LISTING 13.1 SOURCE CODE FOR ShowAddressServlet.java

```
package usingjsp;

import javax.servlet.*;
import java.io.*;

public class ShowAddressServlet extends GenericServlet
{
    public void service(ServletRequest request,
        ServletResponse response)
        throws IOException
    {
// Tell the Web server that the response is HTML
        response.setContentType("text/html");
```

LISTING 13.1 CONTINUED

```
// Get the PrintWriter for writing out the response
        PrintWriter out = response.getWriter();

// Write the HTML back to the browser
        out.println("<HTML>");
        out.println("<BODY>");

        String clientHost = request.getRemoteHost();

        out.println("You are accessing this server from "+
            clientHost);

        out.println("</BODY>");
        out.println("</HTML>");
    }
}
```

The `getProtocol` method returns the name and version of the protocol used to make the request:

```
public String getProtocol()
```

The protocol is returned in the form `protocol/version`, such as `http/1.1`. If you are familiar with the CGI protocol, the protocol is in the same form as the `SERVER_PROTOCOL` server variable.

The `getScheme` method is similar to the `getProtocol` method:

```
public String getScheme()
```

Example schemes would be `http`, `https`, and `ftp`.

You can determine whether the request was made using a secure protocol by calling the `isSecure` method:

```
public boolean isSecure()
```

RETRIEVING REQUEST DATA

As you saw in Chapter 12, "How the Browser Interacts with the Server," an HTTP `POST` or `PUT` request can send data to the server. Most of the time, the data is a list of form variables. There is no restriction on what kind of data can be sent, however. You can upload an image to a servlet or a JSP if you want to. You can find out the size and type of the data that was sent by calling `getContentLength` and `getContentType`:

```
public int getContentLength()
public String getContentType()
```

If the content length is unknown, `getContentLength` returns `-1`. If the content type is unknown, `getContentType` returns `null`.

If the request contains character data, you can find out the kind of character encoding used to write the request. The `getCharacterEncoding` method returns encoding type:

```
public String getCharacterEncoding()
```

If the request doesn't specify a character encoding, `getCharacterEncoding` returns `null`.

To read the request content, use either `getReader` or `getInputStream`:

```
public java.io.BufferedReader getReader()
    throws java.io.IOException
public ServletInputStream getInputStream()
    throws java.io.IOException
```

When the request contains character data, you should use the `BufferedReader` to read the data. It performs any necessary character conversions. To read binary data, use `getInputStream`.

Caution

You can't use both `getReader` and `getInputStream`. If you try to use both methods, the second one will throw an `IllegalStateException`.

HANDLING UPLOADED FILES

The `ServletInputStream` class is useful when you want to upload a file to a servlet or a JSP. There are many ways to upload a file, but the easiest way is through a Java client.

Listing 13.2 shows a servlet that receives a file uploaded from a Java client (or any client that can send data via an HTTP `POST` request).

LISTING 13.2 SOURCE CODE FOR FileReceiverServlet.java

```
package usingjsp;
import javax.servlet.*;
import javax.servlet.http.*;

import java.io.*;
/** Receives a file uploaded using a straight HTTP POST request */public class
FileReceiverServlet extends HttpServlet
{
    public void service(HttpServletRequest request,
        HttpServletResponse response)
        throws java.io.IOException, ServletException
    {
// Get the input stream for reading the file
        InputStream in = request.getInputStream();

// The file is always saved with the same name (just for this demo)
        OutputStream fileOut = new BufferedOutputStream(
            new FileOutputStream("uploaded_file"));

// Create a buffer for reading bytes from the input stream
        byte[] buff = new byte[4096];
        int len;

// Read bytes from the input stream, write them to the file
```

LISTING 13.2 CONTINUED

```
        while ((len = in.read(buff)) > 0)
        {
            fileOut.write(buff, 0, len);
        }
        fileOut.close();

// Send a response back to the client saying the upload was successful
        response.setContentType("text/plain");
        PrintWriter out = response.getWriter();

        out.println("Upload successful!");
    }
}
```

Listing 13.3 shows the Java client class that performs the upload.

LISTING 13.3 SOURCE CODE FOR `Uploader.java`

```
package usingjsp;

import java.net.*;
import java.io.*;

/** Performs an HTTP POST to upload a file to a servlet */
public class Uploader
{
    public static void main(String[] args)
    {
        if (args.length < 1)
        {
            System.out.println("Please supply the name of the file to upload");
            System.exit(1);
        }

        try
        {
            File inFile = new File(args[0]);

// Open the file to be uploaded
            InputStream in = new BufferedInputStream(
                new FileInputStream(inFile));

// Create a URL object for the destination servlet
            URL destination = new URL("http://localhost/servlet/"+
                "usingjsp.FileReceiverServlet");

// Open a connection to the servlet
            URLConnection conn = destination.openConnection();

// Tell the connection that there is output to be sent
            conn.setDoOutput(true);

// Tell the receiver that this is a stream of bytes
            conn.setRequestProperty("Content-type",
                "application/octet-stream");
```

```
// Tell the receiver how many bytes there are
            conn.setRequestProperty("Content-length",
                ""+inFile.length());

            OutputStream out = conn.getOutputStream();

            byte[] buff = new byte[4096];

            int len;

// Copy bytes from the file to the output stream
            while ((len = in.read(buff)) > 0)
            {
                out.write(buff, 0, len);
            }

            InputStream response = conn.getInputStream();

// Read the response back from the receiver servlet
            while ((len = response.read(buff)) > 0)
            {
                System.out.write(buff, 0, len);
            }
        }
        catch (Exception exc)
        {
        }
    }
}
```

You don't always have the luxury of writing a Java client to perform the upload. Sometimes, you must perform a file upload from an HTML page. Listing 13.4 shows a simple HTML page that allows you to select a file to upload.

LISTING 13.4 SOURCE CODE FOR FileUploader.html

```
<html>
<body bgcolor="#ffffff">
<h1>File Uploader</h1>
<form action="/servlet/usingjsp.ReceiveUploadServlet" method="post"
    enctype="multipart/form-data">
Please select a file to upload: <input type="file" name="foo">
<p>
<input type="submit" value="Upload File!">
</form>
</body>
</html>
```


The difficulty with receiving a file uploaded from an HTML form is that the content is of the type "multipart/form-data". When you upload a file in this format, the content type is usually something like

```
multipart/form-data; boundary=------------------
    --------7d03d0287003dc
```

The actual content starts with an additional header, too:

```
-----------------------------7d03d0287003dc
Content-Disposition: form-data; name="foo";
    filename="H:\jspbook\ch13\examples\Uploader.java"
Content-Type: application/octet-stream
```

Because the upload can contain multiple parts, the boundary string is used to separate each part. After the boundary, as shown previously, are several header lines terminated by a blank line. After you read the blank line, the rest of the data is content until you reach another boundary.

Listing 13.5 shows a servlet that can wade through the multipart headers and retrieve an uploaded file.

LISTING 13.5 SOURCE CODE FOR ReceiveUploadServlet.java

```
package usingjsp;

import javax.servlet.*;
import javax.servlet.http.*;
import java.io.*;

public class ReceiveUploadServlet extends GenericServlet
{
    public void service(ServletRequest request,
        ServletResponse response)
        throws IOException
    {
// Get the content type
        String contentType = request.getContentType();

// Set a default for the boundary string length
// Find out where the boundary string starts
        int boundaryIndex = contentType.indexOf("boundary=");

// Get the boundary string
        String boundary = contentType.substring(boundaryIndex+9);
        int boundaryStrLength = boundary.length();

// Get the input stream to read the uploaded file
        ServletInputStream servIn = request.getInputStream();

        DataInputStream in = new DataInputStream(servIn);

// Lop off the headers from the content (read until you get a blank line)
        String line;

        while ((line = in.readLine()) != null)
        {
            getServletContext().log("Got line: "+line);
            if (line.trim().length() == 0) break;
        }

        ByteArrayOutputStream byteOut = new ByteArrayOutputStream(
            request.getContentLength());
```

```
        byte[] buffer = new byte[4096];
        int len;

// Copy the uploaded file to a byte array
        while ((len = in.read(buffer)) > 0)
        {
            byteOut.write(buffer, 0, len);
        }

        byte[] outBytes = byteOut.toByteArray();

        FileOutputStream fileOut = new FileOutputStream("uploaded_file");

// Write the byte array out to the file, trim off the boundary plus some
// padding surrounding the boundary
        fileOut.write(outBytes, 0, outBytes.length - boundaryStrLength - 8);
        fileOut.close();

// Tell the Web server that the response is HTML
response.setContentType("text/html");

// Get the PrintWriter for writing out the response
        PrintWriter out = response.getWriter();

// Write the HTML back to the browser
        out.println("<HTML>");
        out.println("<BODY>");

        String clientHost = request.getRemoteHost();

        out.println("File Accepted, thank you.");

        out.println("</BODY>");
        out.println("</HTML>");
    }
}
```

GETTING LOCALE INFORMATION

When a browser requests a page, it can send a list of locales that it supports. If you are not familiar with the internationalization features of Java, a locale specifies how Java should represent certain data items such as dates and currencies. You can even determine the client's preferred language in case you want to support multiple languages on your Web site.

The `getLocale` method returns the browser's preferred locale, and `getLocales` returns an enumeration of all the locales the browser says it supports:

```
public java.util.Locale getLocale()
public java.util.Enumeration getLocales()
```

THE HttpServletRequest CLASS

The `HttpServletRequest` interfaces add HTTP-specific capabilities to the existing `ServletRequest` interface. If your servlet is an `HttpServlet`, you receive an `HttpServletRequest` object in your servlet's `service` method, or in any of the `doGet`, `doPost`, doPut, and so on methods. In a Java Server Page, the request object is an HttpServletRequest object.

GETTING HEADER VALUES

You sometimes need to examine header values sent in the request. The getHeaderNames method returns an enumeration of all the possible header values:

```
public java.util.Enumeration getHeaderNames()
```

You can retrieve the header objects as strings, using either getHeader for a single value or getHeaders to get all the values for a particular header name:

```
public String getHeader(String name)
public java.util.Enumeration getHeaders(String name)
```

Sometimes a header contains a number or a date. Instead of parsing the value yourself, you can let the request parse the value using either getIntHeader or getDateHeader:

```
public int getIntHeader(String name)
public long getDateHeader(String name)
```

The value returned by getDateHeader is the number of milliseconds since January 1, 1970. If you need a date object, you can create an instance of date like this:

```
Date d = new Date(getDateHeader("If-Modified-Since"));
```

If you are having trouble retrieving header values, see "Header Values," in the "Troubleshooting" section at the end of this chapter.

GETTING THE HTTP METHOD

There are several different kinds of HTTP requests. When a browser just requests a page, it uses a GET method. When the browser needs to send form data in the request body instead of the URL, it uses the POST method. When the browser uploads a file to the server it uses the PUT method. You can find out what method was used to make the request by calling getMethod:

```
public String getMethod()
```

ACCESSING THE QUERY STRING

The list of parameters added to the end of a URL is referred to as the *query string*. You can retrieve the query string, just as it was originally sent, by calling getQueryString:

```
public String getQueryString()
```

Don't forget, even if the browser uses the POST method, it can still pass parameters on the query string. The query string doesn't have to be in the name=value format. You can put any string in the query string of a request.

RETRIEVING COOKIES

The getCookies method returns an array of cookie objects passed in from the browser:

```
public Cookie[] getCookies()
```

Getting Session Information

Sessions are an integral part of servlets and Java Server Pages, so it seems strange that they are only available in the HttpSessionRequest interface and not in the more general SessionRequest interface. Session identifiers are usually stored in cookies, which are specific to the HTTP protocol. The getSession method returns the session associated with the browser and optionally creates a session if it doesn't exist:

```
public Session getSession()
public Session getSession(boolean create)
```

If the create flag is true, getSession creates a new session if one doesn't exist. If a session doesn't exist and create is false, getSession returns null. Calling getSession with no parameter is the same as calling it with a value of true for the create flag.

Although a session identifier is usually stored in a cookie, the servlet API provides a way to keep track of sessions by passing the session ID as a form variable in the URL. You can determine whether the session ID comes from a cookie or from the URL by calling isRequestedSessionIdFromCookie or isRequestedSessionIdFromURL:

```
public boolean isRequestedSessionIdFromCookie()
public boolean isRequestedSessionIdFromURL()
```

If you need to see if the session ID is still valid, call isRequestedSessionIdValid:

```
public boolean isRequestedSessionIdValid()
```

The ServletContext Class

The ServletContext object, available to both JSP and servlets via the getServletContext method, contains information about the servlet engine and the servlet environment.

Getting the Server Version

There are three methods you can use to get information about the server version and the Servlet API version:

```
public int getMajorVersion()
public int getMinorVersion()
public String getServerInfo()
```


If you are running with version 2.1 of the servlet API, getMajorVersion returns 2, and getMinorVersion returns 1. The getServerInfo method returns the name and version of the server separated by slashes. An early version of the Tomcat server returns the following server version:

```
Tomcat Web Server/3.0 (JSP 1.1; Servlet 2.2; Java 1.2.2;
Windows NT 5.0 x86; java.vendor=Sun Microsystems Inc.)
```

Initialization Parameters

The ServletContext object contains the same getInitParameterNames and getInitParameter methods:

```
public java.util.Enumeration getInitParameterNames()
public String getInitParameter(String name)
```

These methods return information for an entire Web application, not just for a specific servlet.

SAVING APPLICATION-WIDE OBJECTS

All the servlets and Java Server Pages within an application can share objects by storing them in the `ServletContext` object. The `getAttribute`, `setAttribute`, and `removeAttribute` methods work just like the ones in the `ServletRequest` class, except that the objects are visible to the entire application:

```
public Object getAttribute(String name)
public void setAttribute(String name, Object attr)
public void removeAttribute(String name)
```

Just as with the `request` object, you can get a list of the attribute names available in the `ServletContext` object by calling `getAttributeNames`:

```
public java.util.Enumeration getAttributeNames()
```

LOGGING MESSAGES

One of the difficulties with debugging a server is that you can't easily see what is going on. After all, with a desktop application, you can see a dialog box pop up with an error message. Most developers writing a server application end up writing their own logging routines so they can gain some visibility into what the server is doing. The `ServletContext` object supplies two logging methods:

```
public void log(String message)
public void log(String message, Throwable throwable)
```

Although these methods are part of the standard Servlet API, the location of the log file varies between servers. When you pass a `Throwable` object to the `log` method, the server prints a stack trace to the log file.

If you are having trouble logging messages, see "Logging Messages," in the "Troubleshooting" section at the end of this chapter.

CALLING OTHER SERVLETS AND JSPS

You use a `RequestDispatcher` object to include or forward to another JSP or servlet. You use the `ServletContext` object to locate the request dispatcher via either the `getRequestDispatcher` or `getNamedDispatcher` methods:

```
public RequestDispatcher getRequestDispatcher(String url)
public RequestDispatcher getNamedDispatcher(String name)
```

The request dispatcher lets you access any resource on the local server. You aren't restricted to just servlets and Java Server Pages. You can include an HTML file if you want. When you use `getRequestDispatcher`, the URL that you pass to the method must start with a `/`. Most of the time, you can think of the path as being relative to the server root. The `/` is actually relative to the context root that the servlet or JSP is running in.

ACCESSING APPLICATION RESOURCES

An application often requires additional resources other than its servlets and Java Server Pages. You might need data files, images files, or sound files. When you install your application, you can just copy all the files into one or more directories, or you can package all the necessary files into a .war file (similar to a .jar file). You can use `getResource` and `getResourceAsStream` to retrieve these resources:

```
public java.net.URL getResource(java.lang.String path)
    throws java.net.MalformedURLException

public java.io.InputStream getResourceAsStream(
    java.lang.String path)
```

THE ServletResponse CLASS

When a servlet needs to send data back to the browser, it uses the `ServletResponse` object. Using this object, you can get an output stream for sending data back, set the content type and length, and set the character encoding if you need to send back character data.

SETTING THE CONTENT TYPE AND LENGTH

You can set the content type and length by calling `setContentType` and `setContentLength`:

```
public void setContentType(String contentType)
public void setContentLength(int contentLength)
```

When you set the content type, you can also set the character encoding. For example, you could set the content type to `text/html; charset=ISO-8859-4`.

OPENING AN OUTPUT STREAM

There are two methods for obtaining an output stream:

```
public ServletOutputStream getOutputStream()
    throws IOException
public PrintWriter getWriter() throws IOException
```

When you need to send character data back to the browser, you should use the `getWriter` method. If you need to send binary data, use `getOutputStream`.

SETTING LOCALE-SPECIFIC INFORMATION

When you send a response back to the browser, you might want to target it to a specific locale, which implies a specific language and possibly country. For example, if you need to write out a date or a currency value, you want to write it in a format that the end user understands. The `ServletRequest` object tells you which locales the browser supports. When you send a request, you can set a locale in the output stream. The locale can imply a particular character encoding and can even change the character encoding based on the content type. To set the locale for the response, call `setLocale`:

```
public void setLocale(Locale aLocale)
```

You can get the locale and character encoding for the response by calling `getLocale` and `getCharacterEncoding`:

```
public Locale getLocale()
public String getCharacterEncoding()
```

RESPONSE BUFFERING

Most of the time, a servlet or JSP response is buffered. You can control the amount of memory used for buffering and also clear out the buffer if you need to. Use `getBufferSize` and `setBufferSize` to control the amount of buffering:

```
public int getBufferSize()
public void setBufferSize(int bufferSize)
```

If you want to change the buffer size, you should do it before you try to send any data back to the browser. After you send data back, or at least write it to the buffer, you can't change the buffer size. If you want to send the current buffer contents back to the browser immediately, call `flush`:

```
public void flush()
```

If you want to clear the contents of the buffer, call `reset`:

```
public void reset()
```

After the response status and headers have been sent back to the browser, the response is said to be "committed." After it is committed, you can't change any header values, which you can normally set in the `HttpServletResponse` object. You can find out whether the response has been committed by calling `isCommitted`:

```
public boolean isCommitted()
```

THE HttpServletResponse CLASS

The `HttpServletResponse` object allows you to set various HTTP-related options in the response to the browser. It is a subclass of `ServletResponse` so it contains all the methods you need to send an HTTP response.

SETTING HEADER VARIABLES

Many of the options you have already encountered, such as content type and content length, are stored in the HTTP header. For header variables that don't have a corresponding response method, use the `setHeader`, `setIntHeader`, or `setDateHeader` methods:

```
public void setHeader(String header, String value)
public void setIntHeader(String header, int value)
public void setDateHeader(String header, Date value)
```

The HTTP header can contain multiple values for the same header name. When you need to store multiple header values, use `addHeader`, `addIntHeader`, or `addDateHeader`:

```
public void addHeader(String header, String value)
public void addIntHeader(String header, int value)
public void addDateHeader(String header, Date value)
```

The `containsHeader` method returns `true` if a header value has already been set:

```
public boolean containsHeader(String header)
```

Redirecting the Browser

When you need to tell the browser to access a different page, use the `sendRedirect` method:

```
public void sendRedirect(String redirectURL)
```

> **Note**
>
> A `redirect` is useful when you need to send the browser to a different server. A `forward` is much more efficient than a `redirect` because the `redirect` must first go back to the browser, which must then request the redirected page. If you are redirecting to a page in the same server, try doing a `forward` instead of a `redirect`.

Returning Status

Unless you need to send a status other than `SC_OK` (HTTP response code 200) indicating a normal response, you don't need to change the status code of the response. If you need to send an abnormal response code, however, you can call `setStatus` or `setError`:

```
public void setStatus(int statusCode)
public void setError(int statusCode)
public void setError(int statusCode, String errorMessage)
    throws IOException
```

Encoding URLs

When you want to send a URL to the browser, either as a link in a Web page or as a redirect request, you should call either `encodeURL` or `encodeRedirectURL`:

```
public String encodeURL(String url)
public String encodeRedirectURL(String url)
```

The main purpose for the encoding is to handle cases when you need to store data in a session but the browser doesn't allow cookies. If the browser doesn't allow cookies, the encode routines append a session ID parameter to the URL. If the browser supports cookies, the encode routines return the URL unchanged.

Sending Cookies

When you need to send a cookie back to the browser, use the `addCookie` method:

```
public void addCookie(Cookie cookie)
```

After it receives them, the browser saves cookies until they expire. You don't need to keep sending the same cookies back to the browser unless their data values change.

THE ServletInputStream CLASS

When the browser does a POST or a PUT request, a servlet or JSP can use ServletInputStream to read the request body. If the posted data contains form variables, you don't need to use the input stream because the Servlet API automatically reads the variables.

The ServletInputStream class is a subclass of InputStream and only adds one extra method. The readLine method reads a line of data into the byte buffer:

```
public int readLine(byte[] buffer, int offset, int length)
```

Note If you are reading character data, however, you should be using a BufferedReader instead of the ServletInputStream because the reader performs character conversions properly.

THE ServletOutputStream CLASS

The ServletOutputStream class is a subclass of the OutputStream class and adds the print and println methods normally found in the PrintStream class:

```
public void print(boolean b)
public void print(char c)
public void print(double d)
public void print(float f)
public void print(int i)
public void print(long l)
public void println()
public void println(boolean b)
public void println(char c)
public void println(double d)
public void println(float f)
public void println(int i)
public void println(long l)
```

Note You are better off using PrintWriter rather than ServletOutputStream because PrintWriter performs the character conversions correctly.

THE HttpSession CLASS

The HttpSession stores information between browser requests. In addition to storing and retrieving objects, you can control when the session is created and how long the session stays active after there has been no activity.

STORING AND RETRIEVING OBJECTS

You can store and retrieve objects in the session that will be available the next time the browser sends a request. Use the `getAttribute`, `setAttribute`, and `removeAttribute` methods to store and retrieve the objects:

```
public Object getAttribute(String name)
public void setAttribute(String name, Object value)
public void removeAttribute(String name)
```

You can get a list of available objects by calling `getAttributeNames`:

```
public Enumeration getAttributeNames()
```

> **Tip**
>
> **In case you haven't noticed, the classes that allow you to store objects with `application`, `session`, `request`, and `page` scope (`ServletContext`, `HttpSession`, `ServletRequest`, and `PageContext`) all use the same methods to get, store, and remove attributes.**

CONTROLLING SESSION TERMINATION

One of the difficulties in dealing with sessions is that the server never knows for sure that the session has ended unless you create some sort of logout mechanism. Because the server and the browser spend most of their time disconnected from each other, the server has no way to know that the user has closed the browser window and is now involved in a killer game of Quake.

Putting a logout mechanism into your Web pages is a great idea if your Web site has the notion of login and logout. When the user logs out, you just invalidate the session by calling the `invalidate` method:

```
public void invalidate()
```

Even with a logout mechanism, you can't be sure that the user will be kind enough to actually log out before shutting down the browser. Whether or not you have a logout mechanism, you can force sessions to terminate after a specified period of inactivity. Typical servlet and JSP engines set the timeout at 30 minutes to begin with. You can usually change the default timeout for all sessions with the server's administration tools, or you can query and change the session timeout by calling `getMaxInactiveInterval` and `setMaxInactiveInterval`:


```
public int getMaxInactiveInterval()
public void setMaxInactiveInterval(int interval)
```

GETTING SESSION STATUS

There are a few aspects of the session that you might be interested in. First, you can get the unique identifier of the session by calling `getId`:

```
public String getId()
```

This identifier is unique across all the sessions within your servlet engine, but not necessarily unique if you are running multiple servlet engines. If you are only using a single servlet engine, you can pass this identifier to other parts of your application (CORBA services, Enterprise Java Beans) to serve as a unique identifier for any session-oriented data stored elsewhere.

If you use the session ID in other parts of your application, you are limiting yourself to using only a single servlet engine. To allow for the possibility of multiple servlet and JSP engines passing session identifiers to other portions of your application, consider putting some unique prefix in front of the session ID before you pass it to another module. For example, you might have an "Internet customer" JSP engine with a consumer-friendly interface. You might also have an "Internal-only" servlet engine that handles internal company data. If both of these engines need to access the same service and pass session IDs, you might prepend "Net" before the Internet customer session IDs and "Int" before the internal customer session IDs.

The `isNew` method tells you whether the session has just been created:

```
public boolean isNew()
```

If a session is new, none of the session information has been sent to the client browser. Remember, the only part of the session that is sent to the browser is the session ID, which is stored in a cookie.

You can find out when a session was created by calling `getCreationTime`:

```
public long getCreationTime()
```

The time value returned by `getCreationTime` is the number of milliseconds since January 1, 1970. You can create a date object from the creation time by passing the time value to the `Date` constructor like this:

```
Date creationTime = new Date(session.getCreationTime());
```

The `getLastAccessedTime` method returns the most recent time that a client browser with this session accessed the server:

```
public long getLastAccessedTime()
```

As with the creation time, the last access time value is the number of milliseconds since January 1, 1970; you can create a `Date` object from this time value by passing the value to the `Date` constructor. The last access time is the value the servlet engine uses to determine when a session has timed out.

Note

Accessing session variables does not change the last access time. The only thing that updates the time is an incoming request from a browser. In other words, you cannot prevent a servlet from timing out by accessing a session variable with the expectation that the access time is updated.

THE `Cookie` CLASS

A cookie is a value stored on the browser and sent from the browser to the server whenever the browser requests a page. Cookies usually store information such as usernames or session IDs. The session ID of the `HttpSession` is sent to the browser as a cookie.

Tip

Most browsers allow the user to disable cookies. If your application requires cookies, make sure you warn the user.

CREATING A NEW COOKIE

When you create a new cookie, you must give the cookie a name and provide an initial value. After the cookie has been created, the value can change but the name must remain the same. The constructor for the `Cookie` class takes the name and value as arguments:

```
public Cookie(String name, String value)
```

The `getName` and `getValue` methods return the name and value of an existing cookie:

```
public String getName()
public String getValue()
```

Note

A cookie's name can only contain printable ASCII characters and cannot contain commas, spaces, or semicolons. A cookie name cannot begin with $.

You can also change the cookie's value by calling `setValue`:

```
public void setValue(String newValue)
```

Note

There are a number of restrictions on the format of cookie values. A cookie value cannot contain spaces, parentheses, brackets, commas, double-quotes, semicolons, at-signs, or several other characters. If you need to store anything besides characters or numbers in a cookie value, consider using an encoding scheme such as Base64.

If you are having trouble storing or retrieving cookies, see "Cookies," in the "Troubleshooting" section at the end of this chapter.

PART II CH 13

SETTING THE DOMAIN AND PATH

A browser doesn't send all its cookies to a server whenever it makes a request. Instead, each cookie is tagged with a domain and path. The browser only sends cookies that match the server's domain and path. For example, if the browser is accessing `http://usingjsp.wutka.com/examples/DemoServlet` and it has a cookie with a domain of `.wutka.com` and a path of `/examples`, it sends that cookie to the server. If it has a cookie with a domain of `.wutka.com` and a path of `/other`, it would not send the cookie because the paths don't match. If is has a cookie with a domain of hackingjava.wutka.com and a path of /examples, it would not send the cookie because the domains don't match.

By default, the domain of a cookie is the server that sent the cookie to begin with. If you have a large environment with multiple servers handling requests, make sure you set the domain on your cookies so it includes all the servers that could process a request.

You can query and set the domain with getDomain and setDomain:

```
public String getDomain()
public void setDomain(String newDomain)
```

You can query and set the path with getPath and setPath:

```
public String getPath()
public void setPath(String newPath)
```

If you want a cookie to match any possible path, use / for the path.

COOKIE AGING

Nobody likes to eat stale cookies, not even a browser. When you send a cookie to the browser, you can give it an expire time. After the expire time has elapsed, the browser gets rid of the cookie. The getMaxAge and setMaxAge methods let you query and set the expire time for a cookie:

```
public int getMaxAge()
public void setMaxAge(int maxAge)
```

When you set the maximum age of a cookie, you are telling the browser how many seconds it should keep the cookie. If the browser should hold on to the cookie for an hour, you would set the maximum age to 3600 seconds. If the age is a positive number, the browser saves the cookie so it will be available even if the user shuts the browser down and starts it up again. If the age is a negative number, the browser holds on to the cookie only as long as the browser is running. When the user shuts the browser down, all cookies with a negative age value disappear. If you set the maximum age to 0, the cookie is immediately removed. If you have stored a cookie on the browser in the past and you want to delete it, the proper way to delete it is to set the age to 0.

SECURE COOKIES

Sometimes a cookie holds sensitive data. When you need to store sensitive data in a cookie and want to ensure that the cookie is only sent to the browser when the connection is secure, you can mark the cookie as secure by calling setSecure:

```
public void setSecure(secureFlag)
```

If a cookie's secureFlag is true, the browser only sends the cookie to the server if it's using a secure protocol such as HTTPS (SSL). You can query the secure flag by calling getSecure:

```
public boolean getSecure()
```

Caution

Resist the temptation to store dangerous information such as credit card numbers in a cookie. Even though the cookie might only be sent over a secure protocol, the cookie might be stored on the user's hard disk. Many people would be unhappy to find their credit card numbers stored on the hard disks. Worse, if the user is on a network and the browser saves the cookie to a network drive, someone snooping the network could see the cookie. In other words, the cookie might still be visible over an insecure network.

Cookie Protocol Versions

The cookie protocol was originally developed by Netscape and then copied by other browser vendors as the use of cookies became more widespread. Since that time, the IETF (the Internet standards body) has created a standard cookie protocol. You can find the standard cookie protocol online at `www.ietf.org` where it is known as RFC 2109.

Note

Internet standards are defined by IETF in the form of Request For Comment documents. You will often see "RFC xxxx" in reference to an Internet standard. There are several online sites that let you search by RFC number or by keywords.

One of the problems with standards that are developed by a committee is that it takes some time for them to be adopted, if they are adopted at all. The officially blessed RFC 2109 cookie protocol adds some additional features that are not yet supported on many browsers. You can get and set the protocol version that your cookie requires by calling `getVersion` and `setVersion`:

```
public int getVersion()
public void setVersion(int version)
```

The original Netscape cookie protocol has a version number of 0, while RFC 2109 has a version number of 1. Unless you have special circumstances in which you know that all the browsers using your system will support RFC 2109, you should stick to version 0 until most of the browser population supports RFC 2109.

Cookie Comments

One of the features added in RFC 2109 is a comment describing the purpose of the cookie. Many browsers have the capability to prompt the user when a server tries to save a cookie. You can use the comment to give the user a clue as to what is being saved in the cookie so they can decide whether they want to accept it. Obviously this is on the honor system. You could easily tell the user that the cookie contains a simple session ID although it actually contains her name, address, and credit card number.

Because the comment field was added in RFC 2109, it is not available in version 0 cookies and is probably not supported by a large number of browsers yet.

Use the `getComment` and `setComment` methods to query and change the cookie's comment:

```
public String getComment()
public void setComment(String comment)
```

TROUBLESHOOTING

HEADER VALUES

Why do some header values only show up on one kind of browser?

There are standard header names, but a browser isn't required to send any header values. Some browser implementations just send more information than others.

Why can't I access a particular header value?

You probably misspelled the name of the header value. The `HttpServletRequest` class is very forgiving when it comes to capitalization, but it does require you to spell the header name correctly. Also, make sure you use hyphens and not underscores for header values like `content-type` and `content-length`.

LOGGING MESSAGES

Where are my log messages going?

Each JSP and servlet engine stores its log messages in a different place. If you are using one of the JSP/servlet engines described in Appendixes C–F, the appendix tells you where log messages go. Otherwise, consult the documentation for your server.

Why aren't my log messages showing up the in log file?

Occasionally, a server might delay logging, either intentionally or unintentionally. This is purely an implementation-specific detail and not related at all to the JSP or servlet specifications. Sometimes you can force the server to write to the log by shutting it down gracefully.

COOKIES

I stored a cookie on the browser; why can't I see it?

First, check to make sure you spelled the cookie name right. Next, make sure the browser has cookies enabled. Also, if you specified a root path for the cookie, make sure that the JSP or servlet reading the cookie is in that path. Remember too, that if you don't give the cookie a specific expiration time, the cookie will vanish when the user shuts the browser down.

CHAPTER 14

Core Java Server Page Components

In this chapter

THE BUILT-IN JSP OBJECTS

Java Server Pages create a simplified layer on top of the servlet API. Aside from making it easy to create HTML output, the Java Server Pages API makes it easy to access common objects such as the `request`, `response`, and `session`. You access these objects through built-in object names.

The built-in object names and their associated implementation classes are shown in Table 14.1:

TABLE 14.1 BUILT-IN JSP OBJECTS AND THEIR IMPLEMENTATION CLASSES

JSP Object	Implementation Class
`request`	`HttpServletRequest`
`response`	`HttpServletResponse`
`out`	`JspWriter`
`session`	`HttpSession`
`application`	`ServletContext`
`pageContext`	`PageContext`
`config`	`ServletConfig`
`page`	`Object`
`exception`	`Throwable`

THE `request` OBJECT

The `request` object represents the current request from the browser and is a subclass of the `ServletRequest` class. For most current implementations of JSP, the `request` object is an instance of `HttpServletRequest`. If your JSP engine supports protocols other than HTTP, you might find that your `request` object is an instance of some other subclass of `ServletRequest`. For instance, there is no reason why someone couldn't come out with a WAP (wireless) version of JSP that had its own `WAPServletRequest` and `WAPServletResponse` objects. In that case, your request object would be an instance of `WAPServletRequest`.

THE `response` OBJECT

Like the `request` object, the `response` object is usually a subclass of the HTTP-specific version of a generic servlet class. In other words, it is usually an instance of `HttpServletResponse`. Again, if you have a JSP engine that is centered around a protocol other than HTTP, the `response` object might be an instance of a different class. The one thing you can count on is that the instance will be a subclass of `ServletResponse`.

THE out OBJECT

The out object is responsible for writing responses back to the browser and is an instance of the JspWriter class. You will learn more about the JspWriter class later in this chapter.

THE session OBJECT

The session object is an instance of HttpSession. Because there is an obvious dependence on the HTTP protocol, this object is only available if your Java Server Pages use the HTTP protocol.

THE application OBJECT

The application object is an instance of the ServletContext object. The names "application" and "ServletContext" don't seem very similar, but when you look at what the ServletContext class does, you'll see that it manages data at the application level.

THE pageContext OBJECT

The pageContext object is an instance of the PageContext class. Many of the items available through built-in variables are also available through the pageContext object. You will learn more about the PageContext class later in this chapter.

THE config OBJECT

The config object gives you access to configuration information for your JSP and is an instance of the ServletConfig class.

THE page OBJECT

The page object is rather peculiar because it is a reference to the current JSP. In other words, it's an alias for the this keyword in Java. Although most Java Server Pages are currently written in Java, the JSP architecture is designed to allow scripting in languages other than Java. These other languages also need to support the built-in objects such as request, response, out, and so on. In those languages, there might not be a this keyword.

THE exception OBJECT

When you create an error page to deal with exceptions that occur during normal JSP page processing, you might need access to the exception that caused the error page to be invoked. You can access that exception through the exception object.

THE JspWriter CLASS

The JspWriter class acts like the PrintWriter class most of the time, except that it is specially tailored to deal with the buffering you need to do in a Java Server Page. If you look at the PrintWriter class, none of the print or println methods throw an IOException. The

JspWriter versions of print and println can and will throw IOException if the buffer fills up and is not automatically flushed.

When you create a Java Server Page, the page is buffered by default and automatically flushes the buffer when the page fills up. You can turn off the automatic buffer flushing by setting autoFlush to false in the page directive.

→ **See** "The autoFlush Option," **p. 262.**

In addition to the print and println methods, the JspWriter class gives you access to information about the buffering. Using this information, you can flush the buffer if necessary or determine how much more you can write to the buffer before it needs to be flushed.

Note

Don't worry if you don't understand the buffering, or if it seems overly complicated. If you use the default settings, you don't have to worry about it at all.

SENDING OUTPUT DATA

Most of the time, you aren't explicitly sending output in your JSP. In other words, you aren't calling the out.print or out.println methods directly. Instead, you just put the text that you want to display directly into the JSP. If you look at the servlet generated from your JSP source file, however, you see that the JSP compiler took that text and converted it into an out.print or out.println statement.

Occasionally, you'll need to write to the output stream from within your Java code. For example, you might have a huge block of Java code that loops through some data to extract some items that you want to display. Rather than closing the code block with a %> tag and using the <%= tag to display the data, you are much better off calling out.print or out.println.

The print and println methods available in the JspWriter class are

```
public void print(boolean b) throws IOException
public void print(char c) throws IOException
public void print(double d) throws IOException
public void print(float f) throws IOException
public void print(int i) throws IOException
public void print(long l) throws IOException
public void println() throws IOException
public void println(boolean b) throws IOException
public void println(char c) throws IOException
public void println(double d) throws IOException
public void println(float f) throws IOException
public void println(int i) throws IOException
public void println(long l) throws IOException
```

Also, instead of calling out.println() to print a blank line, you can call out.newLine().

Because the JspWriter is a subclass of the Writer class, you can also use the write method to write out a string, a single character, or an array of characters:

```
public void write(String str)
public void write(String str, int offset, int length)
public void write(int singleCharacter)
public void write(char[] charArray)
public void write(char[] charArray, int offset, int length)
```

Buffer Control

If you turn off automatic buffer flushing, the most important method to you, aside from `print` and `println`, is the `flush` method:

```
public void flush()
```

If you have a chain of writers set up (that is, if the output of the `JspWriter` is going to another writer) the `flush` method flushes all the writers along the output chain. In other words, calling `flush` ensures that the current contents of the buffer get sent back to the browser, even if they need to go through another writer first.

Instead of flushing the buffer, you might need to clear it out, erasing its current contents. The `clear` or `clearBuffer` methods empty out the contents of the buffer:

```
public void clear() throws IOException
public void clearBuffer() throws IOException
```

It might seem strange to have two methods that appear to do the same thing. The difference is, the `clear` method throws an `IOException` if the buffer has been flushed before. The idea is, when you clear the buffer, the chances are good that you meant to clear out the entire page. If the buffer has been flushed, you aren't clearing out the entire page because some of it has already been sent back to the browser. When that happens, you want the system to let you know that it can't do what you want.

If you want to clear the current contents of the buffer and you don't care if the buffer has been flushed before, use the `clearBuffer` method.

The `getBufferSize` method returns the size of the buffer in bytes, and the `getRemaining` method returns the number of bytes left in the buffer:

```
public int getBufferSize()
public int getRemaining()
```

If buffering is turned off, the `getBufferSize` method returns `0`.

The `isAutoFlush` method returns `true` if the system is handling the automatic flushing of the buffer:

```
public boolean isAutoFlush()
```

If you are having trouble getting the buffering to work correctly, see "Buffering Problems" in the "Troubleshooting" section at the end of this chapter.

Using a PrintWriter

Sometimes, you need a real `PrintWriter` object instead of `JspWriter`. For example, the `printStackTrace` method in the `Throwable` class can print a stack trace to a `PrintStream` or a `PrintWriter`. Unfortunately, `JspWriter` is neither. You can, however, create a new

`PrintWriter` on top of a `Writer` object. Thus, if you absolutely need a `PrintWriter`, just create one around the `JspWriter`. Listing 14.1 shows a JSP that prints a stack trace using the `printStackTrace` method.

LISTING 14.1 SOURCE CODE FOR PrintException.jsp

```
<%@ page language="java" import="java.io.*" %>

<html>
<body bgcolor="#ffffff">
<pre>
<%
    try
    {
        throw new RuntimeException("Print me, please");
    }
    catch (RuntimeException exc)
    {
        PrintWriter pw = new PrintWriter(out);

        exc.printStackTrace(pw);
    }
%>
</pre>
</body>
</html>
```

Figure 14.1 shows the output from the `PrintException` Java Server page.

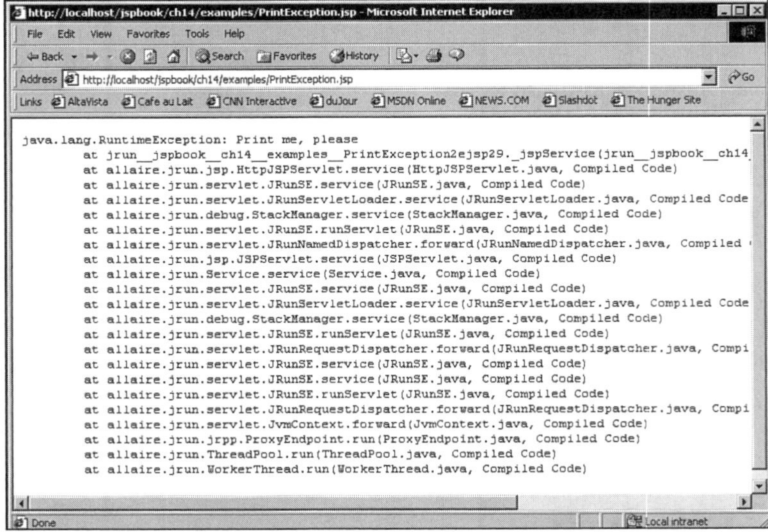

Figure 14.1
You can create a `PrintWriter` to print a stack trace to the browser.

THE PageContext CLASS

The PageContext object acts as a central repository for all the built-in objects a JSP might need to obtain. Typically, the system initializes the built-in variables by calling a method within the PageContext class. For example, if your JSP uses the session object, the generated servlet usually contains a line like

```
HttpSession session = pageContext.getSession();
```

In addition to providing access to the built-in object, the PageContext object has the capability to scan for attributes and attribute names among all the possible scopes (page, request, session, and application).

Finally, the PageContext object contains convenience methods that make it easy to include or forward to another servlet or JSP.

ACCESSING THE BUILT-IN OBJECTS

The objects associated with built-in variables (request, response, out, session, and so on) are available from the PageContext class. In fact, a JSP usually goes to the PageContext class to get these variables. The whole idea of the PageContext class is that it shields a JSP from the intricacies of the servlet API. When a JSP compiler generates a servlet from a Java Server Page, it doesn't need to generate code that goes one place for a ServletContext object and another place for an HttpSession object. Instead, the generated code uses PageContext to get all the objects it needs..

Although there is no technical benefit to this technique, it makes it easier to manage change in the future. If Sun decides to change the way you access the ServletContext object, only the PageContext object needs to change. None of the generated servlets would change, nor would anyone's JSP compiler.

The built-in objects are initialized from the following methods in PageContext:

```
public ServletRequest getRequest()
public ServletResponse getResponse()
public JspWriter getOut()
public HttpSession getSession()
public ServletContext getServletContext()
public ServletConfig getServletConfig()
public Object getPage()
public Throwable getException()
```

ACCESSING ATTRIBUTES FROM THE PageContext CLASS

The PageContext class performs double duty when it comes to storing and retrieving attributes. First, you can store attributes in PageContext explicitly. These objects have a scope of page, meaning that every instance of every JSP page has its own separate PageContext for storing attributes. Any Java beans you create with a page context are stored as attributes in PageContext as well.

The methods for storing, retrieving, and removing attributes in PageContext are similar to their counterparts in ServletRequest, HttpSession, and ServletContext:

```
public Object getAttribute(String name)
public void setAttribute(String name, Object ob)
public void removeAttribute(String name)
```

In addition, you can find out all the attribute names currently in use in the PageContext by calling getAttributeNames:

```
public Enumeration getAttributeNames()
```

The most interesting aspect of PageContext is that it gives you access to attributes in any scope by adding an extra parameter to getAttribute, setAttribute, and removeAttribute:

```
Public Object getAttribute(String name, int scope)
Public void setAttribute(String name, Object object,
    int scope)
public void removeAttribute(String name, int scope)
```

The scope values are contained in the PageContext constants PAGE_SCOPE, REQUEST_SCOPE, SESSION_SCOPE, and APPLICATION_SCOPE. For example, to retrieve an object from a session, you could make the following call:

```
Object ob = PageContext.getAttribute("myObject",
    PageContext.SESSION_SCOPE);
```

You can also locate all the attribute names in a given scope by calling getAttributeNamesInScope:

```
public Enumeration getAttributeNamesInScope(int scope)
```

You can search through all the scopes for a particular object by calling findAttribute:

```
public Object findAttribute(String name)
```

The PageContext object first searches within the page scope, then the request scope, the session scope, and finally the application scope. The search stops at the first scope in which it finds a match. If you have an attribute named myObject stored in the request object and also in the application object, findAttribute("myObject") returns the object stored in the request object.

The getAttributeScope method returns the scope in which it finds a particular name:

```
public int getAttributeScope(String name)
```

For example, if findAttribute finds myObject in the request object, getAttributeScope returns PageContext.REQUEST_SCOPE.

Listing 14.2 shows a JSP that dumps out all the objects it can see in the various scopes.

LISTING 14.2 SOURCE CODE FOR DumpAttributes.jsp

```
<%@ page import="java.util.*" %>
<html>
<body>
This page has access to the following attributes:
<pre>
<%

// Create an array of the possible scopes
    int scopes[] = new int[] {
        PageContext.PAGE_SCOPE,
        PageContext.REQUEST_SCOPE,
        PageContext.SESSION_SCOPE,
        PageContext.APPLICATION_SCOPE };

// Create names for each possible scope
    String scopeNames[] = new String[] {
        "Page", "Request", "Session", "Application"
    };

// Loop through the possible scopes
    for (int i=0; i < scopes.length; i++)
    {
        out.println("In the "+scopeNames[i]+" scope:");

// Get all the attribute names for the current scope
Enumeration e = pageContext.getAttributeNamesInScope(scopes[i]);

        while (e.hasMoreElements())
        {
// Get the attribute name
            Object nameOb = e.nextElement();

// The name should always be a string, but just in case someone put
// some bad data somewhere, you won't get a class cast exception this way
            if (nameOb instanceof String)
            {
// Print out the attribute name and its value
                String name = (String) nameOb;

                out.print(name+": ");
                out.println(pageContext.getAttribute(name, scopes[i]));
            }
            else
            {
                out.println("Oops, the attribute name isn't a string! It's "+
                    nameOb.getClass().getName());
            }
        }
        out.println();
    }
%>
</pre>
</body>
</html>
```

Figure 14.2 shows the output from the DumpAttributes Java Server Page.

FORWARDING AND INCLUDING

Normally you use the `<jsp:include>` and `<jsp:forward>` tags to include or forward to other pages. If you want to do an include or forward in Java code, you can use `ServletContext.getRequestDispatcher` to get the request dispatcher for the page you want to include or forward to. The request dispatcher is a little messy, however. First, you must get the dispatcher for the page you want to call and then invoke either the `include` or the `forward` method in the dispatcher.

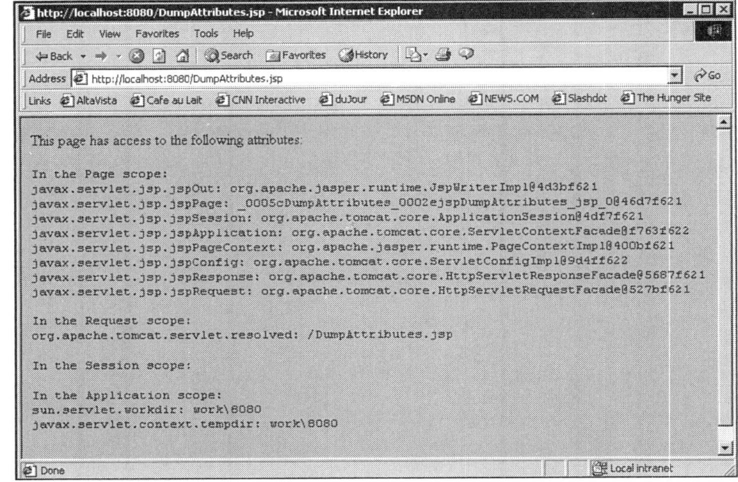

Figure 14.2 The `getAttributeNamesInScope` method is useful for exploring the various scope objects.

The `PageContext` class gives you a nice shortcut for forward and include. You can just call `forward` or `include` and pass the name of the page you are including or forwarding to

```
public void forward(String url)
    throws IOException, ServletException
public void include(String url)
    throws IOException, ServletException
```

For example, in a JSP you could call

```
pageContext.forward("displaySomething.jsp");
```

If you are having trouble forwarding or including, see "Include and Forward Problems" in the "Troubleshooting" section at the end of this chapter.

THE `JspEngineInfo` CLASS

Occasionally, you might want to print out information about the current version of the JSP engine. You might even have code that can adapt itself to various versions of the JSP specification. For example, you might create a JSP that takes full advantage of the features of JSP version 1.1, and another page that runs under JSP 1.0 but doesn't do everything the 1.1 page does. By examining the current version of the JSP engine, you can decide which page to call.

The `JspEngineInfo` class defines just one method, which returns a string containing the current version number of the JSP Engine. The version number is a series of numbers separated by periods, such as 1.1 or 1.2.3.4.5. The `getSpecificationVersion` method returns the current version number:

```
public String getSpecificationVersion()
```

You must take a roundabout path to get to the `JspEngineInfo` object. You must get the object from a `JspFactory` object. The `JspFactory` class is used internally by the JSP engine and by the generated servlets. Typically a single `JspFactory` is used by all the Java Server Pages, which is called the *default factory*. To get the default factory, just call `getDefaultFactory`, like this:

```
JspFactory defaultFactory = JspFactory.getDefaultFactory();
```

After you have the `JspFactory`, you can call `getEngineInfo` to retrieve the `JspEngineInfo` object:

```
JspEngineInfo engineInfo = defaultFactory.getEngineInfo();
```

Listing 14.3 shows a JSP that prints out the version of the JSP specification that the current JSP engine supports.

LISTING 14.3 SOURCE CODE FOR `PrintEngineInfo.jsp`

```
<html>
<body>
The current JSP Engine is:
<%= JspFactory.getDefaultFactory().getEngineInfo().
    getSpecificationVersion() %>
</body>
</html>
```

Figure 14.3 shows the output from PrintEngineInfo.jsp.

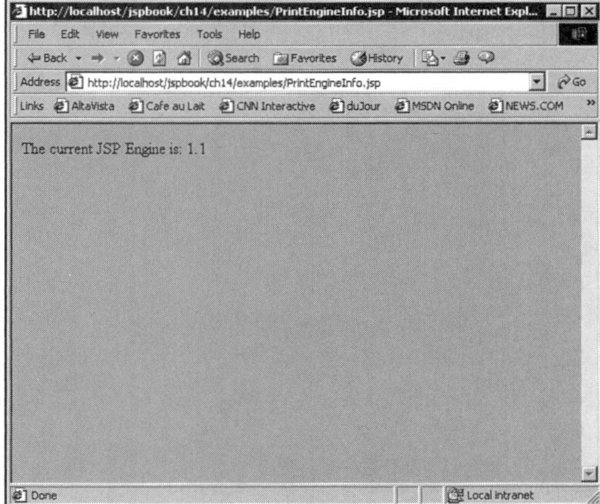

Figure 14.3
You can get the supported JSP version number from the JSP engine.

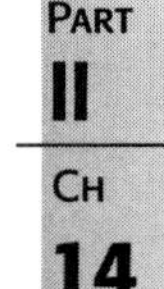

TROUBLESHOOTING

BUFFERING PROBLEMS

I cleared the buffer, so why do I still see part of the old page?

The buffer was probably already flushed. You might need to increase the size of the output buffer, or if you really don't know how big to make it, set `autoflush` to `false`. Be careful, though. You will need to flush the buffer yourself if you set `autoflush` to `false`.

I turned off `autoflush`*, so why do I still see part of the old page?*

You probably included this page from another one. Whenever you include another page at runtime using the `<jsp:include>` tag (as opposed to using the `<%@ include %>` tag), the JSP engine automatically flushes the buffer for the including page. There is no way to stop it. You might need to rethink your design if you need to clear the output from the including page.

INCLUDE AND FORWARD PROBLEMS

Why do I get an error when I try to forward to another page or include another page?

The first thing to check is that you entered the correct filename and that you are using a relative path. If you just enter a filename with no directory names, that file should be in the same directory as the JSP that is including it or forwarding to it. Assuming that the filename is correct, the other thing to check is that the target page compiles correctly on its own. If you forward to or include a bad page, you'll get an error. Try accessing the page manually and see if there is an error.

When I include forward to another page, why do I get an exception referring to the buffer?

When you forward to another page, the JSP engine attempts to clear the output buffer. If the buffer has already been committed, you'll get an error. When you include another page, the JSP engine automatically flushes the output buffer. So, if you include another page and then try to forward, you're almost assured of getting an error. You need to rethink your design to avoid these situations.

CHAPTER 15

JSP Directives

In this chapter

The Java Server Pages specification contains four different types of tags that start with `<%`. The plain `<%` tag begins a block of Java code. The `<%!` tag begins a declaration of class attributes or methods. The `<%=` tag inserts the result of a Java expression in the output. The final `<%` tag is the directive tag, which is `<%@`. There are currently three directives in the JSP specification:

- `page`
- `include`
- `taglib`

The `page` directive is a catchall for various page options that don't really warrant their own directive. The `include` directive allows you to include other files at compile time as opposed to runtime. The `taglib` lets you include an external library of custom JSP tags so you can expand the core set of tags recognized by JSP.

THE page DIRECTIVE

The `page` directive has a number of various options that bear no relation to each other except that they apply to the page. You can have multiple `page` directives, but you can't have the same option in two `page` directives on the same page, with one exception. The `import` option, which lets you specify Java classes to import, can appear as many times as necessary. You can also have multiple options within the same `page` directive, but again only `import` may appear more than once. The options are of the form `name=value` and are separated by spaces. The following is an example `page` directive:

```
<%@ page language="java" import="java.sql.*" %>
```

If you are having trouble putting a page directive in your Java Server Page, see "`Page` Directive Errors" in the "Troubleshooting" section at the end of this chapter.

THE language OPTION

The `language` option lets you specify the language you want to use for scripting in your Java Server Page. For example, because you usually use Java as the scripting language, your `language` option looks like this:

```
<%@ page language="java" %>
```

The Java Server Pages environment was designed to support scripting languages other than Java. You could, for example, use JavaScript as the scripting language if you have a JSP engine such as Resin that supports it. In that case, the `language` option on the page would be

```
<%@ page language="javascript" %>
```

Listing 15.1 shows the familiar "Hello World!" Java Server Page using JavaScript as the scripting language instead of Java. The example works with the Resin JSP engine.

LISTING 15.1 SOURCE CODE FOR JSHello.jsp

```
<%@ page language="javascript" %>
<html>
<body>
<%
    var helloStr = 'Hello World!';
%>
<h1><%=helloStr%></h1>
</body>
</html>
```

THE import OPTION

Of all the options for the page directive, the import option is the one you use the most. You can't use the import keyword within <% %> to import Java packages. Instead, you must use the import option in the page directive. The value for the import option is the name of the package you want to import. For example, to import java.sql.*, use the following page directive:

```
<%@ page import="java.sql.*" %>
```

You can have multiple page directives, so one way to import multiple packages is to have multiple page directives, like this:

```
<%@ page import="java.sql.*" %>
<%@ page import="java.util.*" %>
```

Because you can also have multiple import options in a single page directive, you can also import multiple packages like this:

```
<%@ page import="java.sql.*" import="java.util.*" %>
```

The easiest and most compact method of importing multiple packages, however, is to list them all in one import option, separated by commas, like this:

```
<%@ page import="java.sql.*,java.util.*" %>
```

The JSP compiler reads through the entire JSP file before it generates a servlet, so if you put import statements later on in the code, they still appear at the beginning of the generated servlet where they belong. For example, the Java Server Page shown in Listing 15.2 compiles cleanly and runs even though the import statement is in the middle of the page.

LISTING 15.2 SOURCE CODE FOR TestImport.jsp

```
<HTML>
<BODY>
<PRE>
<%
    out.println("Hello!");
%>
<%@ page import="java.sql.*,java.util.*,java.math.*" %>
</PRE>
</BODY>
</HTML>
```

You may wonder why the JSP compiler doesn't just require you to put the `import` statements at the top. When you include additional code at compile time (using another JSP directive that you will see later in the chapter), that code may contain `import` statements as well. For example, suppose you have one version of a routine that stores information to a text file and another version that stores data in the database. You can include either one of these files at compile time. This is a situation in which the included file is not a JSP or a servlet in its own right, just a single Java routine. Rather than importing java.sql.* in your main JSP, you let the included file import whatever packages it needs, knowing that the JSP compiler will handle it properly.

THE `session` OPTION

The `session` option tells the JSP compiler whether you want to use sessions:

```
<%@ page session="true" %>
```

The default value is `true`, indicating that you do indeed want to use sessions. The only reason for using this option to turn sessions off is for error checking. If you absolutely can't use sessions in your application, set the session value to `false`. The JSP compiler tells you if you accidentally tried to use the session variable anyway.

Tip

It's far better to catch bugs at compile time than it is to catch them at runtime. The `session` option is a specialized tool to help you locate a specific error at compile time.

If you try to store an object in a session and you have turned sessions off for the page, you might get a compile error or a runtime error depending on your JSP engine. For example, Listing 15.3 shows a simple JSP whose only goal is to challenge the `session` option to see if it really has turned sessions off.

LISTING 15.3 SOURCE CODE FOR `UseSession.jsp`

```
<%@ page session="false" %>
<jsp:useBean id="item" class="usingjsp.cart.Item" scope="session"/>
<html>
<body>
</body>
</html>
```

Figure 15.1 shows the response from the Resin JSP engine, giving a compile error because the `session` variable hasn't been defined.

Figure 15.2 shows the response from the Jrun JSP engine, which compiles fine but generates a runtime error when you try to use the `session` object.

THE `buffer` AND `autoFlush` OPTIONS

The `buffer` and `autoFlush` options let you control the buffering of your JSP. To turn the buffering totally off, set the `buffer` option to none, like this:

```
<%@ page buffer="none" %>
```

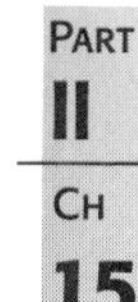

You can also specify the size of the buffer in kilobytes. For example, to set the buffer size to 16KB, you can use either of the following two page directives:

```
buffer="16" %>
<%@ page buffer="16kb" %>
```

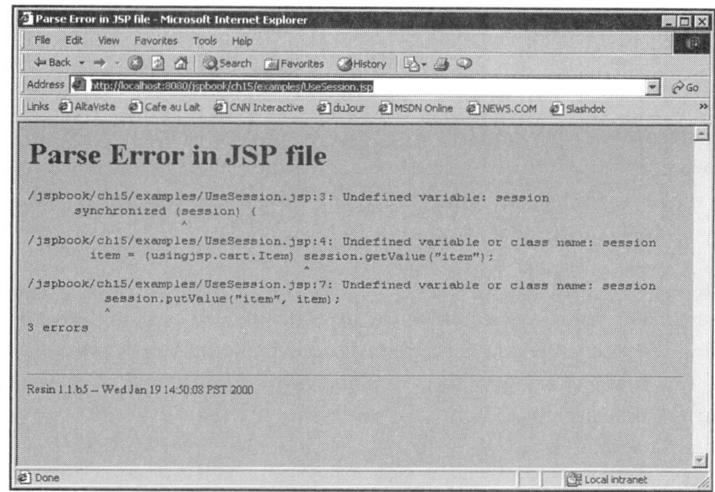

Figure 15.1
Some JSP engines give you a compile error if you try to use a session with sessions disabled.

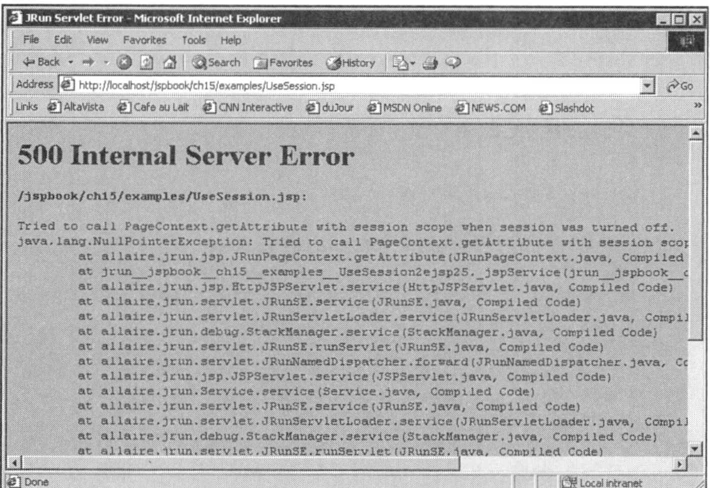

Figure 15.2
Other JSP engines give you a runtime error.

The default buffer size may be no less than 8KB, according to the JSP specification.

Note

The buffer size you specify with the `buffer` option only sets the minimum size for the buffer. The JSP engine may choose a larger buffer size than you requested, but it can never be smaller.

The `autoFlush` option controls whether the buffer is automatically flushed when it fills. The default value is `true`, meaning the buffer is automatically flushed when it is full. If you turn `autoFlush` off and the buffer fills up, the JSP engine throws a runtime exception when you try to write more data to the buffer.

Sometimes, you might want such detailed control over the buffer, but in general, you should leave this option alone.

THE `isThreadSafe` OPTION

The `isThreadSafe` option marks a page as being thread-safe. By default, all Java Server Pages are considered thread-safe. If you set the `isThreadSafe` option to `false`, the JSP engine makes sure that only one thread at a time is executing your JSP. The following `page` directive sets the `isThreadSafe` option to false:

```
<%@ page isThreadSafe="false" %>
```

`isThreadSafe` is a misleading name for this option. It is possible for you to encounter threading issues even if you mark the page as not being thread-safe. For instance, multiple threads can still access any objects that are in the `session` object or the `application` object. You must make sure you synchronize access to any shared resources when you label the JSP as not being thread-safe.

One of the ways you can ensure safe access to shared resources is to synchronize on the various objects where you store data. For example, if you need to create an object and put it in a session, synchronize on the session.

Listing 15.4 shows a JSP that stores a string in the `application` object exactly once.

LISTING 15.4 SOURCE CODE FOR `SingleAccess.jsp`

```
<html>
<body bgcolor="#ffffff">
<%
// See if the object is already in the application

    String storeMe = (String) application.getAttribute("StoreMe");

    if (storeMe == null)
    {
// If the object is null, it must be created
        synchronized (application)
        {
// Check again to make sure only one thread performs the create
            if (application.getAttribute("StoreMe") == null)
            {
                application.setAttribute("StoreMe", "stored");
            }
        }
    }
%>
The application's StoreMe object contains
<%= application.getAttribute("StoreMe") %>
```

```
</body>
</html>
```


Notice that the example in Listing 15.4 checks the `application` object twice, once while unsynchronized and again while synchronized. Traditionally, synchronization has been a slow operation in Java. Because the object is present in the application most of the time, you save time by checking while unsynchronized. After you decide that you need to create the object, checking while synchronized lets you avoid situations in which two threads both discover that they need to create the string.

For example, suppose threads A and B discover they need to create the string. Thread A synchronizes on `application`, while thread B tries to also synchronize. Thread A gets through, creates the string and stores it in the application. When thread A has completed the synchronized block, thread B enters the block, sees that the string has already been created, and then exits the block without creating another string.

Figure 15.3 shows how thread B waits for thread A to complete the synchronized block.

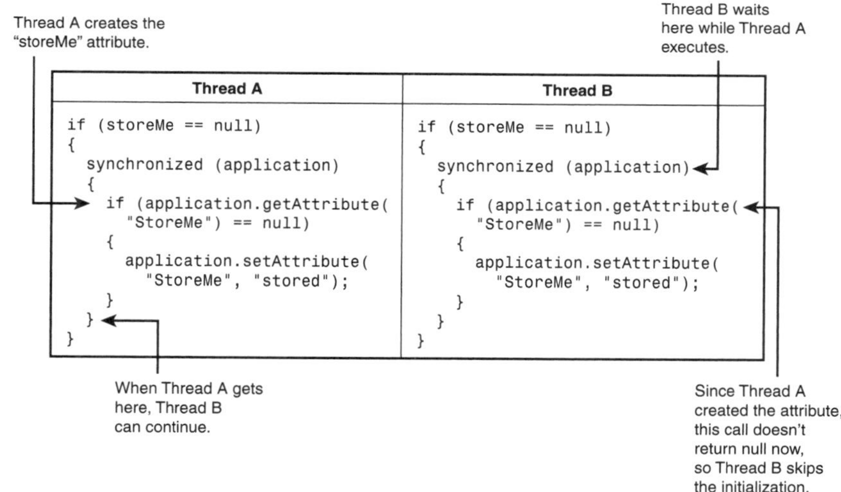

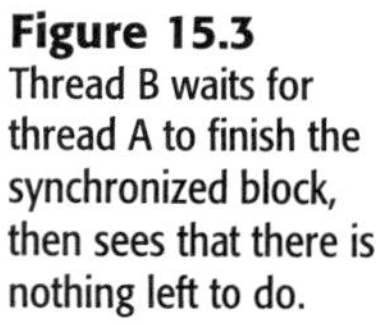
Figure 15.3
Thread B waits for thread A to finish the synchronized block, then sees that there is nothing left to do.

THE errorPage OPTION

The `errorPage` option tells the JSP engine which page to display if there is an error while running the current page. For example, suppose you want to call handleError.jsp if the current page encounters an error. You would use the following `page` directive:

```
<%@ page errorPage="handleError.jsp" %>
```

Caution

Be careful with error pages when you include other pages. When you include another page, the output buffer is automatically flushed. Some JSP engines try to clear the buffer when they call an error page and throw an exception if the buffer has already been flushed. Your best bet is to do the operations that are likely to throw an exception before you get to the included files.

If you are having trouble specifying an error page in your Java Server Page, see "Problems with the Error Page" in the "Troubleshooting" section at the end of this chapter.

THE `isErrorPage` OPTION

The `isErrorPage` option indicates that the current JSP can be used as the error page for another JSP. For example, the handleError.jsp sets the `isErrorPage` option to true because it is supposed to handle errors:

```
<%@ page isErrorPage="true" %>
```

By setting the `isErrorPage` to true, you tell the JSP compiler to create an `exception` object that contains the `Throwable` object that caused the error page to be invoked.

Listing 15.5 shows an error page that prints the message from the exception that caused the error page to be invoked.

LISTING 15.5 SOURCE CODE FOR `ErrorPage.jsp`

```
<%@ page isErrorPage="true" %>
<html>
<body>
<h1>Error</h1>
An error occurred while processing your request.
<p>
The error message is: <%= exception.getMessage() %>.
</body>
</html>
```

Listing 15.6 shows a page that intentionally throws an exception just to invoke the error page shown in Listing 15.5.

LISTING 15.6 SOURCE CODE FOR `ThrowException.jsp`

```
<%@ page errorPage="ErrorPage.jsp" %>
<html>
<body>
You shouldn't see this because I plan
to throw an exception in just a second.
<%
    if (true) throw new RuntimeException("Sorry about that, Chief!");
%>
</body>
</html>
```

Figure 15.4 shows the results of the error page. Notice that none of the text from the original page shows up on the error page.

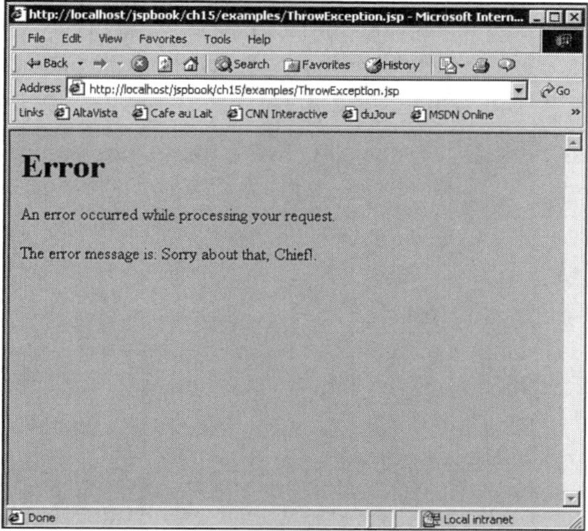

Figure 15.4
The JSP engine clears the output buffer, if possible, before displaying an error page.

THE contentType OPTION

The `contentType` option allows you to specify the kind of data that you are returning to the browser. The default content type is `text/html`, which is the standard content type for HTML pages. If you want to write out XML from your JSP, use the following `page` directive:

```
<%@ page contentType="text/xml" %>
```

THE info OPTION

The `info` option lets you change the value of the info string in the generated servlet. The info string is a description of the servlet that serves no purpose other than to describe the servlet. For example, you may want to indicate what kind of function the JSP performs:

```
<%@ page info="JSP that receives new customer orders" %>
```

THE extends OPTION

The `extends` option lets you specify the superclass for your Java Server Page. Most of the time, you should stick to the superclass that the JSP compiler chooses. If you find that you want to create your own superclass, first ask yourself why you need to.

If, for example, you find several utility routines that your Java Server Pages need to call, consider implementing those routines as static methods in some utility class.

Many times, the superclass for your JSP has been optimized to give you the best performance. If you decide to create your own superclass, you may be throwing away some of the benefits of the JSP engine you are using.

The superclass of a Java Server Page must implement the `JspPage` interface. If your Java Server Pages use the HTTP protocol, as most currently do, the superclass must implement `HttpJspPage`, which extends `JspPage`.

The `JspPage` interface extends the `Servlet` interface, so the superclass of a JSP must also implement all the methods in the `Servlet` interface. You must declare the `Servlet` interface methods in your class as final, meaning the JSP can't override them.

Typically, your superclass extends `HttpServlet`. From there, you need to add only two methods:

```
public void jspInit()
public void jspDestroy()
```

You must call `jspInit` from within your servlet's `init` method and `jspDestroy` from your servlet's `destroy` method. Finally, the `service` method in the servlet must invoke the `_jspService` method in the JSP. The `_jspService` method is defined in the `HttpJspPage` interface and is declared like this:

```
public void _jspService(HttpServletRequest request,
    pttpServletResponse response)
    throws ServletException, IOException
```

Listing 15.7 shows an example servlet that may be used as the superclass for a JSP.

LISTING 15.7 SOURCE CODE FOR `JSPSuperclass.java`

```
package usingjsp;

import javax.servlet.*;
import javax.servlet.http.*;
import javax.servlet.jsp.*;

/** An example superclass for a Java Server Page */

public abstract class JSPSuperclass extends HttpServlet
    implements HttpJspPage
{
// init must be declared as final for this to be a superclass for a JSP
    public final void init(ServletConfig config)
        throws ServletException
    {
// Let the superclass do its initialization
        super.init(config);

// Initialize the JSP
        jspInit();
    }

// destroy must be declared as final for this to be a superclass for a JSP
    public final void destroy()
    {
        super.destroy();

        jspDestroy();
    }
```

```
// getServletConfig must be declared as final for this to
// be a superclass for a JSP
    public final ServletConfig getServletConfig()
    {
        return super.getServletConfig();
    }

// service must be declared as final for this to be a superclass for a JSP
    public final void service(ServletRequest request,
        ServletResponse response)
        throws ServletException, java.io.IOException
    {
        super.service(request, response);
    }


    public final void service(HttpServletRequest request,
        HttpServletResponse response)
        throws ServletException, java.io.IOException
    {
// DEMO ALERT! Put a dummy data item in here to show
// how the subclassing works
request.setAttribute("Demo", "Hello from your superclass");

// Now call the _jspService method to run the JSP
        _jspService(request, response);
    }

// Provide a dummy jspInit method
    public void jspInit()
    {
    }

// Provide a dummy jspDestroy method
    public void jspDestroy()
    {
    }
// The _jspService method is implemented by the servlet generated
// from the JSP page source
    public abstract void _jspService(HttpServletRequest request,
        HttpServletResponse response)
        throws ServletException, java.io.IOException;
}
```

Listing 15.8 shows a JSP that extends the example superclass.

LISTING 15.8 SOURCE CODE FOR TestSubclassing.jsp

```
<%@ page extends="usingjsp.JSPSuperclass"%>
<html>
<body>
I am a subclass of a custom servlet. My parent class
left me a message. Here it is:
<%= request.getAttribute("Demo") %>
</body>
</html>
```

If you are having trouble specifying a superclass in your Java Server Page, see "Superclass Problems" in the "Troubleshooting" section at the end of this chapter.

THE `include` DIRECTIVE

Many programmers who come from the C and C++ world are disappointed with the lack of an `include` keyword in Java. The `include` directive in JSP performs the same service that the C `include` keyword does: It includes a file at compile time as opposed to runtime.

The nice thing about including a file at compile time is that it requires less overhead than a file included at runtime. The included file doesn't need to be a servlet or JSP, either. When the JSP compiler sees an `include` directive, it reads the included file as if it were part of the JSP that's being compiled.

You might have a standard HTML header that you want to put on all your files. For example, to include a file named "header.html", your `include` directive would look like this:

```
<%@ include file="header.html" %>
```

The filename in the `include` directive is actually a relative URL. If you just specify a filename with no associated path, the JSP compiler assumes that the file is in the same directory as your JSP, as in the example with "header.html".

THE `taglib` DIRECTIVE

The Java Server Pages API has an extension mechanism known as a tag library. You can create custom JSP tags that look like HTML or XML tags. By segregating more of your Java code into custom tags, you reduce the amount of Java code that appears in the JSP.

The `taglib` directive loads a tag library for use in the JSP. When you load a tag library, you must specify the URI of the tag library and the prefix for the tags, like this:

```
<%@ taglib uri="http://usingjsp.wutka.com/taglib/testlib"
   prefix="testing" %>
```

When you use a custom tag, it is typically of the form `<prefix:tagname>`. The prefix is the same as the prefix you specify in the `taglib` directive, and the `tagname` is one of the tags implemented in the tag library.

For example, suppose the `testlib` tag library contains a tag called `checkmate`. To use the `checkmate` tag with a prefix of `testing`, your tag would look like `<testing:checkmate>`.

→ For more information on custom tags, including instructions for creating your own tag library, **see** Chapter 29, "Extending JSP with New Tags," **p.551**.

TROUBLESHOOTING

`page` DIRECTIVE ERRORS

Why do I get compile errors on the line with my `page` directive?

The most likely cause of this problem is that you put a space between the `<%` and the `@`. The `<%@` tag used for JSP directives is not the same as the `<%` tag. When you put a space in there, the JSP compiler thinks you want the `<%` tag and the `@` symbol becomes part of the Java code within the `<%` tag.

Why doesn't my import work?

Did you remember the `.*` at the end? Many times you'll mean to import `java.util.*` or `java.sql.*` and forget the `.*` at the end.

PROBLEMS WITH THE ERROR PAGE

Why do I get an exception when I go to an error page?

You probably have already committed the output buffer. When you go to an error page, the JSP engine attempts to clear the output buffer so the error page doesn't contain a mixture of the original page and the error page. This problem occurs most often when you have included another page or forwarded to another page. If you must include or forward, try moving the code that throws the exception as close to the top of the page as you can so you handle any exceptions before you commit the buffer.

Why do I see part of the original page before the error page?

You have most likely already committed the output buffer, but your JSP engine doesn't throw an exception when you try to hit the error page. Some JSP engines will not let you forward to the error page once output has been sent to the browser. Others don't care, but you see part of the original page. Again, try to do things that can throw an exception as early as possible.

SUPERCLASS PROBLEMS

I specified an alternate superclass; why won't my JSP compile?

Are you sure that the superclass is in the classpath?

My JSP compiles; why do I get a runtime error when the page executes?

Make sure your superclass is really a servlet and that it implements the `HttpJspPage` interface. Depending on the JSP engine, the JSP might compile even if the class doesn't implement `HttpJspPage`, but when the JSP engine goes to load the JSP's servlet, it sees that it isn't a JSP servlet because it doesn't implement `HttpJspPage`.

Java Web Application Architecture

CHAPTER 16

Introduction to Application Architecture

In this chapter

Now that you understand the basics of servlets and Java Server Pages, it's time to take a step back and see how these two technologies fit in with the overall structure of an application. Even if you only work on the Web portion of an application, you are still affected by the overall architecture. After all, the architecture defines how and when you access data and what business logic functions you can perform. You can make better decisions if you understand their ramifications beyond the portion you are working on.

If you have little experience with system architecture, this chapter introduces basic concepts and explains how they affect you. Even if you are already familiar with application architecture, this chapter shows you how servlets and JSP integrate with the other components of an application. You can use this information to make better decisions when you design your Web applications.

The Three Layers of an Application

No matter how you slice it, a typical application consists of three layers:

- **Data layer**—Manages the data used by the application. An application that stores its data in data files is said to implement the data layer itself. Many applications use a database to manage the storage of data. The database itself is considered to be the data layer for the application.
- **Business Logic layer**—Contains the various business rules and operations that the application performs on its data. When you store an order, the data section stores the various parts of the order, while the business logic section calculates the price of the order, handles any credit card validation, and verifies that the order has all the required information.
- **Presentation layer**—Interacts with the user in one way or another. GUI screens and Web pages are typical examples of a presentation layer. A report generator is also considered part of the presentation layer.

These three parts of the application are referred to as layers because they build on each other. The data layer is the lowest level of the application and deals with raw data. The business layer sits on top of the data layer and gives life to the data by making it behave according to the business rules. The presentation layer sits on top of the business layer and makes the application useful to the user. Figure 16.1 shows the relationship between the layers.

Application Tiers

Applications are frequently categorized by the number of tiers they have. A *tier* is a grouping of the three layers into a single component of the application. Although there are only three sections (Data, Business Logic, and Presentation) there are actually four categories for an application:

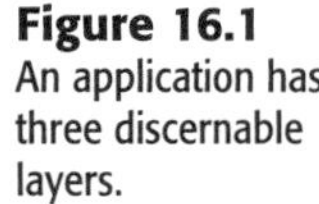

Figure 16.1
An application has three discernable layers.

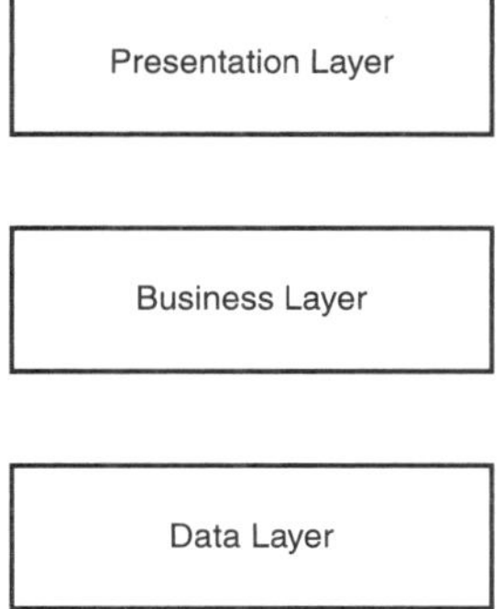

- **Single-tiered applications**—Combine all three sections into a single component (usually an executable program). Many programs that run on your PC and do their own data storage are considered single-tiered applications.
- **Two-tiered applications**—In the traditional sense, combine the presentation and business logic layers into a single component and use a database program for the data layer. Although you could combine the data and business logic layers into a single unit and put the presentation layer in its own separate layer, most applications that separate presentation from the business logic also separate the business logic from the data layer.
- **Three-tiered applications**—Separate the three layers into separate components. These applications typically use distributed object middleware such as CORBA, RMI, or DCOM. For example, you might have a GUI program that uses CORBA to communicate with a server containing the business logic. The CORBA objects on the server then communicate with a database.
- **N-tiered applications**—Similar to three-tiered applications, but they are more distributed than their three-tiered counterparts. An N-tiered application has many distributed objects spread across many machines, again using something such as CORBA, RMI, or DCOM. These objects may have their separate data layers. Many people still refer to N-tiered applications as three-tiered just to indicate that the three layers are separate from each other.

Applications Come Unglued Over Time

If you look at the evolution of computer applications over the last forty years, you see that applications have been coming unglued over time. Computer applications were originally just single-tiered applications running on a mainframe. Databases became popular in the 70s and then exploded in the 80s when the PC entered the scene and hooked up with the local area network. The old single-tiered applications began to separate into two-tiered applications with the database handling the data layer.

At the time, the concept of application "tiers" was not really used. As the local area network gained popularity, the term *client/server* caught on. Originally, a client/server system was a database server and an application client. Soon, applications began to make use of remote procedure calls (RPC), in which a client calls a procedure on a server. Unfortunately, RPC-based systems were also referred to as client/server. Because many RPC-based systems also used databases, the term client/server wasn't descriptive enough.

Eventually, the concept of tiers made its way into the lingo of system designers and it became easier to describe the overall structure of a system. These changes in terminology were necessary because the applications continued to split into different components. In other words, they came unglued.

Physical Versus Logical Tiers

The definition of a *tier* is unfortunately becoming more and more strained. First of all, people often refer to the number of tiers in an application as a count of the number of different machines the application runs on. First, a tier can refer to a logical tier or a physical tier. Just because you can separate the business logic layer from the presentation layer doesn't mean you need to put those layers on separate machines, or even in separate programs. The benefit of working with separate tiers is that it is easy to organize and maintain your code. Some designers automatically assume that if you have separate tiers, those tiers must be physically separated.

If you have a three-tiered application where each tier resides on a separate machine, that is referred to as a *physical three-tiered* model. When you separate your application tiers into three separate programs but run those programs on one or two machines (the business logic layer program running on the same machine as the database server, for example) that application is still a physical three-tiered application.

How Can You Have Half a Tier?

The Web has really thrown a monkey wrench into application design lingo (and application design in general). The problem is that the browser can be thought of as either a dumb terminal or smart platform on which you can execute programs. Remember that a mainframe application is considered a single-tiered application. If you have a program that runs on a Web server, manages its own data and business logic, and generates the HTML it sends back to the browser, is that a single-tiered application or a two-tiered application in which the business logic and data layers are on the Web server and the presentation layer is on the browser?

You could argue that one either way. From a physical standpoint, you could say that it's a two-tiered application. From a logical standpoint, however, you might say it's a single-tiered application because the code to manage all three layers is mingled together. It gets more confusing when you run JavaScript on the browser. You could consider HTML to just be static text just like the characters a mainframe sends to a terminal. After you start executing code on the browser, it becomes more than just a dumb terminal.

One solution to this dilemma is to consider the browser to be a half-tier. You'll see an application described as a "two-and-a-half tiered" application. You have a database for the data layer, a servlet or JSP doing business logic and some presentation, and JavaScript on the browser for some of the presentation. Figure 16.2 shows the layers in a "two-and-a-half tiered" application.

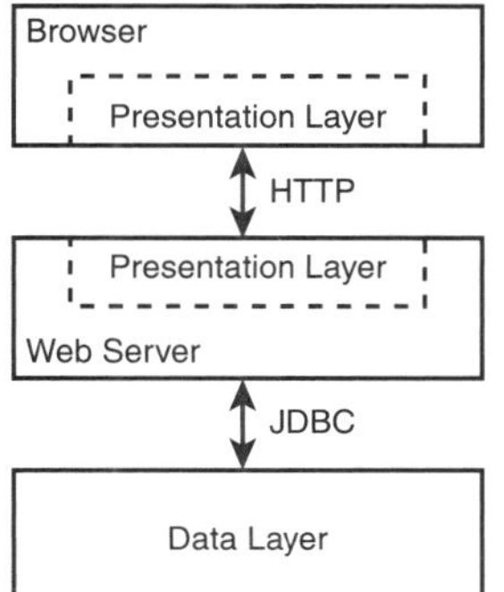

Figure 16.2
In a two-and-a-half-tiered application, some of the presentation is done on the browser and some on the Web server.

Combine the Web server with objects distributed around the network and you have more tiers than you can throw a stick at. You might see the "tier" notation change a little in the future. There will probably be a term distinguishing between the code that runs on a browser and the presentation code on the server. You might even see the use of the term tier diminish as more applications become just a conglomeration of distributed objects. When the a term such as "three-tiered" or "N-tiered" describes almost all the applications you encounter, it will be time for a new term.

What I Mean by "Tier"

As you can see, the use of the term tier is not so cut and dried. One person might call an application two-tiered although another might call it single-tiered or one-and-a-half tiered. This book uses the term tier as a component-level tier. If you separate the data layer from the business logic and presentation layers, that's a two-tiered application. If you manage your data, perform business logic functions, and create the presentation output (including generating HTML) within the same components, that's a single-tiered application. If you separate the presentation layer, the business logic layer, and the data layer into separate components, that's a three-tiered application.

Note

The choice of terminology used here is somewhat arbitrary. If you classify a particular application differently, you aren't wrong, you're just using a different point of view.

Single-Tiered Applications

Many Web applications are single-tiered, often out of necessity. Many Web providers don't provide database access, so applications have had to rely only on local file storage. With the advent of small, cheap database engines such as MySQL, more Web providers are providing database access. There are still plenty of occasions in which a single-tiered application is appropriate. Figure 16.3 shows the structure of a typical single-tiered application.

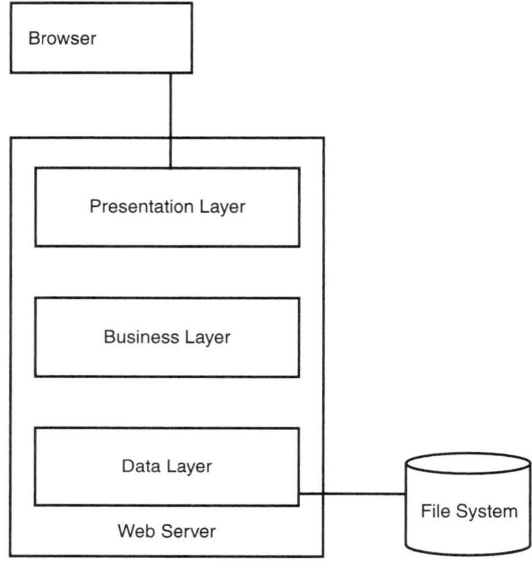

Figure 16.3
A single-tiered application manages presentation, business logic, and data from a single component.

Although single-tiered applications can have a fairly complex presentation layer, you will usually find that they have very simple business logic and data layers. After all, after a data layer becomes complex, you tend to use a database and turn the application into a two- or three-tiered design.

An online survey or poll is a good candidate for a single-tier design because the data and business logic requirements are minimal. An online message board is another good candidate for single-tiered design, although you are probably better off separating the management of the messages from their presentation, even if you store the messages in files rather than in a database.

Two-Tiered Applications

Two-tiered designs usually come about because the data layer is complex. If you must perform queries or maintain relationships between data items, you certainly don't want to write that code yourself. Figure 16.4 shows the structure of a typical two-tiered application.

Although the complexity of the data drives an application from single-tiered to two-tiered design, the complexity of the business logic usually drives a two-tiered design into three tiers. If your application is fairly light on business logic or if you are under extreme time pressure, a two-tiered design might be right for you.

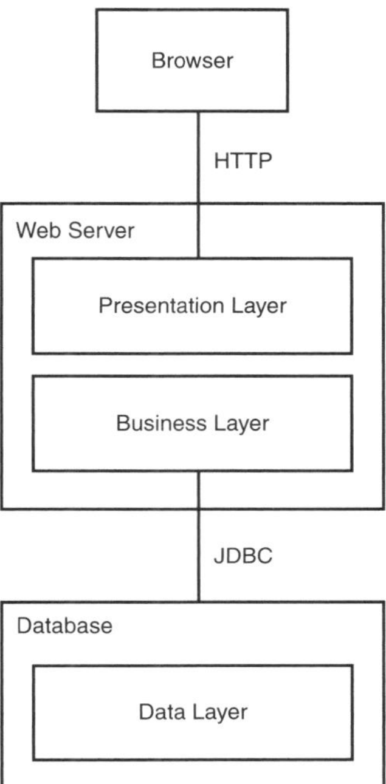

Figure 16.4
A two-tiered design usually puts the data layer into a separate component.

One of the advantages that a two-tiered design still maintains over a three-tiered design is that there are many tools available for designing and accessing the data layer, but there are not many tools for designing and accessing the business logic layer. For example, you can find many object-to-relational mapping tools that help you create a database and map Java objects to database tables. These tools even let you design the database according to the structure of your Java object.

There are few tools that allow you to do the same kind of operation at a higher level. That is, when you need to package your business logic into separate components, there are few tools that help you decide how to perform the separation or how to make data available from these components. Hopefully, as Enterprise Java Beans become more popular, you will find more tools that help you design the business logic layer. Until that time, given the presence of data layer tools combined with the lack of business logic layer tools, a two-tiered application is a better bet when you are really short on time and are willing to make sacrifices in the extensibility and maintainability of your code.

THREE-TIERED APPLICATIONS

A three-tiered design is the most flexible and the most complicated to build. By separating presentation, business logic, and data layers into their own components, you can change the implementation of each layer without affecting the other layers. Figure 16.5 shows the structure of a typical three-tiered application.

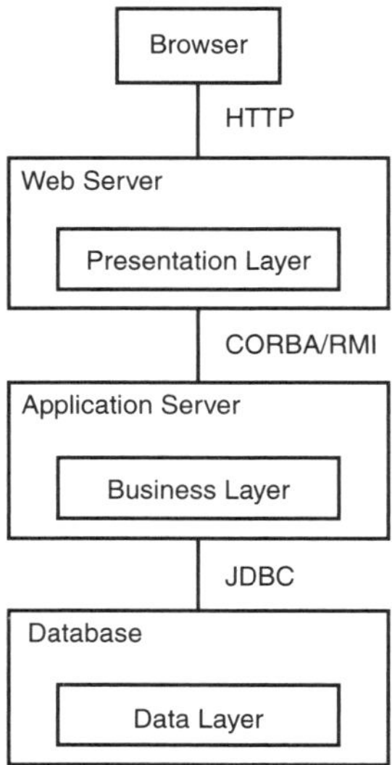

Figure 16.5
A three-tiered application has separate presentation, business logic, and data components.

When you separate the presentation, business logic, and data layers, you must determine how the layers interface with each other. The interface between the business logic and data layers is often determined by using a third-party database tool.

The interface between the presentation and the business logic layers is the difficult part to design, especially when it comes to Web programming. When you create a traditional three-tiered application with a graphical user interface, the coupling between the actual user interface and the business logic layer is a little tighter. The difference is that a graphical user interface can respond immediately to user requests and can perform more frequent interactions. In a Web application, the interaction between the user and the server is much slower.

Suppose, for example, that you have a data entry system that must validate user input against a database. If you use a traditional graphical user interface, you can check the user input immediately and give instant feedback when the user's data isn't valid. With a Web application, you must wait until the user submits a form, making the feedback process much slower.

Note

If the amount of data you need to validate is small, you can always validate it with a JavaScript routine and still give immediate feedback.

You must also make sure that the business logic layer doesn't require a large number of short interactions with the user. In a traditional graphical user interface, you might get away with popping up a series of dialog boxes to ask questions. In a Web application, especially one that might be run over a slow connection, you want to minimize the number of times the user must submit a form to the server. If you need to make a series of business logic layer calls when the user submits a single form, that's fine. Sometimes, however, you just can't make multiple calls using the data from a single form. For example, you might make some sort of survey in which the next survey question depends on the answer from the previous one. In these situations, you must either redesign the application or accept the fact that the user will need to make many short calls to the server.

THE TRADE-OFFS

There is no one-size-fits-all application architecture. When you choose a design, you must evaluate various aspects of the application, your development team, and your schedule to come up with the architecture that strikes a reasonable balance between various factors.

APPLICATION COMPLEXITY

The size and complexity of the application have a tendency to push toward more tiers. That is, the more complex the application, the more tiers you generally have. By partitioning your application into multiple tiers, it becomes easier to manage the complexity because you can focus on each layer individually and also parcel out the work to separate development teams. A single-tiered application is more difficult to split between various development teams because the same section of code may do presentation, business logic, and data at the same time.

MAINTAINABILITY

Some applications are quick, one-time shots that you need to get out quickly and then discard. For example, you might be switching over to a new backend system and you are writing an application to smooth the transition to the new system. After the transition is complete, your application goes away. In those cases, you don't care if it might be tough to make changes later on because the application won't be used. On the other hand, if you are writing an application that will be used for several years and needs to undergo periodic updates, you want to make it easy to modify parts of the system.

Application maintainability tends to push you toward more tiers, because the separation of the various layers allows you to change aspects of one layer without affecting the other layers.

SCHEDULE PRESSURE

Schedule pressure tends to push you toward fewer tiers. It takes time to come up with a good three-tiered design that has a clean separation between the layers. It is often an iterative process in which discoveries made about the presentation layer lead to changes in the interface between the presentation and business layers. Obviously, the more you know up front, the easier it is to make design decisions. Unfortunately, with a short time schedule, you often don't have time to get all the information up front.

Note

Although you can sometimes trim some time off the initial gathering of system requirements, you soon hit a point in which the time you save up front is lost when you need to rework code because of an incorrect assumption or an overlooked requirement.

Although you can gain some development speed by parceling out the work to various development teams, you might also lose some speed because developers of one layer are waiting for parts of another layer to be complete.

DEVELOPMENT TEAM SKILL

The skill of the development team tends to push toward fewer tiers. That is, the less skill a development team has, the less likely it has the capability to implement a three-tiered application. You must take this into account when deciding your application architecture. Although the addition of some key skill sets can enable the team to do the job, you must consider whether your team can handle the job with or without help, and whether you can get the help you need.

MISCELLANEOUS FACTORS

There are miscellaneous factors involved with every project that tend to counteract some of the other factors. For example, if you have a large existing base of code that you can reuse, you might be drawn to use the same architecture as the existing code base. Your management might dictate that you are to use a specific kind of architecture. (Don't laugh; it happens all the time.)

Figure 16.6 shows the various trade-offs you must evaluate and how they push against each other.

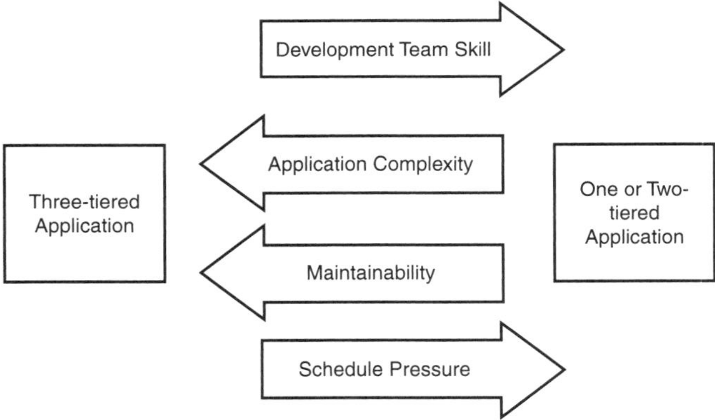

Figure 16.6
Various factors push you in different directions when choosing an architecture.

HYBRID ARCHITECTURES

You don't have to confine yourself to a single architecture for your entire application. Many applications use a mixture of two- and three-tiered designs. When you need to create a database maintenance application to modify the data used by your application, you can create a two-tiered application. The main application can still be three-tiered. You will often find that the amount of effort required to make a three-tiered database maintenance application is excessive, especially if your only goal is to use the same architecture for all parts of your application.

Likewise, you might have a two-tiered application that also needs to access some external data sources. You can create a component that accesses the external system and possibly the database along the way. Although the external system access resembles a three-tiered architecture, the core of your application is still two-tiered. There is something to be said for consistency, but try to focus on the problems at hand first. Don't make huge sacrifices in time and effort just so you can say you used a specific architecture.

CHAPTER 17

Browser-Server Interaction

In this chapter

Designing Your Web Screens

Even after you master Java Server Pages and servlets, many challenges still await you when you lay out your Web pages. When the user submits form data, should you redraw the entire page or just a portion? Do you want to redraw anything at all? Some of these decisions might be out of your control because the overall structure of the Web site and the individual Web pages might be given to you ahead of time.

Your decisions might also be influenced by the amount of data you need to keep on the client. If you need to store data on the client and you don't use cookies, you might not be able to redraw the entire page every time. Whenever you redraw the entire page (as opposed to a single frame) you lose all the information you had stored in scripting variables.

There are many other decisions related to good user interface design. Although this chapter outlines some of the general page structure techniques, it does not discuss any of the issues involving the content itself. There are a number of good graphic design books that will help you with content. Jakob Nielson, one of the gurus of Web design, has written an excellent book entitled *Designing Web Usability: The Practice of Simplicity* (available from New Riders Publishing, ISBN: 1-56205-810-X). You might also enjoy *Information Architecture for the World Wide Web* (available from O'Reilly, ISBN: 1-56592-282-4). There are a number of good tips and essays at Jakob Nielson's Web site, `www.useit.com`.

Redrawing the Entire Page

When you first start working with Java Server Pages and servlets, you usually redraw the entire page whenever the JSP or servlet runs. It certainly makes the most sense, from the standpoint of simplicity. Most users have the idea that they fill in form fields on a page, press a button, and then see a new page.

Chapter 4, "Creating HTML Forms," shows you many ways to arrange your application when you want to redraw entire pages. You have different options as to which pages should be Java Server Pages, which should be HTML, and which should be generated by servlets. Sometimes you need to redisplay a page with notations beside some of the data fields. You might want to label required fields that aren't filled in, for example. Chapter 4 shows you how to do that as well. The two design philosophies you haven't seen yet are multiple frames and hidden frames.

Organizing the Presentation into Frames

If you talk to some of the Web design gurus, they will tell you that frames are evil. Indeed, many Web sites that use frames tend to abuse them. One of the major complaints about frames is that they make navigation a little more difficult. When you hit the Back button on the browser, you can't be sure which frame will change, or if all of them will. Printing is a nuisance with browsers that won't print the entire page but instead only the last frame you clicked on.

Sites that rely on frames for navigation also make book marking difficult because you only bookmark the main page and not necessarily the set of pages you are looking at. In other words, you visit a frame-based site that has navigation links like `Products` and `Services`. You click on the `Products` link and another frame shows a list of products. When you bookmark the page and return some other time, you don't see the products page but the main page you had started from.

Although frames are frowned upon for navigation, they can be invaluable in many interactive Web applications. Suppose you are building a site in which a user can design a personal photo album. The user has a list of photos they can add to the album and when they click on a photo, it is immediately added to the current album page. Suppose that the list of photos is rather long, and instead of providing an indexed interface, you decide to send all the photos on a single page, which might take 20 or 30 seconds to download.

If you redraw the entire page every time the user selects a photo, the user will get pretty tired of waiting for the photo list to load over and over. Instead, you can save time by splitting the screen up into multiple frames in which one frame contains the list of photos and another frame shows the current album page. When the user selects a photo, you only redraw the frame containing the current album page, leaving the list of photos alone. Figure 17.1 shows an example photo album application. The dividing line down the middle separates the two frames.

Figure 17.1
By using frames, you can minimize the amount of time it takes to display form results.

Listing 17.1 shows the HTML file used to set up the two frames.

LISTING 17.1 SOURCE CODE FOR PhotoAlbum.html

```
<html>
<frameset cols="20%,*">
    <frame name="IndexFrame" src="PhotoIndex.jsp">
    <frame name="PhotoFrame" src="ShowAlbum.jsp">
</frameset>
</html>
```

Listing 17.2 shows the Java Server Page that creates the list of photos shown in the frame on the left. Each photo is contained within a hyperlink that references a JSP that adds the photo to the current page. The target attribute in the <a> tag tells the browser to display the results of the JSP in another frame (in this case, the frame on the right).

LISTING 17.2 SOURCE CODE FOR PhotoIndex.jsp

```
<%@ page language="java" import="java.net.*" %>
<html>
<body>

<%!
    class Photo
    {
        public String thumbnailURL;
        public String photoURL;
        public String photoName;

        public Photo(String aThumbnailURL, String aPhotoURL,
            String aPhotoName)
        {
            thumbnailURL = aThumbnailURL;
            photoURL = aPhotoURL;
            photoName = aPhotoName;
        }
    }

    Photo photos[] = new Photo[] {
        new Photo("Sam97.jpg", "Samantha97.jpg", "Sammy 1997"),
        new Photo("Kaity99.jpg", "Kaitlynn99.jpg", "Katy 1999"),
        new Photo("dawnbrian.jpg", "pierce.jpg", "Dawn & Brian"),
        new Photo("Kaity99B.jpg", "Kaitlynn99B.jpg", "Katy #2 1999"),
        new Photo("Sam99.jpg", "Samantha99.jpg", "Sammy 1999")
    };
%>

<table>
<%
    for (int i=0; i < photos.length; i++)
    {
%><tr><td>
<table>
    <tr><td align="center">
       <img src="<%=photos[i].thumbnailURL%>" border="0"></a>
    <tr><td align="center">
```

```
    <tr>
    <table>
    <tr>
<%
        for (int loc=1; loc <= 5; loc++)
        {
%>
       <td>
       <a href="AddPhoto.jsp?photoURL=<%=
        URLEncoder.encode(photos[i].photoURL)%>&photoName=<%=
        URLEncoder.encode(photos[i].photoName)%>&location=<%=loc%>"
        target="PhotoFrame">
       <%=loc%></a>
<%
        }
%>
    </table>
</table>
<%
    }
%>
</table>
</body>
</html>
```


Listing 17.3 shows the AddPhoto.jsp page that adds the selected photo to the current album page and redisplays the current page. The JSP doesn't care that it is being displayed in another frame. In fact, the JSP has no idea what the browser plans to do with it.

LISTING 17.3 SOURCE CODE FOR AddPhoto.jsp

```
<%
    String photoURL = request.getParameter("photoURL");
    String location = request.getParameter("location");

    session.setAttribute(location, photoURL);
%>
<jsp:forward page="ShowAlbum.jsp"/>
```

Listing 17.4 displays the current photo album.

LISTING 17.4 SOURCE CODE FOR ShowAlbum.jsp

```
<%
    String one = (String) session.getAttribute("1");
    if (one == null) one = "one.png";

    String two = (String) session.getAttribute("2");
    if (two == null) two = "two.png";
```

LISTING 17.4 CONTINUED

```
    String three = (String) session.getAttribute("3");
    if (three == null) three = "three.png";

    String four = (String) session.getAttribute("4");
    if (four == null) four = "four.png";

    String five = (String) session.getAttribute("5");
    if (five == null) five = "five.png";
%>
<html>
<body>
<table>
<tr><td><img src="<%=one%>"><td> <td><img src="<%=two%>">
<tr><td> <td><img src="<%=three%>"><td> 
<tr><td><img src="<%=four%>"><td> <td><img src="<%=five%>">
</table>
</body>
</html>
```

SENDING DATA TO A HIDDEN FRAME

Hidden frames are an interesting way to receive results from a JSP or a servlet. The idea is that you aren't sending back visual content, but data. You create a frame set, in which one frame takes 100% of the screen width or height, and the other frame takes the rest, which is 0%. Listing 17.5 shows a Web page that sets up a hidden frame. The blank.html file just contains `<html>` and `<body>` tags.

LISTING 17.5 SOURCE CODE FOR `HiddenFrameset.html`

```
<html>
<frameset rows="100%,*">
    <frame src="InputForm.html">
    <frame src="blank.html" name="TargetFrame">
</frameset>
</html>
```

Now, when you need to interact with the server, you set the target frame for the output to go to the hidden frame. The output usually contains JavaScript, either data or some executable content. For example, you might make a JSP that inserts data into a database and then pops up an alert telling the user that the data has been entered. Listing 17.6 shows a form that allows the user to enter data that will be stored using the hidden frame technique.

LISTING 17.6 SOURCE CODE FOR `InputForm.html`

```
<html>
<body bgcolor="#ffffff">

<form action="ItemInserter.jsp" method="post" target="TargetFrame">
```

```
<table>
<tr><td>Name:<td><input type="text" name="name">
<tr><td>Age:<td><input type="text" name="age">
<tr><td>Phone Number:<td><input type="text" name="phoneNumber">
</table>
<input type="submit" value="Enter">
</form>
</body>
</html>
```

Rather than redrawing the input form, the JSP generates a Web page with a JavaScript function that tells the user either the information has been entered correctly or an error has occurred.

One of the problems with the hidden frame technique is that you don't necessarily know when the server finishes executing your request. Instead, the page returned by the server usually executes some code when it is loaded. Listing 17.7 shows the ItemInserter Java Server Page that inserts the data and then lets the user know via a JavaScript alert.

Listing 17.7 Source Code for ItemInserter.jsp

```
<%
    // You would process the form data here

    String result = "The item has been inserted into the database.";
%>
<html>
<script>

function handleLoad()
{
    alert("<%=result%>");
}

</script>
<body onload="handleLoad()">
</body>
</html>
```

Sending Data to the Browser

Although most Web applications tend to do most of their processing on the server side, JavaScript is a pretty powerful scripting language and can handle client-side processing fairly well. When you put most of the presentation logic on the browser, your servlets and Java Server Pages become data servers. In this kind of model, your application architecture becomes more like the traditional three-tiered application. All the presentation logic runs on the browser, and the Web server sends back only pure data.

Using the same technique that you saw in Listing 17.6, your data page runs a JavaScript function when the page loads. Instead of displaying a dialog box, however, the function invokes a JavaScript function in another frame that receives the data. Your application often has the structure shown in Figure 17.2.

Figure 17.2
When you do all the presentation on the browser, you usually have an invisible frame for code and an invisible frame for data.

Presentation Frame(s)
Client-side code (invisible frame)
Data-exchange frame (invisible frame)

You use two different hidden frames in these types of applications. One hidden frame contains the JavaScript code that handles all the presentation logic. The other hidden frame contains the loaded data. When you invoke a servlet or JSP, you specify the data frame as the target frame. Listing 17.8 shows an HTML page that sets up the frames.

LISTING 17.8 SOURCE CODE FOR `DataFrames.html`

```
<html>
<frameset rows="100%,*">
    <frame src="DataForm.html" name="FormFrame">
    <frame src="DataHandler.html" name="DataFrame">
    <frame src="blank.html" name="TargetFrame">
</frameset>
</html>
```

If you are having trouble setting up a hidden frame, see "Hidden Frames," in the "Troubleshooting" section at the end of this chapter.

Unlike Java, JavaScript doesn't require you to declare the structure of your data ahead of time. You can set up arrays and structures just by declaring data. Listing 17.9 shows an example Java class declaration.

LISTING 17.9 SOURCE CODE FOR `JavaData.java`

```
package usingjsp;

public class JavaData
{
    public String name;
    public int age;
    public String[] children;

    public JavaData()
    {
        name = "Penny Wutka";
        age = 45;
        children = new String[] { "Lira", "Gusgus", "Bandit" };
    }
}
```

Listing 17.10 shows the JavaScript equivalent of the Java class in Listing 17.9. The structure of the data is defined by how you initialize it.

LISTING 17.10 SOURCE CODE FOR JavascriptData.js

```
javaScriptData = {
    name: "Penny Wutka",
    age: 45,
    children: [ "Lira", "Gusgus", "Bandit" ]
};
```

Listing 17.11 shows a servlet that returns structured JavaScript data. Notice the inner class that has the capability to represent itself in JavaScript.

LISTING 17.11 SOURCE CODE FOR DataServlet.java


```
package usingjsp;

import javax.servlet.*;
import javax.servlet.http.*;

import java.io.*;

public class DataServlet extends HttpServlet
{
    public void servlet(HttpServletRequest request,
        HttpServletResponse response)
        throws IOException
    {
        response.setContentType("text/html");

        PrintWriter out = response.getWriter();

        JavaInfo info[] = new JavaInfo[] {
            new JavaInfo("Kaitlynn Tippin", "katy"),
            new JavaInfo("Samantha Tippin", "sammy"),
            new JavaInfo("Edward Alexander", "eddie"),
            new JavaInfo("Norton Alexander", "nortie"),
        };

        out.println("<html><script>");
        out.println("javaInfo = [");
        for (int i=0; i < info.length; i++)
        {
            info[i].writeJavaScript(out);
            out.println(",");
        }
        out.println("};");
        out.println("</script><body
onload=\"top.DataFrame.handleData(javaInfo)\">");
        out.println("</body></html>");
    }

    class JavaInfo
```

LISTING 17.11 CONTINUED

```
    {
        public String name;
        public String nickname;

        public JavaInfo(String aName, String aNickname)
        {
            name = aName;
            nickname = aNickname;
        }

        public void writeJavaScript(PrintWriter out)
        {
            out.println("{ name='"+name+"', nickname:'"+nickname+"' }");
        }
    }
}
```

Listing 17.12 shows the JavaScript code that updates a select box from the data returned by the servlet. When `DataServlet` executes, the resulting page calls the `handleData` function in the `DataHandler` page.

LISTING 17.12 SOURCE CODE FOR `DataHandler.html`

```
<html>

<script>
function handleData(javaInfo)
{
    var nameSelect = top.FormFrame.nameList;

    nameSelect.length = javaInfo.length;

    for (var i=0; i < javaInfo.length; i++)
    {
        nameSelect.options[i].name = javaInfo[i].nickname;
        nameSelect.options[i].text = javaInfo[i].name;
    }
}
</script>
</html>
```

If you are having trouble sending JavaScript data back to the browser, see "JavaScript Data," in the "Troubleshooting" section at the end of this chapter.

HANDLING MULTIPLE CALLS

When you create a really complex user interface with JavaScript, you might find that you need to make multiple calls to the server at the same time. Unfortunately, the browser can't handle multiple calls to the same data frame. If you make a call to a servlet and send the output to a data frame, and then you make another call to a different servlet but still use the same data frame, the browser will stop trying to load the first servlet.

The browser doesn't know you're doing the equivalent of remote procedure calls to the server. It thinks you are just trying to display a Web page. It thinks you have changed your mind about which page you want to display. To handle multiple calls, you must either set up multiple data frames or you must queue up requests so you execute only one at a time.

The big disadvantage of using multiple data frames is that you will inevitably need to add more frames as you expand the application capabilities. You might have a large number of servlets and a complex interface that could need to call any or all the servlets at a given time. Organizing these calls with multiple data frames can be a daunting task.

To queue requests, you need a mechanism to detect when the previous request has completed. Because you are already calling a function when the request completes, you just need to call an additional function to trigger the next request.

Not only do you need to figure out when a request completes, you also need some idea that a request has failed. Because you are skirting around the normal purpose of the browser, you can't expect the browser to give you a lot of help. If your request fails for some reason, none of your functions will be called. Instead, you must resort to a timeout mechanism. If a request hasn't completed within a certain amount of time, you go on to the next request or retry the previous one.

If you need to handle timeouts, chances are you'll be using the `window.setDelay` function. Unfortunately, some browsers can't handle multiple delay requests at the same time. You need to write a scheduler that allows you to handle multiple timeout requests.

If you are having trouble performing multiple calls to the server, see "Multiple Calls," in the "Troubleshooting" section at the end of this chapter.

If you find yourself in a situation in which you need to make multiple requests, you are probably better off using a Java applet to make the requests. Your calls to an applet are synchronous, so you can wait for the results. You also have more flexibility in the kind of calls you make with the applet. For example, you can send XML data to the server with an applet. HTML and JavaScript might be good for displaying information, but they aren't very good for executing remote calls to a server.

TROUBLESHOOTING

HIDDEN FRAMES

How can I do nested frames and still have a hidden frame?

Your best bet is to put the hidden frame in the outermost frame set. When you have many nested frame sets, you often need to rearrange them when redesigning your site. If you refer to the hidden frame from your JavaScript code, you might need to change the references when you rearrange the frames. By putting the hidden frame in the outermost frame set, you always know where it is.

How can I see the data in my hidden frame?

While debugging your application, you should give the hidden frame a small size, maybe just 10 or 20 pixels. You'll see a small frame at the bottom or the far right of your browser. You can then right-click in the frame and select "View Source" or "View Frame Source" to see what information you have sent to the hidden frame.

JAVASCRIPT DATA

Why do I get JavaScript errors when I send back a string containing quotes?

Your JavaScript declaration usually has the form `var myVar="some string";`. When you generate this declaration from a servlet or JSP and the string contains quotes, like `"Hi There,"` your declaration looks like `var myVar=""Hi There"";`. Whenever you send strings back to JavaScript, you should first scan for quote marks and insert backslashes in front of them. The string `"Hi There"` should result in the declaration `var myVar="\"Hi There\"";`.

Why isn't my data handler getting called?

The most likely reason is that you forgot the closing `</script>` tag after the JavaScript data. Without the closing tag, the browser usually interprets the `<body>` tag as being part of the script and reports an error. Sometimes, however, the browser doesn't report an error, but doesn't interpret the `<body>` tag correctly, so it never calls the `onLoad` function.

Why does the browser keep reporting an error around my `<body>` tag?

You probably forgot to close off the script portion with a `</script>` tag.

MULTIPLE CALLS

Why does only the most recent remote call get processed?

Unless you put a scheduling mechanism into your application, making remote calls using the same target frame will not work. Whenever you make a remote call, the browser starts loading the target frame with the results of the remote call. If you make another call while the first one is still executing, the browser assumes that you don't care about the first call since the second call is about to overwrite the frame where the first call's data needs to go. The browser closes the connection for the first call and proceeds with the second one.

I set up a queue for processing calls; why does it seem to hang after a period of time?

With a queuing mechanism, you don't make another call until the current one has finished. If you have an error in the page you are calling, you might never see the current call complete. You should check the error logs of your JSP or servlet engine to see if you are getting any errors. You can also use a timeout mechanism to retry a call after some period of time.

Why does the browser seem to lose some of my `setTimeout` calls?

Some browsers can't handle multiple pending timeout callbacks. You might need to write a scheduler that uses `setTimeout` itself, and instead of using `setTimeout` in your callbacks, use the scheduler.

CHAPTER 18

A Single-Tiered Web Application

In this chapter

Some people will argue that a Web application can't ever be a single-tiered application because the browser is separate from the Web server. From a code standpoint, though, if your servlet or JSP manages data, performs business logic, and generates HTML, you are handling all three tiers within the same component. From one point of view, that constitutes a single-tiered application.

The main feature that distinguishes a single-tiered application from a two- or three-tiered application is that the single-tiered application manages its own data. When the data layer is simple, it is simple to implement the data layer itself. When the data layer is more complex, however, you are much better off using a database.

STORING AND RETRIEVING DATA

When you manage data yourself, you obviously need to decide how to format the data. You might choose to write out the data as a text file, possibly as a comma-delimited list of fields. You could also store your data in XML format, which allows you to structure your data easily. You can also take advantage of existing libraries for reading and writing data. If you don't need to store your data in text format, you can use the Java Serialization API to read and write objects. Like XML, Serialization allows you to store and retrieve complex data structures with relative ease.

Once you decide the format for your data, you must decide how often you need to update it. There are several issues involved in updating the data. If the file is reasonably small and you are sure that you will only be updating the file from a single Web application on a single server, you might consider reading the entire file into memory. When the data changes, you rewrite the file using the copy of the data you have in memory.

If the file is a text file and is fairly large, you'll probably just need to rewrite the entire file. You may need to use some of the locking techniques from Chapter 4, "Creating HTML Forms," if the file can be updated by more than one program. When you rewrite a file, you typically open a new file, then copy the original file line-by-line, changing the lines that you wish to update. Once you finish, you delete the old copy and rename the new copy back to the original name.

If you can allocate fixed-size blocks of data to store each record, you might consider using the `RandomAccessFile` class to access a specific block of data in the file and update it. You must make sure that the block size is large enough to hold the largest possible record, but not so large that you waste a lot of disk space.

LOCKING A FILE

As you saw in Chapter 4, Java doesn't have direct support for locking files. Instead, you can rename files to keep two programs from trying to access a file at the same time. In Chapter 4, you saw the locking code embedded inside a Java Server Page. If you need to work with several different files, it is a waste of time to write the same code over and over. Instead, you can package all the locking code into a single Java class.

There are three ways to update a file when using the file locking technique:

- Append data to the end of the existing file.
- Create a new copy of the file and copy data from the original copy, making changes where necessary.
- Use a `RandomAccessFile` object to update sections of the file.

The file locking class shown in Listing 18.1 allows you to lock a file and update it using any of these techniques. You can create a `FileLock` object by giving it the name of the file you want to lock. To actually lock the file, call the `lock` method. You can specify the number of times to retry the lock before giving up, and also the number of milliseconds to wait before trying again. The default values are `30` tries and `1000` milliseconds (1 second). Once you lock the file, you can call several methods to read and write the file:

- `getInputStream` returns an input stream for reading the locked file. This is useful if you need to create a new file while copying the contents of the original.
- `getOutputStream` returns an output stream for overwriting or appending to the original file. If you specify `true` for the `appendFile` flag, any data you write to the stream is appended to the original file, preserving the contents that were already there. If you overwrite the file instead of appending, none of the original contents are preserved. You should not use `getInputStream` and `getOutputStream` together. If you need to create a new copy of the file and read the original, use `getRewriteOutputStream`.
- `getRewriteOutputStream` returns an output stream for a new copy of the file. You can still use `getInputStream` to read the original file. When you unlock the file, the new copy is renamed back to the original file name and the old copy of the file is deleted.
- `getRandomAccessFile` returns a `RandomAccessFile` object that you can use to update sections of the file directly. You can read and write the same file with a `RandomAccessFile` object.

Listing 18.1 Source Code for `FileLock.java`

```
package usingjsp;

import java.io.*;

// A class that performs file locking by renaming

public class FileLock
{
    protected File mainFile;
    protected File lockedFile;
    protected File tempFile;
    protected boolean rewroteNew;
    protected boolean locked;

/** Create a lock for a named file */
```

LISTING 18.1 CONTINUED

```
    public FileLock(String filename)
    {
        mainFile = new File(filename);
        lockedFile = new File(filename+".lck");
        rewroteNew = false;
        locked = false;
    }

    public boolean lock()
        throws java.io.IOException
    {
        return lock(30, 1000);
    }

    public boolean lock(int maxRetries, int waitTimeMillis)
        throws java.io.IOException
    {
        boolean renameSucceeded = false;

// If the file is already locked, no need to go through the locking
// procedure again
        if (locked) return true;

// Loop until the file is available or there have been too many tries
        for (int i=0; i < maxRetries; i++)
        {

// Make sure the original file exists
            if (mainFile.exists())
            {
               if (mainFile.renameTo(lockedFile))
               {

// If the rename succeeds, the file is locked
                      renameSucceeded = true;
                      break;
               }
            }
            else
            {
// If the original file doesn't exist, try creating it. If the create fails,
// someone must have the file locked already
                if (lockedFile.createNewFile())
                {
                    renameSucceeded = true;
                    break;
                }
            }

// If at this point the rename isn't succeeded, wait for a specified
// period and try again
            try
            {
                Thread.sleep(waitTimeMillis);
            }
```

```
            catch (Exception ignore)
            {
            }
        }

// If the rename failed, return false to indicate that the file
// has been locked
        if (!renameSucceeded)
        {
            return false;
        }

        locked = true;
        rewroteNew = false;

        return true;
    }

/** Unlock the locked file */
    public void unlock()
    {
// If the file hasn't been locked, no need to unlock
        if (!locked) return;

// If the file was rewritten to a temp file, rename the temp file
// back to the original and delete the lock file
        if (rewroteNew)
        {
            lockedFile.delete();
            tempFile.renameTo(mainFile);
        }
        else
        {
// If there was no rewrite, just rename the lock file back to the original
            lockedFile.renameTo(mainFile);
        }

        locked = false;
        rewroteNew = false;
    }

/** Get an input stream to read the locked file */
    public InputStream getInputStream()
        throws IOException
    {
// Only allow reading if the file has been locked
        if (!locked)
        {
            throw new IOException("File not locked");
        }
// Create an input stream to read the locked file
        return new FileInputStream(lockedFile);
    }

/** Get a reader to read the locked file */
    public Reader getReader()
```

LISTING 18.1 CONTINUED

```
        throws IOException
    {
// Only allow reading if the file has been locked
        if (!locked)
        {
            throw new IOException("File not locked");
        }
// Create a reader to read the locked file
        return new FileReader(lockedFile);
    }

/** Get an output stream to write the locked file */
    public OutputStream getOutputStream()
        throws IOException
    {
// By default, rewrite the file instead of append (matches the
// convention for the FileOutputStream constructor)
        return getOutputStream(false);
    }

/** Get an output stream to write or append to the locked file */
    public OutputStream getOutputStream(boolean appendFile)
        throws IOException
    {
// Only allow writing if the file has been locked
        if (!locked)
        {
            throw new IOException("File not locked");
        }
// Create an output stream for writing the file
        return new FileOutputStream(lockedFile.getAbsolutePath(),
            appendFile);
    }

/** Get a writer to write the locked file */
    public Writer getWriter()
        throws IOException
    {
// By default, rewrite the file instead of append (matches the
// convention for the FileOutputStream constructor)
        return getWriter(false);
    }

/** Get a writer to write or append to the locked file */
    public Writer getWriter(boolean appendFile)
        throws IOException
    {
// Only allow writing if the file has been locked
        if (!locked)
        {
            throw new IOException("File not locked");
        }
// Create an output stream for writing the file
        return new FileWriter(lockedFile.getAbsolutePath(),
            appendFile);
    }
```

```
/** Get a stream to create a new copy of the file */
    public OutputStream getRewriteOutputStream()
        throws IOException
    {
// Only allow writing if the file has been locked
        if (!locked)
        {
            throw new IOException("File not locked");
        }

// Create a new file for creating a new copy of the locked file
        tempFile = new File(mainFile.getAbsolutePath()+".tmp");
        rewroteNew = true;

// Create an output stream for writing the new copy
        return new FileOutputStream(tempFile);
    }

/** Get a writer to create a new copy of the file */
    public Writer getRewriteWriter()
        throws IOException
    {
// Only allow writing if the file has been locked
        if (!locked)
        {
            throw new IOException("File not locked");
        }

// Create a new file for creating a new copy of the locked file
        tempFile = new File(mainFile.getAbsolutePath()+".tmp");
        rewroteNew = true;

// Create an output stream for writing the new copy
        return new FileWriter(tempFile);
    }

/** Get a RandomAccessFile object for updating the file */
    public RandomAccessFile getRandomAccessFile()
        throws IOException
    {
// Only allow writing if the file has been locked
        if (!locked)
        {
            throw new IOException("File not locked");
        }

// Create a new RandomAccessFile object for updating the locked file
        return new RandomAccessFile(lockedFile, "rw");
    }
}
```

If you are having trouble with file locking, see "File Locking," in the "Troubleshooting" section at the end of this chapter.

STORING DATA IN A TEXT FILE

There are a number of ways to store data in a text file. The method you choose depends on the kind of data you need to store. If you are storing a list of names or other single items, you can write a Java class to read and write the list. In Chapter 4 you saw examples that wrote text strings to a file with only one data item stored on each line. In the survey program, each line contained a separate field from the survey form. In the online poll, each line contained a count of the number of responses for a particular answer.

You can write Java classes that store all of their data elements into a string, and read data from a string. Once you have the data in a string, you can write it to a text file easily. Listing 18.2 shows a data object that can store itself into a string and read itself out of a string.

LISTING 18.2 SOURCE CODE FOR `Meet.java`

```
package usingjsp;

import java.util.*;

/** Represents a gymnastics meet for the purpose of scheduling judges */

public class Meet implements java.io.Serializable
{
    public String meetName;
    public String gym;
    public String dates;
    public String levels;

    public Vector vaultJudges;
    public Vector barsJudges;
    public Vector beamJudges;
    public Vector floorJudges;

    public Vector carPools;

/** Creates an empty Meet object */
    public Meet()
    {
    }

/** Creates a new Meet object with data elements populated from a string */
    public Meet(String dataString)
    {
// Assume the data elements are separated by |'s
        StringTokenizer tokens = new StringTokenizer(dataString, "|");

// In a production system, you should really check to make sure there are
// mroe tokens, or at least catch a NoSuchElementException
        meetName = tokens.nextToken();
        gym = tokens.nextToken();
        dates = tokens.nextToken();
        levels = tokens.nextToken();

// Use another routine to parse an element that is a list of items
```

```
        vaultJudges = parseStringList(tokens.nextToken());
        barsJudges = parseStringList(tokens.nextToken());
        beamJudges = parseStringList(tokens.nextToken());
        floorJudges = parseStringList(tokens.nextToken());

// The carpool is a list of list, assume each list is separated by ;'s
        if (tokens.hasMoreTokens())
        {
            StringTokenizer carPoolStrings = new StringTokenizer(
                tokens.nextToken(), ";");

            carPools = new Vector();
            while (carPoolStrings.hasMoreTokens())
            {
                carPools.addElement(parseStringList(carPoolStrings.nextToken()));
            }
        }
    }

/** Creates a string representing the data for this class */
    public String toDataString()
    {
        StringBuffer dataBuffer = new StringBuffer();

// Store the fields in the string separated by |'s
        dataBuffer.append(meetName);
        dataBuffer.append("|");
        dataBuffer.append(gym);
        dataBuffer.append("|");
        dataBuffer.append(dates);
        dataBuffer.append("|");
        dataBuffer.append(levels);
        dataBuffer.append("|");

// Store the lists of data
        dataBuffer.append(createStringList(vaultJudges));
        dataBuffer.append("|");
        dataBuffer.append(createStringList(barsJudges));
        dataBuffer.append("|");
        dataBuffer.append(createStringList(beamJudges));
        dataBuffer.append("|");
        dataBuffer.append(createStringList(floorJudges));
        dataBuffer.append("|");

// Store the car pool as a list of lists, with each list separates by ;'s
        Enumeration e = carPools.elements();

        boolean first = true;

        while (e.hasMoreElements())
        {
            if (!first)
            {
                dataBuffer.append(";");
            }
            else
```

LISTING 18.2 CONTINUED

```
            {
                first = false;
            }
            dataBuffer.append(createStringList((Vector) e.nextElement()));
        }

        return dataBuffer.toString();
    }

/** Creates a string containing a list of elements separated by :'s */
    public String createStringList(Vector v)
    {
        StringBuffer dataBuffer = new StringBuffer();

        Enumeration e = v.elements();

        boolean first = true;

        while (e.hasMoreElements())
        {
            if (!first)
            {
                dataBuffer.append(":");
            }
            else
            {
                first = false;
            }
            dataBuffer.append(e.nextElement());
        }

        return dataBuffer.toString();
    }

/** Parses a string of colon-separated items into a vector */
    public Vector parseStringList(String list)
    {
        Vector v = new Vector();

        StringTokenizer tokens = new StringTokenizer(list, ":");

        while (tokens.hasMoreElements())
        {
            v.addElement(tokens.nextToken());
        }

        return v;
    }
}
```

Note

Notice that Meet.java implements `java.io.Serializable` so it can be stored using object serialization as well as by its own string mechanism.

You could keep all of the items in memory, update them, and rewrite the data file whenever the in-memory information changes. The disadvantage of this technique is that you are restricting yourself to a single Java Virtual Machine. If you tried to run multiple copies of the application, each one would have its own unique copy of the data, and whenever the data changed in one application, it would rewrite the data file with its own copy of the data. The other copy of the application wouldn't see these changes; however, when it received an update, it would rewrite the data file again, losing the changes stored by the first copy of the application.

You can make the application a little more scalable by introducing file locking and operating on the data in the file when you need to make a change. Listing 18.3 shows a Java class that manages a file of `Meet` objects, allowing you to add, update, delete, and read all the objects.

LISTING 18.3 SOURCE CODE FOR `MeetManager.java`

```
package usingjsp;

import java.io.*;
import java.util.*;

/** Manages the meet file using the file locking mechanism. */
public class MeetManager
{
    public void updateMeet(Meet meet)
        throws IOException
    {
        FileLock lock = new FileLock("meets");

        if (lock.lock())
        {
            BufferedReader reader = new BufferedReader(
                lock.getReader());

            PrintWriter writer = new PrintWriter(
                lock.getRewriteWriter());

            String line;

// Read each line in the file
            while ((line = reader.readLine()) != null)
            {
// Get the Meet object stored in the string
                Meet currMeet = new Meet(line);

// If this is the meet that is being updated, write out the
// new version of the meet instead of the old one
                if (currMeet.meetName.equalsIgnoreCase(meet.meetName))
                {
                    writer.println(meet.toDataString());
                }
                else
                {
```

LISTING 18.3 CONTINUED

```
// Otherwise, just copy the line
                    writer.println(line);
                }
            }

            writer.close();
            reader.close();
            lock.unlock();
        }
        else
        {
            throw new IOException("Unable to lock Meet file");
        }
    }

    public void deleteMeet(String meetName)
        throws IOException
    {
        FileLock lock = new FileLock("meets");

        if (lock.lock())
        {
            BufferedReader reader = new BufferedReader(
                lock.getReader());

            PrintWriter writer = new PrintWriter(
                lock.getRewriteWriter());

            String line;

// Read each line in the file
            while ((line = reader.readLine()) != null)
            {
// Get the Meet object stored in the string
                Meet currMeet = new Meet(line);

// If this is the meet that is being deleted, just skip the line
                if (currMeet.meetName.equalsIgnoreCase(meetName))
                {
                    continue;
                }
                else
                {
// Otherwise, just copy the line
                    writer.println(line);
                }
            }

            writer.close();
            reader.close();
            lock.unlock();
        }
        else
        {
            throw new IOException("Unable to lock Meet file");
```

```
        }
    }

    public void addMeet(Meet newMeet)
        throws IOException
    {
        FileLock lock = new FileLock("meets");

        if (lock.lock())
        {
// Instead of copying, you can just open the file for append to
// add a new meet
            PrintWriter writer = new PrintWriter(
                lock.getOutputStream(true));    // open for append

            writer.println(newMeet.toDataString());

            writer.close();
            lock.unlock();
        }
        else
        {
            throw new IOException("Unable to lock Meet file");
        }
    }

/** Returns a vector of all the meets in the file */
    public Vector getAllMeets()
        throws IOException
    {
        Vector v = new Vector();

        FileLock lock = new FileLock("meets");

        if (lock.lock())
        {
            BufferedReader reader = new BufferedReader(
                lock.getReader());

            String line;

// Read each line, create a meet from the line,
// then add the meet to the vector
            while ((line = reader.readLine()) != null)
            {
                Meet currMeet = new Meet(line);

                v.addElement(currMeet);
            }

            reader.close();
            lock.unlock();

            return v;
        }
        else
```

LISTING 18.3 CONTINUED

```
            {
                throw new IOException("Unable to lock Meet file");
            }
        }
    }
```

Listing 18.4 shows a JSP that displays a list of the meets known to the `MeetManager` class, allowing you to add, edit, or delete meets.

LISTING 18.4 SOURCE CODE FOR `EditMeetList.jsp`

```
<%@ page language="java" import="usingjsp.*,java.util.*,java.net.*" %>

<html>
<body bgcolor="#ffffff">
<h1>Edit Meets</h1>

<table border=4>
<tr>
<th>Meet<th>Gym<th>Dates<th>Levels
<%
    Vector v = usingjsp.MeetManager.getAllMeets();

    Enumeration e = v.elements();

    while (e.hasMoreElements())
    {
        Meet meet = (Meet) e.nextElement();

%>
<tr>
<td>
<a href="EditMeet.jsp?meetName=<%=URLEncoder.encode(meet.meetName)%>">
    <%=meet.meetName%></a>
<td><%=meet.gym%><td><%=meet.dates%>
<td><%=meet.levels%>
<td>
<a href="DeleteMeet.jsp?meetName=<%=URLEncoder.encode(meet.meetName)%>">
Delete
</a>
<%
    }
%>
</table>

<p>
<a href="EditMeet.jsp">Add a New Meet</a>
</body>
</html>
```

Figure 18.1 shows a list of meets generated by the JSP in Listing 18.4.

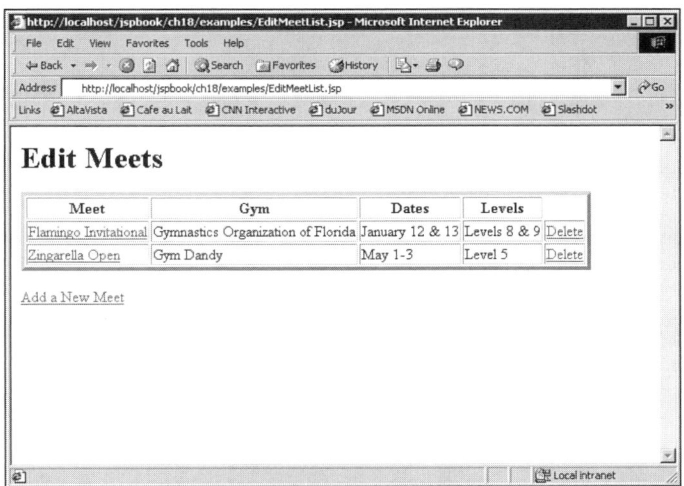

Figure 18.1
A table listing the items in a file may have links to delete or edit the items.

The page to edit a meet is combined with the page to add a new meet. The only thing that can't change during an update is the meet name, because that is used as the unique identifier for the meet. If the edit page is called without a meet name, it makes an input field for the meet name. Otherwise, the meet name is a display-only field. Listing 18.5 shows the JSP for entering a new meet and editing an existing one.

LISTING 18.5 SOURCE CODE FOR EditMeet.jsp

```
<%@ page language="java" import="usingjsp.*,java.net.*,java.util.*" %>
<html>
<body bgcolor="#ffffff">

<form action="SaveMeetChanges.jsp" method="post">
<%
    String meetName = request.getParameter("meetName");

    Meet meet = null;
    boolean isNew = true;

    if (meetName != null)
    {
        Vector v = MeetManager.getAllMeets();

        Enumeration e = v.elements();

        while (e.hasMoreElements())
        {
            Meet currMeet = (Meet) e.nextElement();

            if (currMeet.meetName.equalsIgnoreCase(meetName))
            {
                meet = currMeet;
```

LISTING 18.5 CONTINUED

```
                isNew = false;
                break;
            }
        }
    }

    if (meet == null)
    {
        meet = new Meet();
        meet.gym = "";
        meet.dates = "";
        meet.levels = "";
    }

    String vaultJudges[] = getAssignments(meet.vaultJudges, 2);
    String barsJudges[] = getAssignments(meet.barsJudges, 2);
    String beamJudges[] = getAssignments(meet.beamJudges, 2);
    String floorJudges[] = getAssignments(meet.floorJudges, 2);
%>
<h1>Edit Meet</h1>
<table>
<tr>
<td>Meet Name:
<td>
<%
    if (isNew) {
%><input type="text" name="meetName"><%
    } else {
%><%=meetName%><input type="hidden" name="meetName" value="<%=meetName%>">
<%  } %>
<tr>
<td>Gym: <td><input type="text" name="gym" value="<%=meet.gym%>">
<tr>
<td>Dates: <td><input type="text" name="dates" value="<%=meet.dates%>">
<tr>
<td>Levels: <td><input type="text" name="levels" value="<%=meet.levels%>">
</table>
<p>
<h3>Judging Assignments</h3>
<p>
<table>
<tr>
<td>Vault Assignments
<td><input type="text" name="vaultJudges" value="<%=vaultJudges[0]%>"><br>
<tr>
<td> 
<td><input type="text" name="vaultJudges" value="<%=vaultJudges[1]%>"><br>
<tr>
<td>Bars Assignments
<td><input type="text" name="barsJudges" value="<%=barsJudges[0]%>"><br>
<tr>
<td> 
<td><input type="text" name="barsJudges" value="<%=barsJudges[1]%>"><br>
<tr>
<td>Beam Assignments
```

```
<td><input type="text" name="beamJudges" value="<%=beamJudges[0]%>"><br>
<tr>
<td> 
<td><input type="text" name="beamJudges" value="<%=beamJudges[1]%>"><br>
<tr>
<td>Floor Assignments
<td><input type="text" name="floorJudges" value="<%=floorJudges[0]%>"><br>
<tr>
<td> 
<td><input type="text" name="floorJudges" value="<%=floorJudges[1]%>"><br>
</table>

<h3>Car Pools</h3>
<%
    for (int i=0; i < 4; i++)
    {
        out.println("Car pool #"+(i+1)+":<br>");

        String assignments[] = new String[] { "", "", "", "" };

        if ((meet.carPools != null) && (i < meet.carPools.size()))
        {
            Vector v = (Vector) meet.carPools.elementAt(i);

            assignments = getAssignments(v, 4);
        }

        for (int j=0; j < assignments.length; j++)
        {
%><input type="text" name="<%="carPool"+i%>" value="<%=assignments[j]%>"><br>
<%      }
    }

    if (isNew)
    {
%> <input type="hidden" name="isNew" value="yes"> <%
    }
%>
<p>
<input type="submit" value="Save Changes">
</form>
</body>
</html>
<%!

// Convert a vector into a fixed-size string with empty strings for
// the spots that don't have values
    public static String[] getAssignments(Vector v, int numValues)
    {
        String retval[] = new String[numValues];

        for (int i=0; i < numValues; i++) retval[i] = "";

        if (v != null)
        {
            int vsize = v.size();
```

LISTING 18.5 CONTINUED

```
            for (int i=0; (i < numValues) && (i < vsize); i++)
            {
                retval[i] = (String) v.elementAt(i);
            }
        }

        return retval;
    }
%>
```

Figure 18.2 shows the form generated by the `EditMeet` JSP.

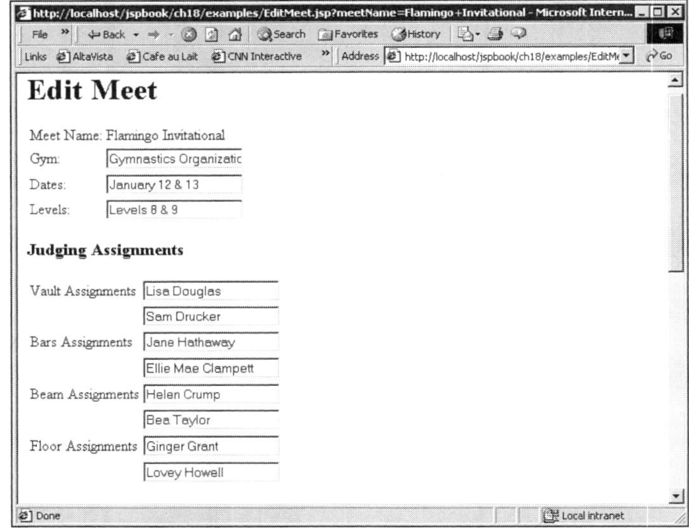

Figure 18.2 You should populate input fields with existing data whenever possible.

The JSP in Listing 18.5 sets up field names to match the names of the elements in the `Meet` object. If the `Meet` class had been implemented as a proper bean, you would be able to copy the fields with the `<jsp:setProperty>` tag. As it is, the SaveMeetChanges.jsp file must copy in each parameter manually, and also do extra work for the parameters that can have multiple values.

Listing 18.6 shows the `SaveMeetChanges` JSP that processes the data from the `EditMeet` JSP and stores the updated/added meet in the meets file.

LISTING 18.6 SOURCE CODE FOR `SaveMeetChanges.jsp`

```
<%@ page language="java" import="usingjsp.*,java.util.*" %>

<html>
<body bgcolor="#ffffff">
<%
```

```
    Meet meet = new Meet();

    meet.meetName = request.getParameter("meetName");
    meet.gym = request.getParameter("gym");
    meet.dates = request.getParameter("dates");
    meet.levels = request.getParameter("levels");

    meet.vaultJudges = getAssignments(
        request.getParameterValues("vaultJudges"));
    meet.barsJudges = getAssignments(
        request.getParameterValues("barsJudges"));
    meet.beamJudges = getAssignments(
        request.getParameterValues("beamJudges"));
    meet.floorJudges = getAssignments(
        request.getParameterValues("floorJudges"));

    meet.carPools = new Vector();

    for (int i=0; i < 4; i++)
    {
        String[] assignments = request.getParameterValues("carPool"+i);

        if (assignments != null)
        {
            Vector v = getAssignments(assignments);
            if (v != null)
            {
                meet.carPools.addElement(v);
            }
        }
    }

    if (request.getParameter("isNew") != null)
    {
        MeetManager.addMeet(meet);
%>
<h1>Meet added!</h1>
<%
    }
    else
    {
        MeetManager.updateMeet(meet);
%>
<h1>Meet updated!</h1>
<%
    }
%>
<p>
<a href="EditMeetList.jsp">Return to Meet List</a>
</body>
</html>

<%!
    public static Vector getAssignments(String[] assignments)
    {
        Vector v = new Vector();
```

LISTING 18.6 CONTINUED

```
        for (int i=0; i < assignments.length; i++)
        {
            if (assignments[i].trim().length() > 0)
            {
                v.addElement(assignments[i]);
            }
        }

        if (v.size() > 0)
        {
            return v;
        }
        else
        {
            return null;
        }
    }
%>
```

Listing 18.7 shows the JSP that allows you to delete an existing meet. As you can see, the delete process is very simple, since it relies on the `MeetManager` class to do all the work.

LISTING 18.7 SOURCE CODE FOR `DeleteMeet.jsp`

```
<%@ page language="java" import="usingjsp.*" %>

<html>
<body bgcolor="#ffffff">

<%
    MeetManager.deleteMeet(request.getParameter("meetName"));
%>
<h1>Meet Deleted!</h1>
<p>
<a href="EditMeetList.jsp">Return to Meet List</a>
</body>
</html>
```

STORING DATA WITH OBJECT SERIALIZATION

The `Meet` class performs some tricky operations when it copies its data into a string. Each data item is separated by a vertical bar. If you want to have a vertical bar in a data item, you need some way to tell whether the bar is part of the data or if it is a separator. For the lists of items, each list item is separated by a colon. Again, if you want to have a colon in the data, you must have some mechanism to tell them apart. Likewise, the list of lists uses a semicolon between each list. As you can see, storing complex data in string form is a difficult process.

If you don't care what the data file looks like, you can use object serialization to store the data items. Serialization can store a wide variety of objects in very complex structures. If you want to store a vector of items, you just serialize the whole vector rather than writing out each element. Listing 18.8 shows how the `MeetManager` class can be modified to use serialization instead of the custom string operations. The real savings would be in the `Meet` class, which would no longer need to have the operations to read itself from a string and write itself to a string.

Listing 18.8 Source Code for `MeetManager2.java`

```
package usingjsp;

import java.io.*;
import java.util.*;

/** Manages the meet file using the file locking mechanism. */
public class MeetManager2
{
    public static void updateMeet(Meet meet)
        throws IOException
    {
        FileLock lock = new FileLock("meets.dat");

        if (lock.lock())
        {
// Get all the available meets
            Vector meets = getMeets(lock);

// Look for one with the same name as this one
            for (int i=0; i < meets.size(); i++)
            {
                Meet currMeet = (Meet) meets.elementAt(i);

                if (currMeet.meetName.equalsIgnoreCase(meet.meetName))
                {
// Replace the old meet with the new version
                    meets.setElementAt(meet, i);
                    break;
                }
            }

// Copy the meets back into the save file
            setMeets(lock, meets);

            lock.unlock();
        }
        else
        {
            throw new IOException("Unable to lock Meet file");
        }
    }

    public static void deleteMeet(String meetName)
        throws IOException
    {
        FileLock lock = new FileLock("meets.dat");
```

LISTING 18.8 CONTINUED

```
        if (lock.lock())
        {
// Get a list of all the meets
            Vector meets = getMeets(lock);

            for (int i=0; i < meets.size(); i++)
            {
                Meet currMeet = (Meet) meets.elementAt(i);

// Look for the meet with the same name as the meet to be deleted
                if (currMeet.meetName.equalsIgnoreCase(meetName))
                {
// Remove the meet from the vector
                    meets.removeElementAt(i);
                    break;
                }
            }

// Copy the vector of meets back to the file
            setMeets(lock, meets);

            lock.unlock();
        }
        else
        {
            throw new IOException("Unable to lock Meet file");
        }
    }

    public static void addMeet(Meet newMeet)
        throws IOException
    {
        FileLock lock = new FileLock("meets.dat");

        if (lock.lock())
        {
// Get a list of all the meets
            Vector meets = getMeets(lock);

// Add the new meet to the vector
            meets.addElement(newMeet);

// Save the new list of meets back to the file
            setMeets(lock, meets);

            lock.unlock();
        }
        else
        {
            throw new IOException("Unable to lock Meet file");
        }
    }

/** Returns a vector of all the meets in the file */
    public static Vector getAllMeets()
```

```
        throws IOException
    {
        FileLock lock = new FileLock("meets.dat");

        if (lock.lock())
        {
            Vector v = getMeets(lock);

            lock.unlock();

            return v;
        }
        else
        {
            throw new IOException("Unable to lock Meet file");
        }
    }

/** Gets a vector containing all the meets */

    public static Vector getMeets(FileLock lock)
        throws IOException
    {
// Get an input stream to read the data file
        InputStream in = lock.getInputStream();

        try
        {

// Try to wrap an object input stream around the normal input stream
// If the file is empty, this operation throws an error, so in order to
// close the file properly, you still need a reference to the file, that's
// why the lock.getInputStream is performed ahead of time.
            ObjectInputStream obIn = new ObjectInputStream(in);

// Read in the vector of objects
            Vector v = (Vector) obIn.readObject();

            in.close();
            return v;
        }
        catch (Exception ignore)
        {
        }

// Make sure the file is closed
        if (in != null)
        {
            in.close();
        }

        return new Vector();
    }

    public static void setMeets(FileLock lock, Vector meets)
        throws IOException
```

LISTING 18.8 CONTINUED

```
    {
        ObjectOutputStream out = new ObjectOutputStream(
            lock.getRewriteOutputStream());

        out.writeObject(meets);

        out.close();
    }
}
```

One of the difficulties you may face if you use serialization is that the serialization code is very strict about object versions. When you save an object, the serialization code computes a special checksum value that encompasses the method and attribute names in the object. When you deserialize an object, the serialization again computes the checksum on the class you are deserializing and compares that value with the checksum stored in the serialized data. If the checksums don't match, you can't deserialize the object. Unfortunately, since the checksum includes method names, if you add even a single method to an object, you make previous serialized copies of the object unreadable, even though the data hasn't changed.

The object serialization code has special rules for matching up data fields to handle cases where a field appears or disappears from one version to the next. You might wonder why it matters if the checksum almost always prevents the deserialization of a slightly different version of the object. The trick is, you can mark an object with a special ID that takes the place of the checksum. Even if you add new methods and new data, if a class has the same ID as the ID stored in a serialized object, the serialization code will attempt to deserialize the object. The name of this special ID is `serialVersionUID`. You must declare it in your class as `static final long`, like this:

```
static final long serialVersionUID = 12345;
```

You can specify anything for the serial version UID, but you should at least try to set the UID of the original version of the class to the checksum that the serialization code would use for that class. You can use the `serialver` command to compute the checksum for a class. The `serialver` command gives you back the declaration for the serial version UID of the class you give it. For example, if you type

```
serialver usingjsp.Meet
```

the `serialver` command will generate the following declaration:

```
static final long serialVersionUID = -8111204589410480230L;
```

Once you include this declaration in the `Meet` class, the current version of the `Meet` class will be compatible with future versions. That is, when you serialize the current version and then change it, the later version will still be able to read the original serialized version.

If you are having trouble storing or retrieving objects using serialization, see "Serialization," in the "Troubleshooting" section at the end of this chapter.

STORING DATA IN A RANDOM ACCESS FILE

One of the disadvantages of both text files and serialized object files is that you must rewrite the entire file whenever you need to make a change. For small files, that's no big deal. When you have a very large file, however, copying the file over and over is a very time consuming process.

If you can calculate a reasonable maximum record size, or create an index file, you can store your objects in a random access file. Using an index file is a complex process, because the records can be of varying lengths. When you delete a record, you leave a hole in the file that can only be filled by a record with the same or smaller size. Managing a file like this is roughly the same as managing memory allocation.

Dealing with fixed record sizes is much easier. You can track objects by their position in the file rather than by some data item. In other words, if you want to update an item, like a `Meet`, you can go directly to where that item is stored rather than looping through the file looking for an item with a particular name.

Listing 18.9 shows the `MeetManager` class modified to use a random access file in conjunction with object serialization.

LISTING 18.9 SOURCE CODE FOR `MeetManager3.java`

```
package usingjsp;

import java.io.*;
import java.util.*;

/** Manages the meet file using the file locking mechanism. */
public class MeetManager3
{
    public static void updateMeet(Meet3 meet)
        throws IOException
    {
        FileLock lock = new FileLock("meets.rnd");

        if (lock.lock())
        {

// Open the locked file as a random-access file
            RandomAccessFile file = lock.getRandomAccessFile();

// Go to the position in the file where this meet is located
            file.seek(meet.meetIndex * Meet3.getMaxSize());

// Convert this meet into an array of bytes
            byte[] meetBytes = getMeetBytes(meet);

// Write the meet into the file
            file.write(meetBytes);

            file.close();
```

LISTING 18.9 CONTINUED

```
            lock.unlock();
        }
        else
        {
            throw new IOException("Unable to lock Meet file");
        }
    }

    public static void deleteMeet(int meetIndex)
        throws IOException
    {
        FileLock lock = new FileLock("meets.rnd");

        if (lock.lock())
        {
// Open the locked file as a random-access file
            RandomAccessFile file = lock.getRandomAccessFile();

// Go to the position in the file where this meet is located
            file.seek(meetIndex * Meet3.getMaxSize());

// Set the value of the object at this location to null (and convert the
// null into an array of bytes)
            byte[] meetBytes = getMeetBytes(null);

// Write the null object back to the file
            file.write(meetBytes);

            file.close();
            lock.unlock();
        }
    }

    public static void addMeet(Meet3 newMeet)
        throws IOException
    {
        FileLock lock = new FileLock("meets.rnd");

        if (lock.lock())
        {
// Open the locked file as a random-access file
            RandomAccessFile file = lock.getRandomAccessFile();

// Calculate the number of meets. The end of the file may be less than
// Meet3.getMaxSize bytes long, so add padding to the file length to make
// sure the calculation comes out right
            int numMeets = (int) ((file.length() + Meet3.getMaxSize() - 1)
                 / Meet3.getMaxSize());

            byte[] buffer = new byte[Meet3.getMaxSize()];

            int newIndex = numMeets;

// Search through the file for any blank spots
            for (int i=0; i < numMeets; i++)
```

```
            {
                file.read(buffer);
                Meet3 currMeet = getMeetFromBytes(buffer);

// If there is a null meet, the new meet can be put there
                if (currMeet == null)
                {
                    newIndex = i;
                    break;
                }
            }

// Store the new meet wherever there was a blank spot, or at the
// end of the file.
            newMeet.meetIndex = newIndex;
            file.seek(newMeet.meetIndex * Meet3.getMaxSize());
            byte[] meetBytes = getMeetBytes(newMeet);
            file.write(meetBytes);

            file.close();
            lock.unlock();
        }
        else
        {
            throw new IOException("Unable to lock Meet file");
        }
    }

/** Returns a vector of all the meets in the file */
    public static Vector getAllMeets()
        throws IOException
    {
        FileLock lock = new FileLock("meets.rnd");

        if (lock.lock())
        {
// Open the locked file as a random-access file
            RandomAccessFile file = lock.getRandomAccessFile();

// Calculate the number of meets. The end of the file may be less than
// Meet3.getMaxSize bytes long, so add padding to the file length to make
// sure the calculation comes out right
            int numMeets = (int) ((file.length() + Meet3.getMaxSize() - 1)
                 / Meet3.getMaxSize());

            byte[] buffer = new byte[Meet3.getMaxSize()];

            Vector v = new Vector();

// Loop through all the meets
            for (int i=0; i < numMeets; i++)
            {
// Read in the byte buffer representing the serialized meet
                file.read(buffer);

// Convert the bytes into an object
```

PART III
CH 18

LISTING 18.9 CONTINUED

```
                Meet3 currMeet = getMeetFromBytes(buffer);

// If the object isn't null, add it to the current list
                if (currMeet != null)
                {
                    v.addElement(currMeet);
                }
            }

            file.close();
            lock.unlock();

            return v;
        }
        else
        {
            throw new IOException("Unable to lock Meet file");
        }
    }

    public static Meet3 getMeet(int meetIndex)
        throws IOException
    {
        FileLock lock = new FileLock("meets.rnd");

        if (lock.lock())
        {

// Open the locked file as a random-access file
            RandomAccessFile file = lock.getRandomAccessFile();

// Go to the position in the file where this meet is located
            file.seek(meetIndex * Meet3.getMaxSize());
            byte[] buffer = new byte[Meet3.getMaxSize()];

// Read in the byte buffer representing the serialized meet
            file.read(buffer);

// Convert the bytes into an object
            Meet3 meet = getMeetFromBytes(buffer);

            file.close();
            lock.unlock();

            return meet;
        }
        else
        {
            throw new IOException("Unable to lock Meet file");
        }
    }

/** Converts a Meet3 object into an array of bytes */

    public static byte[] getMeetBytes(Meet3 meet)
```

```
        throws IOException
    {
// Create a ByteArrayOutputStream that will convert data written to
// a stream into an array of bytes
        ByteArrayOutputStream out = new ByteArrayOutputStream(
            Meet3.getMaxSize());

// Wrap an ObjectOutputStream around the byte array stream
        ObjectOutputStream obOut = new ObjectOutputStream(out);

// Write the object out to the stream
        obOut.writeObject(meet);

// Convert the stream into an array of bytes
        byte[] bytes = out.toByteArray();

// Free up any resources used by the stream
        out.close();
        return bytes;
    }

/** Converts an array of bytes into a Meet3 object */
    public static Meet3 getMeetFromBytes(byte[] bytes)
        throws IOException
    {
// Treat the array of bytes as a stream
        ByteArrayInputStream in = new ByteArrayInputStream(bytes);

// Wrap an ObjectInputStream around the byte stream
        ObjectInputStream obIn = new ObjectInputStream(in);

        Meet3 meet = null;

        try
        {
// Read the object from the stream
            meet = (Meet3) obIn.readObject();
        }
        catch (ClassNotFoundException exc)
        {
            throw new IOException("Invalid class stored in file");
        }

// Free up any resources used by the stream
        in.close();
        return meet;
    }
}
```

TROUBLESHOOTING

FILE LOCKING

Why doesn't locking ever work?

Chances are that you are not allowed to rename the existing file or you have misspelled the name of the file.

Why does locking work for a while and then stop?

If your program crashes while it has the file locked, the file remains locked (that is, it never gets renamed). You will need to rename the file manually to get locking to work again.

SERIALIZATION

Why do I get a `NotSerializableException` when I write an object using `writeObject`?

In order to write an object using the Java Serialization API, you must mark the object as being okay for serialization by declaring that it implements the `java.io.Serializable` interface.

I serialized an object on one computer but I can't read it from another computer; what's wrong?

Obviously, make sure the file hasn't been corrupted to start with. If you transfer the file via FTP, make sure you use BINARY transfer. Beyond that, if you have changed any of the declarations in the class, including adding/removing methods or even method parameters, the classes will be incompatible. The only way you can still recover the data is to set the `serialVersionUID` of the new class to the value from the old class.

I know the class versions are the same and the file is intact; why can I still not read the file?

In almost all cases, the problems reading the file are caused by garbled files or incompatible class versions. Occasionally, however, you also run into problems when you use different Java Virtual Machines. Very old versions of Microsoft's Java VM might not be compatible with some of the later Sun VMs. You shouldn't see any problem going from one hardware platform to another (that is from Intel to Sparc), but virtual machine differences will occasionally cause problems.

CHAPTER 19

Building a Two-Tiered Web Application

In this chapter

Databases play a huge role in a large number of Web sites. Companies frequently keep product information, orders, schedules, and even technical support information in databases. Databases take much of the hassle out of storing and retrieving data. You don't have to worry about converting an object into a string to store it in a file, or using object serialization (unless you store serialized objects in the database). Instead, you get to worry about things like connection pooling and transactions.

In Chapter 7, "Organizing Your Application," you saw a servlet that creates a JDBC connection in its `init` method and disconnects the connection in the `destroy` method. The servlet uses a single connection and relies on the `synchronize` keyword to keep multiple threads from executing queries at the same time. There are a number of problems with this approach. For example, you probably want to share one or more connections between different servlets. You could synchronize on the connection instead of synchronizing the `service` method in the servlet. That would allow multiple servlets to share a connection in a thread-safe manner.

Using a connection pool is an even better approach. A servlet asks the pool for a connection, uses the connection, and then returns it to the pool. You don't need to synchronize because each thread asks for its own connection.

CREATING A CONNECTION POOL

A connection pool is really just a container of connections. The idea is that a connection is expensive to set up, so once you establish a connection, you want to keep it around and use it over again. You pool the connections together so each class doesn't create its own private connection. Some classes need a connection more frequently than others do.

Listing 19.1 shows a very simple connection pool. It keeps the available connections in a stack, and if there are no connections in the pool, it creates a new connection.

LISTING 19.1 SOURCE CODE FOR `SimpleConnectionPool.java`

```
package usingjsp;

import java.sql.*;
import java.util.*;

/** A simple connection pool that allocates new connections where
 *  there are no more connections.
 */
public class SimpleConnectionPool implements IConnectionPool
{
    protected Stack pool;
    protected String connectionURL;
    protected String userName;
    protected String password;

/** Creates a new connection pool that creates connections using
 *  the specified URL, user name and password */
    public SimpleConnectionPool(String aConnectionURL,
```

```
        String aUserName, String aPassword)
    {
        connectionURL = aConnectionURL;
        userName = aUserName;
        password = aPassword;
        pool = new Stack();
    }

/** Gets a connection from the pool or creates one if the pool is empty */
    public synchronized Connection getConnection()
        throws SQLException
    {
// If the pool isn't empty, grab a connection from it
        if (!pool.empty())
        {
            return (Connection) pool.pop();
        }
        else
        {
// Otherwise, create a new connection
            return DriverManager.getConnection(connectionURL,
                userName, password);
        }
    }

/** Returns a connection to the pool */
    public synchronized void releaseConnection(Connection conn)
        throws SQLException
    {
        pool.push(conn);
    }
}
```


Notice that the `SimpleConnectionPool` class extends an interface called `IConnectionPool`. You will see various ways to implement a connection pool in this chapter. The examples refer to the pools through the `IConnectionPool` interface, so the implementation of the connection pool can be changed easily. Listing 19.2 shows the definition of the `IConnectionPool` interface.

LISTING 19.2 SOURCE CODE FOR `IConnectionPool.java`

```
package usingjsp;

import java.sql.*;

/** An interface defining common methods that a connection pool should
 *  implement.
 */
public interface IConnectionPool
{
    public Connection getConnection() throws SQLException;
    public void releaseConnection(Connection conn) throws SQLException;
}
```

Listing 19.3 shows a JSP similar to one of the examples from Chapter 7. It executes a query and displays the results in a table. Notice that the pool is initialized in the `jspInit` method. In practice, you'd need to store the connection pool in the application object and take steps to ensure that there is only one copy of the pool. You will see this demonstrated later in this chapter.

LISTING 19.3 SOURCE CODE FOR `SimplePoolDemo.jsp`

```
<%@ page language="java" import="java.sql.*,java.util.*,usingjsp.*" %>
<%
    Connection conn = null;

    try
    {
        conn = connectionPool.getConnection();

        Statement statement = conn.createStatement();

        ResultSet results = statement.executeQuery("select * from person");

        Vector v = new Vector();

        while (results.next())
        {
            v.addElement(new Person(results));
        }

        request.setAttribute("people", v);

        statement.close();
    }
    finally
    {
        if (conn != null)
        {
            connectionPool.releaseConnection(conn);
        }
    }
%>

<html>
<body bgcolor="#ffffff">

<jsp:include page="/servlet/usingjsp.TableServlet" flush="true">
    <jsp:param name="data" value="people"/>

    <jsp:param name="tableOptions" value="BORDER=4"/>

    <jsp:param name="column" value="name"/>
    <jsp:param name="columnType" value="data"/>
    <jsp:param name="columnHeader" value="Name"/>

    <jsp:param name="column" value="age"/>
    <jsp:param name="columnType" value="data"/>
    <jsp:param name="columnHeader" value="Age"/>
```

```
    <jsp:param name="column" value="city"/>
    <jsp:param name="columnType" value="data"/>
    <jsp:param name="columnHeader" value="City"/>

    <jsp:param name="column" value="state"/>
    <jsp:param name="columnType" value="data"/>
    <jsp:param name="columnHeader" value="State"/>

    <jsp:param name="column" value="country"/>
    <jsp:param name="columnType" value="data"/>
    <jsp:param name="columnHeader" value="Country"/>

    <jsp:param name="column" value="postalCode"/>
    <jsp:param name="columnType" value="data"/>
    <jsp:param name="columnHeader" value="Postal Code"/>

    <jsp:param name="column" value="email"/>
    <jsp:param name="columnType" value="data"/>
    <jsp:param name="columnHeader" value="E-Mail"/>
</jsp:include>
</body>
</html>

<%!
    protected IConnectionPool connectionPool;

    public void jspInit()
    {
        try
        {
            Class.forName("interbase.interclient.Driver");
        } catch (Exception ignore) {}

        connectionPool = new SimpleConnectionPool(
            "jdbc:interbase://localhost/h:/jspbook/database/ibexample",
            "SYSDBA", "masterkey");
    }
%>
```


Note

The `SimplePoolDemo` JSP uses a `finally` block to release its connection. This ensures that the connection is released no matter what kind of errors or exceptions occur. If you aren't careful to release pooled connections, you may either run out of them or allocate them continuously. Always use a `finally` block to release the connection.

If you are having trouble setting up a connection pool, see "Connection Pools," in the "Troubleshooting" section at the end of this chapter.

Mapping Objects to Database Tables

If you do any significant amount of database programming, you will probably find it tedious to work directly with SQL. After using a nice object-oriented language like Java, SQL can be quite a letdown. Many developers map Java objects onto database tables—that is, they make a Java object that represents a row in a database table. When you create a new object, you create one of these data objects, initialize its fields, and tell the object to insert itself into the database. This technique is called object-to-relational mapping, or ORM.

If you can get to the point where you write no SQL, you are doing quite well. There are several commercial packages that perform object-to-relational mapping in a very clean, straightforward way. TOPLink, from The Object People (`www.theobjectpeople.com`), is an excellent ORM framework. One of the benefits of TOPLink is that it caches objects in memory after it has read them, and it provides connection pooling so you don't have to write it. If you access the object again, TOPLink doesn't need to read the object from the database again. Your application usually runs significantly faster when you can cache your data objects.

A Poor-Man's Object-to-Relational Mapping

If you are only working with a few objects and your database structure is fairly simple, you can get away with creating your own object-to-relational mapping, although you may need to write a little SQL code.

Listing 19.4 shows an abstract database object class that simplifies your database coding. Each Java class you map to a database table must supply its own insert, update and delete statements and must be able to read its fields from a `ResultSet` object. The advantage of this base class is that it takes care of creating, executing, and releasing the SQL statement.

Listing 19.4 Source Code for `DatabaseObject.java`

```
package usingjsp;

import java.sql.*;
import java.util.*;

/** A base class for objects that map to database tables */

public abstract class DatabaseObject
{
/** Gets all the objects in a table */
    public Vector getAll(Connection conn)
        throws SQLException
    {
        return getAll(conn, null, null);
    }

/** Gets all the objects in a table matching a specific where clause */
    public Vector getAll(Connection conn, String whereClause)
        throws SQLException
    {
        return getAll(conn, whereClause, null);
    }

/** Gets all the objects in a table matching a specific where clause
    and allows you to specify additional tables that are used in the
    where clause. */
```

```
    public Vector getAll(Connection conn, String whereClause,
        String additionalTables)
        throws SQLException
    {
        Statement s = null;

        try
        {
            s = conn.createStatement();

            Vector v = new Vector();

// Build the query. The basic query is "select <fields> from table"
            String query = "select "+getFieldList()+" from "+getTableName();

// Add the additional tables if needed
            if (additionalTables != null)
            {
                query = query + "," + additionalTables;
            }

// Add the where clause if needed
            if (whereClause != null)
            {
                query = query + " where "+whereClause;
            }

// Perform the query
            ResultSet results = s.executeQuery(query);

// Create a vector of the results
            while (results.next())
            {
                v.addElement(createInstance(results));
            }

            return v;
        }
        finally
        {
            if (s != null)
            {
                try { s.close(); } catch (Exception ignore) {}
            }
        }
    }

/** Executes an arbitrary query string that should return all the
 *  fields in the table just like the other queries. */
    public Vector executeQuery(Connection conn, String query)
        throws SQLException
    {
        Statement s = null;

        try
        {
```

LISTING 19.4 CONTINUED

```
            s = conn.createStatement();

            Vector v = new Vector();

// Execute the query
            ResultSet results = s.executeQuery(query);

// Create a vector containing the results
            while (results.next())
            {
                v.addElement(createInstance(results));
            }

            return v;
        }
        finally
        {
            if (s != null)
            {
                try { s.close(); } catch (Exception ignore) {}
            }
        }
    }

/** Inserts an object into the database */
    public int insert(Connection conn)
        throws SQLException
    {
        PreparedStatement s = null;

        try
        {
// Ask this object to create its own insert statement
            s = conn.prepareStatement(getInsertStatement());

// Populate the insert statement with the data values
            prepareInsertStatement(s);

// Perform the insert
            return s.executeUpdate();
        }
        finally
        {
            if (s != null)
            {
                try { s.close(); } catch (Exception ignore) {}
            }
        }
    }

// Returns a list of the fields in the table (used for select)
    public abstract String getFieldList();

/** Returns a list of fields in the table while specifying a specific
 *  table for the field names, aliasing the table.field names back to the
 *  original name. For example, you might want to query from table A and
```

```
 *  table B, each containing a field F. If you do "select F from A,B ..." you
 *  might get an error because F is ambiguous. You need to do
 *  "select A.F as F from A,B ...". This routine takes the original field
 *  list and creates a list of such aliases.
 */
    public String getFieldList(String tableName)
    {
// Create a tokenizer to parse through the original list
        StringTokenizer fieldList = new StringTokenizer(
            getFieldList(), ",");

// Create the string buffer to hold the resulting list
        StringBuffer newList = new StringBuffer();
        boolean first = true;

        while (fieldList.hasMoreTokens())
        {
            String field = fieldList.nextToken();

            if (!first) newList.append(',');
            first = false;
            newList.append(tableName);
            newList.append('.');
            newList.append(field);
            newList.append(" as ");
            newList.append(field);
        }

        return newList.toString();
    }

/** Creates an insert statement to be used in a PreparedStatement */
    public abstract String getInsertStatement();

/** Stores this object's data in the PreparedStatement returned by
 *  prepareInsertStatement. */
    public abstract void prepareInsertStatement(PreparedStatement s)
        throws SQLException;

/** Updates the database row containing this object */
    public int update(Connection conn)
        throws SQLException
    {
        PreparedStatement s = null;

        try
        {
            s = conn.prepareStatement(getUpdateStatement());

            prepareUpdateStatement(s);

            return s.executeUpdate();
        }
        finally
        {
            if (s != null)
```

LISTING 19.4 CONTINUED

```
            {
                try { s.close(); } catch (Exception ignore) {}
            }
        }
    }

    public abstract String getUpdateStatement();
    public abstract void prepareUpdateStatement(PreparedStatement s)
        throws SQLException;

/** Deletes this object from the database */
    public int delete(Connection conn)
        throws SQLException
    {
        PreparedStatement s = null;

        try
        {
            s = conn.prepareStatement(getDeleteStatement());

            prepareDeleteStatement(s);

            return s.executeUpdate();
        }
        finally
        {
            if (s != null)
            {
                try { s.close(); } catch (Exception ignore) {}
            }
        }
    }

/** Returns the sequence number used to insert this object. This method
 *  is very database-dependent. This version is geared towards the
 *  mySQL database.
 */
    public int getSequenceNumber(Connection conn)
        throws SQLException
    {
        Statement s = null;

        try
        {
            s = conn.createStatement();

            ResultSet results = s.executeQuery(
                "select last_insert_id()");

            if (results.next())
            {
                return results.getInt(1);
            }
            else
            {
                throw new SQLException(
```

```
                    "Unable to generate sequence number");
            }

        }
        finally
        {
            if (s != null)
            {
                try { s.close(); } catch (Exception ignore) {}
            }
        }
    }

    public abstract String getDeleteStatement();
    public abstract void prepareDeleteStatement(PreparedStatement s)
        throws SQLException;

    public abstract String getTableName();
    public abstract DatabaseObject createInstance(ResultSet results)
        throws SQLException;

    public String getSequenceGenerator() { return null; }
}
```

AN EXAMPLE Data OBJECT

Listing 19.5 shows an example of a `data` object. The object is mapped to a table defined by the following SQL statement:

```
create table developer
    ( username varchar(10) not null primary key,
      pword varchar(10),
      developer varchar(50) not null,
      unique(developer))
```

The table is part of a problem reporting system that you will see later in this chapter. A developer logs into the problem reporting system using a username and password defined in the `developer` table. The `developer` column in the table is the full name of the developer associated with the username.

LISTING 19.5 SOURCE CODE FOR Developer.java

```
package usingjsp.problemreport;

import usingjsp.DatabaseObject;
import java.sql.*;

/** A data object representing a developer in the problem reporting
 *  system.
 */
public class Developer extends DatabaseObject
    implements java.io.Serializable
{
```

LISTING 19.5 CONTINUED

```
    public String developer;
    public String userName;
    public String password;

    public Developer()
    {
    }

    public Developer(ResultSet results)
        throws SQLException
    {
        developer = results.getString("developer");
        userName = results.getString("userName");
        password = results.getString("pword");
    }

    public String getDeveloper() { return developer; }
    public void setDeveloper(String aDeveloper)
        { developer = aDeveloper; }

    public String getUserName() { return userName; }
    public void setUserName(String aUserName)
        { userName = aUserName; }

    public String getPassword() { return password; }
    public void setPassword(String aPassword)
        { password = aPassword; }

    public String getTableName() { return "developer"; }

    public DatabaseObject createInstance(ResultSet results)
        throws SQLException
    {
        return new Developer(results);
    }

    public String getFieldList() { return "developer,username,pword"; }

    public String getInsertStatement()
    {
        return "insert into developer (developer, username, pword) "+
            " values (?,?,?)";
    }

    public void prepareInsertStatement(PreparedStatement s)
        throws SQLException
    {
        s.setString(1, developer);
        s.setString(2, userName);
        s.setString(3, password);
    }

    public String getUpdateStatement()
    {
        return "update developer set developer=?, pword=? "+
            " where username=?";
```

```
    }

    public void prepareUpdateStatement(PreparedStatement s)
        throws SQLException
    {
        s.setString(1, developer);
        s.setString(2, password);
        s.setString(3, userName);
    }

    public String getDeleteStatement()
    {
        return "delete from developer where username=?";
    }

    public void prepareDeleteStatement(PreparedStatement s)
        throws SQLException
    {
        s.setString(1, userName);
    }
}
```

Notice that the `Developer` class interacts very little with the JDBC API. Instead, the `Developer` class simply describes how it should be inserted, deleted, and updated in the database. It also describes its table name and its fields. In other words, the `Developer` class takes a passive role in database operations. The `DatabaseObject` class performs the interaction with the JDBC API and calls the various methods `Developer` class to get the database information specific to the `Developer` class.

Listing 19.7 shows a slightly more complicated object, and another part of the problem reporting system. The `ProblemReport` class showing in Listing 19.7 uses a sequence number as its primary key. Listing 19.6 shows the SQL statement that defines the table used by the `ProblemReport` class. The `AUTO_INCREMENT` flag is a feature of the MySQL database package. Other databases have different ways of specifying an automatically generated ID field.

LISTING 19.6 SQL COMMAND TO CREATE THE `problem_report` TABLE

```
create table problem_report
    ( problem_id integer not null primary key auto_increment,
      entered timestamp,
      system varchar(20),
      subsystem varchar(20),
      originator varchar(50),
      description text,
      priority integer,
      status varchar(20),
      ecd date,
      notes blob)
```

The `problem_report` table contains a blob object, which is used to store a Java object using object serialization. While storing Java objects in a blob forces you to use Java to retrieve the object, you can often save a lot of time by using a blob. Typically, a blob works well when the data might otherwise require a large number of joined queries. The blob is also better when you don't need to query the data stored in the blob. That is, if you need to do a "`select…where`" on the data contained in the blob, you probably shouldn't use a blob. Deserializing the object is a fairly expensive operation, and it would take you a good bit of time to deserialize each blob just to perform a query, especially compared to the speed at which the database could perform the query against an ordinary table.

Listing 19.7 shows the `ProblemReport` object that maps to the `problem_report` table.

LISTING 19.7 SOURCE CODE FOR `ProblemReport.java`

```
package usingjsp.problemreport;

import usingjsp.DatabaseObject;
import java.sql.*;
import java.io.*;
import java.util.*;

/** A data object that contains a problem report */
public class ProblemReport extends DatabaseObject
    implements java.io.Serializable
{
    public int problemId;
    public java.util.Date entered;
    public String system;
    public String subsystem;
    public String originator;
    public String description;
    public int priority;
    public String status;
    public java.util.Date estimatedCompletionDate;
    public Vector notes;

    public ProblemReport()
    {
    }

/** Creates an instance of ProblemReport from a result set */
    public ProblemReport(ResultSet results)
        throws SQLException
    {
        problemId = results.getInt("problem_id");
        entered = results.getTimestamp("entered");
        system = results.getString("system");
        subsystem = results.getString("subsystem");
        originator = results.getString("originator");
        description = results.getString("description");
        priority = results.getInt("priority");
        status = results.getString("status");
        estimatedCompletionDate = results.getDate("ecd");
        Object tempNotes = results.getObject("notes");
        if (tempNotes == null)
        {
            notes = new Vector(0);
        }
```

```
// The mySQL driver returns the notes object as an array of bytes. Some
// drivers may see the object as its original type.
        else if (tempNotes instanceof Vector)
        {
            notes = (Vector) results.getObject("notes");
        }
        else if (tempNotes instanceof byte[])
        {
            try
            {
// Convert the byte array into an object
                ObjectInputStream obIn =
                    new ObjectInputStream(new ByteArrayInputStream(
                        (byte[]) tempNotes));
                notes = (Vector) obIn.readObject();
                obIn.close();
            } catch (Exception exc) {
                exc.printStackTrace();
            }
        }
        else
        {
// This really indicates an error
            System.out.println("The notes object is
"+tempNotes.getClass().getName());
        }
    }

    public int getProblemId() { return problemId; }
    public void setProblemId(int aProblemId) { problemId = aProblemId; }

    public java.util.Date getEntered() { return entered; }
    public void setEntered(java.util.Date enteredTime)
        { entered = enteredTime; }

    public String getSystem() { return system; }
    public void setSystem(String aSystem) { system = aSystem; }

    public String getSubsystem() { return subsystem; }
    public void setSubsystem(String aSubsystem) { subsystem = aSubsystem; }

    public String getOriginator() { return originator; }
    public void setOriginator(String anOriginator)
        { originator = anOriginator; }

    public String getDescription() { return description; }
    public void setDescription(String aDescription)
        { description = aDescription; }

    public int getPriority() { return priority; }
    public void setPriority(int aPriority) { priority = aPriority; }

    public String getStatus() { return status; }
    public void setStatus(String aStatus) { status = aStatus; }
```

LISTING 19.7 CONTINUED

```
    public java.util.Date getEstimatedCompletionDate()
        { return estimatedCompletionDate; }
    public void setEstimatedCompletionDate(java.util.Date anECD)
        { estimatedCompletionDate = anECD; }

    public Vector getNotes() { return notes; }
    public void setNotes(Vector newNotes) { notes = newNotes; }

    public String getTableName() { return "problem_report"; }

    public DatabaseObject createInstance(ResultSet results)
        throws SQLException
    {
        return new ProblemReport(results);
    }

/** Overrides the base insert method to grab the sequence number after the
 *  object has been inserted. */

    public int insert(Connection conn)
        throws SQLException
    {
        int numRows = super.insert(conn);

        problemId = getSequenceNumber(conn);

        return numRows;
    }

    public String getFieldList()
    {
        return "problem_id, entered, system, subsystem, originator, "+
            "description, priority, status, ecd, notes";
    }

    public String getInsertStatement()
    {
        return "insert into problem_report (problem_id, entered, "+
            "system, subsystem, originator, description, priority, "+
            "status, ecd, notes) values (?,?,?,?,?,?,?,?,?,?)";
    }

    public void prepareInsertStatement(PreparedStatement s)
        throws SQLException
    {
        s.setInt(1, 0);
        s.setTimestamp(2, new Timestamp(entered.getTime()));
        s.setString(3, system);
        s.setString(4, subsystem);
        s.setString(5, originator);
        s.setString(6, description);
        s.setInt(7, priority);
        s.setString(8, status);
        s.setDate(9, new java.sql.Date(
            estimatedCompletionDate.getTime()));
```

```
        s.setObject(10, notes);
    }

    public String getUpdateStatement()
    {
        return "update problem_report set entered=?, "+
            "system=?, subsystem=?, originator=?, description=?,"+
            " priority=?, status=?, ecd=?, notes=? where problem_id=?";
    }

    public void prepareUpdateStatement(PreparedStatement s)
        throws SQLException
    {
        s.setTimestamp(1, new Timestamp(entered.getTime()));
        s.setString(2, system);
        s.setString(3, subsystem);
        s.setString(4, originator);
        s.setString(5, description);
        s.setInt(6, priority);
        s.setString(7, status);
        s.setDate(8, new java.sql.Date(
            estimatedCompletionDate.getTime()));
        s.setObject(9, notes);
        s.setInt(10, problemId);
    }

    public String getDeleteStatement()
    {
        return "delete from problem_report where problem_id=?";
    }

    public void prepareDeleteStatement(PreparedStatement s)
        throws SQLException
    {
        s.setInt(1, problemId);
    }

    public String getSequenceGenerator()
    {
        return "problem_id_gen";
    }
}
```

If you are having trouble connecting to the database with JDBC, see "Using JDBC," in the "Troubleshooting" section at the end of this chapter.

A Two-Tiered Problem Reporting System

The `ProblemReport` class shown in Listing 19.7 represents the central data item in a problem reporting system. The system allows you to enter problems, bugs, or issues and assign them to several developers. Each problem can have a series of notes, which can represent the history of the problem. For example, if someone in QA enters the problem and sends it to a developer, the developer might make a note in the problem and send it back to QA. QA might then forward the problem to the project manager with another note. The project manager can review the previous notes to help determine what is wrong. In a help-desk situation, the series of notes provides a history to the person answering a call from a frustrated user. The help-desk person can immediately see what the poor user has already gone through.

The one data object that you need before you can implement the problem reporting system is the `ProblemReportDeveloper` object, which links developers to problem reports. The `problem_report_developer` database table is defined using the following SQL statement:

```
create table problem_report_developer
    (problem_id integer not null,
     developer varchar(50) not null,
     primary key (problem_id, developer))
```

Listing 19.8 shows the `ProblemReportDeveloper` class. Because the primary key for the table is composed of all the columns in the table, there is no need to create an updated statement since you must delete and reinsert a database row in order to change it.

LISTING 19.8 SOURCE CODE FOR ProblemReportDeveloper.java

```
package usingjsp.problemreport;

import usingjsp.DatabaseObject;
import java.sql.*;

/** A data object linking a developer to a problem report */

public class ProblemReportDeveloper extends DatabaseObject
    implements java.io.Serializable
{
    public int problemId;
    public String developer;

    public ProblemReportDeveloper()
    {
    }

    public ProblemReportDeveloper(ResultSet results)
        throws SQLException
    {
        problemId = results.getInt("problem_id");
        developer = results.getString("developer");
    }

    public int getProblemId() { return problemId; }
    public void setProblemId(int aProblemId) { problemId = aProblemId; }

    public String getDeveloper() { return developer; }
    public void setDeveloper(String aDeveloper)
        { developer = aDeveloper; }

    public String getTableName() { return "problem_report_developer"; }

    public DatabaseObject createInstance(ResultSet results)
        throws SQLException
    {
```

```
        return new ProblemReportDeveloper(results);
    }

    public String getFieldList() { return "problem_id, developer"; }

    public String getInsertStatement()
    {
        return "insert into problem_report_developer "+
            "(problem_id, developer) values (?,?)";
    }

    public void prepareInsertStatement(PreparedStatement s)
        throws SQLException
    {
        s.setInt(1, problemId);
        s.setString(2, developer);
    }

    public String getUpdateStatement()
    {
        return null;
    }

    public void prepareUpdateStatement(PreparedStatement s) {}

    public String getDeleteStatement()
    {
        return "delete from problem_report_developer where "+
            "problem_id=? and developer=?";
    }

    public void prepareDeleteStatement(PreparedStatement s)
        throws SQLException
    {
        s.setInt(1, problemId);
        s.setString(2, developer);
    }
}
```


You now have all the data elements you need to create a problem reporting system as a two-tiered Web application. The next thing you need to do is figure out the structure of your Web pages.

For a simple problem reporting system, you need to enter new problems, view and edit the problems assigned to you, and possibly view all the outstanding problems. Since each developer needs a different view of the data, you also need a login screen so you can find out who the user is.

Figure 19.1 shows the basic structure of the problem reporting application. After you visit a login page and invoke the login servlet, you go to the main page. From the main page, you can view your problem reports, all problem reports, or enter a new problem. When you are viewing a problem, you can choose to edit it.

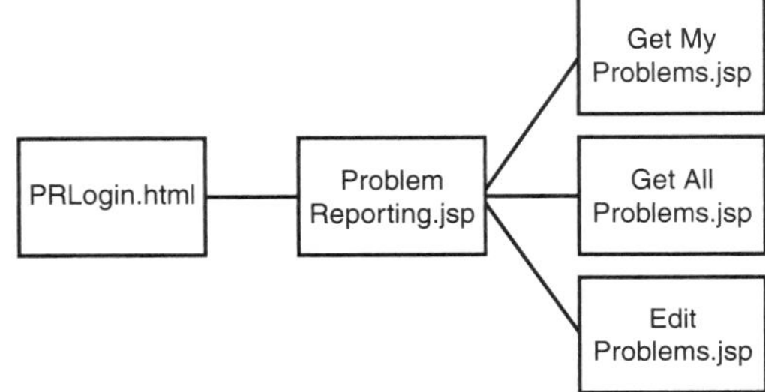

Figure 19.1
The basic structure of the Problem Reporting application.

THE LOGIN SCREEN

Creating a login screen is as simple as throwing a few fields on an HTML form. Listing 19.9 shows the PRLogin.html form.

LISTING 19.9 SOURCE CODE FOR `PRLogin.html`

```
<html>
<body bgcolor="#ffffff">
<h1>Problem Reporting Login</h1>
<form action="usingjsp.problemreport.LoginServlet" method="post">
<table>
<tr>
<td>User Name:<td><input type="text" name="username">
<tr>
<td>Password:<td><input type="password" name="password">
</table>
<p>
<input type="submit" value="Login!">
</form>
</body>
</html>
```

The `LoginServlet` class is where most of the login work is done. Since the login servlet is the entry point into the system, that's where you want to allocate your database connection pool the first time the servlet runs. You can put the connection pool code in the servlet's `init` method, or just create the pool when you realize it isn't there yet. In Listing 19.10, you will see that the `LoginServlet` class creates the connection pool during the `service` method instead of the `init` method. For most applications, you are better off using the `init` method because it is a more natural place to put initialization code and you won't have as much trouble finding the code.

LISTING 19.10 SOURCE CODE FOR `LoginServlet.java`

```
package usingjsp.problemreport;

import javax.servlet.*;
import javax.servlet.http.*;
import usingjsp.*;
import java.sql.*;
```

```
import java.util.*;

/** Validates a user login and then calls the main Problem Reporting page */
public class LoginServlet extends HttpServlet
{
    public void service(HttpServletRequest request,
        HttpServletResponse response)
        throws java.io.IOException, ServletException
    {
// Get the user name and password from the login form
        String username = request.getParameter("username");
        String password = request.getParameter("password");

        if (username == null)
        {
            request.setAttribute("rejectReason",
                "No username specified");

            rejectLogin(request, response);

            return;
        }

        if (password == null)
        {
            request.setAttribute("rejectReason",
                "No password specified");

            rejectLogin(request, response);

            return;
        }

// Get the "application" context
        ServletContext context = getServletContext();

// See if the connection pool has already been created
        IConnectionPool pool = (IConnectionPool) context.getAttribute(
            "connectionPool");

// If not, the pool must be created
        if (pool == null)
        {
// Synchronize on the application object and check one more time
// for the pool just in case another thread is in the process
// of creating the pool

            synchronized(context)
            {
                pool = (IConnectionPool) context.getAttribute(
                    "connectionPool");
                if (pool == null)
                {
// Make sure the database driver is available
                    try {
                        Class.forName("org.gjt.mm.mysql.Driver").
```

LISTING 19.10 CONTINUED

```
                        newInstance();
                } catch (Exception exc) {
                    getServletContext().log(
                        "Error loading JDBC driver", exc);
                }

// Create the connection pool and store it in the application object
                pool = new SimpleConnectionPool(
                    "jdbc:mysql://localhost/usingjsp",
                    "", "");
                context.setAttribute("connectionPool", pool);
            }
        }
    }

    Connection conn = null;

    try
    {
        conn = pool.getConnection();

// Create a dummy developer object for performing a query
        Developer devQuery = new Developer();

// Find the developer object that matches the user name entered on the form
        Vector v = devQuery.getAll(conn, "username='"+
            username.toLowerCase()+"'");

// If the user name doesn't exist, show an error
        if (v.size() != 1)
        {
            request.setAttribute("rejectReason",
                "Invalid username");

            rejectLogin(request, response);

            return;
        }

        Developer d = (Developer) v.elementAt(0);

// Make sure the passwords match
        if (!d.password.equals(password))
        {
            request.setAttribute("rejectReason",
                "Invalid password");

            rejectLogin(request, response);

            return;
        }

        HttpSession session = request.getSession();

        session.setAttribute("username", username);
```

```
            session.setAttribute("developer", d.getDeveloper());

// Send the user on to the main screen
            RequestDispatcher dispatch =
                context.getRequestDispatcher(
                    "/jspbook/ch19/examples/ProblemReporting.jsp");

            dispatch.forward(request, response);
        }
        catch (SQLException exc)
        {
            getServletContext().log(
                "A database error occurred while validating a user",
                exc);

            request.setAttribute("rejectReason",
                "A database error has occurred");

            rejectLogin(request, response);

            return;
        }
        finally
        {
            if (conn != null)
            {
                try
                {
                    pool.releaseConnection(conn);
                }
                catch (Exception ignore)
                {
                }
            }
        }
    }

/** Displays an error if the login fails for any reason */
    public void rejectLogin(HttpServletRequest request,
        HttpServletResponse response)
        throws java.io.IOException, ServletException
    {
        RequestDispatcher dispatch =
            getServletContext().getRequestDispatcher(
                "/jspbook/ch19/examples/RejectLogin.jsp");

        dispatch.forward(request, response);
    }
}
```

Figure 19.2 shows the login page.

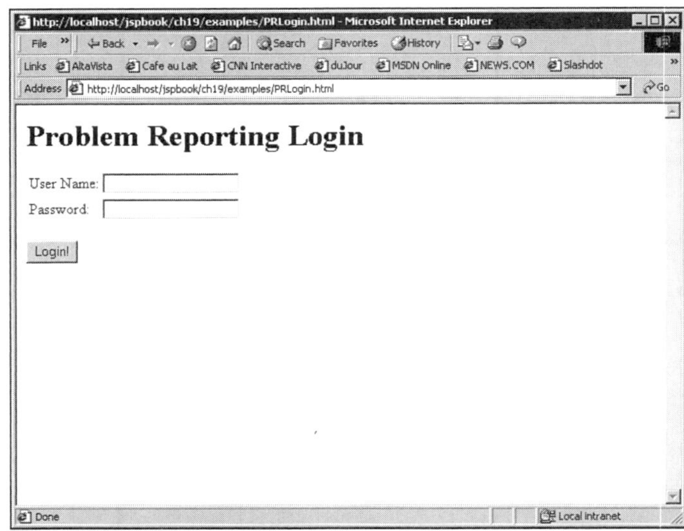

Figure 19.2
The Login screen for the Problem Reporting application is a simple HTML page.

THE MAIN MENU

As in many applications, the main menu simply lists the available options. Some systems customize the menu based on the user's security privileges. Since the problem reporting system doesn't provide any special security capabilities, the menu doesn't change. Listing 19.11 shows the `ProblemReporting` JSP that serves as the main menu.

LISTING 19.11 SOURCE CODE FOR `ProblemReporting.jsp`

```
<html>
<body bgcolor="#ffffff">

<%@ include file="CheckLoggedIn.jsp" %>

<h1>Problem Reporting System</h1>
<p>
You are currently logged in as <%= userName %>.
<p>
Please select an option:
<ul>
    <li><a href="GetMyProblems.jsp">
        Show Problems Assigned To <%= developer %></a>
    <li><a href="GetAllProblems.jsp">
        Show All Problems</a>
    <li><a href="EditProblem.jsp">Enter a New Problem</a>
</ul>

</body>
</html>
```

Figure 19.3 shows the main menu for the problem reporting application.

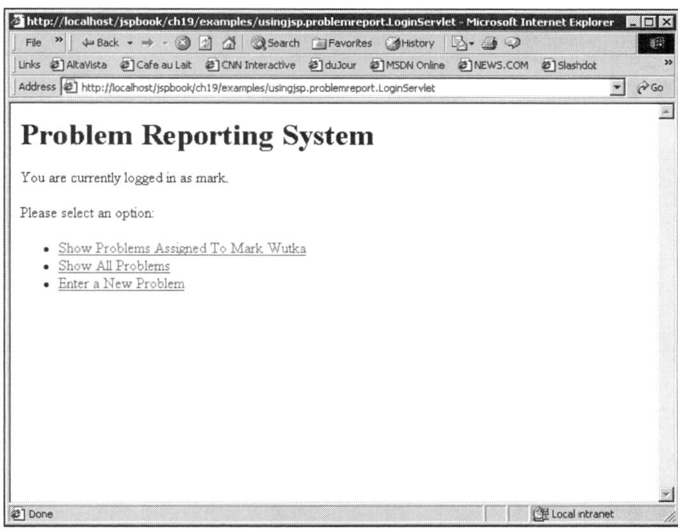

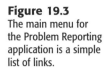

Figure 19.3
The main menu for the Problem Reporting application is a simple list of links.

Querying for Existing Problem Reports

The `DatabaseObject` class handles much of the difficulty involved with querying. The only time you may have problems is when you have to perform a difficult query. For example, in the problem reporting system when you want to display the problem reports assigned to a particular user, you have an interesting situation. You want to query for `ProblemReport` objects, but developers are assigned to a problem report through the `ProblemReportDeveloper` class. In other words, you want to find problem reports where one of the developers in the `problem_report_developer` table is the current developer. In a pure SQL application, your query would look something like this:

```
select distinct pr.* from problem_report pr,
    problem_report_developer prd
where
    pr.problem_id = prd.problem_id and
    prd.developer = 'Mark Wutka'
```

Remember that the `getAll` method in the `DatabaseObject` class allows you to specify an alternate table and a `where` clause. You could almost do the query using the `getAll` method, but you can't specify the `distinct` keyword. Also, notice that you must qualify the `*` in the query. If you just say "`select *`," you may get errors indicating that a particular field is ambiguous. For example, if each table has a `username` field, the database might complain.

The `DatabaseObject` class normally builds a query using the `getFieldNames` method in each data object, which returns a list of the fields that should be used in a query. The `DatabaseObject` class provides a special variation of `getFieldNames` that lets you specify a table name for qualifying the field names. Where you would normally have a field name like `username` in the query, the special variation adds a table name and an alias to make the final field name match the original. In other words, `username` becomes `mytablename.username as username`.

Listing 19.12 shows the `GetMyProblems` JSP that contains a query to fetch the problem reports assigned to the current user. Notice that it uses the `executeQuery` method in the `DatabaseObject` class to create the custom query. It also uses the special version of `getFieldNames` to fully qualify the columns it selects. Once it retrieves the problem reports, it puts them in a table and creates a link that allows you to edit each report.

LISTING 19.12 SOURCE CODE FOR `GetMyProblems.jsp`

```
<%@ page language="java" import="usingjsp.problemreport.*,java.util.*" %>
<%@ page import="usingjsp.*,java.sql.*,java.text.*" %>

<html>
<body bgcolor="#ffffff">

<%@ include file="CheckLoggedIn.jsp" %>

<%
    Connection conn = null;

    IConnectionPool pool =
        (IConnectionPool) application.getAttribute("connectionPool");

    try
    {
        conn = pool.getConnection();

        ProblemReport prQuery = new ProblemReport();

        Vector v = prQuery.executeQuery(conn,
            "select distinct "+prQuery.getFieldList("problem_report")+
            ", problem_report_developer.problem_id as prdprobid"+
            " from problem_report, problem_report_developer "+
            " where problem_report.problem_id = "+
            " problem_report_developer.problem_id and "+
            " problem_report_developer.developer='"+developer+"'");

%>
<h1>Problems Assigned to <%= developer%></h1>
<table border="4">
<tr><th>System<th>Subsystem<th>Originator<th>Description
<th>Priority<th>Status<th>Developers<th>ECD
<%
        ProblemReportDeveloper prdQuery = new ProblemReportDeveloper();

        SimpleDateFormat format = new SimpleDateFormat("MM/dd/yyyy");

        Enumeration e = v.elements();

        while (e.hasMoreElements())
        {
            ProblemReport problem = (ProblemReport) e.nextElement();
%>
<tr><td><%=problem.system%><td><%=problem.subsystem%>
<td><%=problem.originator%><td><%=problem.description%>
<td><%=problem.priority%><td><%=problem.status%>
<td>
```

```
<%
            Vector devs = prdQuery.getAll(conn,
                "problem_id="+problem.problemId);

            Enumeration de = devs.elements();
            boolean first = true;

            while (de.hasMoreElements())
            {
                ProblemReportDeveloper prd = (ProblemReportDeveloper)
                    de.nextElement();

                if (!first) out.print(",");
                first = false;

                out.print(prd.developer);
            }
%>
<td><%=format.format(problem.estimatedCompletionDate)%>
<td><a href="EditProblem.jsp?problemId=<%=problem.problemId%>">Edit</a>
<%
        }
    }
    finally
    {
        try
        {
            pool.releaseConnection(conn);
        } catch (Exception ignore) {}
    }
%>
</table>
<p>
<a href="ProblemReporting.jsp">Return to Main Page</a>
</body>
</html>
```


Figure 19.4 shows a sample list of outstanding problem reports generated by GetMyProblems.jsp.

The only different between displaying the active problem reports for a particular user and those for all users is the initial query. The `GetAllProblems` JSP is identical to GetMyProblems.jsp except that the executeQuery statement in `GetMyProblems` is replaced by the following statement:

```
Vector v = prQuery.getAll();
```

Note

The fact that GetMyProblems.jsp and GetAllProblems.jsp are almost identical should tell you that they should probably be combined into a single file that performs a query based on the presence or absence of some parameter. If you find that you are cutting and pasting a lot of code between two files, you should ask yourself if you can put the common code into a single class.

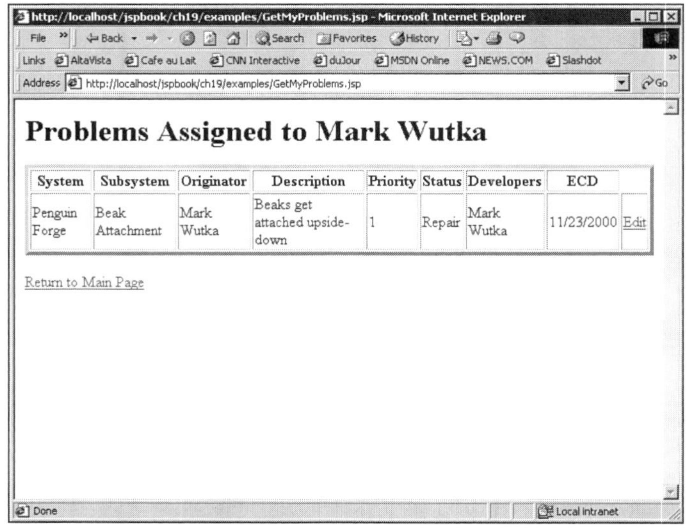

Figure 19.4
The GetMyProblems.jsp page queries the database and displays a list of problem reports.

Creating and Updating Problem Reports

If it weren't for the presence of the `problem_report_developer` table, it would be extremely easy to insert and update problem reports. You would simply update the fields in the `ProblemReport` class and call either the `insert` or `update` method. Because of the link table (`problem_report_developer` links `problem_report` to `developer`) you must insert or delete objects when developers are added to or removed from a problem report.

As you saw earlier in the `ProblemReport` class, the notes assigned to the problem report are stored in a `Vector` object. You may wonder why you couldn't also do the same thing with the developers. The problem is, you need the `problem_report_developer` table when you query for the list of problems assigned to a particular developer. Remember, the rule of thumb for choosing between serialization and separate tables is whether you need to query. In this case, since you need to query, it's better to bite the bullet and write the code to store the assigned developers in a separate table. As it turns out, this isn't such a tough task.

Listing 19.13 shows the `EditProblem` JSP that creates the input form used to make changes to an existing problem report or to enter a new problem report.

Listing 19.13 Source Code for `EditProblem.jsp`

```
<%@ page language="java" import="usingjsp.problemreport.*,java.util.*" %>
<%@ page import="usingjsp.*,java.sql.*,java.text.*" %>

<html>
<body bgcolor="#ffffff">

<%@ include file="CheckLoggedIn.jsp" %>

<form action="SaveProblem.jsp" method="post">
```

```
<%

    Vector developers = null;
    Connection conn = null;

    String problemId = request.getParameter("problemId");

    ProblemReport report = new ProblemReport();
    Vector reports = null;

    IConnectionPool pool = (IConnectionPool)
        application.getAttribute("connectionPool");

    String[] assignedDevelopers = null;

    try
    {

        conn = pool.getConnection();

        Developer devQuery = new Developer();

        developers = devQuery.getAll(conn);

// If there is already a problem id, this is an edit instead of a new
// problem report. Go get the original problem report

        if (problemId != null)
        {
            ProblemReport query = new ProblemReport();

            reports = query.getAll(conn, "problem_id="+problemId);

            if (reports.size() < 1)
            {
%>
The problem you want to edit is no longer in the system. Please
try another report.
<p>
<a href="ProblemReporting.jsp">Return to Main Page</a>
<%
                return;
            }

            report = (ProblemReport) reports.elementAt(0);
%>
<input type="hidden" name="problemId" value="<%=report.problemId%>">
<h1>Edit a Problem Report</h1>
<%

// Get the developers assigned to this problem report

            Vector v = devQuery.executeQuery(conn,
                "select "+devQuery.getFieldList("d")+
                " from developer d, problem_report_developer prd where "+
                "prd.problem_id="+report.problemId+
```

LISTING 19.13 CONTINUED

```
                " and d.developer = prd.developer");

            assignedDevelopers = new String[v.size()];
            for (int i=0; i < assignedDevelopers.length; i++)
            {
                assignedDevelopers[i] = ((Developer) v.elementAt(i)).
                    developer;
            }
        }
        else
        {
// Create a new, blank problem report
            report.entered = new java.util.Date();
            report.system = "";
            report.subsystem = "";
            report.originator = developer;
            report.description = "";
            report.priority = 0;
            report.status = "";
            report.estimatedCompletionDate = new java.util.Date();
            report.notes = new Vector();

            assignedDevelopers = new String[0];
%>
<h1>Enter a New Problem Report</h1>
<%
        }

    }
    finally
    {
        if (conn != null)
        {
            pool.releaseConnection(conn);
        }
    }

    if (developers == null)
    {
        developers = new Vector();
    }

%>

<%
// Preserve the names of the developers previously assigned to this
// problem. That way, the SaveProblem JSP doesn't need to figure it
// out.
    for (int i=0; i < assignedDevelopers.length; i++)
    {
%><input type="hidden" name="prevAssigned"
    value="<%=assignedDevelopers[i]%>"><%
    }
%>
<table>
```

```
<tr>
<td>System:
<td><input type="text" name="system" value="<%=report.system%>">
<td>Subsystem:
<td><input type="text" name="subsystem" value="<%=report.subsystem%>">
<tr><td>Description:
</table>
<textarea name=description rows="4" cols="60"><%=report.description%>
</textarea>
<table>
<tr>
<td>Priority:
<td>
<select name="priority">
<%
    for (int i=1; i <= 10; i++)
    {
        out.print("<option value=\""+i+"\"");
        if (i == report.priority) out.print(" selected");
        out.println(">"+i+"</option>");
    }
%>
<td>Status:
<td><input type="text" name="status" value="<%=report.status%>">
</table>
<table>
<tr>
<td>Estimated Completion Date:
<td><input type="text" name="ecd"
    value="<%= (new SimpleDateFormat("MM/dd/yyyy")).format(
        report.estimatedCompletionDate) %>">
</table>
Assigned Developers:
<table>
<tr>
<%
// Create a select list of the developers that can be assigned to a problem
    for (int i=0; i < 4; i++)
    {
%><td><select name="assigned">
<option value="">None</option>
<%
        for (int j=0; j < developers.size(); j++)
        {
            Developer d = (Developer) developers.elementAt(j);

%><option value="<%=d.developer%>"
<%
            if ((i < assignedDevelopers.length) &&
                (d.developer.equals(assignedDevelopers[i])))
            {
                out.print(" selected");
            }
%>
><%=d.developer%></option><%
        }
```

LISTING 19.13 CONTINUED

```
    }
%>
<tr>
<td>Notes:
</table>
<%
    SimpleDateFormat dateFormat =
        new SimpleDateFormat("mm/dd/yyyy hh:mm:ss");

    Enumeration e = report.notes.elements();
    while (e.hasMoreElements())
    {
        Note note = (Note) e.nextElement();
%>
<%= dateFormat.format(note.date) %> -- <%= note.developer %>
<br>
<%= note.comment %>
<br>
------------------------------------------------------------
<br>
<%
    }
%>
<table>
<tr><td>Enter a New Note:
</table>
<textarea name="newnote" rows="4" cols="60"></textarea>

<p>
<input type="hidden" name="originator" value="<%=report.originator%>">
<input type="submit" value="Save Problem Report">
</form>
</body>
</html>
```

Figure 19.5 shows the `EditProblem` Java Server Page in action.

Notice that the `EditProblem` JSP includes a list of the developers that were previously assigned to a problem report. For a small application like this, you are pretty safe sending data this way. For a more complicated application, however, you are better off performing a query when you save the problem report and getting the old list of developers. It's a subtle point and would probably stem a few lengthy discussions, but you should avoid passing data inside a JSP that doesn't relate specifically to the JSP. The `EditProblem` JSP doesn't need the list of previous developers. When you save the problem report, that information is available.

Listing 19.14 shows the final piece of the `ProblemReporting` application. The `SaveProblem` JSP stores a problem report in the database and also manages the `problem_report_developer` table.

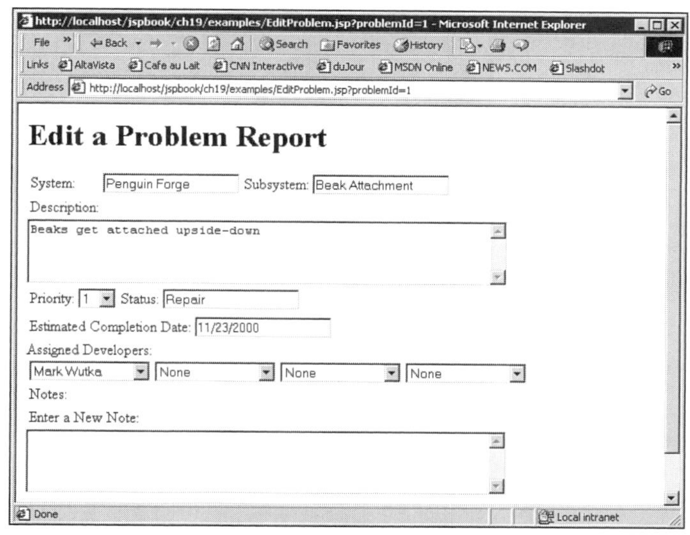

Figure 19.5 The `EditProblem` JSP allows you to make changes to a problem report.

Listing 19.14 Source Code for `SaveProblem.jsp`

```
<%@ page language="java" import="usingjsp.problemreport.*,java.util.*" %>
<%@ page import="usingjsp.*,java.sql.*,java.text.*" %>

<html>
<body bgcolor="#ffffff">

<%@ include file="CheckLoggedIn.jsp" %>

<jsp:useBean id="report" class="usingjsp.problemreport.ProblemReport"
    scope="page"/>
<%
    Connection conn = null;

    IConnectionPool pool =
        (IConnectionPool) application.getAttribute("connectionPool");

    String problemId = request.getParameter("problemId");

    try
    {
        conn = pool.getConnection();

// If this is not a new problem, go find the previous one
        if (problemId != null)
        {
            ProblemReport prQuery = new ProblemReport();

            Vector v = prQuery.getAll(conn, "problem_id="+problemId);

            if (v.size() > 0)
```

LISTING 19.14 CONTINUED

```
            {
                report = (ProblemReport) v.elementAt(0);

// Store the object in the page context so you can treat it like a bean
                pageContext.setAttribute("report", report);
            }
        }
%>
<%-- Copy the attributes of the form into the report --%>
<jsp:setProperty name="report" property="*"/>
<%
// Get the note that was entered
        String newNote = request.getParameter("newnote");

// If there was a note, add it to the list of notes for this problem
        if ((newNote != null) && (newNote.trim().length() > 0))
        {
            Note note = new Note(developer, new java.util.Date(),
                newNote);

            if (report.notes == null)
            {
                report.notes = new Vector();
            }
            report.notes.addElement(note);
        }

        String ecdStr = request.getParameter("ecd");

        if (ecdStr != null)
        {
            SimpleDateFormat fmt = new SimpleDateFormat("MM/dd/yyyy");

            report.estimatedCompletionDate = fmt.parse(ecdStr);
        }

// If this is a new problem, set the date/time that it was entered
        if (problemId == null)
        {
            report.entered = new java.util.Date();
        }

// Do an insert or an update depending on whether this is a new
// problem or an existing one
        if (problemId != null)
        {
            report.update(conn);
        }
        else
        {
            report.insert(conn);
        }

// Get the list of developers that were previously assigned to this problem
        String[] prevAssigned = request.getParameterValues(
            "prevAssigned");
```

```
        if (prevAssigned == null) prevAssigned = new String[0];

// Get the list of developers who are now assigned to this problem
        String[] assigned = request.getParameterValues("assigned");

        Vector deleted = new Vector();

// Loop through the developers who were previously assigned to this problem
        for (int i=0; i < prevAssigned.length; i++)
        {
            if ((prevAssigned[i] == null) ||
                (prevAssigned[i].trim().length() == 0))
            {
                continue;
            }
            boolean found = false;

// See if this developer is still assigned to the problem
            for (int j=0; j < assigned.length; j++)
            {
                if (assigned[j].equals(prevAssigned[i]))
                {
                    found = true;
                    break;
                }
            }
// If the developer is no longer assigned, add them to the list
// of developers that need to be deleted
            if (!found) deleted.addElement(prevAssigned[i]);
        }

        Vector added = new Vector();

// Loop through the developers that are now assigned to the problem
        for (int i=0; i < assigned.length; i++)
        {
            if ((assigned[i] == null) || (assigned[i].trim().length() == 0))
            {
                continue;
            }
            boolean found = false;
// Look through the previously assigned developers to see if this developer
// was previously assigned to the problem
            for (int j=0; j < prevAssigned.length; j++)
            {
                if (assigned[i].equals(prevAssigned[j]))
                {
                    found = true;
                    break;
                }
            }

// If the developer was not previously assigned, add them
// to the list of developers that need to be inserted
            if (!found) added.addElement(assigned[i]);
        }
```

LISTING 19.14 CONTINUED

```
// Create a ProblemReportDeveloper link object to link new developers
// to the problem or remove existing links. The same object can be
// reused to insert and delete multiple links.

        ProblemReportDeveloper prd = new ProblemReportDeveloper();

// The problemId is the same for all developers to be added and deleted
// for this problem
        prd.problemId = report.problemId;

// Delete the developers who are no longer assigned
        for (int i=0; i < deleted.size(); i++)
        {
            prd.developer = (String) deleted.elementAt(i);

            prd.delete(conn);
        }

// Insert the developers who were not previously assigned
        for (int i=0; i < added.size(); i++)
        {
            prd.developer = (String) added.elementAt(i);

            prd.insert(conn);
        }
    }
    finally
    {
        try {
            pool.releaseConnection(conn);
        } catch (Exception ignore) {}
    }
%>
<h1>Success</h1>
<p>
Your problem report has been
<%
    if (problemId != null)
    {
        out.print("updated in the database.");
    }
    else
    {
        out.print("inserted into the database.");
    }
%>
<p>
You may now <a href="ProblemReporting.jsp">return to the Main Page</a>
</body>
</html>
```

Database Locking

If you look at many Web applications, locking doesn't seem to be much of a problem. You often just perform a query or insert a new row into a database. In some situations, however, you may need to lock some part of the database while a user is editing the data.

There are two basic forms of locking—optimistic and pessimistic locking. The optimism and pessimism refer to your view of the likelihood that two users will try to update the same piece of data at the same time. An optimistic view says that it is unlikely that two users will update this data, so allow anyone to change the data. If two people do try to change the data at the same time, the first person to make the change wins. The other person receives an error message.

The pessimistic view says that it is likely that two users will want to change the same piece of data, so go ahead and lock it ahead of time. Unlike optimistic locking, pessimistic locking won't allow others to even try changing the data once a user has indicated they want to make a change.

You should realize that the terms *optimistic* and *pessimistic* aren't philosophies about the general nature of data—they apply to specific cases. You can't simply say that you always take a pessimistic view of data access and therefore will always lock records while you edit them. You sometimes use both locking techniques in the same application. For example, your bank account would probably be updated using optimistic locking, because it is unlikely that you would be trying to access the account from two different places at the same time. If you did manage to do that, you would just find that the second transaction failed to go through.

On the other hand, if you are making an emergency change of flight plans on a commercial airline flight that's already in the air, you probably want to lock the flight plan to let the other flight dispatchers know that you are editing the plan. One dispatcher would be wasting his or her time making changes that will be rejected.

You should strive toward using optimistic locking as much as possible. For one thing, it's easier on the database engine because it doesn't need to maintain any locks on rows or tables. Second, there are many situations where someone pulls up a record on their screen and then goes to lunch or makes a long phone call. If someone else needs to change that record, you don't want to hold them up unnecessarily. With the fickle nature of Web users and Web browsers, you definitely don't want to lock a record from a user who many never come back again.

To implement optimistic locking, you simply need to add an extra column to your database table. Many people label this column `Version` and make it an integer value. Whenever you update a row in the database, increment the version number, but only perform the update if the version number in the database is the same as the version number that you got back. An example update statement would look like this:

```
update people set age=4, version=5 where
    Name='Kaitlynn Tippin' and version=4
```

If the version number is something other than what it was when you received the data, you know that someone else has updated the data. You need to get a fresh copy of the data and tell the users that there was a locking problem and that they should make their changes again. Obviously, the user will not be happy at having to make the changes again. That's where the optimism comes in. You are optimistic that you won't upset too many users.

Instead of just executing a single update statement, some products perform an extra step and examine the current value of the version number before attempting the update. While this results in slightly slower updates, the application can tell the difference between an update failing because of an incorrect version, versus an update failing because the database row no longer exists, or because of some other error in the update statement.

BUILDING A BETTER CONNECTION POOL

The `SimpleConnectionPool` class that you have been using in this chapter is a poor example of a connection pool because it has no upper bound. If your database can handle as many connections as possible, maybe that isn't so bad. Most databases, however, aren't happy with you making 1000 connections and keeping them open all the time.

You really need a connection pool that has the ability to cap the maximum number of connections. When a Java class asks the pool for a connection and there are no connections available, the pool can wait for a connection to become available. Performing the wait and notifying synchronization takes a bit of work because you need to synchronize certain sections of code and keep looping until you get what you need.

Listing 19.15 shows a generic resource pool object that can be used to pool any kind of resource. Using this class as a foundation, you can easily build a connection pool that waits for connections to become available.

LISTING 19.15 SOURCE CODE FOR `ResourcePool.java`

```
package com.wutka.util;

import java.util.*;

/** ResourcePool holds a common set of resources that are given out
    in first-in-first-out order. The pool assumes that all resources
    are equally weighted. Since some resource pools may need to allocate
    additional resources when no more are available, the getOverFlowResource
    method can be overridden to create new ones.
    <P>
    When the resource is allocated, the requesting thread can associate an
    object with the allocated resource. One way to make use of this feature is
    to store the name of the method that is requesting the resource. When
    debugging code, you may want to look at the allocated resources and what
    methods have allocated them. Someties you can find methods that aren't
    releasing resources after allocating them.
    <P>
    If you allocate resources within a try block, you should release them
    in the finally section of the block. That way, the resource is released
    no matter what exception is thrown.
```

```
    @author Mark Wutka
    @version 1.0
*/

public class ResourcePool
{

/** The resources that are currently free */
    protected Vector availableResources;

/** Resources that have been allocated out of the pool */
    protected Vector usedResources;

/** User-defined info about a resource that has been allocated */
    protected Vector usedResourceInfo;

/** Flag to make sure at least one thread has received notification */
    boolean receivedWakeup;

/** The number of threads waiting for notification */
    int numThreadsWaiting;

/** Creates a new resource pool */
    public ResourcePool()
    {
        availableResources = new Vector();
        usedResources = new Vector();
        usedResourceInfo = new Vector();
        receivedWakeup = true;
        numThreadsWaiting = 0;
    }

/** Adds another resource to the pool
 * @param resource The resource being added
 */
    public synchronized void addResource(Object resource)
    {
 // Assume the resource is free, add it to the free list
        availableResources.addElement(resource);
    }

/** Removes a resource from the pool
 * @param resource The resource to be removed
 */
    public synchronized void removeResource(Object resource)
    {
// Remove the resource from the free list
        availableResources.removeElement(resource);

// See if the resources is in the used list
        int pos = usedResources.indexOf(resource);

// If the resource is in the used list, remove it and its associated info
        if (pos >= 0) {
            usedResources.removeElementAt(pos);
            usedResourceInfo.removeElementAt(pos);
```

LISTING 19.15 CONTINUED

```
        }
    }

/** Allocates a resource when the pool is empty. By default, this method
 *    returns null, indicating that the requesting thread must wait. This
 *    allows a thread pool to expand when necessary, allowing for spikes in
 *    activity.
 *    @return A new resource, or null to force the requester to wait
 */
    protected synchronized Object getOverflowResource()
    {
        return null;
    }

/** Requests a resource from the pool, waiting forever if one is not available.
 * No extra information is associated with the allocated resource.
 * @return The allocated resource
 */
    public Object getResource()
    {
        return getResource(null, -1);
    }

/** Requests a resource from the pool, waiting forever if one is not available.
 * @param allocationInfo A value associated with the allocated resource
 * @return The allocated resource
 */
    public Object getResource(Object allocationInfo)
    {
        return getResource(allocationInfo, -1);
    }

/** Requests a resource from the pool, waiting forever if one is not available.
 * @param timeout The maximum amount of time (in milliseconds)
 * to wait for the resource
 * @return The allocated resource
 */
    public Object getResource(long timeout)
    {
        return getResource(null, timeout);
    }

/** Grabs a resource from the free list and moves it to the used list.
 * This method is really the core of the resource pool. The rest of the class
 * deals with synchronization around this method.
 * @param allocationInfo The info to be associated with the allocated resource
 * @return The allocated resource
 */
    protected synchronized Object getResourceFromList(Object allocationInfo)
    {
// See if there is a resource available.
        if (availableResources.size() > 0) {

// Get the first resource from the free list
            Object resource = availableResources.elementAt(0);
```

```
// Remove the resource from the free list
            availableResources.removeElement(resource);

// Add the resource and its associated info to the used list
            usedResources.addElement(resource);
            usedResourceInfo.addElement(allocationInfo);

            return resource;
        }

        return null;
    }

/** Performs a wait for a specified number of milliseconds.
 * @param timeout The number of milliseconds to wait
 * (wait forever if timeout < 0)
 */
    protected synchronized void doWait(long timeout)
    {
        try {
            if (timeout < 0) {
                wait();
            }
            else {
                wait(timeout);
            }
        }
        catch (Exception ignore) {
        }
    }

/** Requests a resource from the pool, waiting forever if one is not available.
 * @param allocationInfo A value associated with the allocated resource
 * @param timeout The maximum amount of time (in milliseconds)
 * to wait for the resource
 * @return The allocated resource
 */
    public Object getResource(Object allocationInfo, long timeout)
    {
// See if there is a resource in the pool already
        Object resource = getResourceFromList(allocationInfo);
        if (resource != null)
        {
            return resource;
        }

// Figure out when to stop waiting
        long endTime = System.currentTimeMillis() + timeout;

        do {

            synchronized(this) {
// See if there are any available resources in the pool
                if (availableResources.size() == 0) {

// Allow subclasses to provide overflow resources
```

Listing 19.15 Continued

```
                    resource = getOverflowResource();

// If there was a resource allocated for overflow, add it to the used list
                    if (resource != null)
                    {
                        usedResources.addElement(resource);
                        usedResourceInfo.addElement(allocationInfo);

                        return resource;
                    }
                }
            }

// Wait for a resource to be allocated

// Figure out the longest time to wait before timing out
            long maxWait = endTime - System.currentTimeMillis();
            if (timeout < 0) maxWait = -1;

// Indicate that there is a thread waiting for a wakeup
            numThreadsWaiting++;

// Wait for a wakeup
            doWait(maxWait);

            numThreadsWaiting--;

// Only mention the received wakeup if the timeout hasn't expired
            if ((timeout < 0) || (System.currentTimeMillis() < maxWait)) {
                receivedWakeup = true;
            }

// See if there is now a resource in the free pool
            resource = getResourceFromList(allocationInfo);
            if (resource != null)
            {
                return resource;
            }

// Keep looping while the timeout hasn't expired (loop forever if there is
// no timeout.
        } while ((timeout < 0) || (System.currentTimeMillis() < endTime));

        return null;
    }

/** Releases a resource back to the pool of available resources
 * @param resource The resource to be returned to the pool
 */
    public void releaseResource(Object resource)
    {
        int pos = -1;

        synchronized(this) {
// Make sure the resource is in the used list
            pos = usedResources.indexOf(resource);
```

```
// If the resource was in the used list, remove it from the used list and
// add it back to the free list
            if (pos >= 0) {
                usedResources.removeElementAt(pos);
                usedResourceInfo.removeElementAt(pos);
                availableResources.addElement(resource);
            }
        }

// If we released a resource, wake up any threads that may be waiting
        if (pos >= 0)
        {
            doWakeup();
        }
    }

/** Performs a notifyAll (which requires a synchronized method) */
    protected synchronized void doNotify()
    {
        try {
            notifyAll();
        }
        catch (Exception ignore) {
        }
    }

    protected void doWakeup()
    {
// Wake up any threads waiting for the resource
        receivedWakeup = false;
        do {
            try {
                    doNotify();
            }
            catch (Exception ignore) {
            }
        }
// Keep looping while there are threads waiting and none have received a wakeup
        while ((numThreadsWaiting > 0) && !receivedWakeup);
    }

/** Return a copy of the resources in the free list
 * @return The resources in the free list
 */
    public synchronized Vector getAvailableResources()
    {
        return (Vector) availableResources.clone();
    }

/** Return a copy of the resources in the used list
 * @return The resources in the used list
 */
    public synchronized Vector getUsedResources()
    {
        return (Vector) usedResources.clone();
    }
```

LISTING 19.15 CONTINUED

```
/** Return a copy of the associated info for the used resources
 * @return The info associated with the allocated resources
 */
    public synchronized Vector getUsedResourceInfo()
    {
        return (Vector) usedResourceInfo.clone();
    }
}
```

Although the `ResourcePool` class provides many options, the only methods you need to worry about for a connection pool are `addResource`, `getResource` and `releaseResource`. Listing 19.16 shows the `ConnectionPool` class that provides an `IConnectionPool` interface and stores its connections in a `ResourcePool` object.

LISTING 19.16 SOURCE CODE FOR `ConnectionPool.java`

```
package usingjsp;

import java.sql.*;
import java.util.*;
import com.wutka.util.*;

/** A connection pool that creates a fixed pool of connections at
 *  startup and waits for connections if they aren't available.
 */
public class ConnectionPool implements IConnectionPool
{
    protected ResourcePool pool;
    protected String connectionURL;
    protected String userName;
    protected String password;

/** Creates a new connection pool that creates connections using
 *  the specified URL, user name and password */
    public ConnectionPool(String aConnectionURL,
        String aUserName, String aPassword, int numConnections)
        throws SQLException
    {
        connectionURL = aConnectionURL;
        userName = aUserName;
        password = aPassword;
        pool = new ResourcePool();

// Create a fixed number of connections and add them to the pool
        for (int i=0; i < numConnections; i++)
        {
            pool.addResource(DriverManager.getConnection(connectionURL,
                userName, password));
        }
    }

/** Gets a connection from the pool */
    public synchronized Connection getConnection()
```

```
        throws SQLException
    {
        return (Connection) pool.getResource();
    }

/** Returns a connection to the pool */
    public synchronized void releaseConnection(Connection conn)
        throws SQLException
    {
        pool.releaseResource(conn);
    }
}
```

Since you have been using the `IConnectionPool` interface in all of your programs, you only need to change one section of code in order to use the new connection pool. The `LoginServlet` class allocates its connection pool and stores the pool in the application object with the following code fragment:

```
// Create the connection pool and store it in the application object
    pool = new SimpleConnectionPool(
        "jdbc:mysql://localhost/usingjsp",
        "", "");
    context.setAttribute("connectionPool", pool);
```

To use the new connection pool, you can just replace these lines with the following code fragment:

```
// Create the connection pool and store it in the application object
    try
    {
        pool = new ConnectionPool(
            jdbc:mysql://localhost/usingjsp",
            "", "", 10);
        context.setAttribute("connectionPool", pool);
    }
    catch (SQLException exc)
    {
        context.log("Error creating connection pool", exc);
    }
```

The only real difference is that the new `ConnectionPool` class can throw an `SQLException` from its constructor because it allocates connections ahead of time. You also must supply the number of connections to allocate.

TROUBLESHOOTING

USING JDBC

Why does the DriverManager tell me that no suitable driver exists?

This usually happens for one of three reasons:

- You mistyped the JDBC URL and the driver manager doesn't recognize the database type.

- They didn't load the JDBC driver class with `Class.forName` and you didn't add it to the `jdbc.drivers` system property.
- The driver class isn't in the classpath.

Why do I get errors saying I can't allocate any more database statements after my program has been running for a few minutes?

If you don't explicitly close your `Statement` objects, they don't get closed until the garbage collector picks them up, which might not occur for a long time. Because a database statement takes up resources in the database as well, or at least in the driver, there is usually a limit to the number of open statements you can have. Under a heavy load, you might end up allocating more statements than the database can handle. The garbage collector only understands memory shortages; it isn't smart enough to clean up old statements when the database can't handle any more.

CONNECTION POOLS

Why can't I allocate multiple connections when I use Microsoft Access?

Access wasn't meant to be a server-side database engine, so it is limited in the number of connections it can accept.

Why do I keep allocating more and more connections?

You probably aren't returning the connections to the pool once you're done with them. This often occurs in applications that don't use the `finally` keyword to set up a block of code to return the connection to the pool. If you return connections to the pool in the `try` block of your routine, and even in the `catch` block, you better make sure you are catching all possible exceptions. You might only be looking for `SQLException`, and when a `NullPointerException` occurs, you never return the connection to the pool. By using the `finally` block, you ensure that the connection is returned to the pool no matter what exception gets thrown (and also during normal execution, of course).

CHAPTER 20

Designing a Three-Tiered Application

In this chapter

In a three-tiered application, the presentation, business logic, and data layers are separated into three separate components. Typically, these layers reside on different machines, although they may also run within the same machine. It isn't necessary to put the components on different machines; the important thing is that you have the *ability* to put them on different machines. Figure 20.1 shows a conceptual model of a three-tiered application.

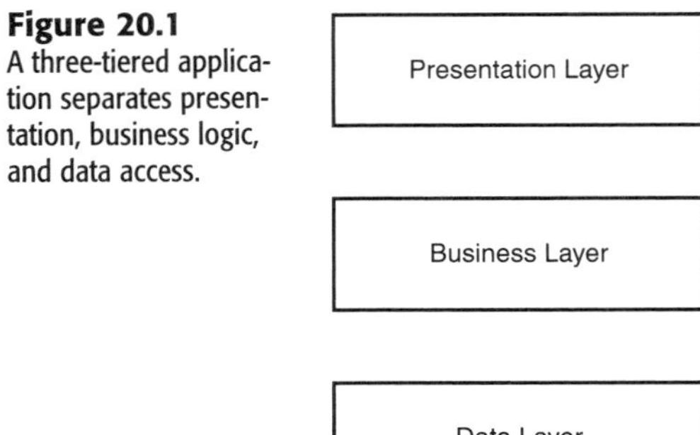

Figure 20.1
A three-tiered application separates presentation, business logic, and data access.

The "glue" between the layers is usually some sort of "middleware." Although there are database middleware products that perform interesting functions such as data replication and synchronization, most Java applications use a JDBC driver as the glue between the business logic and data layers. You may also use an object-to-relational mapping package such as TOPLink or JavaBlend to enhance your interface to the data layer.

The glue between the presentation and business logic layers is usually some sort of distributed object system or a remote procedure call mechanism. There are even ways to use the HTTP protocol as glue between presentation code running directly on the browser and business logic running on the Web server. Under the latter scheme, the code running on the Web server, the servlets and Java Server Pages generate pure data structures and not HTML. All the code to render the data resides on the browser in the form of Java applets or JavaScript routines. Figure 20.2 shows the conceptual 3-tiered model along with the glue between the layers.

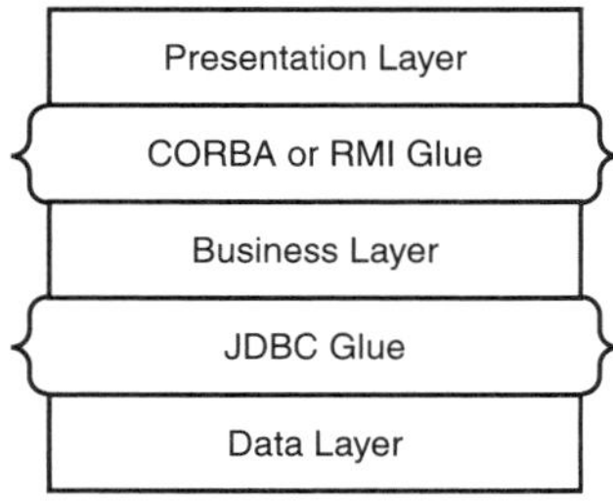

Figure 20.2
A three-tiered application uses middleware "glue" between the layers.

Stubs and Skeletons

If you have used RMI or CORBA for any period of time, you have probably heard the terms *stub* and *skeleton*. When you create a distributed object using either RMI or CORBA, you start with an interface definition. That is, you don't start with the distributed object itself, but by defining how a client talks to the object.

Next, you use a tool that creates a stub and skeleton based on the interface you just defined. The stub acts as a "proxy" for the distributed object. The client code makes calls to the stub just like it makes calls to any other objects in its local memory. The stub packages the call and sends it over to the server where the distributed object is running. The skeleton receives the packaged call from the stub, decodes it, and calls the appropriate method in the distributed object. It then takes any values or exceptions returned by the distributed object, packages them up, and sends them back to the stub. The stub decodes the return value and returns it back to the client. Figure 20.3 illustrates the relationship between the client, distributed object, stub, and skeleton.

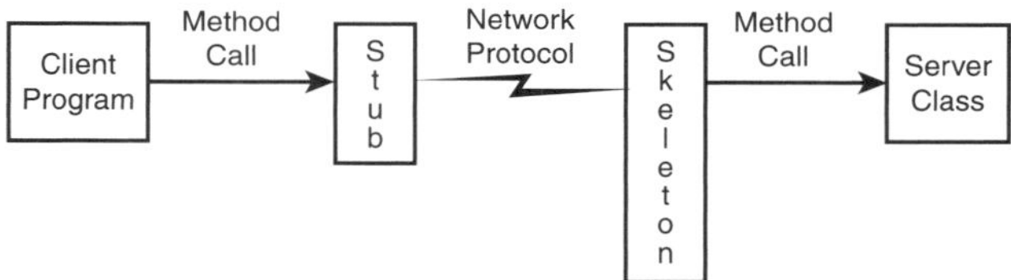

Figure 20.3
The stub and skeleton translate local method calls into a distributed method call.

The stub and the distributed object implement the interface you started with. Because the client talks to the stub through the same interface that the distributed object implements, you could eliminate the stub and skeleton and hook the client directly to the distributed object (running in the same JVM, of course). In other words, you can eliminate the middleware if you want to. Figure 20.4 compares the interaction between client and distributed object with and without the stub and skeleton.

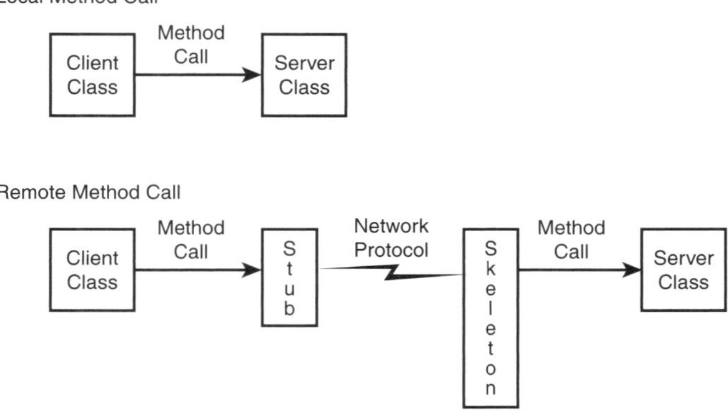

Figure 20.4
Thanks to a uniform interface, a client can talk to a distributed object directly or through a stub.

SINGLE-CLIENT VERSUS MULTI-CLIENT OBJECTS

When you design a three-tiered application, you must determine the relationship between the client and the distributed object. Does each client have its own personal distributed object or does a single distributed object service multiple clients? The determining factor in this decision is the data involved—how much there is, and where it is best to keep it.

If the distributed object doesn't need to keep any data between method calls, it can usually service multiple clients. In these cases, you aren't really doing distributed objects, you're doing remote procedure calls. There isn't anything specifically wrong with remote procedure calls. Sometimes they are called for by the application. Other times, however, the distributed objects need to hold on to data between method calls.

Suppose, for example, you are doing an online shopping cart application and you decide to make the shopping cart a distributed object. You can place objects into the shopping cart using remote method calls. Obviously, the shopping cart needs to remember what items it already has, so it wouldn't be wise to have a shopping cart object service multiple clients. How would it know which items belong to which client? You need each client to have its own shopping cart object.

You could certainly implement portions of the shopping cart as a multi-client object. For example, when you complete the order, you usually send it off to a separate fulfillment application, or at least store the order in a database. You could implement the order completion as a multi-client object. In this case, the client must pass the entire contents of the shopping cart to the distributed object. The client would be responsible for the management of the shopping cart contents before the order is completed.

As with most design issues, the choice between single-client and multi-client objects involves a series of tradeoffs. There is no single right answer to cover all cases. Things generally boil down to a battle between scalability and maintainability.

SCALABILITY

Each distributed object contains a good bit more overhead than a regular Java object. After all, for each distributed object there is also a stub. Depending on the CORBA or RMI implementation, each distributed object may have its own network socket as well, although most implementations are more conservative in their use of network resources. If you can have potentially thousands or tens of thousands of clients that all have their own copy of a distributed object, you are looking at some serious memory usage. In most applications, the distributed objects spend a vast majority of their time just sitting there taking up space waiting for another message from the client. Multi-client objects spend more time servicing client requests because they have more clients.

When you have so many clients, you often need to balance the load across multiple servers. If each client must use a specific distributed object each time, you can't balance the load as easily. Basically, you must perform the load balancing when the client firsts gets a remote reference to the distributed object. After that, if a server gets busy, the only thing you can do is route new clients to another server and hope that things get better. If the client doesn't care which object it talks to, you can balance the load every time the client makes a call.

The bottom line is, multi-client objects tend to scale up better than single-client objects.

MAINTAINABILITY

Remote procedure calls came about before fully distributed objects, and there's a reason why distributed objects were necessary. Take the shopping cart, for example. If you used a remote procedure call to complete the shopping cart order, you would have some code somewhere else to maintain the contents of the cart until checkout time. You have two separate modules that perform shopping cart functions. If you need to change something in the shopping cart, you might have trouble finding which module contains the code you need to change.

Overall, the single-client object is a more object-oriented way of managing your data. One of the things that differentiates OO (Object Oriented) development from procedural development is the melding of methods with data. When you create a multi-client object, you are separating the methods from the data because you pass the data to the method every time you call it. Although the benefits of OO development are sometimes intangible, OO generally leads toward more modular design. Although future maintenance of the code is a big issue, OO code is usually easier to develop in the first place.

The bottom line is, single-client objects tend to be easier to maintain than multi-client objects.

STRIKING A BALANCE

As you design more and more distributed systems, you get a better feel for which way you should go with a particular application. Many times, you get an intuitive feeling that you should go a particular way based on similarities to projects you have already done. One of the difficulties in striking a balance between maintainability and scalability is that your project requirements are pulling hard in both directions. You need to develop the code quickly, make changes quickly and handle many, many users. You might try prototyping the application using each approach, or at least sketch out an initial design and try to evaluate your options based on the potential design. You might also try a hybrid approach. Use some multi-client objects for some of the high-volume, high-use transactions and single-client objects in other places. Unfortunately, there is no one solution that fits every project.

OPTIMIZING DATA ACCESS

A single-client object often has `get/set` methods to manipulate its various data values. When you use CORBA, you can define attributes for a module that are automatically converted into a `get/set` method pair (although the methods don't actually contain the names "get" and "set"). When the object has a large number of attributes, setting each attribute with a separate remote method call can take a long time. Each network call has a fixed amount of overhead in addition to the data being passed. For a large request, the overhead makes up a small percentage of the overall network traffic. For a short call, the overhead makes up a larger percentage. If you must set a large number of attributes on a busy network, you are clogging up your network with overhead.

In cases like these, you might consider creating methods to set a group of attributes at one time. In CORBA, that might involve the creation of a struct to contain the attributes you want to set. In RMI, you might create a pass-by-value object (a non-RMI object) containing the data.

When you need to read a lot of attributes, you can create view objects that represent all or a subset of the attributes in the object. This is especially useful if the overall data structure is complex. For example, in a shopping cart, if each item in the cart is a distributed object, you need a way to loop through the cart, get a reference to each item, and then use remote calls to fetch the attributes in each item. On the other hand, the cart could gather the information itself, package the data into some CORBA structs or data objects and pass the data back to the client. Many projects use these techniques when getting and setting attribute data.

DATABASE LOCKING

Database locking is another issue you frequently encounter in a three-tiered application. Locking is more of an issue when the clients can update existing data. If your application involves only querying and inserting new records, you probably don't need to worry about locking too much. Unfortunately, many applications involve updating.

You have three types of locking to choose from: optimistic, pessimistic, and non-existent. You were introduced to optimistic and pessimistic locking in Chapter 19, "Building a Two-Tiered Web Application." The third option, *non-existent* locking, means that you don't care and will happily overwrite changes that someone else made. Although this third option may sound horrible, it actually works for some applications in which you can assume that the most recent update must contain the correct data. This mostly occurs in systems in which the data reflects some real-life situation. It doesn't do any good to reject a new update that contains the current situation just because someone else was modifying the previous version of the information.

When the data arrives frequently, you also rarely need to perform locking. For example, for aircraft positions, you may receive updates every 5 minutes or even every 30 seconds. You may want to update the current position with no regard to locking because even if you cause the information to be incorrect, it will only be incorrect for a short period of time. Obviously, this technique is for systems in which the correctness of the data doesn't affect the operation of the system. An air traffic controller needs absolutely accurate information. A passenger watching a flight tracking display doesn't require 100% correct information all the time.

Generally speaking, three-tiered applications work best with optimistic locking. There are always exceptions to this, but generally, companies seem to be more willing to accept someone having to re-key data than they are to allow someone to open up a record, lock it, and go take a 20-minute break while no one else can update the record.

If you create a three-tiered application with pessimistic locking, you should consider adding `lock` and `unlock` methods for records to allow clients to pull up a record without locking it, and unlock a locked record without applying any changes.

When you use optimistic locking, you must look at where the data resides. For a single-client object, you can keep the object's version number (if you use version numbers) in the distributed object. If you have a multi-client object in which the clients pass all the data as method parameters, you must include the object's version number in the data being passed. Some applications don't use a version number, but instead keep an original copy of the object and compare the original copy to the version currently stored in the database. A scheme like this is much more difficult to handle with a multi-client object because the client must keep track of the original copy of the data as well. If you have a choice, use something like a version number as your optimistic locking flag.

In fact, for large objects, you may have multiple version flags that allow you to optimistically lock a portion of the data. For example, suppose you have a very large database object that represents information about an airline flight. Some of the attributes involve the flight crew, whereas others involve the number of passengers and the total cargo weight. Many different clients may update this object, where each client is updating only a subset of the data. You might create a version number for the flight crew information, another for the cargo, and a third for the passenger data. A client can update the flight crew data while another updates the cargo information without invalidating each other's copy of the object.

THREE-TIERED APPLICATION WITH ENTERPRISE JAVABEANS

The Enterprise JavaBeans specification is an excellent blueprint for three-tiered applications. An EJB container (think of a container as a server) provides the glue between presentation and business logic as well as the glue between business logic and data. You have the option with EJB to allow the container to handle the database chores. You just update the attributes in your Java beans and let the container make the database calls to save the object. This option is called *Container Managed Persistence* or CMP. You can also write your own database code to store your Java beans. If the beans save themselves to the database, they are performing *Bean Managed Persistence* or BMP.

There are two types of Enterprise JavaBeans: session beans and entity beans. The *entity* beans represent persistent data and are typically stored in a database. *Session* beans contain methods that typically relate to business logic functions. A client can make remote method calls to both session and entity beans. Most of the time, session beans are single-client objects. You can, however, create a stateless session bean that acts as a multi-client object. Because an entity bean represents persistent data, it typically has a single client. When a client uses an EJB server, it first gets a reference to a session bean. It can then initiate a series of method calls that represent a transaction. If the client decides to roll back the transaction, no changes are saved to the database. When the client commits the transaction, any changes are stored to the database. If an entity bean had multiple clients, one client's changes could end up in another client's transaction.

You will learn more about using EJBs with servlets and Java Server Pages in Chapter 23, "Using Enterprise JavaBeans in a Web Application."

CHAPTER 21

Using RMI in a Web Application

In this chapter

The Java Remote Method Invocation (RMI) package is a very natural way to do a three-tiered application. Because RMI is so tightly integrated with Java, it gives you a very natural feel. Calling a method in a remote Java object is just like calling a method in a local object, except that there is always the possibility of the call failing because of network problems.

When you use RMI in a Java Web application, the main thing you need to be concerned with is how you manage your remote object references. That is, you need to know when to create a connection to a remote object, how many connections you need, and when to release a connection.

USING A SINGLE RMI OBJECT FOR ALL REQUESTS

If you use a single RMI object or a small group of RMI objects to handle all your requests, you are probably using the stateless server model introduced in Chapter 20, "Designing a Three-Tiered Application." That is, you don't keep session-oriented information in the remote object. Instead, you pass the information every time you make a request. As you know from Chapter 20, the stateless server model usually scales up better than the stateful server, but you lose many benefits of a distributed object system. You have actually taken a step backward into the world of remote procedure calls.

Creating the connection to the remote object (normally referred to as *binding*) can be done in a servlet's `init` method or in a `jspInit` method. Listing 21.1 shows an example of a remote interface that you can use from a JSP.

LISTING 21.1 SOURCE CODE FOR `MOTD.java`

```
package usingjsp.rmi;

import java.rmi.*;

/** Describes the Message-Of-The-Day (MOTD) interface */
public interface MOTD extends Remote
{
    public String getMOTD() throws RemoteException;
}
```

Listing 21.2 shows a simple implementation of the Message-Of-The-Day service described in Listing 21.1.

LISTING 21.2 SOURCE CODE FOR `MOTDImpl.java`

```
package usingjsp.rmi;

import java.io.*;
import java.rmi.*;
import java.rmi.server.UnicastRemoteObject;

/** An implementation of the Message-Of-The-Day remote interfcae. */

public class MOTDImpl extends UnicastRemoteObject
```

```
    implements MOTD
{
/** The name of the file containing the message */
    protected String motdFileName;

/** Creates a new instance of the MOTD server assigned to a
 *  specific filename.
 */
    public MOTDImpl(String aMotdFileName)
        throws RemoteException
    {
        motdFileName = aMotdFileName;
    }

/** Returns the Message-Of-The-Day */
    public String getMOTD()
    {
        try
        {
// Open the message file
            BufferedReader reader = new BufferedReader(
                new FileReader(motdFileName));

// Create a buffer to hold the resulting message
            StringBuffer buffer = new StringBuffer();

            String line;

// Read all the lines in the file
            while ((line = reader.readLine()) != null)
            {
// Put each line into the buffer separated by newlines
                buffer.append(line);
                buffer.append("\n");
            }

            reader.close();

// Return the message
            return buffer.toString();
        }
        catch (IOException exc)
        {
// If there's an error, just return an empty message
            return "";
        }
    }

/** Activates the MOTD service */
    public static void main(String[] args)
    {
        String motdFile = System.getProperty("file", "motd.txt");
        String motdService = System.getProperty("service",
            "MessageOfTheDay");

// Must assign an RMI security manager
```

LISTING 21.2 CONTINUED

```
        if (System.getSecurityManager() == null)
        {
            System.setSecurityManager(new RMISecurityManager());
        }

        try
        {
// Create an instance of the MOTD service
            MOTDImpl impl = new MOTDImpl(motdFile);

// Register the service with the RMI registry
            Naming.rebind("//localhost/"+motdService, impl);

        }
        catch (Exception exc)
        {
            exc.printStackTrace();
        }
    }
}
```

Don't forget that after you compile the MOTDImpl.java file, you need to run the `rmic` compiler to create the stub and skeleton for the RMI implementation. An example of an `rmic` command would be:

```
rmic -d . usingjsp.rmi.MOTDImpl
```

If you are having trouble running `rmic`*, see "Running* `rmic`*" in the "Troubleshooting" section at the end of this chapter.*

When you run the server, you need to supply a security policy to allow you to create the remote object and register it with the naming service. As long as you are not on a live production system, you can create a security policy that allows all access. Listing 21.3 shows a dummy security policy file that you can use for testing.

LISTING 21.3 SOURCE CODE FOR `motd.policy`

```
grant {
        // Allow everything for now
            permission java.security.AllPermission;
};
```

Caution

The `motd.policy` file circumvents the Java security model. Make sure you only use it on a test system that is reasonably secure.

When you start your server, you must supply the name of the security policy file by setting the `java.security.policy` property, like this:

```
java -Djava.security.policy=motd.policy usingjsp.rmi.MOTDImpl
```

Note

Make sure you have already started the `rmiregistry` program before you run the server.

Listing 21.4 shows a Java Server Page that uses the MOTD interface to display a banner at the top of the page. Notice that it binds to the RMI service in the `jspInit` method and stores the remote reference in the application object.

LISTING 21.4 SOURCE CODE FOR `ShowMOTD.jsp`

```
<%@ page language="java" import="java.rmi.*,usingjsp.rmi.*" %>
<html>
<body bgcolor="#ffffff">
<table>
<tr><td bgcolor="#000080">
<font color="#ffffff">
<%= ((MOTD)application.getAttribute("MOTD")).getMOTD() %>
</font>
</table>
<h1>Welcome</h1>
Welcome to the Site
</body>
</html>

<%!
    public void jspInit()
    {
        try
        {
            MOTD motdRef = (MOTD) Naming.lookup(
                "//localhost/MessageOfTheDay");

            application.setAttribute("MOTD", motdRef);
        }
        catch (Exception exc)
        {
            application.log("Error binding to MOTD service", exc);
        }
    }
%>
```

Figure 21.1 shows the output from the `ShowMOTD` Java Server Page.

Remember to make the stub class available to the JSP engine by putting it somewhere in the JSP engine's classpath. If you already have a classpath entry pointing to your servlets, you may want to put the stubs and skeletons in the same directory. For example, if you have been putting your servlets in `c:\jspstuff\servlets`, you should generate a stub for that directory by typing:

```
rmic -d c:\jspstuff\servlets usingjsp.rmi.MOTDImpl
```

If you are having trouble running an RMI program, see "Running RMI Programs" in the "Troubleshooting" section at the end of this chapter.

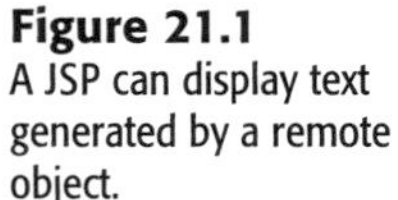

Figure 21.1
A JSP can display text generated by a remote object.

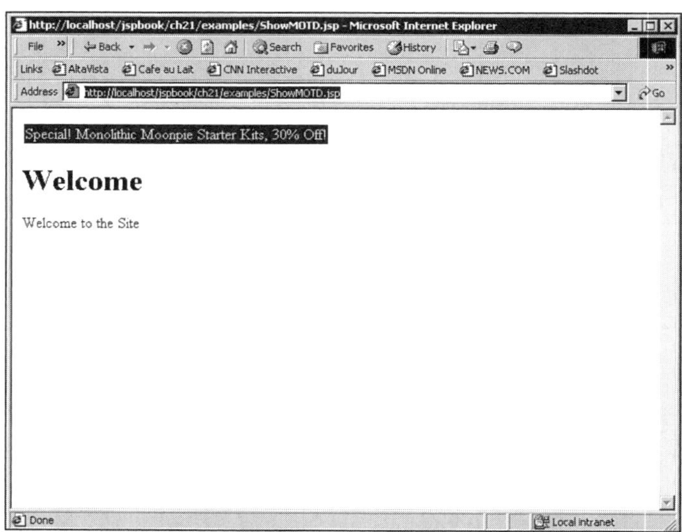

USING ONE OBJECT PER BROWSER SESSION

The remote procedure call approach to RMI really robs you of some of the benefits of RMI. The thing that distinguishes RMI and CORBA from remote procedure calls is that you can keep state information on the server. That is, each client can talk to its own private version of an object and that object can keep its own local data.

For example, in Chapter 8, "More About Saving Data," you saw a shopping cart example that stored the shopping cart information inside the `session` object. You can make an RMI shopping cart that keeps its information in the RMI object instead of on the Web server. This allows you to access the shopping cart in many different ways, rather than forcing you to use servlets or JSP.

When you create a stateful server and access it from a servlet or a Java Server Page, you typically store your remote references in the session object. That way, each browser session has its own separate remote objects in the RMI server.

When you need to create a new remote object, you don't usually just create the object directly. Instead, you use a factory object, as you saw in Chapter 20. You invoke a method in the factory object to create a new instance of a remote object. The example application you are about to see uses both a stateless and stateful remote object. The stateless object also acts as a factory for the stateful objects.

AN EXAMPLE RMI APPLICATION

Suppose you want to write a Web application that allows you to enter and edit service requests. The request contains the originator of the request, a brief description, and the complete details. You could put more information into the service request, of course, but for the purposes of demonstrating RMI, the following should be a sufficient set of data items.

THE DATABASE INTERFACE

The requests are stored in a database table defined by the following SQL statement:

```
create table service_request
    ( request_id int not null primary key auto_increment,
      originator varchar(50),
      title varchar(50),
      details text);
```

Using the `DatabaseObject` class from Chapter 19, "Building a Two-Tiered Web Application," you can easily create a class to read, insert, update, and delete items in the `service_request` table. Listing 21.5 shows you the `ServiceRequest` Java class that performs the database operations you will need.

LISTING 21.5 SOURCE CODE FOR `ServiceRequest.java`

```
package usingjsp.service;

import usingjsp.DatabaseObject;
import java.util.*;
import java.sql.*;

/** Provides data access to the service_request database table */

public class ServiceRequest extends DatabaseObject
    implements java.io.Serializable
{
    public int requestId;
    public String originator;
    public String title;
    public String details;

    public ServiceRequest()
    {
    }

/** Populates the data items from a database row */
    public ServiceRequest(ResultSet results)
        throws java.sql.SQLException
    {
        requestId = results.getInt("request_id");
        originator = results.getString("originator");
        title = results.getString("title");
        details = results.getString("details");
    }

    public int getRequestId() { return requestId; }
    public void setRequestId(int aRequestId) { requestId = aRequestId; }

    public String getOriginator() { return originator; }
```

LISTING 21.5 CONTINUED

```
    public void setOriginator(String anOriginator)
        { originator = anOriginator; }

    public String getTitle() { return title; }
    public void setTitle(String aTitle) { title = aTitle; }

    public String getDetails() { return details; }
    public void setDetails(String theDetails) { details = theDetails; }

/** Returns a list of fields to be used in a select statement */
    public String getFieldList()
    {
        return "request_id,originator,title,details";
    }

/** Returns the name of the table this class is mapped to */
    public String getTableName() { return "service_request"; }

/** Creates a new instance of this object populated with
 *  data from a database table.
 */
    public DatabaseObject createInstance(ResultSet results)
        throws SQLException
    {
        return new ServiceRequest(results);
    }

/** Inserts this object in the database and then updates the request
 *  id with the value automatically generated by the database.
 */
    public int insert(Connection conn)
        throws SQLException
    {
        int numRows = super.insert(conn);

        requestId = getSequenceNumber(conn);

        return numRows;
    }

/** Returns the SQL statement used to insert this object into the database */
    public String getInsertStatement()
    {
        return "insert into service_request (request_id, originator, "+
            "title, details) values (?,?,?,?)";
    }

/** Stores this object's data into the insert statement */
    public void prepareInsertStatement(PreparedStatement s)
        throws SQLException
    {
        s.setInt(1, 0);
        s.setString(2, originator);
        s.setString(3, title);
        s.setString(4, details);
    }
```

```
/** Returns the SQL statement used to update this object in the database */
    public String getUpdateStatement()
    {
        return "update service_request set originator=?, "+
            "title=?, details=? where request_id=?";
    }

/** Stores this object's data into the update statement */
    public void prepareUpdateStatement(PreparedStatement s)
        throws SQLException
    {
        s.setString(1, originator);
        s.setString(2, title);
        s.setString(3, details);
        s.setInt(4, requestId);
    }

/** Returns the SQL statement used to delete this object from the database */
    public String getDeleteStatement()
    {
        return "delete from service_request where request_id=?";
    }

/** Stores this object's primary key into the delete statement */
    public void prepareDeleteStatement(PreparedStatement s)
        throws SQLException
    {
        s.setInt(1, requestId);
    }
}
```

The Remote Interfaces

You need to perform two main tasks in the service request application. First of all, you must be able to get a list of service requests. Second, you must be able to insert, update, or delete an existing request. These two main tasks lead you to two separate RMI interfaces. The first interface, shown in Listing 21.6, allows you to get a list of all the service requests, locate a specific one, or create an empty request.

Listing 21.6 Source Code for `ServiceRequests.java`

```
package usingjsp.service;

import java.rmi.*;

public interface ServiceRequests extends Remote
{
    public RemoteServiceRequest[] getAll()
        throws RemoteException;
    public RemoteServiceRequest[] getAllByOriginator(String originator)
        throws RemoteException;
    public RemoteServiceRequest getByRequestId(int requestId)
        throws RemoteException;
```

LISTING 21.6 CONTINUED

```
    public RemoteServiceRequest create()
        throws RemoteException;
}
```

As you will soon see, the `ServiceRequests` implementation is a stateless object. You don't need a separate copy of this object for each browser session.

Listing 21.7 shows the `RemoteServiceRequest` interface, which serves two purposes. First, it acts as a remote wrapper around the bean property methods in the `ServiceRequest` class. That is, all of the `get` and `set` methods may be invoked via RMI through the `RemoteServiceRequest` interface. Second, it provides methods to let you save (which implies either insert or update) and delete the service request.

LISTING 21.7 SOURCE CODE FOR `RemoteServiceRequest.java`

```
package usingjsp.service;

import java.rmi.*;

public interface RemoteServiceRequest extends Remote
{
    public int getRequestId()
        throws RemoteException;
    public void setRequestId(int requestId)
        throws RemoteException;

    public String getOriginator()
        throws RemoteException;
    public void setOriginator(String originator)
        throws RemoteException;

    public String getTitle()
        throws RemoteException;
    public void setTitle(String aTitle)
        throws RemoteException;

    public String getDetails()
        throws RemoteException;
    public void setDetails(String theDetails)
        throws RemoteException;

    public void save()
        throws RemoteException;
    public void delete()
        throws RemoteException;
}
```

IMPLEMENTING THE `ServiceRequests` INTERFACE

The `ServiceRequests` interface calls for only a few operations, most of which are already implemented by the `DatabaseObject` class. All you need to do is invoke the proper method in DatabaseObject. The other thing you need is a main method that creates the lone instance of the ServiceRequestsImpl class and registers it with the RMI registry. Listing 21.8 shows the ServiceRequestsImpl class.

Listing 21.8 Source Code for ServiceRequestsImpl.java

```
package usingjsp.service;

import java.rmi.*;
import java.rmi.server.UnicastRemoteObject;
import java.sql.*;
import java.util.*;
import usingjsp.IConnectionPool;
import usingjsp.ConnectionPool;

public class ServiceRequestsImpl extends UnicastRemoteObject
    implements ServiceRequests
{
    protected IConnectionPool pool;

    public ServiceRequestsImpl()
        throws RemoteException
    {
// Force the JDBC driver to load
        try
        {
            Class.forName("org.gjt.mm.mysql.Driver").newInstance();
        }
        catch (Exception exc)
        {
            throw new RemoteException(
                "Error loading JDBC driver: "+exc.toString());
        }

// Create the connection pool
        try
        {
            pool = new ConnectionPool(
                "jdbc:mysql://localhost/usingjsp",
                "", "", 10);
        }
        catch (SQLException exc)
        {
            throw new RemoteException(
                "Error creating connection pool: "+exc.toString());
        }
    }

/** Returns an array of all the service request */
    public RemoteServiceRequest[] getAll()
        throws RemoteException
    {
        return doQuery(null);
    }
```

Listing 21.8 Continued

```
/** Returns an array of all service request with a
 *  specific originator */
    public RemoteServiceRequest[] getAllByOriginator(String originator)
        throws RemoteException
    {
        return doQuery("originator = '"+originator+"'");
    }

/** Locates a service request by its request id */
    public RemoteServiceRequest getByRequestId(int requestId)
        throws RemoteException
    {
        RemoteServiceRequest[] reqs = doQuery("request_id="+requestId);

        if (reqs.length == 1) return reqs[0];
        return null;
    }

/** Creates a new, empty service request */
    public RemoteServiceRequest create()
        throws RemoteException
    {
        return new RemoteServiceRequestImpl(pool);
    }

/** Performs the actual database query (using DatabaseObject.getAll) */
    protected RemoteServiceRequest[] doQuery(String whereClause)
        throws RemoteException
    {
        Connection conn = null;

        try
        {
// Allocate a connection from the pool
            conn = pool.getConnection();

// Create a dummy object for performing a query
            ServiceRequest query = new ServiceRequest();

// Perform the query
            Vector v = query.getAll(conn, whereClause);

// Create an array to hold the results
            RemoteServiceRequest remotes[] = new
                RemoteServiceRequest[v.size()];

// Loop through the results
            for (int i=0; i < remotes.length; i++)
            {
// Wrap each ServiceRequest object with a remote version
                remotes[i] = new RemoteServiceRequestImpl(
                    (ServiceRequest) v.elementAt(i), pool);
            }
```

```
            return remotes;
        }
        catch (SQLException exc)
        {
            throw new RemoteException(
                "Got exception while performing query: "+exc.toString());
        }
        finally
        {
            if (conn != null)
            {
                try
                {
                    pool.releaseConnection(conn);
                }
                catch (Exception ignore) {}
            }
        }
    }

    public static void main(String[] args)
    {
// Must assign an RMI security manager
        if (System.getSecurityManager() == null)
        {
            System.setSecurityManager(new RMISecurityManager());
        }

        try
        {
// Create an instance of the Service Request service
            ServiceRequestsImpl impl = new ServiceRequestsImpl();

// Register the service with the RMI registry
            Naming.rebind("//localhost/ServiceRequests", impl);

        }
        catch (Exception exc)
        {
            exc.printStackTrace();
        }
    }
}
```

Remember the discussion about using a factory method when you want to use separate items for each browser session? The `ServiceRequestsImpl` class acts like a factory. When you want to create a new `RemoteServiceRequest` object, you call the create method in the `ServiceRequests` interface. `ServiceRequestsImpl` will, in turn, create a new instance of `RemoteServiceRequestImpl` and return it back to you. You can also consider the queries to work like factories. They do create new instances of remote objects, but their data is populated from pre-existing data in the database. It gets confusing, though, if you think of the server as "creating" the objects when they already exist in the database.

IMPLEMENTING THE RemoteServiceRequest INTERFACE

Once again, most of the work required to implement the `RemoteServiceRequest` interface has already been done. You just need to know which methods to invoke. The `RemoteServiceRequest` interface includes methods that map directly to the bean property methods in the `ServiceRequest` object. You must relay the remote version of the methods on to the real methods in `ServiceRequest`. To do that, your implementation contains a `ServiceRequest` object. Each `get` and `set` method in the remote interface calls the corresponding `get` and `set` method in the `ServiceRequest` object.

The `save` and `delete` methods also act as passthrough methods, although they must also acquire a database connection before calling the `insert`, `update`, and `delete` methods in the `ServiceRequest` object. Listing 21.9 shows the `RemoteServiceRequestImpl` class.

LISTING 21.9 SOURCE CODE FOR RemoteServiceRequestImpl.java

```
package usingjsp.service;

import java.rmi.*;
import java.rmi.server.UnicastRemoteObject;
import java.sql.*;
import usingjsp.IConnectionPool;

/** Provides a remote interface for manipulating a ServiceRequest object */

public class RemoteServiceRequestImpl extends UnicastRemoteObject
    implements RemoteServiceRequest
{
/** The real service request this object provides access to */
    protected ServiceRequest request;

/** A pool of database connections */
    protected IConnectionPool pool;

/** Creates a new, empty service request */
    public RemoteServiceRequestImpl(IConnectionPool aPool)
        throws RemoteException
    {
        pool = aPool;
        request = new ServiceRequest();
    }

/** Creates a wrapper around an existing service request */
    public RemoteServiceRequestImpl(ServiceRequest aRequest,
        IConnectionPool aPool)
        throws RemoteException
    {
        request = aRequest;
        pool = aPool;
    }

// The following get/set methods just invoke their corresponding
// get/set methods in the real ServiceRequest object
```

```
    public int getRequestId() { return request.getRequestId(); };
    public void setRequestId(int id) { request.setRequestId(id); }

    public String getOriginator() { return request.getOriginator(); }
    public void setOriginator(String o) { request.setOriginator(o); }

    public String getTitle() { return request.getTitle(); }
    public void setTitle(String t) { request.setTitle(t); }

    public String getDetails() { return request.getDetails(); }
    public void setDetails(String d) { request.setDetails(d); }

/** Inserts or updates a ServiceRequest object depending on whether
 *  the requestId field has been initialized or not
 */
    public void save()
        throws RemoteException
    {
        Connection conn = null;

        try
        {
            conn = pool.getConnection();

            if (request.getRequestId() <= 0)
            {
                request.insert(conn);
            }
            else
            {
                request.update(conn);
            }
        }
        catch (SQLException exc)
        {
            throw new RemoteException(
                "Got exception while saving object: "+exc.toString());
        }
        finally
        {
            if (conn != null)
            {
                try
                {
                    pool.releaseConnection(conn);
                } catch (Exception ignore) {
                }
            }
        }
    }

/** Deletes the service request from the database */
    public void delete()
        throws RemoteException
    {
        Connection conn = null;
```

LISTING 21.9 CONTINUED

```
        try
        {
            conn = pool.getConnection();

            request.delete(conn);
        }
        catch (SQLException exc)
        {
            throw new RemoteException(
                "Got exception while deleting object: "+exc.toString());
        }
        finally
        {
            if (conn != null)
            {
                try
                {
                    pool.releaseConnection(conn);
                } catch (Exception ignore) {
                }
            }
        }
    }
}
```

CREATING THE WEB INTERFACE

The Web interface for the service request application isn't too different from the interface for the problem reporting application, except it is a little simpler. First of all, there is no login screen. Anyone can use the system. Second, the main entry page displays a list of all the service requests and allows you to insert, edit and delete directly from the main page. Listing 21.10 shows the main page for the service requests application.

LISTING 21.10 SOURCE CODE FOR ServiceRequests.jsp

```
<%@ page language="java" import="java.rmi.*,usingjsp.service.*" %>
<html>
<body bgcolor="#ffffff">
<h1>Service Requests</h1>
<%
// Get a list of all the requests
    RemoteServiceRequest[] requests =
        ((ServiceRequests) application.getAttribute("serviceRequests")).
            getAll();

// Only show the table heading if there are requests to display
    if (requests.length > 0)
    {
%>
<table border="4">
<tr><th>Title<th>Originator
<%
```

```
// Loop through all the requests
        for (int i=0; i < requests.length; i++)
        {
%>
<tr><td><%=requests[i].getTitle()%><td><%=requests[i].getOriginator()%>
<td>
<a href="EditServiceRequest.jsp?requestId=<%=requests[i].getRequestId()%>">
Edit</a>
<td>
<a href=
"DeleteServiceRequestConf.jsp?requestId=<%=requests[i].getRequestId()%>">
Delete</a>
<%
        }
%>
</table>
<%
    }
%>
<p>
<a href="EditServiceRequest.jsp">Enter a New Service Request</a>
</body>
</html>

<%!
    public void jspInit()
    {
        try
        {
// Locate the remote application
            ServiceRequests req = (ServiceRequests) Naming.lookup(
                "//localhost/ServiceRequests");

// Store it in the application object for everyone to use
            application.setAttribute("serviceRequests", req);
        }
        catch (Exception exc)
        {
            application.log(
                "Error binding to Service Request service");
        }
    }
%>
```

Figure 21.2 shows the main screen of the service request application.

Editing Service Requests

The service request application is a mixture of stateless and stateful objects. The `ServiceRequestsImpl` class is a stateless object, while the `RemoteServiceRequest` is a stateful object. In addition, the Web portion of the application acts as a stateful server, because it keeps a copy of the object you are editing. That is, when you say you want to edit an object, it stores the object in your session. Once you save the edited object, it retrieves the object from the session and copies your changes into the object. While you don't really gain anything when you create the edit page, the save page is remarkably short and simple.

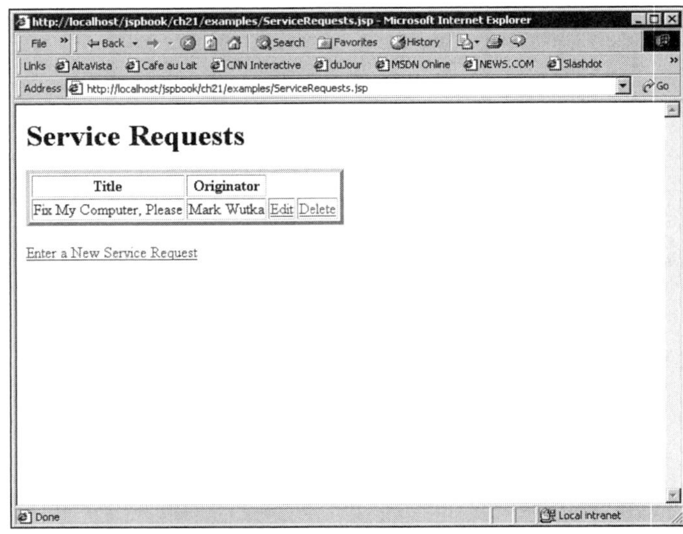

Figure 21.2
The main screen of the Service Request application uses RMI to locate the current requests.

Listing 21.11 shows the `EditServiceRequest` Java Server Page.

LISTING 21.11 SOURCE CODE FOR `EditServiceRequest.jsp`

```
<%@ page language="java" import="java.rmi.*,usingjsp.service.*" %>
<html>
<body bgcolor="#ffffff">
<%
    String requestIdStr = request.getParameter("requestId");

    RemoteServiceRequest remoteRequest = null;

// Locate the remote service in the application object
    ServiceRequests requests = (ServiceRequests)
        application.getAttribute("serviceRequests");

// If there was a requestId parameter passed in, locate the object
// it refers to
    if (requestIdStr != null)
    {
        int requestId = Integer.parseInt(requestIdStr);

        remoteRequest = requests.getByRequestId(requestId);
    }

// If there was no request id or the object no longer exists,
// create a new, empty object
    if (remoteRequest == null)
    {
        remoteRequest = requests.create();
%><h1>Enter a New Service Request</h1><%
    }
    else
```

```
    {
%><h1>Edit Service Request</h1><%
    }

// Store the current object so the SaveRequest.jsp page can get at it
    session.setAttribute("currentRequest", remoteRequest);
%>
<form action="SaveRequest.jsp" method="post">
<table>
<tr>
<td>Originator: <td><input type="text" name="originator"
    value="<%= nullToSpace(remoteRequest.getOriginator())%>">
<tr>
<td>Title: <td><input type="text" name="title"
    value="<%= nullToSpace(remoteRequest.getTitle())%>"><br>
<tr>
<td>Details:
</table>
<textarea name="details" rows=4 cols=60>
<%= nullToSpace(remoteRequest.getDetails()) %>
</textarea>
<p>
<input type="submit" value="Save!">
</form>
<p>
<a href="ServiceRequests.jsp">Return to Main Page</a>
</body>
</html>

<%!
/** Keeps null strings from appearing as "null" in text fields */
    public static String nullToSpace(String str)
    {
        if (str == null) return "";
        return str;
    }
%>
```

Figure 21.3 shows the EditServiceRequest JSP in action.

Listing 21.12 shows the SaveRequest JSP. Because the object is stored in the session, and it contains get and set methods like the underlying ServiceRequest class, you can use <jsp:useBean> and <jsp:setProperty> to do almost all the work for you. The only thing left is to call the save method.

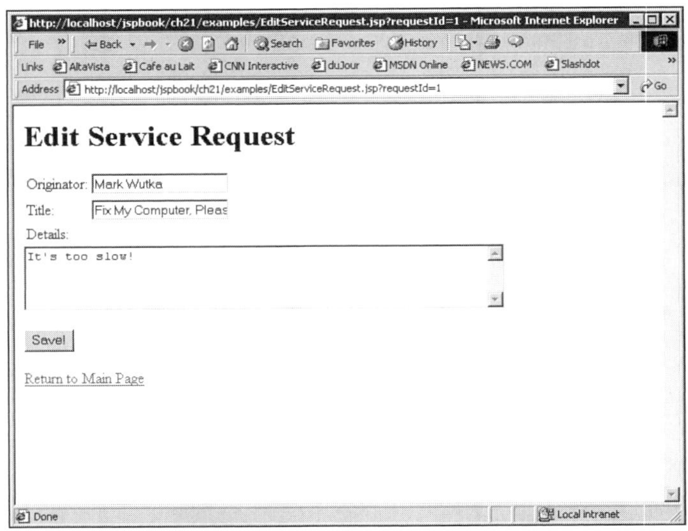

Figure 21.3
The `EditServiceRequest` page uses RMI to change values in an object on the RMI server.

LISTING 21.12 SOURCE CODE FOR `SaveRequest.jsp`

```
<%@ page language="java" import="usingjsp.service.*" %>
<html>
<body bgcolor="#ffffff">
<jsp:useBean id="currentRequest" type=
    "usingjsp.service.RemoteServiceRequest" scope="session"/>
<jsp:setProperty name="currentRequest" property="*"/>
<% currentRequest.save(); %>
<h1>Success</h1>
Your service request has been entered into the database.
<p>
<a href="ServiceRequests.jsp">Return to Main Page</a>
</body>
</html>
```

TROUBLESHOOTING

RUNNING `rmic`

Where's `rmic`? I installed Java but it's not here.

Make sure you have installed the Java JDK and not the Java JRE. If you can run `javac`, `rmic` should be there, too. If you are using Microsoft's Java SDK, Microsoft conveniently omitted any RMI support from their Java implementation. Your best bet is to use Sun's JDK when using RMI.

Why doesn't `rmic` find my class files?

`Rmic` is usually very good at finding class files; if it can't, they must not be in the path, or you typed the name wrong. Remember to use the fully qualified classname (that is, include the package name).

RUNNING RMI PROGRAMS

Why do I get security exceptions when I run my RMI program?

You need to set the security policy for your application in order to use RMI.

Why can't my RMI client find the server?

Make sure the `rmiregistry` program is running. The `rmiregistry` program acts as a directory lookup so clients can find the servers they need.

CHAPTER 22

Using CORBA in a Web Application

In this chapter

CORBA is, of course, the Common Object Request Broker Architecture and is a language-neutral system for inter-object communication. When CORBA first appeared on the scene, it was hailed as a great unifying technology that would bridge the gap between different programming languages and different operating systems. CORBA may have failed to live up to its potential to some extent, but it is still a useful technology. While many Java applications lean toward RMI, which is more tightly integrated with Java, and Enterprise Java Beans, which uses RMI as the underlying transport, other applications still use CORBA for a variety of reasons.

One of the attractions of CORBA is the fact that it works across multiple programming languages. You can write CORBA services in C++ and access them from Java. There are even CORBA language bindings for scripting languages like Python and Perl, allowing you to create scripts to access your CORBA services. This multilanguage capability is especially useful for accessing legacy systems. You may not be able to run Java on some of your systems, but you might be able to run CORBA on them. You can use CORBA to expose legacy systems to your Java applications, allowing you to develop new applications without adding more complexity to the legacy systems.

When a project first starts, many developers go through numerous debates deciding whether to use CORBA, RMI or some other distributed solution. RMI is tightly integrated with Java, making the development a bit easier and more seamless. CORBA gives you better options for system interconnection. Although RMI and CORBA take different approaches when it comes to defining your remote interface, they are essentially the same when it comes to your overall application architecture. As with RMI, when you use CORBA you must decide whether each browser session will talk to its own separate object or share the same object with the other sessions.

Using One CORBA Object for All Sessions

You can use the same CORBA object to service requests from all your browser sessions. When used this way, CORBA is little more than a remote procedure call mechanism. In situations like this, your server is typically stateless. This is the same situation you saw at the beginning of Chapter 21, "Using RMI in a Web Application," where all browser sessions accessed a single RMI object.

Listing 22.1 shows the CORBA IDL file for a simple CORBA service that returns a Message-Of-The-Day similar to the application in Chapter 21.

Listing 22.1 Source Code for MOTD.idl

```
module usingjsp
{
    module motd
    {
        interface MOTD
        {
            string getMOTD();
```

```
        };
    };
};
```

If you are having trouble compiling IDL files, see "Compiling IDL Files," in the "Troubleshooting" section at the end of this chapter.

Listing 22.2 shows the CORBA service that implements the Message-Of-The-Day service.

Listing 22.2 Source Code for MOTDImpl.java

```
package usingjsp.motd;

import org.omg.CosNaming.*;
import org.omg.CosNaming.NamingContextPackage.*;
import org.omg.CORBA.*;

import java.io.*;

public class MOTDImpl extends _MOTDImplBase
{
/** The name of the file containing the message */
    protected String motdFileName;

/** Creates a new instance of the MOTD server assigned to a
 *  specific filename.
 */
    public MOTDImpl(String aMotdFileName)
    {
        motdFileName = aMotdFileName;
    }

    public String getMOTD()
    {
        try
        {
// Open the message file
            BufferedReader reader = new BufferedReader(
                new FileReader(motdFileName));

// Create a buffer to hold the resulting message
            StringBuffer buffer = new StringBuffer();

            String line;

// Read all the lines in the file
            while ((line = reader.readLine()) != null)
            {
// Put each line into the buffer separated by newlines
                buffer.append(line);
                buffer.append("\n");
            }

            reader.close();

// Return the message
```

LISTING 22.2 CONTINUED

```
            return buffer.toString();
        }
        catch (IOException exc)
        {
// If there's an error, just return an empty message
            return "";
        }
    }

    public static void main(String[] args)
    {
        String motdFile = System.getProperty("file", "motd.txt");
        String motdService = System.getProperty("service",
            "MessageOfTheDay");
        try
        {
// Create a reference to the CORBA orb
            ORB orb = ORB.init(args, null);

// Create an instance of the MOTD implementation
            MOTDImpl impl = new MOTDImpl(motdFile);

// Register the MOTD implementation with the ORB
            orb.connect(impl);

// Locate the CORBA naming service
            org.omg.CORBA.Object objRef =
                orb.resolve_initial_references("NameService");

// Cast the CORBA Object to NamingContext using the narrow method
            NamingContext ncRef = NamingContextHelper.narrow(objRef);

// Create a NameComponent representing the path for the MOTD service
            NameComponent nc = new NameComponent(motdService, "");
            NameComponent[] path = new NameComponent[] { nc };

// Register the MOTD implementation with the naming service
            ncRef.rebind(path, impl);

// Go into an infinite loop while the ORB services requests
            java.lang.Object sync = new java.lang.Object();
            synchronized (sync)
            {
                sync.wait();
            }
        }
        catch (Exception exc)
        {
            exc.printStackTrace();
        }
    }
}
```

To run `MOTDImpl`, you must first start the CORBA naming service. The naming service that comes with JDK 1.2 is called `tnameserv`. You must start it with the following command:

```
tnameserv -ORBInitialPort 1050
```

To run the `MOTDImpl` service, you must also specify the `ORBInitialPort` parameter on the command line, like this:

```
java usingjsp.motd.MOTDImpl -ORBInitialPort 1050
```

Listing 22.3 shows a Java Server Page that binds to the Message-Of-The-Day service if necessary and displays the message.

Listing 22.3 Source Code for ShowMOTD.jsp

```
<%@ page language="java" import="org.omg.CORBA.*,usingjsp.motd.*" %>
<%@ page import="org.omg.CosNaming.*" %>
<html>
<body bgcolor="#ffffff">
<table>
<tr><td bgcolor="#000080">
<font color="#ffffff">
<%= ((MOTD)application.getAttribute("MOTD")).getMOTD() %>
</font>
</table>
<h1>Welcome</h1>
Welcome to the Site
</body>
</html>

<%!
    public void jspInit()
    {
        try
        {
// Create an instance of the CORBA orb
            ORB orb = ORB.init(
                new String[] { "-ORBInitialPort", "1050" }
                , null);

// Locate the CORBA naming service
            org.omg.CORBA.Object objRef =
                orb.resolve_initial_references("NameService");

// Instead of using the Java cast operator, the correct way to convert
// a CORBA Object into a specific type is to use that type's helper
            NamingContext ncRef = NamingContextHelper.narrow(objRef);

// Create a name component path for locating the MOTD service
            NameComponent nc = new NameComponent("MessageOfTheDay", "");
            NameComponent path[] = new NameComponent[] { nc };

// Locate the MOTD service and narrow (i.e. cast) the reference
// to an object of type MOTD
            MOTD motdRef = MOTDHelper.narrow(ncRef.resolve(path));

// Put the MOTD object in the application object
            getServletContext().setAttribute("MOTD", motdRef);
        }
```

LISTING 22.3 CONTINUED

```
        catch (Exception exc)
        {
            getServletContext().log("Error binding to MOTD service", exc);
        }
    }
%>
```

You can access CORBA services from servlets too. Listing 22.4 shows the servlet equivalent of the JSP from Listing 22.4.

LISTING 22.4 SOURCE CODE FOR ShowMOTDServlet.java

```
package usingjsp.motd;

import org.omg.CORBA.*;
import org.omg.CosNaming.*;

import javax.servlet.*;
import javax.servlet.http.*;
import java.io.*;

public class ShowMOTDServlet extends HttpServlet
{
    public void service(HttpServletRequest request,
        HttpServletResponse response)
        throws IOException, ServletException
    {
        try
        {
            MOTD motd = (MOTD) getServletContext().getAttribute("MOTD");

            String motdMessage = motd.getMOTD();

            response.setContentType("text/html");

            PrintWriter out = response.getWriter();

            out.println("<html><body bgcolor=\"#ffffff\">");
            out.println("<table><tr><td bgcolor=\"#000080\">");
            out.println("<font color=\"#ffffff\">");
            out.println(motdMessage);
            out.println(" </font></table><h1>Welcome</h1>");
            out.println("Welcome to the Site");
            out.println("</body></html>");
        }
        catch (Exception exc)
        {
            throw new ServletException("Got exception: "+exc.toString());
        }
    }

    public void init()
    {
        try
```

```
        {
// Create an instance of the CORBA orb
            ORB orb = ORB.init(
                new String[] { "-ORBInitialPort", "1050" }
                , null);

// Locate the CORBA naming service
            org.omg.CORBA.Object objRef =
                orb.resolve_initial_references("NameService");

// Instead of using the Java cast operator, the correct way to convert
// a CORBA Object into a specific type is to use that type's helper
            NamingContext ncRef = NamingContextHelper.narrow(objRef);

// Create a name component path for locating the MOTD service
            NameComponent nc = new NameComponent("MessageOfTheDay", "");
            NameComponent path[] = new NameComponent[] { nc };

// Locate the MOTD service and narrow (i.e. cast) the reference
// to an object of type MOTD
            MOTD motdRef = MOTDHelper.narrow(ncRef.resolve(path));

// Put the MOTD object in the application object
            getServletContext().setAttribute("MOTD", motdRef);
        }
        catch (Exception exc)
        {
            getServletContext().log("Error binding to MOTD service", exc);
        }
    }
}
```

Figure 22.1 shows the output from the MOTD servlet.

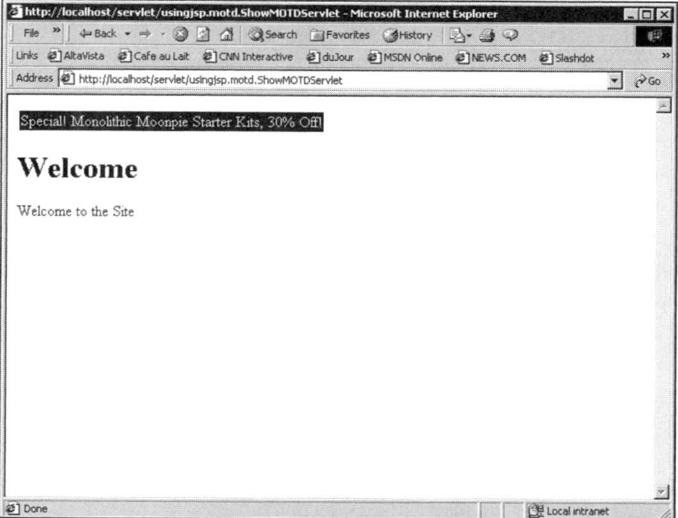

Figure 22.1 Servlets and Java Server Pages can display results from CORBA services

If you're having trouble running CORBA programs, see "Running CORBA Programs," in the "Troubleshooting" section at the end of this chapter.

USING SEPARATE CORBA OBJECTS FOR EACH SESSION

When you use a single CORBA object to handle all requests, you are going against the spirit of CORBA. Like RMI, CORBA represents a step above remote procedure calls. You can often make better use of CORBA by treating it like a distributed object system. Allow your servlets and Java Server Pages to have their own CORBA objects. You will often reduce the complexity of your Web classes when they no longer need to keep track of the data that is now being kept in CORBA objects .

As usual, there are tradeoffs involved with the fully distributed object architecture. Object attributes, like the ones defined in the CORBA IDL file shown in Listing 22.5, often lead to slow systems.

LISTING 22.5 SOURCE CODE FOR ManyAttributes.idl

```
module usingjsp
{
    interface Person
    {
        attribute string firstName;
        attribute string middleName;
        attribute string lastName;
        attribute short age;
        attribute string address1;
        attribute string address2;
        attribute string city;
        attribute string state;
        attribute string zip;
        attribute string homePhoneNumber;
        attribute string workPhoneNumber;
    };
};
```

The reason for the slowdown is that when you get or set a CORBA attribute, you make a remote call to the CORBA server. When you need to display many attributes, you make many calls. In a Web application, the slowdown may not be as noticeable as with a GUI application. A GUI frequently demands immediate access to the data, and when you use CORBA attributes you often see delays in updating the screen. With a Web application, you don't show the data to the user until you have retrieved it all. Although it may take longer to show the page, the user sees all the data at once when the page is finally displayed.

USING CORBA STRUCTS

Some applications store data elements in CORBA structures instead of defining them as attributes. You define a CORBA struct that represents all the data you want to send to an object and pass that structure in a single CORBA method call. For a large number of attributes, this method is much more efficient. Unfortunately, it also has its drawbacks:

- You must write code to copy data out of and possibly into structs. That's another piece of code that you must edit whenever you add new attributes.

- Structs are data-only. You can't invoke a method on a struct. You lose the OO advantages of combining methods with data.
- It is difficult, sometimes impossible, to represent complex data structures in CORBA structs. For example, it is not easy to define a linked list with CORBA structs.

Despite these disadvantages, you may still find yourself gravitating toward the struct approach. Listing 22.6 shows an IDL file for a simple struct-based application.

LISTING 22.6 SOURCE CODE FOR `PhoneBook.idl`

```
module usingjsp
{
    module phonebook
    {
        struct PhoneBookEntry
        {
            string firstName;
            string middleName;
            string lastName;
            string address1;
            string address2;
            string city;
            string state;
            string zip;
            string homePhone;
            string workPhone;
            string mobilePhone;
            string notes;
        };

        typedef sequence<PhoneBookEntry> PhoneBookEntries;

        interface PhoneOps
        {
            PhoneBookEntries getAll();
            PhoneBookEntries search(in string lastName);

            void add(in PhoneBookEntry newEntry);
            void update(in PhoneBookEntry newEntry);
            void delete(in PhoneBookEntry newEntry);
        };
    };
};
```

DEALING WITH NULL STRINGS

You don't need to work with CORBA structs long to see one of the most irritating limitations. You can't have null strings in CORBA. If you use many structures, it won't take long before you start seeing problems with uninitialized strings. These problems occur more often after you have gone back and added more fields to an existing structure. Although it is something of a brute force method, you can write a small Java function to loop through the fields in a CORBA struct and change all null strings to blanks. Listing 22.7 shows such a utility class.

LISTING 22.7 SOURCE CODE FOR `NullToBlank.java`

```
package usingjsp;

import java.lang.reflect.*;
import org.omg.CORBA.portable.*;

public class NullToBlank
{
// Keep a copy of the string class object handy
// String.class is shorthand for Class.forName("java.lang.String"), it's
// better to keep a copy of it statically than to regenerate it with
// every call.

    public static Class stringClass = String.class;

/** Examines an object changing any null strings to blanks. If the object
 *  contains any nested CORBA structures, will examine those too.
 */
    public static void nullToBlank(Object ob)
    {
// If the object is an array, loop through the members
        if (ob instanceof Object[])
        {
            Object[] obArray = (Object[]) ob;
            for (int i=0; i < obArray.length; i++)
            {
// Convert nulls to an empty string in each element
                nullToBlank(obArray[i]);
            }
            return;
        }

// Get the list of fields in this object
        Field[] obFields = ob.getClass().getFields();

        for (int i=0; i < obFields.length; i++)
        {
            try
            {
// Get the object's value
                Object obValue = obFields[i].get(ob);

// See if the object is null
                if (obValue != null)
                {
// If it is an array or a CORBA object, loop through the object's fields
                    if ((obValue instanceof IDLEntity) ||
                        (obValue instanceof Object[]))
                    {
                        nullToBlank(obValue);
                    }
                    continue;
                }

// Get the object's class
                Class obClass = obFields[i].getType();
```

```
// See if this object is supposed to be a string. You can't use
// instanceof in this case because the value is null so you don't
// know what its real class is supposed to be
                if (obClass.equals(stringClass))
                {
                    obFields[i].set(ob, "");
                }
            }
            catch (IllegalAccessException ignore) {}
        }
    }
}
```

ALTERNATIVES TO NULL

While changing a null string value may be a workable solution for you, there are times when you need something like a null. You may have a structure containing a lot of information but you only want to use the structure when it contains valid information. For example, you might have an `Employee` struct that contains a struct called `ManagerInfo`. The `ManagerInfo` struct contains manager-specific information only if the employee is a manager. You can add an `isManager` flag to the employee struct to indicate that the `ManagerInfo` struct is valid. In Java, however, you might want to use a null for the `ManagerInfo` struct. Unfortunately, CORBA structs can't be null. If you want to keep the notion of a null structure, you can store your structures in a sequence. In other words, you can use a null to replace something like

```
ManagerInfo mgrInfo;
```

You would declare a `ManagerInfoSeq` sequence by typing

```
typedef sequence<ManagerInfo> ManagerInfoSeq;
```

and to declare `mgrInfo` as a `ManagerInfoSeq` use

```
ManagerInfoSeq mgrInfo;
```

Now, when you want to indicate that there is no value for `mgrInfo`, you would assign it an empty array:

```
mgrInfo = new ManagerInfo[0];
```

AN EXAMPLE CORBA APPLICATION

You have already seen an example application that uses CORBA as a remote procedure call mechanism. Allowing browser sessions to have their own copies of CORBA objects, however, lets you use CORBA the way it was meant to be used.

When each browser session has its own set of CORBA objects, the CORBA objects act like an extension of the `session` object. That is, you store information specific to the session in the CORBA objects. The `session` object, in turn, holds references to the CORBA objects being used by the browser session. You may wonder why you should bother storing data in the CORBA objects when you can put it in the session and get it out easily. CORBA gives you an extra layer of separation between your application components. If your application performs a lot of work from within a JSP or servlet, you will find it difficult to use the same application code in a traditional GUI application. If you use CORBA, you can access the application code from a GUI and from a Web application at the same time.

Listing 22.8 shows the IDL for an online shopping cart application, much like the one you saw in Chapter 8, "More About Saving Data."

Listing 22.8 Source Code for `ShoppingCart.idl`

```
module usingjsp
{
    module cart
    {
        module corba
        {
            struct ItemInfo
            {
                string productCode;
                string description;
                double price;
                long quantity;
            };

            typedef sequence<ItemInfo> ItemInfoSeq;

            struct BillingInfo
            {
                string nameOnCard;
                string creditCardType;
                string creditCardNumber;
                string creditCardExpiration;
            };

            struct ShippingInfo
            {
                string name;
                string address1;
                string address2;
                string city;
                string state;
                string country;
                string postalCode;
                string email;
            };

            exception ShoppingCartException { string message; };

            interface IShoppingCart
            {
                void addItem(in ItemInfo item);
                void removeItem(in long itemIndex);
                ItemInfoSeq getItems();

                string completeOrder(in ShippingInfo shipping,
                    in BillingInfo billing)
```

```
                    raises (ShoppingCartException);
            };

            interface IShoppingCartFactory
            {
                IShoppingCart createShoppingCart();
            };
        };
    };
};
```

Listing 22.9 shows the implementation of the online shopping cart. Notice that the implementation works on top of the same shopping cart objects from Chapter 8. You can see now why the original shopping cart was written as a separate Java class. If it had been written directly into a JSP or a servlet, you couldn't use it to implement this CORBA service.

LISTING 22.9 SOURCE CODE FOR `ShoppingCartImpl.java`

```
package usingjsp.cart;

import usingjsp.cart.corba.*;
import org.omg.CORBA.*;
import java.util.*;

public class ShoppingCartImpl extends _IShoppingCartImplBase
{
    protected ShoppingCart cart;

    public ShoppingCartImpl()
    {
        cart = new ShoppingCart();
    }

/** Adds an item to the shopping cart */
    public void addItem(ItemInfo itemInfo)
    {
        Item item = new Item(itemInfo.productCode,
            itemInfo.description, itemInfo.price,
            itemInfo.quantity);

        cart.addItem(item);
    }

/** Removes an item from the shopping cart */
    public void removeItem(int itemIndex)
    {
        cart.removeItem(itemIndex);
    }

/** Returns an array of the items in the shopping cart */
    public ItemInfo[] getItems()
    {
// Get the items from the cart
        Vector items = cart.getItems();
```

LISTING 22.9 CONTINUED

```
// Create an array for returning the values
        ItemInfo[] itemInfos = new ItemInfo[items.size()];

        for (int i=0; i < itemInfos.length; i++)
        {
// Get the item from the vector
            Item item = (Item) items.elementAt(i);

// Create a CORBA version of the item
            itemInfos[i] = new ItemInfo(item.productCode,
                item.description, item.price,
                item.quantity);
        }

        return itemInfos;
    }

/** Asks the shopping cart to complete the order */
    public String completeOrder(ShippingInfo shippingInfo,
        BillingInfo billingInfo)
        throws usingjsp.cart.corba.ShoppingCartException
    {
// Copy the CORBA version of the billing information into a Billing object
        Billing billing = new Billing();

        billing.nameOnCard = billingInfo.nameOnCard;
        billing.creditCardType = billingInfo.creditCardType;
        billing.creditCardNumber = billingInfo.creditCardNumber;
        billing.creditCardExpiration = billingInfo.creditCardExpiration;

// Copy the CORBA version of the shipping information into a Shipping object
        Shipping shipping = new Shipping();
        shipping.name = shippingInfo.name;
        shipping.address1 = shippingInfo.address1;
        shipping.address2 = shippingInfo.address2;
        shipping.city = shippingInfo.city;
        shipping.state = shippingInfo.state;
        shipping.country = shippingInfo.country;
        shipping.postalCode = shippingInfo.postalCode;
        shipping.email = shippingInfo.email;

        try
        {
            return cart.completeOrder(shipping, billing);
        }
        catch (usingjsp.cart.ShoppingCartException exc)
        {
            throw new usingjsp.cart.corba.ShoppingCartException(
                exc.getMessage());
        }
    }
}
```

You may recall the discussion of factory objects in Chapter 21. When you want to create many instances of an object that will each be used by a single client, you create a single service that creates new instances. In other words, to create a shopping cart, you use a shopping cart factory. Listing 22.10 shows the shopping cart factory, which also acts as the main class for the CORBA server.

Listing 22.10 Source Code for `ShoppingCartFactoryImpl.java`

```
package usingjsp.cart;

import org.omg.CosNaming.*;
import org.omg.CosNaming.NamingContextPackage.*;
import org.omg.CORBA.*;
import usingjsp.cart.corba.*;

public class ShoppingCartFactoryImpl extends _IShoppingCartFactoryImplBase
{
    static ORB orb;

    public ShoppingCartFactoryImpl()
    {
    }

/** Creates a new shopping cart */
    public IShoppingCart createShoppingCart()
    {
        IShoppingCart cart = new ShoppingCartImpl();

        orb.connect(cart);

        return cart;
    }

    public static void main(String[] args)
    {
        String factoryService = System.getProperty("service",
            "ShoppingCartFactory");
        try
        {
// Create a reference to the CORBA orb
            orb = ORB.init(args, null);

// Create an instance of the MOTD implementation
            ShoppingCartFactoryImpl impl =
                new ShoppingCartFactoryImpl();

// Register the MOTD implementation with the ORB
            orb.connect(impl);

// Locate the CORBA naming service
            org.omg.CORBA.Object objRef =
                orb.resolve_initial_references("NameService");

// Cast the CORBA Object to NamingContext using the narrow method
            NamingContext ncRef = NamingContextHelper.narrow(objRef);
```

LISTING 22.10 CONTINUED

```
// Create a NameComponent representing the path for the MOTD service
            NameComponent nc = new NameComponent(factoryService, "");
            NameComponent[] path = new NameComponent[] { nc };

// Register the shopping cart factory implementation
            ncRef.rebind(path, impl);

// Go into an infinite loop while the ORB services requests
            java.lang.Object sync = new java.lang.Object();
            synchronized (sync)
            {
                sync.wait();
            }
        }
        catch (Exception exc)
        {
            exc.printStackTrace();
        }
    }
}
```

Listing 22.11 shows the servlet that creates the initial shopping cart object and stores it in the session object.

LISTING 22.11 SOURCE CODE FOR `ShoppingCartServlet.java`

```
package usingjsp.cart;

import org.omg.CORBA.*;
import org.omg.CosNaming.*;

import javax.servlet.*;
import javax.servlet.http.*;
import java.io.*;

import usingjsp.cart.corba.*;

public class ShoppingCartServlet extends HttpServlet
{
    IShoppingCartFactory factory = null;

    public void service(HttpServletRequest request,
        HttpServletResponse response)
        throws IOException, ServletException
    {
        try
        {
// Create a new shopping cart for this session
            IShoppingCart cart = factory.createShoppingCart();

            request.getSession().setAttribute("ShoppingCart", cart);

// Forward to the product catalog
            RequestDispatcher dispatcher =
```

```
                getServletContext().getRequestDispatcher(
                    "/jspbook/ch22/examples/ShowProductCatalog.jsp");

            dispatcher.forward(request, response);
        }
        catch (Exception exc)
        {
            throw new ServletException("Got exception: "+exc.toString());
        }
    }

    public void init()
    {
        try
        {
// Create an instance of the CORBA orb
            ORB orb = ORB.init(
                new String[] { "-ORBInitialPort", "1050" }
                , null);

// Locate the CORBA naming service
            org.omg.CORBA.Object objRef =
                orb.resolve_initial_references("NameService");

// Instead of using the Java cast operator, the correct way to convert
// a CORBA Object into a specific type is to use that type's helper
            NamingContext ncRef = NamingContextHelper.narrow(objRef);

// Create a name component path for locating the MOTD service
            NameComponent nc = new NameComponent(
                "ShoppingCartFactory", "");
            NameComponent path[] = new NameComponent[] { nc };

// Locate the shopping cart factory service and narrow (i.e. cast)
// the reference to an object of type IShoppingCartFactory
            factory = IShoppingCartFactoryHelper.narrow(
                ncRef.resolve(path));
        }
        catch (Exception exc)
        {
            getServletContext().log(
                "Error binding to ShoppingCartFactory service", exc);
        }
    }
}
```

Listing 22.12 shows the servlet that adds an item to the shopping cart. It is almost identical to the servlet from Chapter 8 except that it uses CORBA to talk to the shopping cart.

LISTING 22.12 SOURCE CODE FOR `AddToShoppingCartServlet.java`

```
package usingjsp.cart.corba;

import javax.servlet.*;
import javax.servlet.http.*;
```

LISTING 22.12 CONTINUED

```
import java.io.*;

public class AddToShoppingCartServlet extends HttpServlet
{
    public void service(HttpServletRequest request,
        HttpServletResponse response)
        throws IOException, ServletException
    {

// First get the item values from the request
        String productCode = request.getParameter("productCode");
        String description = request.getParameter("description");
        int quantity = Integer.parseInt(
            request.getParameter("quantity"));
        double price = Double.parseDouble(
            request.getParameter("price"));

// Now create an item to add to the cart
        ItemInfo item = new ItemInfo(productCode, description,
            price, quantity);

        HttpSession session = request.getSession();

// Get the cart
        IShoppingCart cart = (IShoppingCart) session.
            getAttribute("ShoppingCart");

        cart.addItem(item);

// Now display the cart and allow the user to check out or order more items
        response.sendRedirect(response.encodeRedirectURL(
            "/jspbook/ch22/examples/ShowCartAfterAdd.jsp"));
    }
}
```

Listing 22.13 shows the Java Server Page that displays the contents of the shopping cart. Again, the code is very similar to the shopping cart code in Chapter 8.

LISTING 22.13 SOURCE CODE FOR ViewShoppingCart.jsp

```
<%@ page language="java" import="usingjsp.cart.corba.*,java.util.*" %>
<%@ page import="java.text.*" %>

<%-- Show the header with the shopping cart image --%>
<table border="0">
<tr><td><img src="cart4.png"><td><h1>Shopping Cart</h1>
</table>

<%
// Get the current shopping cart from the user's sessoin
    IShoppingCart cart = (IShoppingCart) session.getAttribute("ShoppingCart");

// Get the items from the cart
    ItemInfo[] items = cart.getItems();
```

```
// If there are no items, tell the user that the cart is empty
    if (items.length == 0)
    {
        out.println("<h3>Your shopping cart is empty.</h3>");
    }
    else
    {
%>
<%-- Display the header for the shopping cart table --%>
<br>
<table border=4>
<tr><th>Description</th><th>Quantity</th><th>Price</th></tr>
<%

// Get a formatter to write out currency values
        NumberFormat currency = NumberFormat.getCurrencyInstance();

        for (int i=0; i < items.length; i++)
        {
            ItemInfo item = items[i];

// Print the table row for the item
            out.print("<tr><td>");
            out.print(item.description);
            out.print("</td><td>");
            out.print(item.quantity);
            out.print("</td><td>");
            out.print(currency.format(item.price));

// Print out a link that allows the user to delete an item from the cart
            out.println("</td><td>"+
                "<a href=\"/servlet/usingjsp.cart.corba.RemoveItemServlet?"+
                    "item="+i+"\">Remove</a></td></tr>");
        }
    }
%>
</TABLE>
```

Finally, Listing 22.14 shows the servlet that performs the shopping cart checkout function.

LISTING 22.14 SOURCE CODE FOR CheckoutServlet.java

```
package usingjsp.cart.corba;

import javax.servlet.*;
import javax.servlet.http.*;
import java.io.*;
import java.net.*;
import usingjsp.cart.*;

public class CheckoutServlet extends HttpServlet
{
    public void service(HttpServletRequest request,
        HttpServletResponse response)
        throws IOException, ServletException
```

Listing 22.14 Continued

```
    {

// First get the shipping values from the request
        ShippingInfo shipping = new ShippingInfo();

        shipping.name = request.getParameter("name");
        shipping.address1 = request.getParameter("address1");
        shipping.address2 = request.getParameter("address2");
        shipping.city = request.getParameter("city");
        shipping.state = request.getParameter("state");
        shipping.postalCode = request.getParameter("postalCode");
        shipping.country = request.getParameter("country");
        shipping.email = request.getParameter("email");

// Next, get the billing values
        BillingInfo billing = new BillingInfo();

        billing.nameOnCard = request.getParameter("nameOnCard");
        billing.creditCardType = request.getParameter("creditCardType");
        billing.creditCardNumber = request.getParameter(
            "creditCardNumber");
        billing.creditCardExpiration = request.getParameter(
            "creditCardExpiration");

        HttpSession session = request.getSession();

// Get the cart
        IShoppingCart cart = (IShoppingCart) session.
            getAttribute("ShoppingCart");

        try
        {
            String confirmation = cart.completeOrder(shipping, billing);

// Now display the cart and allow the user to check out or order more items
            response.sendRedirect(response.encodeRedirectURL(
                "/jspbook/ch22/examples/ShowConfirmation.jsp"+
                "?confirmationNumber="+URLEncoder.encode(confirmation)));
        }
        catch (ShoppingCartException exc)
        {
            PrintWriter out = response.getWriter();

            out.println("<html><body><h1>Error</h1>");
            out.println("The following error occurred while "+
                "processing your order:");
            out.println("<pre>");
            out.println(exc.getMessage());
            out.println("</pre>");
            out.println("</body></html>");
            return;
        }
    }
}
```

The shopping cart application presented here is not quite complete. Since you have already seen a complete shopping cart in Chapter 8, you know the other parts that need to be filled in. You can use the code from this chapter as a template for completing the shopping cart application if you decide to implement it.

TROUBLESHOOTING

COMPILING IDL TO JAVA

Where is `idltojava`?

Prior to JDK 1.3, Java did not ship with an IDL-to-Java compiler. Starting with JDK 1.3 the JDK includes an IDL-to-Java compiler called `idlj`. If you are still running JDK 1.2, you can get `idltojava` from `http://java.sun.com`.

Why does `idltojava` fail, saying it can't preprocess input?

For some reason, `idltojava` needs a C preprocessor installed on your system. If you don't have a C preprocessor, you must include the `–fno-cpp` option when you run `idltojava`.

RUNNING CORBA PROGRAMS

Why can't my clients access the server?

You probably aren't running the naming service. If you're using the CORBA support built in to the JDK, you want to run `tnameserv`. If you are using another CORBA product, consult the documentation for that product. Visibroker users should run `osagent`. Also, if the client and server are on two different networks, you might have issues with some name services. Visibroker, for instance, uses network broadcasts to locate services. Most network routers limit broadcasts to the local network, so clients and servers running on different network segments often have trouble communicating.

Why do I keep getting null-value exceptions from CORBA?

You probably aren't initializing a value in one of your CORBA structures. Remember that CORBA doesn't allow null values at all, so you must make sure that all your strings and sequences have been initialized.

Why do I get CORBA UNKNOWN errors when I use another CORBA implementation?

Starting with JDK 1.2, Java ships with built-in CORBA support. Sometimes, however, the built-in classes clash with classes in third-party libraries. When you start your program, you must tell it the classnames for the ORB and ORBSingleton classes. Consult the documentation for your ORB for further information.

CHAPTER 23

USING ENTERPRISE JAVABEANS IN A WEB APPLICATION

In this chapter

WHAT IS ENTERPRISE JAVABEANS?

Enterprise JavaBeans (EJB) is a framework for creating high-performance applications in Java. Most business applications have several common features. They access a database or some kind of persistent data store, execute transactions on the data, and often have some kind of mapping layer between the database and the Java classes.

When you create a mapping layer between a database and Java classes, you almost always end up with two kinds of objects: data objects and business logic objects. The EJB standard formalizes many of these concepts into a standard framework. The benefit of a standard framework is that you can now choose from a number of application servers and write code that is easily ported between servers. Ideally, you should be able to run code on any EJB server with no changes, but in practice, you often use server-specific objects that may not be available on all servers.

ENTITY AND SESSION BEANS

Enterprise JavaBeans comes in two flavors: entity beans and session beans. *Entity beans* represent the data items that are the core of your application. A typical entity bean might be `Customer`, `Order`, `OrderItem`, or `Product`. *Session beans*, on the other hand, represent logical operations and usually operate on the entity beans. A typical session bean might be named `OrderEntry` or `PaymentAuthorization`.

A session bean is typically the main bean that an application uses, although an application might manipulate the entity beans directly in many circumstances. For example, an application might create an `Order` entity bean and an `OrderItem` entity bean and initialize their values. It would then use the `OrderEntry` session bean to store the order.

CONTAINERS

The term *container* is frequently confusing for Java developers who are unfamiliar with Enterprise JavaBeans. You often see the phrase "EJB container" and think that it must be a container class like a `Vector` or a `Hashtable`. In this context, however, a container is more like a server. A server might actually support multiple separate containers, so the container is more like a virtual server running inside an EJB server. Sun also makes references to servlet containers, which are essentially servlet engines like Tomcat or JRun. Again, the term *container* essentially means *server*.

PERSISTENCE

Saving and retrieving entity beans is extremely important in an EJB application. EJB persistence comes in two flavors: Container-Managed Persistence (CMP) and Bean-Managed Persistence (BMP). With *Bean-Managed Persistence*, each entity bean is responsible for saving itself and retrieving itself from the database. The bean must have methods to insert itself, update itself, read itself, and do a few other housekeeping methods.

Container-Managed Persistence is one of the most exciting features of EJB because the EJB container itself handles the bean persistence. Ideally, you can write entity and session beans that just do business logic: that is, they get to concentrate on what they're good at. The container handles the database operations.

Transactions

Operations in a session bean typically take place within the scope of a transaction, just as they do in a typical two-tiered database application. The difference is, the EJB container manages the transactions (although the session bean does have some control over the transaction). You can tell the EJB container what kind of transaction scope is needed for each session bean method. For instance, you can indicate that a particular method always begins a new transaction, or that a method can only be called after a transaction has been started. As with the Container-Managed Persistence, the transaction features let you concentrate on the business logic and leave the transaction housekeeping to the server.

Connection Pooling

The EJB container even handles database connection pooling, relieving you of yet another housekeeping chore. After you configure the container, telling it how to create a database connection, it grabs a connection for you automatically. If you use CMP, you might never need to use the database connection directly. Even if you use BMP, you don't need to worry about getting a connection from the pool and returning it when you're done. The container handles that for you.

Object Pooling

An EJB server can also pool Enterprise JavaBeans. The advantage to pooling the beans is that EJB setup can take a lot of time, depending on the bean. For beans that you use frequently, you may want to tell the EJB server to keep a pool of the beans handy because you'll need them often.

How EJB, Servlets, and Java Server Pages Fit Together

Enterprise JavaBeans, servlets, and Java Server Pages are part of the Java 2 Enterprise Edition (J2EE) suite of APIs. These three technologies represent the core of J2EE because they are the parts of J2EE that function as servers. The other APIs—JDBC, JNDI, RMI, CORBA, Java Transaction Service (JTS), Java Message Service (JMS), J2EE Connector Architecture (JCA), Java Authentication and Authorization Service (JAAS), and XML—help support EJB, servlets, and JSP servers.

EJB is flexible enough to use for both Web applications and standard GUI applications. Obviously for Web applications, you should use JSP and servlets to interact with the browser. EJB concentrates solely on the back-end processing: the part that doesn't interact with the user. Servlets and JSP make an attractive mechanism for developing the user interface because many applications are going to a Web-based approach.

You will find Web-centric applications becoming more popular as more devices become Internet-enabled. Already, you are seeing cell phones with Web access. Soon you will have small Web terminals in your car and in various parts of your house. It's much easier to write an application once, for the Web, rather than make a separate standalone application for every type of device a user might have. The possibility of so many Web-enabled devices makes the combination of EJB, servlets, and Java Server Pages a potent development tool.

CREATING AN ENTITY BEAN

One thing you quickly notice about Enterprise JavaBeans is that they are considerably more time-consuming to create than normal Java beans. For every entity bean, you must create two different Java interfaces as well as the implementation class for the bean itself.

Note

As Enterprise JavaBeans becomes more popular, you can expect various Java development tools to make EJB development easier. Borland's JBuilder 3.5 will even generate Remote and Home interfaces for you.

CREATING THE ENTITY BEAN IMPLEMENTATION

If you want to use Container Managed Persistence, you can create an entity bean a lot faster than usual. You define the fields that will be stored in the database: some methods to manipulate the contents of the bean and a few standard methods defined in the `EntityBean` interface, most of which are empty when using CMP. You must still define the Home and Remote interfaces for the bean, but you don't need to write any database code.

The methods in the `EntityBean` interface are

```
public void ejbActivate()
    throws EJBException, java.rmi.RemoteException
public void ejbLoad()
    throws EJBException, java.rmi.RemoteException
public void ejbPassivate()
    throws EJBException, java.rmi.RemoteException
public void ejbRemove()
    throws EJBException, RemoveException, java.rmi.RemoteException
public void ejbStore()
    throws EJBException, java.rmi.RemoteException
public void setEntityContext(EntityContext entContext)
    throws EJBException, java.rmi.RemoteException
public void unsetEntityContext()
   throws EJBException, java.rmi.RemoteException
```

An entity bean that uses CMP is easier to write than it is to describe. It's better to look at one first, and then see what the individual pieces actually do. Listing 23.1 shows an entity bean that uses CMP for persistence.

Listing 23.1 Source Code for AddressEJB.java

```
package usingjsp.ejb;

import usingjsp.DatabaseObject;
import javax.ejb.*;


/** A data object representing an Address for an address book database
 */
public class AddressEJB
    implements EntityBean, java.io.Serializable
{
    public String firstName;
    public String middleName;
    public String lastName;
    public String homePhoneNumber;
    public String workPhoneNumber;
    public String mobilePhoneNumber;
    public String address1;
    public String address2;
    public String city;
    public String state;
    public String zip;
    public String email;

    private EntityContext context;

    public AddressEJB()
    {
    }

    public AddressKey ejbCreate(String aFirstName, String aMiddleName,
        String aLastName)
        throws CreateException
    {
        if ((firstName == null) && (lastName == null))
        {
            throw new CreateException(
                "You must supply at least a first or last name");
        }

        firstName = aFirstName;
        middleName = aMiddleName;
        lastName = aLastName;

        return null;
    }

    public String getFirstName() { return firstName; }
    public void setFirstName(String theFirstName)    {
        firstName = theFirstName;
    }

    public String getMiddleName() { return middleName; }
    public void setMiddleName(String theMiddleName)    {
        middleName = theMiddleName;
```

LISTING 23.1 CONTINUED

```
    }

    public String getLastName() { return lastName; }
    public void setLastName(String theLastName)    {
        lastName = theLastName;
    }

    public String getHomePhoneNumber() { return homePhoneNumber; }
    public void setHomePhoneNumber(String theHomePhoneNumber)    {
        homePhoneNumber = theHomePhoneNumber;
    }

    public String getWorkPhoneNumber() { return workPhoneNumber; }
    public void setWorkPhoneNumber(String theWorkPhoneNumber)    {
        workPhoneNumber = theWorkPhoneNumber;
    }

    public String getMobilePhoneNumber() { return mobilePhoneNumber; }
    public void setMobilePhoneNumber(String theMobilePhoneNumber)    {
        mobilePhoneNumber = theMobilePhoneNumber;
    }

    public String getAddress1() { return address1; }
    public void setAddress1(String theAddress1)    {
        address1 = theAddress1;
    }

    public String getAddress2() { return address2; }
    public void setAddress2(String theAddress2)    {
        address2 = theAddress2;
    }

    public String getCity() { return city; }
    public void setCity(String theCity)    {
        city = theCity;
    }

    public String getState() { return state; }
    public void setState(String theState)    {
        state = theState;
    }

    public String getZip() { return zip; }
    public void setZip(String theZip)    {
        zip = theZip;
    }

    public String getEmail() { return email; }
    public void setEmail(String theEmail)    {
        email = theEmail;
    }

    public void ejbActivate()
    {
    }
```

```
    public void ejbPassivate()
    {
    }

    public void ejbLoad()
    {
    }

    public void ejbStore()
    {
    }

    public void ejbRemove()
    {
    }

    public void setEntityContext(EntityContext aContext)
    {
        context = aContext;
    }

    public void unsetEntityContext()
    {
        context = null;
    }
}
```


As you can see, the bean contains some public attributes that will be stored in a database table. It also has some accessor methods that let you manipulate the attribute values.

The various `finder` methods let you locate entity beans based on certain values. This technique of defining `finder` methods is not as powerful as a full-blown query language such as SQL or OQL, but it does make things easier. When you use CMP, you don't write the finger methods yourself. Instead, you tell the EJB server how to perform queries when you configure the bean.

The `ejbCreate` method creates a new instance of the bean and stores it in the database. When you use CMP, the `ejbCreate` method only needs to initialize the bean's attributes and possibly throw a `CreateException` if there is an error in any of the parameters that were passed in. When you use BMP, the `ejbCreate` method must insert a copy of the entity bean into the database.

Finally, you see the methods defined in the `EntityBean` interface. The EJB container calls `setEntityContext` just after it creates an instance of an entity bean in memory (after you ask it to create a new bean or locate an existing bean in the database). If an entity bean needs to access its associated context, it must store the context in a local variable. The `EntityContext` object returns a reference to the entity bean it's associated with (that is, the entity bean itself) and also the entity bean's primary key. The `unsetEntityContext` method informs the bean that it no longer has a context and is no longer being used by the EJB container.

The `ejbLoad` method is responsible for loading the entity bean in the database. When you use CMP, the `ejbLoad` method might be empty, or it might contain code to do any processing of data after it has been loaded from the database. When performing CMP, the EJB container calls `ejbLoad` after it has loaded the bean from the database.

The `ejbStore` method is responsible for storing the entity bean in the database. When you use CMP, the `ejbStore` method might be empty, or it might contain code to prepare some of the data elements for storage in the database. When performing CMP, the EJB container calls `ejbStore` before it stores the bean in the database.

The `ejbRemove` method is responsible for removing an entity bean from the database. When you use CMP, the `ejbRemove` method can perform any cleanup that might be required before removing the object. If you are using CMP and you want to keep the object from being removed, throw a `RemoveException`.

The EJB container might keep a pool of entity bean objects ready to handle any incoming requests. Whenever the container pulls a bean out of the pool and gets ready to use it, it calls the bean's `ejbActivate` method. Likewise, when the container returns a bean to the pool it calls the bean's `ejbPassivate` method. You don't need to do anything in these methods unless you have some specific requirements.

Listing 23.2 shows the same bean as Listing 23.1, only this time using BMP. Notice that the main differences are in the `ejbCreate`, `ejbLoad`, `ejbStore`, `ejbRemove`, and the `find` methods.

LISTING 23.2 SOURCE CODE FOR `AddressEJBBMP.java`

```
package usingjsp.ejb;

import javax.ejb.*;
import java.sql.*;
import javax.sql.*;
import javax.naming.*;
import java.util.*;

/** A data object representing an Address for an address book database
 */
public class AddressEJBBMP
    implements EntityBean, java.io.Serializable
{
    public String firstName;
    public String middleName;
    public String lastName;
    public String homePhoneNumber;
    public String workPhoneNumber;
    public String mobilePhoneNumber;
    public String address1;
    public String address2;
    public String city;
    public String state;
    public String zip;
    public String email;
```

```
private EntityContext context;
private Connection conn;
private static String dbName = "java:comp/env/jdbc/AddressDB";

public AddressEJBBMP()
{
}

public AddressKey ejbCreate(String aFirstName, String aMiddleName,
    String aLastName)
    throws CreateException
{
    firstName = aFirstName;
    middleName = aMiddleName;
    lastName = aLastName;

    if ((firstName == null) && (lastName == null))
    {
        throw new CreateException(
            "You must supply at least a first or last name");
    }

    PreparedStatement insertStmt = null;

    try
    {
        insertStmt = conn.prepareStatement(
            "insert into address (firstName, middleName, lastName) "+
            "values (?,?,?)");

        insertStmt.setString(1, firstName);
        insertStmt.setString(2, middleName);
        insertStmt.setString(3, lastName);

        if (insertStmt.executeUpdate() == 1)
        {
            return new AddressKey(firstName, middleName, lastName);
        }
        else
        {
            throw new CreateException(
                "Address:firstName="+firstName+",middleName="+
                middleName+",lastName="+lastName);
        }
    }
    catch (SQLException sqlExc)
    {
        throw new EJBException(sqlExc.toString());
    }
    finally
    {
        try
        {
            insertStmt.close();
        }
        catch (SQLException ignore)
        {
```

LISTING 23.2 CONTINUED

```
            }
        }
    }

    public void ejbPostCreate(String aFirstName, String aMiddleName,
        String aLastName)
    {
    }

    public String getFirstName() { return firstName; }
    public void setFirstName(String theFirstName)    {
        firstName = theFirstName;
    }

    public String getMiddleName() { return middleName; }
    public void setMiddleName(String theMiddleName)    {
        middleName = theMiddleName;
    }

    public String getLastName() { return lastName; }
    public void setLastName(String theLastName)    {
        lastName = theLastName;
    }

    public String getHomePhoneNumber() { return homePhoneNumber; }
    public void setHomePhoneNumber(String theHomePhoneNumber)    {
        homePhoneNumber = theHomePhoneNumber;
    }

    public String getWorkPhoneNumber() { return workPhoneNumber; }
    public void setWorkPhoneNumber(String theWorkPhoneNumber)    {
        workPhoneNumber = theWorkPhoneNumber;
    }

    public String getMobilePhoneNumber() { return mobilePhoneNumber; }
    public void setMobilePhoneNumber(String theMobilePhoneNumber)    {
        mobilePhoneNumber = theMobilePhoneNumber;
    }

    public String getAddress1() { return address1; }
    public void setAddress1(String theAddress1)    {
        address1 = theAddress1;
    }

    public String getAddress2() { return address2; }
    public void setAddress2(String theAddress2)    {
        address2 = theAddress2;
    }

    public String getCity() { return city; }
    public void setCity(String theCity)    {
        city = theCity;
    }
```

```
public String getState() { return state; }
public void setState(String theState)    {
    state = theState;
}

public String getZip() { return zip; }
public void setZip(String theZip)    {
    zip = theZip;
}

public String getEmail() { return email; }
public void setEmail(String theEmail)    {
    email = theEmail;
}

public void ejbActivate()
{
}

public void ejbPassivate()
{
}

public void ejbLoad()
{
    PreparedStatement loadStmt = null;

    try
    {
        loadStmt = conn.prepareStatement(
            "select homePhoneNumber, workPhoneNumber,"+
            "mobilePhoneNumber,address1,address2,city,state,zip,email"+
            " from address where firstName=? and middleName=?"+
            " and lastName=?");

        loadStmt.setString(1, firstName);
        loadStmt.setString(2, middleName);
        loadStmt.setString(3, lastName);

        ResultSet results = loadStmt.executeQuery();

        if (results.next())
        {
            homePhoneNumber = results.getString(1);
            workPhoneNumber = results.getString(2);
            mobilePhoneNumber = results.getString(3);
            address1 = results.getString(4);
            address2 = results.getString(5);
            city = results.getString(6);
            state = results.getString(7);
            zip = results.getString(8);
            email = results.getString(9);
        }
        else
        {
            throw new NoSuchEntityException(
                "Address:firstName="+firstName+",middleName="+
                middleName+",lastName="+lastName);
```

LISTING 23.2 CONTINUED

```
            }
        }
        catch (SQLException sqlExc)
        {
            throw new EJBException(sqlExc.toString());
        }
        finally
        {
            try
            {
                loadStmt.close();
            }
            catch (SQLException ignore)
            {
            }
        }
    }

    public void ejbStore()
    {
        PreparedStatement updateStmt = null;

        try
        {
            updateStmt = conn.prepareStatement(
                "update address set homePhoneNumber=?, workPhoneNumber=?,"+
                "mobilePhoneNumber=?,address1=?,address2=?,city=?,"+
                "state=?,zip=?,email=? where firstName=? and "+
                "middleName=? and lastName=?");

            updateStmt.setString(1, homePhoneNumber);
            updateStmt.setString(2, workPhoneNumber);
            updateStmt.setString(3, mobilePhoneNumber);
            updateStmt.setString(4, address1);
            updateStmt.setString(5, address2);
            updateStmt.setString(6, city);
            updateStmt.setString(7, state);
            updateStmt.setString(8, zip);
            updateStmt.setString(9, email);
            updateStmt.setString(10, firstName);
            updateStmt.setString(11, middleName);
            updateStmt.setString(12, lastName);

            if (updateStmt.executeUpdate() == 0)
            {
                throw new EJBException(
                    "Unable to store "+
                    "Address:firstName="+firstName+",middleName="+
                    middleName+",lastName="+lastName);
            }
        }
        catch (SQLException sqlExc)
        {
            throw new EJBException(sqlExc.toString());
        }
```

```
    finally
    {
        try
        {
            updateStmt.close();
        }
        catch (SQLException ignore)
        {
        }
    }
}

public void ejbRemove()
{
    PreparedStatement deleteStmt = null;

    try
    {
        deleteStmt = conn.prepareStatement(
            "delete from address where firstName=? and "+
            "middleName=? and lastName=?");

        deleteStmt.setString(1, firstName);
        deleteStmt.setString(2, middleName);
        deleteStmt.setString(3, lastName);

        if (deleteStmt.executeUpdate() == 0)
        {
            throw new EJBException(
                "Unable to delete "+
                "Address:firstName="+firstName+",middleName="+
                middleName+",lastName="+lastName);
        }
    }
    catch (SQLException sqlExc)
    {
        throw new EJBException(sqlExc.toString());
    }
    finally
    {
        try
        {
            deleteStmt.close();
        }
        catch (SQLException ignore)
        {
        }
    }
}

public void setEntityContext(EntityContext aContext)
{
    context = aContext;
    try
    {
        InitialContext iContext = new InitialContext();
        DataSource dataSource = (DataSource) iContext.lookup(dbName);
```

LISTING 23.2 CONTINUED

```
            conn = dataSource.getConnection();
        }
        catch (Exception exc)
        {
            throw new EJBException(exc.toString());
        }
    }

    public void unsetEntityContext()
    {
        context = null;
    }

    public AddressKey ejbFindByPrimaryKey(AddressKey key)
        throws FinderException
    {
        PreparedStatement findStmt = null;

        try
        {
            findStmt = conn.prepareStatement(
                "select firstName, lastName, middleName "+
                "from address where firstName=? and "+
                "middleName=? and lastName=?");

            findStmt.setString(1, key.firstName);
            findStmt.setString(2, key.middleName);
            findStmt.setString(3, key.lastName);

            ResultSet results = findStmt.executeQuery();

            if (results.next())
            {
                return key;
            }
            else
            {
                throw new ObjectNotFoundException(
                    "Unable to locate "+
                    "Address:firstName="+firstName+",middleName="+
                    middleName+",lastName="+lastName);
            }
        }
        catch (SQLException sqlExc)
        {
            throw new EJBException(sqlExc.toString());
        }
        finally
        {
            try
            {
                findStmt.close();
            }
            catch (SQLException ignore)
            {
```

```
        }
    }
}

public Collection ejbFindByLastName(String lastName)
{
    return find("lastName = ?", lastName);
}

public Collection ejbFindByEmail(String email)
{
    return find("email = ?", email);
}

public Collection ejbFindByHomePhoneNumber(String homePhone)
{
    return find("homePhoneNumber = ?", homePhone);
}

public Collection ejbFindByWorkPhoneNumber(String workPhone)

{
    return find("workPhoneNumber = ?", workPhone);
}

public Collection ejbFindByMobilePhoneNumber(String mobilePhone)
{
    return find("mobilePhoneNumber = ?", mobilePhone);
}

public Collection find(String whereClause, String parameter)
{
    PreparedStatement findStmt = null;

    try
    {
        findStmt = conn.prepareStatement(
            "select firstName, lastName, middleName "+
            "from address where "+whereClause);

        findStmt.setString(1, parameter);

        ResultSet results = findStmt.executeQuery();

        ArrayList retval = new ArrayList();

        while (results.next())
        {
            String firstName = results.getString(1);
            String middleName = results.getString(2);
            String lastName = results.getString(3);

            AddressKey key = new AddressKey(firstName,
                middleName, lastName);

            retval.add(key);
        }
```

LISTING 23.2 CONTINUED

```
                return retval;
            }
            catch (SQLException sqlExc)
            {
                throw new EJBException(sqlExc.toString());
            }
            finally
            {
                try
                {
                    findStmt.close();
                }
                catch (SQLException ignore)
                {
                }
            }
        }

}
```

CREATING THE HOME INTERFACE

The Home interface of an Enterprise Java Bean contains methods for creating new instances of the bean and for locating existing instances. It must contain an ejbCreate with the same method signature as the ejbCreate method in the entity bean itself, except that it must also declare that it can throw java.rmi.RemoteException. The Home interface must also contain the finder method declarations from the entity bean, again declaring that they can also throw `java.rmi.RemoteException` and also `FinderException`.

Listing 23.3 shows the Home interface for the bean from Listings 23.1 and 23.2. The Home interface is the same whether you use Container-Managed Persistence or Bean-Managed Persistence.

LISTING 23.3 SOURCE CODE FOR `AddressHome.java`

```
package usingjsp.ejb;

import javax.ejb.*;
import java.rmi.RemoteException;
import java.util.*;

public interface AddressHome extends EJBHome
{
    public Address create(String firstName, String middleName,
        String lastName)
        throws RemoteException, CreateException;

    public Address findByPrimaryKey(AddressKey key)
        throws FinderException, RemoteException;
```

```
    public Collection findByLastName(String lastName)
        throws FinderException, RemoteException;

    public Collection findByEmail(String email)
        throws FinderException, RemoteException;

    public Collection findByHomePhoneNumber(String number)
        throws FinderException, RemoteException;

    public Collection findByWorkPhoneNumber(String number)
        throws FinderException, RemoteException;

    public Collection findByMobilePhoneNumber(String number)
        throws FinderException, RemoteException;
}
```


Creating the Remote Interface

An EJB's Remote interface defines the methods that clients can invoke on the bean. Typically you'll define the bean's accessor methods in the Remote interface as well as any business logic methods. As with the methods in the Home interface, all the methods in the Remote interface should have corresponding methods in the entity bean class, except that the methods in the Remote interface must be able to throw `java.rmi.RemoteException`.

Listing 23.4 shows the Remote interface for the bean shown earlier in Listing 23.1. As with the Home interface, the Remote interface is the same whether you use CMP or BMP.

Listing 23.4 Source Code for `Address.java`

```
package usingjsp.ejb;

import javax.ejb.EJBObject;
import java.rmi.RemoteException;

public interface Address extends EJBObject
{

    public String getFirstName() throws RemoteException;
    public void setFirstName(String theFirstName) throws RemoteException;

    public String getMiddleName() throws RemoteException;
    public void setMiddleName(String theMiddleName)    throws RemoteException;

    public String getLastName() throws RemoteException;
    public void setLastName(String theLastName)    throws RemoteException;

    public String getHomePhoneNumber() throws RemoteException;
    public void setHomePhoneNumber(String theHomePhoneNumber)
        throws RemoteException;

    public String getWorkPhoneNumber() throws RemoteException;
    public void setWorkPhoneNumber(String theWorkPhoneNumber)
        throws RemoteException;
```

LISTING 23.4 CONTINUED

```
    public String getMobilePhoneNumber() throws RemoteException;
    public void setMobilePhoneNumber(String theMobilePhoneNumber)
        throws RemoteException;

    public String getAddress1() throws RemoteException;
    public void setAddress1(String theAddress1)    throws RemoteException;

    public String getAddress2() throws RemoteException;
    public void setAddress2(String theAddress2)    throws RemoteException;

    public String getCity() throws RemoteException;
    public void setCity(String theCity)    throws RemoteException;

    public String getState() throws RemoteException;
    public void setState(String theState)throws RemoteException;

    public String getZip() throws RemoteException;
    public void setZip(String theZip)throws RemoteException;

    public String getEmail() throws RemoteException;
    public void setEmail(String theEmail)throws RemoteException;
}
```

CREATING A SESSION BEAN

A session bean usually implements business logic and is not stored in the database. Although entity beans can be shared between multiple clients, each EJB client has its own instance of a session bean. Although session beans are not stored in the database, they can have their own member variables representing the current state of the session.

For example, you might have a shopping cart bean that keeps a vector of the items in the cart. Although the items will eventually be stored in the database, you might choose to hold on to them in the session bean until the user decides to complete the order.

A session bean must implement the `SessionBean` interface, which defines several of the same methods as the `EntityBean` interface. These methods are

```
public void ejbActivate()
    throws EJBException, java.rmi.RemoteException
public void ejbPassivate()
    throws EJBException, java.rmi.RemoteException
public void ejbRemove()
    throws EJBException, java.rmi.RemoteException
public void setSessionContext(SessionContext sessContext)
    throws EJBException, java.rmi.RemoteException
```

A session bean must also implement an `ejbCreate` method that is executed when you create a session bean.

A session bean also requires Home and Remote interfaces just like an entity bean. Again, the Home interface defines any methods for creating the session bean. The entity bean also had `find` methods in the Home interface, but because session beans aren't persistent, there's no notion of finding them. You just create them.

Like the Remote interface for the entity bean, the Remote interface for a session bean defines the business logic methods available in the bean. A client can only invoke methods in the Home and Remote interfaces.

CREATING A STATELESS SESSION BEAN

If you have ever used Microsoft Transaction Server, the stateless session bean concept should be familiar because the MTS model calls for only stateless components. Stateless beans are, obviously, beans that have no state. More specifically, a stateless bean doesn't need to remember anything between method invocations. If you create a stateless shopping cart bean, you store the shopping cart items in the database instead of the shopping cart, because the cart isn't allowed to hold on to the items between method invocations.

The advantage of stateless session beans is that the server can manage them much more efficiently.

You don't really do anything different for a stateless session bean, at least not from an API standpoint. The most important thing is that you change your approach to coding the bean. You can't assume that any information from the last method call is available in the current one. Ideally, you don't have member variables in a stateless session bean. Practically speaking, however, you usually need member variables; otherwise you must pass massive amounts of data from one method to another. Just be careful that you don't rely on the member variables being initialized to sane values when a client invokes a remote method.

ACCESSING EJBS FROM JAVA SERVER PAGES

There are several ways you can access EJBs from servlets and Java Server Pages. You can create an EJB from a Web application the same way you would from a standalone GUI application. You use the `javax.naming` API to locate the bean.

Listing 23.5 shows a Java Server Page that creates a new instance of an Enterprise JavaBean.

LISTING 23.5 SOURCE CODE FOR `CreateAddress.jsp`

```
<%@ page language="java" import="javax.naming.*,usingjsp.ejb.*" %>
<%@ page import="javax.rmi.PortableRemoteObject,java.util.*" %>

<html>
<body>
<pre>
<%
    try
    {
```

Listing 23.5 Continued

```
        Context initial = new InitialContext();

        Object addressRef = initial.lookup("Address");

        usingjsp.ejb.AddressHome home =
            (usingjsp.ejb.AddressHome) PortableRemoteObject.narrow(
            addressRef, usingjsp.ejb.AddressHome.class);

        Address addr = home.create("Samantha", "Lauren", "Tippin");

        out.println("Address inserted");
    }
    catch (Exception exc)
    {
        exc.printStackTrace(new PrintWriter(out));
    }
%>
</pre>
</body>
</html>
```

The JSP in Listing 23.5 is more like a servlet than a JSP because it doesn't display much HTML. Sun often recommends writing a wrapper Java bean (not an EJB) to act as a front-end for your JSP. That way, you can use the `<jsp:useBean>` tag to eventually connect with an EJB.

The problem with writing a front-end Java bean is that it takes some time. Writing an EJB, a home interface and a remote interface is enough of a hassle, why should you have to write yet another class?

Listing 23.6 shows you a way to create an EJB and then access it with the `<jsp:useBean>` tag without writing a custom wrapper.

Listing 23.6 Source Code for `SaveAddress.jsp`

```
<%@ page language="java" import="javax.naming.*,usingjsp.ejb.*" %>
<%@ page import="javax.rmi.PortableRemoteObject,java.util.*" %>
<%
    try
    {
        Context initial = new InitialContext();

        Object addressRef = initial.lookup("Address");

        usingjsp.ejb.AddressHome home =
            (usingjsp.ejb.AddressHome) PortableRemoteObject.narrow(
            addressRef, usingjsp.ejb.AddressHome.class);

        String firstName = request.getParameter("firstName");
        String middleName = request.getParameter("middleName");
        String lastName = request.getParameter("lastName");
```

```
        Address addr = home.create(firstName, middleName, lastName);

        pageContext.setAttribute("address", addr);
    }
    catch (Exception exc)
    {
        exc.printStackTrace(new PrintWriter(out));
    }
%>
<html>
<body bgcolor="#ffffff">
<jsp:useBean id="address" scope="page" type="usingjsp.ejb.Address"/>
<jsp:setProperty name="address" property="*"/>
Your new address entry has been saved.
</body>
</html>
```


Listing 23.7 shows the HTML front-end for SaveAddress.jsp.

LISTING 23.7 SOURCE CODE FOR EnterAddress.html

```
<html>
<body bgcolor="#ffffff">
<form action="SaveAddress.jsp" method="post">
<table>
<tr><td align="right">First Name:</td>
<td><input type="text" name="firstName"></td></tr>
<tr><td align="right">Middle Name:</td>
<td><input type="text" name="middleName"></td></tr>
<tr><td align="right">Last Name:</td>
<td><input type="text" name="lastName"></td></tr>
<tr><td align="right">Home Phone Number:</td>
<td><input type="text" name="homePhoneNumber"></td></tr>
<tr><td align="right">Work Phone Number:</td>
<td><input type="text" name="workPhoneNumber"></td></tr>
<tr><td align="right">Mobile Phone Number:</td>
<td><input type="text" name="mobilePhoneNumber"></td></tr>
<tr><td align="right">Address Line 1:</td>
<td><input type="text" name="address1"></td></tr>
<tr><td align="right">Address Line 2:</td>
<td><input type="text" name="address2"></td></tr>
<tr><td align="right">City:</td>
<td><input type="text" name="city"></td></tr>
<tr><td align="right">State:</td>
<td><input type="text" name="state"></td></tr>
<tr><td align="right">Zip:</td>
<td><input type="text" name="zip"></td></tr>
</table>
<p>
<input type="submit" value="Save Address">
</form>
</body>
</html>
```

PACKAGING A COMPLETE EJB AND JSP APPLICATION

Writing the code for the various EJB and Web components is only half the battle when it comes to an EJB-based application. You must get everything installed on the EJB server, too. Don't even think about trying to create the installation files by hand; there are too many places to make mistakes. Most, hopefully all, EJB servers come with some sort of deployment tool, even the sample EJB server shipped with the J2EE Software Development Kit from Sun. The J2EE SDK deployment tool is called deploytool and after you get used to it, it makes EJB installation pretty painless.

When you start deploytool, you see a screen like the one shown in Figure 23.1. Choose File, New Application to create a new EJB/Web application.

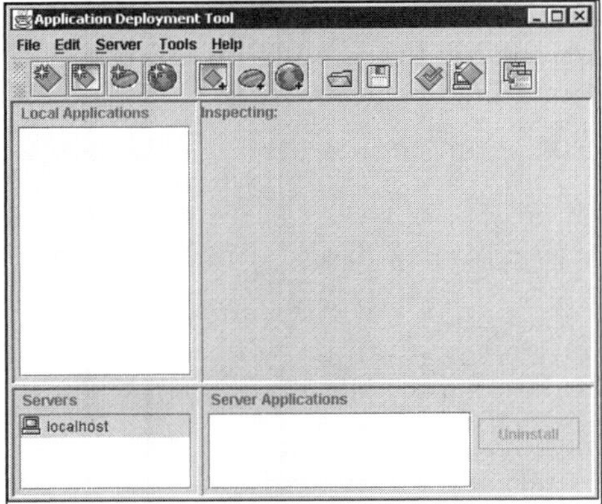

Figure 23.1
Deploytool makes it easy to install EJB and Web components.

After you enter the name of your deployment file (the .ear file) and the name of your application, you are ready to add components. For this example, you need the Address EJB, the SaveAddress Java Server Page and the EnterAddress HTML page.

To add the Address EJB, choose File, New Enterprise Bean. On the first screen where you can enter data, you must add at least the list of Java class files that make up the EJB. Figure 23.2 shows you the screen after the class files for Address have been added.

Next, enter the names for the various parts of the EJB (the EJB class, the home interface, and the remote interface) as well as a display name. The display name is only used within the deployment tool; you can call it whatever you like. Don't forget to indicate whether the EJB is an entity bean or a session bean, and if it's a session bean, whether it's stateful or stateless. Figure 23.3 shows the screen where you enter the classnames.

On the next screen, you must indicate whether the bean uses Container-Managed Persistence or Bean-Managed Persistence. For this example, you must use the Bean-Managed Persistence version of the Address EJB, because the deploytool doesn't handle multi-valued keys very well. Don't forget to enter `usingjsp.ejb.AddressKey` for the classname of the key at the bottom of the screen. Figure 23.4 shows the persistence screen.

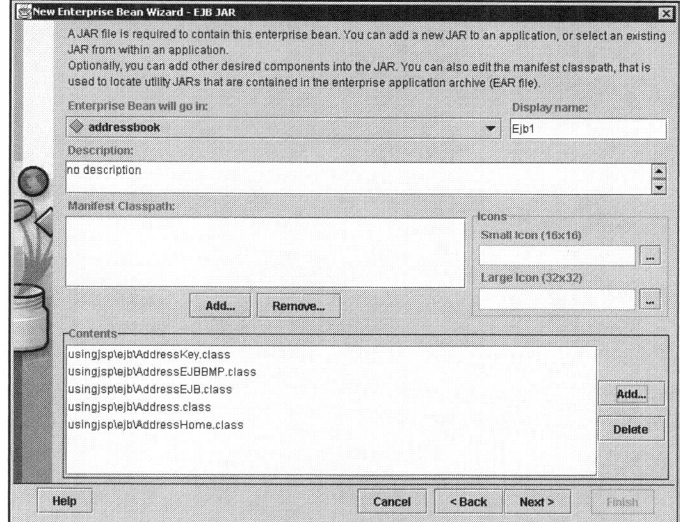

Figure 23.2
Add all the EJB class files to the deployment descriptor.

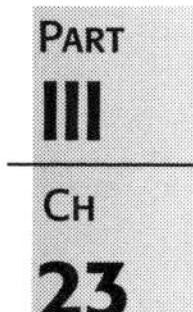

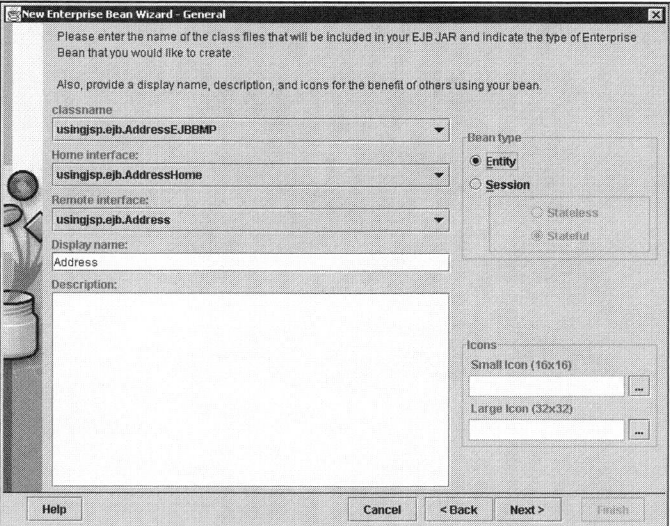

Figure 23.3
Enter the names of the various implementation classes.

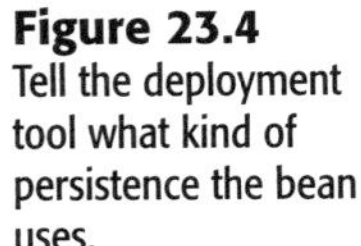

Figure 23.4
Tell the deployment tool what kind of persistence the bean uses.

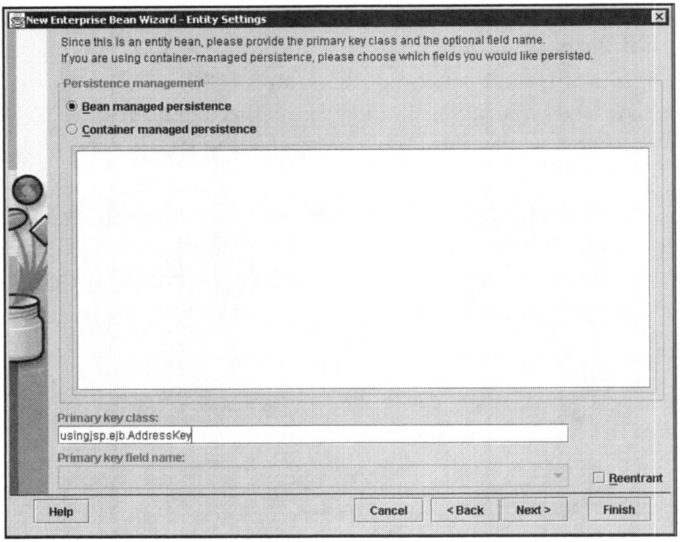

The next screen where you need to enter data is titled Resource References, and you should have to skip over two screens to get to it. Click the Add button on the right and enter **`jdbc/AddressDB`** for the coded name (it should match the last part of the `dbName` value from AddressEJBBMP.java). Make sure the type is `javax.sql.DataSource` and that the Authentication is `Container`.

Next, skip over to the Transaction Management screen and change the transaction type for every method in the bean to `Required` as shown in Figure 23.5.

Figure 23.5
Mark all the methods as requiring transactions.

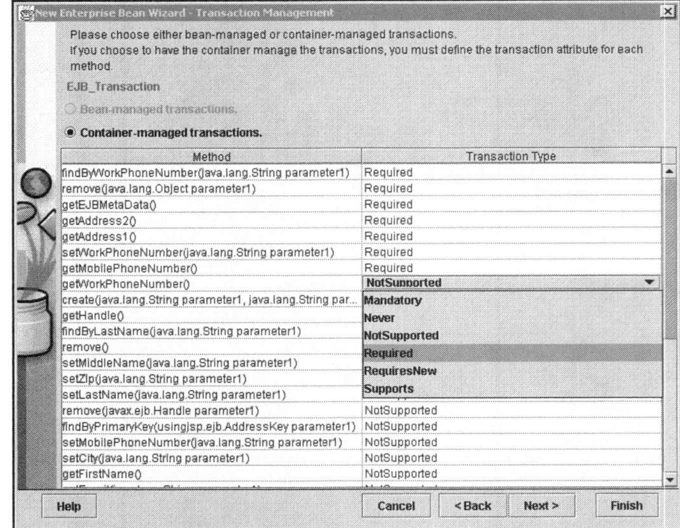

After you finish configuring the transactions, go to the next screen and click Finish. You are now ready to add the Web component.

From the main deploytool window, choose File, New Web Component. On the first screen where you can enter data, enter the display name for the Web component (the name is just used by deploytool and can be whatever you like). Next, click the Add button to add the files that make up the Web component.

In the Add Content Files screen, the first window lets you select the files that make up the Web component. Select EnterAddress.html and SaveAddress.jsp, as shown in Figure 23.6.

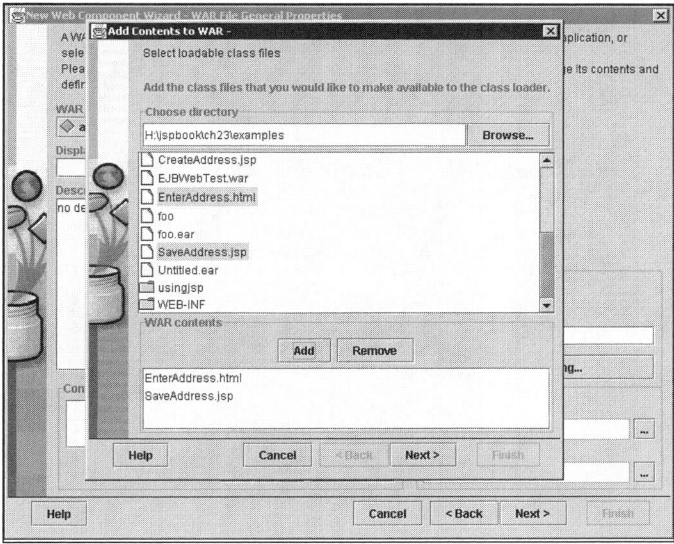

Figure 23.6
Enter the files that make up the Web component.

After you have selected the files, click Next and then Finish and you'll be back at the initial screen for creating the WAR file (the Web Archive file). Click Next and indicate that this component is a JSP, and then click Next again. Now you must enter the name of the JSP and give it a display name (again used just by deploytool). Now just keep clicking Next until you can click Finish; you've added the Web component successfully.

There are a few extra cleanup items you need to take care of before you deploy the Web application. From the main screen, select the JNDI Names tab and set the JNDI name for the `jdbc/AddressDB` component to `jdbc/Cloudscape`. Figure 23.7 shows the screen after you have added the JNDI name.

Now, click the Web Context tab and enter a root name for the Web application. Figure 23.8 shows a possible configuration for the Web application. The context root path you enter is the root path for the URL to access the Web application without the host name or port number.

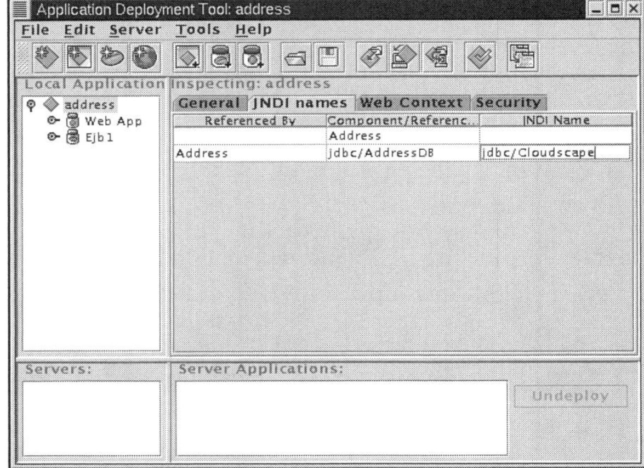

Figure 23.7 Assign a JNDI name to the `jdbc/AddressDB` component.

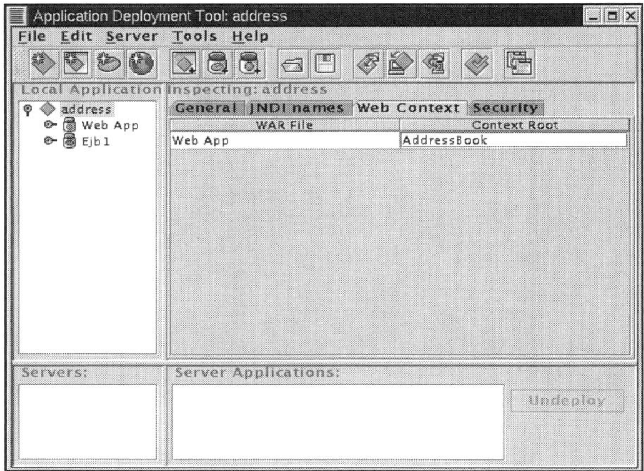

Figure 23.8 Enter the context root for the Web application.

Finally, click Tools, Deploy Application to deploy your application on the EJB server. Before you can access the EJB, you must make sure you create the Address table in the Cloudscape database. Listing 23.8 shows the SQL command to create the table.

LISTING 23.8 SOURCE CODE FOR `create_address.sql`

```
create table address
    ( firstName varchar(30),
      middleName varchar(30),
      lastName varchar(30),
      homePhoneNumber varchar(30),
      workPhoneNumber varchar(30),
      mobilePhoneNumber varchar(30),
      address1 varchar(50),
      address2 varchar(50),
      city varchar(30),
      state varchar(2),
```

```
    zip varchar(9),
    email varchar(30),
    primary key(firstName, middleName, lastName))
```

The J2EE SDK comes with an interactive SQL tool called cloudIJ. The 1.2.1 release of the J2EE SDK has cloudIJ embedded way down in the documentation directory under doc/guides/ejb/examples/util. You must edit the file first to tell it the root directory of the J2EE installation. After that, you can just type `cloudIJ < create_address.sql`.

After you have everything installed, you should be able to point your browser to the internal Web server running inside the j2ee server. If the context root of the application is `AddressBook`, you should enter a URL of `http://localhost:8000/AddressBook/EnterAddress.html`. If your browser is running on a different host than the EJB server, make sure you use the host name of the EJB server instead of `localhost`. If everything is working, you should see a form where you can enter values for the address table and then click Save Address to run the SaveAddress Java Server Page.

Enterprise Java Beans are very powerful, although fairly cumbersome to set up. If EJB development proceeds the same way Microsoft's COM/MTS development has, you should expect more wizard-type tools to handle a lot of the tedious setup for you. After you get the tedious part out of the way, EJBs and JSP/servlets make a very potent combination.

TROUBLESHOOTING

EJB PROBLEMS

Why does my entity bean access the database so frequently?

When you make a remote call to a method in an entity bean and the method call is not performed as part of a larger transaction, the EJB server loads the bean from the database and saves it after you call the method. There are many solutions to this problem. If you invoke the methods as part of a larger transaction, you won't hit the database as much, although transactions also involve some overhead. You might also consider reducing the number of remote calls you make to the entity beans or even eliminate entity beans altogether. Issues like this are really beyond the scope of this book, however. EJB design and optimization is a complex subject worthy of its own book.

Why does my EJB application run so slowly?

There are any number of reasons why this might be happening. You might be accessing the database so frequently that it can't keep up. You might be performing too many remote calls, which are considerably slower than local calls. Some EJB servers also have problems with transaction locking and might slow down considerably under heavy use. Again, this is a complex subject. The J2EE Web site at `http://java.sun.com/j2ee` has several white papers on EJB design and optimization.

JSP and EJB Problems

Why won't my JSP compile when I use EJB?

Assuming you don't have any obvious syntax errors, the problem might be that you don't have either the classes for your EJBs in your classpath, or the EJB libraries themselves might not be in your classpath. If you are installing your JSP on a fully J2EE compliant server, it's probably not a classpath problem. You usually see these problems when you are using a JSP server that doesn't also support EJB.

Why can't my servlets or Java Server Pages locate my EJBs?

You probably misspelled the name of the bean either when you deployed the beans or when you tried to access the bean.

PART IV

Taking JSP and Servlets Beyond HTML

CHAPTER 24

Creating an XML Application

In this chapter

The Extensible Markup Language (XML) represents an important step in data representation. In the past, programs used many different formats for storing data. There have been text files with comma-delimited or pipe-delimited fields, binary files in any number of formats, and even plain ASCII text. Unfortunately, most programs use slightly different ways to store data, even if the overall format is similar. For example, when you save data using comma-separated fields, how do you specify what each field is? You might save the first name followed by the last name. Another developer might save the last name and then the first name. How do you know the format of the file, other than by someone telling you? You could put a line at the top of the file explaining what each field is, but even that might have different formats.

Another problem you encounter when storing data is that most representations tend to be tabular in nature. That is, when you write data into a file, you typically put all the information for a particular data element on a single line in the file. What happens when the data you want to write is a Java object with many nested data structures? How can you store all those data structures within a single line, especially if you must stick to a prescribed set of fields?

XML solves this problem by defining a standard way to represent data, a standard way to tag the data with its type, and a standard way to describe the overall data structure. XML *is* very simple, easy to read, and easy to understand. There are a few things XML *is not*:

- XML is not a replacement for HTML. Although there is an XML-compliant version of HTML, XML does not define how to represent data on a Web browser.
- XML is not a cure for all the data format ills. Various software vendors and the business sector must still agree on a common representation for data. For example, the travel industry needs a standard format to represent a reservation. The banking industry needs a standard format to represent account information.
- XML is not a programming language. XML lets you describe data, but it doesn't let you describe how to process the data.

A "HELLO WORLD" XML PAGE

In a minimal XML page you need two things: a heading identifying the page as an XML page, and a single pair of tags that represents the root of the data. Think of the root tags as being like the `<HTML> </HTML>` tags in an HTML document. They enclose everything else. An XML document might have only one pair of root tags. Everything else in the document must be within those two tags.

Listing 24.1 shows a "Hello World" XML page.

LISTING 24.1 SOURCE CODE FOR `HelloWorld.xml`

```
<?xml version=_1.0_?><greeting>   Hello World_</greeting>
```

The `<?xml version="1.0"?>` tag must be present in any XML file. The `<greeting>` `</greeting>` tag pair is the root of the document.

SENDING XML FROM A JAVA SERVER PAGE

You can create XML Java Server Pages the same way you create HTML pages. The only difference is that you must set the content type of your page to `text/xml`. To set the content type, use the `<%@page%>` tag, like this:

```
<%@ page contentType="text/xml" %>
```

Listing 24.2 shows the "Hello World" XML page as a Java Server Page.

LISTING 24.2 SOURCE CODE FOR XMLHelloWorld.jsp

```
<%@ page contentType="text/xml" %>

<?xml version="1.0"?>
<greeting>
    Hello World!
</greeting>
```


Figure 24.1 shows the `XMLHelloWorld` Java Server Page from Internet Explorer 5. As you can see, Internet Explorer shows you the XML source code.

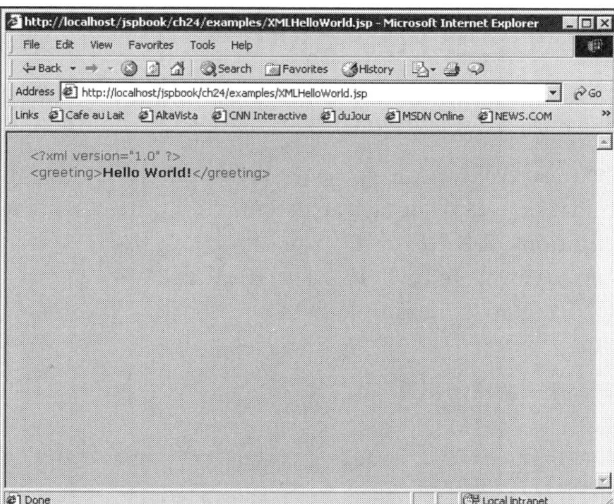

Figure 24.1 Internet Explorer shows you XML source code.

SENDING XML FROM A SERVLET

Sending XML from a servlet is just as easy as sending HTML. The only difference is that you must set the content type to `text/xml` as you did with the JSP. Because you always need to set the content type in a servlet (unless you don't send a response at all), sending XML is just as easy as sending HTML.

Listing 24.3 shows a servlet that generates the "Hello World" XML page.

LISTING 24.3 SOURCE CODE FOR `XMLHelloWorldServlet.java`

```
package usingjsp;
import javax.servlet.*;
import javax.servlet.http.*;
import java.io.*;

public class XMLHelloWorldServlet extends HttpServlet
{
    public void service(HttpServletRequest request,
        HttpServletResponse response)
        throws ServletException, IOException
    {
        response.setContentType(_text/xml_);

        PrintWriter out = response.getWriter();

        out.println(_<?xml version=\_1.0\_?>_);
        out.println(_<greeting>_);
        out.println(_    Hello World__);
        out.println(_</greeting>_);
    }
}
```

A FEW SIMPLE RULES FOR XML

You already know that an XML page must start with the `<?xml?>` tag and must contain a single root tag. There are a few additional rules that dictate how you create an XML page.

First, when you create an XML page, you have the option of specifying a Document Type Definition (DTD) that defines what tags are permitted in the XML page. DTDs let you create standard definitions of XML pages. You can use an XML validator to check an XML page to make sure it conforms to its DTD. Use the `<!DOCTYPE>` tag to specify the DTD for your page. Listing 24.4 shows an example DTD.

LISTING 24.4 SOURCE CODE FOR `Simple.dtd`

```
<!ELEMENT person (first-name? | middle-name? | last-name?)+>
<!ELEMENT first-name (#PCDATA)>
<!ELEMENT middle-name (#PCDATA)>
<!ELEMENT last-name (#PCDATA)>
<!ELEMENT number-name (#PCDATA)>
```

Creating a DTD is more complex than creating an XML page. You should consult the W3C Web site at `http://www.w3c.org` for pointers on how to create a DTD. Listing 24.5 shows an XML page that conforms to the DTD in Listing 24.4.

Listing 24.5 Source Code for `Simple.xml`

```
<?xml version="1.0"?>
<!DOCTYPE Simple SYSTEM "http://localhost/Simple.dtd">
<person>
<first-name>Samantha</first-name>
   <middle-name>Lauren</middle-name>
    <last-name>Tippin</last-name>
</person>
```

A DTD is optional, of course. You can create an XML page with any set of tags you want. For each opening tag you must have a closing tag. The exception to this rule is that you can end a tag with `/>` to indicate that it doesn't need a closing tag. Remember the `<jsp:include/>` and `<jsp:forward/>` tags end with `/>` and thus take no closing tag. You can't interleave tags, either. In other words, if tag B starts within tag A, then tag B must be closed before tag A closes. The following combination of tags is illegal in XML:

```
<foo>
   <bar>
</foo>
    </bar>
```

Because the `<bar>` tag starts inside the `<foo>` tag, it must also close within the `<foo>` tag.

You can also specify attributes within a tag. Although HTML is lenient about quotes in attributes, XML requires that the value of every attribute is enclosed in quotes. In other words, you might have an HTML tag like this:

```
<img src="katy.jpg" width=140 height=150>
```

A valid XML version of the `<IMG>` tag would look like this:

```
<img src="katy.jpg" width="140" height="150"/>
```

Notice that the XML version of `<IMG>` ends with `/>` because it doesn't need a closing tag.

Why Use XML with JSP and Servlets?

If you are new to the XML world, you are probably wondering why you would care about using XML from servlets and JSPs. After all, you are sending output to a browser and the browser understands HTML, not XML. One thing you often find when you create applications that need to send data to other applications is that there are often firewalls sitting between the applications. This is especially true when one business sends data to another business. You would think that RMI or CORBA would be the technologies of choice for exchanging data between businesses, but when it comes to firewalls, many developers take the path of least resistance: HTTP. There are products that allow you to send CORBA over a firewall, and RMI even supports HTTP tunneling, but because most firewalls already support HTTP and HTTPS (HTTP over SSL), you can use the `URL` and `URLConnection` classes to communicate with servlets and JSPs with little or no extra work.

When you pass XML data via HTTP, it makes sense to use servlets to handle incoming XML and Java Server Pages to generate outgoing XML. Java has several good XML parsers for handling incoming XML. You might need to perform additional work to copy the XML values into Java classes, however.

Automatically Generated XML

The simple, uniform structure of XML makes it very computer-friendly. The nested structure of XML makes it an ideal format for storing complex data structures. In fact, XML makes a nice format for serializing Java objects. There are several different ways to serialize Java objects into XML. Some approaches choose to define an XML DTD that describes a Java object. For example, you might have XML that looks like this:

```
<class>
    <class-name>usingjsp.TestClass</class-name>
    <attribute>
        <attribute-name>myAttribute</attribute-name>
        <attribute-value>Foo</attribute-value>
    </attribute
</class>
```

Although this method is good, it is very Java-centric. XML allows you to describe a huge variety of data structures, so wouldn't it be nice if you could easily map those data structures into Java as well? Conversely, it would be nice to generate XML from these Java classes.

You can use a package called JOX (Java Objects in XML), available at `http://www.wutka.com/jox`, to serialize Java objects into XML. Listing 24.6 shows an example Java bean suitable for serialization.

Listing 24.6 Source Code for `TestBean.java`

```
package com.wutka.jox.test;

import com.wutka.jox.*;
import java.util.*;

public class TestBean implements java.io.Serializable
{
    protected int foo;
    protected String bar;
    protected java.util.Date baz;
    protected Vector thingies;
    protected TestSubbean subbean;

    public TestBean()
    {
        bar = "";
        baz = new Date();
        thingies = new Vector();
    }

    public int getFoo() { return foo; }
    public void setFoo(int aFoo) { foo = aFoo; }
```

```
    public String getBar() { return bar; }
    public void setBar(String aBar) { bar = aBar; }

    public java.util.Date getBaz() { return baz; }
    public void setBaz(java.util.Date aBaz) { baz = aBaz; }

    public TestSubbean getSub() { return subbean; }
    public void setSub(TestSubbean aSub) { subbean = aSub; }

    public String[] getThingies()
    {
        String[] retThingies = new String[thingies.size()];
        if (thingies.size() > 0) thingies.copyInto(retThingies);

        return retThingies;
    }

    public void setThingies(String[] newThingies)
    {
        thingies = new Vector(newThingies.length);
        for (int i=0; i < newThingies.length; i++)
        {
            thingies.addElement(newThingies[i]);
        }
    }

    public String getThingies(int i)
    {
        return (String) thingies.elementAt(i);
    }

    public void setThingies(int i, String thingy)
    {
        thingies.setElementAt(thingy, i);
    }

    public String toString()
    {
        StringBuffer ret = new StringBuffer(
            "foo="+foo+";bar="+bar+";baz="+baz.toString()+
            ";thingies=");
        for (int i=0; i < thingies.size(); i++)
        {
            if (i > 0) ret.append(",");
            ret.append((String) thingies.elementAt(i));
        }

        ret.append(";sub=");
        ret.append(subbean.toString());

        return ret.toString();
    }
}
```

Listing 24.7 shows the XML generated by JOX.

LISTING 24.7 SOURCE CODE FOR TestBean.xml

```
<?xml version="1.0"?>
<MarkTest>
<thingies>Moe</thingies>
<thingies>Larry</thingies>
<thingies>Curly</thingies>
<thingies>Shemp</thingies>
<thingies>Curly Joe</thingies>
<foo>5</foo>
<baz>5/15/00 5:59 PM</baz>
<bar>This is the bar value</bar>
<sub>
<age>35</age>
<name>Mark</name>
</sub>
</MarkTest>
```

Listing 24.8 shows a servlet that displays the contents of a bean using the JOX library.

LISTING 24.8 SOURCE CODE FOR BeanXMLServlet.java

```
package usingjsp.xml;import com.wutka.jox.*;
import com.wutka.jox.test.*;
import javax.servlet.*;
import javax.servlet.http.*;
import java.io.*;

public class BeanXMLServlet extends HttpServlet
{
    public void service(HttpServletRequest request,
        HttpServletResponse response)
        throws IOException, ServletException
    {

// Create the bean and populate it
        TestBean bean = new TestBean();

        bean.setThingies(
            new String[] { "Moe", "Larry", "Curly", "Shemp",
                "Curly Joe" });

        bean.setFoo(5);
        bean.setBar("This is the bar value");
        bean.setBaz(new java.util.Date());

        TestSubbean sub = new TestSubbean();
        sub.setName("Mark");
        sub.setAge(35);

        bean.setSub(sub);

// Set the content type for the response
        response.setContentType("text/xml");

// Get the Writer for sending the response
```

```
        Writer out = response.getWriter();

// Wrap a JOXBeanWriter around the output writer
        JOXBeanWriter beanOut = new JOXBeanWriter(out);

// Write out the object as XML with a root tag of <MarkTest>
        beanOut.writeObject("MarkTest", bean);
    }
}
```

PARSING XML WITH SAX AND DOM

When you use servlets and Java Server Pages to generate XML for application-to-application communication, the client on the other end must be able to interpret the XML and turn it into useful data structures. More importantly, if a client sends XML to your JSP or servlet, you must be able to parse the XML document. You can use any of several different parsers to turn XML documents into Java data structures.

There are two different approaches for parsing XML in Java: SAX and DOM. SAX stands for Simple API for XML and allows you to handle XML tags in the data as the parser encounters them. In other words, when the parser locates an XML tag, it calls a Java method to handle the tag. It's up to you to decide what to do with it. DOM, or Document Object Model, isn't strictly an API; it's an object model describing how an XML document is organized. When you parse an XML document using a DOM parser, the parser reads the entire document and passes you back a `Document` object containing everything that was defined in the XML document.

Each of these approaches has its advantages and disadvantages, and you certainly don't need to choose one over the other. You can use whichever one makes sense for your situation. For example, if you are parsing very large files (in the 10-15MB range and higher), you probably want to use SAX, because a DOM parser will first read the entire file into memory before you can begin processing it. The Java XML API from Sun supports both SAX and DOM.

PARSING XML USING SAX

SAX uses an event-driven model for parsing. The SAX parser reads the XML and when it finds something interesting, it calls a method in a handler class. The handler class is something that you must write, although there is a skeleton base class that you can start with. SAX will tell you when it finds the beginning of a document, the end of a document, an opening tag, a closing tag, or character data within an element. It will also tell you when it finds an error.

SAX is most useful when you need to read through a very large XML file but you might not need much of the data in the file. If you need to search through a file for a particular tag or data value, SAX is generally much quicker.

Listing 24.9 shows a servlet that reads an XML file sent to it and searches for a particular tag. After it finds the tag, it looks for character data.

LISTING 24.9 SOURCE CODE FOR SaxParseServlet.java

```
package usingjsp.xml;

import java.io.*;

import javax.servlet.*;
import javax.servlet.http.*;

import javax.xml.parsers.*;
import org.xml.sax.*;

public class SaxParseServlet extends HttpServlet
{
    public void doPost(HttpServletRequest request,
        HttpServletResponse response)
        throws ServletException, IOException
    {
        try
        {
// Create a parser factory
            SAXParserFactory factory = SAXParserFactory.newInstance();

// Ask the parser factory to create a new parser
            SAXParser parser = factory.newSAXParser();

// This servlet just sends a plain text response
            response.setContentType("text/plain");

// Create an input source around the request reader, ask the parser
// to parse the input source and invoke methods in the XMLHandler class
// when it finds XML elements
            parser.parse(new InputSource(request.getReader()),
                new XMLHandler(request, response));
        }
        catch (ParserConfigurationException exc)
        {
            throw new ServletException(exc.toString());
        }
        catch (SAXException exc)
        {
            throw new ServletException(exc.toString());
        }
    }

    class XMLHandler extends HandlerBase
    {
        protected HttpServletRequest request;
        protected HttpServletResponse response;

        protected boolean handlingFirstName;
        protected boolean handlingLastName;
        protected boolean inName;

        protected String firstName;
        protected String lastName;
```

```
        public XMLHandler(HttpServletRequest aRequest,
            HttpServletResponse aResponse)
        {
            request = aRequest;
            response = aResponse;

            inName = false;
            handlingFirstName = false;
            handlingLastName = false;
        }

        public void startElement(String name, AttributeList attributes)
        {
// Look for a <name> element
            if (name.equals("name"))
            {
                inName = true;
                firstName = null;
                lastName = null;
            }
// If inside a <name> element, look for <first>
            else if (name.equals("first"))
            {
                if (!inName) return;

                handlingFirstName = true;
            }
// If inside a <name> element, look for <last>
            else if (name.equals("last"))
            {
                if (!inName) return;

                handlingLastName = true;
            }
        }

        public void characters(char[] chars, int start, int length)
        {
// If these characters are occurring inside a <first> element, save them
            if (handlingFirstName)
            {
                firstName = new String(chars, start, length);
            }
// If these characters are occurring inside a <last> element, save them
            else if (handlingLastName)
            {
                lastName = new String(chars, start, length);
            }
            else
            {
                return;
            }
        }

        public void endElement(String name)
            throws SAXException
```

LISTING 24.9 CONTINUED

```
        {
            if (name.equals("name"))
            {
// After the end of the name element, if there's a first and a last name,
// print them separated by a space
                if ((firstName != null) && (lastName != null))
                {
                    try
                    {
                        PrintWriter out = response.getWriter();

                        out.println(firstName+" "+lastName);
                    }
                    catch (IOException ioExc)
                    {
                        throw new SAXException(ioExc.toString());
                    }
                }
                inName = false;
            }
            else if (name.equals("first"))
            {
                if (!inName) return;
                handlingFirstName = false;
            }
            else if (name.equals("last"))
            {
                if (!inName) return;
                handlingLastName = false;
            }
        }
    }
}
```

Listing 24.10 shows a test client program that sends the XML file to the servlet from Listing 24.9.

LISTING 24.10 SOURCE CODE FOR `XMLTestClient.java`

```
import java.io.*;
import java.net.*;
public class XMLTestClient
{
    public static void main(String[] args)
    {
        try
        {
// args[1] is the name of the file to sendFile f = new
File(args[1]);
            int contentLength = (int) f.length();

// args[0] is the URL to send the file to
            URL url = new URL(args[0]);
            URLConnection conn = url.openConnection();
```

```
// Tell the URLConnection that this is an XML file
            conn.setDoOutput(true);
            conn.setRequestProperty("content-type", "text/xml");
            conn.setRequestProperty("content-length", ""+contentLength);

            FileInputStream in = new FileInputStream(f);

            byte[] buffer = new byte[4096];
            int len;

            OutputStream out = conn.getOutputStream();

// Send the XML file to the servlet
            while ((len = in.read(buffer)) > 0)
            {
                out.write(buffer, 0, len);
            }

            InputStream resp = conn.getInputStream();

// Read the response back from the servlet
            while ((len = resp.read(buffer)) > 0)
            {
                System.out.write(buffer, 0, len);
            }
        }
        catch (Exception exc)
        {
            exc.printStackTrace();
        }
    }
}
```


PARSING XML USING DOM

A DOM parser reads an XML file in its entirety before passing any information to you. It creates a representation of the XML contents using a set of Java classes. An XML file is structured like a tree. The main document tag is the base of the tree, and each nested tag is a branch of the tree. The document model used by a DOM parser is also structured like a tree. You receive a `Document` object, which returns a list of `Node` objects.

The `Node` class is really an interface, not a class. DOM has a number of classes that implement the `Node` interface. The one you deal with most often is the `Element` class, which represents a tag or tag pair from an XML document. You might also find `Comment` nodes, `Text` nodes, `CDATASection` nodes, `Character` nodes, and several others. The `Element` class might contain a list of child nodes representing the tags and data contained between the element's opening and closing tags.

Listing 24.11 shows a servlet that uses a DOM parser to parse through the same file as the servlet in Listing 24.9. You can see how different a DOM parser is from a SAX parser. Although SAX is a bit faster, DOM tends to be a bit easier to use when you need to preserve the structure of the document.

LISTING 24.11 SOURCE CODE FOR DomParseServlet.java

```
package usingjsp.xml;

import java.io.*;

import javax.servlet.*;
import javax.servlet.http.*;

import javax.xml.parsers.*;
import org.xml.sax.*;
import org.w3c.dom.*;

public class DomParseServlet extends HttpServlet
{
    public void doPost(HttpServletRequest request,
        HttpServletResponse response)
        throws ServletException, IOException
    {
        try
        {
// Create a parser factory
            DocumentBuilderFactory factory = DocumentBuilderFactory.
                newInstance();

// Ask the parser factory to create a new parser
            DocumentBuilder parser = factory.newDocumentBuilder();

// This servlet just sends a plain text response
            response.setContentType("text/plain");

            PrintWriter out = response.getWriter();

// Create an input source around the request reader, ask the parser
// to parse the input source
            Document doc = parser.parse(new InputSource(request.getReader()));

// Get all the Name elements
            NodeList names = doc.getElementsByTagName("name");

            int numNames = names.getLength();

            for (int i=0; i < numNames; i++)
            {
                Element e = (Element) names.item(i);

                String firstName = null;

// See if there is a first name
                NodeList firstNameList = e.getElementsByTagName("first");
                if (firstNameList.getLength() > 0)
                {
                    Element firstNameNode = (Element) firstNameList.item(0);

// Make the really bold assumption that <first> has a child and that
// it is text. You really should check first, though.
                    CharacterData nameText = (CharacterData)
                        firstNameNode.getFirstChild();
```

```
                    firstName = nameText.getData();
                }

                String lastName = null;

// See if there is a last name
                NodeList lastNameList = e.getElementsByTagName("last");
                if (lastNameList.getLength() > 0)
                {
                    Element lastNameNode = (Element) lastNameList.item(0);

// Make the really bold assumption that <last> has a child and that
// it is text. You really should check first, though.
                    CharacterData nameText = (CharacterData)
                        lastNameNode.getFirstChild();

                    lastName = nameText.getData();
                }

                if ((firstName != null) && (lastName != null))
                {
                    out.println(firstName+" "+lastName);
                }
            }
        }
        catch (ParserConfigurationException exc)
        {
            throw new ServletException(exc.toString());
        }
        catch (SAXException exc)
        {
            throw new ServletException(exc.toString());
        }
    }
}
```


PARSING XML USING JOX

The JOX library uses a DOM parser to parse through XML. The main reason to use JOX instead of using DOM directly is that JOX automatically copies values from the XML document into a Java bean. Also, JOX is geared towards reading and writing files and fits very well within the servlet framework.

Listing 24.12 shows a servlet that uses JOX to read an XML file and copy its values into a Java bean.

LISTING 24.12 SOURCE CODE FOR JOXParseServlet.java

```
package usingjsp.xml;

import java.io.*;

import javax.servlet.*;
```

LISTING 24.12 CONTINUED

```
import javax.servlet.http.*;

import com.wutka.jox.*;
import com.wutka.jox.test.*;

public class JOXParseServlet extends HttpServlet
{
    public void doPost(HttpServletRequest request,
        HttpServletResponse response)
        throws ServletException, IOException
    {
        TestBean newBean = new TestBean();

        JOXBeanReader reader = new JOXBeanReader(request.getReader());

        reader.readObject(newBean);

// This servlet just sends a plain text response
        response.setContentType("text/plain");

        PrintWriter out = response.getWriter();

        out.println(newBean.toString());
    }
}
```

TROUBLESHOOTING

GENERATING XML FROM A JSP

Why doesn't the browser recognize my JSP as an XML file?

You probably forgot to change the content type to "text/xml".

USING THE SUN XML LIBRARIES

Why can't the Java compiler find the XML libraries?

Make sure that both jaxp.jar and parser.jar are in your classpath.

My program compiles okay, why does it tell me it can't find the parser library?

You must have both jaxp.jar and parser.jar in your classpath. The jaxp.jar file defines the standard interfaces for SAX and DOM but doesn't contain any of the implementation classes. You can compile a program using only jaxp.jar but when you run the program, you need to include an actual XML parser in the classpath.

USING JOX

Why do I get a `ClassNotFoundException` *when I use the JOX library?*

JOX also requires the Sun XML libraries, so you must also include jaxp.jar and parser.jar in your classpath. Make sure that the JOX jar file is also in your classpath.

CHAPTER 25

Adding XSL Stylesheets to Enhance an XML Application

In this chapter

What Is XSL?

Although XML has been gathering heaps of praise as the next "big thing," the Extensible Style Language (XSL) has been lurking quietly, waiting to be noticed. XSL is a language for translating XML from one format into another. For example, you might have a set of XML tags that describe a person (`<firstName>`, `<lastName>`, and so on) and you want to represent those tags with HTML. You can create a stylesheet to tell the XSL processor how to translate the person XML into HTML.

> **Note**
>
> There are actually two distinctly different kinds of XSL. The XSL Transformation language is the kind of XSL discussed in this chapter. You will often see the XSL Transformation language referred to as XSLT. There is also an XSL formatting language that is more of a layout language like HTML with Cascading Style Sheets (CSS). This chapter does not address the XSL formatting language at all.

In some ways, XSL looks like a competitor to Java Server Pages. XSL can process data in XML form and render a Web page. Many people tout XSL as the solution for creating Web applications and wireless Web applications using the same set of data. You write two stylesheets, one to generate HTML and one to generate WML (the markup language for wireless Web applications).

As you will see, however, XSL isn't really a competitor to JSP. Instead, it complements JSP and servlets nicely by giving you a template language for formatting XML. As you will soon see, XSL is not the prettiest language in the world. It isn't easy to read and is frequently difficult to write. There are cases where you would be better off using Java Server Pages to format your data. Still, adding XSL to your toolchest is a wise decision.

A Simple XSL Stylesheet

The best way to get a feel for how XSL stylesheets work is to see one in action. Listing 25.1 shows an XML file describing two people. Notice the `<?xsl-stylesheet?>` tag that specifies the name of the XSL stylesheet that accompanies this XML file.

Listing 25.1 Source Code for `Person.xml`

```
<?xml version="1.0"?>
<?xml-stylesheet type="text/xsl" href="PersonToHTML.xsl"?>
<people>
    <person>
        <firstName>Samantha</firstName>
        <middleName>Lauren</middleName>
        <lastName>Tippin</lastName>
        <age>7</age>
    </person>
    <person>
        <firstName>Kaitlynn</firstName>
        <middleName>Dawn</middleName>
```

```
        <lastName>Tippin</lastName>
        <age>4</age>
    </person>
</people>
```

Listing 25.2 shows the PersonToHTML.xsl stylesheet that translates the XML definitions into HTML.

Listing 25.2 Source Code for PersonToHTML.xsl

```
<?xml version="1.0"?>
<xsl:stylesheet
    xmlns:xsl="http://www.w3.org/1999/XSL/Transform"
    version="1.0">
    <xsl:template match="people">
        <html>
        <body bgcolor="#ffffff">
        <table border="4">
            <tr><th>First Name</th><th>Middle Name</th><th>Last Name</th>
            <th>Age</th></tr>

        <xsl:apply-templates/>

        </table>
        </body>
        </html>
    </xsl:template>

    <xsl:template match="person">
        <tr>
            <td>
                <xsl:value-of select="firstName"/>
            </td>
            <td>
                <xsl:value-of select="middleName"/>
            </td>
            <td>
                <xsl:value-of select="lastName"/>
            </td>
            <td>
                <xsl:value-of select="age"/>
            </td>
        </tr>
    </xsl:template>
</xsl:stylesheet>
```

XSL might look a little odd at first, but it's really not so bad after you get used to it. Because an XSL stylesheet is a value XML document, it must start with the `<?xml?>` tag. The root tag for an XSL stylesheet is `<xsl:stylesheet>` which includes a reference to the XSL namespace (the `xmlns:xsl=...`).

Probably the most common XSL tag you'll see is `<xsl:template>`. In an XSL stylesheet, you set up templates that match various XML tags. For instance, `<xsl:template match="people"/>` defines the actions the XSL processor should take when it encounters a `<people>` tag.

In Listing 25.2 shown earlier, the action for the `<people>` tag is to set up the beginning of the HTML document by defining the `<html>` and `<body>` tags and then begin a table. The `<xsl:apply-templates/>` tag tells the XSL processor to look for templates that apply to the body of the `<people>` tag. In other words, look at all the child tags of `<people>` and see if there is an `<xsl:template>` tag defined for any of them. If so, apply the template and insert the output right here. After the `<xsl:apply-templates/>` tag, you see that the template closes off the table, the body, and the HTML page. The other template handles the rest of the output.

Note

Keep in mind that although a template can match multiple items in the XML file, the XSL processor executes the template once for each match. You don't need to worry about what happens if there are multiple matches.

The second template in the stylesheet makes use of another handy tag, `<xsl:value-of>`. The template for the `<person>` tag starts a row in the HTML table, and then creates `<td>` tags for each of the four child tags. The `<xsl:value-of>` tag lets you insert the text from a child tag into the current output.

Listing 25.3 shows the HTML output from the combination of the Person.xml data file and the PersonToHTML.xsl stylesheet.

LISTING 25.3 HTML OUTPUT FROM `PersonToHTML.xsl` STYLESHEET

```
!DOCTYPE html PUBLIC '-//W3C/DTD HTML 4.0 Frameset//EN'
    'http://www.w3c.org/TR/REC-html40/frameset.dtd'>
<html>
  <body bgcolor="#ffffff">
    <table border="4">
      <tr>
        <th>First Name</th>
        <th>Middle Name</th>
        <th>Last Name</th>
        <th>Age</th>
      </tr>
    <tr>
        <td>Samantha</td>
        <td>Lauren</td>
        <td>Tippin</td>
        <td>7</td>
      </tr>
    <tr>
        <td>Kaitlynn</td>
        <td>Dawn</td>
        <td>Tippin</td>
        <td>4</td>
      </tr>
</table>
  </body>
</html>
```

Figure 25.1 shows the page as displayed by the browser.

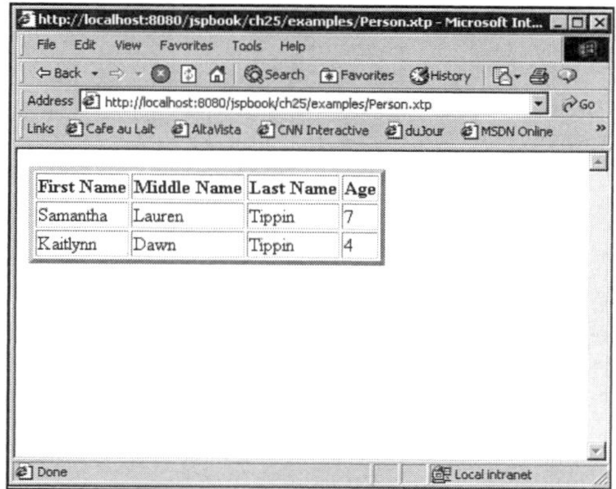

Figure 25.1 You can generate HTML from an XSL stylesheet.

Note

The Resin Web Server from `http://www.caucho.com` has a built-in XSL stylesheet processor that makes it easy to add XSL to your existing JSP/Servlet applications. The only thing you need to do to run the XSL processor is rename your .xml files to .xtp. For example, to view the Person.xml file, just rename it Person.xtp.

Rather than using `<xsl:value-of>` to match the values of the child tags, you can set up additional `<xsl:template>` tags. When you want to insert the value of the current tag into the output, use `<xsl:value-of select="."/>`. Listing 25.4 shows an alternate version of PersonToHTML.xsl that displays the output in exactly the same format, but matches the children of `<person>` with separate templates.

Listing 25.4 Source Code for PersonToHTML2.xsl

```
<?xml version="1.0"?>
<xsl:stylesheet
    xmlns:xsl="http://www.w3.org/1999/XSL/Transform"
    version="1.0">

    <xsl:template match="people">
        <html>
        <body bgcolor="#ffffff">
        <table border="4">
            <tr><th>First Name</th><th>Middle Name</th><th>Last Name</th>
            <th>Age</th></tr>

        <xsl:apply-templates/>

        </table>
        </body>
        </html>
    </xsl:template>

    <xsl:template match="person">
        <tr>
            <xsl:apply-templates/>
        </tr>
</xsl:template>
```

LISTING 25.4 CONTINUED

```
    <xsl:template match="firstName">
        <td><xsl:value-of select="."/></td>
    </xsl:template>

    <xsl:template match="middleName">
        <td><xsl:value-of select="."/></td>
    </xsl:template>

    <xsl:template match="lastName">
        <td><xsl:value-of select="."/></td>
    </xsl:template>

    <xsl:template match="age">
        <td><xsl:value-of select="."/></td>
    </xsl:template>

</xsl:stylesheet>
```

NAVIGATING AN XML DOCUMENT WITH XPATH

The XPath standard defines how you refer to an element in an XML page relative to another element. For example, if you want to refer to the `<firstName>` element that is a child of the `<person>` element, you can use the XPath expression `person/firstName`. In some ways, it is similar to the convention you use for naming files. XPath is more than just a naming standard; however, it is used for pattern matching. You use XPath expressions in the `match` attribute of the `<xsl:template>` tag. So far, all you have seen are tag names for the match target, but you can look for far more interesting items.

Suppose you have several tags in your document that have a child node of `<name>`. If you want to handle the `<name>` tag differently depending on its parent tag, you must use an XPath expression to match the name. For example, to create a template that matches only `<name>` tags that are children of `<company>` tags, you would use the following `<xsl:template>` tag:

```
<xsl:template match="company/name"/>
```

You can also use to match all children. For example, in the previous Listing 25.4, there are templates to match each child node of `<person>`, but the templates are doing the same thing. You can reduce the four separate templates down to a single template by specifying `match="person/*"` as shown in Listing 25.5.

LISTING 25.5 SOURCE CODE FOR `PersonToHTML3.xsl`

```
<?xml version="1.0"?>
<xsl:stylesheet
    xmlns:xsl="http://www.w3.org/1999/XSL/Transform"
    version="1.0">
    <xsl:template match="people">
        <html>
        <body bgcolor="#ffffff">
        <table border="4">
            <tr><th>First Name</th><th>Middle Name</th><th>Last Name</th>
            <th>Age</th></tr>
```

```
        <xsl:apply-templates/>

        </table>
        </body>
        </html>
    </xsl:template>

    <xsl:template match="person">
        <tr>
            <xsl:apply-templates/>
        </tr>
    </xsl:template>

    <xsl:template match="person/*">
        <td><xsl:value-of select="."/></td>
    </xsl:template>

</xsl:stylesheet>
```

XPath has two types of syntax representation: abbreviated and unabbreviated. The syntax you have seen so far is abbreviated. The unabbreviated syntax for matching a tag named `<person>` is `match="self::person"`. The syntax for matching all children of the `<person>` node is `match="self::person/child::*"`. Listing 25.6 shows the unabbreviated version of PersonToHTML.xsl.

LISTING 25.6 SOURCE CODE FOR `PersonToHTML4.xsl`

```
<?xml version="1.0"?>
<xsl:stylesheet
    xmlns:xsl="http://www.w3.org/1999/XSL/Transform"
    version="1.0">
    <xsl:template match="self::people">
        <html>
        <body bgcolor="#ffffff">
        <table border="4">
            <tr><th>First Name</th><th>Middle Name</th><th>Last Name</th>
            <th>Age</th></tr>

        <xsl:apply-templates/>

        </table>
        </body>
        </html>
    </xsl:template>

    <xsl:template match="self::person">
        <tr>
            <xsl:apply-templates/>

        </tr>
    </xsl:template>

    <xsl:template match="self::person/child::*">
        <td><xsl:value-of select="self"/></td>
    </xsl:template>

</xsl:stylesheet>
```

Table 25.1 shows the abbreviated and unabbreviated syntax for various common patterns that you might want to match against with XPath.

Table 25.1 Abbreviated and Unabbreviated Syntax Examples for XPath

Abbreviated	Unabbreviated	Description
`elem`	`child::elem`	Selects all children of the current node named `elem`.
`*`	`child::*`	Selects all children of the current node.
`text()`	`child::text()`	Selects all text nodes that are children of the current node.
`@attr`	`attribute::attr`	Selects attribute named `attr` from the current node.
`@*`	`attribute::*`	Selects all attributes from the current node.
`elem[1]`	`child::elem[position()=1]`	Selects first child of the current node named `elem`.
`*/elem`	child::*/child::elem	Selects all grandchildren of the current node named `elem`.
`elem[@attr="foo"]`	`child::elem [attribute::attr="foo"]`	Selects all children of the current node whose `attr` attribute has the value of `"foo"`.
`elem[something]`	`child::elem[child::something]`	Selects all children named `elem` that have children named `something`.
`elem[foo or bar]`	`child::elem [child::foo or child::bar]`	Selects all children named `elem` that have children named either `foo` or `bar`.

Applying XSL Templates on the Browser

Internet Explorer 5 has a built-in XSL processor that can apply templates on the client side. This gives you a lot of flexibility because you can generate XML from a Java Server Page and have the browser apply the stylesheet to the XML. There are some things you must change in the XSL namespaceto use IE as the stylesheet processor. Internet Explorer uses the namespace `http://www.w3.org/TR/WD-xsl`, so you must change the `xmlns:xsl` reference in the `<xsl:stylesheet>` tag. Second, IE doesn't support default rules for items that don't match any of your templates. Believe it or not, there is an element in the Person.xml document that doesn't match any of the templates in PersonToHTML.xsl—the document root. You must add the following template to match the document root:

```
<xsl:template match="/">
    <xsl:apply-templates/>
</xsl:template>
```

The advantage of processing the stylesheet on the browser is that you have much more flexibility on your server, and the server isn't bogged down processing stylesheets for every user. The main disadvantage is that Internet Explorer 5 is the only browser as of August 2000 that supports XSL. If your application must support general Web users, you'll still need to apply the stylesheet on the server.

APPLYING XSL TEMPLATES FROM A SERVLET

XSL becomes a powerful tool when you combine it with the power of servlets and Java Server Pages. You can create XML documents within your server-side Java code and use a stylesheet to format the XML into something the client understands.

To apply an XSL stylesheet to an XML document from a servlet or JSP, you must have an XSL processor installed in your servlet engine's classpath. The Apache Group's Xalan XSL processor (`http://xml.apache.org`) is an excellent XSL processor and works well in a servlet environment. IBM's LotusXSL processor, available from `http://www.alphaworks.ibm.com`, is also good.

Listing 25.7 shows a servlet that takes an XML document or a filename from the `request` object along with a stylesheet filename and applies a stylesheet to the document. As an added bonus, it checks to see if the request came from a wireless application and if so, it applies a different stylesheet. The servlet assumes that the HTML stylesheets are in a subdirectory named `html` and the wireless WML stylesheets are in a subdirectory named `wml`.

➔ For more information on Wireless Web applications, **see** Chapter 26, "Creating a Wireless Web Application," **p. 489**.

LISTING 25.7 SOURCE CODE FOR `XSLServlet.java`

```
package usingjsp.xsl;

import java.io.*;

import javax.servlet.*;
import javax.servlet.http.*;

import org.apache.xalan.xslt.*;
import org.w3c.dom.*;
import org.xml.sax.*;

public class XSLServlet extends HttpServlet
{
    public void service(HttpServletRequest request,
        HttpServletResponse response)
        throws IOException, ServletException
    {

// Get the XML source passed in the request
        Object source = request.getAttribute("source");
```

LISTING 25.7 CONTINUED

```
        XSLTInputSource xmlSource = null;

// See if the source is an XML document
        if (source instanceof Document)
        {
            xmlSource = new XSLTInputSource((Document) source);
        }
// Otherwise see if it is a file or a filename
        else if ((source instanceof File) || (source instanceof String))
        {
            if (source instanceof File)
            {
                xmlSource = new XSLTInputSource(
                    new FileReader((File) source));
            }
            else
            {
                xmlSource = new XSLTInputSource(
                    new FileReader((String) source));
            }
        }

// Get the URL for the stylesheet (assume for now that it's local)
        String stylesheet = (String) request.getAttribute("stylesheet");

        String stylesheetPath = null;

// If the request came from a wireless application, pull the stylesheet
// from the wml directory, otherwise use the html directory
        if (isWML(request))
        {
            stylesheetPath = "wml"+File.separator+stylesheet;
            response.setContentType("text/vnd.wap.wml");
        }
        else
        {
            stylesheetPath = "html"+File.separator+stylesheet;
            response.setContentType("text/html");
        }

// Create an input source for reading the stylesheet (use the servlet
// context to get an input stream for the stylesheet)

        XSLTInputSource stylesheetSource = new XSLTInputSource(
            getServletContext().getResourceAsStream(stylesheetPath));


// Create a result target that writes to the servlet's output stream
        XSLTResultTarget target = new XSLTResultTarget(response.getWriter());

// Create an XSL processor and process the XML source and the stylesheet
        try
        {
            XSLTProcessor processor = XSLTProcessorFactory.getProcessor();

            processor.process(xmlSource, stylesheetSource, target);
        }
        catch (SAXException exc)
        {
```

```
            throw new ServletException(exc);
        }
    }

    public static boolean isWML(HttpServletRequest request)
    {
// Checks to see if the request came from a wireless app (from chapter 26)
        String accept = request.getHeader("Accept");
        if (accept == null) return false;

        if (accept.indexOf("text/vnd.wap.wml") >= 0)
        {
            return true;
        }

        return false;
    }
}
```

Listing 25.8 shows a Java server page that creates an XML document on-the-fly and then passes it to the XSL servlet using the `<jsp:forward>` tag.

Listing 25.8 Source Code for TestXSL.jsp

```
<%@ page import="org.w3c.dom.*,org.apache.xerces.dom.*" %>
<%

/* The following statement creating a Document object is not
 * part of the standard DOM API. In order to pass a Document
 * object to the Xalan stylesheet processor, the Document must
 * be from the Xerces (Apache's XML parser) implementation.
 * If you have the Sun XML parser installed, which you need for
 * Tomcat, you won't be able to create a Document object that
 * Xalan understands.
 */
    Document doc = new DocumentImpl();

// Create the root element
    Element root = doc.createElement("mainpage");

    doc.appendChild(root);

// Create the greeting
    Element greeting = doc.createElement("greeting");

    greeting.appendChild(doc.createTextNode("Welcome to the Demo!"));

    root.appendChild(greeting);

// Create the main menu
    Element menu = doc.createElement("menu");

    Element menuItem1 = doc.createElement("item");
    menuItem1.setAttribute("name", "Products");
    menuItem1.setAttribute("link", "products.jsp");
    menu.appendChild(menuItem1);

    Element menuItem2 = doc.createElement("item");
```

Listing 25.8 Continued

```
menuItem2.setAttribute("name", "Services");
    menuItem2.setAttribute("link", "service.jsp");
    menu.appendChild(menuItem2);

    Element menuItem3 = doc.createElement("item");
    menuItem3.setAttribute("name", "Support");
    menuItem3.setAttribute("link", "support.jsp");
    menu.appendChild(menuItem3);

    root.appendChild(menu);

    request.setAttribute("source", doc);
    request.setAttribute("stylesheet", "mainpage.xsl");
%><jsp:forward page="XSLServlet"/>
```

The JSP in Listing 25.8 creates an XML document that would look like this, if written to a file:

```
<mainpage>
    <greeting>Welcome to the Demo!</greeting>
    <menu>
        <item name="Products" link="products.jsp"/>
        <item name="Services" link="services.jsp"/>
        <item name="Support" link="support.jsp"/>
    </menu>
</mainpage>
```

By using stylesheets, you can display this XML any number of ways. Listing 25.9 shows a stylesheet that converts the XML document into an HTML document.

Listing 25.9 Source Code for HTML Version of `mainpage.xsl`

```
<?xml version="1.0"?><xsl:stylesheet
xmlns:xsl="http://www.w3.org/1999/XSL/Transform"
    version="1.0">

    <xsl:template match="/">
        <xsl:apply-templates/>
    </xsl:template>

    <xsl:template match="mainpage">
        <html>
        <body bgcolor="#ffffff">
            <xsl:apply-templates/>
        </body>
        </html>
    </xsl:template>

    <xsl:template match="greeting">
        <h1><xsl:value-of select="."/></h1>
        <p></p>
    </xsl:template>

    <xsl:template match="menu">
        <p>Please choose from the following menu options:</p>
        <bl>
```

```
            <xsl:apply-templates/>
        </bl>
    </xsl:template>

    <xsl:template match="item">
        <li><a>
            <xsl:attribute name="href">
                <xsl:value-of select="@link"/>
            </xsl:attribute>
            <xsl:value-of select="@name"/>
            </a></li>
    </xsl:template>
</xsl:stylesheet>
```

Figure 25.2 shows the output of XSLServlet when it applies the stylesheet to the XML document for HTML output.

Figure 25.2
You can use an XSL stylesheet from a servlet to generate HTML.

Listing 25.10 shows a stylesheet that formats the same XML document as the stylesheet in Listing 25.9, only the target format is WML, the markup language for wireless Web applications.

LISTING 25.10 SOURCE CODE FOR WML VERSION OF `mainpage.xsl`

```
<?xml version="1.0"?>
<xsl:stylesheet
    xmlns:xsl="http://www.w3.org/1999/XSL/Transform"
    version="1.0">

    <xsl:output doctype-public="-//WAPFORUM//DTD WML 1.1//EN"
        doctype-system="http://www.wapforum.org/DTD/wml_1.1.xml"/>

    <xsl:template match="/">
        <xsl:apply-templates/>
    </xsl:template>

    <xsl:template match="mainpage">
        <wml>
        <card id="mainpage">
```

LISTING 25.10 CONTINUED

```
            <xsl:apply-templates/>
        </card>
        </wml>
    </xsl:template>

    <xsl:template match="greeting">
        <p><xsl:value-of select="."/></p>
    </xsl:template>

    <xsl:template match="menu">
            <p>
            <xsl:apply-templates/>
            </p>
    </xsl:template>

    <xsl:template match="item">
        <a>
            <xsl:attribute name="href">
                <xsl:value-of select="@link"/>
            </xsl:attribute>
            <xsl:attribute name="title">
                <xsl:value-of select="@name"/>
            </xsl:attribute>
            <xsl:value-of select="@name"/>
            </a>
    </xsl:template>
</xsl:stylesheet>
```

JSP OR STYLESHEETS?

There is some level of overlap between the features of Java Server Pages and XSL stylesheets. You might be wondering how to decide which one to use.

XSL works best when you already have XML files, or when you generate an XML document as part of your normal processing. There are now applications that can query a database and return an XML document representing the data. XSL is ideal for formatting these documents.

JSP is better when you are working with pure Java objects, which is probably what you'll be using most of the time. Even if you read in XML data, if you do any processing on it, you'll likely be converting the XML into a Java object and then invoking methods on the Java object. If you have Java objects and want to use XSL stylesheets, you must first take the extra step of representing your Java objects as XML documents, which is not a pleasant task.

TROUBLESHOOTING

TRANSLATOR PROBLEMS

My stylesheet works under `Resin`*; why won't it work under Internet Explorer?*

Don't forget to change the namespace URI to `http://www.w3.org/TR/WD-xsl` when using IE.

Why won't Resin apply my XSL stylesheet to my XML file?

Resin doesn't realize it needs to run the XSL processor unless you change the extension to .xtp.

Why doesn't the XSL processor process tags contained within one of the tags I defined in my stylesheet?

You probably forgot the `<xsl:apply-templates>` tag.

Why doesn't the XSL processor do anything with my XML file?

Some XSL processors, notably IE, require you to specify a rule for "`/`" to match the document itself.

CHAPTER 26

Creating a Wireless Web Application

In this chapter

Over the past few years, mobile phone networks have been switching from analog to digital transmission. In addition to getting better reception, digital Personal Communications Service (PCS) phone users are finding that their little phone is more than just a glorified walkie-talkie. Digital transmission makes it much easier for the phone network to pass data as well as voice traffic through the airwaves. Although this was possible with an analog system, it was much more complicated.

PCS phones now come with tiny Web browsers that work over a "wireless Web." This wireless Web is not quite the same as the Web you use from your home computer. Although there are gateways bridging the two, the data traffic on the wireless web uses the Wireless Application Protocol (WAP) to transmit data. Without getting bogged down in the details, the wireless networks don't have the same data capacity as the rest of the Internet. WAP was designed to accommodate the low bandwidth and reduced connectivity restrictions of wireless networks.

Figure 26.1 shows how a typical Web browser interacts with a Web server. By now, you can probably draw this picture in your sleep.

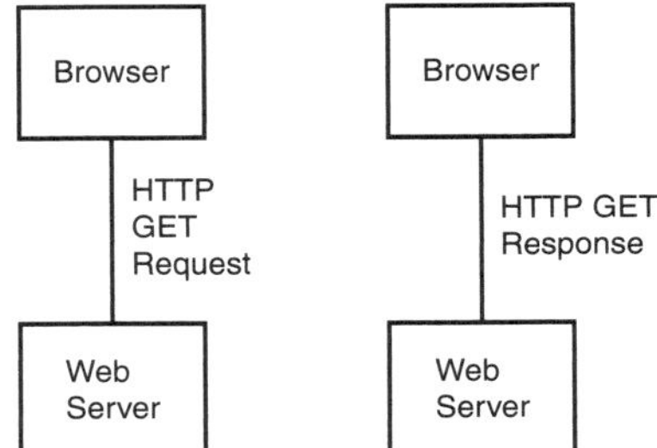

Figure 26.1
A Web browser uses the TCP/IP to communicate with a Web server.

Figure 26.2 shows the path that a PCS phone takes to get to that same Web server. The WAP gateway sits between the wireless network and the TCP/IP network and serves as the bridge between the two networks.

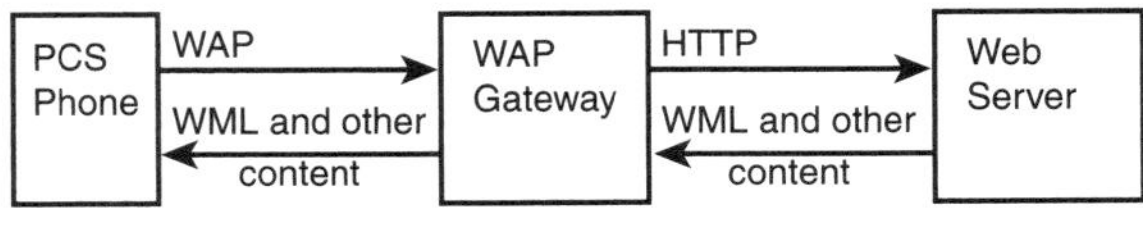

Figure 26.2
The WAP gateway passes requests between a wireless network and a TCP/IP network.

Most wireless Web sites use the Wireless Markup Language (WML), which is a form of XML. That is, WML is defined using an XML Document Type Definition (DTD) and is specifically designed to accommodate the small browsers embedded inside PCS phones. Because many Web providers aren't yet willing to take the time to create a WML version of their site, it is possible to create an HTML→WML translator to make most of the Web available to PCS phones. Unfortunately, although this idea sounds good, very few Web sites translate well because of their layout. It is better to create a scaled-down version with WML.

One of the disadvantages of the gateway approach is that the WAP gateway can become a huge bottleneck. All the requests from the wireless network must funnel through the WAP gateway, which must keep track of connections on both networks. It is possible to create a WAP server that serves WML directly to the wireless network without using a TCP/IP network, as shown in Figure 26.3.

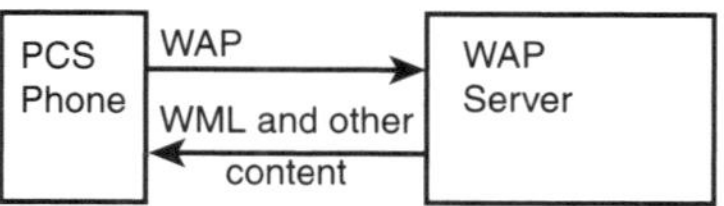

Figure 26.3
A WAP server provides content directly to the wireless network.

Although no WAP servers yet provide a servlet API, you might soon be able to write servlets and JSPs specifically for wireless networks. In the meantime, however, you can use JSP and servlets to create WML content that is accessed through a WAP gateway.

A WIRELESS "HELLO WORLD" PAGE

Listing 26.1 shows the ubiquitous "Hello World" application for a wireless device.

LISTING 26.1 SOURCE CODE FOR `WirelessHello.jsp`

```
<%@ page language="java" contentType="text/vnd.wap.wml" %>
<?xml version="1.0"?>
<!DOCTYPE wml PUBLIC "-//WAPFORUM//DTD WML 1.1//EN"
    "http://www.wapforum.org/DTD/wml_1.1.xml">

<wml>
<card id="hello">
<p>
Hello Wireless World!
</p>
</card>
</wml>
```


The first thing you might notice in WirelessHello.jsp is that the content type is not `text/html`. Of course, it isn't `text/wml` either, which would probably make a lot more sense than `text/vnd.wap.wml`, but that's the way it is.

After you get past the `<%@page` line, the file looks like a typical XML file. You must always have the `<?xml` header. The `<!DOCTYPE` tag isn't strictly necessary for all XML pages, but if there is a DTD defined for the XML you are generating, you should include it.

Now you get into the actual WML code. The `<wml>` tag is the root tag of a WML document. Everything else must be enclosed within it. As you will see in a moment, a WML page consists of a number of cards, which are really like little pages. The `WirelessHello` page contains a single card named hello. The one tag that is familiar from the HTML world is the <p> tag defining a paragraph.

Tip

Remember that because WML is an XML-based markup language, a tag must always have a closing tag or end with />. You must remember to use a closing </p> tag for paragraphs, and put a / in the <br/> tag to insert a line break.

VIEWING THE WIRELESS HELLO PAGE

You don't need a wireless Web-enabled phone to test out your wireless Web pages. You can get a WAP phone simulator from some of the vendors that make phones and phone software. Phone.com provides the wireless Web browser software for a number of phone manufacturers and also makes a WAP gateway. You can download its UP.SDK development kit that includes a nice phone simulator at http://www.phone.com. Follow the link for developers to see what Phone.com has to offer.

Figure 26.4 shows the WirelessHello page running in the Phone.com simulator.

Figure 26.4
A phone simulator lets you debug wireless Web pages without paying for wireless Web time.

Note

In case you're wondering why Phone.com's SDK is called UP.SDK, the company was once called Unwired Planet, thus the *UP* in UP.SDK.

Nokia, the well-known phone manufacturer, also has a phone simulator. Go to http://www.forum.nokia.com, then follow the link for WAP developers. The Nokia phone simulator is in the Nokia WAP toolkit. Figure 26.5 shows the WirelessHello page running in the Nokia phone simulator.

Figure 26.5
Nokia's phone simulator shows you the WML it is displaying.

A BRIEF INTRODUCTION TO WML

As you now know, WML is based on XML and is optimized for low-bandwidth transactions. One of the optimizations in WAP and WML is that a server can return multiple display pages in a single request. These display pages are referred to as cards. When you return a response to a WAP phone (or other device), the response can contain a series of `<card>` tags. The phone displays the first card in the response, and it is up to you to provide navigation to the other cards. Figure 26.6 illustrates the layout of a response.

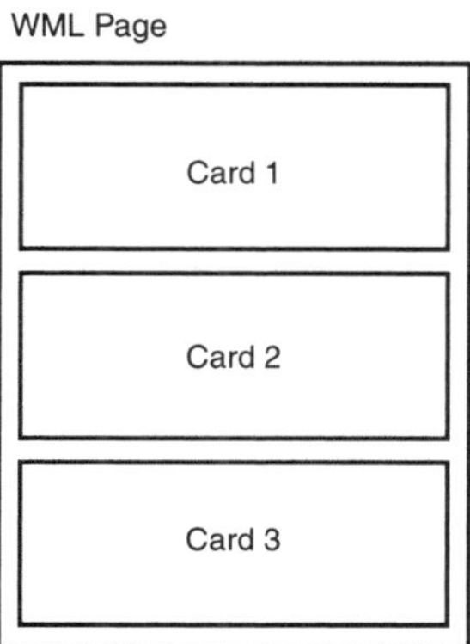

Figure 26.6
A response can contain multiple "pages" organized into cards.

Navigating Between Cards

There are two main ways to navigate between cards. You can use the `<a>` tag, which creates a hyperlink just like in HTML, or you can use the `<do>` tag, which lets you perform an action when the user presses a particular key or activates some other feature of the device.

Listing 26.2 shows an example page with four cards. The main card contains three hyperlinks to the other cards. In a WML hyperlink, the text after the `#` in a URL indicates the card name. For example, `href="#moe"` refers to the card with an ID of `moe`.

Listing 26.2 Source Code for `Hyperlinks.jsp`

```
<%@ page language="java" contentType="text/vnd.wap.wml" %>
<?xml version="1.0"?>
<!DOCTYPE wml PUBLIC "-//WAPFORUM//DTD WML 1.1//EN"
    "http://www.wapforum.org/DTD/wml_1.1.xml">

<wml>

<card id="main">
    <p>
        <a href="#moe" title="Moe">Moe Howard</a>
        <a href="#larry" title="Larry">Larry Fine</a>
        <a href="#curly" title="Curly">Curly Howard</a>
    </p>
</card>

<card id="moe">
    <p>
        Moe Howard<br/>
        Why I oughta...
    </p>
</card>

<card id="larry">
    <p>
        Larry Fine<br/>
        Ow! Ow! Ow!
    </p>
</card>

<card id="curly">
    <p>
        Curly Howard<br/>
        Woob woob woob woob<br/>
        Nyuk nyuk nyuk
    </p>
</card >
</wml>
```

Figure 26.7 shows the main menu running in the Phone.com simulator.

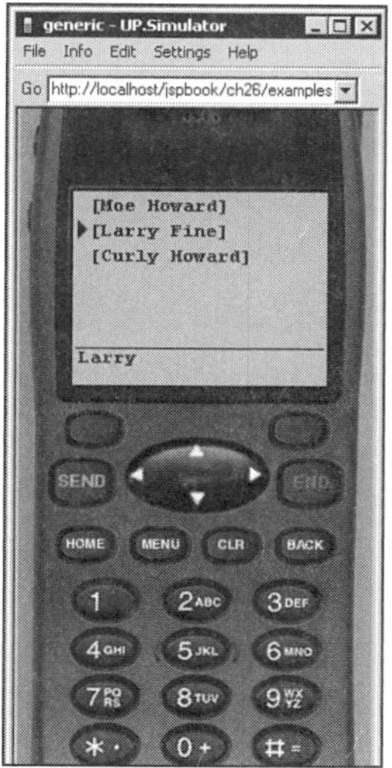

Figure 26.7
The phone displays only the first card. You must navigate to the others.

In addition to hyperlinks, you can control navigation based on the keys the user presses. When you control navigation by keypresses, you can look for the keys either within a particular card or within the entire deck.

Tip

A WML page is referred to as a deck because it usually consists of a number of cards.

Listing 26.3 shows a Web page similar to Hyperlinks.jsp, except that you use the Accept keys to navigate forward through the list.

Listing 26.3 Source Code for Next.jsp

```
<%@ page language="java" contentType="text/vnd.wap.wml" %>
<?xml version="1.0"?>
<!DOCTYPE wml PUBLIC "-//WAPFORUM//DTD WML 1.1//EN"
    "http://www.wapforum.org/DTD/wml_1.1.xml">

<wml>

<card id="moe">
    <!-- If the user presses Accept, display the Larry card -->
    <do type="accept" label="Larry">
        <go href="#larry"/>
    </do>
    <p>
        Moe Howard<br/>
        Why I oughta...
    </p>
</card>
```

LISTING 26.3 CONTINUED

```
<card id="larry">
    <!-- If the user presses Accept, display the Curly card -->
    <do type="accept" label="Curly">
        <go href="#curly"/>
    </do>

    <p>
        Larry Fine<br/>
        Ow! Ow! Ow!
    </p>
</card>

<card id="curly">
    <!-- If the user presses Accept, display the Moe card -->
    <do type="accept" label="Moe">
        <go href="#moe"/>
    </do>
    <p>
        Curly Howard<br/>
        Woob woob woob woob<br/>
        Nyuk nyuk nyuk
    </p>
</card >
</wml>
```

Note

The Accept key is usually directly below the display. On some phones, it's on the right although on others it's on the left. The phone usually gives you a clue by placing the label string on the side where the Accept key is.

Remember, too, that not all phones have a Back key. You need to make sure that users can navigate around from whatever card they are on. For example, in the Hyperlinks example, you can't get back from any of the specific cards unless you have a Back key. Figure 26.8 shows the Curly card running in the Nokia phone simulator. There's no way out!

CREATING INPUT FORMS

Although WML doesn't have a `<form>` tag like HTML, you can still create input forms and process them as if they were HTML forms. The `<input>` tag creates an input field much like its HTML equivalent. When you create an input field, you must give the field a name, but all other attributes of the tag are optional. You might specify `size` and `maxlength` just like in HTML. The `type` attribute might be `text` or `password`, with `text` being the default. One of the interesting options is that you can specify a format.

The format is a list of characters indicating what kinds of values can be entered at each position in the field. The format characters are `A`, `a`, `M`, `m`, `N`, `X`, and `x` as shown in Table 26.1.

Figure 26.8
Watch your navigation! Don't leave any dead ends for people with no Back button.

TABLE 26.1 FORMAT TYPES FOR INPUT FIELDS

Format	Function
A	Permits any uppercase character except a number
a	Allows any lowercase character except a number
M	Allows any character (including symbols and numbers) and defaults the first character to uppercase
m	Allows any character and defaults the first character to lowercase
N	Allows only numbers, plus any symbols or numbers
X	Allows any uppercase characters, plus any symbols or numbers
x	Allows any lowercase characters, plus any symbols or numbers

Normally, a format character represents a single position in the field. For example, if you specify a format of NANA, you require the first and third characters to be numbers and the second and fourth to be letters.

If you put an asterisk before a character, you allow any number of those characters. For example, if you want a format that allows a single letter followed by any number of digits, use A*N. If you want a format that allows any character but requires at least one, use M*M. Remember, the * can represent 0 characters.

Tip

When creating format strings for an input field, remember that the * is associated with the character to its right, not its left. In most other wildcard formats, the * is associated with the character to its left.

You can also use a specific count instead of the *. For example, if you want to require exactly four letters, you could use either AAAA as a format or 4A.

> **Note**
>
> The * and the count format options can only be applied to the last format character. In other words, you can't do something like A*AN.

The following <input> tag allows only letters and requires at least two:

```
<input name="atleasttwo" format="AA*A">
```

You can also insert fixed characters in the format text by preceding that character with a \. For example, a field that allows you to enter a Social Security number looks like this:

```
<input name="ssn" format="NNN\-NN\-NNNN">
```

You can also create select lists using the <select> and <option> tags like you do in HTML. Here is a select list that allows you to pick a color:

```
<select name="color">
    <option value="r">Red</option>
    <option value="g">Green</option>
    <option value="b">Blue</option>
</select>
```

PROCESSING FORM INPUT

One of the unique things about WML is that it makes the values of input and select fields available within the deck. You can reference the value of a field by putting a $ in front of the field name. Listing 26.4 shows a single-card deck with a text input field and a select list. In between the input field and the select list, it prints out the value from the input field.

LISTING 26.4 SOURCE CODE FOR Input.jsp

```
<%@ page language="java" contentType="text/vnd.wap.wml" %>
<?xml version="1.0"?>
<!DOCTYPE wml PUBLIC "-//WAPFORUM//DTD WML 1.1//EN"
    "http://www.wapforum.org/DTD/wml_1.1.xml">

<wml>

<card id="fieldfun">
<p>Type something:
    <input name="ssn" format="NNN\-NN\-NNNN"/>
    $ssn
    <select name="colors">
        <option value="r">Red</option>
        <option value="g">Green</option>
        <option value="b">Blue</option>
    </select>
</p>
</card>
</wml>
```

The `$ssn` symbol directly before the `<select>` tag inserts the value from the text field into the output from the card. In the Phone.com simulator, it displays the value directly above the select field, as shown in Figure 26.9.

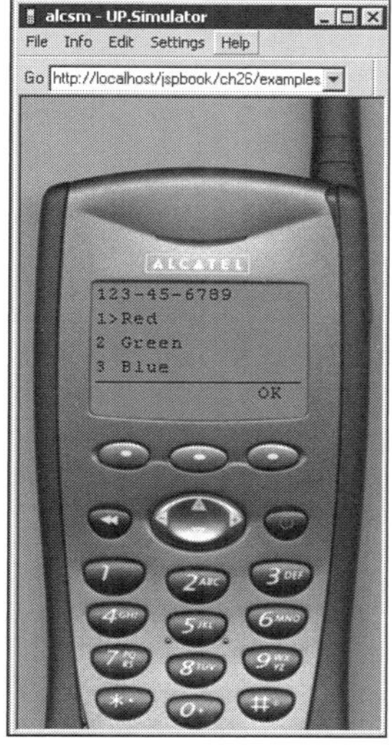

Figure 26.9
You can display input values in other parts of the deck.

Note

Notice that the phone image in the Phone.com simulator is different than the one you saw before. The Phone.com simulator comes with different configurations so you can see what a page would look like in several different phones.

To post a form to a Web server, use the `<do>` tag to define an action for a keypress and a `<go>` tag to define the action to be taken. Within the `<go>` tag, you use `<postfield>` tags to specify the values you want to send. Listing 26.5 shows how you would post the values from Input.jsp back to a Web page called HandleInput.jsp.

Listing 26.5 Source Code for `Input2.jsp`

```
<%@ page language="java" contentType="text/vnd.wap.wml" %>
<?xml version="1.0"?>
<!DOCTYPE wml PUBLIC "-//WAPFORUM//DTD WML 1.1//EN"
    "http://www.wapforum.org/DTD/wml_1.1.xml">

<wml>

<card id="fieldfun">
<do type="accept">
    <go href="HandleInput.jsp" method="post">
       <postfield name="ssn" value="$(ssn)"/>
       <postfield name="colors" value="$(colors)"/>
```

LISTING 26.5 CONTINUED

```
    </go>
</do>

<p>Type something:
    <input name="ssn" format="NNN\-NN\-NNNN"/>
    $ssn
    <select name="colors">
        <option value="r">Red</option>
        <option value="g">Green</option>
        <option value="b">Blue</option>
    </select>
</p>
</card>
</wml>
```

The form input is delivered to your servlet or JSP exactly the same way it is when it comes from a browser.

DETECTING WIRELESS CLIENTS IN A JSP OR SERVLET

You can write a JSP or servlet that services requests from wireless phones and Web browsers at the same time, especially when you are handling form input. When you send a response back, of course, you want to know whether you should send HTML or WML. When the browser or the phone makes a request, it passes the Web server a list of the kinds of content it will accept. You can retrieve the list by making the following method call:

```
String accept = request.getHeader("Accept");
```

For a wireless client, you should see `text/vnd.wap.wml` somewhere in the accept string. You can test for it this way:

```
if (accept.indexOf("text/vnd.wap.wml") >= 0)
{
    // handle a wireless client
}
else
{
    // handle a regular web client
}
```

A WIRELESS SCORE ENTRY AND REPORTING SYSTEM

As an avid Scrabble player, I go to several tournaments a year. Scrabble is not exactly a spectator sport, so the only way my family knows how I am doing is when I call them and tell them. Wouldn't it be nice to enter the results using a wireless phone and post them on a Web page for all to see? That sounds like a good application for JSP and servlets!

The winner of a Scrabble tournament is the person with the most wins. In case of a tie, the winner is the one whose cumulative win-loss spread is the highest. In other words, you take the total number of points you won by in all your games and subtract the total number of points you lost by and that's the cumulative spread. Winning 500 to 400 is the same as winning 350 to 250. You get a win and add 100 points to your cumulative spread.

The five core elements you need to represent a result from a Scrabble tournament game are

- The round the game was played
- The player's name
- The player's score
- The opponent's name
- The opponent's score

You can compute a won-lost record and a cumulative spread from the results, so there's no need to store them. You can represent these items in a database with a SQL table like this:

```
create table scores
    ( round int not null,
      player varchar(30) not null,
      opponent varchar(30) not null,
      player_score int not null,
      opponent_score int not null,
      primary key (round, player) );
```

Note

This application makes the assumption that you are tracking the performance of a single player, thus the "player" column in the table is the player you are tracking. For a more general application, you would need to do a little more work.

Listing 26.6 shows a database object that represents a score in the database.

Listing 26.6 Source Code for `Score.java`

```
package usingjsp.scores;

import usingjsp.DatabaseObject;
import java.sql.*;
import java.io.*;
import java.util.*;

/** A class to contain scores */
public class Score extends DatabaseObject
    implements java.io.Serializable
{
    public int round;
    public String player;
    public String opponent;
    public int playerScore;
    public int opponentScore;
```

LISTING 26.6 CONTINUED

```
    public Score()
    {
    }

    public Score(ResultSet results)
        throws SQLException
    {
        round = results.getInt("round");
        player = results.getString("player");
        opponent = results.getString("opponent");
        playerScore = results.getInt("player_score");
        opponentScore = results.getInt("opponent_score");
    }

    public int getRound() { return round; }
    public void setRound(int aRound) { round = aRound; }

    public String getPlayer() { return player; }
    public void setPlayer(String aPlayer) { player = aPlayer; }

    public String getOpponent() { return opponent; }
    public void setOpponent(String aOpponent)
        { opponent = aOpponent; }

    public int getPlayerScore() { return playerScore; }
    public void setPlayerScore(int aPlayerScore)
        { playerScore = aPlayerScore; }

    public int getOpponentScore() { return opponentScore; }
    public void setOpponentScore(int aOpponentScore)
        { opponentScore = aOpponentScore; }

/** Returns the name of the table containing scores */
    public String getTableName() { return "scores"; }

/** Returns a list of the table fields this class uses */
    public String getFieldList()
    {
        return "round,player,opponent,player_score,opponent_score";
    }

/** Creates a new instance of this object from a database row */
    public DatabaseObject createInstance(ResultSet results)
        throws SQLException
    {
        return new Score(results);
    }

/** Returns the SQL statement used to insert this object into
 *  the database */
    public String getInsertStatement()
    {
        return "insert into scores "+
            "(round,player,opponent,player_score,opponent_score) "+
```

```
            " values (?,?,?,?,?)";
    }

/** Populates an insert statement with this object's data */
    public void prepareInsertStatement(PreparedStatement s)
        throws SQLException
    {
        s.setInt(1, round);
        s.setString(2, player);
        s.setString(3, opponent);
        s.setInt(4, playerScore);
        s.setInt(5, opponentScore);
    }

/** Returns the SQL statement used to update this object in
 *  the database */
    public String getUpdateStatement()
    {
        return "update scores set "+
            "opponent=?,player_score=?,opponent_score=? "+
            " where round=? and player=?";
    }

/** Populates an update statement with this object's data */
    public void prepareUpdateStatement(PreparedStatement s)
        throws SQLException
    {
        s.setString(1, opponent);
        s.setInt(2, playerScore);
        s.setInt(3, opponentScore);
        s.setInt(4, round);
        s.setString(5, player);
    }

/** Returns the SQL statement used to delete this object from
 *  the database */
    public String getDeleteStatement()
    {
        return "delete from scores where round=? and player=?";
    }

/** Populates a delete statement with this object's data */
    public void prepareDeleteStatement(PreparedStatement s)
        throws SQLException
    {
        s.setInt(1, round);
        s.setString(2, player);
    }
}
```

When you break it down, there are three main functions this application needs to perform:

- Insert new scores into the database
- Compute the player's won-lost record and cumulative point spread
- List the results from each game

Inserting a score in the database should work the same way whether the data was entered from a browser or from a phone. Computing the player's record and fetching the scores are also display-independent tasks. Using the notion of handling display tasks in JSPs and non-display tasks in servlets, it makes sense to use servlets to perform the major system tasks and then use JSPs to display the results.

Listing 26.7 shows the servlet that receives a score and inserts it into the database.

LISTING 26.7 SOURCE CODE FOR RegisterScoreServlet.java

```
package usingjsp.scores;

import javax.servlet.*;
import javax.servlet.http.*;
import java.io.*;
import java.sql.*;

import usingjsp.*;

public class RegisterScoreServlet extends HttpServlet
{
    public void service(HttpServletRequest request,
        HttpServletResponse response)
        throws IOException, ServletException
    {
        Connection conn = null;
        IConnectionPool pool = null;

        try
        {
// Require the user to enter a secret numeric code just to keep
// other people from entering fake scores
            String passCode = request.getParameter("passcode");

            if (!passCode.equals("12345")) // same code as my luggage!
            {
                throw new RuntimeException("Invalid passcode!");
            }

// Get a reference to the connection pool
            pool = ScoreSupport.getConnectionPool(getServletContext());

// Allocate a database connection
            conn = pool.getConnection();

// Create a new score object and populate its fields
            Score score = new Score();
            score.round = Integer.parseInt(
                request.getParameter("round"));
            score.player = request.getParameter("player");
            score.playerScore = Integer.parseInt(
                request.getParameter("score"));
            score.opponent = request.getParameter("opponent");
            score.opponentScore = Integer.parseInt(
                request.getParameter("opponentscore"));
```

```
// Insert the score into the database
            score.insert(conn);

// Assume that the client is using HTML
            String destPage = "/ScoreMenuHTML.jsp";

// If the client is using WML, send them to a different page
            if (ScoreSupport.isWML(request))
            {
                destPage = "/ScoreMenuWML.jsp";
            }

            getServletContext().getRequestDispatcher(destPage).forward(
                request, response);
        }
        catch (Exception exc)
        {
            String errorPage = "/ErrorHTML.jsp";

            if (ScoreSupport.isWML(request))
            {
                errorPage = "/ErrorWML.jsp";
            }

            request.setAttribute("exception", exc);

            exc.printStackTrace();

            getServletContext().getRequestDispatcher(errorPage).forward(
                request, response);
        }
        finally
        {
            if (conn != null)
            {
                try
                {
                    pool.releaseConnection(conn);
                } catch (Exception ignore) {}
            }
        }
    }
}
```

All the core servlets need to use the database pool, and there is no way to know which one will be called first. Each of the servlets needs to see if the pool has been created, and if not, create it. Rather than duplicate the code, you just put it into a utility class. Likewise, each servlet needs to figure out if the client supports HTML or WML. Again, the utility class is the way to go.

Listing 26.8 shows the `ScoreSupport` utility class that performs some commonly used functions.

LISTING 26.8 SOURCE CODE FOR ScoreSupport.java

```
package usingjsp.scores;

import javax.servlet.*;
import javax.servlet.http.*;
import java.sql.*;
import usingjsp.*;

public class ScoreSupport
{
    public static IConnectionPool getConnectionPool(
        ServletContext application)
        throws SQLException
    {
        IConnectionPool pool =
            (IConnectionPool) application.getAttribute(
                "ScoresConnectionPool");

        if (pool == null)
        {
            synchronized (application)
            {
                pool = (IConnectionPool) application.getAttribute(
                        "ScoresConnectionPool");
                if (pool == null)
                {
                    try
                    {
                        Class.forName("org.gjt.mm.mysql.Driver").
                            newInstance();
                    }
                    catch (Exception exc)
                    {
                        application.log("Error loading JDBC driver", exc);
                    }

                    pool = new ConnectionPool(
                        "jdbc:mysql://localhost/usingjsp", "", "", 3);

                    application.setAttribute("ScoresConnectionPool",
                        pool);
                }
            }
        }

        return pool;
    }

    public static boolean isWML(HttpServletRequest request)
    {
        String accept = request.getHeader("Accept");
        if (accept == null) return false;

        if (accept.indexOf("text/vnd.wap.wml") >= 0)
        {
            return true;
```

```
        }

        return false;
    }
}
```

The score input form for a Web browser is rather mundane and you could certainly write one in a matter of minutes. The input form for a wireless phone is much more interesting.

You really need only six input fields for entering a score and sending it to `RegisterScoreServlet`. The input form isn't too different from Input2.jsp; there are just a few more fields. Listing 26.9 shows the WML version of the score input form.

Listing 26.9 Source Code for `RegisterScoreWML.jsp`

```
<%@ page language="java" contentType="text/vnd.wap.wml" %>

<?xml version="1.0"?>
<!DOCTYPE wml PUBLIC "-//WAPFORUM//DTD WML 1.1//EN"
    "http://www.wapforum.org/DTD/wml_1.1.xml">

<wml>
<card id="regscore">
<do type="accept">
    <go href="RegisterScoreServlet"
        method="post">
        <postfield name="passcode" value="$(passcode)"/>
        <postfield name="round" value="$(round)"/>
        <postfield name="player" value="$(player)"/>
        <postfield name="score" value="$(score)"/>
        <postfield name="opponent" value="$(opponent)"/>
        <postfield name="opponentscore" value="$(opponentscore)"/>
    </go>
</do>
<p>Passcode:
<input type="text" name="passcode" maxlength="6" format="N*N"/>
</p>
<p>Round:
<input type="text" name="round" maxlength="2" format="N*N"/>
</p>
<p>Player:
<input type="text" name="player" maxlength="20" format="*m" value="Mark"/>
</p>
<p>Score:
<input type="text" name="score" maxlength="4" format="N*N"/>
</p>
<p>Opponent:
<input type="text" name="opponent" maxlength="20" format="*m"/>
</p>
<p>Opp. Score:
<input type="text" name="opponentscore" maxlength="4" format="N*N"/>
</p>
</card>
</wml>
```

Now, you have everything you need to enter a score. The next thing you need to do is display the won-lost record. Because the database object takes much of the pain out of database queries, the `ShowScoresServlet` class doesn't need to do much work.

Listing 26.10 shows the `ShowScoresServlet` class, which fetches the list of scores for all players or a particular player and calls the appropriate display JSP.

LISTING 26.10 SOURCE CODE FOR `ShowScoresServlet.java`

```
package usingjsp.scores;

import javax.servlet.*;
import javax.servlet.http.*;
import java.io.*;
import java.sql.*;
import java.util.*;

import usingjsp.*;

public class ShowScoresServlet extends HttpServlet
{
    public void service(HttpServletRequest request,
        HttpServletResponse response)
        throws IOException, ServletException
    {
        Connection conn = null;
        IConnectionPool pool = null;

// See if there is a specific player whose scores should be shown
        String whichPlayer = request.getParameter("player");

        try
        {
            pool = ScoreSupport.getConnectionPool(getServletContext());

            conn = pool.getConnection();

            Score query = new Score();

// By default, use a dummy where clause that would retrieve all scores
            String whereClause = "round > 0";

// If the query should search for a specific player, change the where clause
            if (whichPlayer != null)
            {
                whereClause = "player = '"+whichPlayer+"'";
            }

// Do the query and add an "order by" clause to make display easier
            Vector v = query.getAll(conn,
                whereClause + " order by round, player");

// Put the list in the request so the JSP can get at it
            request.setAttribute("scoreList", v);

            String destPage = "/ShowScoresHTML.jsp";
```

```
            if (ScoreSupport.isWML(request))
            {
                destPage = "/ShowScoresWML.jsp";
            }

            getServletContext().getRequestDispatcher(destPage).forward(
                request, response);
        }
        catch (Exception exc)
        {
            String errorPage = "/ErrorHTML.jsp";

            if (ScoreSupport.isWML(request))
            {
                errorPage = "/ErrorWML.jsp";
            }

            request.setAttribute("exception", exc);

            exc.printStackTrace();

            getServletContext().getRequestDispatcher(errorPage).forward(
                request, response);
        }
        finally
        {
            if (conn != null)
            {
                try
                {
                    pool.releaseConnection(conn);
                } catch (Exception ignore) {}
            }
        }
    }
}
```


Although there are many ways to arrange the output, it makes sense to put the results from a particular round into a card. The deck of cards from `ShowScoresWML` would represent all the scores from the tournament. Listing 26.11 shows the `ShowScoresWML` Java Server Page that displays the list of scores.

Listing 26.11 Source Code for `ShowScoresWML.jsp`

```
<%@ page language="java" contentType="text/vnd.wap.wml" %>
<%@ page import="java.net.*,java.util.*,usingjsp.scores.*" %>

<?xml version="1.0"?>
<!DOCTYPE wml PUBLIC "-//WAPFORUM//DTD WML 1.1//EN"
    "http://www.wapforum.org/DTD/wml_1.1.xml">

<wml>
<%
    Vector scoreList = (Vector) request.getAttribute("scoreList");
```

LISTING 26.11 CONTINUED

```
    int currRound = 0;
    int numElements = scoreList.size();
    int maxRound = 0;

// Figure out which round is the last one
    for (int i=0; i < numElements; i++)
    {
        Score s = (Score) scoreList.elementAt(i);

        if (s.round > maxRound) maxRound = s.round;
    }

    for (int i=0; i < numElements; i++)
    {
        Score s = (Score) scoreList.elementAt(i);

// If this score starts a new round, start a new card
        if (s.round != currRound)
        {
            if (currRound != 0) out.println("</card>");
            out.println("<card id=\"round"+s.round+"\">");
            currRound = s.round;
        }

// By default, the next link goes back to the main menu
        String dest="Scores.jsp";

// If there are more rounds to go, make the next link go to the next round
        if (s.round < maxRound)
        {
            dest="#round"+(s.round+1);
        }
%>
<do type="accept" label="Next">
    <go href="<%=dest%>"/>
</do>
<p>
Round: <%= s.round %><br/>
<%= s.player %>: <%= s.playerScore %>
    (<%= s.playerScore > s.opponentScore ? "W" : "L"%>)<br/>
<%= s.opponent %>: <%= s.opponentScore %>
    (<%= s.opponentScore > s.playerScore ? "W" : "L"%>)<br/>
Spread: <%= s.playerScore - s.opponentScore %>

</p>
<%
    }
%>
</card>
</wml>
```

Figure 26.10 shows a card generated by the `ShowScoresWML` JSP.

Figure 26.10
Cards usually display a logical grouping of your data.

The `ShowScoresServlet` has the capability to filter on a particular player. If you do enter scores for all the players in the tournament, you would have a tough time scanning through them all on your phone. From a Web browser, it's easy to see the entire list. To reduce the clutter on a phone, this application lets you list the records for each player, and then examine the list of scores for that player. If you're on a Web browser, you can get the complete list of scores directly.

Listing 26.12 shows the final of the three core servlets: `ShowRecordsServlet`. Like `ShowScoresServlet`, it fetches data and then calls an appropriate JSP to render the output.

Listing 26.12 Source Code for `ShowRecordsServlet.java`

```
package usingjsp.scores;

import javax.servlet.*;
import javax.servlet.http.*;
import java.io.*;
import java.sql.*;
import java.util.*;

import usingjsp.*;

public class ShowRecordsServlet extends HttpServlet
{
    public void service(HttpServletRequest request,
        HttpServletResponse response)
        throws IOException, ServletException
    {
        Connection conn = null;
        IConnectionPool pool = null;
```

LISTING 26.12 CONTINUED

```
        try
        {
            pool = ScoreSupport.getConnectionPool(getServletContext());

            conn = pool.getConnection();

            Score query = new Score();

// Get all the scores
            Vector v = query.getAll(conn);

// Create a table to keep track of each player
            Hashtable playerRecords = new Hashtable();

            Enumeration e = v.elements();

            while (e.hasMoreElements())
            {
                Score s = (Score) e.nextElement();

// Get the player's wins, losses and cumulative spread
                int[] playerRecord = (int[]) playerRecords.get(
                    s.player);

// If this player isn't in the table, create a blank entry
                if (playerRecord == null)
                {
                    playerRecord = new int[] { 0, 0, 0 };
                    playerRecords.put(s.player, playerRecord);
                }

// If the player won this game, increment the wins
                if (s.playerScore > s.opponentScore)
                {
                    playerRecord[0]++;
                }
                else
                {
// Otherwise increment the losses (a bug here: a tie shows up as a loss)
                    playerRecord[1]++;
                }
// Update the cumulative spread
                playerRecord[2] += (s.playerScore - s.opponentScore);
            }

// Put the table in the request so the JSP can get at it
            request.setAttribute("recordTable", playerRecords);

            String destPage = "/ShowRecordsHTML.jsp";

            if (ScoreSupport.isWML(request))
            {
                destPage = "/ShowRecordsWML.jsp";
            }
```

```
            getServletContext().getRequestDispatcher(destPage).forward(
                request, response);
        }
        catch (Exception exc)
        {
            String errorPage = "/ErrorHTML.jsp";

            if (ScoreSupport.isWML(request))
            {
                errorPage = "/ErrorWML.jsp";
            }

            request.setAttribute("exception", exc);

            exc.printStackTrace();

            getServletContext().getRequestDispatcher(errorPage).forward(
                request, response);
        }
        finally
        {
            if (conn != null)
            {
                try
                {
                    pool.releaseConnection(conn);
                } catch (Exception ignore) {}
            }
        }
    }
}
```

Listing 26.13 shows the Java Server Page that shows the various player records. Each player is displayed on a separate card and each card contains a link to the `ShowScoresServlet` to show that player's scores.

Listing 26.13 Source Code for ShowRecordsWML.jsp

```
<%@ page language="java" contentType="text/vnd.wap.wml" %>
<%@ page import="java.net.*,java.util.*,usingjsp.scores.*" %>

<?xml version="1.0"?>
<!DOCTYPE wml PUBLIC "-//WAPFORUM//DTD WML 1.1//EN"
    "http://www.wapforum.org/DTD/wml_1.1.xml">

<wml>
<%
    Hashtable recordTable = (Hashtable) request.getAttribute(
        "recordTable");

    Enumeration keys = recordTable.keys();

    int playerNumber = 0;
```

LISTING 26.13 CONTINUED

```
    while (keys.hasMoreElements())
    {
        String playerName = (String) keys.nextElement();

        int[] playerRecord = (int[]) recordTable.get(playerName);

        playerNumber++;
%>
<card id="ply<%=playerNumber%>">
<p><%=playerName%><br/>
W: <%=playerRecord[0]%><br/>
L: <%=playerRecord[1]%><br/>
Cume: <%=playerRecord[2]%><br/>
<a href="ShowScoresServlet?player=<%=URLEncoder.encode(playerName)%>"
    title="Scores">Scores</a>
</p>
</card>
<%
    }
%>
</wml>
```

Figure 26.11 shows a card generated by ShowRecordsWML.jsp.

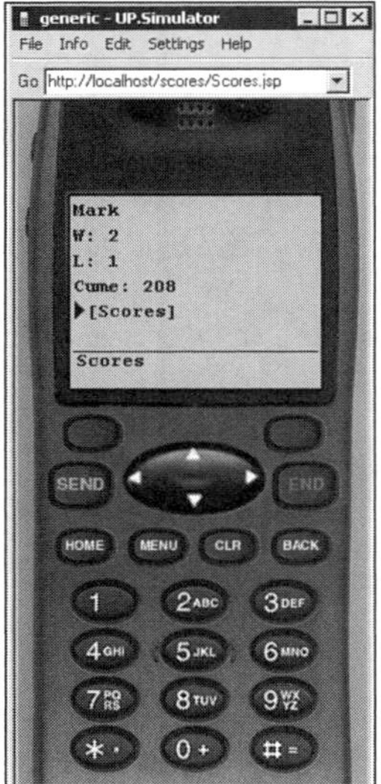

Figure 26.11
A card can link to a JSP or servlet to retrieve additional data.

Last, but not least, Listing 26.14 shows the main menu page for the WML version of the application.

Listing 26.14 Source Code for ScoreMenuWML.jsp

```
<%@ page language="java" contentType="text/vnd.wap.wml" %>

<?xml version="1.0"?>
<!DOCTYPE wml PUBLIC "-//WAPFORUM//DTD WML 1.1//EN"
    "http://www.wapforum.org/DTD/wml_1.1.xml">

<wml>
<card id="scoremenu">
<p>
<a href="ShowRecordsServlet" title="Show Records">Show Records</a><br/>
<a href="RegisterScoreWML.jsp" title="Enter Score">Enter Score</a>
</p>
</card>
</wml>
```

Figure 26.12 shows the main menu running in a simulator.

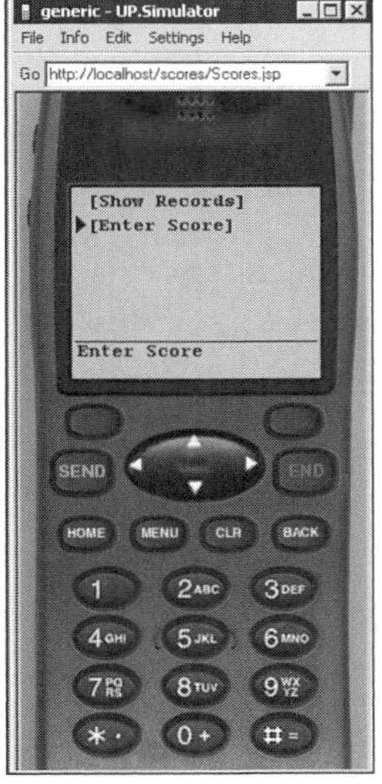

Figure 26.12 The main menu for the Scores application is shown.

Deploying the Scores Application

The Scores application strives to be a reasonably well-structured servlet/JSP application. It delegates display functions to Java Server Pages and performs nondisplay work in servlets. The final piece to make the application complete is a Web Archive (WAR) file that contains all the pieces of the application.

The WAR file contains all the JSPs at the root level, a WEB-INF directory containing the web.xml deployment descriptor, and a directory containing all the compiled Java classes. To create the WAR file, assuming you have all the JSP and Java files in your current directory, you would enter the following two commands:

```
javac -d WEB-INF\classes *.java
jar cvf scores.war *.jsp WEB-INF
```

You should also make sure that the web.xml file is in the WEB-INF directory before you create the WAR file.

Listing 26.15 shows the web.xml file for the Scores application.

Listing 26.15 Source Code for `web.xml`

```
<web-app>
    <display-name>Scores Application</display-name>
    <description>An application for entering and displaying scores</description>
    <servlet>
        <servlet-name>RegisterScoreServlet</servlet-name>
        <servlet-class>usingjsp.scores.RegisterScoreServlet</servlet-class>
    </servlet>
    <servlet>
        <servlet-name>ShowScoresServlet</servlet-name>
        <servlet-class>usingjsp.scores.ShowScoresServlet</servlet-class>
    </servlet>
    <servlet>
        <servlet-name>ShowRecordsServlet</servlet-name>
        <servlet-class>usingjsp.scores.ShowRecordsServlet</servlet-class>
    </servlet>
    <servlet-mapping>
        <servlet-name>RegisterScoreServlet</servlet-name>
        <url-pattern>/RegisterScoreServlet</url-pattern>
    </servlet-mapping>
    <servlet-mapping>
        <servlet-name>ShowScoresServlet</servlet-name>
        <url-pattern>/ShowScoresServlet</url-pattern>
    </servlet-mapping>
    <servlet-mapping>
        <servlet-name>ShowRecordsServlet</servlet-name>
        <url-pattern>/ShowRecordsServlet</url-pattern>
    </servlet-mapping>
    <welcome-file-list>
        <welcome-file>Scores.jsp</welcome-file>
    </welcome-file-list>
</web-app>
```

After the WAR file is created, you can deploy it in your Web server using whatever management tools the Web server provides.

Troubleshooting

Running with the Simulator

Why does the simulator report an error when reading my WML files?

There are four major possibilities for this. First, your JSP or servlet may be reporting an error. You can test this by pointing your browser to the same URL you are trying to access from the phone simulator. If the browser doesn't report an error, you're probably okay there. The next possibility is that you forgot to set the content type to "text/vnd.wap.wml". The third possibility is that your WML contains an error. The phone.com simulator has a separate window that shows any error messages that occur as a result of parsing the WML output. Likewise, the Nokia simulator shows you any parsing errors in a source code window. The last possibility is that the WML file is too large. Some phones and simulators may only accept about 1,500 bytes of data.

RUNNING WITH A REAL PHONE

Why does my phone report an error when the simulator had no problem?

Unfortunately, the simulators are not 100% accurate. They often handle errors that the phones do not. Also, the simulators usually support the most recent additions to the WML specification. Because the browser is embedded into the phone's firmware, it can't be changed easily and lags behind the standard.

CHAPTER 27

Creating On-the-Fly Graphics

In this chapter

IMAGES AREN'T JUST STATIC FILES

By now you know that you can generate all kinds of output from servlets and Java Server Pages. So far, the one common denominator in the various forms of output has been the fact that they are all readable text. You might be surprised to discover, however, that you can send images from a servlet! Sending an image from a servlet is not the same thing as sending an `<img>` tag back in an HTML response. Instead, you create an actual JPEG image from inside the servlet and send it back.

Image processing is not something you want to include in every Web application, however. It takes a lot of CPU time and memory. For an extremely busy Web site, you need a number of extremely powerful servers to keep up with the demand. Still, for many applications, server-side image generation is a huge plus. For example, you might need to generate custom maps or graphs. You might be writing a weather map that must interpret special map formats and render them as images. You might even be writing an online photo studio that allows you to customize digital photos using interesting digital effects.

SENDING IMAGES FROM A SERVLET

As long as you have access to the Java AWT on the server, you can generate images using the libraries that ship with Java2. The technique revolves around the `BufferedImage` class, which is an in-memory representation of an image. You create a `Graphics` object from the image and use the methods in the `Graphics` object to create the image. You can also manipulate the pixel values of the image directly, which is useful when you want to perform digital image processing.

The other key part of the technique is the `JPEGImageEncoder` class, which takes the in-memory image and writes it in JPEG format to an output stream. Although you might be able to find other image encoders, `JPEGImageEncoder` is currently the only one that ships with the Java2 JDK.

Listing 27.1 shows a unique twist on the familiar "Hello World" theme, writing the message to a JPEG image and returning it.

LISTING 27.1 SOURCE CODE FOR `ImageRenderServlet.java`

```
package usingjsp;

import java.awt.*;
import java.awt.image.*;import java.io.*;
import com.sun.image.codec.jpeg.*;
import javax.servlet.*;

public class ImageRenderServlet extends GenericServlet
{
    public void service(ServletRequest request, ServletResponse response)
        throws IOException
    {
// Create the in-memory image
        BufferedImage buffImage = new BufferedImage(
            500, 200, BufferedImage.TYPE_INT_RGB);
```

```
// Create a graphics object from the image
        Graphics2D graphics = (Graphics2D) buffImage.getGraphics();

// Draw "Hello World" on the image
        graphics.setFont(new Font("Times", Font.BOLD, 36));
        graphics.drawString("Hello World! ", 10, 160);

// Tell the browser this servlet is returning a JPEG image
        response.setContentType("image/jpeg");

// Create an encoder to convert the image into JPEG format, using
// the servlet's output stream as the stream for writing the image
        JPEGImageEncoder encoder = JPEGCodec.createJPEGEncoder(
            response.getOutputStream());

// Convert the image to JPeg
        encoder.encode(buffImage);

    }
}
```

Figure 27.1 shows the output from the servlet as displayed by Internet Explorer.

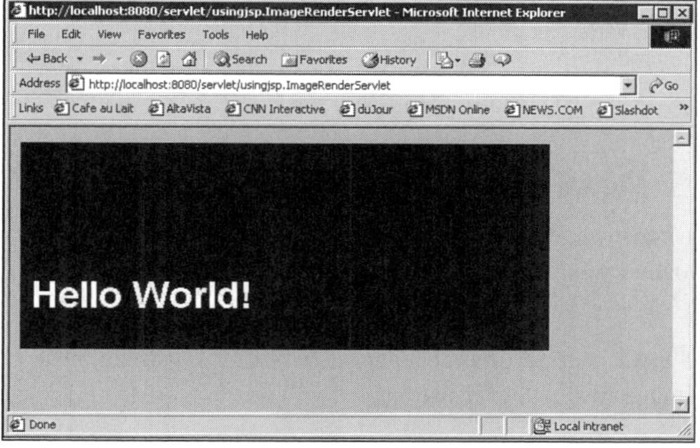

Figure 27.1
Using the AWT, you can generate images from a servlet.

Technically, you can also generate images from a Java Server Page. You just need to change the content type and reset the output stream before writing the image. Listing 27.2 shows the JSP version of `ImageRenderServlet` and, although it is technically possible for you to generate images from a JSP, it doesn't make much sense. You're really treating the JSP like a servlet instead of taking advantage of the template-nature of JSP. Why confuse things by making a JSP do things that are meant for pure servlets? Keep it simple.

LISTING 27.2 SOURCE CODE FOR `ImageRender.jsp`

```
<%@ page language="java" import="java.awt.*,java.awt.image.*"%><%@ page
    import="java.io.*,com.sun.image.codec.jpeg.*,javax.servlet.*"
    contentType="image/jpeg" %><%
```

LISTING 27.2 CONTINUED

```
// Reset the response in order to get a byte-oriented output stream
// Many JSP engines will have already gotten a character stream
// at this point
    response.reset();

// Create the in-memory image
    BufferedImage buffImage = new BufferedImage(
        500, 200, BufferedImage.TYPE_INT_RGB);

// Create a graphics object from the image
    Graphics2D graphics = (Graphics2D) buffImage.getGraphics();

// Draw "Hello World" on the image
    graphics.setFont(new Font("Times", Font.BOLD, 36));
    graphics.drawString("Hello World! ", 10, 160);

// Tell the browser this servlet is returning a JPEG image
    response.setContentType("image/jpeg");

// Create an encoder to convert the image into JPEG format, using
// the servlet's output stream as the stream for writing the image
    JPEGImageEncoder encoder = JPEGCodec.createJPEGEncoder(
        response.getOutputStream());

// Convert the image to JPEG
    encoder.encode(buffImage);
%>
```

UPLOADING IMAGES TO A SERVLET FROM JAVA

In addition to creating images from a servlet, you can accept uploaded images. The ability to accept uploaded images and also generate new images gives you the power to perform online image transformations.

Listing 27.3 shows a servlet that accepts a JPEG image using a basic HTTP post and decodes the image into a `BufferedImage`.

LISTING 27.3 SOURCE CODE FOR `ReceiveImageServlet.java`

```
package usingjsp;

import javax.servlet.*;
import javax.servlet.http.*;

import java.io.*;
import java.net.*;

import java.awt.image.*;
import com.sun.image.codec.jpeg.*;

/** Receives an image uploaded using a straight HTTP POST request */

public class ReceiveImageServlet extends HttpServlet
{
```

```
    public void doPost(HttpServletRequest request,
        HttpServletResponse response)
        throws java.io.IOException, ServletException
    {
        HttpSession session = request.getSession();

        BufferedImage currImage =
            (BufferedImage) session.getAttribute("image");
        if (currImage != null)
        {
            currImage.flush();
        }

// Get the input stream for reading the file
        InputStream in = request.getInputStream();

// Create a decoder for JPEG data streams
        JPEGImageDecoder decoder = JPEGCodec.createJPEGDecoder(in);

// Decode the JPEG
        BufferedImage image = decoder.decodeAsBufferedImage();

// Save the image so other servlets can access it
        session.setAttribute("image", image);

// Go to the image menu
        response.sendRedirect(
            "/jspbook/ch27/examples/ImageMenu.jsp?url="+
            URLEncoder.encode(
                "/servlet/usingjsp.ShowOriginalImageServlet"));
    }
}
```

Notice that the `ReceiveImageServlet` in Listing 27.3 stores the image in the session. This allows you to continue working on the image from page to page and send back different versions.

If you want to upload images to `ImageReceiverServlet`, you can use the `Uploader.java` program from Chapter 13, "Core Servlet Components."

UPLOADING IMAGES TO A SERVLET FROM A BROWSER

If you want your Web application to be available to most users, you can't count on them being able to run a Java client to upload images. Instead, you must use the browser's upload capability. Listing 27.4 shows a servlet that accepts an image sent using the browser's upload capability.

LISTING 27.4 SOURCE CODE FOR `ReceiveImageUpload.java`

```
package usingjsp;

import javax.servlet.*;
import javax.servlet.http.*;
import java.io.*;
import java.net.*;
```

Listing 27.4 Continued

```
import java.awt.image.*;
import com.sun.image.codec.jpeg.*;

public class ReceiveImageUpload extends HttpServlet
{
    public void doPost(HttpServletRequest request,
        HttpServletResponse response)
        throws IOException, ServletException
    {
        HttpSession session = request.getSession();

        BufferedImage currImage =
            (BufferedImage) session.getAttribute("image");
        if (currImage != null)
        {
            currImage.flush();
        }

// Get the content type
        String contentType = request.getContentType();

// Set a default for the boundary string length
// Find out where the boundary string starts
        int boundaryIndex = contentType.indexOf("boundary=");

// Get the boundary string
        String boundary = contentType.substring(boundaryIndex+9);
        int boundaryStrLength = boundary.length();

// Get the input stream to read the uploaded file
        ServletInputStream servIn = request.getInputStream();

        DataInputStream in = new DataInputStream(servIn);

// Lop off the headers from the content (read until you get a blank line)
        String line;

        while ((line = in.readLine()) != null)
        {
            if (line.trim().length() == 0) break;
        }

// Create a decoder for JPEG data streams
        JPEGImageDecoder decoder = JPEGCodec.createJPEGDecoder(in);

// Decode the JPEG
        BufferedImage image = decoder.decodeAsBufferedImage();

// Save the image so other servlets can access it
        session.setAttribute("image", image);


// Go to the image menu
        response.sendRedirect(
            "/jspbook/ch27/examples/ImageMenu.jsp?url="+
            URLEncoder.encode(
                "/servlet/usingjsp.ShowOriginalImageServlet"));
    }
}
```

As with the servlet in Listing 27.3, the `ReceiveImageUpload` servlet stores the image in the session. Listing 27.5 shows a Web page that allows you to upload an image to the `ReceiveImageUpload` servlet.

Listing 27.5 Source Code for `UploadImage.html`

```
<html>
<body bgcolor="#ffffff">
<h1>File Uploader</h1>
<form action="/servlet/usingjsp.ReceiveImageUpload" method="post"
    enctype="multipart/form-data">
Please select a JPEG to upload: <input type="file" name="jpegImage">
<p>
<input type="submit" value="Upload File!">
</form>
</body>
</html>
```

Performing Online Image Processing

Now that you can send and receive images, you can make a Web site for manipulating images. You just need to come up with some image processing techniques that might be interesting to a user.

The tricky part of this whole operation is that the servlet is returning only an image and not the surrounding HTML. You can't create an HTML page and supply the image inside it as a whole operation. Instead, you must display the HTML page and include a link to the image processing servlet as part of an `<img>` tag.

Listing 27.6 shows a Java Server Page that displays a processed image as well as a menu for performing various image-manipulation techniques. When you invoke the JSP, you pass it parameters that it should send to the image processing servlet. When the browser displays the HTML generated by the JSP, it sees the `<img>` tag and invokes the image processing servlet. In other words, the image processing isn't performed until after the JSP has executed and returned its HTML page to the browser.

Listing 27.6 Source Code for `ImageMenu.jsp`

```
<html>
<body bgcolor="#ffffff">
<table border="0">
<tr><th>Original Image</th><th>Modified Image</th></tr>
<tr>
<td>
<img src="/servlet/usingjsp.ShowOriginalImageServlet">
</td>
<td>
<%
    String imageSrc = request.getParameter("url");
    if (imageSrc == null)
```

LISTING 27.6 CONTINUED

```
    {
        imageSrc = "/servlet/usingjsp.ShowOriginalImageServlet";
    }
%>
<img src="<%=imageSrc%>?<%=request.getQueryString()%>">
</td>
</tr>
</table>
<p>What do you want to do?</p>
<bl>
<li><a href="UploadImage.html">Upload a New Image</a></li>
<li><a href="ImageCaption.html">Add a caption to an image</a></li>
<li><a href="LightingEffects.html">Add lighting effects</a></li>
<li><a href="ImageMenu.jsp?url=/servlet/usingjsp.EmbossImageServlet">
Emboss the image</a></li>
<li><a href="ImageMenu.jsp?url=/servlet/usingjsp.EdgeDetectServlet">
Perform edge detection</a></li>
</bl>
</body>
</html>
```

ADDING CAPTIONS TO IMAGES

The first image-processing technique is quite simple: applying a caption to an image. Because the image is stored in the session, you can add new image processing techniques just by adding new servlets that manipulate the image already stored in the servlet.

Listing 27.7 shows an HTML page that allows you to specify the caption and various aspects of the font before displaying the processed image. Notice that the form invokes the ImageMenu.jsp file from Listing 27.7. You use the same technique for all image effects.

LISTING 27.7 SOURCE CODE FOR `ImageCaption.html`

```
<html>
<body bgcolor="#ffffff">
<p>Please enter a caption:</p>
<form action="ImageMenu.jsp"
   method="get">
<input type="hidden" name="url" value="/servlet/usingjsp.ImageCaptionServlet">
<input type="text" name="caption">
<p>
<table border=0>
<tr><td>Font:</td>
<td>
<select name="font">
    <option value="timesroman">Times-Roman</option>
    <option value="courier">Courier</option>
    <option value="arial">Arial</option>
    <option value="helvetica">Helvetica</option>
</select>
</td></tr>
<tr><td>Font style:</td>
```

```
<td>
<select name="style">
    <option value="normal">Normal</option>
    <option value="bold">Bold</option>
    <option value="italic">Italic</option>
</select>
</td></tr>
<tr><td>Font size:</td>
<td>
<select name="size">
    <option value="8">8</option>
    <option value="10">10</option>
    <option value="12">12</option>
    <option value="14">14</option>
    <option value="16">16</option>
    <option value="18">18</option>
    <option value="20">20</option>
    <option value="24">24</option>
    <option value="36">36</option>
    <option value="48">48</option>
</select>
</td></tr>
<tr><td>Font color:</td>
<td>
<select name="color">
    <option value="0x000000">Black</option>
    <option value="0xffffff">White</option>
    <option value="0xff0000">Red</option>
    <option value="0x00ff00">Green</option>
    <option value="0x0000ff">Blue</option>
</select>
</td></tr>
<tr><td>Caption location:</td>
<td>
<select name="location">
    <option value="top">Top</option>
    <option value="bottom">Bottom</option>
</select>
</td></tr>
</table>
<input type="submit" value="Show Caption">
</form>
</body>
</html>
```


Listing 27.8 shows the `ImageCaptionServlet` program that adds a caption to an image.

LISTING 27.8 SOURCE CODE FOR `ImageCaptionServlet.java`

```
package usingjsp;

import java.awt.*;
import java.awt.image.*;
import java.awt.geom.*;import java.io.*;
import com.sun.image.codec.jpeg.*;
import javax.servlet.*;
import javax.servlet.http.*;
```

LISTING 27.8 CONTINUED

```
public class ImageCaptionServlet extends HttpServlet implements ImageObserver
{
    public void doGet(HttpServletRequest request,
        HttpServletResponse response)
        throws IOException
    {
// Make sure the browser calls this servlet every time
        response.setHeader("Cache-Control", "no-cache");
        response.setHeader("Pragma", "no-cache");
        response.setHeader("Expires", "0");

        HttpSession session = request.getSession();

// Get the in-memory image
        BufferedImage buffImage =
            (BufferedImage) session.getAttribute("image");

// If there's no image, create a blank one
        if (buffImage == null)
        {
            buffImage = new BufferedImage(100, 100,
                BufferedImage.TYPE_INT_RGB);
        }

// Create a new image to hold the original image plus the caption
        BufferedImage outputImage =
            new BufferedImage(buffImage.getWidth(),
                buffImage.getHeight(), BufferedImage.TYPE_INT_RGB);

// Get a graphics context for drawing to the new image
        Graphics2D g = (Graphics2D) outputImage.getGraphics();

// Copy the old image onto the new one
        g.drawImage(buffImage, 0, 0, this);

// Get the captioning parameters
        String caption = request.getParameter("caption");
        if (caption == null) caption = "<<caption>>";

        String location = request.getParameter("location");
        if (location == null) location = "bottom";

        String fontStr = request.getParameter("font");
        if (fontStr == null) fontStr = "times";

        int style = Font.PLAIN;
        String styleStr = request.getParameter("style");
        if (styleStr.equals("italic")) style = Font.ITALIC;
        if (styleStr.equals("bold")) style = Font.BOLD;

        int size = 8;
        String sizeStr = request.getParameter("size");

        if (sizeStr != null)
        {
            try
```

```
            {
                size = Integer.parseInt(sizeStr);
            }
            catch (Exception ignore) {}
        }

        int color = 0xffffff;
        String colorStr = request.getParameter("color");
        if (colorStr != null)
        {
            try
            {
                color = Integer.parseInt(colorStr);
            }
            catch (Exception ignore) {}
        }

        Color fontColor = new Color(color);
        Font font = new Font(fontStr, style, size);

// See how big the caption will be on the image
        Rectangle2D bounds = font.getStringBounds(
            caption, g.getFontRenderContext());

// The X value is computed to make the text appear centered
        int x = (int) ((outputImage.getWidth() - bounds.getWidth()) / 2);

// Put the text at the top by default
        int y = (int) (bounds.getHeight());

// .. but allow the user to put it at the bottom
        if (location.equals("bottom"))
        {
            y = outputImage.getHeight()-1;
        }

        g.setColor(fontColor);
        g.setFont(font);

// Draw the caption
        g.drawString(caption, x, y);

        response.setContentType("image/jpeg");

// Create an encoder to convert the image into JPEG format, using
// the servlet's output stream as the stream for writing the image
        JPEGImageEncoder encoder = JPEGCodec.createJPEGEncoder(
            response.getOutputStream());

// Convert the image to JPEG
        encoder.encode(outputImage);

    }
    public boolean imageUpdate(Image img, int infoFlags, int x, int y,
        int width, int height)
    {
        return false;
    }
}
```

Tip

Notice the three response headers (`Cache-Control`, `Pragma`, and `Expires`) at the beginning of `ImageCaptionServlet`. You can use these values to keep the browser from caching data from a servlet. This is especially important when you generate dynamic images.

Figure 27.2 shows a captioned image. To generate the caption, you invoke the upload page from Listing 27.5 and then the ImageCaption.html page from Listing 27.7. Better yet, use the ImageMenu.jsp page as the start page for all the operations in this chapter.

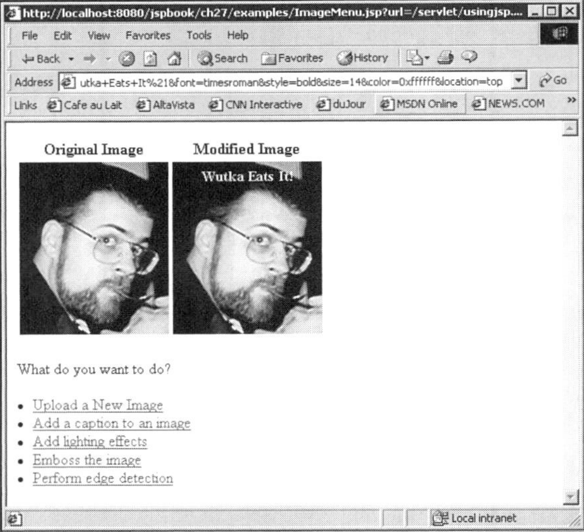

Figure 27.2
You can add captions to images on-the-fly.

EMBOSSING IMAGES

The image embossing technique makes an image look like it has been embossed into a sheet of metal, and takes on a 3D effect. The technique looks at pixels in relation to the pixels around them and computes an imaginary altitude based on the brightness of each pixel.

Interestingly, the emboss technique doesn't change the existing image, but starts from scratch with a solid gray image—almost as if it starts with a fresh sheet of metal for embossing. For each pixel in the image, it looks at the pixel colors to the upper left and lower right of the current pixel. The brighter of the two pixels has the higher "altitude." The current pixel is then lightened or darkened depending on the altitude difference between the upper-left and lower-right pixels.

Listing 27.9 shows the `EmbossImageServlet` that performs the image emboss.

Listing 27.9 Source Code for EmbossImageServlet.java

```
package usingjsp;

import java.awt.*;
import java.awt.image.*;
import java.io.*;
import com.sun.image.codec.jpeg.*;
import javax.servlet.*;
import javax.servlet.http.*;

public class EmbossImageServlet extends HttpServlet
{
    public void doGet(HttpServletRequest request,
        HttpServletResponse response)
        throws IOException
    {
// Make sure the browser calls this servlet every time
        response.setHeader("Cache-Control", "no-cache");
        response.setHeader("Pragma", "no-cache");
        response.setHeader("Expires", "0");

        HttpSession session = request.getSession();

// Get the in-memory image
        BufferedImage buffImage =
            (BufferedImage) session.getAttribute("image");

// If there's no image, create a blank one
        if (buffImage == null)
        {
            buffImage = new BufferedImage(100, 100,
                BufferedImage.TYPE_INT_RGB);
        }

// Create a blank image to hold the embossed image
        BufferedImage outputImage =
            new BufferedImage(buffImage.getWidth(),
                buffImage.getHeight(), BufferedImage.TYPE_INT_RGB);

// Perform the emboss
        embossImage(buffImage, outputImage);

// Create an encoder to convert the image into JPEG format, using
// the servlet's output stream as the stream for writing the image
        JPEGImageEncoder encoder = JPEGCodec.createJPEGEncoder(
            response.getOutputStream());

// Convert the image to JPEG
        encoder.encode(outputImage);

    }

// To emboss an image, you start with a completely gray destination image.
// For each pixel in the source image, look at the pixels to the upper-left and
// lower-right. Figure out the change in red, green, and blue between the
// upper-left and lower-right and look at the maximum change (either maximum
```

LISTING 27.9 CONTINUED

```
// positive or maximum negative) for any color component. For example,
// if the green changed by -5, blue changed by 10, and red changed by
// -100, the maximum change would be -100 (the red, which changed the most).
//
// Now, add the amount of change to 128 (the gray level) and create a
// pixel in the destination image with red, green, and blue values equal
// to the new gray level. Make sure you adjust the gray level so it can't
// be less than 0 or more than 255.
//
//
    public void embossImage(BufferedImage srcImage, BufferedImage destImage)
    {

        int width = srcImage.getWidth();
        int height = srcImage.getHeight();

// Loop through every pixel

        for (int i=0; i < height; i++) {
            for (int j=0; j < width; j++) {

// Assume that the upper left and lower right are 0
                int upperLeft = 0;
                int lowerRight = 0;

// If the pixel isn't on the upper or left edge, get the upper-left
// pixel (otherwise, the upper-left for edge pixels is the default of 0)

                if ((i > 0) && (j > 0)) {

// The & 0xffffff strips off the upper 8 bits, which is the transparency

                    upperLeft = srcImage.getRGB(j-1, i-1)
                        & 0xffffff;
                }

// If the pixel isn't on the bottom or right edge, get the lower-right
// pixel (otherwise, the lower-right for edge pixels is the default of 0)

                if ((i < height-1) && (j < width-1)) {

// The & 0xffffff strips off the upper 8 bits, which is the transparency
                    lowerRight = srcImage.getRGB(j+1, i+1)
                        & 0xffffff;
                }

// Get the differences between the red, green, and blue pixels

                int redDiff = ((lowerRight >> 16) & 255) -
                    ((upperLeft >> 16) & 255);
                int greenDiff = ((lowerRight >> 8) & 255) -
                    ((upperLeft >> 8) & 255);
                int blueDiff = (lowerRight & 255) -
                    (upperLeft & 255);
```

```
// Figure out which color had the greatest change

                int diff = redDiff;
                if (Math.abs(greenDiff) > Math.abs(diff))
                    diff=greenDiff;
                if (Math.abs(blueDiff) > Math.abs(diff))
                    diff=blueDiff;

// Add the greatest change to a medium gray
                int greyColor = 128 + diff;

// If the gray is too high or too low, make it fit in the 0-255 range
                if (greyColor > 255) greyColor = 255;
                if (greyColor < 0) greyColor = 0;

// Create the new color, and don't forget to add in a transparency
// of 0xff000000 making the image completely opaque

                int newColor = 0xff000000 + (greyColor << 16) +
                    (greyColor << 8) + greyColor;

                destImage.setRGB(j, i, newColor);
            }
        }
    }
}
```

Figure 27.3 shows the image before and after the emboss.

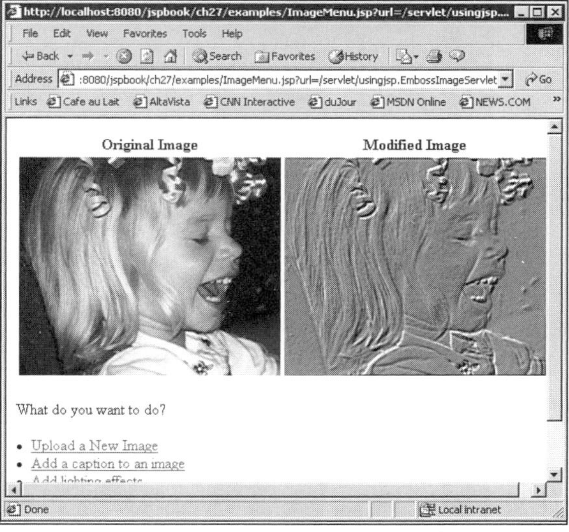

Figure 27.3
The digital emboss effect gives an image a 3D appearance.

EDGE DETECTION

The edge detection effect is similar mathematically to the emboss effect, but the result is quite different. The edge detect algorithm starts with a black image and again looks at the pixels to the upper left and lower right of the current pixel. This time, however, it just looks for places where the colors actually change. The end effect tends to highlight the edges of various objects in the picture.

Listing 27.10 shows the source code for the `EdgeDetectServlet` program.

LISTING 27.10 SOURCE CODE FOR `EdgeDetectServlet.java`

```
package usingjsp;

import java.awt.*;
import java.awt.image.*;
import java.io.*;
import com.sun.image.codec.jpeg.*;
import javax.servlet.*;
import javax.servlet.http.*;

public class EdgeDetectServlet extends HttpServlet
{
    public void doGet(HttpServletRequest request,
        HttpServletResponse response)
        throws IOException
    {
// Make sure the browser asks for this file every time
        response.setHeader("Cache-Control", "no-cache");
        response.setHeader("Pragma", "no-cache");
        response.setHeader("Expires", "0");

        HttpSession session = request.getSession();

// Get the in-memory image
        BufferedImage buffImage =
            (BufferedImage) session.getAttribute("image");

// If there's no image, create a blank one
        if (buffImage == null)
        {
            buffImage = new BufferedImage(100, 100,
                BufferedImage.TYPE_INT_RGB);
        }

// Create an image to hold the edge-detected image
        BufferedImage outputImage =
            new BufferedImage(buffImage.getWidth(),
                buffImage.getHeight(), BufferedImage.TYPE_INT_RGB);

// Create a matrix for performing an edge-detection
               float matrix[] = { -5, 0, 0, 0, 0, 0, 0, 0, 5 };

               Kernel kernel = new Kernel(3, 3, matrix);

               ConvolveOp op = new ConvolveOp(kernel,
```

```
                    ConvolveOp.EDGE_ZERO_FILL, null);

// Perform the edge-detect
            op.filter(buffImage, outputImage);

// Create an encoder to convert the image into JPEG format, using
// the servlet's output stream as the stream for writing the image
        JPEGImageEncoder encoder = JPEGCodec.createJPEGEncoder(
            response.getOutputStream());

// Convert the image to JPEG
        encoder.encode(outputImage);

    }
}
```

Figure 27.4 shows a picture before and after the edge-detection effect.

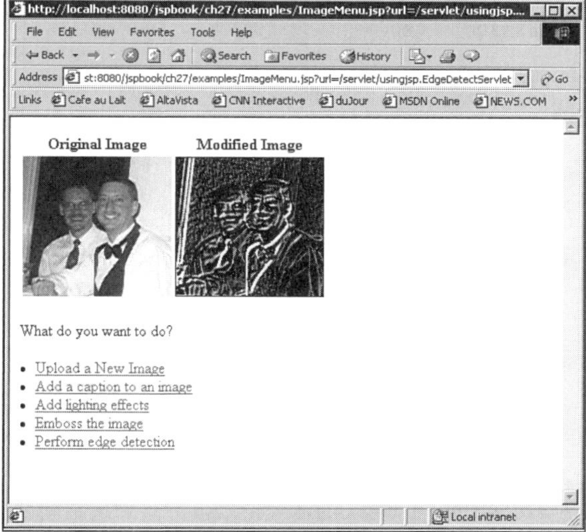

Figure 27.4 The edge-detect effect highlights the edges of objects.

Lighting Effects

The final interesting effect is a simple lighting effect. You can make portions of an image brighter or dimmer depending on the distance from an imaginary lighting point, making it look like there is a light shining on the image. The servlet shown in Listing 27.11 takes an X,Y coordinate and a radius and shines an imaginary spotlight on the image, centered around the X,Y coordinate.

Listing 27.11 Source Code for `LightingEffectsServlet.java`

```
package usingjsp;

import java.awt.*;
```

LISTING 27.11 CONTINUED

```
import java.awt.image.*;
import java.awt.geom.*;
import java.io.*;
import com.sun.image.codec.jpeg.*;
import javax.servlet.*;
import javax.servlet.http.*;

public class LightingEffectsServlet extends HttpServlet
{
    public void doGet(HttpServletRequest request,
        HttpServletResponse response)
        throws IOException
    {
// Make sure the browser calls this servlet every time
        response.setHeader("Cache-Control", "no-cache");
        response.setHeader("Pragma", "no-cache");
        response.setHeader("Expires", "0");

        HttpSession session = request.getSession();

// Get the in-memory image
        BufferedImage buffImage =
            (BufferedImage) session.getAttribute("image");

// If there's no image, create a blank one
        if (buffImage == null)
        {
            buffImage = new BufferedImage(100, 100,
                BufferedImage.TYPE_INT_RGB);
        }

// Get the lighting parameters
        int centerX = Integer.parseInt(request.getParameter("centerX"));
        int centerY = Integer.parseInt(request.getParameter("centerY"));
        int radius = Integer.parseInt(request.getParameter("radius"));
        double intensity = Double.parseDouble(
            request.getParameter("intensity"));
        double fade = Double.parseDouble(
            request.getParameter("fade"));

// Can't have an intensity less than 0, an intensity of 0 is total darkness
// "How much blacker could it be? The answer is 'none more black'." -N.Tufnel
        if (intensity < 0.0) intensity = 0.0;

        int width = buffImage.getWidth();
        int height = buffImage.getHeight();

// Create a blank image to hold the new filtered image
        BufferedImage outputImage = new BufferedImage(
            width, height, BufferedImage.TYPE_INT_RGB);

// Loop through all the pixels in the image
        for (int x=0; x < width; x++)
        {
            for (int y=0; y < height; y++)
```

```
            {
// Get the current pixel value, compute its lighting value
                int rgb = buffImage.getRGB(x, y);
                rgb = filterRGB(x, y, rgb, centerX, centerY, radius,
                    intensity, fade);

// .. then copy it to the new image
                outputImage.setRGB(x, y, rgb);
            }
        }

        response.setContentType("image/jpeg");

// Create an encoder to convert the image into JPEG format, using
// the servlet's output stream as the stream for writing the image
        JPEGImageEncoder encoder = JPEGCodec.createJPEGEncoder(
            response.getOutputStream());

// Convert the image to JPEG
        encoder.encode(outputImage);

    }

    public int filterRGB(int x, int y, int rgb, int centerX,
        int centerY, int radius, double intensity, double fade)
    {
// Save the pixel's transparency value
        int trans = rgb & 0xff000000;

// Compute the distance from the edge of the circle (distance from center
// - radius).
        double dist = Math.sqrt((x-centerX)*(x-centerX) +
            (y-centerY)*(y-centerY)) - radius;
        if (dist < 0.0) dist = 0.0;

// Compute the intensity based on distance and fade
        double intense = intensity - dist * fade;

// Again, none more black than 0.0
        if (intense < 0.0) intense = 0.0;

// Adjust the colors based on the new intensity
        int red = (int)(((rgb >> 16) & 0xff) * intense);
// Max color value for each component is 255
        if (red > 255) red = 255;

        int green = (int)(((rgb >> 8) & 0xff) * intense);
        if (green > 255) green = 255;

        int blue = (int)((rgb & 0xff) * intense);
        if (blue > 255) blue = 255;

// Return the new color
        return trans + (red << 16) + (green << 8) + blue;
    }
}
```

Figure 27.5 shows an image with a lighting effect applied.

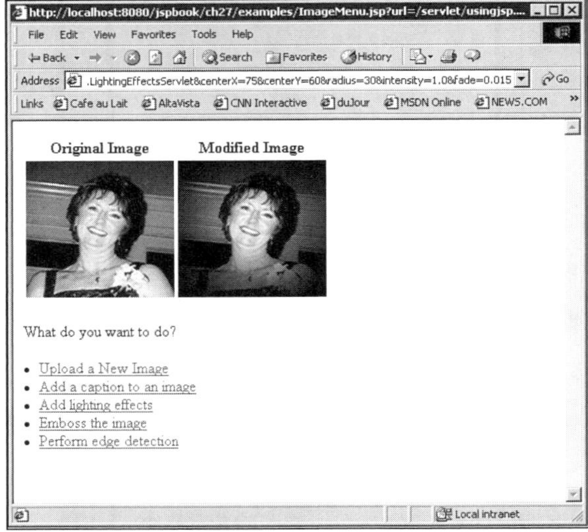

Figure 27.5
Lighting effects let you focus on specific parts of an image.

Using these and various other image manipulation techniques, you can create interesting, dynamic images from a servlet.

TROUBLESHOOTING

REFRESH PROBLEMS

Why doesn't the image change when I refresh the page?

The browser is probably caching the image. Make sure you set the `Cache-Control`, `Pragma`, and `Expires` header values to insure that the browser doesn't cache the image.

PERFORMANCE PROBLEMS

Why does the image processing run so slowly?

Because the graphics libraries are geared toward drawing to the screen, you might find that on some systems the libraries perform poorly when you are doing in-memory operations. You might be able to find a memory-only graphics library for Java, or you might consider running a different Java Virtual Machine or using a different hardware platform where the JVM has better graphics support.

Why does the server report resource shortages after I process a lot of images?

Although most Java Virtual Machines should have no problem with memory-only images, some might still allocate operating system resources that might be in limited supply. Make sure you call the `flush` method on your images when you're done with them. The `flush` method releases any resources that the image might be holding on to.

PART V

Advanced Techniques

CHAPTER 28

Packaging a JSP Application

In this chapter

You might have noticed that servlets and Java Server Pages don't mix well when it comes to naming. So far, most of the servlets you have used are accessed using the `/servlet/` prefix. The problem with that is, when the servlet needs to invoke a JSP, it must include the full pathname of the JSP. Although that might be fine for testing, in a real-world application, you shouldn't have to rewrite a JSP or a servlet just because you want to move your application to a different directory.

The servlet API defines a way for you to package together your JSPs, Java classes, and servlets into a single bundle that you can deploy on a Web server. This bundle is called a *Web Archive*, or *WAR file*.

A SIMPLE WAR FILE EXAMPLE

When you create a WAR file, you must include a web.xml file that describes the application. Usually, you will at least need descriptions of the various servlets in your application. Listing 28.1 shows a crude servlet that calls a Java Server Page.

LISTING 28.1 SOURCE CODE FOR `ExampleWARServlet.java`

```
package usingjsp.warexample;

import javax.servlet.*;
import javax.servlet.http.*;

import java.io.*;

public class ExampleWARServlet extends HttpServlet
{
    public void service(HttpServletRequest request,
        HttpServletResponse response)
        throws ServletException, IOException
    {
// Just call the JSP
        RequestDispatcher dispatcher =
            getServletContext().getRequestDispatcher(
                "/ExampleWARJSP.jsp");

        dispatcher.forward(request, response);
    }
}
```

Without a WAR file, you would need to put the ExampleWARJSP.jsp file in your Web server's root directory. Listing 28.2 shows ExampleWARJSP.jsp.

LISTING 28.2 SOURCE CODE FOR `ExampleWARJSP.jsp`

```
<html>
<body>

<h1>Hello From the WAR!</h1>
```

```
<p>
This page was invoked by ExampleWARServlet!
</body>
</html>
```

The web.xml file for the example application assigns a name to the example servlet and sets up a URL mapping. The mapping is relative to the base path of the installed application. In other words, if the mapping says that the servlet's name is `/ExampleWARServlet` and the base path is /example, the full path for the example servlet would be /example/ExampleWARServlet.

Listing 28.3 shows the web.xml file.

Listing 28.3 Source Code for `web.xml`

```
<!DOCTYPE web-app PUBLIC
    "-//Sun Microsystems, Inc.//DTD Web Application2.2//EN"
    "http://java.sun.com/j2ee/dtds/web-app_2_2.dtd">
<web-app>
    <display-name>WARExample</display-name>
    <description>
        A skeletal application to demonstrate WAR files
    </description>
    <servlet>
        <servlet-name>ExampleWARServlet</servlet-name>
        <servlet-class>usingjsp.warexample.ExampleWARServlet</servlet-class>
    </servlet>
    <servlet-mapping>
        <servlet-name>ExampleWARServlet</servlet-name>
        <url-pattern>/ExampleWARServlet</url-pattern>
    </servlet-mapping>
</web-app>
```

You will soon learn what each of the elements in the web.xml file mean. Most of them are probably obvious because their names are descriptive.

When you create the WAR file, the web.xml file must be in a directory named WEB-INF, and any Java classes you need, like the servlet, must be in a classes directory under WEB-INF. If you have ExampleWARJSP.jsp, ExampleWARServlet.java, and web.xml in the same directory, you can use the following Windows commands to create example.war:

```
mkdir WEB-INF
copy web.xml WEB-INF
mkdir WEB-INF\classes
javac -d WEB-INF\classes ExampleWARServlet.java
jar cvf example.war *.jsp WEB-INF
```

If you are running UNIX or Linux, the procedure is almost identical:

```
mkdir WEB-INF
cp web.xml WEB-INF
mkdir WEB-INF/classes
javac -d WEB-INF/classes ExampleWARServlet.java
jar cvf example.war *.jsp WEB-INF
```

INSTALLING A WAR FILE UNDER TOMCAT

As this book is being written, the Tomcat Web server from Apache does not have an automatic WAR installation utility. To install your WAR file in Tomcat, you just copy it to the webapps directory underneath the main Tomcat directory.

Tomcat automatically assigns a base path for the application based on the name of the WAR file. Because the example here is named example.war, Tomcat assigns the application a prefix of `/example`. Figure 28.1 shows the results of the application running under Tomcat.

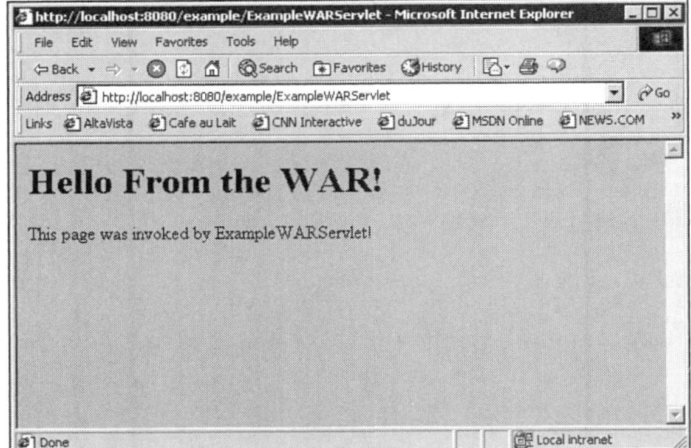

Figure 28.1
Tomcat automatically assigns the application name based on the WAR filename.

INSTALLING A WAR FILE UNDER JRUN

JRun has a nice WAR file installation utility. From the JRun management console, select the server on which you want to deploy the WAR file. The server screen on the right has a hyperlink for WAR deployment. After you click the WAR deployment link, you see a screen like the one in Figure 28.2.

The first field in the screen is the name of the directory or the WAR file of the application you are installing. Had you not created the WAR file, you could enter the name of the directory where you created the WAR file. It's much better to create the file, however, because you can then move it from one server to another easily.

Next, you select the server where the application will run. After that, you give the application a name. This name is the name that will appear in the JRun Management Console underneath the Web Applications heading.

The Application Host list box lets you limit the hosts that this application is available on. You only care about this box if you are running a multi-homed server in which several host names are mapped to one server.

The application URL is the base path of the application. If you enter /example in this box, the application will have the same base path as it did under Tomcat.

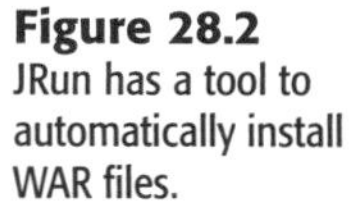

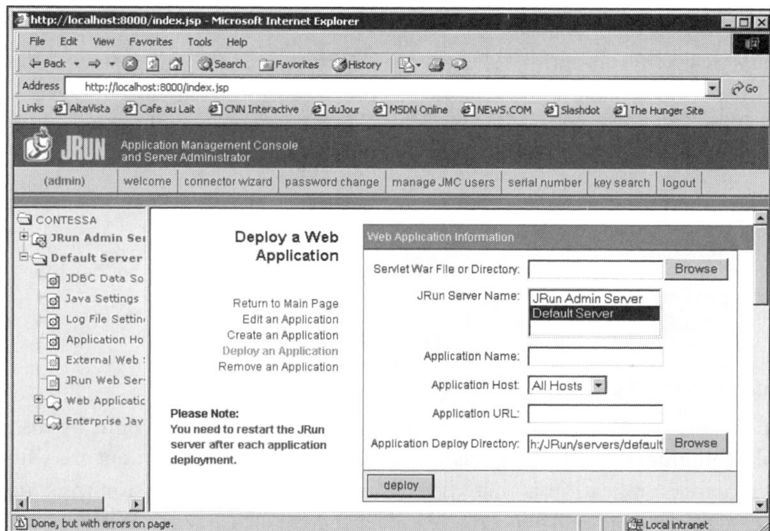

Figure 28.2
JRun has a tool to automatically install WAR files.

Finally, the application deploy directory is a directory where JRun will unpack the WAR file so it can work with the files. Typically, you use the root directory for the server plus the application pathname. For example, if your JRun is installed in c:\JRun, you are adding the application to the default server, and the base path for your application is /example, the deploy directory should be c:\JRun\servers\default\example.

WAR Configuration Options

There are a number of different elements that might appear in the web.xml file. Although most of them are discussed here, some of them are discussed in Chapter 29, "Extending JSP with New Tags," and some in Chapter 31, "Security."

General Application Options

The general application options deal with the parts of the application that are above a servlet. For example, the description of the application, the initial startup file, and the various error pages to use.

`display-name`

The `display-name` option is a short description of the application. It is intended to be the kind of name you would expect to see in a GUI tool. It is similar to the Application Name option in the JRun WAR deployment screen.

Example:

```
<display-name>ExampleWAR</display-name>
```

description

The `description` option is the long description of the application. When this option is a direct child of `<web-app>` it describes the application; otherwise, it describes the item it is a child of. That is, other things can have a description, so when you see a `<description>` tag, don't assume that it's a description of the application.

Example:

```
<description>
This application demonstrates how you use a WAR file to deploy
an application in different Web servers.
</description
```

distributable

The `distributable` option indicates that this application might be distributed across multiple containers (servlet engines). One of the things you must ensure when you create a distributable application is that all the items you place in a session must implement the `java.io.Serializable` interface, indicating that they can be serialized. The container might need to copy objects from one session object to another if a browser session accesses a different server.

Example:

```
<distributable/>
```

context-param

The `context-param` option lets you set initialization parameters that are accessible through the `ServletContext` class. Use the `<param-name>` and `<param-value>` tags to set the parts of the context parameter. You can also include an optional description tag.

Example:

```
<context-param>
    <param-name>initParam1</param-name>
    <param-value>Foo!</param-value>
    <description>A simple init parameter</description>
</context-param>
```

mime-mapping

You might find it odd that you can set mime mappings for files in a WAR file, because most of the time you set content types in a servlet or a JSP. If you forward to a non-servlet, non-JSP resource, however, the content type for the response will be the mime type of the resource you are returning. The `mime-mapping` option allows you to control those content types.

Example:

```
<mime-mapping>
    <extension>wml</extension>
```

```
    <mime-type>text/vnd.wap.wml>
</mime-mapping>
```

welcome-file-list

When you access a Web site , you rarely enter a filename. For instance, you might enter `http://www.slashdot.org` without entering a filename such as index.html or default.html. The `welcome-file-list` option lets you specify the possible names for the default application file. In other words, if the application is named example and you go to `http://localhost/example`, the welcome file list indicates the possible files that you might run. If the list includes index.html, index.htm, and default.jsp, and if the only file in the application is default.jsp, that's what you'll see.

Example:

```
<welcome-file-list>
    <welcome-file>index.html</welcome-file>
    <welcome-file>index.htm</welcome-file>
    <welcome-file>default.jsp</welcome-file>
</welcome-file-list>
```

error-page

The `error-page` option allows you to specify the pages that handle various errors that might occur. You can map HTTP errors to specific error pages and also map Java exceptions to specific error pages. To map a HTTP error, use the `<error-code>` tag and specify the error number, such as 404. To map a Java exception, make sure you use the fully qualified classname of the exception, such as `java.lang.NullPointerException`.

Example:

```
<error-page>
    <error-code>404</error-code>
    <location>Handle404Error.jsp</location>
</error-page>
<error-page>
    <exception-type>java.lang.NullPointerException
        </exception-type>
    <location>HandleNullPointerServlet</location>
</error-page>
```

session-config

The `session-config` option lets you change various settings related to sessions created by the application. Under the current servlet specification, the only option you can change is the session timeout, which is specified in minutes .

Servlet Options

Servlet options allow you to change the options at the servlet level. Although there are several servlet options, they are all specified within one of two tags, either `<servlet>` or `<servlet-mapping>` .

servlet

The servlet option is the main option for changing the attributes of a servlet. You can specify a servlet's name, class, description, initialization parameters, and startup information.

The <servlet-name> tag lets you specify the name of the servlet. This name can be used in the <servlet-mapping> tag to create a URL mapping for the servlet. The servlet name alone is not enough to specify the name you use to access the servlet.

The <servlet-class> tag specifies the fully qualified pathname for the servlet. Instead of a servlet class, you might specify the name of a JSP file for this servlet by using the <jsp-file> tag.

Only the <servlet-name> and either <servlet-class> or <jsp-file> tags are required for the <servlet> tag; all others are optional.

The <display-name> tag specifies the short name of the servlet and might be used in a GUI tool. Likewise, the <description> tag specifies the long description of the servlet.

The <init-param> tag allows you to specify any number of initialization parameters for the servlet, which are passed in to the servlet via the ServletConfig class. The <init-param> tag must contain a single <param-name> and a single <param-value> tag and might optionally contain a <description> tag.

The <load-on-startup> tag indicates that you want the servlet to be loaded when the Web server first starts up. The data value associated with the tag is a priority number that allows you to specify an order for servlet startup. The lowest numbers are started first.

Example:

```
<servlet>
    <servlet-name>MyServlet</servlet-name>
    <servlet-class>com.wutka.MyServlet</servlet-class>
    <display-name>MyVeryOwnServlet</display-name>
    <description>It's mine, all mine!</description>
    <init-param>
        <param-name>owner</param-name>
        <param-value>me</param-value>
    </init-param>
    <init-param>
        <param-name>belongsTo</param-name>
        <param-value>me</param-value>
    </init-param>
    <load-on-startup>1</load-on-startup>
</servlet> .
```

servlet-mapping

The servlet-mapping option lets you map URLs to servlets. At a minimum, you can use the servlet's name as the URL pattern, like this:

```
<servlet-mapping>
    <servlet-name>MyServlet</servlet-name>
    <url-pattern>MyServlet</url-pattern>
</servlet-mapping>
```

You can also map a servlet so it handles any path that starts with a certain pattern. For example, when a path starts with /servlet, the Web server runs a special invoker servlet that extracts the servlet name from the rest of the path and executes it. The `<servlet-mapping>` definition for the invoker looks like this:

```
<servlet-mapping>
    <url-pattern>/servlet/*</url-pattern>
    <servlet-name>invoker</servlet-name>
</servlet-mapping>
```

You can also use servlet mapping to handle various file extensions. For example, the Resin server has a special servlet that handles requests for Java Server Pages. The server maps any URL ending with `.jsp` to this servlet using the following servlet mapping:

```
<servlet-mapping>
    <url-pattern>*.jsp</url-pattern>
    <servlet-name>com.caucho.jsp.JspServlet</servlet-name>
</servlet-mapping>
```

OTHERS

There are other config options dealing with security and custom tag libraries. You will learn more about these options in the next few chapters.

TROUBLESHOOTING

INSTALLATION PROBLEMS

Why doesn't the Resin Servlet Engine use my WAR file?

As of July 2000, Resin does not unpack WAR files automatically. You must unpack the file in Resin's doc directory and when you restart the server, it will see the application.

Why isn't Tomcat unpacking my WAR file?

If you have already installed a WAR file, Tomcat may not unpack it again, even if you have changed the WAR file. When you install a new WAR file, make sure you delete the directory where Tomcat unpacked the previous version. Then you can be sure Tomcat will unpack the WAR file when it restarts.

I reinstalled my WAR file in Jrun; why hasn't anything changed?

You still need to restart the server. All the old class files (servlets and JSPs) are still present in the Java Virtual Machine.

CHAPTER 29

EXTENDING JSP WITH NEW TAGS

In this chapter

Many times, you need a Web designer to design your Java Server Pages. The designer might be an expert with HTML, but might not know anything about Java. The `<jsp:useBean>`, `<jsp:setProperty>`, and `<jsp:getProperty>` tags allow you to make parts of your application accessible through tags, but you can't invoke bean methods without using either the `<%` or `<%=` tags. You can also provide some additional flexibility with the `<jsp:include>` and `<jsp:forward>` tags, but these tags are often overkill. You need a way to allow a Web designer to perform a specific operation without knowing any Java.

JSP Tag Extensions let you create new tags that a Web designer can insert directly into a Java Server Page. Through Tag Extensions, you can define tags that let you insert data into the output stream, include sections of a page only if certain conditions are met, and even modify the contents of the page itself before they are sent back to the browser.

A "HELLO WORLD" TAG

To create a custom JSP tag, you must first create a Java class that acts as a tag handler. Whenever your custom tag appears in a Java Server Page, the JSP engine invokes your tag handler. If your custom tag doesn't care about the body text between its opening and closing tags, you can use the simple `TagSupport` class, which implements the `Tag` interface. If you need to access and possibly change the body text within the opening and closing tags, you must subclass the `BodyTagSupport` class instead. The `BodyTagSupport` class implements the `BodyTag` interface, which allows you to access body text.

For example, suppose you define a custom tag named `<mytags:DoSomething>` and you use it this way:

```
<mytags:DoSomething>
   Here is some text
</mytags:DoSomething>
```

If your tag handler only implements the Tag interface, it can't see the body text (that is, "Here is some text"). All it can do is decide whether you can see the body text or not. Your custom tag can also generate its own output.

Listing 29.1 shows the `HelloWorldTagHandler` class that inserts the familiar "Hello World!" message into the JSP response. Because it doesn't need to access its body text, it subclasses `TagSupport`.

LISTING 29.1 SOURCE CODE FOR `HelloWorldTag.java`

```
import javax.servlet.jsp.tagext.*;
import javax.servlet.jsp.*;
import java.io.*;

public class HelloWorldTag extends TagSupport
{
    public int doStartTag()
        throws JspException
```

```
    {
        try
        {
            JspWriter out = pageContext.getOut();

            out.println("<h1>Hello World!</h1>");
        }
        catch (IOException ioExc)
        {
            throw new JspException(ioExc.toString());
        }

        return SKIP_BODY;
    }

public int doEndTag()
    {
        return EVAL_PAGE;
    }
}
```

Note

Don't worry about the `SKIP_BODY` and `EVAL_PAGE` return values just yet. You'll see what they mean shortly.

Listing 29.2 shows a JSP that calls `HelloWorldTag` via a tag named `<mytag:hello>`. At this point, you don't know how to relate `HelloWorldTag` to `<mytag:hello>`. You will see that in the next section.

LISTING 29.2 SOURCE CODE FOR TestHello.jsp

```
<%@ taglib uri="/hello" prefix="mytag" %>
<html>
<body>
<mytag:hello/>
</body>
</html>
```

Figure 29.1 shows the output from TestHello.jsp.

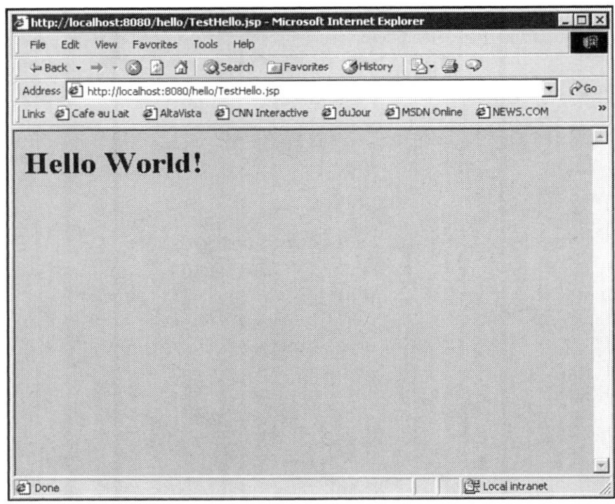

Figure 29.1
Custom tags can insert text into the response.

PACKAGING AND INSTALLING A TAG

When you create a custom tag library you must also create a Tag Library Descriptor (TLD) that describes each tag in your tag library. Listing 29.3 shows the TLD for the `HelloWorldTag` Java class.

LISTING 29.3 SOURCE CODE FOR `hello.tld`

```
<?xml version="1.0"?>
<!DOCTYPE taglib
    PUBLIC "-//Sun Microsystems, Inc.//DTD JSP Tag Library 1.1//EN"
    "http://java.sun.com/j2ee/dtds/web-jsptaglibrary_1_1.dtd">

<taglib>
    <tlibversion>1.0</tlibversion>
    <jspversion>1.1</jspversion>
    <shortname>hello</shortname>
    <uri></uri>
    <info>
        An example Hello World tag
    </info>

    <tag>
        <name>hello</name>
        <tagclass>HelloWorldTag</tagclass>
    </tag>
</taglib>
```

The first few lines of hello.tld are pretty standard for an XML file. You must start with the `<?xml?>` tag, of course. The next line defines the location of the Document Type Definition for this kind of document. The `<!DOCTYPE` tag should be the same for all your TLDs.

`<taglib>` is the root tag for a TLD and encloses all the other tags. Remember an XML document has a single root tag that encloses everything else in the document. The next few tags describe the tag library.

The `<tlibversion>` tag describes the version number of the tag library, and the `<jspversion>` tag indicates which version of JSP the tag library requires. The `<shortname>` tag gives a short name for the tag library that might be used within a JSP Page Authoring tool. The idea is that you would load various tag libraries and see a list of the available libraries. The short name is the name you would see in the list. The `<info>` tag gives the long description of the tag library. Finally, the `<uri>` tag gives the normal URI for this tag library. Again, the URI is handy for a page authoring tool where you might have a local copy of the library, but when you build a JSP that uses the tag library, you might want to put the normal URI into the library. In other words, the page authoring tool might see the tag library on the hard drive with a path like c:\taglibs\hello.tld. You don't want the JSP to refer to the tag library with a URI of file:///c/taglibs/hello.tlb, because the JSP might be deployed on a machine that doesn't have a c:\taglibs directory. You want a URI that works no matter where the JSP is deployed.

After the initial information describing the tag library, you can list the tags contained in the library. This tag library contains a single tag with a name of `hello` (as indicated by the `<name>` tag). The tag name, along with the prefix for the tag library, make up the full tag that you put in the JSP. In other words, you take the tag name `hello` and combine it with the prefix specified in the JSP (`mytag` in Listing 29.1) to get the full name of the tag, which is `<mytag:hello>`.

> **Note**
>
> The reason for splitting the naming into two parts is that several people might make a tag named `hello` in their tag libraries. You need a way to specify which tag you mean, so you must use a prefix to indicate which library you are referring to.

Finally, the `<tagclass>` tag indicates the fully qualified pathname of the class that implements this tag.

Now that you have created the TLD file, you must deploy the tag library and your test Web page as a Web application. Create a directory called WEB-INF and in the WEB-INF directory, create a file called web.xml that looks like the file in Listing 29.4.

Listing 29.4 Source Code for `web.xml`

```
<?xml version="1.0"?>
<!DOCTYPE web-app
    PUBLIC "-//Sun Microsystems, Inc.//DTD Web Application 2.2//EN"
    "http://java.sun.com/j2ee/dtds/web-app_2.2.dtd">

<web-app>
    <display-name>Tag Demo</display-name>
    <description>An application for testing custom tags</description>
    <taglib>
```

Listing 29.4 Continued

```
        <taglib-uri>/hello</taglib-uri>
        <taglib-location>/WEB-INF/tld/hello.tld</taglib-location>
    </taglib>
</web-app>
```

Most of the web.xml file should be familiar from the example in Chapter 28, "Packaging a JSP Application," where you packaged a Web application into a WAR file. There are a few tags that you haven't seen before, however. The `<taglib>` tag defines a tag library that the Web application uses. The `<taglib-uri>` tag defines the name that a JSP would use as the URI for this tag library. Look back at Listing 29.2 and you can see that TestHello.jsp specifies /hello as the URI for the tag library, which matches what you see in web.xml. The `<taglib-location>` tag specifies the location of the hello.tld file, which is the file from Listing 29.3. According to the web.xml file, hello.tld should be stored in a directory called tld that is below the WEB-INF directory.

Now, under the WEB-INF directory, create a classes directory and copy the HelloWorldTag.class file to the classes directory. Make sure that TestHello.jsp is in the same directory as the WEB-INF directory. Now, create a file called tagdemo.war by going to the directory where WEB-INF and TestHello.jsp are located and entering the following command:

```
jar cvf tagdemo.war WEB-INF TestHello.jsp
```

The `jar` command should respond with something like this:

```
added manifest
adding: WEB-INF/(in = 0) (out= 0)(stored 0%)
adding: WEB-INF/classes/(in = 0) (out= 0)(stored 0%)
adding: WEB-INF/classes/HelloWorldTag.class(in = 839) (out= 486)(deflated 42%)
adding: WEB-INF/tld/(in = 0) (out= 0)(stored 0%)
adding: WEB-INF/tld/hello.tld(in = 457) (out= 268)(deflated 41%)
adding: WEB-INF/web.xml(in = 441) (out= 262)(deflated 40%)
adding: TestHello.jsp(in = 87) (out= 68)(deflated 21%)
```

Now follow the procedure from Chapter 28 to install the WAR file in your Web server. After the file is installed, you should be able to access TestHello.jsp and see the output shown previously in Figure 29.1.

If you are having trouble installing your custom tag library, see "Install Problems" in the "Troubleshooting" section at the end of this chapter.

Conditional Includes Using Custom Tags

Earlier in Listing 29.1, you saw that the `doStartTag` method in the custom tag returns a value of `SKIP_BODY` and the `doEndTag` method returns a value of `EVAL_PAGE`. These values tell the JSP engine how to handle the content between the start and end of the custom tag, and also whether to continue evaluating the rest of the page after the custom closing tag. When `doStartTag` returns `SKIP_BODY`, it tells the JSP engine to ignore the content between the start and end of the custom tag. If the `doStartTag` returns `EVAL_BODY_INCLUDE`, the data between the start and end tags is copied to the response and any nested tags are evaluated.

When `doEndTag` returns `EVAL_PAGE`, it tells the JSP engine to continue evaluating the rest of the page. If `doEndTag` returns `SKIP_PAGE`, the JSP engine ignores everything else in the JSP after the closing tag and returns the response to the browser.

Because you can control whether the JSP engine includes body text between the start and end of a tag, you can create tags that include text only if certain conditions are met.

Listing 29.5 shows a custom tag that only includes its content when the time of day is between 6 a.m. and 6 p.m.

Listing 29.5 Source Code for DayTag.java

```
import javax.servlet.jsp.tagext.*;
import javax.servlet.jsp.*;
import java.util.*;

public class DayTag extends TagSupport
{
    public int doStartTag()
        throws JspException
    {
// Get the time of day
        GregorianCalendar currTime = new GregorianCalendar();

// Get the hour of day
        int hour = currTime.get(Calendar.HOUR_OF_DAY);

// If the time is between 6AM and 6PM, tell the JSP engine to
// include the text between the start and end tag
        if ((hour >= 6) && (hour <= 18))
        {
            return EVAL_BODY_INCLUDE;
        }
        else
        {
// Otherwise, ignore the body text
            return SKIP_BODY;
        }
    }

    public int doEndTag()
    {
        return EVAL_PAGE;
    }
}
```

You can easily make a `NightTag` class that does the same test except that it only includes the body content when the hour is less than 6 or greater than 18. Listing 29.6 shows the daynight.tld file describing the `DayTag` class and its companion `NightTag` class.

LISTING 29.6 SOURCE CODE FOR `daynight.tld`

```
<?xml version="1.0"?>
<!DOCTYPE taglib
    PUBLIC "-//Sun Microsystems, Inc.//DTD JSP Tag Library 1.1//EN"
    "http://java.sun.com/j2ee/dtds/web-jsptaglibrary_1_1.dtd">

<taglib>
    <tlibversion>1.0</tlibversion>
    <jspversion>1.1</jspversion>
    <shortname>daynight</shortname>
    <uri></uri>
    <info>
        day tag to include text between 6am and 6pm, night to include
        text otherwise
    </info>

    <tag>
        <name>day</name>
        <tagclass>DayTag</tagclass>
    </tag>

    <tag>
        <name>night</name>
        <tagclass>NightTag</tagclass>
    </tag>
</taglib>
```

The daynight.tld file should seem pretty familiar now. It doesn't contain any tags that you haven't already seen from the hello.tld file; it just defines two tags instead of one. Listing 29.7 shows a JSP that tests the day and night tags to make sure they work.

LISTING 29.7 SOURCE CODE FOR `TestDayNight.jsp`

```
<%@ taglib uri="/daynight" prefix="dn" %>
<html>
<body>

<dn:day>
<h1>My, what a beautiful day it is!</h1>
</dn:day>

<dn:night>
<h1>I hate night, it's too dark for golf!</h1>
</dn:night>

</body>
</html>
```

Figure 29.2 shows the output from TestDayNight.jsp when run during the day.

Figure 29.3 shows the output from TestDayNight.jsp when run at night. Notice that the text between the `<dn:day>` and `</dn:day>` doesn't show up.

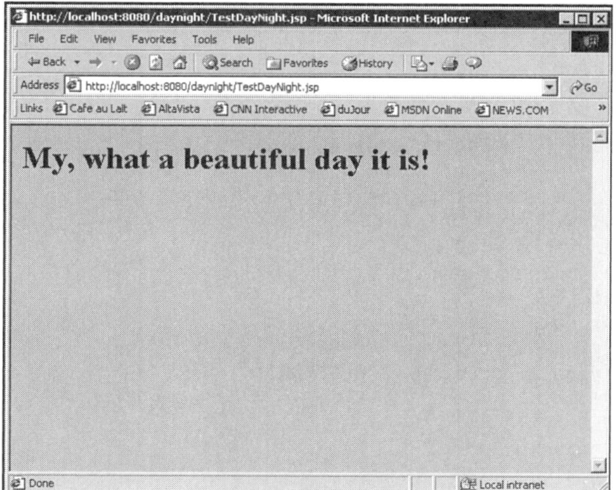

Figure 29.2
A custom tag can choose whether to include its body content.

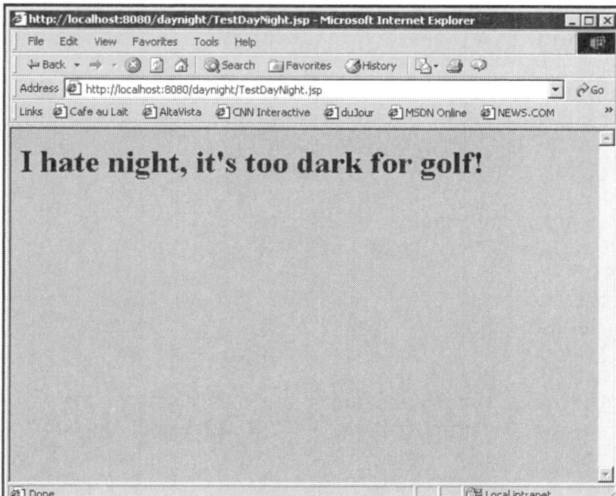

Figure 29.3
The `<xx:night>` tag only shows up at night.

Accessing Tag Attributes

Just like regular tags, custom tags can have attribute values. You need to provide `get` and `set` methods for each attribute. Although you enclose each attribute in quotes, you can have numeric attributes in your custom tag. The JSP engine performs the conversion automatically. Listing 29.8 shows a custom tag to display a checkerboard. The board has several options that can be changed by various attributes in the `<xx:checkerboard>` tag.

LISTING 29.8 SOURCE CODE FOR CheckerboardTag.java

```
import javax.servlet.jsp.tagext.*;
import javax.servlet.jsp.*;
import java.io.*;
public class CheckerboardTag extends TagSupport
{
// Variables to hold the attributes for the checkerboard

    protected int width = 40;
    protected int height = 40;
    protected int rows = 8;
    protected int cols = 8;
    protected String darkColor = "#000040";
    protected String lightColor = "#FFFFC0";

    public int doStartTag()
        throws JspException
    {
        try
        {
            JspWriter out = pageContext.getOut();

            out.println("<table>");

// Count down so the bottom row is row 0 (it helps for
// calculating the colors, the bottom left should be dark)

            for (int i=rows-1; i >= 0; i—)
            {
// Start a new row with the specified height
                out.print("<tr height=\""+height+"\">");

// Loop through the columns
                for (int j=0; j < cols; j++)
                {

// Start making the cell for this square
                    out.print("<td width=\""+width+"\" bgcolor=\"");

// If row+column is even, make the square dark. The lower-left
// corner should always be dark

                    if ((i + j) % 2 == 0)
                    {
                        out.print(darkColor);
                    }
                    else
                    {
                        out.print(lightColor);
                    }
                    out.print("\"> </td>");
                }
                out.println("</tr>");
            }
            out.println("</table>");
        }
        catch (IOException ioExc)
```

```
        {
            throw new JspException(ioExc.toString());
        }

        return SKIP_BODY;
    }

    public int doEndTag()
    {
        return EVAL_PAGE;
    }

// Get/set methods, just like in a bean

    public int getHeight() { return height; }
    public void setHeight(int aHeight) { height = aHeight; }

    public int getWidth() { return width; }
    public void setWidth(int aWidth) { width = aWidth; }

    public int getRows() { return rows; }
    public void setRows(int aRows) { rows = aRows; }

    public int getCols() { return cols; }
    public void setCols(int aCols) { cols = aCols; }

    public String getDarkColor() { return darkColor; }
    public void setDarkColor(String aDarkColor)
    {
        darkColor = aDarkColor;
    }

    public String getLightColor() { return lightColor; }
    public void setLightColor(String aLightColor)
    {
        lightColor = aLightColor;
    }
}
```

Now, just putting the attributes in the tag is not enough. You must also configure the attributes in the TLD file. Each attribute is defined using an `<attribute>` tag. Within the `<attribute>` tag there is a `<name>` tag defining the name of the attribute, a `<required>` tag indicating whether the attribute is required, and a tag called `<rtexprvalue>`. You might have noticed other JSP examples where the value of a tag attribute was specified using a JSP expression (the `<%=` tag). Evaluating custom tags where the attribute value can be generated at runtime is a difficult task for the JSP engine. Rather than allow all attribute expressions to be computed at runtime, the JSP engine wants you to explicitly mark the attributes whose values can be generated at runtime. Set the value of `<rtexprvalue>` to `yes` or `true` if you need the attribute to be evaluated at runtime. The value is `false` by default.

For the `<required>` tag, you can use values of `yes`, `no`, `true`, or `false`. The `<required>` tag is `false` by default, meaning that if you don't explicitly say otherwise, an attribute is optional.

Listing 29.9 shows the TLD file for the `CheckerboardTag` class.

LISTING 29.9 SOURCE CODE FOR checkerboard.tld

```
<?xml version="1.0"?>
<!DOCTYPE taglib
    PUBLIC "-//Sun Microsystems, Inc.//DTD JSP Tag Library 1.1//EN"
    "http://java.sun.com/j2ee/dtds/web-jsptaglibrary_1_1.dtd">

<taglib>
    <tlibversion>1.0</tlibversion>
    <jspversion>1.1</jspversion>
    <shortname>checkerboard</shortname>
    <uri></uri>
    <info>
        A tag that prints out a checkerboard pattern
    </info>

    <tag>
        <name>checkerboard</name>
        <tagclass>CheckerboardTag</tagclass>
        <attribute>
            <name>width</name>
            <required>no</required>
        </attribute>
        <attribute>
            <name>height</name>
            <required>no</required>
        </attribute>
        <attribute>
            <name>rows</name>
            <required>no</required>
        </attribute>
        <attribute>
            <name>cols</name>
            <required>no</required>
        </attribute>
        <attribute>
            <name>darkColor</name>
            <required>no</required>
        </attribute>
        <attribute>
            <name>lightColor</name>
            <required>no</required>
        </attribute>
    </tag>
</taglib>
```

The checkerboard.tld file is similar to the other TLD files you have seen except that this one defines attributes for its tag. Listing 29.10 shows a JSP that tests out the `CheckerboardTag` class.

LISTING 29.10 SOURCE CODE FOR `TestCheckerboard.jsp`

```
<%@ taglib uri="/checkerboard" prefix="cb" %>
<html>
<body>
<cb:checkerboard width="50" height="50" rows="8" cols="8"
    darkColor="#000000" lightColor="#ffffff"/>

</body>
</html>
```


Figure 29.4 shows the output from TestCheckerboard.jsp.

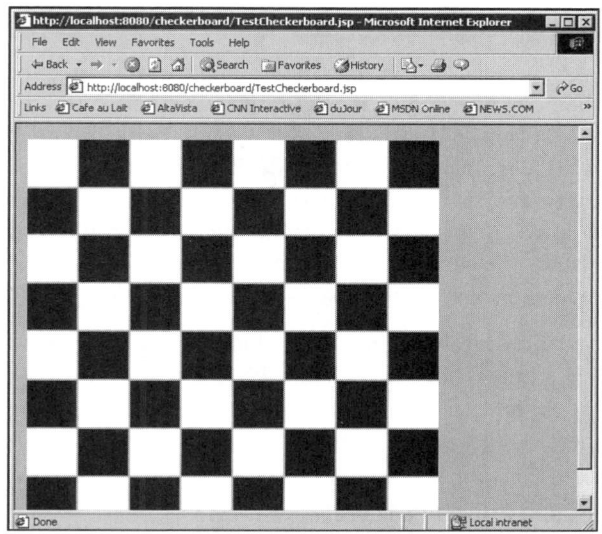

Figure 29.4 You can use attributes to change the behavior of a custom tag.

If you are having trouble setting attribute values in a custom tag, see "Attribute Values" in the "Troubleshooting" section at the end of this chapter.

PROCESSING BODY CONTENT WITH A CUSTOM TAG

One of the most interesting features of the JSP tag extension mechanism is that the tags can access their own body content. That is, a tag can see the text contained between its begin and end tags and even modify that text.

Processing body text is a little more involved and requires a specialized tag interface. A basic tag implements an interface called `Tag` and usually inherits from the `TagSupport` class. A tag that processes its body text must implement the `BodyTag` interface and usually inherits from `BodyTagSupport`.

Because the BodyTag interface extends the Tag interface, it includes the doStartTag and doEndTag methods. A tag implementing the BodyTag interface might still return SKIP_BODY from the doStartTag method to indicate that the JSP engine should not evaluate the text between the beginning and end of the tag. Instead of returning EVAL_BODY_INCLUDE, however, a body tag must return EVAL_BODY_TAG to include its body text.

Note

A custom tag that implements the BodyTag must not return EVAL_BODY_INCLUDE, otherwise the JSP engine reports an error. If a custom tag that only implements the Tag interface returns EVAL_BODY_TAG, the JSP engine also reports an error. In other words, EVAL_BODY_INCLUDE can only be used with non-body tags and EVAL_BODY_TAG can only be used with a body tag.

Body tags have a very peculiar way of operating on body text. When the JSP engine first starts evaluating the body text, it calls the doInitBody method in the custom tag. There is no return value for doInitBody and it is intended for you to perform initialization in this method. After the JSP engine evaluates the body content, it calls doAfterBody in the custom tag. Whenever doAfterBody is called, the custom tag can access the current body content by calling getBodyContent. The peculiar thing is that if doAfterBody returns EVAL_BODY_TAG, the JSP engine re-evaluates the current body content and calls doAfterBody again! The JSP engine finally accepts the content after doAfterBody returns SKIP_BODY.

That sounds very counter-intuitive, and it is. Before delving into some of the complexities, take a look at a very minimal body tag. Listing 29.11 shows a body tag that prints its body text to the response (in other words, it shows the text between its begin and end tags as if the tags weren't there).

LISTING 29.11 SOURCE CODE FOR TestBodyTag.java

```
import javax.servlet.jsp.tagext.*;
import javax.servlet.jsp.*;
import java.io.*;

public class TestBodyTag extends BodyTagSupport
{
    public int doStartTag()
        throws JspException
    {
        return EVAL_BODY_TAG;
    }

    public int doEndTag()
    {
        return EVAL_PAGE;
    }

    public void doInitTag()
    {
    }
```

```
    public int doAfterBody()
        throws JspException
    {
// Get the current body content
        BodyContent body = getBodyContent();

        try
        {
// Ask the body content to write itself out to the response
            body.writeOut(body.getEnclosingWriter());
        }
        catch (IOException exc)
        {
            throw new JspException(exc.toString());
        }
// Tell the JSP engine that the body content has been evaluated
        return SKIP_BODY;
    }
} java
```

If you are having trouble getting a body tag to work, see "Body Tags" in the "Troubleshooting" section at the end of this chapter.

In Listing 29.11, you see that you can write the body content into the response by calling `body.writeOut(body.getEnclosingWriter())`. The `body.writeOut` method writes the contents of the body to any `Writer` object. The `getEnclosingWriter` method returns the writer for the section of the response that this body tag is contained in. You can use `body.getReader` to get a `Reader` object that lets you read the contents of the body, or just call `body.getString` to get the contents as a string. In fact, an alternate way to write out the contents of a body is

```
body.getEnclosingWriter().println(body.getString());
```

Caution

Make sure you always have a case where your `doAfterBody` method returns `SKIP_BODY`. If you only return `EVAL_TAG_BODY`, the JSP engine will get stuck in an infinite loop calling your `doAfterBody` method over and over.

The odd looping behavior with `doAfterBody` gets even more confusing with the fact that the JSP engine does not re-parse the body content after each call to `doAfterBody`. In other words, if you write out some additional text or tags, those do not get added to the current body content. Why have this looping structure at all, then? Why can't you just use a for-loop? The reason for the looping behavior is that you might have a body tag with some nested custom tags that change the values of some variables, like this java:

```
<xx:bodyTag>
   Some HTML text
   <xx:computeNewValue/>
   Some more text
</xx:bodyTag>
```

In this example, the `<xx:computeNewValue>` tag calculates some value that helps determine when the `<xx:bodyTag>` tag should stop looping. It doesn't really matter what the values are; the important point is that the tag handler for `<xx:computeNewValue>` is called every time the body text is re-evaluated. If you tried to do a for-loop to print out the body text, you wouldn't have a way to call the tag handler for `<xx:computeNewValue>` java.

ADDING SCRIPTING VARIABLES

Your custom tags can define scripting variables that are accessible to your Java Server Pages. In fact, you can even get the JSP engine to add a Java variable to the generated servlet to hold the value of your script variable. All you need to do is create a special `TagExtraInfo` class that describes the scripting variables your tag might define.

Listing 29.12 shows a subclass of `TagExtraInfo` that defines a scripting variable called `scriptVar`.

LISTING 29.12 SOURCE CODE FOR `ScriptExtraInfo.java`

```
import javax.servlet.jsp.tagext.*;
public class ScriptExtraInfo extends TagExtraInfo
{
public VariableInfo[] getVariableInfo(TagData data)
    {
        return new VariableInfo[] {
                new VariableInfo("scriptVar", "java.lang.String",
                true, VariableInfo.AT_END) };
    }
}
```

The tag itself doesn't need to know about the extra info class, but it does need to put the scripting variables into the page context so the Java Server Page can extract the value of each variable and place it in a local Java variable. Listing 29.13 shows a custom tag that puts a value into the page context.

LISTING 29.13 SOURCE CODE FOR `ScriptTag.java`

```
import javax.servlet.jsp.tagext.*;
import javax.servlet.jsp.*;
import java.io.*;
public class ScriptTag extends TagSupport
{
    public int doStartTag()
        throws JspException
    {
        pageContext.setAttribute("scriptVar", "This is the script variable");

        return SKIP_BODY;
    }

    public int doEndTag()
    {
        return EVAL_PAGE;
    }
}
```

Listing 29.14 shows a Java Server Page that calls the `ScriptTag` custom tag and then accesses `scriptVar` as if it were a local variable.

Listing 29.14 Source Code for TestScriptTag.jsp

```
<%@ taglib uri="/scripttag" prefix="xx" %>
<html>
<body>
<xx:setVar/>
<h1><%= scriptVar %></h1>
</body>
</html>
```

Note

You might be wondering how a value gets from the page context into a Java variable automatically. It isn't as automatic as you might think. According to the JSP specification, the JSP engine is responsible for getting the value from the page context and copying it to the local variable. If you examine the servlet generated from a JSP using a tag-generated scripting variable, you'll see a line that copies the value out of the page context.

To match a `TagExtraInfo` class to its associated tag, you must include a `<teiclass>` tag in the Tag Library Descriptor for the custom tag. Listing 29.15 shows the TLD for the `ScriptTag` class.

Listing 29.15 Source Code for scripttag.tld

```
<?xml version="1.0"?>
<!DOCTYPE taglib
    PUBLIC "-//Sun Microsystems, Inc.//DTD JSP Tag Library 1.1//EN"
    "http://java.sun.com/j2ee/dtds/web-jsptaglibrary_1_1.dtd">

<taglib>
    <tlibversion>1.0</tlibversion>
    <jspversion>1.1</jspversion>
    <shortname>scripttag</shortname>
    <uri></uri>
    <info>
        An example scripting variable tag
    </info>

    <tag>
        <name>setVar</name>
        <tagclass>ScriptTag</tagclass>
        <teiclass>ScriptExtraInfo</teiclass>
    </tag>
</taglib>
```

If you are having trouble defining scripting variables, see "Scripting Variables" in the "Troubleshooting" section at the end of this chapter.

The TagExtraInfo class actually serves two purposes. In addition to defining scripting variables, it has an isValid method that allows you to validate attribute values at JSP compile time. The isValid method takes an argument of type TagData and returns true if the combination of attributes in TagData is valid, or false if there is an error in the attributes. The idea here is that you can't define what constitutes a good attribute value or a good set of values without evaluating the values. By evaluating them when the JSP is compiled, you avoid any unnecessary runtime overhead.

The TagData class contains the following methods for examining the attributes for a tag:

```
Object getAttribute(String attrName)
Enumeration getAttributes()
String getAttributeString(String attrName)
String getId()
void setAttribute(String attrName, Object value)
```

Most of these methods are self-explanatory. The getId method is a shortcut for getAttributeString("id").

Because some attribute values must be evaluated at request time instead of compile time, the getAttribute method returns a special object named TagData.REQUEST_TIME_VALUE for any value that must be evaluated at request time. A request time attribute value is a value that can be described using the <%= %> tag pair.

TROUBLESHOOTING

INSTALL PROBLEMS

Why do I see my custom tag in the HTML output?

You most likely forgot to put the taglib directive at the top of the page. You also might not have remembered to use the prefix you defined in the taglib directive, or you mistyped the prefix or the tag name.

Why do I get a compile error when I use a custom tag?

Well, the first thing to check is that it's really the tag that's causing the problem. Try removing the tag and see if that clears up the problem. Next, make sure that you have installed the tag library on the Web server. The class files should be under the WEB-INF/classes directory (WEB-INF must be capitalized, so don't count on web-inf working the same way). Also make sure you have a TLD file and that the web.xml file in the WEB-INF directory has the correct pathname for the TLD. Because custom tags are a very recent addition, not all JSP engines implement them the same way (some might not even implement them correctly). You might need to consult the documentation for your JSP engine to see if there are any additional notes for installing custom tag libraries.

ATTRIBUTE VALUES

Why do I get a runtime error when I try to set an attribute value?

There is probably some mismatch between the attribute type in the custom tag and the attribute value you are trying to set. For instance, trying to store the string "Fred" into an integer value isn't going to work.

I created `get` and `set` methods, so why doesn't the JSP engine recognize my attributes?

Don't forget that you must also define the names of the attributes in the TLD file.

BODY TAGS

When I use a body tag, why does the JSP engine stop responding?

You are probably stuck in an infinite loop caused by your `doAfterBody` method returning `EVAL_BODY_TAG` over and over instead of returning `SKIP_BODY`.

I tried to write out some code in `<% %>` and re-evaluated the body text; why do the `<% %>` tags show up in the output?

Remember, the JSP engine only parses the body text one time. It might evaluate custom tags in the body text multiple times, but after the text is parsed, that's it.

I rewrote the body text and returned `EVAL_BODY_TAG`; why do I still see the original body text?

Again, the JSP engine only parses the body text once. You will always receive the original body text in `doAfterBody`.

SCRIPTING VARIABLES

I put a value in the page context, so why doesn't the JSP have a variable to hold the value?

You might have forgotten to create the `TagExtraInfo` object, or you forgot to link the `TagExtraInfo` object to the tag class by adding a `<teiclass>` item in the TLD file.

CHAPTER 30

INTERNATIONALIZATION

In this chapter

The Internet has had a huge impact on software development. Now developers and users from countries around the world can share information almost instantaneously. Oddly enough, developers rarely consider the fact that the people who use their software might be in another country. At least, this is often the case in the United States.

Java provides reasonable support for internationalization, some of which happens behind the scenes. When a Java program starts, it examines the locale configured in the operating system and sets up a default locale. Several Java classes use the locale for formatting dates and currencies. You can also define sets of resources, called *resource bundles*, which are locale-dependent. By confining your locale-specific data to resource bundles, you can support multiple locales in your programs without hard-coding every possible locale variation.

> **Note**
>
> **You might have seen "internationalization" abbreviated as I18N. The abbreviation is a clever acknowledgment of the fact that there are 18 letters between the *I* and the *N* in internationalization.**

DETECTING THE BROWSER'S PREFERRED LOCALE

As you saw in Chapter 12, "How the Browser Interacts with the Server," the browser sends a number of header fields in each request indicating certain preferences. One of these preferences is a list of languages that the browser prefers for Web pages. The `ACCEPT-LANGUAGE` header value contains a list of languages that the browser is prepared to handle. Using this header value, you can locate a locale that you are prepared to support and deliver content targeted toward that locale.

For example, suppose you have a Web site that is in both German and English. Although each version contains links to allow you to change languages at any time, you might want to default the user to the language his browser prefers. For example, if you see `de-DE` as the preferred language, you send the user to the German version of the page, and if you see `en-US` or `en-UK`, you send the user to the English version.

Listing 30.1 shows a JSP that detects the preferred language sent by the browser and chooses one of two possible pages.

LISTING 30.1 SOURCE CODE FOR `MyPage.jsp`

```
<%
    String lang = request.getHeader("ACCEPT-LANGUAGE");

    String whatPage = "MyPage_En.html";

    if (lang.startsWith("de"))
    {
        whatPage = "MyPage_De.html";
    }
%><jsp:forward page="<%=whatPage%>"/>
```

Figure 30.1 shows the JSP when viewed from a browser with a preferred language setting of English (en/US) and Figure 30.2 shows the JSP viewed from a browser that prefers German (de/DE) .

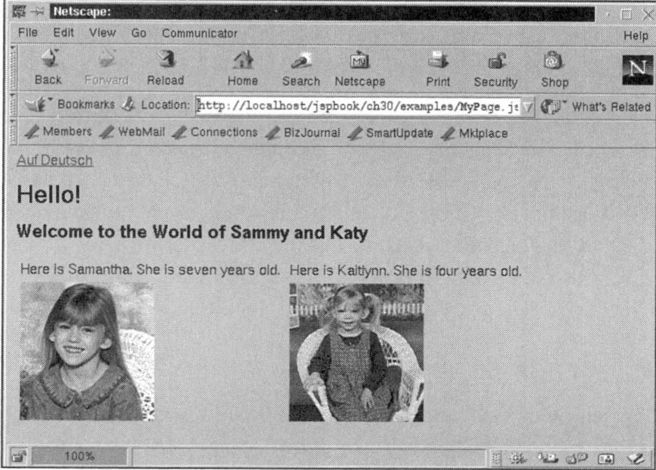

Figure 30.1
You can create a multilingual Web site by detecting the preferred language.

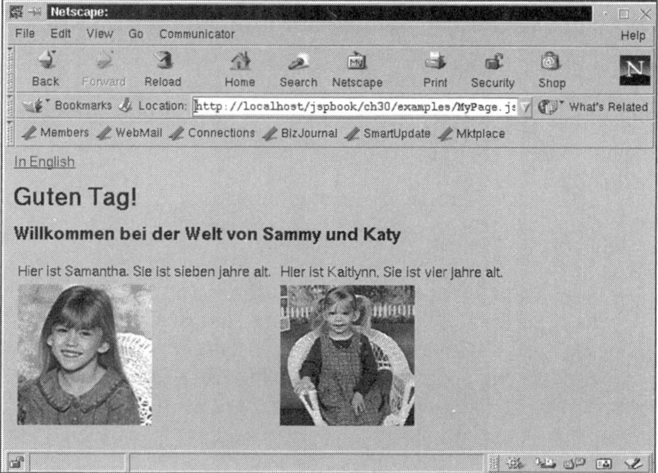

Figure 30.2
When you provide alternate language pages, include links to see the other language versions.

Tip

Both Netscape and Internet Explorer let you set the preferred language for your browser. These settings allow you to view your alternate language pages without changing the language setting for the entire operating system.

USING LOCALE-BASED TEXT FORMATTERS

Java relies on the `java.text` package for providing locale-based formatting. A locale represents both a language and a country, because two countries might share the same language but still format numbers, dates, and currencies differently. For example, the United States and the United Kingdom share the same language, but they format currencies differently because the United States uses a $ symbol and the UK uses the £ symbol.

In a Java application, you normally rely on the default locale, which the Java virtual machine detects by querying the operating system. Because you can assume that users have configured their systems with the locale they prefer, your application can safely rely on the default locale. In a Web application, however, the problem is more complicated. The application is running on a Web server, and the user is using a browser on another computer, possibly halfway around the world. You must create a locale object that conforms to the user's preference.

CREATING A LOCALE OBJECT

To create a locale object, you need at least a language for the locale, and preferably a country as well. There are also variant settings for a locale that are vendor- and browser-specific. If you don't know the country code for a locale, just use a blank string. You can still format dates and numbers without a country, but currencies will not have the correct currency symbol.

The following code fragment creates a locale for French, but does not specify a country code:

```
Locale french = new Locale("fr", "");
```

This code fragment creates a locale for German with a country code for Austria:

```
Locale germanAustria = new Locale("de", "AT");
```

Caution

Resist the temptation to use `Locale.setDefault` to set the current locale to be the browser's locale. You wouldn't need to pass the locale to all the formatting routines that way, but for a Web application, you introduce an ugly threading problem. Two servlets might set the default locale at the same time. One servlet might set the locale to English-US and another might immediately change it to German-Germany. The servlet that wanted English would suddenly find it was using the German format.

FORMATTING DATES

You might have used the `SimpleDateFormat` class in the `java.text` package to format dates. Although it might provide an easy way to specify date formats, you lose some of the locale-independence when you use it. When you create an instance of `SimpleDateFormat`, you must supply a basic pattern for the date. You might pick a format like `MM/dd/yyyy`, for example. Unfortunately, many countries write dates in the form `dd/MM/yyyy`.

The `DateFormat` class doesn't give you the leeway that `SimpleDateFormat` does, but it does protect you from various locale-dependent formats. The `DateFormat` class has several factory methods that create a DateFormat object for you. You don't use the constructor. Instead, you call getDateInstance, getDateTimeInstance, or getTimeInstance, depending on whether you want to display dates only, dates and times, or times only.

When you create a DateFormat, you must specify one of four formats: SHORT, MEDIUM, LONG, or FULL. You can also give the locale for the format, and if you omit the locale, you'll get the default locale. For getDateInstance and getTimeInstance, you need to specify only one format. For getDateTimeInstance, you must specify SHORT, MEDIUM, LONG, or FULL for both the date and the time. You might choose to write out the date in long format but the time in full format.

Listing 30.2 shows a Java Server Page that displays the date using the four format options. The locale is not included in this example, however. You will see how to include it later in this chapter.

Listing 30.2 Source Code for ShowDates.jsp

```
<%@ page language="java" import="java.text.*,java.util.*" %>
<%

    DateFormat dtShort = DateFormat.getDateTimeInstance(
        DateFormat.SHORT, DateFormat.SHORT);

    DateFormat dtMedium = DateFormat.getDateTimeInstance(
        DateFormat.MEDIUM, DateFormat.MEDIUM);

    DateFormat dtLong = DateFormat.getDateTimeInstance(
        DateFormat.LONG, DateFormat.LONG);

    DateFormat dtFull = DateFormat.getDateTimeInstance(
        DateFormat.FULL, DateFormat.FULL);
%>
<html>
<body>
A short date/time looks like: <%=dtShort.format(new Date())%><p>
A medium date/time looks like: <%=dtMedium.format(new Date())%><p>
A long date/time looks like: <%=dtLong.format(new Date())%><p>
A full date/time looks like: <%=dtFull.format(new Date())%><p>
</body>
</html>
```

Figure 30.3 shows the output of the ShowDates Java Server page.

Formatting Currency

Formatting currency values is much more involved than formatting dates and times. It's not that there's anything difficult about formatting a currency value; the problem is that you can rarely just switch from one currency to another without performing some sort of conversion. The NumberFormat class will format a specific value like 12.34 into dollars as $12.34 or into Deutschmarks as 12,34DM, but 12,34DM is not the same amount of money as $12.34. Java does not provide any way to convert from one currency to another.

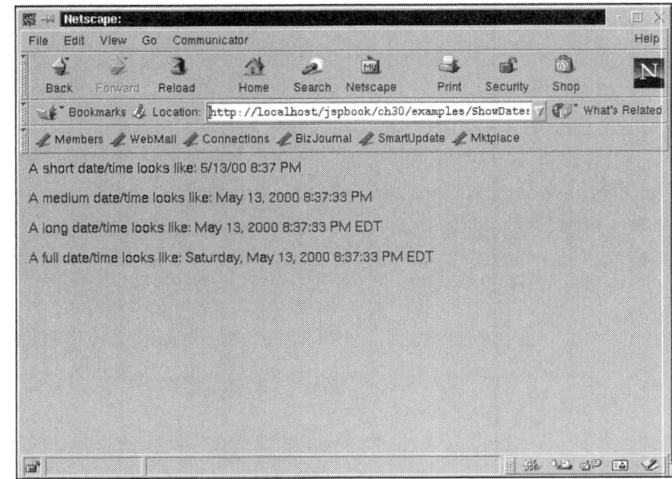

Figure 30.3
You can choose between four basic styles of date and time.

When you think about it, it's almost impossible to make a standard API for converting currencies because currencies are traded at various rates. Imagine trying to make an API that lets you get the price of a stock or the price of a car. There would be too many places to go for the information and too many different formats for the data. You have the same problem trying to convert currencies. Perhaps one day all the currency traders will publish rates using a standard XML format and you can perform reasonable conversions. Even so, because the rates fluctuate, you must still worry about how stale the information is. The conversion rate for an unstable currency might plummet over the course of a day or two.

By now you see that the capability to display currency values for different locales is not such a useful feature. If you do find that you need to display currency values, you can call `NumberFormat.getCurrencyInstance` and pass it the locale whose currency you want to display:

```
NumberFormat currencyFormat =
    NumberFormat.getCurrencyInstance(someLocale);
```

Getting a Locale for a Browser's Preferred Language

When you examine the `ACCEPT-LANGUAGE` header value, you will find a list of locale codes consisting of a two-letter language code, possibly a country code, and even variant options after the country code. Each locale code is separated by a comma. When you just want the preferred language (the browser sends the locales in order of preference), you need to grab the first one in the list.

Listing 30.3 shows a Java Server Page that parses the `ACCEPT-LANGUAGE` header value and gets a locale value for the preferred local.

Listing 30.3 Source Code for TestLocale.jsp

```
<%@ page language="java" import="java.text.*,java.util.*" %>
<%

// Get the default locale in case you can't determine the
// user's locale
    Locale locale = Locale.getDefault();

// Get the browser's preferred language
    String acceptLangString = request.getHeader("ACCEPT-LANGUAGE");

// If there is an ACCEPT-LANGUAGE header, parse it
    if (acceptLangString != null)
    {

// The accepted languages should be separated by commas, but also
// add space as a separator to eliminate whitespace
        StringTokenizer localeParser = new StringTokenizer(
            acceptLangString, " ,");

// See if there is a language in the list (you only need the first one)
        if (localeParser.hasMoreTokens())
        {
// Get the locale
            String localeStr = localeParser.nextToken();

// The locale should be in the format ll-CC where ll is the language
// and CC is the country, like en-US for English in the U.S. and
// de-DE for German in Germany. Allow the browser to use _ instead
// of -, too.
            StringTokenizer localeSplitter = new StringTokenizer(
                localeStr, "_-");

// Assume both values are blank
            String language = "";
            String country = "";

// See if there is a language specified
            if (localeSplitter.hasMoreTokens())
            {
                language = localeSplitter.nextToken();
            }

// See if there is a country specified (there won't always be one)
            if (localeSplitter.hasMoreTokens())
            {
                country = localeSplitter.nextToken();

            }

// Create a locale based on this language and country (if country is
// blank, you'll still get locale-based text, but currencies won't
// display correctly.
            locale = new Locale(language, country);
        }
```

Listing 30.3 Continued

```
    }
%>
<html>
<body>
Your locale language is <%=locale.getLanguage()%>.<p>
Your locale country is <%=locale.getCountry()%>.<p>
<%
// Get a formatter to display currency
    NumberFormat currencyFormatter =
        NumberFormat.getCurrencyInstance(locale);

// Get a formatter to display dates and times
    DateFormat dateFormatter =
        DateFormat.getDateTimeInstance(
            DateFormat.FULL, DateFormat.FULL, locale);
%>
A currency in your locale looks like this:
    <%= currencyFormatter.format(12.34) %><p>
A date in your locale looks like this:
    <%= dateFormatter.format(new Date()) %><p>
</body>
</html>
```

Figure 30.4 shows the `TestLocale` Java Server Page running with a locale of en-US (English - U.S.).

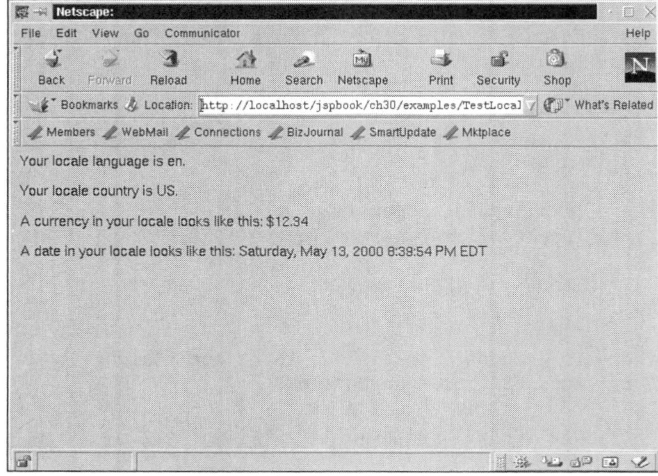

Figure 30.4
The java.text package can format dates and currencies.

Figure 30.5 shows the `TestLocale` Java Server Page running with a locale of de (German) and no country code. Notice the odd looking character in the currency. If you don't specify a country you'll see this odd symbol. Also notice that the currency formatter still uses the German convention of using a comma where English text uses a period. Although the currency formatter doesn't know the currency symbol, it uses the number formatter to format the currency value, and the number formatter doesn't need to know the country.

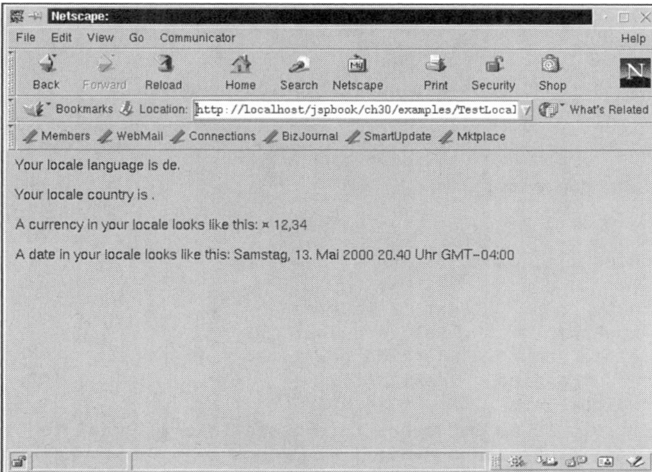

Figure 30.5
If you don't specify a country for a locale, the currency symbol isn't correct.

USING RESOURCE BUNDLES IN WEB PAGES

The Java's I18N support includes objects known as *resource bundles*. When you create a multilingual application or Web site, you don't always want to make separate screens or pages for each language. For example, when you create an HTML form, the prompt strings can be in different languages, but the HTML for defining the form itself is the same no matter what language you use.

By using resource bundles, you can group various prompt strings and other objects that are locale-dependent. When you create a resource bundle class, you decide on a base classname and then define each locale's resources in a class whose name is formed by adding the locale to the end of the classname.

For example, you might store some resources in a class called `SomeResources`. The French version of the resources would be in a class called `SomeResources_fr`, and the German version would be in a class called `SomeResources_de`. If you need to make a special German version of the resources tailored to Austria, you can put them in a class called `SomeResources_de_AT`.

Because writing resource bundles can be tedious, Java gives you some prebuilt framework classes. The `ListResourceBundle` class allows you to store the resources in an array of objects. Listing 30.4 shows an example `ListResourceBundle`. Notice that there is no locale at the end of the classname. That makes this class the default bundle if there is no bundle for the browser's locale.

LISTING 30.4 SOURCE CODE FOR `TestResources.java`

```
package usingjsp;

import java.text.*;
import java.util.*;

public class TestResources extends ListResourceBundle
{
    public Object[][] getContents()
    {
        return contents;
    }

    final Object[][] contents =
    {
        { "namePrompt", "What is your name: " },
        { "agePrompt", "How old are you: " },
        { "placePrompt", "Where do you live: " },
        { "greetHeading", "Hello!" },
        { "welcomeText",
            "Welcome to our web site. Please take a moment to "+
            "fill out our survey" },
        { "submitButtonText", "Submit" }
    };
}
```

Listing 30.5 shows the German version of the `TestResources` resource bundle.

LISTING 30.5 SOURCE CODE FOR `TestResources_de.java`

```
package usingjsp;

import java.util.*;
import java.text.*;

public class TestResources_de extends ListResourceBundle
{
    public Object[][] getContents()
    {
        return contents;
    }

    final Object[][] contents =
    {
        { "namePrompt", "Wie heißen Sie" },
        { "agePrompt", "Wie alt sind Sie: " },
        { "placePrompt", "Wo wohnen Sie: " },
        { "greetHeading", "Guten Tag!" },
        { "welcomeText",
            "Willkommen bei unserer Web-Site. Bitte, dauern Sie einen "+
            "Moment Um unsere Umfrage auszufüllen" },
        { "submitButtonText", "Senden" }
    };
}
```

Listing 30.6 shows a Java Server Page that displays an HTML form using the prompts from the `TestResources` resource bundle. Notice that you don't need separate pages for each language. Only the prompts need to change.

Listing 30.6 Source Code for ResourceBundles.jsp

```
<%@ page language="java" import="java.text.*,java.util.*" %>
<%

// Get the default locale in case you can't determine the
// user's locale
    Locale locale = Locale.getDefault();

// Get the browser's preferred language
    String acceptLangString = request.getHeader("ACCEPT-LANGUAGE");

// Allow the user to override the browser's language setting. This
// lets you test with tools like Babelfish (which isn't that great
// at translating to begin with).
    String override = request.getParameter("langOverride");

    if (override != null)
    {
        acceptLangString = override;
    }

// If there is an ACCEPT-LANGUAGE header, parse it
    if (acceptLangString != null)
    {

// The accepted languages should be separated by commas, but also
// add space as a separator to eliminate whitespace
        StringTokenizer localeParser = new StringTokenizer(
            acceptLangString, " ,");

// See if there is a language in the list (you only need the first one)
        if (localeParser.hasMoreTokens())
        {
// Get the locale
            String localeStr = localeParser.nextToken();

// The locale should be in the format ll-CC where ll is the language
// and CC is the country, like en-US for English in the U.S. and
// de-DE for German in Germany. Allow the browser to use _ instead
// of -, too.
            StringTokenizer localeSplitter = new StringTokenizer(
                localeStr, "_-");

// Assume both values are blank
            String language = "";
            String country = "";
```

LISTING 30.6 CONTINUED

```
// See if there is a language specified
            if (localeSplitter.hasMoreTokens())
            {
                language = localeSplitter.nextToken();
            }

// See if there is a country specified (there won't always be one)
            if (localeSplitter.hasMoreTokens())
            {
                country = localeSplitter.nextToken();

            }

// Create a locale based on this language and country (if country is
// blank, you'll still get locale-based text, but currencies won't
// display correctly).
locale = new Locale(language, country);
        }
    }

// Get the bundle of resource strings for this locale
    ResourceBundle resources = ResourceBundle.getBundle(
        "usingjsp.TestResources", locale);
%>
<html>
<body>
<h1><%= resources.getString("greetHeading")%></h1>
<p>
<%= resources.getString("welcomeText")%>:
<p>
<form action="your_form_handler_here" method="post">

<%=resources.getString("namePrompt")%>
<input type="text" name="name"><br>

<%=resources.getString("agePrompt")%>
<input type="text" name="age"><br>

<%=resources.getString("placePrompt")%>
<input type="text" name="place"><br>

<p>
<input type="submit" value="<%=resources.getString("submitButtonText")%>">
</form>
</body>
</html>
```

Figure 30.6 shows the `ResourceBundles` JSP running in a browser with a preferred language of English.

Figure 30.7 shows the `ResourceBundles` JSP running in a browser with a preferred language of German.

Although the `ListResourceBundle` class makes it easy to customize various items in a Web page, the `PropertyResourceBundle` class makes it even easier. The `PropertyResourceBundle` class lets you store locale-specific strings in a properties file instead of a Java class, making it much easier to customize the resources. All you need to do to use the `PropertyResourceBundle` class is to create a properties file with lines of the form `name=value`. Listing 30.7 shows a properties file defining the same resource names as TestResources.java. Make sure the properties file ends with ".properties". The `ResourceBundle` class specifically looks for files with the ".properties" extension.

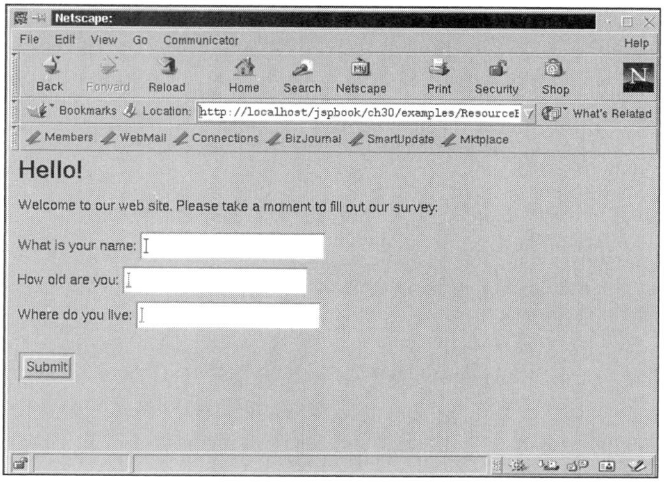

Figure 30.6
Resource bundles let you customize parts of a JSP or servlet.

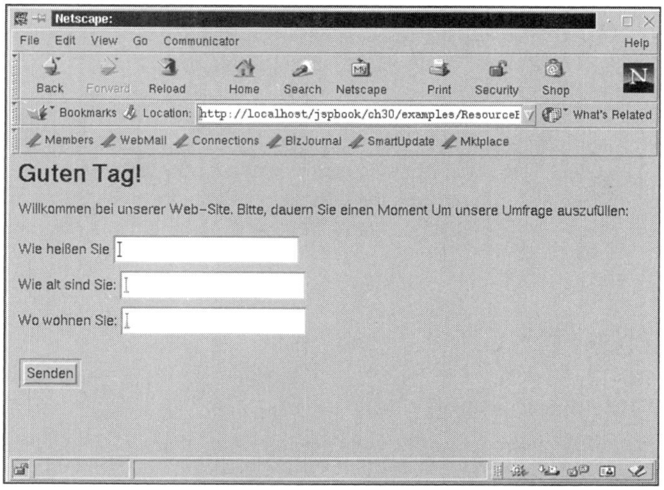

Figure 30.7
The `ResourceBundle` class locates a resource bundle for a particular locale.

LISTING 30.7 SOURCE CODE FOR `TestResourceProps.properties`

```
namePrompt=What is your name:
agePrompt=How old are you:
placePrompt=Where do you live:
greetHeading=Hello!
welcomeText=Welcome to our Web site.
➥Please take a moment to fill out our survey
submitButtonText=Submit
```

Listing 30.8 shows the German version of the properties file. Notice that you just need to append the language to the end of the name of the properties file, right before the ".properties" extension.

LISTING 30.8 SOURCE CODE FOR `TestResourceProps_de.properties`

```
namePrompt=Wie heißen Sie:
agePrompt=Wie alt sind Sie:
placePrompt=Wo wohnen Sie:
greetHeading=Guten Tag!
welcomeText= Willkommen bei unserer Web-Site.
➥Bitte, dauern Sie einen Moment Um unsere Umfrage auszufüllen
submitButtonText=Senden
```

The beauty of the `PropertyResourceBundle` class is that it treats the files as if they were classnames. That is, you just need to put the properties files somewhere in your classpath and call `ResourceBundle.getBundle` using the base name of the properties file (such as `TestResourceProps`).

You only need to change one line in ResourceBundles.jsp to support properties files instead of using the `TestResources` class:

```
ResourceBundle resources = ResourceBundle.getBundle(
    "TestResourceProps", locale);
```

Note

If you have a properties file named TestResourceProps.properties and a class named `TestResourceProps`, the class takes precedence over the properties file. The `ResourceBundle` class loads the `TestResourceProps` class instead of the properties file.

TROUBLESHOOTING

TESTING MULTI-LINGUAL WEB SITES

How can I tell if my Web site actually works for other languages?

You can change the language setting for your browser to specify a different preferred language.

LOCATING RESOURCE BUNDLES

Why can't the resource bundle find my properties file?

Treat the properties file like a .class file. It must be visible somewhere along your classpath. Also, make sure that the browser is requesting a language that you support. If not, make sure you have a default properties file (one without a language on the end).

CHAPTER 31

Security

In this chapter

In Chapter 5, "Saving Data Between Requests," you saw how to create a login form and keep track of a user with the `session` object. The servlet container gives you an alternative to creating your own login form. By adding additional information to the deployment descriptor for your Web application, you can force the user to log in to the application without writing specific code for login authentication.

ROLE-BASED SECURITY

The authentication mechanism in the servlet specification uses a technique called *role-based security*. The idea is that rather than restricting resources at the user level, you create groups of users called *roles* and restrict the resources by role. A single user can have more than one role. For example, a company might have employees and contractors, so you can have an application that permits different operations depending on whether you are an employee or a contractor. You might also have a manager role. If a contractor happens to be a manager, he would have two roles: contractor and manager.

There are no predefined roles. You can come up with role names as you see fit. As far as creating users and roles, each servlet engine has its own method for defining users and roles. See Appendixes C–F for instructions on creating users and roles for several common servlet engines, or consult the documentation for your servlet engine.

BASIC AUTHENTICATION

The servlet specification provides several ways to authenticate users. Although servlet engines are not required to implement the authentication features, you should expect most of the top servlet engines to support them.

The HTTP protocol has a built-in authentication protocol. When you log in to a page that requires authentication, the Web server first sends back a message telling the browser to send authentication information. The browser then prompts you for a username and password to send to the server. After the browser sends the username and password, assuming they are correct, the Web server displays the requested page. The browser holds on to the authentication information in case the Web server asks for it again.

To set up basic authentication for a Web application, you must add several new tags to your web.xml file. Listing 31.1 shows a basic web.xml file that uses authentication.

LISTING 31.1 SOURCE CODE FOR `web.xml` FOR THE `authtest` APPLICATION

```
<!DOCTYPE web-app PUBLIC "-//Sun Microsystems, Inc.//DTD WebApplication 2.2//EN"
"http://java.sun.com/j2ee/dtds/web-app_2_2.dtd">
<web-app>
    <display-name>authtest</display-name>
    <description>A test of authentication</description>
    <security-constraint>
        <web-resource-collection>
            <web-resource-name>Test</web-resource-name>
```

```
            <url-pattern>/*</url-pattern>
            <http-method>GET</http-method>
            <http-method>POST</http-method>
        </web-resource-collection>
        <user-data-constraint>
            <transport-guarantee>NONE</transport-guarantee>
        </user-data-constraint>
        <auth-constraint>
            <role-name>manager</role-name>
        </auth-constraint>
    </security-constraint>
    <login-config>
        <auth-method>BASIC</auth-method>
    </login-config>
</web-app>
```

The two main tags that have been added to the basic deployment descriptor are `<security-constraint>` and `<login-config>`.

The `<security-constraint>` Tag

The `<security-constraint>` tag tells the servlet engine what security requirements your application has. You can have more than one security constraint if necessary. Within the security constraint, you must specify a Web resource collection with the `<web-resource-collection>` tag.

A Web resource collection is a collection of URL patterns that the security constraint applies to. For instance, you might want to restrict only a single directory in your application. The `<url-pattern>` tag in your resource collection would then contain a pattern matching the directory you want to restrict. The pattern `/*` in Listing 31.1 means that the security constraint applies to all URLs in the application's directory. The `<web-resource-name>` tag specifies the name for the Web resource collection. There is no connection between the name and any of the URLs within it. The name serves little purpose, but can be useful for various development and configuration tools.

The other tag you find in the Web resource collection is the `<http-method>` tag. This specifies which HTTP methods require authentication. If you do not specify an HTTP method, the security applies to all HTTP methods. You might, for example, want to perform authentication for an HTTP `POST`, but not for a `GET`. You might also want to perform different kinds of authentication for `GET` and `POST`. In the latter case, you specify two separate security constraints, one with an HTTP method of `GET` and the other with an HTTP method of `POST`.

The `<user-data-constraint>` tag tells the servlet engine what kind of data security your application needs. You can include a `<description>` tag to describe the constraint, but it is optional. The `<transport-guarantee>` tag indicates the kind of transport-level data security your application needs. The value for the `<transport-guarantee>` tag can be one of three values:

- **NONE**—Indicates that the application doesn't require any special data security.
- **INTEGRAL**—Indicates the client and server should ensure that the data can't be changed by anyone. Although you would typically use an encrypted protocol such as SSL for this level of security, `INTEGRAL` does not require that the data can't be observed by a third party. You could send digitally signed, unencrypted messages back and forth and still meet the requirements for `INTEGRAL`.
- **CONFIDENTIAL**—Requires that a third party can't tamper with the data or read it. You will almost always use SSL for this level unless you have another encryption transport protocol available.

The `<auth-constraint>` tag lets you specify the various roles this security constraint applies to. The `<role-name>` tag lets you specify a specific role. You can include multiple `<role-name>` tags within a single `<auth-constraint>` tag.

THE <login-config> TAG

The `<login-config>` tag lets you control the type of authentication you want the servlet engine and browser to perform. You specify the type of authentication through the `<auth-method>` tag. There are four kinds of authentication methods supported by the servlet specification:

- **BASIC**—Causes the browser to prompt the user for a username and password and then send them to the server without encrypting them first. If you use `BASIC` authentication over an SSL (encrypted) connection, the username and password are encrypted by the SSL protocol itself. The password is encoded using base64 encoding, which isn't really a form of encryption.
- **DIGEST**—Causes the browser to encrypt the password before sending it. Although this method can prevent someone from reading the password as it travels over the network, this method is not as secure as using a fully encrypted session.
- **FORM**—Just like the `BASIC` authentication method except the server sends back a login form rather than using the browser's built-in form. The username and password are transmitted as form variables.
- **CLIENT-CERT**—Requires the user to provide a public key certificate for authentication. This method is frequently too cumbersome for general users because they rarely have their own digital certificates, but does offer a reasonably high level of security, even over an unencrypted connection.

For basic authentication, you can specify a realm name using the `<realm-name>` tag. The realms help organize various sections of a Web site that might need authentication. By grouping applications into separate realms, you can require the user to log in to each application. The realm name isn't configured anywhere other than in the `<realm-name>` tag, so you don't need to worry about setting up different realms. The realm is little more than a name passed back and forth between the browser and the server.

Listing 31.1 uses basic authentication. Figure 31.1 shows the login prompt for a page in the `authtest` application running under Internet Explorer.

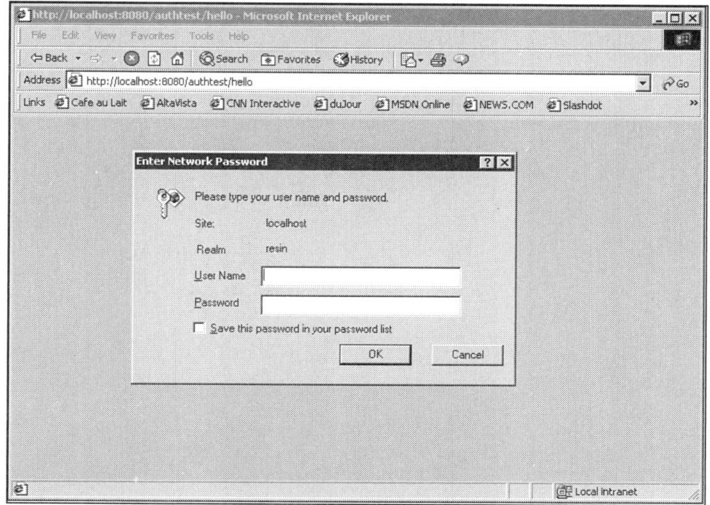

Figure 31.1 The browser prompts for a username and password for basic authentication.

CREATING A CUSTOM LOGIN FORM

When you use the `FORM` authentication method, you must supply a login form to prompt the user for a username and password. The login form must contain form elements named `j_username` and `j_password`. The action in the `<form>` tag must be `j_security_check`. Listing 31.2 shows the HTML source for an example login form.

LISTING 31.2 SOURCE CODE FOR LoginForm.html

```
<html>
<body bgcolor="#ffffff">
<center><img src="banner.jpg"></center>
<form action="j_security_check">
<center>
<table border="0">
<tr>
<td><img src="login.jpg"></td>
<td><input type="text" name="j_username"></td>
</tr>
<tr>
<td><img src="password.jpg"></td>
<td><input type="password" name="j_password"></td>
</tr>
</table>
<input type="submit" value="Login!">
</center>
</form>
</body>
</html>
```

Figure 31.2 shows the example login form after the user has tried to access a page that requires authentication.

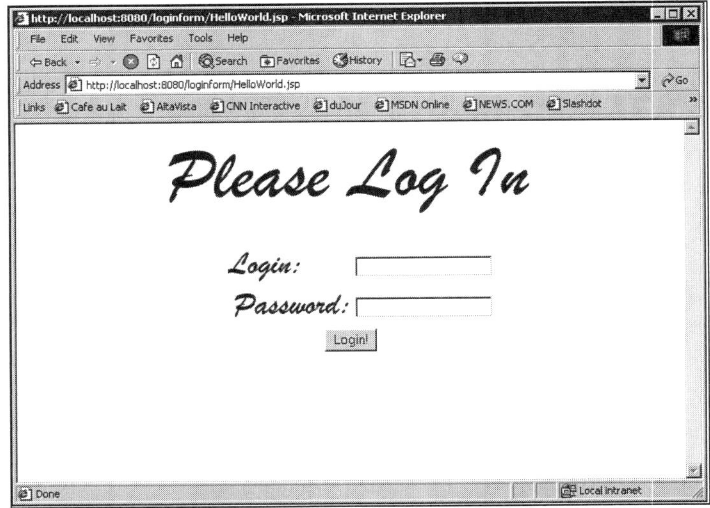

Figure 31.2
You can supply your own custom login form.

You can also create an error page that displays when there is an error in performing the authentication. Listing 31.3 shows a simple error page.

LISTING 31.3 SOURCE CODE FOR LoginErr.html

```
<html>
<body bgcolor="#ffffff">
<h1>Sorry</h1>
An error occurred during authorization.
<p>
</body>
</html>
```

Figure 31.3 shows the simple error page in action.

When you supply your own custom login form, you must supply the name of the login form and the name of the error form inside the `<login-config>` tag. The `<form-login-page>` tag specifies the location of the login page, while the `<form-error-page>` tag specifies the location of the error page. The `<form-login-page>` and `<form-error-page>` tags are contained within the `<form-login-config>` tag. Listing 31.4 shows an example web.xml file for authentication with a custom login form.

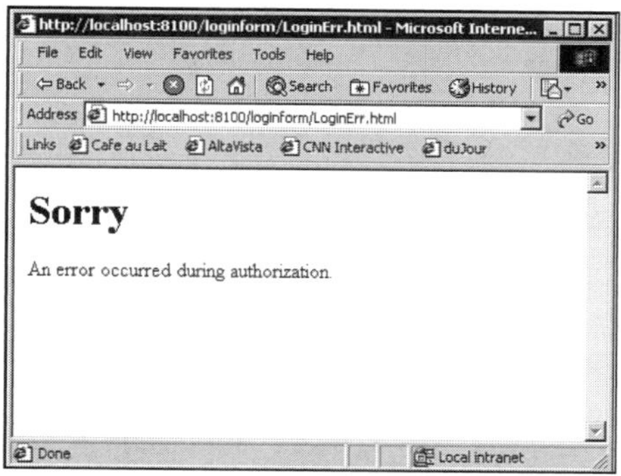

Figure 31.3
You can supply your own custom error page for handling authentication errors.

PART V CH 31

LISTING 31.4 `web.xml` **FOR** `loginform` **APPLICATION**

```
<!DOCTYPE web-app PUBLIC "-//Sun Microsystems, Inc.//DTD WebApplication 2.2//EN"
"http://java.sun.com/j2ee/dtds/web-app_2_2.dtd">
<web-app>
    <display-name>loginform</display-name>
    <description>A test of custom login forms</description>
    <security-constraint>
        <web-resource-collection>
            <web-resource-name>Test</web-resource-name>
            <url-pattern>/*.jsp</url-pattern>
            <http-method>GET</http-method>
            <http-method>POST</http-method>
        </web-resource-collection>
        <user-data-constraint>
            <transport-guarantee>NONE</transport-guarantee>
        </user-data-constraint>
        <auth-constraint>
            <role-name>manager</role-name>
        </auth-constraint>
    </security-constraint>
    <login-config>
        <auth-method>FORM</auth-method>
        <form-login-config>
            <form-login-page>/LoginForm.html</form-login-page>
            <form-error-page>/LoginErr.html</form-error-page>
        </form-login-config>
    </login-config>
</web-app>
```

CHECKING SECURITY ROLES PROGRAMMATICALLY

Role-based authentication is nice when you can partition pages based on a role, but you can rarely make this kind of authentication seamless. Suppose you want to set up pages that can only be run by someone in a `manager` role. Obviously you can group the pages into a separate Web resource collection and specify a role name of `manager` in the `<auth-config>` tag for the collection. The problem is, where do you put the links to the manager-only pages?

If you put them on a page that everyone can access, the non-manager users might click the link and see an error page. Although this mechanism does secure your application, it doesn't make it pretty.

Tip

If you want your site to look professional, a user should never see an error page as part of the normal operation of the site.

Rather than presenting the user with an ugly error page, you can check the user's role programmatically by calling the `isUserInRole` method in the `request` object. For example, in a Java Server Page that links to pages for managers, you might have the following code:

```
<% if (request.isUserInRole("manager")) { %>
<a href="managers/mgrreport.jsp">Manager Report</a>
<a href="managers/personnel.jsp">Personnel Records</a>
<% } %>
```

By checking the user's role in a JSP or servlet, you can customize the Web page to only show the user the items she can access.

If you need the name of the user as it was entered in the authentication form, you can call `getRemoteUser` in the `request` object.

Listing 31.4 shows the source for a custom tag that lets you specify a required role for all the text contained in the tag body. The beauty of the custom tag is that it is more compact and more readable than using Java code embedded inside `<% %>` tags.

LISTING 31.4 SOURCE CODE FOR `RequireRoleTag.java`

```
import javax.servlet.jsp.tagext.*;
import javax.servlet.jsp.*;
import javax.servlet.http.*;
import java.util.*;

public class RequireRoleTag extends TagSupport
{
    protected String role = null;

    public int doStartTag()
        throws JspException
    {
        HttpServletRequest request =
            (HttpServletRequest) pageContext.getRequest();

        if ((role != null) && request.isUserInRole(role))
        {
            return EVAL_BODY_INCLUDE;
        }
        else
        {
            return SKIP_BODY;
        }
    }
```

```
    public int doEndTag()
    {
        return EVAL_PAGE;
    }

    public String getRole() { return role; }
    public void setRole(String aRole) { role = aRole; }
}
```

Listing 31.5 shows a Java Server Page that tests the custom tag in Listing 31.4.

Listing 31.5 Source Code for CheckRole.jsp

```
<%@ taglib uri="/rolecheck" prefix="rc" %>
<html>
<body>

<h1>Welcome</h1>

Here are the things you can do:<br>
<a href="complain.jsp">Complain</a><br>
<a href="checkstocks.jsp">Check Your Stocks</a><br>
<a href="clock.jsp">Look At The Clock</a><br>
<rc:require-role role="manager">
    <a href="fire.jsp">Fire Someone At Random</a><br>
    <a href="meeting.jsp">Call A 10-Hour Meeting</a><br>
</rc:require-role>
</body>
</html>
```


Listing 31.6 shows the rolecheck.tld file used to define the custom tag library.

Listing 31.6 Source Code for rolecheck.tld

```
<?xml version="1.0"?>
<!DOCTYPE taglib
    PUBLIC "-//Sun Microsystems, Inc.//DTD JSP Tag Library 1.1//EN"
    "http://java.sun.com/j2ee/dtds/web-jsptaglibrary_1_1.dtd">

<taglib>
    <tlibversion>1.0</tlibversion>
    <jspversion>1.1</jspversion>
    <shortname>rolecheck</shortname>
    <uri></uri>
    <info>
        A tag to require a specific authentication role for its body
    </info>

    <tag>
        <name>require-role</name>
        <tagclass>RequireRoleTag</tagclass>
    </tag>
</taglib>
```

Listing 31.7 shows the web.xml file that describes the application.

LISTING 31.7 web.xml **FILE FOR** rolecheck **APPLICATION**

```
<!DOCTYPE web-app PUBLIC "-//Sun Microsystems, Inc.//DTD Web
Application 2.2//EN" "http://java.sun.com/j2ee/dtds/web-app_2_2.dtd">
<web-app>
    <display-name>authtest</display-name>
    <description>A test of authentication</description>
    <taglib>
        <taglib-uri>/rolecheck</taglib-uri>
        <taglib-location>/WEB-INF/tld/rolecheck.tld</taglib-location>
    </taglib>
    <security-constraint>
        <web-resource-collection>
            <web-resource-name>Test</web-resource-name>
            <url-pattern>/*</url-pattern>
            <http-method>GET</http-method>
            <http-method>POST</http-method>
        </web-resource-collection>
        <user-data-constraint>
            <transport-guarantee>NONE</transport-guarantee>
        </user-data-constraint>
        <auth-constraint>
            <role-name>manager</role-name>
        </auth-constraint>
    </security-constraint>
    <login-config>
        <auth-method>BASIC</auth-method>
    </login-config>
</web-app>
```

USING CLIENT CERTIFICATES FOR AUTHENTICATION

There are at least two ways to use client certificates for authentication, but only one is likely to be supported by most servlet engines. The safest way to do certification authentication is to set the authentication method in the `<auth-method>` tag to `CLIENT-CERT`.

After the client has been authenticated, you can access the `java.security.Principal` object that represents the user by calling `getUserPrincipal`.

Note

Because certificate authentication is rarely used in typical applications, you might have difficulty finding a servlet engine that supports certificate authentication.

Your second option is to not use the normal authentication mechanism and go back to checking authentication manually, like you did in Chapter 5. If you use an SSL-enabled servlet engine, you might be able to access the client's certificate by accessing the `javax.servlet.request.X509Certificate` attribute in the `request` object.

The idea is that you keep a database of valid certificate numbers and when a user accesses your site, you check the certificate number against the list of valid numbers. If the numbers match, you allow the user in. Because a trusted certificate authority digitally signs the certificates, it is almost impossible to forge a certificate.

Listing 31.5 shows a segment of code that accesses the client's certificate.

LISTING 31.5 CODE TO ACCESS A CLIENT CERTIFICATE

```
    X509Certificate cert = (X509Certificate) request.
        GetAttribute("javax.servlet.request.X509Certificate");

    if (cert != null)
    {
        String serialNumber = cert.getSerialNumber().toString();
        String issuer = cert.getIssuerDN().getName();

// validate the serialNumber/issuer against a valid list here...
    }
```

The serial number alone is not necessarily unique. The serial number is only required to be unique for a single certificate authority. For extra safety, you should check both the serial number and the name of the certificate issuer to make sure that you have the correct certificate.

TROUBLESHOOTING

AUTHENTICATION PROBLEMS

Why doesn't the servlet engine prompt me for authentication information?

Most likely it's because the servlet engine doesn't support the kind of authentication you want. If the servlet engine doesn't support authentication, you might still be able to use the Web server's authentication if the servlet engine is just acting as a plug-in for a Web server like Apache or Netscape. Another possibility is that even though you changed the servlet configuration to require authentication, you might have forgotten to restart the servlet engine to pick up the changes.

CERTIFICATE PROBLEMS

Why doesn't the servlet engine pass me the certificate information when I use SSL?

Very few servlet engines support the certificate attribute. The Java Web Server from Sun does, but as of August 2000, neither JRun, ServletExec, Tomcat, or Resin support it. When the servlet engine acts as a plug-in to a Web server, you are less likely to get the certificate information because the Web server probably isn't passing the information to the servlet engine in the first place.

CHAPTER 32

XML Syntax for JSP

In this chapter

In Chapter 24, "Creating an XML Application," you learned how to create an XML page from a Java Server Page. The JSP specification includes an interesting syntax alternative to the typical `<% %>` tags you have been using. This alternate syntax allows you to create Java Server Pages that are XML documents to begin with. That is, they are already XML documents before they are parsed.

Although that might sound interesting, when you see the XML syntax, you'll realize that it's not an efficient way to create Java Server Pages. The syntax is cumbersome and difficult to read. The thing to remember is, although the syntax is cumbersome for you, it's incredibly easy for a program to read. There are dozens of XML parsers available on the Internet, and every one of them can read a JSP in its XML form. If you wanted to read a JSP file in the original JSP syntax, you would have a hard time finding a JSP parser that wasn't tightly integrated into a JSP engine.

Now you're probably wondering why you would even care about parsing a JSP outside of a JSP engine. If you're writing a tool for creating and editing Java Server Pages, it's much easier for you to read and write XML than it is for you to parse the regular JSP syntax. That's really the key to the XML syntax for JSP—it's not for human consumption. Still, it's good to know, especially if you want to write a program to create and edit Java Server Pages.

THE XML JSP SYNTAX

When you step back and look at the various parts of Java Server Pages, you realize that there are really only a few special syntax elements. There are four basic JSP elements: `<%`, `<%=`, `<%!`, and `<%@`. The first three elements contain Java code. The last one contains JSP directives.

Mapping these elements into XML is simple. Table 32.1 shows the XML equivalents for each JSP element.

TABLE 32.1 XML EQUIVALENTS FOR JSP ELEMENTS

JSP Element	XML Element
`<%`	`<jsp:scriptlet>`
`<%=`	`<jsp:expression>`
`<%!`	`<jsp:declaration>`
`<%@`	`<jsp:directive>`

The `<jsp:directive>` tag requires a little more explanation. All the JSP directives except for the `taglib` directive can be rewritten with the `<jsp:directive>` tag. For each directive, you append `.directivename` to the end of the XML tag name and then include the JSP attributes in the tag as XML attributes.

For example, take the following JSP directive:

```
<%@ page language="java" import="java.util.*" %>
```

You append `.page` to the end of `jsp:directive` to get a tag name of `<jsp:directive.page>`. Then, you include the JSP attributes as XML attributes to get the following XML tag:

```
<jsp:directive.page language="java" import="java.util.*"/>
```

In keeping with the XML standard of having a single body tag that encompasses the entire document, you must enclose the entire document with a `<jsp:root> </jsp:root>` tag pair. You must include the JSP XML namespace in the `<jsp:root>` tag like this:

```
<jsp:root xmlns:jsp=
    "http://java.sun.com/products/jsp/dtd/jsp_1_0.dtd">
```

Remember that the `taglib` directive is the one directive that doesn't map to a `<jsp:directive>`. When you think about it, a `taglib` directive defines the equivalent of an XML namespace. That is, it defines a specific prefix for a set of tags and a URI indicating where to get the tag definitions. Every `taglib` directive in a JSP becomes an `xmlns` declaration in the `<jsp:root>` tag. For example, the following `taglib` declaration

```
<%@ taglib uri="http://usingjsp.wutka.com/taglibs/test"
    prefix="test" %>
```

causes the `<jsp:root>` tag to look like this:

```
<jsp:root xmlns:jsp=
    "http://java.sun.com/products/jsp/dtd/jsp_1_0.dtd"
    xmlns:test=" http://usingjsp.wutka.com/taglibs/test">
```

Part V Ch 32

To round things out, here is the typical XML header information for an XML JSP page:

```
<?xml version="1.0">
<!DOCTYPE root PUBLIC "-//Sun Microsystems Inc.//DTD
➥JavaServer Pages Version 1.1//EN"
    "http://java.sun.com/products/jsp/dtd/jspcore_1_0.dtd">
```

The HelloWorld JSP in XML

Listing 32.1 shows the famous HelloWorld Java Server Page in pure XML syntax.

Listing 32.1 Source Code for `HelloWorld.jsp`

```
<?xml version="1.0"?>
<!DOCTYPE root PUBLIC "-//Sun Microsystems Inc.//DTD JavaServer Pages Version
1.1//EN"
    "http://java.sun.com/products/jsp/dtd/jspcore_1_0.dtd">
<jsp:root xmlns:jsp="http://java.sun.com/products/jsp/dtd/jsp_1_1.dtd">
    <jsp:directive.page language="java"/>

    <jsp:scriptlet>
        out.println("<html><body><h1>Hello World!</h1></body></html>");
    </jsp:scriptlet>
</jsp:root>
```

TRANSLATING XML JSP SYNTAX

Not all JSP engines support the XML syntax for Java. Resin supports it, but can't handle `<![CDATA[` tags embedded in the page. JRun doesn't like the `xmlns:jsp` specifier in the `<jsp:root>` tag. Because XML is easy to parse and because there are so few changes to make to map the XML JSP syntax to the classic JSP syntax, it's simple to make a Java program that reads in the XML file and writes out the classic JSP version.

You can use the translation program for cases where your JSP engine doesn't handle the XML syntax but you still need to use it. Just translate the XML files into the classic syntax and them give them to your JSP engine. As more developers demand support for the XML syntax, you should see an improvement in the support provided by the various vendors.

Listing 32.2 shows the `XMLToJSP.java` class that performs the translation from XML to classic JSP syntax.

LISTING 32.2 SOURCE CODE FOR `XMLToJSP.java`

```
import javax.xml.parsers.*;
import org.w3c.dom.*;
import org.xml.sax.*;
import java.io.*;

/** Converts an XML file with JSP syntax into a regular JSP file */

public class XMLToJSP implements EntityResolver
{
    public XMLToJSP()
    {
    }

/** Looks for references to the JSP DTD which Sun has not put on its
 *  Web site even though it's in the JSP spec. Substitutes a local
 *  copy of the JSP DTD. */
public InputSource resolveEntity(String publicId, String systemId)
    {
        if (systemId.startsWith("http://java.sun.com/products/jsp/dtd"))
        {
            try
            {
                return new InputSource(new FileReader("jsp.dtd"));
            }
            catch (IOException exc)
            {
                exc.printStackTrace();
            }
            return null;
        }
        else
        {
            return null;
        }
    }
```

```
    public static void main(String[] args)
    {
        if (args.length < 1)
        {
            System.out.println("Please supply an XML file");
        }

// Figure out the root name of the file
// read from zzz.xml, write to zzz.jsp
        String xmlFileName = args[0];
        if (!xmlFileName.toLowerCase().endsWith(".xml"))
        {
            xmlFileName = xmlFileName + ".xml";
        }
        String jspFileName = xmlFileName.substring(0,
            xmlFileName.indexOf(".xml"))+".jsp";

        try
        {
// Create a DocumentBuilderFactory
            DocumentBuilderFactory fact =
                DocumentBuilderFactory.newInstance();

// Create a Document Builder to parse the XML file
            DocumentBuilder builder = fact.newDocumentBuilder();

// Set up an entity resolver to weed out reference to the
// phantom JSP DTD mentioned in the JSP spec
            builder.setEntityResolver(new XMLToJSP());

// Open the XML input file
            BufferedReader xmlFile =
                new BufferedReader(new FileReader(
                    xmlFileName));

// Parse the input file
            Document doc = builder.parse(
                new InputSource(xmlFile));

            xmlFile.close();

            if (doc == null)
            {
                    System.out.println("No document available");
                    System.exit(1);
            }

            PrintWriter out = new PrintWriter(
                new FileWriter(jspFileName));

// Write out the JSP file from the XML document object
            writeJSPChildren(doc, out);

            out.close();

        } catch (Exception exc) {
```

LISTING 32.2 CONTINUED

```
            exc.printStackTrace();
        }
    }

    public static void writeJSP(Node n, PrintWriter out)
    {
// If this is a text node, print out its value
        if ((n.getNodeType() == Node.CDATA_SECTION_NODE) ||
            (n.getNodeType() == Node.TEXT_NODE))
        {
            CharacterData textNode = (CharacterData) n;
            out.print(textNode.getData());
            return;
        }
// Ignore everything else that isn't an element or a document
        else if ((n.getNodeType() != Node.ELEMENT_NODE) &&
                (n.getNodeType() != Node.DOCUMENT_NODE))
        {
            return;
        }

// Get the name of the tag
        String nodeName = n.getNodeName();

// For JSP root, look for xmlns tags and create <%@ taglib directives
        if (nodeName.equals("jsp:root"))
        {
            NamedNodeMap attrs = n.getAttributes();

            int numAttrs = attrs.getLength();

            for (int i=0; i < numAttrs; i++)
            {
                Node attr = attrs.item(i);

                if (attr.getNodeName().startsWith("xmlns:"))
                {
                    String ns = attr.getNodeName().substring(6);
                    if (ns.equals("jsp")) continue;

                    out.println("<%@ taglib uri=\""+attr.getNodeValue()+
                        "\" prefix=\""+ns+"\" %>");
                }
            }

            writeJSPChildren(n, out);
        }

// For a directive, get the directive name then print out the attributes
        else if (nodeName.startsWith("jsp:directive."))
        {
            out.print("<%@ "+nodeName.substring(14));
            NamedNodeMap attrs = n.getAttributes();

            int numAttrs = attrs.getLength();
```

```
            for (int i=0; i < numAttrs; i++)
            {
                Node attr = attrs.item(i);

                out.print(" "+attr.getNodeName()+"=\""+
                    attr.getNodeValue()+"\"");
            }
            out.println(" %>");
        }
// For a scriptlet, just print out the <% %> tags
        else if (nodeName.equals("jsp:scriptlet"))
        {
            out.println("<%");
            writeJSPChildren(n, out);
            out.println("%>");
        }
// For an expression, just print out the <%= %> tags
        else if (nodeName.equals("jsp:expression"))
        {
            out.print("<%= ");
            writeJSPChildren(n, out);
            out.print(" %>");
        }
// For a declaration, just print out the <%! %> tags
        else if (nodeName.equals("jsp:declaration"))
        {
            out.println("<%!");
            writeJSPChildren(n, out);
            out.println("%>");
        }
// For anything else, assume it's part of the document and print it out
        else
        {
            out.print("<"+nodeName);
            NamedNodeMap attrs = n.getAttributes();

            int numAttrs = attrs.getLength();

            for (int i=0; i < numAttrs; i++)
            {
                Node attr = attrs.item(i);

                out.print(" "+attr.getNodeName()+"=\""+
                    attr.getNodeValue()+"\"");
            }
            out.print(">");
            writeJSPChildren(n, out);
            out.print("</"+nodeName+">");
        }
    }

// Write out the elements contained within a particular node
    public static void writeJSPChildren(Node n, PrintWriter out)
    {
        NodeList children = n.getChildNodes();
```

LISTING 32.2 CONTINUED

```
            int numChildren = children.getLength();

            for (int i=0; i < numChildren; i++)
            {
                writeJSP(children.item(i), out);
            }
        }
    }
```

The XMLToJSP program uses the JAXP parsing API from Sun. One of the problems you might encounter with the XML syntax for JSP is that the DTD for the XML syntax is not available from Sun even though a URL for it is in the Java specification. To combat the problem (by the time you are reading this, Sun might have finally corrected the problem), the XMLToJSP program substitutes a local copy of the DTD when it finds a reference to the DTD for JSP. Listing 32.3 shows the local copy of the DTD used by XMLToJSP.

If you are having trouble running the XMLToJSP program, see "Running the XMLToJSP Program" in the "Troubleshooting" section at the end of this chapter.

LISTING 32.3 SOURCE CODE FOR jsp.dtd

```
<!ENTITY % jsp.body "(#PCDATA
        |jsp:directive.page
        |jsp:directive.include
        |jsp:scriptlet
        |jsp:declaration
        |jsp:expression
        |jsp:include
        |jsp:forward
        |jsp:useBean
        |jsp:setProperty
        |jsp:getProperty
        |jsp:plugin
        |jsp:fallback
        |jsp:params
        |jsp:param)*
        ">

<!ELEMENT jsp:useBean %jsp.body;>

<!ATTLIST jsp:useBean
        id ID #REQUIRED
        class CDATA #REQUIRED
        scope (page|session|request|application) "page">

<!ELEMENT jsp:setProperty EMPTY>

<!ATTLIST jsp:setProperty
        name IDREF #REQUIRED
        property CDATA #REQUIRED
        value CDATA #IMPLIED
        param CDATA #IMPLIED>
```

```
<!ELEMENT jsp:getProperty EMPTY>

<!ATTLIST jsp:getProperty
        name IDREF #REQUIRED
        property CDATA #REQUIRED>

<!ELEMENT jsp:include EMPTY>

<!ATTLIST jsp:include
        flush (true|false) "false"
        page CDATA #REQUIRED>

<!ELEMENT jsp:forward EMPTY>

<!ATTLIST jsp:forward
        page CDATA #REQUIRED>

<!ELEMENT jsp:scriptlet (#PCDATA)>

<!ELEMENT jsp:declaration (#PCDATA)>

<!ELEMENT jsp:expression (#PCDATA)>

<!ELEMENT jsp:directive.page EMPTY>

<!ATTLIST jsp:directive.page
        language CDATA "java"
        extends CDATA #IMPLIED
        contentType CDATA "text/html; ISO-8859-1"
        import CDATA #IMPLIED
        session (true|false) "true"
        buffer CDATA "8kb"
        autoFlush (true|false) "true"
        isThreadSafe (true|false) "true"
        info CDATA #IMPLIED
        errorPage CDATA #IMPLIED
        isErrorPage (true|false) "false">

<!ELEMENT jsp:directive.include EMPTY>

<!ATTLIST jsp:directive.include
        file CDATA #REQUIRED>

<!ELEMENT jsp:useBean %jsp.body;>

<!ATTLIST jsp:useBean
        id ID #REQUIRED
        class CDATA #REQUIRED
        scope (page|session|request|application) "page">

<!ELEMENT jsp:setProperty EMPTY>

<!ATTLIST jsp:setProperty
        name IDREF #REQUIRED
        property CDATA #REQUIRED
        value CDATA #IMPLIED
        param CDATA #IMPLIED>
```

LISTING 32.3 CONTINUED

```
<!ELEMENT jsp:getProperty EMPTY>

<!ATTLIST jsp:getProperty
        name IDREF #REQUIRED
        property CDATA #REQUIRED>

<!ELEMENT jsp:include EMPTY>
<!ATTLIST jsp:include
        flush (true|false) "false"
        page CDATA #REQUIRED>

<!ELEMENT jsp:forward EMPTY>

<!ATTLIST jsp:forward
        page CDATA #REQUIRED>

<!ELEMENT jsp:scriptlet (#PCDATA)>

<!ELEMENT jsp:declaration (#PCDATA)>

<!ELEMENT jsp:expression (#PCDATA)>

<!ELEMENT jsp:directive.page EMPTY>

<!ATTLIST jsp:directive.page
        language CDATA "java"
        extends CDATA #IMPLIED
        contentType CDATA "text/html; ISO-8859-1"
        import CDATA #IMPLIED
        session (true|false) "true"
        buffer CDATA "8kb"
        autoFlush (true|false) "true"
        isThreadSafe (true|false) "true"
        info CDATA #IMPLIED
        errorPage CDATA #IMPLIED
        isErrorPage (true|false) "false">

<!ELEMENT jsp:directive.include EMPTY>

<!ATTLIST jsp:directive.include
        file CDATA #REQUIRED>

<!ELEMENT jsp:root %jsp.body;>

<!ATTLIST jsp:root
        xmlns:jsp CDATA #FIXED "http://java.sun.com/products/jsp/dtd/jsp_1_0.dtd">
```

TROUBLESHOOTING

RUNNING XML-JSP FILES DIRECTLY

How do I get my JSP engine to parse my XML file as a JSP?

Unfortunately, since the XML-JSP syntax is only optional, most JSP engines have chosen not to support it. If your file ends with .jsp instead of .xml and the JSP engine doesn't parse it correctly, you can assume that your JSP engine doesn't support the alternate syntax.

RUNNING THE `XMLToJSP` PROGRAM

Why do I get a `ClassNotFoundException` when I try to run `XMLToJSP`?

You must have the JAXP XML parser from Sun installed on your system. You must either include parser.jar and jaxp.jar in your CLASSPATH variable, specify them with the –classpath option at runtime, or copy them to the jre/lib/ext directory where your Java Virtual Machine is installed.

APPENDIX A

JSP Syntax and API Reference

In this appendix

JSP Syntax

The basic JSP syntax is the same no matter what scripting language you are using. If you are familiar with Active Server Pages, the JSP syntax should look very familiar.

Code Scriptlets

The `<% %>` tags enclose any number of lines that are interpreted as executable code. Any code within the `<% %>` tags is placed in the main service method of the JSP.

Example:

```
<%
   for (int i=0; i < 10; i++)
   {
        out.println("Hello");
   }
%>
```

Expressions

The `<%= %>` tags enclose an expression whose value is inserted into the output stream.

Example:

```
Welcome back, <%= getFirstName() %>!
```

Declarations

The `<%! %>` tags enclose a series of declarations that are placed outside the main service method.

Example:

```
<%!
    public String getFirstName()
    {
        Person pers = (Person) session.getAttribute("person");
        return pers.firstName;
    }
%>
```

Comments

The `<%— —%>` tags enclose comment text. The JSP compiler completely ignores the comment text. Comments cannot be nested. After the JSP compiler sees `—%>`, the comment is ended, no matter how many times it has seen `<%—`.

Example:

```
<%—
   This is the section where the personnel
   records are displayed in an HTML table.
—%>
```

DIRECTIVES

The `<%@ %>` tags enclose a JSP directive. A directive is an instruction to the JSP compiler and does not contain any code. The format for a directive tag is

```
<%@ directive attribute="value" attribute="value" … %>
```

THE page DIRECTIVE

The page directive specifies different options specific to the JSP page. The allowable attributes for the page directive are shown in Table A.1.

TABLE A.1 page DIRECTIVE ATTRIBUTES

Attribute Name	Attribute Value
autoflush	true if buffer should be flushed automatically, false otherwise. The default value is true.
buffer	none for no buffering or *nnn*kb to specify the buffer size in kilobytes. If buffer=none, autoFlush must be false. The default value is 8kb.
contentType	The MIME type for the response. Default is text/html.
errorPage	The URL of the page to execute if an error occurs in this page.
extends	Defines an alternate superclass for the servlet generated by this JSP.
import	A list of Java packages to import. You can either list the packages separated by commas or use multiple import attributes.
info	A string describing the JSP. When the JSP is compiled into a servlet, the info string is returned by the servlet's getServletInfo method.
isErrorPage	true if this page can be used as an error page by another JSP. The default value is false.
isThreadSafe	true if this page can be executed by multiple threads at once. If false, only one thread at a time can execute the page. The default value is true.
language java.	Specifies the scripting language used in the JSP. The default value is
session	true if this page needs to store or retrieve data from the session object. If false, this JSP can't access the session object. The default value is true.

Example:

```
<%@ page language="java" import="java.util.*" %>
```

THE include DIRECTIVE

The include directive inserts an external file into the JSP at compile time. The only attribute allowed for import is file:

```
<%@ import file="header.html" %>
```

APP
A

THE `taglib` DIRECTIVE

The `taglib` directive defines a tag library used by this JSP. The `uri` attribute gives the location of the tag library itself and the `prefix` attribute specifies a prefix to be used in front of each tag from the library.

Example:

```
<%@ taglib uri="/tags" prefix="mytag" %>
```

BUILT-IN OBJECTS

Every JSP has access to several built-in Java objects. These built-in objects appear as Java variables within scriptlets (`<% %>`) and expressions (`<%= %>`) but not declarations (`<%! %>`). Table A.2 shows the built-in objects.

TABLE A.2 BUILT-IN JSP OBJECTS

Object	Java Class	Purpose
`application`	`javax.servlet.ServletContext`	Contains data shared by all servlets within a particular application.
`config`	`javax.servlet.ServletConfig`	The configuration information for this JSP.
`exception`	`java.lang.Throwable`	The error or exception that caused this error page to be invoked.
`out`	`javax.servlet.jsp.JspWriter`	The `Writer` used to send a response to the browser.
`page`	`java.lang.Object`	The current Java Server Page. In Java, it's the same as the `this` variable. Other scripting languages might not support `this`, so `page` represents the equivalent for those other languages.
`pageContext`	`javax.servlet.jsp.PageContext`	Contains references to most of the objects a JSP might need and also has some useful utilities such as `include` and `forward`.
`request`	`javax.servlet.http.HttpServletRequest`	Stores information about the incoming request, including form variables.
`response`	`javax.servlet.http.HttpServletResponse`	Contains information about the response, including header variables, cookies, and content type.
`session`	`javax.servlet.http.HttpSession`	Contains data associated with a particular browser session.

ACTIONS

Java Server Pages can use certain built-in tags, referred to as *actions*, to perform various tasks. Between the built-in tags and the tag library extensions, you can almost eliminate code from a JSP.

Be sure to follow the XML tag rules as far as always having a closing tag, or using `/>` to terminate a tag with no closing tag.

`<jsp:forward>`

Changes which JSP is being displayed. The `page` attribute is the page being forwarded to. The current JSP's buffer is cleared and the page is replaced with the one being forwarded to. A JSP can forward to another JSP, a servlet, or any other kind of page (HTML, XML, and so on).

Example:

```
<jsp:forward page="newpage.jsp"/>
```

`<jsp:getProperty>`

Retrieves a property from a bean and inserts it into the output stream. The `name` attribute is the name of the bean whose property is being retrieved. The `property` attribute is the name of the bean property to retrieve.

Example:

```
Welcome back, <jsp:getProperty name="person"
    property="firstName"/>!
```

`<jsp:include>`

Calls another JSP, servlet, or static page and includes its output in the current JSP. The `page` attribute is the name of the other page that is being included.

Example:

```
<jsp:include page="menu.jsp">
```

`<jsp:param>`

Passes additional parameters inside the `<jsp:forward>`, `<jsp:include>`, and `<jsp:plugin>` tags. The `name` attribute specifies the name of the parameter, while the `value` attribute specifies the parameter's value. During an `include` or a `forward`, these parameters look like form variables that were passed in from the browser. The `<jsp:param>` tag must appear between the opening and closing tags for the tag it is being used with.

Example:

```
<jsp:forward page="register.jsp">
   <jsp:param name="passwordRequired" value="true"/>
   <jsp:param name="registrationType" value="guest"/>
</jsp:forward>
```

<jsp:plugin>

Embeds a Java applet or bean into the output page. The <jsp:plugin> tag automatically detects the browser type and generates whatever HTML is necessary to use the Java plug-in as a runtime environment for the applet or bean. Use the <jsp:fallback> tag to insert text into the page when a plugin can't be loaded (for older or incompatible browsers) .

Table A.3 shows the attributes supported by the <jsp:plugin> tag.

TABLE A.3 <jsp:plugin> ATTRIBUTES

Attribute	Purpose
type	bean or applet, the type of object in the plugin (required)
code	The class name for the plugin object (required)
codebase	The location of the class object and supporting objects (required)
align	HTML align attribute
archive	The archive file containing the object's code
height	HTML height attribute
hspace	HTML hspace attribute
iepluginurl	The location of the JRE Plugin for IE (only used to override the default)
jreversion	The minimum version of JRE required by the plugin object (default is "1.1")
name	HTML name attribute
nspluginurl	The location of the JRE Plugin for Netscape (only used to override the default)
vspace	HTML vspace attribute
width	HTML width attribute

Example:

```
<jsp:plugin type="applet" code="Buzzy.class"
    codebase="/buzzy">
   <jsp:param name="foreground" value="yellow"/>
   <jsp:param name="background" value="black"/>
   <jsp:fallback>
      Sorry, Buzzy is afraid to fly in this browser.
   </jsp:fallback>
</jsp:plugin>
```

<jsp:setProperty>

Sets a property in a bean, possibly copying the property value from a form variable. The name attribute is the name of the bean whose property is being set. The property attribute is the name of the property to be set. If the property value is "*", the tag loops through all the form parameters, copying any that match the name of a property in the bean. The param attribute is the name of the form variable containing the value to be stored in the property.

The `value` attribute is the value to be stored. You cannot specify both a `param` and a `value` for the same property.

Example:

```
<jsp:setProperty name="Person" property="name" value="Kaitlynn"/>
```

`<jsp:useBean>`

Defines a bean for use in the JSP, creating the bean only if it doesn't already exist. The `id` attribute specifies the name that this bean will be known by within the JSP. The `scope` attribute specifies the scope of the bean (`page`, `request`, `session`, `attribute`). The default scope is `page`. If the bean already exists in a particular scope, no other attributes are necessary. Otherwise, you must specify one of three combinations:

- `class` and `type`
- `beanName` and `type`
- `type`

The `type` attribute is the type of the JSP variable that refers to the bean. It must either be the same class as the bean, or a superclass of the bean (you must be able to assign the bean to a variable of that type). The `class` attribute is the actual class name of the bean. You use `type` and `class` together in situations in which you want an abstract reference to an object, such as `Person`, and you need to create a concrete instance, such as `Employee`. The `beanName` allows you to instantiate a bean using the `java.beans.Beans.instantiate` method.

XML Syntax

JSP supports an alternate XML-compliant syntax. Although the syntax is harder to read and write, it is very machine friendly and is intended for use in automated tools.

Root Document

Every XML page requires a single root document tag. The root tag for JSP is `<jsp:root>`. In the `<jsp:root>` tag you must include a reference to the JSP namespace.

Example:

```
<jsp:root xmlns:jsp="http://java.sun.com/products/jsp/dtd/jsp_1_1.dtd">
```

Code Scriptlets

The `<jsp:scriptlet> </jsp:scriptlet>` tags enclose any number of lines that are interpreted as executable code. Any code within the `<jsp:scriptlet> </jsp:scriptlet>` tags is placed in the main service method of the JSP.

Example:

```
<jsp:scriptlet>
   for (int i=0; i < 10; i++)
   {
```

```
        out.println("Hello");
    }
</jsp:scriptlet>
```

EXPRESSIONS

The `<jsp:expression> </jsp:expression>` tags enclose an expression whose value is inserted into the output stream.

Example:

```
Welcome back,
<jsp:expression> getFirstName() </jsp:expression>!
```

DECLARATIONS

The `<jsp:declaration> </jsp:declaration>` tags enclose a series of declarations that are placed outside the main service method.

Example:

```
<jsp:declaration>
    public String getFirstName()
    {
        Person pers = (Person) session.getAttribute("person");
        return pers.firstName;
    }
</jsp:declaration>
```

DIRECTIVES

The `<jsp:directive>` tag specifies a JSP directive. A directive is an instruction to the JSP compiler and does not contain any code. The format for the `<jsp:directive>` tag is

```
<jsp:directive.directive attribute="value" attribute="value" ... />
```

The names of the directives and their attribute values are the same as for the `<%@ %>` tag pair, except for the `taglib` directive, which is specified as part of the root document tag.

TAG LIBRARIES

In the JSP XML syntax, tag libraries are specified as additional namespaces in the `<jsp:root>` tag. Take the prefix for the tag library and put `xmlns:` in front of it for the attribute name, and then the value is the URI of the tag library.

Example:

```
<jsp:root
    xmlns:jsp="http://java.sun.com/products/jsp/dtd/jsp_1_1.dtd"
    xmlns:mytag="/mytaglibrary">
```

JAVA SERVER PAGES API

Because Java Server Pages eventually become servlets, most of the core classes used by JSPs are in the servlet API. The JSP API does include some special utility classes, as well as support for tag libraries.

javax.servlet.jsp

The `javax.servlet.jsp` package contains support classes for Java Server Pages. Although most of the classes you use from within a Java Server Page are in the `javax.servlet` and `javax.servlet.http` packages, there are a few classes like `PageContext` that you may use frequently.

INTERFACES

`HttpJspPage` Extends: `JspPage`

The `HttpPage` interface defines the methods that an HTTP Java Server Page must implement. Almost all current implementations of JSP only support HTTP. In the future, as wireless protocols like WAP become more prevalent, you might see other interfaces like `WAPPage`.

- `_jspService`

  ```
  public void _jspService(HttpServletRequest request
                          HttpServletResponse response)
      throws ServletException, java.io.IOException
  ```

  This is the main service method for the JSP. It contains any scriptlets and expressions embedded in the page as well as any support code needed to display the JSP. This method is automatically generated by the JSP compiler. You should *never* implement this method yourself.

`JspPage` **EXTENDS:** `Servlet`

The `JspPage` interface defines two of the three methods required of all Java Server Page servlets. The third method, `_jspService`, must be defined by a protocol-specific version of this interface, such as `HttpJspPage`.

- `jspDestroy`

  ```
  public void jspDestroy()
  ```

  Invoked when the JSP is about to be destroyed. Put any necessary cleanup code here (release database connections, close open files, and so on).

- `jspInit`

  ```
  public void jspInit()
  ```

  Invoked when the JSP is initialized.

CLASSES

`JspEngineInfo` The `JspEngineInfo` class returns information about the current JSP engine. There are very few methods in this class that are useful to a JSP author. Most of them are used by the JSP engine itself.

- `getSpecificationVersion`

  `public String getSpecificationVersion()`

  Returns the version of the JSP specification implemented by this JSP engine. The specification number is a series of numbers separated by periods. It might be of the form `"1.1"` or a long series of numbers like `"1.1.6.5.4.3.2"`.

`JspFactory` The `JspFactory` class implements a number of utility methods used mostly by the JSP engine for initializing a JSP.

- `getDefaultFactory`

  `public static JspFactory getDefaultFactory()`

  Returns the default JSP factory for this implementation.

- `getEngineInfo`

  `public JspEngineInfo getEngineInfo()`

  Returns the `JspEngineInfo` object that describes the current JSP implementation.

- `getPageContext`

  ```
  public PageContext getPageContext(Servlet servlet,
                                    ServletRequest request,
                                    ServletResponse response,
                                    String errorPageURL,
                                    boolean needsSession,
                                    int buffer,
                                    boolean autoFlush)
  ```

  Creates a new `PageContext` object. This method is typically used only by the JSP engine and placed in the `_jspService` method of the JSP's servlet.

- `releasePageContext`

  `public void releasePageContext(PageContext context)`

  Releases a page context that had been allocated by `getPageContext`. This method is usually only used by the JSP engine and is placed near the end of the `_jspService` method of the JSP's servlet.

- `setDefaultFactory`

  `public void setDefaultFactory(JspFactory factory)`

  Sets the default `JspFactory` for this JSP implementation. This method should only be called by the JSP engine itself.

`JspWriter`

- `DEFAULT_BUFFER`

  `public static final int DEFAULT_BUFFER`

A constant indicating that buffering should be on and that the buffer size should be the default size. This constant is used internally and is not used as an argument or return value for any of the public methods of `JspWriter`.

- `NO_BUFFER`

  `public static final int NO_BUFFER`

  A constant indicating that buffering should be off. This constant is used internally and is not used as an argument or return value for any of the public methods of `JspWriter`.

- `UNBOUNDED_BUFFER`

  `public static final int UNBOUNDED_BUFFER`

  A constant indicating that buffering should be on and that the buffer should be allowed to grow without bound. This constant is used internally and is not used as an argument or return value for any of the public methods of `JspWriter`.

- `clear`

  `public void clear() throws java.io.IOException`

  Clears the contents of the output buffer. If the buffer has already been flushed, this method throws an `IOException`. The exception is useful in cases where you need to know that data has already been sent back to the browser.

- `clearBuffer`

  `public void clear() throws java.io.IOException`

  Clears the contents of the output buffer. This method does the same thing as the `clear` method except that it doesn't throw an exception if the buffer has been flushed.

- `close`

  `public void close() throws java.io.IOException`

  Flushes and closes the output stream. Any further flushes or writes to the stream cause an `IOException`. You will not get an exception if you call `close` on a closed stream, however.

- `flush`

  `public void flush() throws java.io.IOException`

  Flushes the output stream, forcing data to be sent back to the browser. This method forces the entire chain of writers or streams to be flushed. If there's any data at all to write to the browser, it will be written when you call `flush`.

- `getBufferSize`

  `public int getBufferSize()`

  Returns the total size of the buffer in bytes. If the writer is unbuffered, this method returns `0`.

- `getRemaining`

  `public int getRemaining()`

  Returns the number of unused bytes remaining in the buffer. If the writer is unbuffered, this method returns `0`.

- `isAutoFlush`

  ```
  public boolean isAutoFlush()
  ```

  Returns `true` if the buffer will be flushed whenever it is full.

- `newLine`

  ```
  public void newLine() throws java.io.IOException
  ```

  Writes a newline to the output buffer.

- `print`

  ```
  public void print(boolean b) throws java.io.IOException
  public void print(char ch) throws java.io.IOException
  public void print(char[] chars) throws java.io.IOException
  public void print(double d) throws java.io.IOException
  public void print(float f) throws java.io.IOException
  public void print(int i) throws java.io.IOException
  public void print(long l) throws java.io.IOException
  public void print(Object ob) throws java.io.IOException
  public void print(String s) throws java.io.IOException
  ```

  Prints an item to the output stream.

- `println`

  ```
  public void println(boolean b) throws java.io.IOException
  public void println(char ch) throws java.io.IOException
  public void println(char[] chars) throws java.io.IOException
  public void println(double d) throws java.io.IOException
  public void println(float f) throws java.io.IOException
  public void println(int i) throws java.io.IOException
  public void println(long l) throws java.io.IOException
  public void println(Object ob) throws java.io.IOException
  public void println(String s) throws java.io.IOException
  ```

  Prints an item to the output stream and appends a newline.

`PageContext` The `PageContext` class is a utility used by Java Server Pages to access most of the built-in objects.

- `APPLICATION`

  ```
  public static final String APPLICATION
  ```

  Internal name used to refer to the `application` object.

- `APPLICATION_SCOPE`

  ```
  public static final int APPLICATION_SCOPE
  ```

  Constant used to refer to attributes with application scope.

- `CONFIG`

  ```
  public static final String CONFIG
  ```

  Internal name used to refer to the `config` object.

- `EXCEPTION`

  ```
  public static final String EXCEPTION
  ```

  Internal name used to refer to the `exception` object.

- `OUT`

  `public static final String OUT`

  Internal name used to refer to the `out` object.

- `PAGE`

  `public static final String PAGE`

  Internal name used to refer to the `page` object.

- `PAGE_SCOPE`

  `public static final int PAGE_SCOPE`

  Constant used to refer to attributes with page scope.

- `PAGECONTEXT`

  `public static final String PAGECONTEXT`

  Internal name used to refer to the page context itself.

- `REQUEST`

  `public static final String REQUEST`

  Internal name used to refer to the `request` object.

- `REQUEST_SCOPE`

  `public static final int REQUEST_SCOPE`

  Constant used to refer to attributes with request scope.

- `RESPONSE`

  `public static final String RESPONSE`

  Internal name used to refer to the `response` object.

- `SESSION`

  `public static final String SESSION`

  Internal name used to refer to the `session` object.

- `SESSION_SCOPE`

  `public static final int SESSION_SCOPE`

  Constant used to refer to attributes with session scope.

- `findAttribute`

  `public Object findAttribute(String name)`

  Searches first through the page scope, then the request scope, then the session scope, and finally the application scope and returns the first attribute with the specified name. If there is no such attribute in any scope, this method returns `null`.

- `forward`

  ```
  public void forward(String relativeURL)
      throws ServletException, java.io.IOException
  ```

  Forwards the current request to the new URL, clearing the current output buffer. If the URL starts with a `"/"`, the URL is interpreted relative to the root directory for this JSP. If the JSP is part of a deployed Web application, the root directory is the root directory for the application. If the JSP is not part of any application, the root directory is usually the root directory for the Web server. If the output buffer has already been flushed, this method should throw an `IOException`.

This method should only be used by a JSP.

- `getAttribute`

  ```
  public Object getAttribute(String name)
  public Object getAttribute(String name, int scope)
  ```

  Searches for an attribute in a particular scope. If no scope is given, `getAttribute` searches the page scope. Use the `PAGE_SCOPE`, `REQUEST_SCOPE`, `SESSION_SCOPE`, and `ATTRIBUTE_SCOPE` constants for the value of the `scope` parameter.

- `getAttributeNamesInScope`

  ```
  public java.util.Enumeration getAttributeNamesInScope(int scope)
  ```

  Returns an enumeration of all the attributes stored with a particular scope. Use the `PAGE_SCOPE`, `REQUEST_SCOPE`, `SESSION_SCOPE`, and `ATTRIBUTE_SCOPE` constants for the value of the `scope` parameter.

- `getAttributesScope`

  ```
  public int getAttributesScope(String name)
  ```

  Returns the scope of the attribute with the specified name. This method first looks in the page scope, then request, session, and application in that order. The value returned will be either `PAGE_SCOPE`, `REQUEST_SCOPE`, `SESSION_SCOPE`, or `ATTRIBUTE_SCOPE`.

- `getException`

  ```
  public Exception getException()
  ```

  Returns the built-in `exception` object.

- `getOut`

  ```
  public JspWriter getOut()
  ```

  Returns the built-in `out` object.

- `getPage`

  ```
  public Object getPage()
  ```

  Returns the built-in `page` object.

- `getRequest`

  ```
  public ServletRequest getRequest()
  ```

  Returns the built-in `request` object.

- `getResponse`

  ```
  public ServletResponse getResponse()
  ```

  Returns the built-in `response` object.

- `getServletConfig`

  ```
  public ServletConfig getServletConfig()
  ```

  Returns the `ServletConfig` object for this page.

- `getServletContext`

  ```
  public ServletContext getServletContext()
  ```

  Returns the `ServletContext` object for this page.

- getSession

```
public HttpSession getSession()
```

Returns the built-in session object.

- handlePageException

```
void handlePageException(Exception exc)
    throws ServletException, java.io.IOException
```

Callback to handle any uncaught exceptions. This method either calls an error-handling page or takes some implementation-defined default action if there is no error-handling page defined.

- include

```
public void include(String relativeURL)
    throws ServletException, java.io.IOException
```

Includes the contents of the specified URL in the current page. The buffer is flushed before the page is included. If the URL starts with a "/", the URL is interpreted relative to the root directory for this JSP. If the JSP is part of a deployed Web application, the root directory is the root directory for the application. If the JSP is not part of any application, the root directory is usually the root directory for the Web server.

This method should only be used by a JSP.

- initialize

```
public void initialize(Servlet servlet,
                       ServletRequest request,
                       ServletResponse response,
                       String errorPageURL,
                       boolean needsSession,
                       int bufferSize,
                       boolean autoFlush)
    throws java.io.IOException, IllegalStateException,
           IllegalArgumentException
```

Initializes this PageContext object. This method is usually called by a JspFactory object and should not be called by a JSP.

- popBody

```
public JspWriter popBody()
```

Returns the previous JspWriter stored on the body content stack. This method is used by the tag extension mechanism.

- pushBody

```
public BodyContent pushBody()
```

Temporarily stores the current JspWriter on a stack and returns a new BodyContent for writing out information from a custom tag.

- release

```
public void release()
```

Frees any resources used by this PageContext. This method should not be called by a JSP.

- `removeAttribute`

  ```
  public Object removeAttribute(String name)
  public Object removeAttribute(String name, int scope)
  ```

  Removes an attribute from a particular scope. If no scope is given, `removeAttribute` searches the page scope. Use the `PAGE_SCOPE`, `REQUEST_SCOPE`, `SESSION_SCOPE`, and `ATTRIBUTE_SCOPE` constants for the value of the `scope` parameter.

- `setAttribute`

  ```
  public Object setAttribute(String name, Object obj)
  public Object setAttribute(String name, Object obj, int scope)
  ```

  Stores an attribute in a particular scope. If no scope is given, `setAttribute` uses the page scope. Use the `PAGE_SCOPE`, `REQUEST_SCOPE`, `SESSION_SCOPE`, and `ATTRIBUTE_SCOPE` constants for the value of the `scope` parameter.

EXCEPTIONS

`JspException` The `JspException` represents an exception known by the JSP engine.

- `JspException Constructor`

  ```
  public JspException()
  public JspException(String message)
  ```

  Constructs a new `JspException` with an optional message.

`JspTagException` The `JspTagException` is used by the tag extension mechanism to tell the JSP that there is an error with the tag. The JSP itself should catch and process these exceptions.

- `JspTagException Constructor`

  ```
  public JspTagException()
  public JspTagException(String message)
  ```

  Constructs a new `JspTagException` with an optional message.

javax.servlet.jsp.tagext

The `javax.servlet.jsp.tagext` package contains classes for creating custom JSP tags. You don't use these classes at all if you aren't creating a custom tag.

INTERFACES

`BodyTag` Extends: `Tag`

The `BodyTag` interface must be implemented by custom tag handlers that want to process body text.

- `EVAL_BODY_TAG`

  ```
  public static final int EVAL_BODY_TAG
  ```

  Constant returned from `doStartTag` and `doAfterBody` to tell the JSP engine that this class wants to interpret the body text.

- `doAfterBody`

  `public int doAfterBody() throws JspException`

  Called by the JSP engine after the tag's body text has been parsed and evaluated. If this method returns `EVAL_BODY_TAG`, the JSP engine re-evaluates the body text (but does not reparse) and calls `doAfterBody` again. When this method returns `SKIP_BODY`, the JSP engine goes on to process the data after the end tag.

- `doInitBody`

  `public void doInitBody() throws JspException`

  Called by the JSP engine to tell the tag handler that the body text is about to be evaluated. This method can perform any necessary initialization.

- `setBodyContent`

  `public void setBodyContent(BodyContent content)`

  Gives the current body content (containing the body text) to this tag handler. If there is no body text, this method isn't called.

`Tag` The `Tag` interface defines the minimum set of methods for a tag handler. Tag handlers that want to process body text must implement `BodyTag`, which extends the `Tag` interface.

- `EVAL_BODY_INCLUDE`

  `public static final int EVAL_BODY_INCLUDE`

  Constant returned by `doStartTag` to tell the JSP engine to include the tag's body text in the output.

- `EVAL_PAGE`

  `public static final int EVAL_PAGE`

  Constant returned by `doEndTag` to tell the JSP engine to continue evaluating the page.

- `SKIP_BODY`

  `public static final int SKIP_BODY`

  Constant returned by `doStartTag` to tell the JSP engine to skip the tag's body text.

- `SKIP_PAGE`

  `public static final int SKIP_PAGE`

  Constant returned by `doEndTag` to tell the JSP engine to skip the rest of the page.

- `doEndTag`

  `public int doEndTag()`

  Called by the JSP engine to tell the tag handler that the engine has finished evaluating the tag. If this method returns `SKIP_PAGE`, the JSP engine will stop processing the page. This method should normally return `EVAL_PAGE` to tell the JSP engine to continue evaluating the page.

- `doStartTag`

  `public int doStartTag()`

  Called by the JSP engine to tell the tag handler that the engine is evaluating the tag. If this method returns `SKIP_BODY`, the JSP engine won't include the tag's body text in the response. If the method returns `EVAL_BODY_TAG`, the tag's body text will be copied to the output stream.

- `getParent`

  `public Tag getParent()`

  Returns the current parent for this tag (the tag this one is contained within). The value is set by `setParent`.

- `release`

  `public void release()`

  Tells the tag handler it is no longer needed and it can release any resources it has allocated (database connections, open files, and so on).

- `setPageContext`

  `public void setPageContext(PageContext context)`

  Gives the tag handler the current page context so it can access items such as the request and the session.

- `setParent`

  `public void setParent(Tag parent)`

  Tells this tag handler who its parent is.

CLASSES

`BodyContent` Extends: `JspWriter`

A special instance of `JspWriter` used by body tags to read and write body content.

- `clearBody`

  `public void clearBody()`

  Clears the contents of the current body tag.

- `flush`

  `public void flush() throws java.io.IOException`

  A body tag isn't allowed to flush the output. This method overrides `flush` to throw an exception if you call it.

- `getEnclosingWriter`

  `public JspWriter getEnclosingWriter()`

  Returns the writer for the text that encloses this tag. This is the writer you need to write to if you want to put something in the response.

- `getReader`

  `public Reader getReader()`

  Returns a reader for examining the body content. At this point, the body content has been evaluated by the JSP engine, so any scriptlets, expressions, and custom tags contained in the body have already been evaluated.

- `getString`

  `public String getString()`

Returns the body content as a `String`. As with `getReader`, any scriptlets, expresssions, or custom tags in the body have already been evaluated.

- `writeOut`

  `public void writeOut(Writer out) throws java.io.IOException`

  Writes this body content out to the specified writer. Usually used as `writeOut(getEnclosingWriter())`.

`BodyTagSupport` Extends: `TagSupport`

Implements: `BodyTag`

The `BodyTagSupport` class is a handy base class for body tag implementations. It takes care of some of the housekeeping chores you would need to handle if you just implemented the `BodyTag` interface directly.

- `doAfterBody`

  `public int doAfterBody() throws JspException`

  Called by the JSP engine after the tag's body text has been parsed and evaluated. If this method returns `EVAL_BODY_TAG`, the JSP engine re-evaluates the body text (but does not reparse) and calls `doAfterBody` again. When this method returns `SKIP_BODY`, the JSP engine goes on to process the data after the end tag.

- `doEndTag`

  `public int doEndTag()`

  Called by the JSP engine to tell the tag handler that the engine has finished evaluating the tag. If this method returns `SKIP_PAGE`, the JSP engine will stop processing the page. This method should normally return `EVAL_PAGE` to tell the JSP engine to continue evaluating the page.

- `doInitBody`

  `public void doInitBody() throws JspException`

  Called by the JSP engine to tell the tag handler that the body text is about to be evaluated. This method can perform any necessary initialization.

- `doStartTag`

  `public int doStartTag()`

  Called by the JSP engine to tell the tag handler that the engine is evaluating the tag. If this method returns `SKIP_BODY`, the JSP engine won't include the tag's body text in the response. If the method returns `EVAL_BODY_TAG`, the tag's body text will be copied to the output stream.

- `getBodyContent`

  `public BodyContent getBodyContent()`

  Returns the current body content.

- `getPreviousOut`

  `public JspWriter getPreviousOut()`

  Shortcut for `getBodyContent().getEnclosingWriter()`.

- `release`

  `public void release()`

  Tells the tag handler it is no longer needed and it can release any resources it has allocated (database connections, open files, and so on).

- `setBodyContent`

  `public void setBodyContent(BodyContent content)`

  Gives the current body content (containing the body text) to this tag handler. If there is no body text, this method isn't called.

`TagAttributeInfo` The `TagAttributeInfo` class contains information about the attributes that a tag supports.

- `ID`

  `public static final String ID`

  Constant defining the attribute name for the `id` attribute. `ID` is the one attribute name hard-coded into the tag extension mechanism.

- `canBeRequestTime`

  `public boolean canBeRequestTime()`

  Returns `true` if this attribute can be set at request time (if the value can contain a `<%= %>` expression).

- `getIdAttribute`

  ```
  public static TagAttributeInfo getIdAttribute(
      TagAttributeInfo[] attributes)
  ```

  Handy utility to search for the `id` attribute.

- `getName`

  `public String getName()`

  Returns the name of the attribute.

- `getTypeName`

  `public String typeName()`

  Returns the attribute's type.

- `isRequired`

  `public boolean isRequired()`

  Returns `true` if this attribute is required.

- `toString`

  `public String toString()`

  Returns a string representation of this attribute.

`TagData` The `TagData` class allows you to get and set the attributes for a particular tag.

- `REQUEST_TIME_VALUE`

  `public static final Object REQUEST_TIME_VALUE`

A special value returned from `getAttribute` during compile time to indicate that the value is only available at request time.

- `getAttribute`

  `public Object getAttribute(String attributeName)`

  Returns the value of the named attribute, or `null` if the attribute doesn't exist. If this request is made at compile time and the attribute is only available at request time, this method returns `REQUEST_TIME_VALUE`.

- `getAttributes`

  `public java.util.Enumeration getAttributes()`

  Returns an enumeration of all the available attributes.

- `getAttributeString`

  `public String getAttributeString(String attributeName)`

  Returns the value of an attribute as a string.

- `getId`

  `public String getId()`

  Returns the value of the `id` attribute. This is the same as `getAttributeString(TagData.ID)`.

- `setAttribute`

  `public void setAttribute(String attributeName, Object value)`

  Sets the value of the specified attribute.

`TagExtraInfo` The `TagExtraInfo` class is similar to a `BeanInfo` class in that it provides extra information about a tag. You can use this class to tell the JSP engine what scripting variables a tag creates and also to verify attribute values at compile time.

- `getTagInfo`

  `public TagInfo getTagInfo()`

  Returns a `TagInfo` object describing the tag this `TagExtraInfo` belongs to. The `TagInfo` value is set automatically by the `setTagInfo` method.

- `getVariableInfo`

  `public VariableInfo[] getVariableInfo()`

  Returns an array of `VariableInfo` structures describing the scripting variables this tag uses.

- `isValid`

  `public boolean isValid(TagData data)`

  Evaluates the values of the attributes in the `TagData` structure and returns `true` if the attributes are valid. Sometimes you want to create a mutually exclusive pair of attributes. You can use this method to make sure that someone doesn't specify both attributes at the same time. Because `isValid` is called at compile time, you can catch errors earlier.

- `setTagInfo`

  `public void setTagInfo(TagInfo info)`

Sets the `TagInfo` structure for this `TagExtraInfo`. This method is called automatically by the JSP engine.

`TagInfo` The `TagInfo` class describes various aspects of a tag. The information stored in this class comes from the Tag Library Descriptor (TLD) file.

- `BODY_CONTENT_EMPTY`

  `public static final String BODY_CONTENT_EMPTY`

  Constant to indicate that the tag normally doesn't have body content.
- `BODY_CONTENT_JSP`

  `public static final String BODY_CONTENT_JSP`

  Constant to indicate that the tag normally has JSP content in its body.
- `BODY_CONTENT_TAG_DEPENDENT`

  `public static final String BODY_CONTENT_TAG_DEPENDENT`

  Constant to indicate that the tag's body depends on the tag itself.
- `getAttributes`

  `public TagAttributeInfo[] getAttributes()`

  Returns information about the attributes supported by this tag, or `null` if there is no information.
- `getBodyContent`

  `public String getBodyContent()`

  Returns a string indicating what kind of body content the tag normally has (`BODY_CONTENT_JSP`, for example).
- `getInfoString`

  `public String getInfoString()`

  Returns the info string from the TLD file.
- `getTagClassName`

  `public String getTagClassName()`

  Returns the name of the tag handler class for this tag.
- `getTagExtraInfo`

  `public TagExtraInfo getTagExtraInfo()`

  Returns the `TagExtraInfo` class for this tag or `null` if there isn't one.
- `getTagLibrary`

  `public TagLibraryInfo getTagLibrary()`

  Returns information about the tag library this tag belongs to.
- `getTagName`

  `public String getTagName()`

  Returns the name of this tag.
- `getVariableInfo`

  `public VariableInfo getVariableInfo(TagData data)`

Returns information about the scripting variables created by this object. If this tag has no `TagExtraInfo` object, this method returns `null`; otherwise it returns the value returned by the `getVariableInfo` method in the `TagExtraInfo` object.

- `isValid`

  `public boolean isValid(TagData data)`

  Evaluates the values of the attributes in the `TagData` structure and returns `true` if the attributes are valid. Sometimes you want to create a mutually exclusive pair of attributes. You can use this method to make sure that someone doesn't specify both attributes at the same time. Because `isValid` is called at compile time, you can catch errors earlier.

- `toString`

  `public String toString()`

  Returns a string representation of this object for debugging purposes.

`TagLibraryInfo` The `TagLibraryInfo` object describes the information stored in a Tag Library Descriptor (TLD) file.

- `getInfoString`

  `public String getInfoString()`

  Returns the value of the `<info>` tag from the TLD.

- `getPrefixString`

  `public String getPrefixString()`

  Returns the value of the prefix string specified in the `<%@ taglib %>` tag.

- `getReliableURN`

  `public String getReliableURN()`

  Returns the name of a reliable URN for this TLD (specified by the `<uri>` tag in the TLD).

- `getRequiredVersion`

  `public String getRequiredVersion()`

  Returns the minimum version of JSP required for this tag library.

- `getShortName`

  `public String getShortName()`

  Returns the value of the `<shortname>` tag from the TLD.

- `getTag`

  `public TagInfo getTag(String shortName)`

  Returns information about a specific tag defined in the TLD.

- `getTags`

  `public TagInfo[] getTags()`

  Returns information about all the tags defined in the TLD.

- `getURI`

  `public String getURI()`

  Returns the URI specified in the `<%@ taglib %>` tag.

`TagSupport` Implements: `Tag`

The `TagSupport` class is a handy base class for implementing tags that don't need to access their body content. This class handles much of the housekeeping work that you would need to implement yourself if you just implemented the `Tag` interface.

- `doEndTag`

  `public int doEndTag()`

  Called by the JSP engine to tell the tag handler that the engine has finished evaluating the tag. If this method returns `SKIP_PAGE`, the JSP engine will stop processing the page. This method should normally return `EVAL_PAGE` to tell the JSP engine to continue evaluating the page.

- `doStartTag`

  `public int doStartTag()`

  Called by the JSP engine to tell the tag handler that the engine is evaluating the tag. If this method returns `SKIP_BODY`, the JSP engine won't include the tag's body text in the response. If the method returns `EVAL_BODY_TAG`, the tag's body text will be copied to the output stream.

- `findAncestorWithClass`

  `public static Tag findAncestorWithClass(Tag from, Class whichClass)`

  Uses the `getParent` method for a tag to search backward, looking for a tag handler whose class is `whichClass`. Returns `null` if no matching tag can be found. This method is useful when you have a tag that expects to be contained by another tag and you want to find the instance of that other tag.

- `getId`

  `public String getId()`

  Returns the value if this tag's `id` attribute, or `null` if there is no `id`.

- `getParent`

  `public Tag getParent()`

  Returns the current parent for this tag (the tag this one is contained within). The value is set by `setParent`.

- `getValue`

  `public Object getValue(String valueName)`

  Returns an object stored in this tag instance. This method is similar to the `getAttribute` methods in some of the built-in JSP variables. The idea is that you associate values with this tag instance that other tags can retrieve (that's why `findAncestorWithClass` is important).

- `getValues`

  `public java.util.Enumeration getValues()`

  Returns an enumeration of the names of all the values stored in this tag.

- `release`

  `public void release()`

  Tells the tag handler it is no longer needed and it can release any resources it has allocated (database connections, open files, and so on).

- `removeValue`

  `public String removeValue(String valueName)`

  Removes a value associated with this tag.

- `setPageContext`

  `public void setPageContext(PageContext context)`

  Gives the tag handler the current page context so it can access items such as the request and the session.

- `setParent`

  `public void setParent(Tag parent)`

  Tells this tag handler who its parent is.

- `setValue`

  `public void setValue(String valueName, Object value)`

  Associates a value with this tag.

`VariableInfo` The `VariableInfo` class describes the scripting variables created by a tag.

- `AT_BEGIN`

  `public static final int AT_BEGIN`

  Constant used to indicate that a scripting variable is available starting from the beginning of the tag and extending through the rest of the page.

- `AT_END`

  `public static final int AT_END`

  Constant used to indicate that a scripting variable is available after the closing tag and extending through the rest of the page.

- `NESTED`

  `public static final int NESTED`

  Constant used to indicate that a scripting variable is only available between a tag's begin and end tags.

- `getClassName`

  `public String getClassName()`

  Returns the class name of the scripting variable that will be created.

- `getDeclare`

  `public boolean getDeclare()`

  Indicates whether the JSP compiler should declare a variable in the servlet to hold the value for this variable.

- `getScope`

  `public int getScope()`

  Returns the scope for this variable (use the constants from the `PageContext` class for the possible return values).

- `getVarName`

  `public String getVarName()`

  Returns the name of this variable.

APPENDIX

SERVLET API REFERENCE

In this appendix

THE javax.servlet API

The javax.servlet API covers most of the basic features that any servlet needs. It is protocol-independent, allowing for future expansion into new protocols such as the Wireless Application Protocol (WAP). The HTTP-specific servlet features are provided by a separate javax.servlet.http package.

Most of the commonly used items in this API are defined as interfaces and not as concrete classes. Each servlet engine has the flexibility to implement these interfaces as it sees fit.

INTERFACES

RequestDispatcher

The RequestDispatcher interface is the entryway for calling another servlet, JSP or other Web resource, either by inclusion or by forwarding. When you include or forward to another resource, you must get the RequestDispatcher for that object (a service provided by the ServletContext interface).

forward

```
public void forward(ServletRequest request,
                    ServletResponse response)
    throws ServletException, java.io.IOException
```

Forwards the current request to another resource on this same server. Because the new resource replaces the current one, the output buffer for the current servlet or JSP must not have been committed. After data has been returned to the browser, the forward mechanism doesn't work because there is no way to tell the browser to ignore what it has already received. If you try to do a forward after data has been committed, you will receive an IllegalStateException.

include

```
public void include(ServletRequest request,
                    ServletResponse response)
    throws ServletException, java.io.IOException
```

Includes another resource in the current servlet's output. This include is performed at runtime. Unlike the forward method, the output buffer might already be committed when you perform an include because the current servlet is still part of the output sent to the browser.

Servlet

This interface defines the minimum set of methods that every servlet must implement.

destroy

```
public void destroy()
```

When the servlet engine is about to take a servlet out of service, it calls the `destroy` method. This allows a servlet to clean up any resources that can't wait until garbage collection time. You usually need to release database connections and close open files in a `destroy` method because you never know how long it will take before the garbage collector cleans up those resources.

getServletConfig

```
public ServletConfig getServletConfig()
```

Returns the `ServletConfig` item that was passed to the servlet via the `init` method. The `ServletConfig` object contains information about the servlet itself and its initialization parameters.

getServletInfo

```
public String getServletInfo()
```

Returns information about the servlet. The Servlet API specification suggests that this string contain the author, version, and copyright. You can't put any HTML/XML tags in this string.

init

```
public void init(ServletConfig config)
    throws ServletException
```

When the servlet engine loads a servlet, it first creates a new instance of the servlet and then calls the servlet's `init` method, passing it a `ServletConfig` object. The servlet must hold on to the `ServletConfig` object because there is no other way to get it.

If the servlet does not want to be brought into service (if a required database is down, for instance), it can either throw an exception or just not return from the `init` method for a specific period of time. The timeout period for the `init` method is implementation-specific.

The `GenericServlet` and `HttpServlet` classes implement a parameterless `init` method that is called after the base class safely tucks away the `ServletConfig` object. You should use the convenience `init` method if it's available.

service

```
public void service(ServletRequest request,
                    ServletResponse response)
    throws ServletException, java.io.IOException
```

The servlet engine calls this method to allow the servlet to process a request. This method will not be called until the `init` method has been called, so you can be sure that any initialization you perform in your `init` method will have been completed by the time this method is called. Because the servlet engine can be multi-threaded, this method might be called multiple times at once by different threads. If you use any resources that are not thread-safe, you must synchronize access to those resources.

`ServletConfig`

The `ServletConfig` interface defines a set of methods for retrieving information about a servlet and its configuration. The servlet engine creates a `ServletConfig` item for each servlet and passes it to the servlet's `init` method during startup.

`getInitParameter`

```
public String getInitParameter(String parameterName)
```

This method returns the value of the named initialization parameter, or `null` if the parameter doesn't exist. You can set servlet initialization parameters from the servlet's deployment descriptor or possibly from the servlet engine's administration tool.

`getInitParameterNames`

```
public Enumeration getInitParameterNames()
```

Returns an enumeration of the names of all the init parameters for the servlet.

`getServletContext`

```
public ServletContext getServletContext()
```

Returns the `ServletContext` object for this servlet. The `ServletContext` interface allows the servlet to access various features provided by the servlet engine, such as logging, request dispatching, and objects stored with an application-level scope.

`getServletName`

```
public String getServletName()
```

Returns the name of this servlet. The servlet name is usually specified in the servlet's deployment descriptor or configured with the servlet engine's administration tool. If no name has been configured, the servlet name is just the classname of the servlet.

`ServletContext`

The `ServletContext` interface gives a servlet access to various features provided by the servlet engine.

getAttribute

```
public Object getAttribute(String attributeName)
```

Returns an object stored with an application scope or `null` if there is no object in the application scope with the specified name.

getAttributeNames

```
public Enumeration getAttributeNames()
```

Returns an enumeration of the names of the attributes stored with an application scope.

getContext

```
public ServletContext getContext(String uri)
```

Returns the `ServletContext` for a specific servlet. This method allows applications to exchange data by storing data in each other's `ServletContexts`. The URI for the requested context must be an absolute path starting with `'/'`. For security reasons, the servlet engine might choose to return `null` rather than allow a servlet to access another servlet's `ServletContext`.

getInitParameter

```
public String getInitParameter(String name)
```

Returns the value of an initialization parameter configured for the entire servlet engine as opposed to an `init` parameter for an individual servlet.

getInitParameterNames

```
public Enumeration getInitParameterNames()
```

Returns an enumeration of the names of all the initialization parameters for the entire servlet engine.

getMajorVersion

```
public int getMajorVersion()
```

Returns the major version number of the servlet API that the servlet engine supports.

getMimeType

```
public String getMimeType(String file)
```

Returns the mime type associated with a particular filename. The mime types are specified in the servlet engine's configuration. For a filename of foobar.jpg you would expect the mime type to be `image/jpeg`. If there is no mime type associated with the filename, this method returns `null`.

getMinorVersion

```
public int getMinorVersion()
```

Returns the minor version number of the servlet API that the servlet engine supports.

getNamedDispatcher

```
public RequestDispatcher getNamedDispatcher(String servletName)
```

Returns a request dispatcher for the named servlet. You give a servlet a name by setting it in the servlet engine's configuration file, or by using the engine's administration tool. If there is a problem creating a request dispatcher for the servlet, this method returns `null`.

getRealPath

```
public String getRealPath(String virtualPath)
```

Returns the actual operating system path associated with the given virtual path. For example, /examples/HelloWorld.jsp might have a real path of c:\myjspfiles\examples\HelloWorld.jsp. If there is no specific path for the file, this method returns `null`.

getRequestDispatcher

```
public RequestDispatcher getRequestDispatcher(String resourcePath)
```

Returns a request dispatcher for the given resource. Unlike `getNamedDispatcher`, this method returns a dispatcher for any kind of resource, not just servlets. If the server can't return a request dispatcher for the resource, this method returns `null`.

getResource

```
public URL getResource(String path) throws MalformedURLException
```

Returns a URL object that points to a particular resource. The resource might be located on the local server or on a remote server. If there is no mapping for the specified path, this method returns `null`.

The resource returned is always returned directly as file content. If you load a JSP file, you get the JSP source and not the JSP output.

getResourceAsStream

```
public InputStream getResourceAsStream(String path)
```

Returns the contents of the named resource as an input stream. As with the `getResource` method, the resource might be located on the local server or on a remote server. If there is no mapping for the specified path, this method returns `null`.

Again, the resource is returned directly, so when you access a JSP file, you get the original source file.

getServerInfo

```
public String getServerInfo()
```

Returns the name and version of the servlet engine in the form *server name/server version*.

getServlet

```
public Servlet getServlet(String name) throws ServletException
```

Returns a reference to the named servlet.

This method was deprecated in version 2.1 of the servlet API. You shouldn't count on it being available.

getServletNames

```
public Enumeration getServletNames()
```

Returns an enumeration of the names of all the servlets in the servlet engine.

This method was deprecated in version 2.1 of the servlet API. You shouldn't count on it being available.

getServlets

```
public Enumeration getServlets()
```

Returns an enumeration of the names of all the servlets in the servlet engine.

This method was deprecated in version 2.1 of the servlet API. You shouldn't count on it being available.

log

```
public void log(String message)
public void log(String message, Throwable throwable)
public void log(Exception exc, String message)
```

Logs a message and an optional exception to the servlet engine's log file.

The `log(Exception, String)` version of this method is deprecated as of version 2.1 of the servlet API. Use the version that accepts a `Throwable` if you want to log an exception.

removeAttribute

```
public void removeAttribute(String name)
```

Removes a named attribute stored at the application context level.

setAttribute

```
public void setAttribute(String name, Object object)
```

Stores an attribute at the application context level.

ServletRequest

The `ServletRequest` interface defines methods that a servlet can use to access information about an incoming request.

getAttribute

```
public Object getAttribute(String name)
```

Returns an object stored with a request context. Normally, the only objects stored at the request context level are objects that you put there with the `setAttribute` method. The servlet engine can also store attributes in the request context. Certain servlet engines, such as Sun's Java Web Server, store incoming HTTPS certificates with an attribute name of `javax.servlet.request.X509Certificate`.

getAttributeNames

```
public Enumeration getAttributeNames()
```

Returns an enumeration of the names of the objects stored at the request context level.

getCharacterEncoding

```
public String getCharacterEncoding()
```

Returns the character encoding used in the request. The browser usually specifies the encoding, and if no encoding has been specified, this method returns `null`.

getContentLength

```
public int getContentLength()
```

Returns the number of bytes in the incoming request content. This method returns `-1` if the content length isn't known.

getContentType

```
public String getContentType()
```

Returns the mime type of the incoming request, or `null` if the mime type isn't known.

getInputStream

```
public ServletInputStream getInputStream()
    throws java.io.IOException
```

Returns an input stream used for reading the request content as a stream of bytes. You can't use this method if you have already called `getReader`. You can't read the content as a character stream and a binary stream at the same time.

getLocale

```
public java.util.Locale getLocale()
```

Returns the preferred locale specified by the browser. If the browser doesn't specify a preferred language (via the Accept-Language header value), this method returns the default locale.

getLocales

```
public Enumeration getLocales()
```

Returns an enumeration of all the locales the browser says it supports. If the browser doesn't send any locale information in the request, this method returns an enumeration containing only the default locale.

getParameter

```
public String getParameter(String name)
```

Returns the value of an incoming parameter as a string. If there is no such parameter specified in the request, this method returns `null`.

getParameterNames

```
public Enumeration getParameterNames()
```

Returns an enumeration of the names of all the parameters in the request.

getParameterValues

```
public String[] getParameterValues(String name)
```

Returns an array of the values of all the parameters with a specific name. This allows you to access parameters when there are multiple occurrences of the same name. This method returns `null` if there are no parameters with the specified name.

getProtocol

```
public String getProtocol()
```

Returns the name and version of the protocol used to make the request. For example, HTTP version 1.0 would be represented as HTTP/1.0.

getReader

```
public BufferedReader getReader() throws java.io.IOException
```

Returns a reader used for reading the content data sent from the browser. Unlike the input stream returned by `getInputStream`, this method performs any necessary character translation.

You can't use this method if you have already called `getInputStream`. You can't read the content as a binary stream and as a character stream at the same time.

`getRealPath`

```
public String getRealPath(String virtualPath)
```

Returns the operating system path for the specified virtual path. This method is deprecated as of version 2.1 of the servlet specification. Use `ServletContext.getRealPath` instead.

`getRemoteAddr`

```
public String getRemoteAddr()
```

Returns a string containing the numeric IP address of the client making the request.

`getRemoteHost`

```
public String getRemoteHost()
```

Returns the name of the host making the request. If the host name is unknown, this method returns the numeric IP address of the host.

`getRequestDispatcher`

```
public RequestDispatcher getRequestDispatcher(String resourcePath)
```

Returns a request dispatcher for the given resource. Unlike `getNamedDispatcher`, this method returns a dispatcher for any kind of resource, not just servlets. If the server can't return a request dispatcher for the resource, this method returns `null`.

This version of `getRequestDispatcher` can take a relative path.

`getScheme`

```
public String getScheme()
```

Returns the name of the scheme used to make the request. A scheme is essentially a protocol. Example schemes are `ftp`, `http`, and `https`.

`getServerName`

```
public String getServerName()
```

Returns the host name of the server that received the request. Remember that a single server service can be available through multiple host names. This method lets you determine which host name the request was sent to.

getServerPort

```
public int getServerPort()
```

Returns the port number that the request was sent to. For normal HTTP traffic, the standard port number should be 80. For normal HTTPS traffic, the standard port number is 443.

isSecure

```
public boolean isSecure()
```

Returns `true` if the request was made using a secure protocol (like HTTPS).

removeAttribute

```
public void removeAttribute(String name)
```

Removes the named attribute from the request context.

setAttribute

```
public void setAttribute(String name, Object value)
```

Stores the named value in the request context.

ServletResponse

The `ServletResponse` class gives you control over the response sent back to the browser.

flushBuffer

```
public void flushBuffer() throws java.io.IOException
```

Flushes any output currently in the output buffer. This method commits the response, so if you try to forward to another page after calling this method, you might get an error or see parts of both pages on the browser.

getBufferSize

```
public int getBufferSize()
```

Returns the size of the response buffer. If there is no buffering, this method returns 0.

getCharacterEncoding

```
public String getCharacterEncoding()
```

Returns the character encoding used for the response. The default character encoding is `ISO-8859-1` (Latin-1).

getLocale

```
public java.util.Locale getLocale()
```

Returns the locale for this response (set by the `setLocale` method). You usually set the locale to support international clients. If you do not explicitly set a locale, this method returns the default locale.

getOutputStream

```
public ServletOutputStream getOutputStream()
    throws java.io.IOException
```

Returns a byte-oriented output stream for writing the response. You can't use this method if you have already called `getWriter` because you can't write both byte-oriented and character-oriented data. If you have called `getWriter` and then change your mind and need to call `getOutputStream`, call `reset` first. Of course, you can't call `reset` if the response has already been committed.

getWriter

```
public PrintWriter getWriter() throws java.io.IOException
```

Returns a writer for writing character data to the response. Make sure you set the content type and locale (if necessary) before calling this method, because the character encoding used might depend on both of those settings.

You can't call `getWriter` if you have already called `getOutputStream` unless you clear out the response by calling `reset` first.

isCommitted

```
public boolean isCommitted()
```

Returns `true` if the response has already been committed. You can't call `reset` if this method returns `true`. When the response is committed, data has been sent back to the browser. There is no way to clear out the data the browser has already received.

reset

```
public void reset()
```

Clears out the response, including headers. You can't call `reset` if the response has already been committed. If you do try to call `reset` when the buffer has been committed, you'll get an `IllegalStateException`.

setBufferSize

```
public void setBufferSize(int size)
```

Sets the preferred buffer size for the response. The servlet engine might choose to use a larger buffer than the one you specify with this method, but it will never be smaller. You can get the actual buffer size by calling `getBufferSize`.

You must call this method before the response has been committed, otherwise you'll get an `IllegalStateException`.

setContentLength

```
public void setContentLength(int contentLength)
```

Sets the content length in the response header. This method doesn't actually control the number of bytes you write in the response content; it's up to you to make sure you write the correct number of bytes. The `Content-Length` header value is set as a courtesy to the browser to let it know how many bytes to expect.

setContentType

```
public void setContentType(String contentType)
```

Sets the `Content-Type` header value for the response. The content type also dictates what kind of character encoding is used if you call `getWriter`.

setLocale

```
public void setLocale(java.util.Locale locale)
```

Sets the locale for this response. Setting the locale might change the character encoding used in the response and might also set various HTTP header values.

SingleThreadModel

This interface has no methods; it simply exists as an indicator for the servlet engine that a servlet should be single threaded. If a servlet implements the method, the servlet engine must ensure that only one thread at a time can call the servlet's `service` method.

CLASSES

GenericServlet

This class is a general base class for writing a servlet. A servlet only needs to implement the `Servlet` interface, but there are many housekeeping chores that a servlet must perform. This class handles most of those chores, making it much easier to implement a servlet.

destroy

```
public void destroy()
```

When the servlet engine is about to take a servlet out of service, it calls the `destroy` method. This allows a servlet to clean up any resources that can't wait until garbage collection time. You usually need to release database connections and close open files in a `destroy` method, because you never know how long it will take before the garbage collector cleans up those resources.

getInitParameter

```
public String getInitParameter(String parameterName)
```

This method returns the value of the named initialization parameter, or `null` if the parameter doesn't exist. You can set servlet initialization parameters from the servlet's deployment descriptor or possibly from the servlet engine's administration tool.

getInitParameterNames

```
public Enumeration getInitParameterNames()
```

Returns an enumeration of the names of all the `init` parameters for the servlet.

getServletConfig

```
public ServletConfig getServletConfig()
```

Returns the `ServletConfig` item that was passed to the servlet via the `init` method. The `ServletConfig` object contains information about the servlet itself and its initialization parameters.

getServletContext

```
public ServletContext getServletContext()
```

Returns the `ServletContext` object for this servlet. The `ServletContext` interface allows the servlet to access various features provided by the servlet engine, such as logging, request dispatching, and objects stored with an application-level scope.

getServletInfo

```
public String getServletInfo()
```

Returns information about the servlet. The Servlet API specification suggests that this string contain the author, version, and copyright. You can't put any HTML/XML tags in this string.

getServletName

```
public String getServletName()
```

Returns the name of this servlet. The servlet name is usually specified in the servlet's deployment descriptor or configured with the servlet engine's administration tool. If no name has been configured, the servlet name is just the classname of the servlet.

init

```
public void init() throws ServletException
public void init(ServletConfig config)
    throws ServletException
```

When the servlet engine loads a servlet, it first creates a new instance of the servlet and then calls the servlet's `init` method, passing it a `ServletConfig` object. The servlet must hold on to the `ServletConfig` object because there is no other way to get it.

You should use the parameterless version of this method, however, because the `GenericServlet` implementation of the other `init` method takes care of saving the `ServletConfig` object.

If the servlet does not want to be brought into service (if a required database is down, for instance), it can either throw an exception or just not return from the `init` method for a specific period of time. The timeout period for the `init` method is implementation-specific.

log

```
public void log(String message)
public void log(String message, Throwable throwable)
```

Logs a message and an optional exception to the servlet engine's log file.

service

```
public void service(ServletRequest request,
                    ServletResponse response)
    throws ServletException, java.io.IOException
```

The servlet engine calls this method to allow the servlet to process a request. This method will not be called until the `init` method has been called, so you can be sure that any initialization you perform in your `init` method will have completed by the time this method is called. Because the servlet engine can be multi-threaded, this method might be called multiple times at once by different threads. If you use any resources that are not thread-safe, you must synchronize access to those resources.

ServletInputStream

Extends: `java.io.InputStream`

The `ServletInputStream` class let you read binary data from the request. Typically, you use this method when reading data from an HTTP `POST` or `PUT`. On an HTTP `GET`, there is nothing to read.

This method only adds one method beyond those defined in the `InputStream` base class.

readLine

```
public int readLine(byte[] buffer, int offset, int len)
    throws java.io.IOException
```

Reads a line from the input stream and copies it into the buffer. The return value is the number of bytes read, or `-1` if the method hits the end of the input stream.

`ServletOutputStream`

Extends: `java.io.OutputStream`

This class adds `print` and `println` methods similar to those found in the `PrintStream` class.

print

```
public void print(boolean b) throws java.io.IOException
public void print(char ch) throws java.io.IOException
public void print(double d) throws java.io.IOException
public void print(float f) throws java.io.IOException
public void print(int i) throws java.io.IOException
public void print(long l) throws java.io.IOException
public void print(String s) throws java.io.IOException
```

Prints an item to the output stream.

println

```
public void println() throws java.io.IOException
public void println(boolean b) throws java.io.IOException
public void println(char ch) throws java.io.IOException
public void println(double d) throws java.io.IOException
public void println(float f) throws java.io.IOException
public void println(int i) throws java.io.IOException
public void println(long l) throws java.io.IOException
public void println(String s) throws java.io.IOException
```

Prints an item to the output stream and appends a newline.

EXCEPTIONS

`ServletException`

ServletException CONSTRUCTOR

```
public ServletException()
public ServletException(String message)
public ServletException(String message, Throwable rootCause)
public ServletException(Throwable rootCause)
```

The `rootCause` parameter in the `ServletException` constructor is the exception that cause the servlet to throw the `ServletException`. This allows you to "chain" exceptions. You don't have to declare that the servlet throws a different kind of exception (in fact, you can't), but you can still tell the servlet engine what kind of exception caused the original problem.

getRootCause

```
public Throwable getRootCause()
```

Returns the root cause throwable specified in the constructor.

`UnavailableException`

Extends: `ServletException`

The `UnavailableException` indicates that the servlet is either temporarily or permanently unavailable.

`UnavailableException` CONSTRUCTOR

```
public UnavailableException(String message)
public UnavailableException(String message, int seconds)
```

Creates a new exception indicating that the servlet is unavailable. If you do not specify a number of seconds, the servlet is considered permanently unavailable. Otherwise, the `seconds` parameter is the estimated number of seconds that the servlet is unavailable.

`getUnavailableSeconds`

```
public int getUnavailableSeconds()
```

Returns the number of seconds the servlet expects to be unavailable (it might be unavailable for a longer period).

`isPermanent`

```
public boolean isPermanent()
```

Returns `true` if the servlet is permanently unavailable.

THE `javax.servlet.http` API

INTERFACES

`HttpServletRequest`

The `HttpServletRequest` class provides methods for accessing HTTP-specific portions of the incoming request.

`getAuthType`

```
public String getAuthType()
```

Returns the name of the authentication scheme used for authenticating access to this servlet. If there is no authentication, this method returns `null`.

`getContextPath`

```
public String getContextPath()
```

Returns the context portion of the servlets URI. For a URI of `http://localhost/myservlets/personal/HiCeal` the context path would be `/myservlets/personal`.

getCookies

```
public Cookie[] getCookies()
```

Returns an array of all the cookies contained in the request, or `null` if there are no cookies.

getDateHeader

```
public long getDateHeader(String name)
```

Interprets a header value as a date and returns the date's time value. To convert this value to a date, do this:

```
Date d = new Date(request.getDateHeader("startDate"));
```

The servlet engine ignores capitalization when searching for header names.

If there is no such header, this method returns `-1`. If the header exists but can't be converted to a date, this method throws an `IllegalArgumentException`.

getHeader

```
public String getHeader(String name)
```

Returns a header value as a string or `null` if there is no such header name. The servlet engine ignores capitalization when searching for header names.

getHeaderNames

```
public Enumeration getHeaderNames()
```

Returns an enumeration of all the header names in the request. If there are no headers, the enumeration is empty. If the servlet container doesn't allow servlets to access headers, this method returns `null`.

getHeaders

```
public Enumeration getHeaders(String name)
```

Returns an enumeration of all the header values with a specific name, or `null` if the request doesn't contain any headers with the specified name.

getIntHeader

```
public int getIntHeader(String name)
```

Interprets the specified header value as an `int` and returns the value. If there is no such header, this method returns `null`. If the header exists but can't be converted to an `int`, this method throws a `NumberFormatException`.

getMethod

```
public String getMethod()
```

Returns the HTTP method used to make the request (`GET`, `POST`, `PUT`, and so on).

getPathInfo

Returns the extra path information in the URL (information after the servlet name but before the query string). When you configure a servlet, you can specify a URL path for the servlet. When a browser invokes the servlet, it can add extra information to the servlet's path. This information is returned by `getPathInfo`.

For example, you might want to create a servlet to manage virtual directories. The servlet might handle all paths starting with `/virtual/`. For a path of `/virtual/mark/foo.c`, this method would return `/mark/foo.c`.

If there is no extra path information, this method returns `null`.

getPathTranslated

```
public String getPathTranslated()
```

This method is similar to `getPathInfo` but it translates the extra path information into a real operating system path.

If there is no extra path information, this method returns `null`.

getQueryString

```
public String getQueryString()
```

Returns the query string portion of the URL (the portion following the `?`). If there is no query string, this method returns `null`.

getRemoteUser

```
public String getRemoteUser()
```

Returns the name the used to authenticate this user. This is not the same as the user's login name on his home system. When you use authentication, the user must enter a username and password. This method returns the username entered for authentication, or `null` if the user hasn't been authenticated.

getRequestedSessionId

```
public String getRequestedSessionId()
```

Returns the session ID that the client requested when making the request, or `null` if the client didn't request a session. The requested session ID might not be the same as the actual session ID. If the old session has expired, or if the servlet explicitly creates a new session, the session IDs won't match.

getRequestURI

```
public String getRequestURI()
```

Returns the URI portion of the first line of the HTTP request. For example, if the first line is

```
GET /HelloWorld.jsp HTTP/1.0
```

this method would return

```
/HelloWorld.jsp.
```

getServletPath

```
public String getServletPath()
```

Returns the portion of the path used to invoke the servlet, not including the extra path info. If a servlet is configured to handle all paths starting with `/virtual`, this method returns `/virtual` for the path `/virtual/mark/foo.c`.

getSession

```
public HttpSession getSession()
public HttpSession getSession(boolean create)
```

This method returns the current session, creating a new one if necessary. If the `create` flag is `false`, this method does not create a new session and returns `null` if a session doesn't already exist.

getUserPrincipal

```
public java.security.Principal getUserPrincipal()
```

Returns the principal object used when authenticating this user, or `null` if the user hasn't been authenticated.

isRequestedSessionFromCookie

```
public boolean isRequestedSessionFromCookie()
```

Returns `true` if the requested session ID came in as a cookie.

isRequestedSessionFromURL

```
public boolean isRequestSessionFromURL()
```

Returns `true` if the requested session ID came in as part of the URL.

isRequestedSessionIdValid

```
public boolean isRequestedSessionIdValid()
```

Returns `true` if the requested session ID still refers to a valid session.

isUserInRole

```
public boolean isUserInRole(String role)
```

Returns `true` if the user has been authenticated with a particular role name. If the user hasn't been authenticated at all, this method returns `false`.

HttpServletResponse

The `HttpServletResponse` interface provides methods for setting HTTP-specific portions of the response.

addCookie

```
public void addCookie(Cookie cookie)
```

Adds a cookie to the response.

addDateHeader

```
public void addDateHeader(String name, long date)
```

Adds a date header value to the response. If there are already headers with the same name, this method just adds to the existing ones.

To add a `java.util.Date` value, call the `getTime` method in the date to get the value to pass to this method.

addHeader

```
public void addHeader(String name, String value)
```

Adds a header value to the response. If there are already headers with the same name, this method just adds to the existing ones.

addIntHeader

```
public void addHeader(String name, int value)
```

Adds an `int` header value to the response. If there are already headers with the same name, this method just adds to the existing ones.

containsHeader

```
public boolean containsHeader(String name)
```

Returns `true` if there is already a header with the specified name.

encodeRedirectURL

```
public String encodeRedirectURL(String url)
```

Encodes a URL for performing a redirect, adding the session ID as a parameter if the browser doesn't support cookies.

encodeURL

```
public String encodeURL(String url)
```

Encodes a URL, adding the session ID as a parameter if the browser doesn't support cookies. Any time you return a URL from a servlet or a JSP, you should encode it in case the browser doesn't support cookies.

sendError

```
public void sendError(int statusCode)
public void sendError(int statusCode, String message)
```

Makes this response an error response and returns the specified status code and optional message.

sendRedirect

```
public void sendRedirect(String URL) throws java.io.IOException
```

Sends a redirect response back to the browser. If the response has already been committed, this method throws an `IllegalStateException`.

Make sure you return immediately after calling this method. The act of calling this method does not automatically terminate a servlet or JSP.

setDateHeader

```
public void setDateHeader(String name, long date)
```

Sets a date header value to the response. If there are already headers with the same name, this method replaces the existing ones.

To set a `java.util.Date` value, call the `getTime` method in the date to get the value to pass to this method.

setHeader

```
public void addHeader(String name, String value)
```

Sets a header value in the response. If there are already headers with the same name, this method replaces the existing ones.

setIntHeader

```
public void setHeader(String name, int value)
```

Sets an `int` header value in the response. If there are already headers with the same name, this method replaces the existing ones.

setStatus

```
public void setStatus(int statusCode)
```

Sets the status code for this response.

HttpSession

The `HttpSession` class contains information about a client's session and also contains objects stored in the session context.

getAttribute

```
public Object getAttribute(String name)
```

Returns an object stored at the session context level, or `null` if no such object exists.

getAttributeNames

```
public Enumeration getAttributeNames()
```

Returns an enumeration of all the objects stored in the session.

getCreationTime

```
public long getCreationTime()
```

Returns the time the session was created.

getId

```
public String getId()
```

Returns the session's unique ID.

getLastAccessedTime

```
public long getLastAccessedTime()
```

Returns the last time a client accessed this session.

getMaxInactiveInterval

```
public int getMaxInactiveInterval()
```

Returns the number of seconds since the last request that the servlet engine will wait before deciding that the session can be closed. This is basically the timeout period for a session.

invalidate

```
public void invalidate()
```

Marks a session as invalid and releases any objects bound to it.

isNew

```
public boolean isNew()
```

Returns `true` if the client doesn't know about this session (if it hasn't been sent the session ID).

removeAttribute

```
public void removeAttribute(String name)
```

Removes an attribute stored in the session.

setAttribute

```
public void setAttribute(String name, Object value)
```

Stores an object in the session.

setMaxInactiveInterval

```
public void setMaxInactiveInterval(int interval)
```

Sets the amount of time (in seconds) since the last request that the servlet engine will wait before deciding that a session can be closed. In other words, this sets the timeout period for a session.

HttpSessionBindingListener

The `HttpSessionBindingListener` interface defines methods that an object must implement if it wants to be notified when it is bound to a session and unbound. This lets objects detect how many sessions they belong to.

valueBound

```
public void valueBound(HttpSessionBindingEvent event)
```

Tells the current object that is has been bound by a session.

valueUnbound

```
public void valueUnbound(HttpSessionBindingEvent event)
```

Tells the current object that is has been unbound by a session.

CLASSES

Cookie

The `Cookie` class represents a cookie value that can be sent to a browser or has been received from a browser.

`Cookie` CONSTRUCTOR

`public Cookie(String name, String value)`

Creates a new cookie with the specified name and value.

`clone`

`public Object clone()`

Creates a full copy of a cookie.

`getComment`

`public String getComment()`

Returns the cookie's comment value, or `null` if there is no comment.

`getDomain`

`public String getDomain()`

Returns the domain name for this cookie.

`getMaxAge`

`public int getMaxAge()`

Returns the maximum age in seconds for the cookie. An age of `-1` means that the cookie stays on the browser until the browser is shut down.

`getName`

`public String getName()`

Returns the cookie's name.

`getPath`

`public String getPath()`

Returns the cookie's path.

`getSecure`

`public boolean getSecure()`

Returns `true` if this cookie should only be sent using a secure protocol.

`getValue`

`public String getValue()`

Returns the cookie's value.

getVersion

```
public int getVersion()
```

Returns the version number of the cookie protocol that this cookie supports. Version 0 is the original Netscape specification supported by most browsers. Version 1 is the official RFC 2109 standard that is not widely used yet.

setComment

```
public void setComment(String comment)
```

Stores a comment about the cookie.

setDomain

```
public void setDomain(String domain)
```

Sets the domain this cookie is restricted to.

setMaxAge

```
public void setMaxAge(int age)
```

Sets the maximum age in seconds for a cookie. A value of `0` causes the cookie to be deleted immediately. A value of `-1` means the cookie will be deleted only when the browser is shut down.

setPath

```
public void setPath(String path)
```

Specifies a path that must be present at the start of the URL for the browser to send this cookie.

setSecure

```
public void setSecure(boolean secureFlag)
```

If `secureFlag` is `true`, this cookie should only be sent when using a secure protocol.

setValue

```
public void setValue(String value)
```

Changes the cookie's value.

setVersion

```
public void setVersion(int version)
```

Sets the version number of the cookie protocol that this cookie supports. Version 0 is the original Netscape specification supported by most browsers. Version 1 is the official RFC 2109 standard that is not widely used yet.

HttpServlet

The HttpServlet class is a handy base class for creating HTTP servlets. Instead of implementing a service method, an HTTP servlet should implement methods to handle specific HTTP methods such as GET, POST, and PUT.

doDelete

```
protected void doDelete(HttpServletRequest request,
    HttpServletResponse response)
    throws ServletException, java.io.IOException
```

This method is called whenever the client issues an HTTP DELETE request, which usually indicates that the client wants the Web server to delete a document.

doGet

```
protected void doGet(HttpServletRequest request,
    HttpServletResponse response)
    throws ServletException, java.io.IOException
```

This method is called whenever the client issues an HTTP GET request or HTTP HEAD request. This method is by far the most common method used in an HTTP servlet.

doOptions

```
protected void doOptions(HttpServletRequest request,
    HttpServletResponse response)
    throws ServletException, java.io.IOException
```

This method automatically returns a list of HTTP methods supported by this servlet, which is what the HTTP OPTIONS request is used for. You don't need to override this method unless you want to change the behavior of an options request.

doPost

```
protected void doPost(HttpServletRequest request,
    HttpServletResponse response)
    throws ServletException, java.io.IOException
```

This method is called whenever the client issues an HTTP POST request and is the second most-used method after doGet. This method usually receives form data that is too big to put in an HTTP GET request or shouldn't be included in the URL for security reasons.

doPut

```
protected void doPut(HttpServletRequest request,
    HttpServletResponse response)
    throws ServletException, java.io.IOException
```

This method is called whenever the client issues an HTTP PUT request and is normally used by the client to upload a file to the Web server.

doTrace

```
protected void doTrace(HttpServletRequest request,
    HttpServletResponse response)
    throws ServletException, java.io.IOException
```

This method is called when the browser performs an HTTP `TRACE` request, which is used for debugging. You don't need to override this method unless you want to change the behavior of a trace request.

getLastModified

```
protected long getLastModified(HttpServletRequest req)
```

This method returns the time the request was last modified. It is usually used to help support browser caching. If the servlet is sending back files, it can compare the last modified time of the request to the last modified time of the file and send back the file only if the file is newer than the request.

service

```
public void service(ServletRequest request,
    ServletResponse response)
    throws ServletException, java.io.IOException
protected void service(HttpServletRequest request,
    HttpServletResponse response)
    throws ServletException, java.io.IOException
```

The servlet engine calls this method to allow the servlet to process a request. This method will not be called until the `init` method has been called, so you can be sure that any initialization you perform in your `init` method will have completed by the time this method is called. Because the servlet engine can be multi-threaded, this method might be called multiple times at once by different threads. If you use any resources that are not thread-safe, you must synchronize access to those resources.

Although you can override these methods in an `HttpServlet`, it is better to override the individual *doXXX* methods instead.

HttpSessionBindingEvent

The `HttpSessionBindingEvent` contains information about an object being bound to a particular session.

`HttpSessionBindingEvent` CONSTRUCTOR

```
public HttpSessionBindingEvent(HttpSession session, String name)
```

Creates a new `HttpSessionBindingEvent` with a specific session and object name.

getName

```
public String getName()
```

Returns the name that the object is being bound to or unbound from.

getSession

```
public HttpSession getSession()
```

Returns the session where the object is being bound or unbound.

HttpUtils

The `HttpUtils` object contains a few handy utility methods, frequently used by the other HTTP classes.

getRequestURL

```
public static StringBuffer getRequestURL(HttpServletRequest request)
```

Pieces together the original request URL using various methods in the request object. The URL is returned as a `StringBuffer` to make it easy for you to add information to the end of it.

parsePostData

```
public static Hashtable parsePostDate(int len, ServletInputStream in)
```

Automatically parses request form data sent with a content type of `application/x-www-form-urlencoded` and returns a hash table containing names and values.

parseQueryString

```
public static Hashtable parseQueryString(String queryString)
```

Automatically parses form data from a query string and returns a hash table containing names and values.

APPENDIX C

APACHE AND TOMCAT

In this appendix

The Tomcat servlet engine is an open-source package developed as part of the Apache Software Foundation's Jakarta project. Sun Microsystems originally developed Tomcat as part of the Java Server Web Development Kit and has turned the Tomcat source code over to Apache for further development.

Tomcat can act as a standalone Web server and also as a servlet/JSP engine for other Web servers. When you download the Tomcat server, you really get two packages: Tomcat and Jasper. Tomcat is really only a servlet engine and Jasper is the JSP engine. Most people refer to both of these packages collectively as Tomcat, however.

Note

To use Tomcat, you will need a full Java Development Kit (JDK) installed on your system. The smaller Java Runtime Environment (JRE) does not include a Java compiler, which is necessary for compiling Java Server Pages. If you get an error telling you there is no compiler, you probably have the JRE edition.

WHERE TO GET TOMCAT

The Tomcat Web site is at `http://jakarta.apache.org`. Figure C.1 shows the Jakarta-Tomcat Web site as of late August 2000.

Figure C.1
The Jakarta Project is an open-source implementation of JSP and servlets.

To download Tomcat, click the Binaries link under Download on the left side of the page. Unless you are really adventurous, you should stick with the release builds. These have been tested thoroughly and deemed to be relatively stable. The milestone builds typically have newer features and bug fixes, but haven't been tested enough to be considered a release.

The nightly builds are snapshots of the very latest version of the code. Because there are a number of developers working on Tomcat, you might find that the nightly builds vary greatly in quality as new changes make their way into the code. It often takes several iterations before a new set of changes becomes stable.

When you click the Release Builds link, you get a list of files to download. For Windows, you should download the jakarta-tomcat.zip file. For Linux, you can use jakarta-tomcat.tar.Z, jakarta-tomcar.tar.gz, or jakarta-tomcat.zip. For other UNIX systems, use either jakarta-tomcat.tar.Z or jakarta-tomcat.tar.gz. If you don't have gunzip on your system, download the .tar.Z version. Unlike Linux, many commercial UNIX distributions do not come with an unzip program.

Figure C.2 shows the release download page.

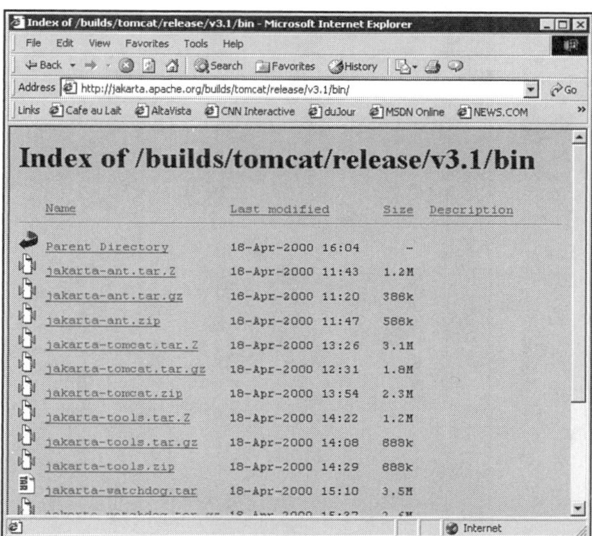

Figure C.2
The Tomcat server is packaged in several different formats.

If you want to use Tomcat purely as a servlet/JSP engine for Netscape, Apache, or IIS, you must also download a connector DLL or library for your Web server. As of August 2000, Tomcat includes only prebuilt connectors for Windows and Linux running on an Intel platform. For Windows, there are connectors for Netscape, IIS, and Apache, although for Linux there is only an Apache connector.

The connectors are in the linux and win32 directories off the main release download page. Table C.1 shows the connectors available for Windows.

TABLE C.1 PRE-BUILT CONNECTORS FOR TOMCAT

Web Server	Connector
Netscape	nsapi_redirect.dll
IIS	isapi_redirect.dll
Apache	ApacheModuleJServ.dll

Figure C.3 shows the download page for the connectors.

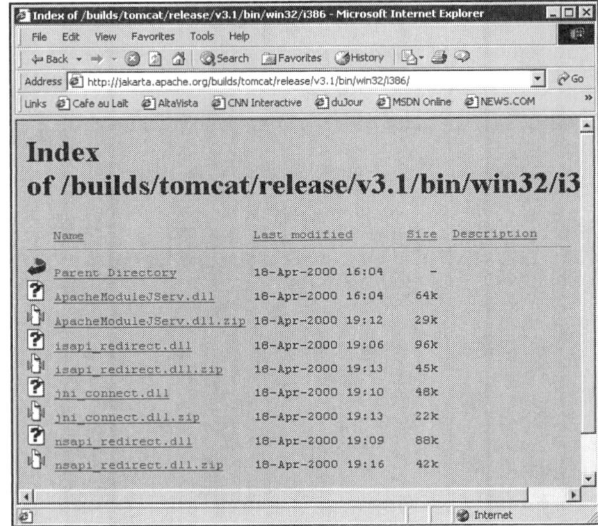

Figure C.3
Tomcat provides several connector modules to integrate with other Web servers.

The only connector in binary available for Linux is mod_jserv.so; it's only for Apache.

INSTALLING TOMCAT

Unlike several commercial JSP implementations, Tomcat doesn't have a graphical installer. Instead, you must install it manually.

INSTALLING TOMCAT ON WINDOWS

You need an unzip program to unpack Tomcat for Windows. You can use either WinZip from `www.winzip.com` or Info-ZIP from `ftp://ftp.freesoftware.com/pub/infozip/Info-ZIP.html`. WinZip is a commercial product, but is the most popular zip utility for Windows. Info-ZIP is a command-line tool available for wide variety of systems and is 100% free. After you unpack Tomcat, it is basically installed except for configuring any connectors.

UNPACKING TOMCAT WITH WINZIP

To install Tomcat from WinZip, run Windows Explorer, go to the directory where you downloaded Tomcat and double-click on jakarta-tomcat.zip. WinZip shows you a screen that looks like the one in Figure C.4. Click the Extract button.

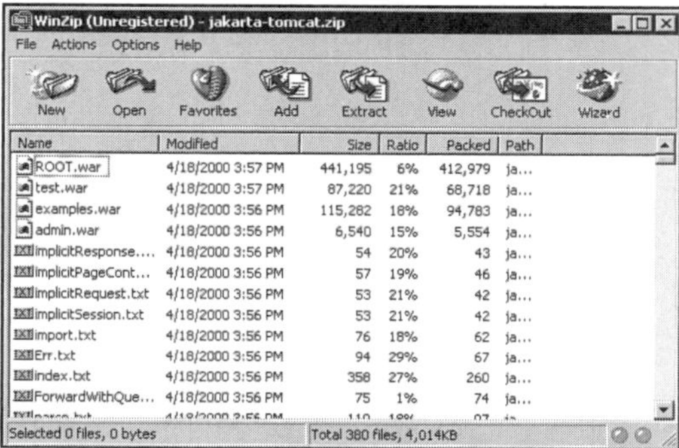

Figure C.4
WinZip makes it easy to unpack Tomcat.

After you click Extract, you'll see a window similar to the one shown in Figure C.5. Select the directory where you want to install Tomcat. Keep in mind that Tomcat will be placed in a subdirectory named jakarta-tomcat off of whatever directory you choose. In other words, if you ask WinZip to install Tomcat in c:\tomcat, you will end up installing Tomcat in c:\tomcat\jakarta-tomcat.

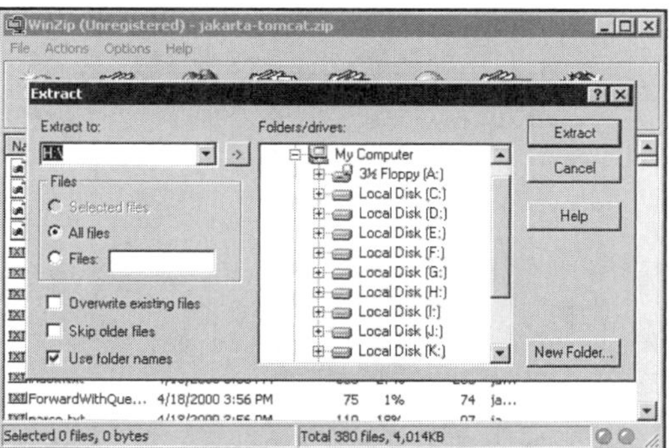

Figure C.5
WinZip allows you to choose where to unpack a file.

UNPACKING TOMCAT FROM THE COMMAND LINE

If you want to unpack Tomcat using a command-line unzip program such as Info-ZIP, bring up a command window (DOS prompt), go to the directory where you want to install Tomcat, and unzip jakarta-tomcat.zip. Remember, when you unpack Tomcat, it will be placed in a directory named jakarta-tomcat below the directory where you unpack it. If you want Tomcat to be installed in c:\jakarta-tomcat, you must unpack it from c:\. If you unpack it from c:\tomcat, it will be installed in c:\tomcat\jakarta-tomcat.

TESTING THE INSTALLATION

Although it isn't required to run Tomcat, you should set the TOMCAT_HOME environment variable to point to the directory where you installed Tomcat. Some of the other Tomcat tools make use of TOMCAT_HOME.

To try out your new Tomcat installation, go to the directory where you installed Tomcat, then go to the bin directory, and type **startup**. You should see a window like the one shown in Figure C.6.

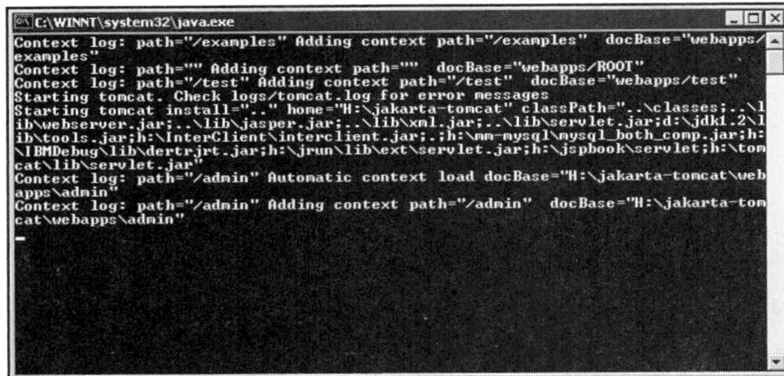

Figure C.6
You see several status messages when Tomcat starts up.

By default, Tomcat starts on port 8080. Point your browser to http://localhost:8080 and you should see a screen like the one shown in Figure C.7. If you installed Tomcat on a machine other than the one where your browser is, use the hostname of the machine where Tomcat is running instead of localhost.

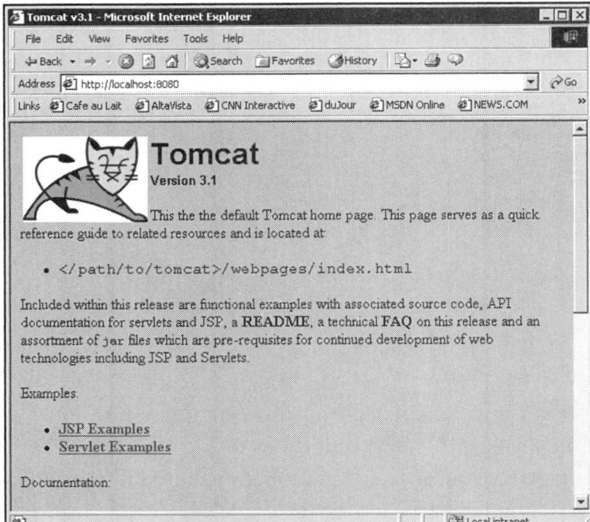

Figure C.7
This is the default Tomcat home page.

INSTALLING TOMCAT ON LINUX OR UNIX

To install Tomcat on Linux or UNIX, go to the directory where you want to install Tomcat. You don't need to be root to install Tomcat, unless you are installing it in a protected directory such as /usr/local. No matter which file you downloaded, the .zip, .tar.Z, or .tar.gz, Tomcat will be installed in a subdirectory called jakarta-tomcat from wherever you unpack it. If you want to install it in /usr/local/jakarta-tomcat, you must unpack it from the /usr/local directory.

If you download jakarta-tomcat.tar.Z, you unpack Tomcat with this command:

```
zcat /home/mark/download/jakarta-tomcat.tar.Z | tar xvf -
```

Remember to change `/home/mark/download` to the path where you downloaded Tomcat.

If you downloaded jakarta-tomcat.tar.gz, you can unpack it this way:

```
gunzip -c /home/mark/download/jakarta-tomcat.tar.gz | tar xvf -
```

Make sure you have gunzip on your machine. If you are running Linux or have the GNU version of tar, you can unpack the file like this:

```
tar xvzf /home/mark/download/jakarta-tomcat.tar.gz
```

If you downloaded jakarta-tomcat.zip, unpack it with this command:

```
unzip /home/mark/download/jakarta-tomcat.zip
```

After you unpack Tomcat, you are ready to try it out. Go to the bin directory under the jakarta-tomcat directory and type **`./startup.sh`**. You should see some startup messages like the ones shown in Figure C.8.

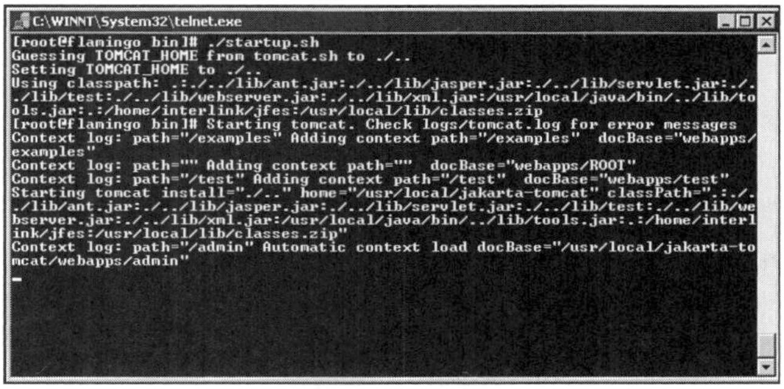

```
C:\WINNT\System32\telnet.exe
[root@flamingo bin]# ./startup.sh
Guessing TOMCAT_HOME from tomcat.sh to ./..
Setting TOMCAT_HOME to ./..
Using classpath: .:./../lib/ant.jar:./../lib/jasper.jar:./../lib/servlet.jar:./.
./lib/test:./../lib/webserver.jar:./../lib/xml.jar:/usr/local/java/bin/../lib/to
ols.jar:.:/home/interlink/jfes:/usr/local/lib/classes.zip
[root@flamingo bin]# Starting tomcat. Check logs/tomcat.log for error messages
Context log: path="/examples" Adding context path="/examples"  docBase="webapps/
examples"
Context log: path="" Adding context path=""  docBase="webapps/ROOT"
Context log: path="/test" Adding context path="/test"  docBase="webapps/test"
Starting tomcat install="./.." home="/usr/local/jakarta-tomcat" classPath=".:./.
./lib/ant.jar:./../lib/jasper.jar:./../lib/servlet.jar:./../lib/test:./../lib/we
bserver.jar:./../lib/xml.jar:/usr/local/java/bin/../lib/tools.jar:.:/home/interl
ink/jfes:/usr/local/lib/classes.zip"
Context log: path="/admin" Automatic context load docBase="/usr/local/jakarta-to
mcat/webapps/admin"
```

Figure C.8
Tomcat prints several status messages when it starts up.

Although it isn't required to run Tomcat, you should set the `TOMCAT_HOME` environment variable to point to the directory where you installed Tomcat. Some of the other Tomcat tools make use of `TOMCAT_HOME`.

As with the Windows version, Tomcat starts on port 8080 by default. Point your browser to `http://localhost:8080` and you should see a screen like the one shown previously in Figure C.7. If you installed Tomcat on a machine other than the one where your browser is, use the hostname of the machine where Tomcat is running instead of `localhost`.

Note

After you get past the installation issues, Tomcat works identically under Windows, UNIX, and Linux because it is 100% Java.

RUNNING TOMCAT STANDALONE

If you have successfully started Tomcat with the `startup` command, you know almost everything you need to know about running Tomcat standalone. The shutdown.bat file for Windows or the shutdown.sh file for UNIX/Linux stops the Tomcat server.

If you want to change the port number for the server (the default for HTTP is 80), see "Tomcat Configuration" later in this appendix.

RUNNING TOMCAT UNDER NETSCAPE SERVER FOR WINDOWS

You can set up the Netscape Web server to pass certain directory names to Tomcat for processing. In essence, you can use Netscape as your main Web server and use Tomcat as a servlet and JSP engine. Unfortunately, the mapping between Tomcat and Netscape is a fairly manual process. If you want to add directories to the set of directories handled by Tomcat, you must edit the Netscape configuration files manually.

Note

Adding Tomcat support to Netscape is a tedious, error-prone process. Make absolutely sure that you need to hook these two products together before proceeding. Commercial products such as JRun have an automated script that makes it easy to hook up to Netscape.

To hook Netscape and Tomcat together, you need the nsapi_redirect.dll file from the Jakarta Web site. If you don't know where to get nsapi_redirect.dll, see "Where to Get Tomcat" earlier in this appendix. Copy nsapi_redirect.dll to the jakarta-tomcat/bin directory.

If you are running the iPlanet 4 Web server (the next generation of Netscape Web servers) or another Netscape server that supports servlets, make sure you disable servlets first. Go to the Web server administration Web page and select Servlets. Make sure the No option button is selected for both Activate the Servlet Engine and JSP Enabled. Figure C.9 shows the servlet administration page with both options disabled.

Note

You are probably asking yourself why you need to even install Tomcat if the iPlanet Web server supports JSP and servlets. If your version of iPlanet supports at least version 2.2 of the Servlet specification and at least version 1.1 of the JSP specification, go ahead and use the built-in servlet/JSP support. As of July 2000, iPlanet is woefully behind in its support of servlets and JSP.

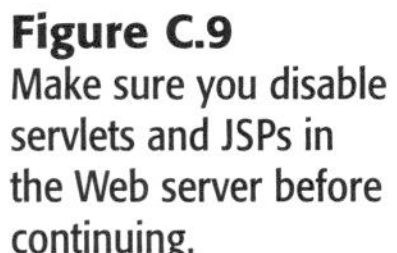

Figure C.9
Make sure you disable servlets and JSPs in the Web server before continuing.

Now that you have disabled servlets and JSP in the Web server, go to the Web server's config directory. For iPlanet 4 with a server name of usingjsp.wutka.com, and iPlanet installed in f:\Netscape\server4, the path for the config directory is F:\Netscape\server4\https-USINGJSP.wutka.com\config.

In this config directory you will find a file called obj.conf. Go to the top of the obj.conf file and look for some lines that start with `"Init fn="`. After the last of these `init` lines, add the following two lines:

```
Init fn="load-modules" funcs="jk_init,jk_service"
➥shlib="h:/jakarta-tomcat/bin/nsapi_redirect.dll"
Init fn="jk_init"
➥ worker_file="h:/jakarta-tomcat/conf/workers.properties"
➥log_level="debug" log_file="h:/jakarta-tomcat/nsapi.log"
```

In this example, Tomcat is installed just below H: in H:\jakarta-tomcat. Make sure you change these lines to match your own configuration.

Next, go down to the line:

```
<Object name="default">
```

Add the following two lines immediately after:

```
NameTrans fn="assign-name" from="/servlet/*" name="servlet"
NameTrans fn="assign-name" from="/examples/*" name="servlet"
```

Finally, go to the section where you see parameters grouped between `<Object> </Object>` tags. After any `</Object>` tag, add the following declaration:

```
<Object name="servlet">
ObjectType fn="force-type" type="text/plain"
Service fn="jk_service" worker="ajp12"
</Object>
```

APP C

Note

If there is already a declaration with `<Object name="servlet">`, change it to match the declaration shown previously. Make sure there aren't two objects with a name of "servlet".

Your final configuration file should look something like the file shown in Listing C.1.

LISTING C.1 obj.conf FILE FOR IPLANET 4 WEB SERVER

```
# Sun Netscape Alliance - obj.conf
# You can edit this file, but comments and formatting changes
# might be lost when the admin server makes changes.

# Use only forward slashes in pathnames—backslashes can cause
# problems. See the documentation for more information.

Init fn="flex-init" access="f:/Netscape/Server4/https-
USINGJSP.wutka.com/logs/access" format.access="%Ses->client.ip% - %Req->vars.auth-
user% [%SYSDATE%] \"%Req->reqpb.clf-request%\" %Req->srvhdrs.clf-status%
%Req->srvhdrs.content-length%"
Init fn="load-types" mime-types="mime.types"
Init fn="load-modules" funcs="jk_init,jk_service" shlib="h:/jakarta-
tomcat/bin/nsapi_redirect.dll"
Init fn="jk_init" worker_file="h:/jakarta-tomcat/conf/workers.properties"
log_level="debug" log_file="h:/jakarta-tomcat/nsapi.log"

<Object name="default">
NameTrans fn="assign-name" from="/servlet/*" name="servlet"
NameTrans fn="assign-name" from="/examples/*" name="servlet"
NameTrans fn="pfx2dir" from="/ns-icons" dir="f:/Netscape/Server4/ns-icons"
name="es-internal"
NameTrans fn="pfx2dir" from="/mc-icons" dir="f:/Netscape/Server4/ns-icons"
name="es-internal"
NameTrans fn="pfx2dir" from="/help" dir="f:/Netscape/Server4/manual/https/ug"
name="es-internal"
NameTrans fn="pfx2dir" from="/manual" dir="f:/Netscape/Server4/manual/https"
name="es-internal"
NameTrans fn="document-root" root="f:/Netscape/Server4/docs"
PathCheck fn="nt-uri-clean"
PathCheck fn="check-acl" acl="default"
PathCheck fn="find-pathinfo"
PathCheck fn="find-index" index-names="index.html,home.html"
ObjectType fn="type-by-extension"
ObjectType fn="force-type" type="text/plain"
Service method="(GET|HEAD)" type="magnus-internal/imagemap" fn="imagemap"
Service method="(GET|HEAD)" type="magnus-internal/directory" fn="index-common"
Service method="(GET|HEAD|POST)" type="*~magnus-internal/*" fn="send-file"
AddLog fn="flex-log" name="access"
</Object>

<Object name="cgi">
ObjectType fn="force-type" type="magnus-internal/cgi"
Service fn="send-cgi"
</Object>
```

```
<Object name="servlet">
ObjectType fn="force-type" type="text/plain"
Service fn="jk_service" worker="ajp12"
</Object>

<Object name="jsp092">
ObjectType fn="type-by-extension"
ObjectType fn="change-type" type="magnus-internal/jsp092" if-type="magnus-
internal/jsp"
Service fn="NSServletService" type="magnus-internal/jsp092"
</Object>

<Object name="ServletByExt">
ObjectType fn="force-type" type="magnus-internal/servlet"
Service type="magnus-internal/servlet" fn="NSServletService"
</Object>

<Object name="es-internal">
PathCheck fn="check-acl" acl="es-internal"
</Object>
```

If you need to map additional pathnames so they will run under Tomcat, add additional `NameTrans` lines. For example, if you want `/jspbook` to pass through to Tomcat, add the following line:

```
NameTrans fn="assign-name" from="/jspbook/*" name="servlet"
```

Running Tomcat Under IIS

You can set up Internet Information Server (IIS) or its smaller companion Personal Web Server (PWS) to call Tomcat to handle certain directories. Unlike commercial implementations (such as JRun), which have nice, simple installation procedures, Tomcat's plugin for IIS is a tedious, manual process.

Because the IIS installation requires you to edit your Registry manually and perform several configuration steps inside the Web server administration tool, you should avoid trying to hook Tomcat and IIS together. Instead, either use a different servlet/JSP engine such as Resin or JRun, or use a different Web server such as Apache.

Running Tomcat Under Apache

If you have tried to run Apache under Netscape or IIS, you will find the Tomcat-Apache integration to be a breath of fresh air.

Running Tomcat with Apache for Windows

For the Windows version of Apache, you need to download the ApacheModuleJServ.dll file from the Jakarta Web site (see "Where to Get Tomcat" at the beginning of this appendix if you don't know where to get the file) .

Now, copy the ApacheModuleJServ.dll file into the modules directory in your Apache installation. If you installed Apache into c:\apache, the modules directory is c:\apache\modules.

After you copy the file, you need to edit the httpd.conf file, which is under c:\apache\conf (if Apache is installed in c:\apache). At the end of the file, add the following line:

```
Include h:/jakarta-tomcat/conf/tomcat-apache.conf
```

Obviously, you must replace h:/jakarta-tomcat with the name of the directory where you have installed Tomcat. Make sure Tomcat is already running, because it creates the tomcat-apache.conf file when it starts up, and then restart Apache. You should now be able to access servlets and Java Server Pages.

RUNNING TOMCAT WITH APACHE FOR LINUX

For the Linux version of Apache, you need to download the mod_jserv.so file from the Jakarta Web site (see "Where to Get Tomcat" at the beginning of this appendix if you don't know where to get the file) .

Now, copy the mod_jserv.so file into the modules directory in your Apache installation. If you installed Apache into /opt/apache, the modules directory is /opt/apache/modules.

Note

If you are running a recent distribution of Red Hat Linux, the Apache installation has been split across several locations. The modules directory is /etc/httpd/modules, and the configuration directory is /etc/httpd/conf.

After you copy the file, you need to edit the httpd.conf file, which is under /opt/apache/conf (again assuming an installation directory of /opt/apache). At the end of the file, add the following line:

```
Include /usr/local/jakarta-tomcat/conf/tomcat-apache.conf
```

Again, you must replace /usr/local/jakarta-tomcat with the name of the directory where you have installed Tomcat. Make sure Tomcat is already running, because it creates the tomcat-apache.conf file when it starts up, and then restart Apache. You should now be able to access servlets and Java Server Pages.

TOMCAT CONFIGURATION

Tomcat configuration is very straightforward. In the conf directory, there is a file called server.xml. Most of the directives in server.xml deal with logging and various worker classes within the Tomcat server. The part of the file you might want to edit is the section that defines contexts.

If you want to add a virtual directory that you can access through Tomcat, you must set up a context for it. Suppose, for example, you have a directory h:\jspbook and you want to access it from Tomcat via the URL `http://localhost/jspbook`. You would add a context mapping to the server.xml file like this:

```
<Context path="/jspbook" docBase="h:/jspbook" debug="0" reloadable="true" >
</Context>
```

You must restart Tomcat to pick up any additional contexts. If you are using the Apache-Tomcat integration, Tomcat automatically adds any new contexts to its tomcat-apache.conf file, so when you restart Apache, it will also know about the new directory.

The web.xml file contains the configuration for the default Web application. The format of the file is identical to the format used for Web Archive (WAR) files. You can find more information on the format of WAR files from Chapter 28, "Packaging a JSP Application."

WORKING DIRECTORY

When you work with files in a servlet or JSP, you sometimes need to know the default working directory for the servlet engine. For servers such as JRun, there is a specific directory that is the same every time. For Tomcat, however, the current working directory is the working directory at the time startup was run.

For example, if you go to c:\jakarta-tomcat\bin and then type **`startup`**, the working directory is c:\jakarta-tomcat\bin. If, on the other hand, you go to c:\windows and type **`c:\jakarta-tomcat\bin\startup`**, the working directory is c:\windows.

LOGGING

Unlike most other JSP/servlet engines, Tomcat doesn't log `System.out` and `System.err` output to a file. You see the output in the window where you started Tomcat. If you redirect Tomcat's output to a file, the `System.out` and `System.err` messages appear in the file.

For other log messages, Tomcat has a logs directory containing tomcat.log, servlet.log, and jasper.log. The servlet.log and jasper.log files contain log messages from the servlet and JSP engines. They do not contain log messages about individual servlets and Java Server Pages, however. All messages about servlets and Java Server Pages go to the tomcat.log file, including any JSP compilation errors.

SETTING THE CLASSPATH

Tomcat typically uses the same classpath settings as your Java Virtual Machine. If you are running Windows, you can set the classpath environment variable from the control panel. Under Unix and Linux, you just change the `CLASSPATH` environment variable from your login shell.

AUTHENTICATION

Unfortunately, as of August 2000, Tomcat doesn't support user-level authentication in its standalone mode. If you use Tomcat with another Web server, you can always use the authentication facilities of the other Web server.

Special Tomcat Features

Although Tomcat was one of the first JSP/servlet engines to support version 2.2 of the servlet specification and version 1.1 of the JSP specification, it doesn't include many additional features.

WAR File Installation

Tomcat doesn't have any special tool for installing WAR files, but it does recognize them if you place them in jakarta-tomcat/webapps. When you restart Tomcat, it automatically unpacks any new WAR files. If you need to update a WAR file, however, you must delete the directory Tomcat creates.

For example, if you copy a file named tagdemo.war into the webapps directory, Tomcat creates a directory named tagdemo the next time it starts and unpacks the contents of tagdemo.war into the directory. If you want to install a new tagdemo.war, make sure you remove the tagdemo directory.

JSP Compiler

One of the niftiest add-on features of Tomcat is a command-line JSP compiler. You can precompile a single JSP file or an entire directory. The compiler is in the jakarta-tomcat/bin directory and is called `jspc`. Before running `jspc`, you must ensure that the `TOMCAT_HOME` environment variable is set and that it points to the directory where Tomcat is installed.

To run `jspc`, just type

```
jspc filename.jsp
```

where `filename` is the name of the JSP you want to compile. The `jspc` program will create a file called *filename*.java containing the servlet that would normally be generated behind the scenes. You can also precompile all the servlets in a directory by typing

```
jspc -webapp directoryname
```

Although the JSP engine compiles Java Server Pages automatically, you might find that it is useful to precompile some JSPs. For example, when you package your application in a WAR file, you might want to configure a JSP as a servlet so you can change various settings using servlet configuration tags.

If you are just precompiling so the pages are always ready, you might consider the precompilation protocol discussed back in Chapter 10, "Performance."

APPENDIX

JRun

In this appendix

The JRun server from Allaire has been a popular JSP and servlet engine for the past few years. Recently, JRun version 3 added EJB capabilities to become a full-fledged J2EE server. JRun is easy to configure, easy to administer, and comes with a wide variety of features. It is available for Windows, Solaris, Linux, and HPUX.

WHERE TO FIND JRUN

Unlike Tomcat, JRun is a commercial product, so you can't just download a free copy and run it in a production system. Like most good software vendors, however, Allaire lets you download JRun and try it out free. You can get JRun at `http://www.allaire.com`.

INSTALLING JRUN FOR WINDOWS

JRun comes packaged as a single executable program that you simply run to start the install procedure. When you start the installation, the first thing you need to decide is where you want to install JRun. After agreeing to the software license and verifying your name and company, you will see the dialog box shown in Figure D.1.

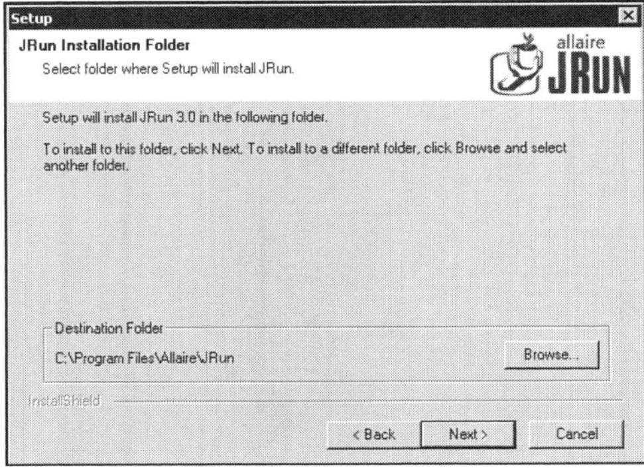

Figure D.1
The first thing you must decide is where to install JRun.

Click the Browse button if you want to change the installation directory; otherwise click Next.

The next choice you have is the type of installation: Full, Minimal, or Custom. Unless you are really short on disk space, go ahead and select the full installation (see Figure D.2).

Next, JRun gives you the option of changing the folder for JRun on the programs menu. You can change this if you want to keep your programs menu organized; otherwise just click Next. After the programs menu choice, the JRun install unpacks all its files and if you are running Windows NT or Windows 2000, it asks if you want to install JRun as a service, as shown in Figure D.3.

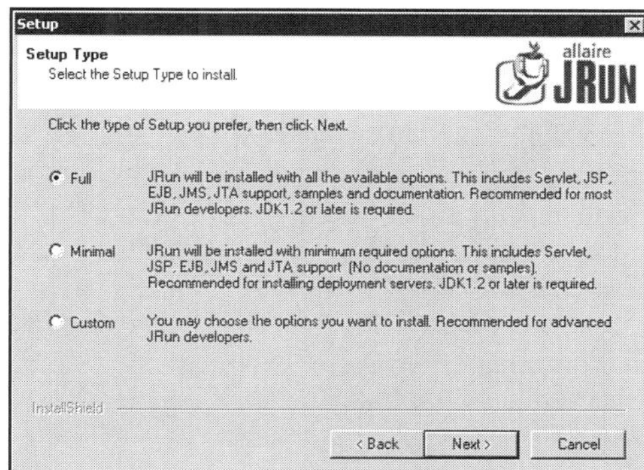

Figure D.2
Choose Full install if you have enough space.

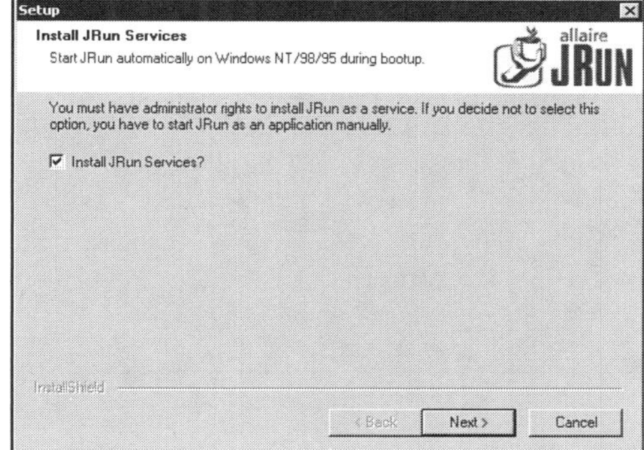

Figure D.3
If you have Administrator rights, you can install JRun as a service under Windows NT or Windows 2000.

Now you must tell JRun where your Java Runtime Environment (JRE) or Java Development Kit (JDK) is installed. It automatically searches your system and gives you a list of likely candidates, as shown in Figure D.4.

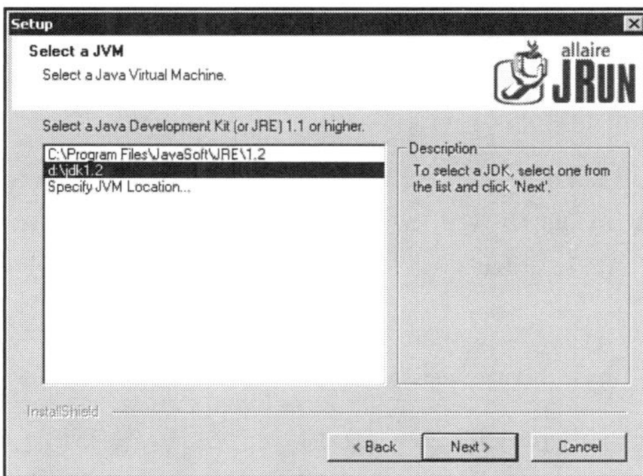

Figure D.4
JRun helps you figure out where your JRE or JDK is installed.

JRun is pretty specific about which versions of the JDK or JRE it will accept. The Windows installation of JRun includes a JRE installation in case you don't have a supported JRE.

After you select your JRE, you are given the option to change the port number for the admin server. If the port number displayed in the dialog box conflicts with another program you are running, or if you are installing a second copy of JRun on the same machine, you need to change the port number. Otherwise, leave it alone.

After the admin port dialog box, you see a dialog box that lets you set the admin password for the administration server. You must enter the password twice to make sure you typed correctly. Figure D.5 shows the password dialog.

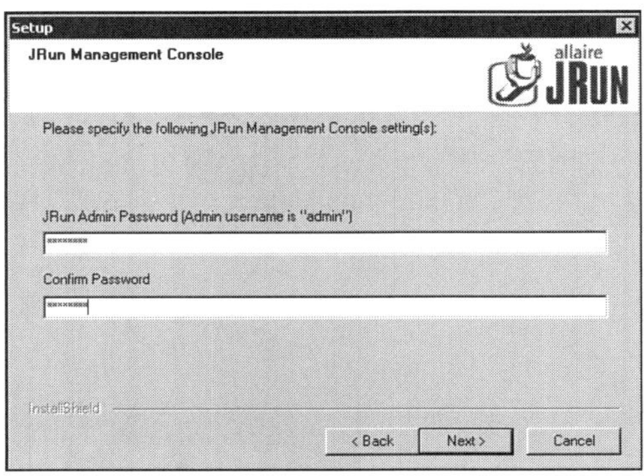

Figure D.5
Make sure you pick a good admin password.

After JRun performs a few more setup tasks, you have one last option. You can configure a connection to an existing Web server. Web server connections are discussed later in this appendix.

INSTALLING JRUN FOR LINUX

To install JRun for Linux, you don't need to be root unless you want to install to a directory where you don't otherwise have access, or unless you need to configure a connector to Netscape or Apache.

After you run the installation script, you are prompted to enter the name of the directory where you want to install JRun, as shown in Figure D.6. Press Enter to accept the default directory or type in a different directory.

Next you have a choice of whether you want just Servlet/JSP support, just EJB/JMS support, or a full install. If you have enough disk space, go ahead and do a full install.

After the JRun install unpacks some files, it asks you where your Java Development Kit (JDK) or Java Runtime Environment (JRE) is located. The install program first looks for a likely candidate (probably by finding where in the path the `java` command is located) and offers you that directory as the default. Figure D.7 shows the installation program prompting for the location of the JDK/JRE.

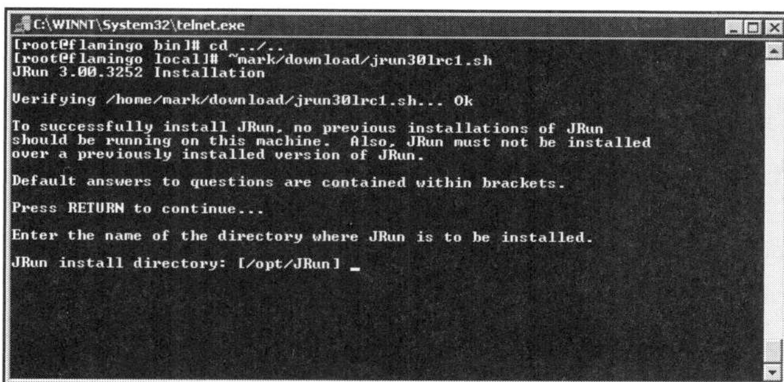

Figure D.6
Press Enter to accept the default directory, or type in a different one.

```
C:\WINNT\System32\telnet.exe
JRun 3.00 Configuration

This script will configure JRun to bootstrap the web-based JRun
Management Console (JMC).  The JMC will then be used to complete the
installation.

Suggested answers to the questions are contained within brackets.
You may accept the suggested answer by just pressing ENTER at the
prompt.

It is highly recommended that you do not install JRun on top of any
existing JRun 2.x.x or JRun 3.0 beta directories.

Copyright (c) 2000 Allaire Corporation

---

JRun requires either a Java Runtime Environment (JRE) or Java
Development Kit (JDK) version 1.1.6 or higher.  A Java Development
Kit is required for developing JavaServer Pages applications. JDK
1.2 or higher is required for developing EJBs.
Enter the absolute path to the JRE or JDK directory.
JRE/JDK directory [/usr/local/java]: _
```

Figure D.7
The installation program tries to figure out where the JDK/JRE is located before it asks you.

Next you must choose the admin password for the administration server. You must enter the password twice just to make sure you didn't make a typo.

After you enter the admin password, you have the option to change the port number for the admin server. If you have another program that uses the default port, or you are installing a second copy of JRun on the same machine, you'll need to change the port number, otherwise just leave it alone.

Finally, JRun performs its final setup tasks and starts the admin server.

Starting JRun

Under Windows NT, JRun should start up when you reboot. If you need to start it manually, go to the Start menu, select JRun, and then select JRun Server. Under UNIX or Linux, go to the bin directory wherever you installed JRun (/opt/JRun/bin for example) and type the following:

```
jrun -start default &
```

You might even want to start it with the `nohup` command just to make sure it doesn't terminate when you log off:

```
nohup jrun -start default &
```

JRUN ADMINISTRATION

JRun uses a Web-based administration tool, managed by the admin server. If you installed JRun under Windows, your Start menu should have a JRun entry and under that, an entry for JRun Management Console. Otherwise, just point your browser to the host where JRun is running and use the port number for the admin server (the default is 8000). For example, if you installed JRun on a Linux machine called mrpengy.wutka.com, you would access the JRun admin server with the URL `http://mrpengy.wutka.com:8000`.

When you first bring up the management console, you are greeted with a login screen. Use the username admin and the password you specified when you installed JRun (unless you have changed it since). Figure D.8 shows the admin login screen.

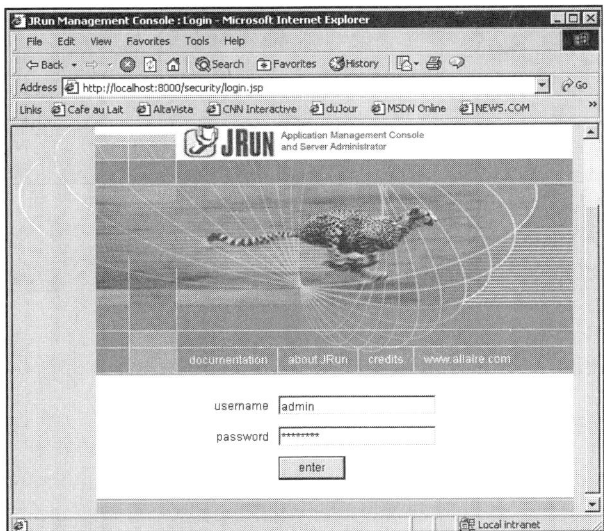

Figure D.8
Use the username admin to administer JRun.

After you successfully log in, you should see the main admin screen shown in Figure D.9.

If you get an error when you try to access the admin server, it may be because the server isn't running. If you are running Windows, go to your start menu, select JRun and then select JRun Admin Server. Then try hitting the admin server page again.

Under UNIX or Linux, go to the directory where you installed JRun and then to the bin directory underneath the main JRun directory. Type the following:

```
jrun -start admin
```

Then try to access the admin server again.

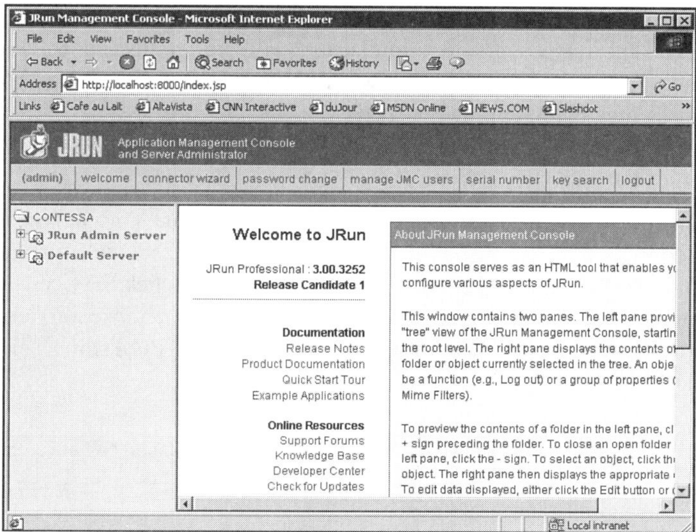

Figure D.9
The main admin screen for JRun has many options.

CONNECTING JRUN TO OTHER WEB SERVERS

No matter what Web server you want to connect JRun to, you use the same screen in the management console. From the main admin screen, click Connector Wizard. You should then see the screen shown in Figure D.10.

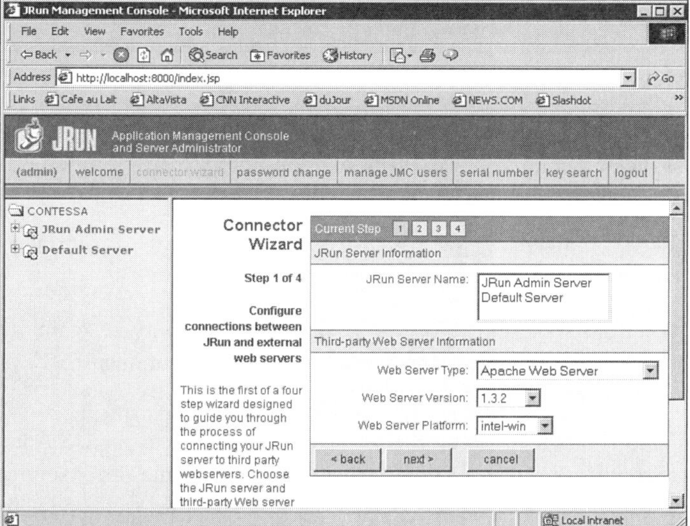

Figure D.10
The JRun Connector Wizard makes it easy to hook into other Web servers.

You want to set up the connector for the default server, so highlight Default Server and then choose the Web server, version, and platform you are connecting to. The Web server must be running on the same machine as JRun. Make sure the default server is running before you set up a new connection.

CONNECTING JRUN TO IIS OR PWS

After you choose Internet Information Server or Personal Web Server as the server you want to connect to, you must shut down the Web server before continuing. If you are running Windows NT, go to the control panel and double-click Services. In Windows 2000, go to the Start menu, select Administrative Tools, and then choose Services. Scroll to the bottom of the screen and you should see World Wide Web Publishing Service, as shown in Figure D.11.

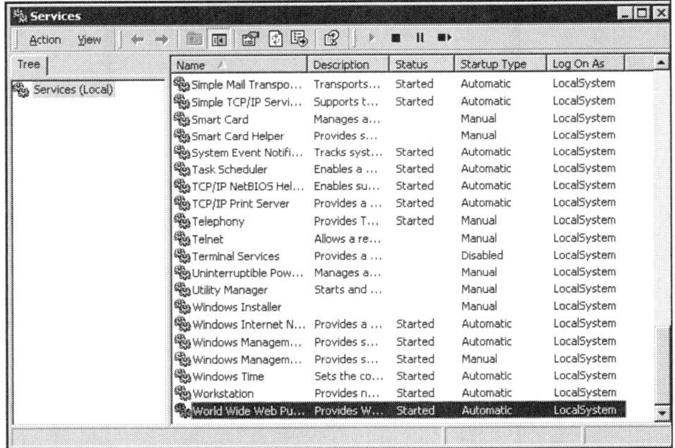

Figure D.11
You can stop IIS or PWS by stopping the World Wide Web Publishing service.

After you stop the Web server, you must select the port number for the JRun connector. You must pick a port number that doesn't conflict with anything else. In Figure D.12, you can see the port number will be 8081.

Next, you must enter the name of your IIS/PWS scripts directory. This directory is typically C:\InetPub\Scripts.

Finally, you must start up the World Wide Publishing Service again. Try running `http://localhost/servlet/SnoopServlet` to see if the connector is working. If not, try restarting the IIS Admin service.

Under Windows NT, bring up the services window, select the IIS Admin service, and then click the Stop button. It will tell you that it will stop some other services, one of which should be the World Wide Web Publishing service. After the service has been stopped, click the Start button to start it again. You will need to start the other stopped services (such as World Wide Web Publishing) manually.

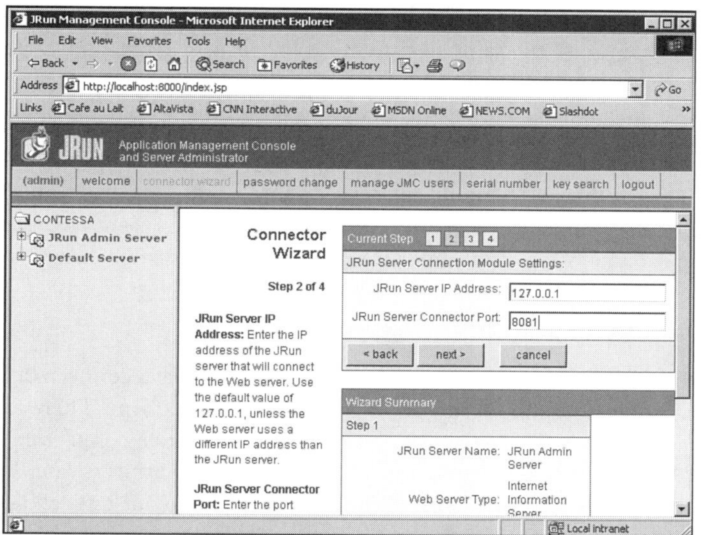

Figure D.12
Set the connector port to a value that isn't used by other programs.

Under Windows 2000, you can restart the IIS Admin service and all its subordinate services by selecting IIS Admin from the services screen and clicking the restart button (it looks like a square and a triangle together) as shown in Figure D.13.

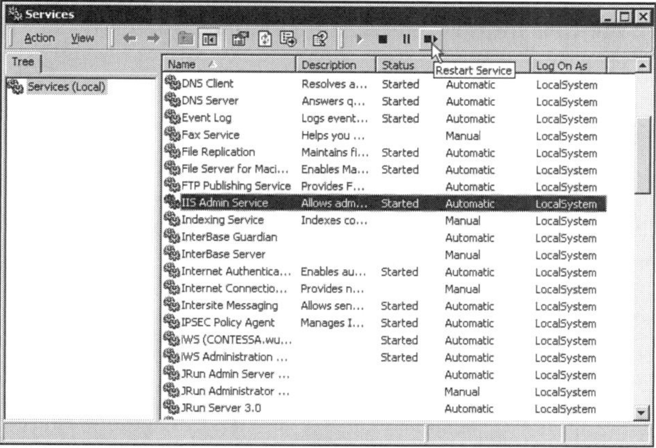

Figure D.13
Windows 2000 lets you restart services with a single button click.

If you still can't access `SnoopServlet`, try rebooting. If that doesn't work, you might need to run through the Connector Wizard again.

Connecting JRun to Netscape Web Server

After you choose either Netscape FastTrack Server or Netscape Enterprise Server in the Connector Wizard, you must shut down the Netscape Web Server. Go to the admin screen for Netscape, select the server you want to shut down and click the Stop button.

Now, select the port number for the JRun connector. If you run multiple connectors, you should be able to use the same port number for all your connectors. The connector port screen was shown in Figure D.13.

Next you must select the directory where the Web server information is stored. Netscape usually names the Web server by prepending either http or https to the host name, although you have the option of changing the server name. If the server is named `mrpengy.wutka.com`, the web server is stored in a directory named `https-mrpengy.wutka.com` under the main Netscape directory. You must enter the full path name for this directory into the Connector Wizard. For example, the full name for the mrpengy Web server is

```
F:\Netscape\server4\https-mrpengy.wutka.com
```

You also have a choice of using a native connector or a Java connector. Because JRun is a pure Java product, it should run on any Java-enabled platform. There are a limited number of officially supported platforms, and Allaire supplies native connectors for the Web servers on these platforms. If you are on one of the supported platforms, use the native connector, it should be much faster. Otherwise, the Java connector is your only choice.

If you entered the pathname for the Web server correctly, JRun should now tell you to restart your Web server. After you bring the Netscape server back up, try hitting `http://localhost/servlet/SnoopServlet` to make sure that JRun and Netscape are working together.

Connecting JRun to Apache

After you choose the Apache Web Server in the Connector Wizard, you must stop your Apache server. If you are running Windows NT, you should be able to stop the server from the Start menu. If you are running a recent installation of Red Hat Linux, you should be able to stop it by typing

```
/etc/rc.d/rc3.d/S85httpd stop
```

Now, select the port number for the JRun connector. If you run multiple connectors, you should be able to use the same port number for all your connectors. The connector port screen was shown in Figure D.13.

Next, enter the name of the Apache conf directory. Normally, this directory is just below the main directory where you installed Apache. On recent Red Hat Linux installations, the directory is /etc/httpd/conf.

After JRun tells you the connector has been installed successfully, start your Apache Web server back up and then try to access `http://localhost/servlet/SnoopServlet`.

Using JRun as a Standalone Web Server

You can use JRun as a standalone Web server. In fact, the default installation starts up a Web server on port 8100. Try pointing your browser to `http://localhost:8100` and see what

happens. You can change the port number by going to the main admin screen, clicking Default Server, and then clicking JRun Web Server. You should see a screen like the one shown in Figure D.14.

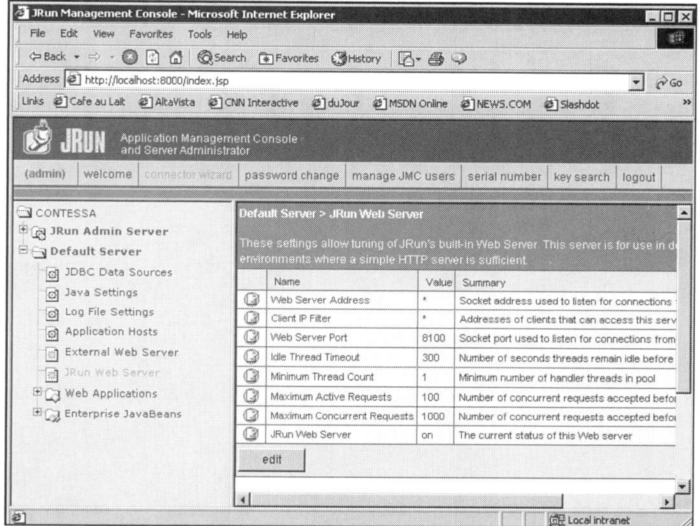

Figure D.14
JRun comes with a built-in Web server that you can run standalone.

On the right, there is a configuration item named Web Server Port. If you want to use JRun as the main Web server for your machine, change this port number to 80, and then stop and start the JRun server. Make sure you aren't running any other Web servers on this port, of course.

WORKING DIRECTORY

The default working directory for any servlets or Java Server Pages running under JRun is the root directory for the server they are running under. If you just stick to the basic JRun configuration and use the Default Server for all your applications, the working directory will be `<JRun directory>/servers/default`.

INSTALLING WEB APPLICATIONS

JRun has excellent support for Web applications and makes installation a breeze. From the main management console, click Default Server on the left-hand side of the screen. You should then see a screen like the one shown in Figure D.15.

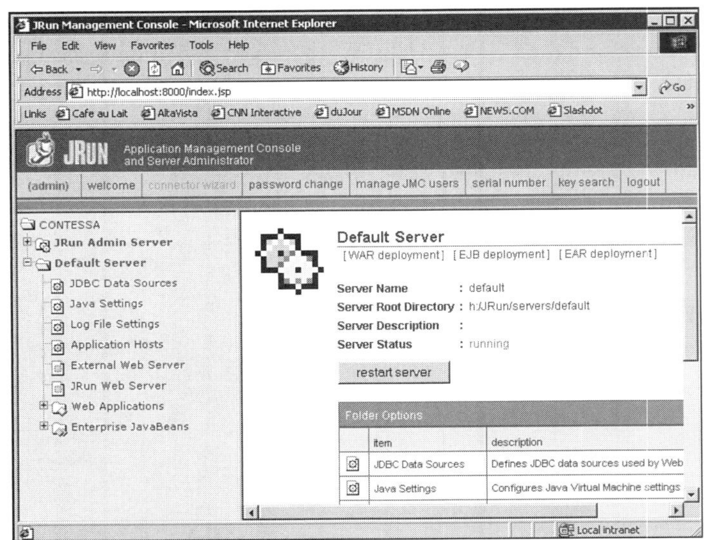

Figure D.15
JRun makes it easy to install a Web application.

On the top right-hand side of the screen, just below Default Server, you should see a link named WAR Deployment. Click the link and you'll get a screen like the one shown in Figure D.16.

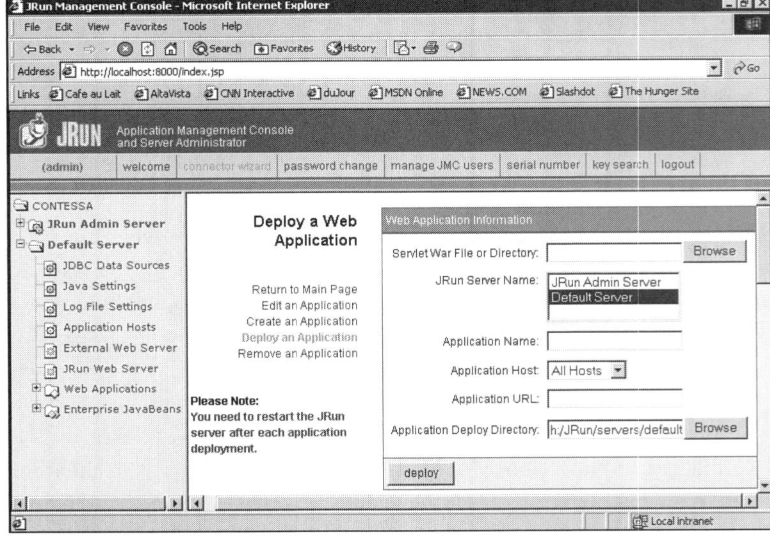

Figure D.16
To deploy a Web application, just fill in a few fields and click Deploy.

You must tell JRun where the WAR file is, which server to use (it's almost always Default Server), the name of the application, the application host (leave this one alone), the URL (the root path for the application), and the directory where JRun should unpack the WAR file.

Most of these items are self-explanatory. For the last item, the directory where it should unpack the WAR file, you should consider putting it under `<JRUNdirectory>/servers/default/<your app name>`. For example, if JRun is installed in `h:/JRun` and your application is named `myapp`, tell JRun to unpack the WAR file in `h:/JRun/servers/default/myapp`.

Setting the Classpath

JRun uses its own settings for the Java classpath rather than using the CLASSPATH environment variable. From the JRun management tool, you can select "JVM Settings" to change various aspects of the Java Virtual Machine, including the classpath and also various command-line switches.

Log Files

JRun stores its log files in the logs directory just below the main JRun directory. The log files are named *xxx*-err.log, *xxx*-out.log, and *xxx*-event.log where *xxx* is the name of the JRun server, like admin or default. The err and out files contain data sent to System.err and System.out. The event file contains various event notifications generated by JRun.

JRun Special Features

JRun version 3 is a full Java2 Enterprise Edition (J2EE) server. In addition to supporting JSP and servlets, it also supports EJB, JMS (Java Message Service), JNDI, and several other required J2EE packages. You may have noticed when you installed a WAR file that JRun can install EAR files (Enterprise Application Archive) just as easily.

Allaire also makes a companion product called JRun Studio, which is a development environment for creating and deploying servlets and Java Server Pages. JRun Studio handles many of the tedious deployment tasks, such as creating the web.xml and TLD files.

APPENDIX

SERVLETEXEC

In this appendix

ServletExec is a JSP and servlet engine that can operate as an external server, or operate as an in-process ISAPI or NSAPI library. As you may recall from Chapter 1, "The Evolution of the Web Server," ISAPI and NSAPI are library interfaces that let you extend the capabilities of the Web server similar to the way you do with servlets. The ISAPI/NSAPI versions of ServletExec are easy to install and configure. Because they run as part of IIS or Netscape, you don't need to start a separate server process.

The disadvantage of the ISAPI/NSAPI approach is that you are limited to a single Java virtual machine to handle all requests. Many JSP/servlet engines allow you to run multiple Java virtual machines, which can improve performance and security. Most Web providers that support JSP and servlets allow you to run your application in a separate Java virtual machine. That way, when you change classes and need to restart the JVM, you don't affect any other users. Second, you don't run the risk of someone sabotaging your server with malicious Java classes running in the same JVM.

Note

ServletExec was originally produced by New Atlanta Communications, which has since been bought by Unify.

WHERE TO GET SERVLETEXEC

ServletExec is a commercial product, but you can download an evaluation copy from `http://www.servletexec.com`. You have a choice of downloading one of the in-process servers (either ISAPI or NSAPI) or an out-of-process server that supports IIS, Netscape, and Apache. The in-process versions are available for IIS and PWS running under the following:

- Windows 98
- Windows NT
- Windows 2000

You can also get an in-process version for Netscape running under the following:

- Windows NT
- Windows 2000
- Solaris 2.6 (or later)

The out-of-process server works with IIS/PWS on the following:

- Windows 98
- Windows NT
- Windows 2000

It also works with Netscape on the following:

- Windows NT
- Windows 2000
- Solaris 2.6
- HPUX 11
- AIX 4.3.3
- Linux systems with kernel version 2.0 and higher (which would include most recent distributions of Red Hat, Debian, Caldera, SuSE, Slackware, Mandrake, and so on)

ServletExec also supports Apache on all the platforms in which it supports Netscape, and also on Windows 98.

Installing the ServletExec ISAPI Plug-In

To install the ServletExec ISAPI plug-in, you must first stop your Web server. On Windows NT or Windows 2000, go to the Services dialog box and stop the IIS Admin service.

Next, run the ServletExec ISAPI install program that you downloaded from Unify. If you haven't shut down IIS Admin yet, the installer will remind you.

The only thing you need to do, other than agree to the software license, is select the directory where you want to install ServletExec. It handles the rest. Figure E.1 shows the dialog bog where you can change the directory.

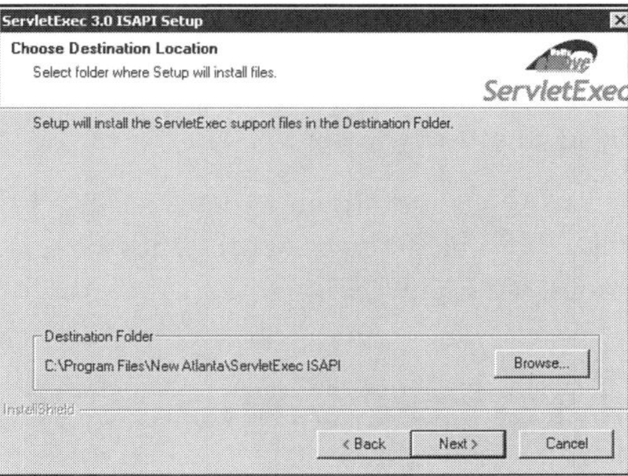

Figure E.1
You only need to select the install directory; ServletExec handles the rest.

After the installation completes, you must start the IIS Admin service and also the World Wide Web Publishing service. On Windows 2000, you may also need to start the FTP Publishing service and the Simple Mail Transport Protocol service. As soon as the World Wide Web Publishing service starts, you should be able to go to `http://localhost/servlet/TestServlet` and see the output shown in Figure E.2.

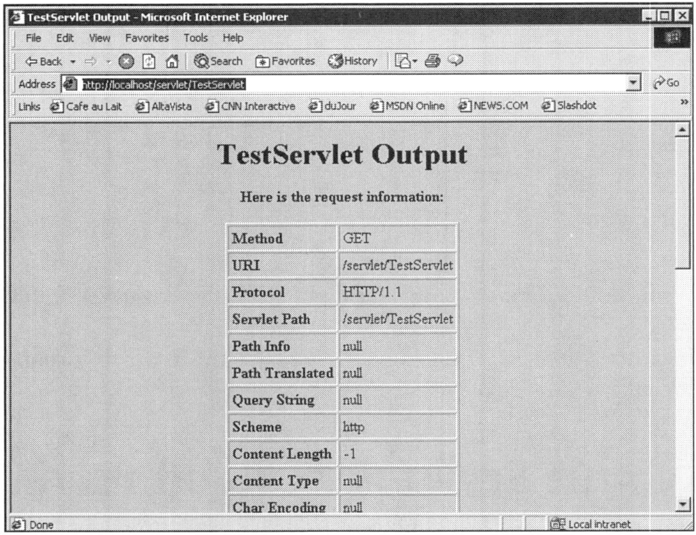

Figure E.2
The TestServlet confirms that servlet support is working in IIS/PWS.

Installing the ServletExec NSAPI Plug-In

To install the ServletExec NSAPI plug-in, just run the ServletExec NSAPI install program you downloaded from Unify. You may want to change the directory where you install ServletExec using the dialog box shown previously in Figure E.1. After you decide on the directory, you must select which instance of Netscape you want to install ServletExec in. Unless you're running a big site, you probably only have one instance of Netscape.

After you pick the instance, ServletExec performs the install. When it asks if you want it to modify the obj.conf file, let it. ServletExec makes a backup copy in case something goes wrong. Don't edit that file by hand unless you absolutely need to.

After the install finishes, go to the Netscape admin screen and restart the server. When the server comes back up, you should be able to go to `http://localhost/servlet/TestServlet` and see the page shown previously in Figure E.2.

Installing the ServletExec Standalone Server for Windows

To install the ServletExec standalone server, just run the installation program you downloaded from Unify. The install program can install the server itself and also create new connections to Web servers. Figure E.3 shows the choices you have when you start the install process.

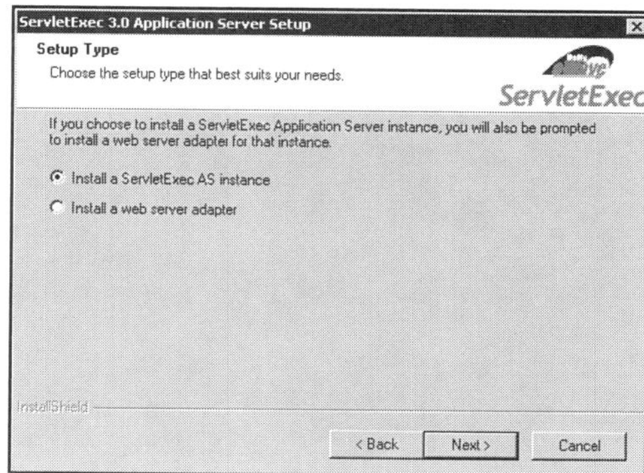

Figure E.3
You can install an application server or connect the application server to an existing Web server.

If this is the first time you've run the installation, install a new ServletExec instance.

After you agree to the software license, you have the option to modify the name of the directory where you will install ServletExec. Refer to Figure E.1 to see the screen that lets you modify the directory.

Next you must choose a name for this server instance. The default is the name of the host. Figure E.4 shows the screen where you choose the instance name.

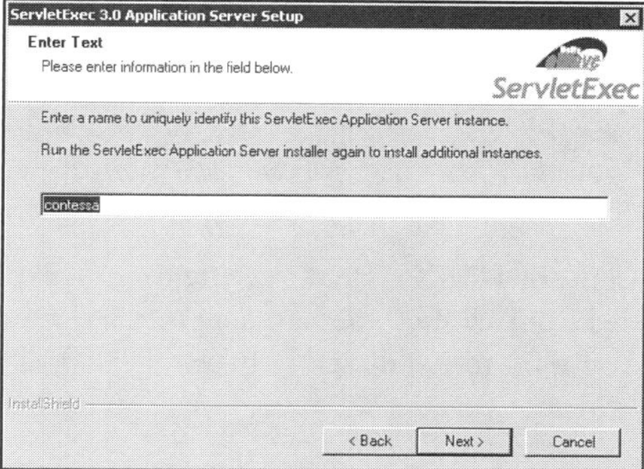

Figure E.4
You must give each instance of ServletExec its own unique name.

Now you pick a Web server to connect this instance of ServletExec to. Figure E.5 shows your choices.

After the installation completes, you should be able to access `http://localhost/servlet/TestServlet` to see if the installation worked.

Caution

The ServletExec server uses port 8888 by default, which is also the default admin port for Netscape. If you are running Netscape, you need to change the port number used by the Netscape admin server or change ServletExec's port number.

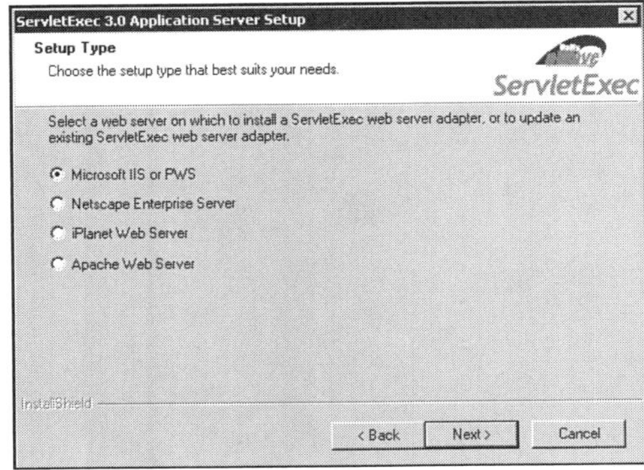

Figure E.5
You must connect ServletExec to an existing Web server.

INSTALLING THE SERVLETEXEC STANDALONE SERVER FOR LINUX/UNIX

Before you start the installation, if you are running Red Hat Linux and you intend to connect to the Apache Web server, make sure you have the apache-devel package installed. Look for a file named /usr/sbin/apxs. If it's already on your system, you already have apache-devel installed. Otherwise, load it from your Red Hat installation disk. The ServletExec installer needs the apxs to install its connector.

Note

You will most likely need to be root to complete the installation of ServletExec. If you have write access to the Web server configuration directory and write access to the directory where you want to install ServletExec, you can get by without becoming the superuser.

To install ServletExec on a Linux or UNIX system, execute the install program (it should end with .bin) you downloaded from Unify. After agreeing to the software license, you must choose the directory where you want to install ServletExec. The default is /usr/local/NewAtlanta.

Next, choose the Web server you want ServletExec to connect to. Figure E.6 shows the choices for a Red Hat 6.2 Linux system.

As with the Windows version of the installation, you have a choice of installing a new server instance and a Web connector, or just a new Web connector. If this is your first time running the install, install a new server instance.

If you install a Web connector for Apache and you're running a recent version of Red Hat Linux, use /etc/httpd as the directory for the Apache.

Now you must enter a unique name for this instance of the ServletExec server. The default is the hostname.

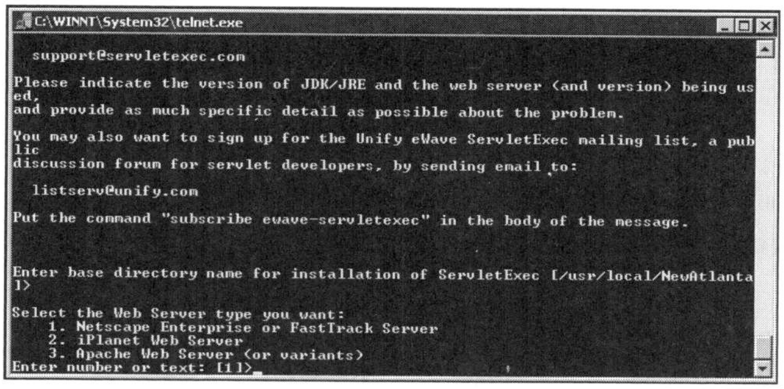

Figure E.6
The UNIX install is text-only.

```
C:\WINNT\System32\telnet.exe

  support@servletexec.com

Please indicate the version of JDK/JRE and the web server (and version) being us
ed,
and provide as much specific detail as possible about the problem.

You may also want to sign up for the Unify eWave ServletExec mailing list, a pub
lic
discussion forum for servlet developers, by sending email to:

  listserv@unify.com

Put the command "subscribe ewave-servletexec" in the body of the message.


Enter base directory name for installation of ServletExec [/usr/local/NewAtlanta
]>

Select the Web Server type you want:
    1. Netscape Enterprise or FastTrack Server
    2. iPlanet Web Server
    3. Apache Web Server (or variants)
Enter number or text: [1]>
```


If you are installing a connector for Apache, you must indicate where the apxs program is located. For many Apache installations, it's in the bin directory below where you installed Apache. For Red Hat Linux, it's /usr/sbin/apxs, but it's only installed if you install the apache-devel package.

After the connector has been configured, you must tell the installer where your Java Development Kit is installed. After that, when the installer asks you whether you want to complete the installation automatically, select Yes.

Before you can test out the ServletExec installation, you must start the ServletExec application server. If you installed ServletExec in /usr/local/NewAtlanta, `cd` to /usr/local/NewAtlanta/ServletExecAS. From here, you must `cd` to the directory containing the server instance you created. The directories are named by prepending `se-` to the instance name you specified. For instance, if you named the instance usingjsp, the directory name would be se-usingjsp.

Caution

The ServletExec server uses port 8888 by default, which is also the default admin port for Netscape. If you are running Netscape, you need to change the port number used by the Netscape admin server or change ServletExec's port number.

Now you can start the server instance with this command:

```
StartServletExec &
```

If you ever need to shut the server down, go to the same directory and type the following:

```
StopServletExec
```

Finally, you must restart your Web server. If you are running the Netscape Web server, go to the Netscape admin page and stop/start the server.

If you're running Red Hat Linux, you can restart the Web server with the following two commands:

```
/etc/rc.d/rc3.d/S85httpd stop
/etc/rc.d/rc3.d/S85httpd start
```

After the Web server has been restarted, go to `http://localhost/servlet/TestServlet` to see if the installation worked. If your Web browser is running on a machine other than the one where you installed ServletExec, use the hostname of the other machine instead of `localhost`.

SERVLETEXEC ADMINISTRATION

ServletExec has a nice Web-based administration tool. If you're running Windows, there should be a menu option for ServletExec admin under Programs/New Atlanta/ServletExec AS on your Start menu. Figure E.7 shows the ServletExec admin screen.

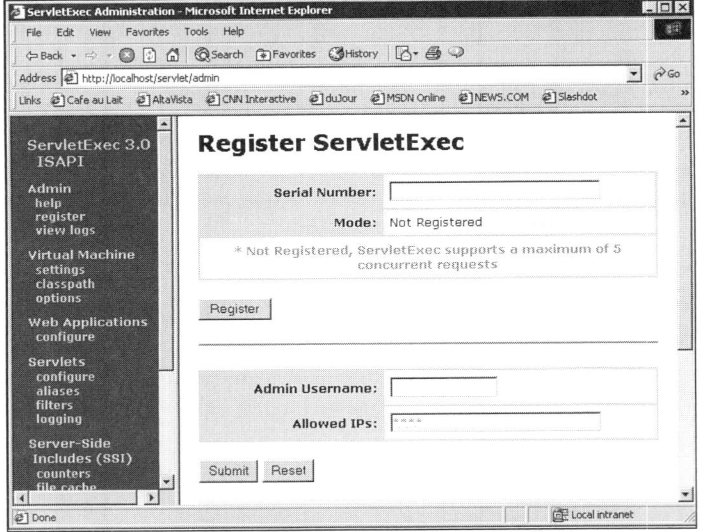

Figure E.7
The ServletExec admin screen makes it easy to manage your Web applications.

If you aren't running Windows or you need to administer the ServletExec instance on another machine, you can access the admin application directly with the URL `http://hostname/servlet/admin`.

WORKING DIRECTORY

ServletExec doesn't have a specific default working directory. The working directory is wherever the ServletExec server instance was started. On a Windows NT machine, don't be surprise to find that c:\winnt\system32 is the working directory.

INSTALLING WEB APPLICATIONS

ServletExec makes it easy to install a Web application. Just go to the admin screen, and under Web Applications on the left side, click Configure. If you want to add a new application, click the Add Web Application button.

You only need to enter three fields to install a Web application in ServletExec: the name of the application, the root URL of the application, and the location of the application's WAR file. Figure E.8 shows the Add Web Application screen.

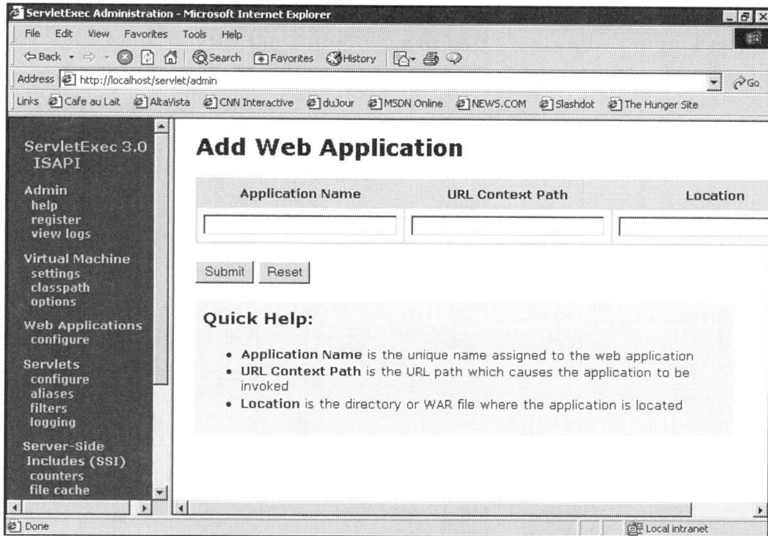

Figure E.8
Adding a Web application is as easy as filling out three fields.

After you have added an application, you can remove or reload it from the Configure Web Applications screen, as shown in Figure E.9.

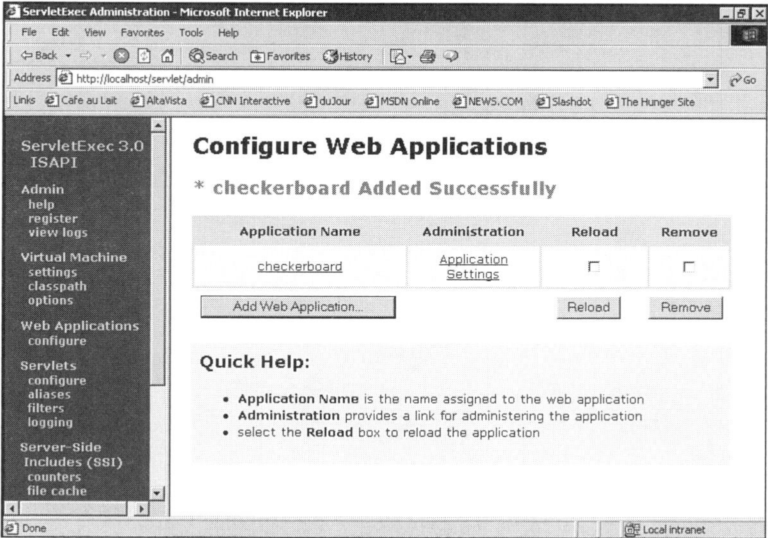

Figure E.9
You can reload or remove an application by clicking the appropriate button.

LOG MESSAGES

ServletExec places all log messages in a directory named Servlet Logs under the main installation directory. If you have installed any web applications, each web application has its own separate logging directory under the main logging directory. All messages logged with the servlet logging API are written to a file called Servlet.log as are all messages written to System.out and System.err.

SETTING THE CLASSPATH

The ServletExec admin page allows you to add additional entries to your classpath. Just select "classpath" under "Virtual Machine" and add your additional entries. Figure E.10 shows the screen that allows you to set the classpath.

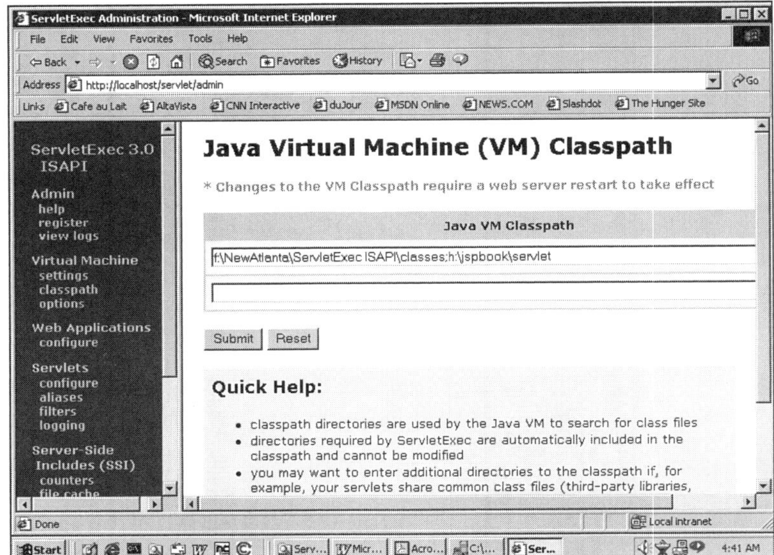

Figure E.10
You can set the classpath using the admin tool.

SERVLETEXEC SPECIAL FEATURES

ServletExec doesn't come with many extraneous features; it is a good servlet/JSP engine and little more. It does include support for server-side includes (SSI) in case your Web server doesn't support them. Despite the lack of extras, ServletExec is an excellent servlet and JSP engine. It is easy to install, use, and administer.

APPENDIX F

RESIN

In this appendix

The Resin Web Server is an open-source Web server from Caucho Technology. Although Resin is an open-source project, Caucho still requests that you buy a license from them. A license entitles you to better support and faster upgrades. Legally, you aren't required to buy a license. As Caucho says, you aren't required to tip in restaurants. However, if you make any money from your use of Resin, you should buy a license to support further development.

Resin provides many features above and beyond the core JSP and servlet functionality. Resin lets you use JavaScript as the scripting language in your JSPs. It also has excellent support for XSL templates.

Where to Get Resin

You can download Resin from the Caucho Web site at `http://www.caucho.com`. Although Resin comes in a 100% pure Java variety, the Windows version gives you the ability to run the Resin Web Server and the Resin servlet engine (which plugs into other Web servers) as a Windows NT service. If you are installing Resin for Windows, download the Windows zip version of Resin. For Linux and UNIX platforms, download the tar.gz version.

Installing Resin on Windows

You need an unzip program to unpack Resin for Windows. You can use either WinZip from `www.winzip.com` or Info-ZIP from `ftp://ftp.freesoftware.com/pub/infozip/Info-ZIP.html`. WinZip is a commercial product, but is the most popular zip utility for Windows. Info-ZIP is a free command-line tool available for a wide variety of systems. After you unpack Resin, it's basically installed except for configuring any connectors.

Note

As of July 2000, the current version of Resin is 1.1.2. Wherever you see resin-1.1.2, remember that you'll most likely have a more recent version.

Unpacking Resin with WinZip

To install Resin from WinZip, run Windows Explorer, go to the directory where you downloaded Resin, and double-click resin-1.1.2.zip. WinZip shows you a screen that looks like the one shown in Figure F.1. Click the Extract button.

After you click on Extract, you'll see a window similar to the one shown in Figure F.2. Select the directory where you want to install Resin. Keep in mind that Resin will be placed in a subdirectory named resin1.1 off of whatever directory you choose. In other words, if you ask WinZip to install Tomcat in c:\resin, you will end up installing Tomcat in c:\resin\resin1.1.

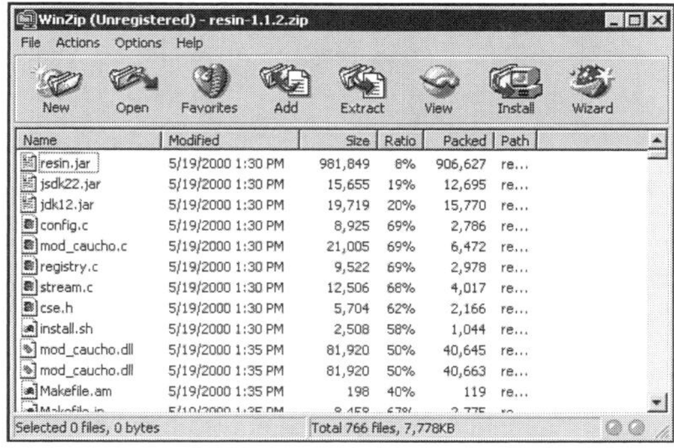

Figure F.1
WinZip makes it easy to unpack Resin.

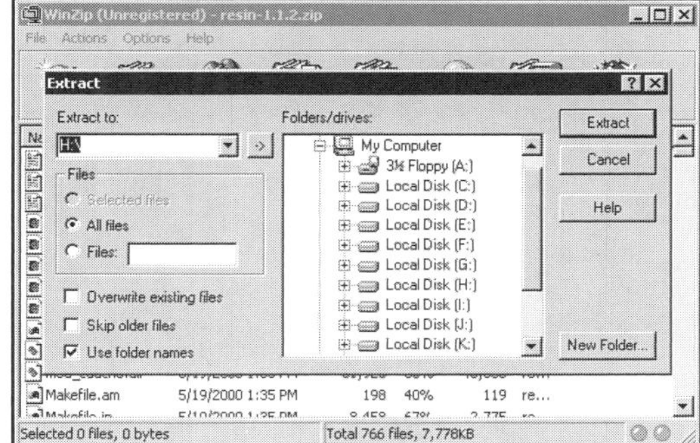

Figure F.2
WinZip allows you to choose where to unpack a file.

UNPACKING RESIN FROM THE COMMAND LINE

If you want to unpack Resin using a command-line unzip program such as Info-ZIP, bring up a command window (DOS prompt), go to the directory where you want to install Resin, and unzip resin-1.1.2.zip. Remember, when you unpack Resin, it is placed in a directory named resin1.1 below the directory where you unpack it. If you want Resin to be installed in c:\resin1.1, you must unpack it from c:\. If you unpack it from c:\resin, it is installed in c:\resin\resin1.1.

TESTING THE INSTALLATION

After you unpack Resin, it's ready to run. Go to the bin directory under the Resin directory and type **`httpd`**. You should see a control window similar to the one shown in Figure F.3.

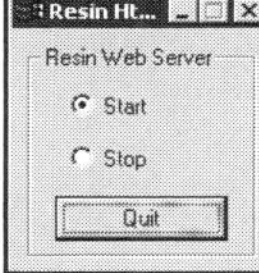

Figure F.3
Resin has a control window that enables you to stop and start the Web server.

The Resin Web Server starts on port 8080 by default, so when you point your browser to `http://localhost:8080`, you should see a response from the Resin Web Server similar to the one shown in Figure F.4.

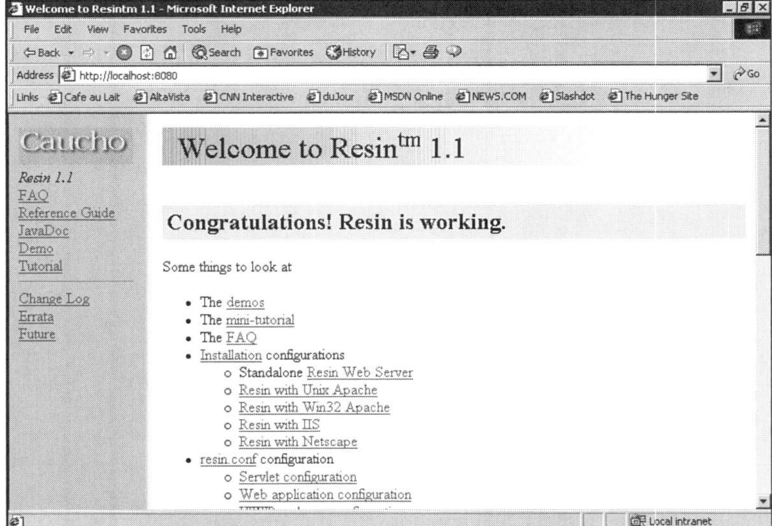

Figure F.4
Resin comes with a built-in Web server.

INSTALLING RESIN ON LINUX/UNIX

To install Resin on Linux or UNIX, go to the directory where you want to install Resin. You don't need to be root to install Resin, unless you are installing it in a protected directory such as /usr/local. Resin is installed in a subdirectory called resin1.1 from wherever you unpack it. If you want to install it in /usr/local/resin1.1, you must unpack it from the /usr/local directory.

On most recent Linux distributions, you can unpack Resin with a command like

```
tar xvzf /tmp/resin-1.1.2.tar.gz
```

On most UNIX systems, the `tar` command doesn't have built-in gzip support, so you must use `gunzip` to decompress the file and then `tar` to unpack it. You can combine the operations into a single command, however:

```
gunzip -c /tmp/resin-1.1.2.tar.gz | tar xvf -
```

To test your installation, follow the same procedure that you would for Windows. Go to resin1.1/bin and type **`httpd.sh`**. You won't see any output; the command will just sit there looking like the command line in Figure F.5.

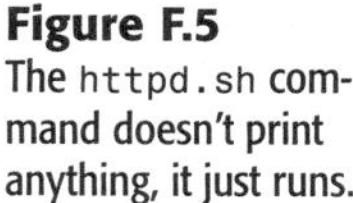

Figure F.5
The `httpd.sh` command doesn't print anything, it just runs.

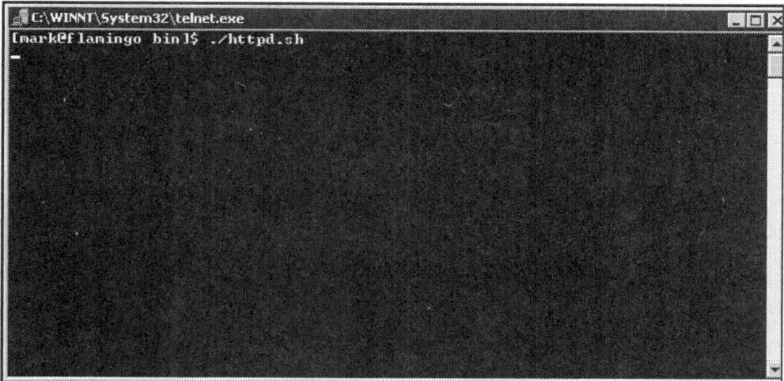

After you start httpd, you should be able to point your browser to `http://localhost:8080` and see the response shown previously in Figure F.4. If you are running Resin on a host other than the one where you browser is running, use the name of the host running Resin instead of localhost.

APP F

RUNNING RESIN STANDALONE

Resin works fine as a standalone Web server. The one thing you may want to change is the port number it uses. If you want Resin to be the main Web server, go to the resin1.1/conf directory and edit the resin.conf file. Look for a line like this:

```
<httpd-port>8080</httpd-port>
```

Change the 8080 to 80 and restart Resin. Now the URL for your Resin Web server is `http://localhost` (or `http://nameofyourhost`).

RUNNING RESIN UNDER ANOTHER WEB SERVER

You can use Resin as the servlet/JSP engine for an existing Web server. Under Windows, Resin can act as a servlet/JSP engine for IIS/PWS, Netscape, and Apache. Just run resin1.1/bin/setup and tell Resin which Web servers you want it to connect to. Figure F.6 shows the dialog box from the setup program.

Figure F.6
Resin can install itself under several Web servers.

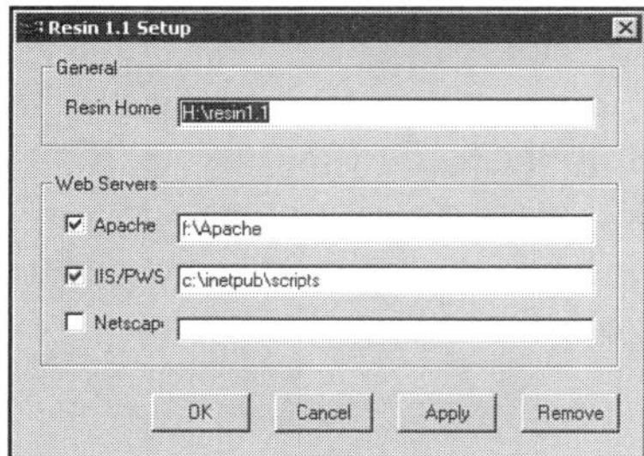

You need to restart whatever Web servers you run Resin under and also start the Resin servlet engine, resin1.1/bin/srun. The `httpd` program is the standalone Resin Web Server, while `srun` is the servlet/JSP engine for an existing Web server.

Running httpd or srun as Windows NT Services

You probably don't want to run `httpd` or `srun` manually every time you restart your computer. If you're running Windows NT or Windows 2000, you can install the programs as services that will start automatically the next time you reboot. To install `httpd` as a service, just type

```
httpd -install
```

Likewise, to install `srun` as a Windows NT service, type

```
srun -install
```

If you want to remove either of these programs from the list of services, type

```
httpd -remove
```

or

```
srun -remove
```

Resin Administration

Resin doesn't have a nice administration Web service like JRun or ServletExec. If you need to change Resin's configuration, you must edit the resin1.1/conf/resin.conf file manually. The resin.conf file is in XML format, but many of the tags are Resin-specific. It does, however, support the `<Web-app>` tag and the various tags, such as `<servlet-mapping>`, that you use for configuring Web applications.

Working Directory

The default working directory for Resin is the directory where you installed it (that is, the resin1.1 directory).

Installing Web Applications

Resin isn't very helpful when it comes to installing a Web application. You must unpack the WAR file yourself and edit the resin.conf file to add your new application. To install an application, go to the resin1.1/doc directory and create a new directory to hold your application. For example, suppose you are installing an application named testapp. You would create a directory under resin1.1/doc named testapp.

Next, go to the testapp directory and unpack your testapp.war file.

Finally, edit the resin1.1/conf/resin.conf file. Toward the bottom of the file, you should see some <web-app> tags. Add a tag for your application like this:

```
<web-app id="testapp"/>
```

Logging

Resin writes out all its logging information to files in the log directory under the main installation directory. Any output sent to System.out is written to a file called stdout.log, while data written to System.err goes to a file called stderr.log. In addition, any compile errors or execution errors are written to error.log.

Setting the Classpath

Resin typically uses the same classpath settings as your Java Virtual Machine. If you are running Windows, you can set the `classpath` environment variable from the control panel. Under UNIX and Linux, you just change the `CLASSPATH` environment variable from your login shell.

Adding Authentication Users

Resin has an interesting way of configuring users for servlet authentication. You must either create a special Java class to authenticate users or use the built-in `JDBCAuthenticator` class that reads users from the database. You can find out more about the authenticator in the Resin documentation, but the basic configuration information is shown in Listing F.1.

Listing F.1 Configuration Information for Resin Authentication

```
<db-pool id="my-db-pool"
driver="org.gjt.mm.mysql.Driver"
url="jdbc:mysql://localhost:3306/test"
user=""
password=""/>

<authenticator id='com.caucho.server.http.JdbcAuthenticator'>
<password-query>
SELECT password FROM LOGIN WHERE username=?
</password-query>
</authenticator>
```

The basic idea is that you store usernames and passwords in a database table and provide Resin with a way to verify the password. The `db-pool` information lets Resin know how to access the database.

RESIN SPECIAL FEATURES

Resin doesn't have the prettiest installation procedure, and installing Web applications is a manual process, but Resin manages to include some really nice extra features.

JAVASCRIPT JAVA SERVER PAGES

You probably know by now that Java Server Pages are not necessarily written in Java. The JSP specification allows for the use of languages other than Java. Most JSP engines available today only support Java, but Resin lets you use JavaScript as a scripting language as well. Resin even provides a good set of library routines to help your JavaScript along. There is an XML parser, a Database interface, and even a file access library. When you can't find a JavaScript routine to do what you need, you can use Java classes from your JavaScript code.

The documentation included with Resin gives you all the information you need to write JSPs with JavaScript.

XSL

As you saw in Chapter 25, "Adding XSL Stylesheets to Enhance an XML Application," XSL is both an alternative to Java Server Pages and an enhancement to JSP. Resin supports XSL and some interesting variations. For example, you can use XSL to create custom JSP tags that you can call from the Java Server Pages. Because the tags are driven by an XSL template instead of pure Java code like JSP tags, you can change the XSL tags easily.

Because XSL can be cumbersome to use (it's difficult to even read, almost as bad as Perl!), Resin includes an XSLT-lite syntax that makes XSL much more readable.

Resin even combines some of its extra features to give you some powerful options. You can use JavaScript in your XSL templates to make dynamic XSL. You get much of the power of JSP this way.

If you are looking to get into XSL as well as JSP, give Resin a try. It gives you the best of both worlds.

INDEX

Symbols

A

B

H

J

K-L

Q

R

S

W

X-Z

This handy card serves as your quick reference for the syntax and major objects of JSP.

Table 1 JSP Syntax

<table>
<tr><th>Command</th><th>Description</th></tr>
<tr><td><% Java code %></td><td>Executes Java code</td></tr>
<tr><td><%= Java expression %></td><td>Evaluates a Java expression</td></tr>
<tr><td><%! Java declarations %></td><td>Declares a method or field</td></tr>
<tr><td><%-- comment --></td><td>Inserts a comment</td></tr>
</table>

Table 2 JSP Directives

<table>
<tr><th>Directive</th><th>Options</th></tr>
<tr><td><%@ page options %></td><td>autoFlush="true|false"
buffer="none|sizekb"
contentType="content_type"
errorPage="error_url"
extends="className"
import="imports"
info="info"
isErrorPage="true|false"
isThreadSafe="true|false"
language="scripting_language"
session="true|false"</td></tr>
<tr><td><%@ include options %></td><td>file="file"</td></tr>
<tr><td><%@ taglib options %></td><td>uri="taglib_uri"
prefix="tag_prefix"</td></tr>
</table>

Table 3 JSP Actions

<table>
<tr><th>Action</th><th>Options</th></tr>
<tr><td><jsp:useBean></td><td>class="class" |
class="class" type="type" |
beanName="name" type="type" |
type="type"
id="name"
scope="page|request|session|application"</td></tr>
<tr><td><jsp:setProperty></td><td>property="*" |
property="propertyName" |
property="prop" param="param"|
property="prop" value="value"
name="beanName"</td></tr>
</table>

Table 3 Continued

Action	Options
<jsp:getProperty>	name="*beanName*" property="*propertyName*"
<jsp:include>	page="*page_url*" flush="true"
<jsp:forward>	page="*page_url*" flush="true"
<jsp:param>	name="*name*" value="*value*"
<jsp:plugin>	type="bean|applet" code="*objectCode*" codebase="*objectCodebase*" align="*alignment*" archive="*archiveList*" height="*height*" hspace="*hspace*" jreversion="*jre_version*" name="*componentName*" vspace="*vspace*" width="*width*" nspluginurl="*url*" iepluginurl="*url*"

Table 4 JSP Built-In Objects

Object	Java Type
request	javax.servlet.ServletRequest typically: javax.servlet.HttpServletRequest
response	javax.servlet.ServletResponse typically: javax.servlet.HttpServletResponse
pageContext	javax.servlet.jsp.PageContext
session	javax.servlet.http.HttpSession
application	javax.servlet.ServletContext
out	javax.servlet.jsp.JspWriter
config	javax.servlet.ServletConfig
page	java.lang.Object
exception	java.lang.Throwable